CADOGAN GUIDES

"Cadogan Guides really need no introduction and are mini-encyclopaedic on the countries covered . . . they give the explorer, the intellectual or cultural buff – indeed any visitor – all they need to know to get the very best from their visit . . . it makes a good read too by the many inveterate armchair travellers."

—*The Book Journal*

"Rochelle Jaffe, owner and manager of Travel Books Unlimited in Bethesda, Maryland, attributes [Cadogan Guides'] popularity to both their good, clean-looking format and the fact that they include 'information about everything for everyone' . . . . These guides are one of the most exciting series available on European travel."

—*American Bookseller* magazine

"The Cadogan Guide to Italy is the most massive, literate, and helpful guide to Italy in years."

—*International Travel News*, USA

"*Italy*, by Dana Facaros and Michael Pauls is an absolute gem of a travel book, humorous, informed, sympathetic, as irresistible as that land itself."

—Anthony Clare, Books of the Year, *The Sunday Times*, 1988–89

Other titles in the Cadogan Guide series:

AUSTRALIA
BALI
THE CARIBBEAN
GREEK ISLANDS
INDIA
IRELAND
ITALIAN ISLANDS
ITALY
NORTHEAST ITALY
NORTHWEST ITALY
MOROCCO
PORTUGAL
ROME
SCOTLAND
SOUTH ITALY
SPAIN
THAILAND & BURMA
TURKEY

Forthcoming:

ECUADOR,
THE GALAPAGOS
& COLOMBIA
MEXICO
NEW YORK
NEW ORLEANS
TUNISIA
VENICE

ABOUT THE AUTHORS

From their base in a tiny Umbrian village, travel writers DANA FACAROS and MICHAEL PAULS have researched and written a string of *Cadogan Guides* to Italy: a big fat tome on the whole country, *Italy*; regional guides to *Northwest Italy*, *Northeast Italy*, *South Italy* and this revised version of *Tuscany and Umbria* with an additional chapter on *The Marches*; a city guide to *Rome*; and an update to their successful guide to the *Italian Islands*.

They have also written a highly acclaimed series for *The Observer* magazine on 'Hidden Italy'.

They have finally torn themselves and their two children away from the pasta and have moved on to foie gras and a tiny French village in the Lot.

Dear Readers,

Please, please help us to keep this book up to date. We would be delighted to receive any additional information or suggestions. Please write to us or fill in the form on the last page of this book. Writers of the best letters will be acknowledged in future editions, and will receive a free copy of the Cadogan Guide of their choice.

The Publisher

CADOGAN GUIDES

TUSCANY, UMBRIA & THE MARCHES

DANA FACAROS and MICHAEL PAULS

Illustrations by Pauline Pears

CADOGAN BOOKS
London

THE GLOBE PEQUOT PRESS
Chester, Connecticut

Cadogan Books Ltd
Mercury House, 195 Knightsbridge, London SW7 1RE

The Globe Pequot Press
138 West Main Street, Chester, Connecticut 06412

Cover design by Keith Pointing
Cover illustration by Povl Webb
Maps © Cadogan Books Ltd,
drawn by Thames Cartographic Services Ltd

Series Editors: Rachel Fielding and Paula Levey

First published in 1989
Second Edition 1990

British Library Cataloguing in Publication Data

Facaros, Dana
Tuscany, Umbria & the Marches. – 2nd ed. – (Cadogan guides).
1. Italy, Tuscany. – Visitors' guides. 2. Italy, Umbria. – Visitors' guides.
I. Title II. Pauls, Michael III. Facaros, Dana. Tuscany & Umbria.
914.5509429

ISBN 0–947754–21–0

Library of Congress Cataloging-in-Publication Data

Facaros, Dana
Tuscany & Umbria & the Marches / Dana Facaros and Michael Pauls. – 2nd ed.

p. cm. – (Cadogan guides)
Rev. ed. of: Tuscany & Umbria, *c.* 1989.
Includes bibliographical references and index.
ISBN 0–87106–393–X
1. Tuscany (Italy) – Description and travel – 1981 – Guide-books.
2. Umbria (Italy) – Description and travel – 1981 – Guide-books.
3. Marches (Italy) – Description and travel – Guide-books.
I. Pauls, Michael. II. Title. III. Title: Tuscany, Umbria and the Marches. IV. Series.
DG732.F27 1990 914.5—dc20 90–3850 CIP

Photoset in Ehrhardt on a Linotron 202
Printed and bound in Great Britain by Redwood Press Limited,
Melksham, Wiltshire

CONTENTS

LIST OF MAPS

ACKNOWLEDGEMENTS

We would particularly like to thank Michael Davidson and Brian Walsh, whose unfailing good humour helped us through the darkest corners of Italy, and who have contributed substantially to this book by updating all the practical information. We would like to thank the Italian National Tourist Office, and all the local and municipal tourist boards throughout Tuscany, Umbria and The Marches for their kind assistance in writing this book. Special thanks go to Paola Greco, in London, and the Terni tourist office for their kind help to Michael and Brian. We would also like to thank the 49 residents of Rosciano for their innumerable kindnesses, courgettes, and bottles of wine, especially Anna, the late Tito, Fiorella, Mario, Alessandra, and Sara, Flavia, and Augusto; Michael and Brian, Clare, Anne, Santino, and Stefanie who make us laugh even when the Umbrian storm clouds gather, and whose suggestions and comments were invaluable; Carolyn, Chris, Marge, and Mila who crossed the ocean to cheer us up; Paula and Rachel, our publishers, who have worked as hard as we have (well, nearly) to put out this book. And a very special thanks to Fred Rainer, lay Catholic expert extraordinaire, who loaned us his Italian library, delivered our dayly five litres, and told us a hundred monkish secrets.

The publishers would particularly like to thank Dorothy Groves and Stephen and Meg Davies for respectively copy-editing, proof-reading and indexing.

INTRODUCTION

A glass of wine before dinner on the garden terrace, the olives glinting in the last flash of the setting sun as the curling geometric vineyards lose their rigid order in the melting darkness, and only the black daggers of the cypresses on the hills stand out—where could you be but Tuscany? It needs no introduction, this famous twilit land, where Titans of art 500 years ago copied, and then outdid nature, and where nature gets her gentle revenge by rivalling art. Umbria is perhaps most familiar as the land of St Francis and Assisi, and indeed many have found it a mystic place, one that 'speaks in silences'. These days it is becoming popular because it has so much in common with Tuscany—wine, art, and lavish natural beauty, but perhaps most of all because it is filled with the same remarkable sense of continuity, of a land and people in perfect agreement.

Travellers have been coming to this region ever since the Middle Ages, to learn, to see, and to understand. Most have come with their Baedekers or Ruskins or Berensons in hand, and even today it is often hard to escape the weight of generations of Tuscan opinions or to avoid treading on those same old grapes of purple prose. After all, most of what we call Western Civilization and culture was either rediscovered or invented here; at times it seems as if the artists of the early 1400s descended from outer space with their secret messages for the imagination. Anyway, to the mass of opinion, we've added ours, for better or worse, but mostly in the hope of provoking some of your own.

But at the end of the day—or as we are at the twilight of the 20th century, when times seem to be changing faster than we can or care to—the enduring charm of Tuscany and Umbria is in that dreamy glass of wine, in those hills that look exactly as they did when Piero and Perugino painted them, in the bartender who's a dead ringer for Lorenzo de' Medici, in those bewitching Etruscan smiles that seem to have been smiled only yesterday. Things have stayed the same way for centuries not by any accident, or economic reason, or by divine decree of some Tuscan National Trust, but because that's the way people like them. Tuscans and Umbrians make as few concessions to the 20th century as possible, and their Brigadoon may not be for everyone. They're not catching up with the world; the world's catching up with them.

NOTE: little hamlets outside Italian towns are called *frazioni*, or fractions, and in this new edition of the guide we've included the region of the Marches, in many ways a 'fraction' of Tuscany and Umbria. Undeservedly overshadowed by its neighbours, the Marches shares many of their best features: transcendent Renaissance art, wine, hill-towns, and a few surprises—but receives only a fraction of their visitors, too: altogether a quiet but seductive slice of Central Italian gentility.

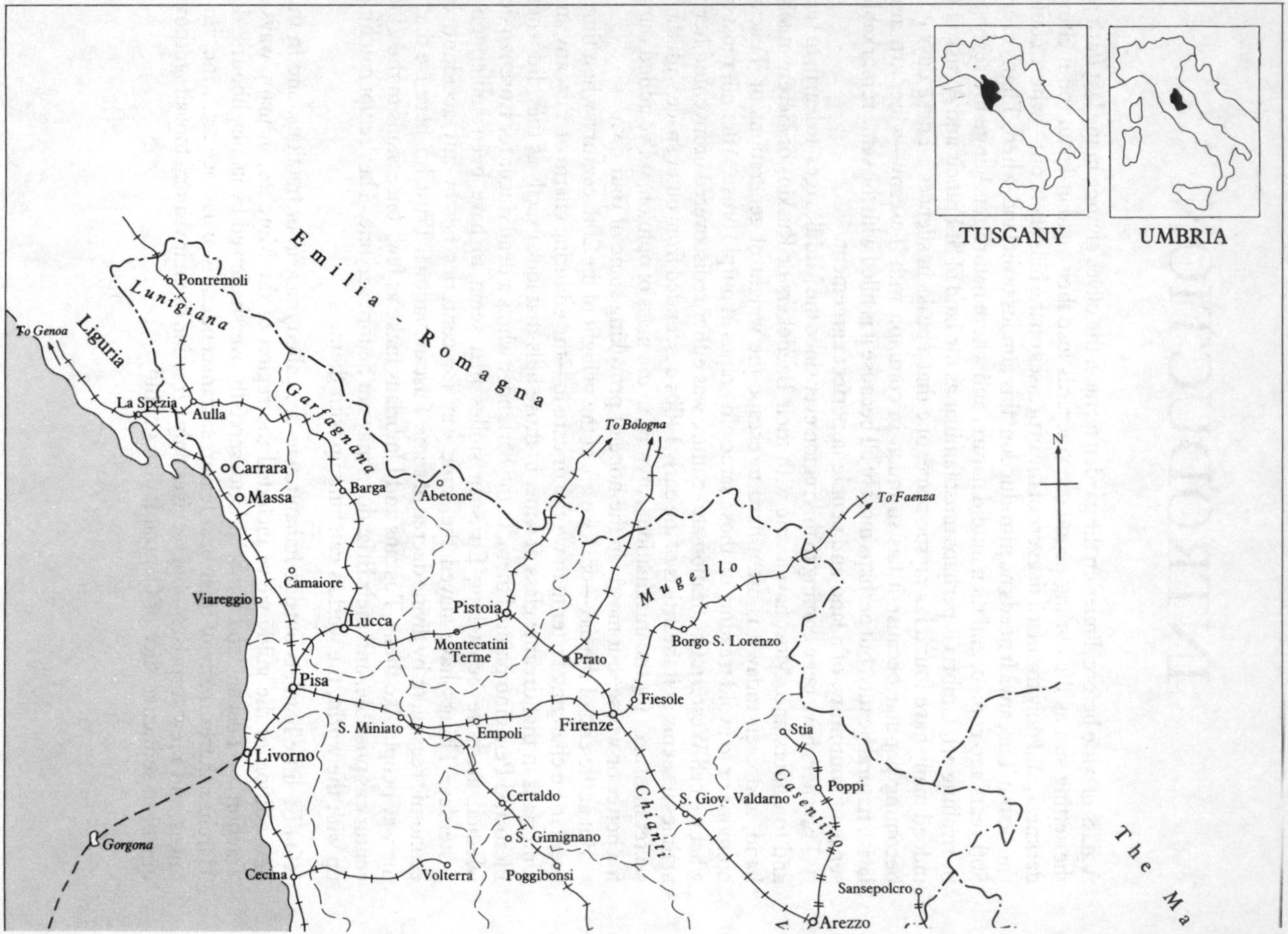
TUSCANY
UMBRIA
N
To Genoa
Liguria
Lunigiana
Pontremoli
Emilia - Romagna
La Spezia
Aulla
Garfagnana
Carrara
Massa
Barga
Abetone
To Bologna
To Faenza
Mugello
Camaiore
Viareggio
Pistoia
Lucca
Montecatini Terme
Prato
Borgo S. Lorenzo
Pisa
Fiesole
S. Miniato
Empoli
Firenze
Stia
Livorno
Casentino
Poppi
Certaldo
Chianti
S. Giov. Valdarno
S. Gimignano
Gorgona
Cecina
Volterra
Poggibonsi
Sansepolcro
Arezzo
The Ma

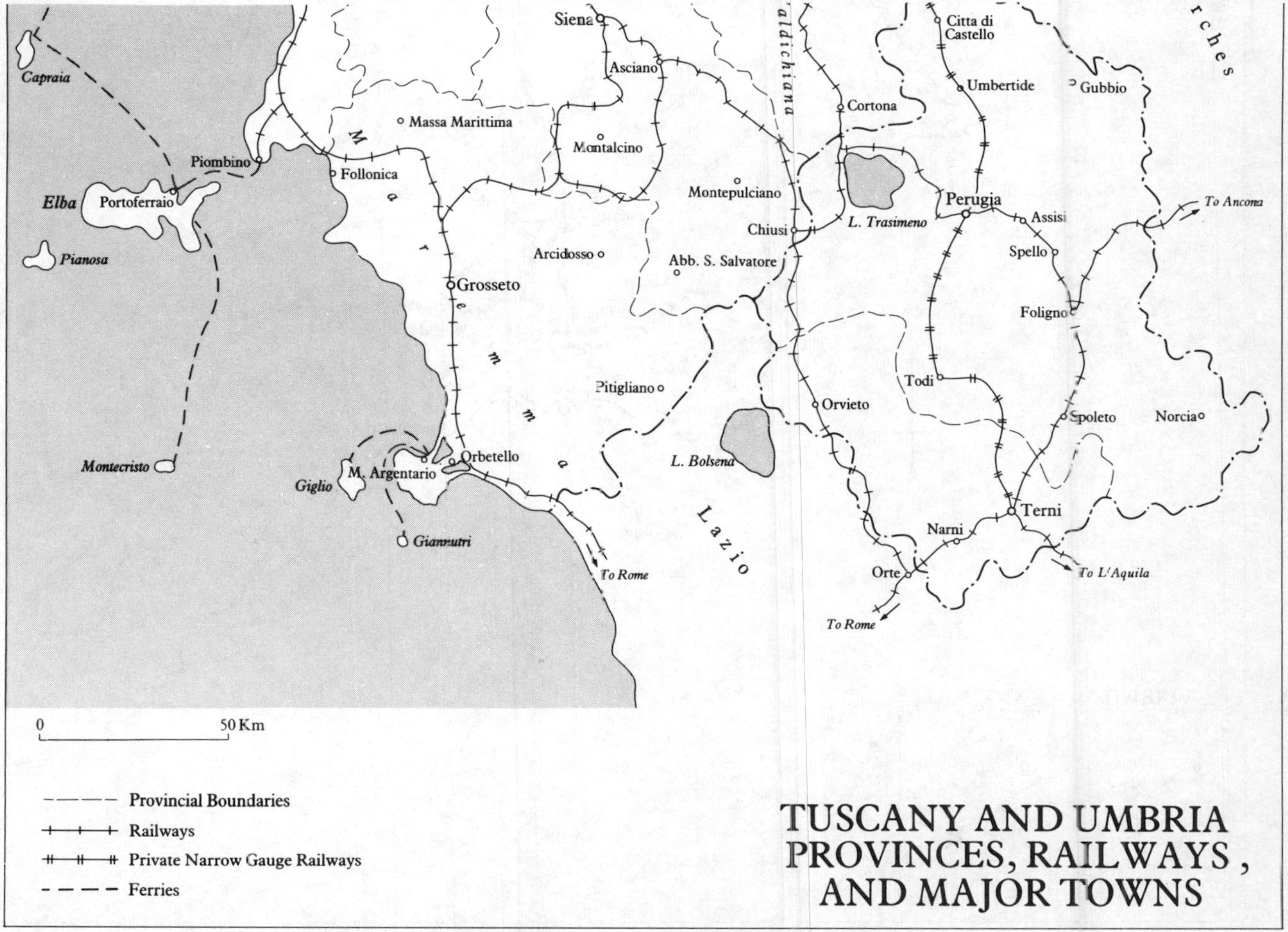

TUSCANY AND UMBRIA PROVINCES, RAILWAYS , AND MAJOR TOWNS

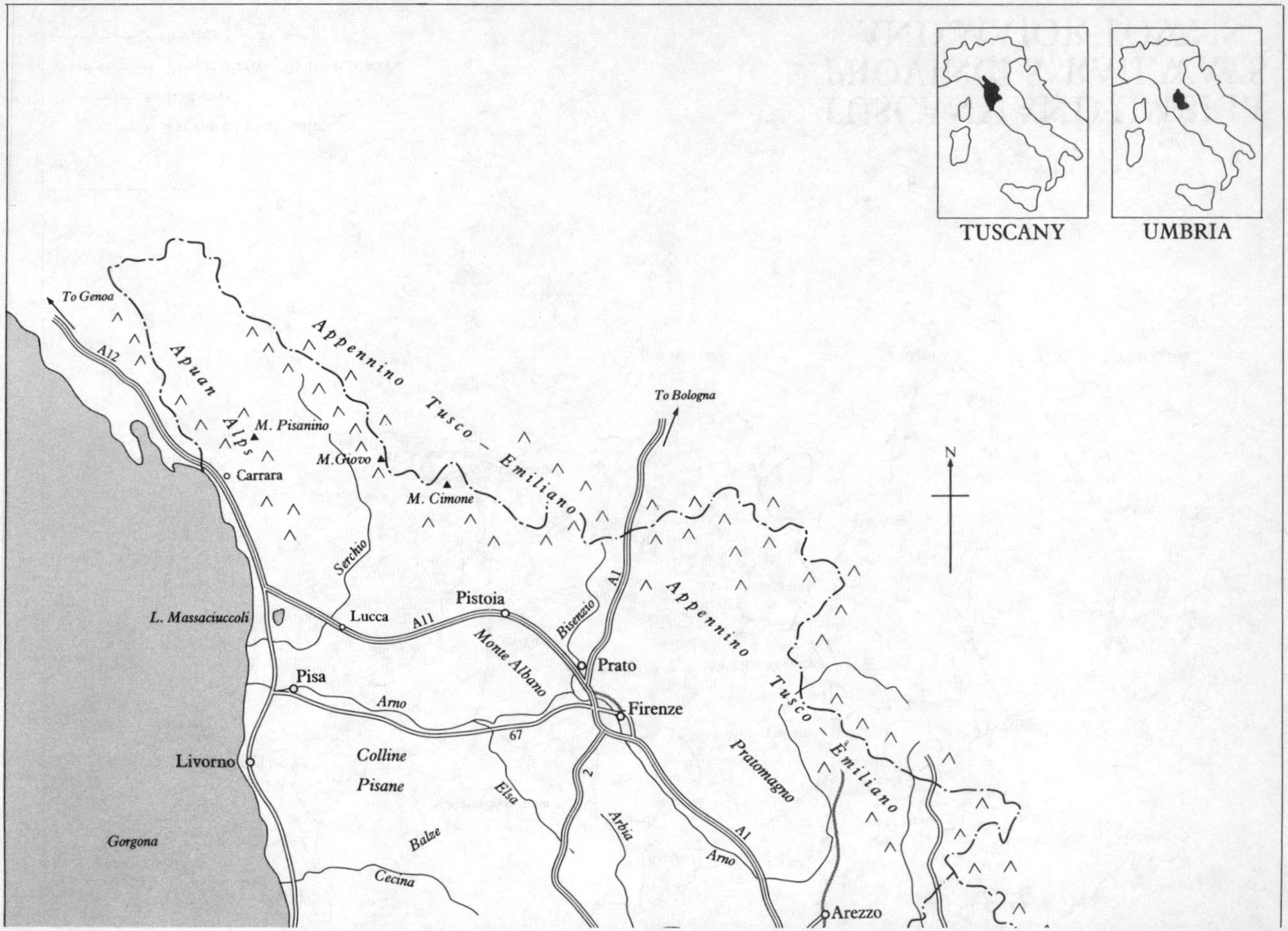
TUSCANY
UMBRIA
N
To Genoa
A12
Apuan Alps
M. Pisanino
Carrara
Appennino Tusco-Emiliano
M. Giovo
M. Cimone
Serchio
To Bologna
A1
L. Massaciuccoli
Lucca
A11
Pistoia
Bisenzio
Monte Albano
Prato
Pisa
Arno
Firenze
67
Livorno
Colline Pisane
Elsa
2
Arbia
Pratomagno
Gorgona
Balze
Cecina
Arno
Arezzo

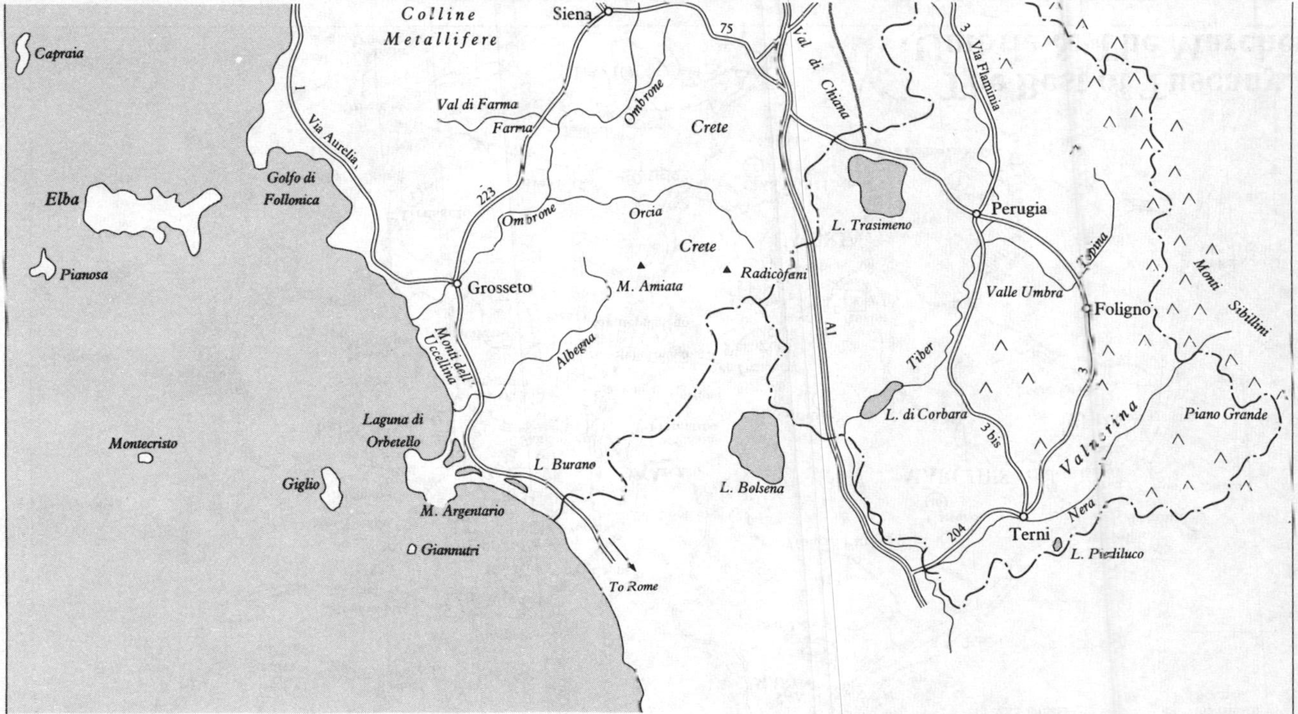

TUSCANY AND UMBRIA NATURAL FEATURES AND MAIN HIGHWAYS

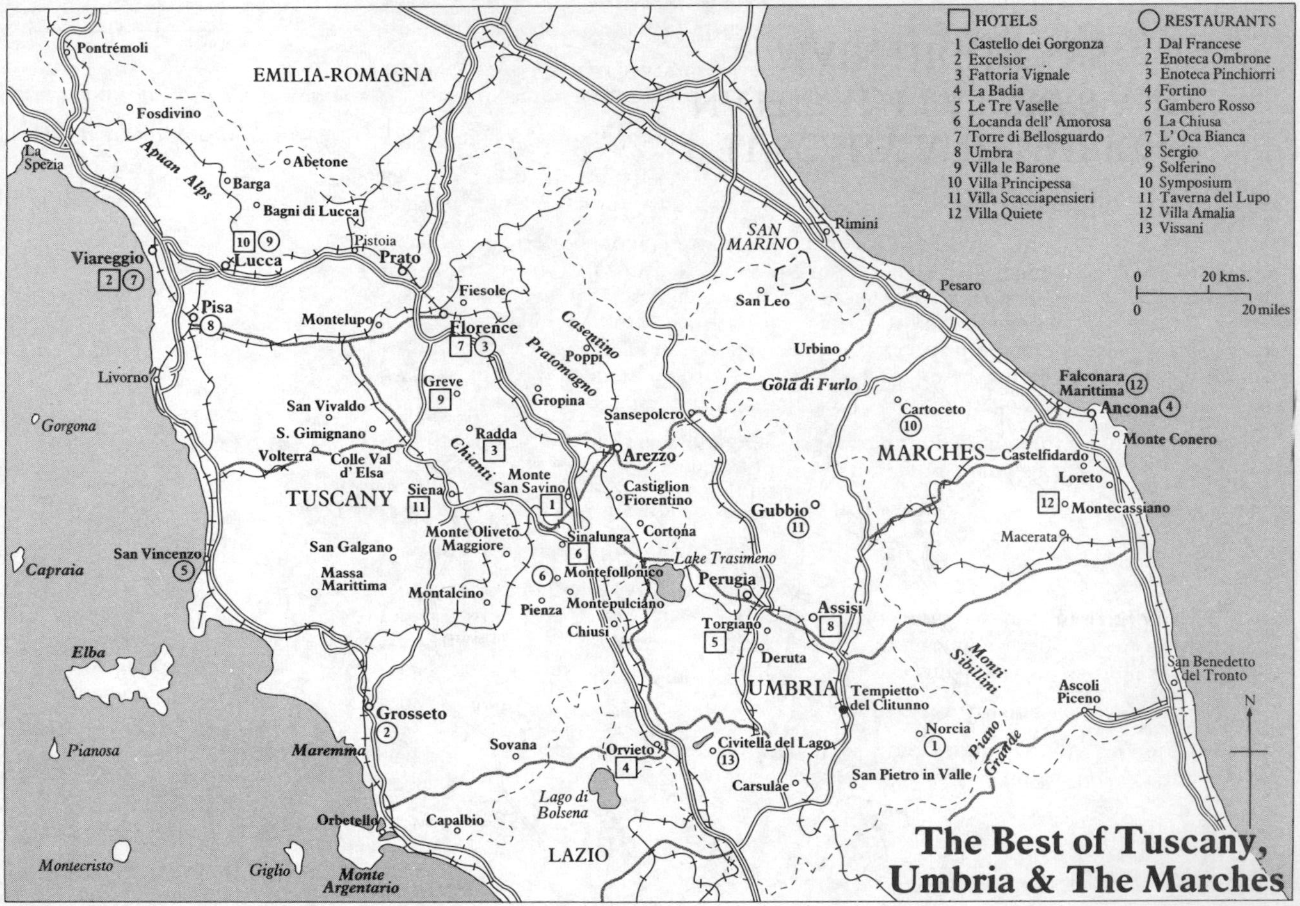
HOTELS
1 Castello dei Gorgonza
2 Excelsior
3 Fattoria Vignale
4 La Badia
5 Le Tre Vaselle
6 Locanda dell' Amorosa
7 Torre di Bellosguardo
8 Umbra
9 Villa le Barone
10 Villa Principessa
11 Villa Scacciapensieri
12 Villa Quiete
RESTAURANTS
1 Dal Francese
2 Enoteca Ombrone
3 Enoteca Pinchiorri
4 Fortino
5 Gambero Rosso
6 La Chiusa
7 L' Oca Bianca
8 Sergio
9 Solferino
10 Symposium
11 Taverna del Lupo
12 Villa Amalia
13 Vissani
0 20 kms.
0 20 miles
N
EMILIA-ROMAGNA
Pontrémoli
Fosdivino
La Spezia
Apuan Alps
Abetone
Barga
Bagni di Lucca
Pistoia
Prato
Lucca
Viareggio
Pisa
Fiesole
Florence
Montelupo
Livorno
Gorgona
Casentino
Poppi
Pratomagno
Greve
Gropina
San Vivaldo
S. Gimignano
Radda
Chianti
Volterra
Colle Val d' Elsa
TUSCANY
Siena
Monte San Savino
Arezzo
Sansepolcro
Castiglion Fiorentino
Cortona
Monte Oliveto Maggiore
San Galgano
Sinalunga
Montefollonico
Lake Trasimeno
Massa Marittima
Montalcino
Pienza
Montepulciano
Chiusi
San Vincenzo
Capraia
Elba
Pianosa
Montecristo
Grosseto
Maremma
Sovana
Orvieto
Lago di Bolsena
Capalbio
Orbetello
Giglio
Monte Argentario
LAZIO
SAN MARINO
Rimini
San Leo
Pesaro
Urbino
Gola di Furlo
Cartoceto
MARCHES
Castelfidardo
Falconara Marittima
Ancona
Monte Conero
Loreto
Montecassiano
Macerata
Gubbio
Perugia
Assisi
Torgiano
Deruta
UMBRIA
Tempietto del Clitunno
Civitella del Lago
Carsulae
Monti Sibillini
Norcia
Piano Grande
San Pietro in Valle
Ascoli Piceno
San Benedetto del Tronto
The Best of Tuscany, Umbria & The Marches

The Best of Tuscany, Umbria and the Marches

Antiquities: Etruscan sites and museums in **Chiusi, Perugia, Volterra, Cortona, Florence** and **Fiesole**, also Romans at **Carsulae**; prehistoric menhirs of **Pontrémoli; Tempietto del Clitunno**.

Beaches: island of **Capraia**, several on **Elba. Monte Conero**, near **Ancona**.

Best-Kept Secrets: Italy's Sword in the Stone, **San Galgano**; Niki de Sant-Phalle's Giardino dei Tarocchi, **Capalbio**; the exquisite tiny city of **Massa Marittima**; ceramic chapels of the **monastery of San Vivaldo**; 18th-century spa of **Bagni di Lucca**; Dark Age abbey of **San Pietro in Valle**; the accordion museum of **Castelfidardo**.

Castles: **San Leo, Castiglion Fiorentino, Prato, Fosdinovo**.

Ceramic towns: **Gubbio, Deruta, Montelupo**.

Festivals: Renaissance theatre and barrel-rolling in **Montepulciano; Siena's** Palio; race of the 'candles' in **Gubbio**; carnival in **Viareggio**; the Quintana, jousting in **Ascoli Piceno**.

Hotels: Villa Scacciapensieri, **Siena**; La Badia, **Orvieto**; Torre di Bellosguardo, **Florence**; Villa le Barone, **Greve**; Umbra, **Assisi**; Locanda dell'Amorosa, **Sinalunga**; Villa Principessa, **Lucca**; Excelsior, **Viareggio**; Castello dei Gargonza, **Monte San Savino**; Le Tre Vaselle, **Torgiano**; Fattoria Vignale, **Radda**; Villa Quiete, **Montecassiano**.

Landscapes: classic Tuscan in **Chianti**, and almost as immaculately elegant in the **Casentino** and **Pratomagno**; the hills **south of Siena**, and the triangle between **Sansepolcro, Cortona** and **Perugia**; the canyon of **Gola di Furlo** south of Urbino on the Marches

Coastal scenery: the **Maremma, Elba** and **Monte Argentario**. Also: **Piano Grande** and the **Monti Sibillini**, and the marbly **Apuan Alps**.

Medieval art and architecture: Pisa, **Siena, Perugia, Florence, Assisi, Lucca, Gubbio**.

Renaissance art and architecture: Besides **Florence**, of course, **Urbino, Siena, San Gimignano, Arezzo, Pienza, Montepulciano, Monte Oliveto Maggiore, Loreto, Orvieto**, and **Perugia**.

Restaurants: Enoteca Pinchiorri, **Florence**; Vissani, **Civitella del Lago**; Sergio, **Pisa**; Fortino, **Ancona**; Enoteca Ombrone, **Grosseto**; Solferino, **Lucca**; L'Oca Bianca, **Viareggio**; La Chiusa, **Montefollonico**; Gambero Rosso, **San Vincenzo**; Taverna del Lupo, **Gubbio**; Dal Francese, **Norcia**; Symposium, **Cartoceto**; Villa Amalia, **Falconara Marittima**.

Part I

GENERAL INFORMATION

Etruscan Reliefs, Chiusi

Before You Go

A little preparation can make your trip many times more enjoyable (or at least less frustrating). Although this book was designed to be especially useful to frequent visitors who are ready to poke into some of Italy's nooks and crannies, it will also get you around the major sights if this is your first trip; check the suggested itineraries (p. 39) and the list of festivals (p. 21) to get some idea of where you want to be and when. There are several tour operators who specialize in holidays to Italy. In the UK Citalia (tel (081) 686 5533 or (071) 434 3844) probably has the widest range. (See also p. 30 for Self-Catering Holidays and p. 19 for Special Interest Holidays). You can pick up free hints, brochures, maps, and information from the Italian National Tourist Offices, at the following addresses; an especially useful booklet to request is the annually updated *Travellers' Handbook*, which has loads of good information and current prices.

UK: 1 Princes Street, London W1R 8AY (tel (071) 408 1254; telex 22402).
Eire: 47 Merrion Square, Dublin 2, Eire (tel (001) 766397; telex 31682).
USA:
630 Fifth Avenue, Suite 1565, New York, NY 10111 (tel (212) 245 4961; telex 236024).
500 N. Michigan Avenue, Chicago, Ill. 60611 (tel (312) 644 0990/1; telex 0255160).
360 Post Street, Suite 801, San Francisco, California 94108 (tel (415) 392 6206; telex 67623).

Canada: Store 56, Plaza 3, Place Ville Marie, Montreal, Quebec (tel (514) 866 7667; telex 525607).

You can pick up more detailed information by writing directly to any of the city or provincial tourist offices. These are usually very helpful in sending out lists of flats, villas, or farmhouses to hire, or at least lists of agents who handle the properties.

For a wide range of maps, try Stanford's 12–14 Long Acre, London WC2E 9LP, tel (071) 836 1321: the green Italian Touring Club map of Tuscany and the combined map of Umbria and the Marches are the most detailed.

Getting to Tuscany and Umbria

By Air

The main international airports serving the region are Pisa and Rome, though others of possible interest include Genoa (for the Lunigiana) and Bologna (just over the Apennines from the Mugello or Casentino); if you're bound for the Marches, connecting flights will whisk you to Ancona or Rimini (just north of Pesaro). Alitalia and British Airways offer direct flights from London to Pisa, Rome, Genoa, or Bologna, and from Manchester to Rome. The real challenge is finding a bargain, especially in the high season (mid-May–mid-September); start hunting around a few months in advance, or if you're a gambler, at the last minute. Most of the cheap flights from London are on cryptic Third World airlines destined for Africa, the Middle East and beyond that stopover in Rome.

From North America the major carriers are Pan Am, TWA, and Air Canada, with flights to Rome or Milan, though British Airways has just begun a new New York–London–Pisa service called the Manhattan Express that departs at 9 pm and has you in Florence by 4 pm the next day. Fares from Canada are often much higher than they are from the states. Also, it's worthwhile checking into budget fares to London (especially if Virgin Atlantic stays around), Brussels, Paris, Frankfurt, or Amsterdam; these routes are more competitive than the Italian ones, and you may save money by either flying or riding the rails to Italy from there.

There are advantages in paying an airline's normal fare, mainly that it does not impose any restrictions on when you go or return; most are valid for a year. To sweeten the deal, Alitalia in particular often has promotional perks like rental cars (Jetdrive), or discounts on domestic flights within Italy, on hotels, or on tours. Ask your travel agent. Children under the age of two travel for 10 per cent of the adult fare on British Airways flights; Alitalia have a nominal charge of £20. Children between 2 and 12 travel for half fare, and bona fide students with proof of age and school attendance between the ages of 12 and 25 receive a 25 per cent discount on British Airways flights, and a 20 per cent discount on Alitalia.

The same carriers listed above have a variety of discounts for those who book in advance or are able to decide their departure and return dates in advance. If you're travelling from Europe, you can save quite a tidy sum by paying for your ticket when you make your reservations (Eurobudget); an extra advantage is that the return date is left open. Travellers from anywhere can save money by swallowing a little alphabet soup—

PEX, APEX, and SUPERPEX, which like Eurobudget require reservations and payment at the same time on return-only flights. PEX (or APEX) fares have fixed arrival and departure dates, and the stay in Italy must include at least one Saturday night; from North America the restrictions are at least a week's stay but not more than 90 days. SUPERPEX, the cheapest normal fares available, have the same requirements as PEX, but must be purchased at least 14 days (or sometimes 21 days in North America) in advance. Disadvantages of PEXing are that there are penalty fees if you change your flight dates. At the time of writing, the lowest APEX return fare between London and Pisa in the off-season is £184; the lowest mid-week SUPERPEX between New York and Rome (via Milan) in the off-season is $685.

Other advantages of taking a regular flight over a charter are an increase in reliability in dates and in punctuality, and you're not out of a wad of cash if you miss your flight. Also, if you live in neither London nor New York, they will often offer big discounts to get you from your home airport to the international one. If you live in the US boondocks, you can dial some '800' numbers to check out prices on your own: Alitalia's number is 800 223 5730.

Both Pisa's Galileo airport and Rome's international airport, Leonardo da Vinci/Fiumicino are now linked to their respective central rail stations by train or bus.

Charter Flights

These aren't as much of a bargain to Italy as they are to other Mediterranean destinations, though they're certainly worth looking into—check ads in the travel section of your newspaper (*Sunday Times* and *Time Out* are especially good) and your travel agent. From London, Pilgrim Air (44 Goodge St, tel (071) 637 5333) has regularly scheduled charters to Milan; from the US, CIEE has regular charters from New York to Rome (tel 800 223 7402). Other charter flights are usually booked by the big holiday companies. To find out about extra seats on these and on commercial flights, visit your local bucket shop (in the USA, call Access (tel 800 333 7280) or Air Hitch for similar services—check listings in the *Sunday New York Times*). Pickings are fairly easy in the off season, and tight in the summer months, but not impossible. You take your chances, but you can save some of your hard-earned dough. The cheapest fare from London to Rome at the time of writing is £120, from New York $610.

The problem with charters is they are delayed more often than not, and since the same plane is usually commuting back and forth it can mean arriving at Rome's charter airport Ciampino at 3 am, which must be one of the lower rings in Dante's *Inferno*. Another disadvantage is you have to accept the given dates, and if you miss your flight (bus and train strikes in Italy do make this a distinct possibility) there's no refund. Most travel agencies, however, offer traveller's insurance that includes at least a partial refund of your charter fare if strikes and illness keep you from the airport.

Students

Besides saving 25 per cent on regular flights, students under 26 have the choice of flying on special discount charters. From the US, CIEE (see above) is a good place to start looking. From Canada, contact Canadian Universities Travel Services, 44 St George St, Toronto, Ontario M55 2E4, tel (416) 979 2406. From London, check out STA Travel, 117 Euston Road, NW1 or 86 Old Brompton Rd, SW7, for telephone enquiries for

European destinations ring (071) 937 9921; WST, 6 Wrights Lane W8, tel (071) 938 4362 or USIT, 52 Grosvenor Gardens, SW1, tel (071) 730 8518.

By Train

From Victoria Station to Florence it's about 23 hours, will set you back around £75 one way second class, £105 first class. These trains require reservations and a couchette and on the whole are a fairly painless way of getting there. Discounts are available for families travelling together, for children—free under age 4 and 40 per cent discount between the ages of 4 and 8. Under 26-ers, students or not, can save up to 40 per cent and over on second-class seats by purchasing Eurotrain tickets available in the UK from any student travel office, many high street travel agents or direct from Eurotrain, tel (071) 730 3402. Eurotrain also has a kiosk at Victoria Station which is open from 8 am to 8 pm seven days a week. Eurotrain tickets are available throughout Europe at student travel offices (CTS in Italy) in main railway stations. Any rail tickets purchased in Britain for Italy are valid for two months and allow any stopovers you care to make on the way.

Rail travel to Italy becomes an even more attractive option if you intend to purchase an Inter-Rail pass (in Europe), or a EurRail pass (from North America). Inter-Rail cards (about £155) are sold by British Rail to people under 26 and offer discounts of over 30 per cent in Britain and 30 or 50 per cent on Channel Ferries, and free rail passage on the Continent, and are valid for a month. Inter-Rail Senior cards offer similar discounts to people over 60. EurRail passes must be purchased before leaving for Europe, and are valid for anywhere from 15 days to 3 months of unlimited first-class travel. These passes are a good deal if you plan to do lots and lots of rail travel and can't be bothered to buy tickets, etc. They seem rather less rosy if your travelling is limited to Italy, where domestic rail tickets are one of the few bargains available. Within Italy itself there are several discount tickets available (see below, travelling within Italy), which you can inquire about at CIT Italian State railways offices before you leave home:

UK: 50 Conduit St, London, W1, tel (071) 434 3844
also at Wasteels Travel, 121 Wilton Rd, London SW1, tel (071) 834 7066 or at any branch of Thomas Cook Ltd
USA: 666 Fifth Ave, New York, NY 10103, tel (212) 223 0230
There's also an 800 number you can call from anywhere: (800) 223 0230
Canada: 2055 Peel St, Suite 102, Montreal, Quebec H3A 1VA, tel (514) 845 9101

By Coach

This is the cheapest way (but just barely, compared with the trains) to get to Italy from London and not too much torture if you get off at Milan, a little worse if you go on to Florence. There are, again, discounts for students, senior citizens, and children. Contact National Express, Victoria Coach Station, London SW1, tel (071) 730 0202 for times and bookings.

By Car

Driving to Italy from the UK is a rather lengthy and expensive proposition, and if you're only staying for a short period figure your costs against Alitalia's or other airlines' fly-drive scheme. Depending on how you cross the Channel, it is a good two-day trip—about 1600 km from Calais to Rome. Ferry information is available from the Continental Car Ferry Centre, 52 Grosvenor Gardens, London SW1. You can cut many of the costly motorway tolls by going from Dover to Calais, through France, to Basle, Switzerland, and then through the Gotthard Tunnel over the Alps; in the summer you can save the steep tunnel tolls by taking one of the passes. You can avoid some of the driving by putting your car on the train (although again balance the sizeable expense against the price of hiring a car for the period of your stay): Express Sleeper Cars run to Milan from Paris or Boulogne, and to Bologna from Boulogne. Services are drastically cut outside the summer months, however. For more information, contact the CIT offices listed above.

To bring your car into Italy, you need your car registration (log book), valid driving licence, and valid insurance (a Green Card is not necessary, but you'll need one if you go through Switzerland). Make sure everything is in excellent working order or your slightly bald tyre may enrich the coffers of the Swiss or Italian police—it's not uncommon to be stopped for no reason and have your car searched until the police find something to stick a fine on. Also beware that spare parts for non-Italian cars are difficult to come by, almost impossible for pre-1988 Japanese models. If you're coming to live in Italy, remember that cars with foreign plates are obliged to leave the country every six months for a hazily defined period of time.

One advantage of driving your own car is that you can save about 10–15 per cent on expensive Italian petrol and motorway tolls by purchasing **Petrol Coupons**, issued to owners of GB-registered vehicles by London's CIT office (see above), at Wasteels Travel, 121 Wilton Rd, London SW1, tel (071) 834 7066, or at your local AA or RAC office (though ring them first to make sure they have the coupons in stock) or at the frontier from Italian Auto Club offices. Coupons are sold only in person to the car-owner with his or her passport and car registration, and cannot be paid for in Italian lire—prices are tagged to current exchange rates, and unused coupons may be refunded on your return. Along with the coupons and motorway vouchers, you get a *Carta Carburante* which entitles you to breakdown services provided by the Italian Auto Club (ACI) (for local offices, see p. 12). At the time of writing motorway tunnel tolls are:

Mont Blanc Tunnel, from Chamonix (France) to Courmayeur: small car or motorcycle L15 000 single, L19 000 return. Medium-sized car (axle distance 2.31–2.63 m) L23 000 single, L29 000 return. Large cars (axle distance 2.64–3.30) or cars with caravans L31 000 single or L38 000 return.

Fréjus Tunnel, from Modane (France) to Bardonécchia: same as above except for large cars or cars with caravans (trailers) L28 000 single, L36 000 return.

Gran San Bernardo, from Bourg St Pierre (Switzerland) to Aosta: small car or motorcycle: L13 500 single, L19 000 return. Medium car L20 000 single, L28 000 return. Large car or car with caravan L27 000 single, L38 000 return.

Traveller's Insurance and Health

You can insure yourself for almost any possible mishap—cancelled flights, stolen or lost baggage, and health. While national health coverage in the UK and Canada takes care of their citizens while travelling, the US doesn't. Check your current policies to see if they cover you while abroad, and under what circumstances, and judge whether you need a special traveller's insurance policy. Travel agencies sell them, as well as insurance companies; they are not cheap.

Minor illnesses and problems that crop up in Italy can usually be handled free of charge in a public hospital clinic or *ambulatorio*. If you need minor aid, Italian pharmacists are highly trained and can probably diagnose your problem; look for a *Farmacia* (they all have a list in the window detailing which ones are open during the night and on holidays). Extreme cases should head for the *Pronto Soccorso* (First Aid services). The emergency number from anywhere in Italy is 113.

Most Italian doctors speak at least rudimentary English, but if you can't find one, contact your embassy or consulate for a list of English-speaking doctors.

What to Pack

You simply cannot overdress in Italy; whatever grand strides Italian designers have made on the international fashion merry-go-round, most of their clothes are purchased domestically, prices be damned. Now whether or not you want to try to keep up with the natives is your own affair and your own heavy suitcase—you may do well to compromise and just bring a couple of smart outfits for big nights out. It's not that the Italians are very formal; they simply like to dress up with a gorgeousness that adorns their cities just as much as those old Renaissance churches and palaces. The few places with dress codes are the major churches and basilicas (no shorts or sleeveless shirts), and some of the smarter restaurants.

After agonizing over fashion, remember to pack small and light: trans-Atlantic airlines limit baggage by size (two pieces are free, up to 62 inches in height and width; in second class you're allowed one of 62 inches and another up to 44 inches). Within Europe limits are by weight: 20 kilos (44 lbs) in second class, 30 kilos (66 lbs) in first. You may well be penalized for anything bigger. If you're travelling mainly by train, you'll especially want to keep bags to a minimum: jamming big suitcases in overhead racks in a crowded compartment isn't much fun for anyone. Never take more than you can carry, but do bring the following: any prescription medicine you need, an extra pair of glasses or contact lenses if you need them, a pocket knife and corkscrew (for picnics), a flashlight (for dark frescoed churches and hotel corridors), a travel alarm (for those early trains) and a pocket Italian-English dictionary (for flirting and other emergencies; outside the main tourist centres you may well have trouble finding someone who speaks English). If you're a light sleeper, you may want to invest in ear plugs. Your electric appliances will work in Italy if you adapt and convert them to run on 220 AC with two round prongs on the plug. Of course, what you bring depends on when and where you go . . .

Climate

The climate in Tuscany, Umbria and the Marches is temperate along the coasts and in the valleys, and considerably cooler up in the mountains; the higher Apennines and Monte Amiata have enough snow to support skis until April. Summers are hot and humid; in August the Florentines, Sienese, and Pisans hand their cities over to the tourist (even the good restaurants tend to close) and seek relief by the sea or in the mountains. Spring days, especially in the month of May, when it rains less, are pleasantly and not insufferably warm, and the fields and gardens are brimming with flowers. Autumn, too, is a classic time to visit, in October and November; before the winter rains begin and the air is clear, the colours of the countryside are brilliant and rare. The hills of Tuscany and Umbria are always beautiful, but in October, they're extraordinary.

Winter can be an agreeable time to visit the indoor attractions of the cities and avoid crowds, particularly in Florence, where it seldom snows but may rain for several days at a time. Umbria is not called the Green Heart of Italy for its arid climate, and it can be hung over with mists for weeks at a time, which depending on how one looks at it, can be terribly romantic or a big bore. The mountains, especially the Apuan Alps along the coast, also get a considerable amount of rain, with 80–120 inches a year.

Average Temperatures in °C (°F)

	January	*April*	*July*	*October*
Ancona	6 (42)	14 (56)	25 (77)	17 (62)
Florence	6 (42)	13 (55)	25 (77)	16 (60)
Livorno	9 (47)	15 (59)	24 (75)	15 (59)
Siena	5 (40)	12 (54)	25 (77)	15 (59)
Perugia	5 (40)	11 (52)	24 (75)	13 (55)
Terni	5 (40)	13 (55)	25 (77)	15 (59)

Average monthly rainfall in millimetres (inches)

	January	*April*	*July*	*October*
Ancona	68 (3)	57 (2)	28 (1)	101 (4)
Florence	61 (3)	74 (3)	23 (1)	96 (4)
Livorno	71 (3)	62 (3)	7 (0)	110 (4)
Siena	70 (3)	61 (3)	21 (1)	112 (4)
Perugia	60 (3)	70 (3)	30 (1)	115 (4)
Terni	68 (3)	85 (3)	43 (2)	123 (5)

Passports and Customs Formalities

To get into Italy you need a valid passport or a British Visitor's Card. Nationals of the UK, Ireland, USA, Canada, and Australia do not need visas for stays up to three months. (However, if you're not an EEC national and mean to reach Italy through France, see if you need to pick up a French transit visa.) If you mean to stay longer than three months in Italy, get a visa from your Italian consulate or face the prospect of having to get a *Visa di Soggiorno* at the end of three months—possible only if you can prove a source of income and are willing to spend a couple of exasperating days at some provincial Questura office filling out forms.

According to Italian law, you must register with the police within three days of your arrival. If you check into a hotel this is done automatically. If you come to grief in the mesh of rules and forms, you can at least get someone to explain it to you in English by calling the Rome Police Office for visitors, tel (06) 4686, ext. 2858.

Italian Customs are usually benign, though how the frontier police manage to recruit such ugly, mean-looking characters to hold the submachine guns and drug-sniffing dogs from such a good-looking population is a mystery, but they'll let you be if you don't look suspicious and haven't brought along more than 150 cigarettes or 75 cigars, or not more than a litre of hard drink or three bottles of wine, a couple of cameras, a movie camera, 10 rolls of film for each, a tape-recorder, radio, phonograph, one canoe less than 5.5 m, sports equipment for personal use, and one TV (though you'll have to pay for a licence for it at Customs). Pets must be accompanied by a bilingual Certificate of Health from your local Veterinary Inspector. You can take the same items listed above home with you without hassle—except of course your British pet. US citizens may return with $400 worth of merchandise—keep your receipts. British subjects are permitted £200 worth of dutiable merchandise.

There are no limits to how much money you bring into Italy: legally you may not transport more than L400 000 in Italian banknotes, though they rarely check.

On Arrival

Money

It's a good idea to bring some Italian lire with you; unforeseen delays and unexpected public holidays may foul up your plans to change at a bank when you arrive. Travellers' cheques or Eurocheques remain the most secure way of financing your holiday in Italy; they are easy to change and insurance against unpleasant surprises. Credit cards (American Express, Diner's Club, Mastercard, Access, Eurocard, Barclaycard, Visa) are usually only accepted in hotels, restaurants, and shops (but never at any petrol stations) frequented by foreign tourists—Italians themselves rarely use them—and it is not unknown for establishments to fiddle with the exchange rates and numbers on your bill once you've left. Use them with discretion.

There's been a lot of loose talk about knocking three noughts off the Italian lira, but it never seems to happen; as it is, everybody can be a 'millionaire'. It is also confusing to the visitor unaccustomed to dealing with rows of zeros, and more than once you'll think you're getting a great deal until you realize you've simply miscounted the zeros on the price tag. Some unscrupulous operators may try to take advantage of the confusion when you're changing money, so do be careful. Notes come in denominations of L100 000, L50 000, L10 000, L5 000, L2 000, and L1 000; coins are in L500, L200, L100, L50, L20, all the way down to the ridiculous and practically worthless aluminium coinage of L10, L5 and L1. Telephone tokens (*gettoni*) may be used as coins as well and are worth L200.

The easiest way to have money sent to you in Italy is for someone from home to get a bank to telex the amount to an Italian bank, and for you to go and pick it up. Technically, it shouldn't take more than a couple of days to arrive, but make sure the telex includes the number of your passport, ID card, or driver's licence, or the Italians may not give you your money. Save all the receipts of your currency exchanges.

Banking hours in Italy are usually 8:30 am–1:20 pm, and one hour in the afternoon (from 3–4 or 4–5 pm). They are closed on Saturdays, Sundays, and national holidays. Some banks are worth visiting for their space capsule doors alone!

Getting Around

The republic has an excellent network of airports, railways, highways, and byways, and you'll find getting around fairly easy—unless one union or another takes it into its head to go on strike (to be fair, this rarely happens during the main holiday season). There's plenty of talk about passing a law to regulate strikes, but don't count on it happening soon. Instead learn how to recognize the word in Italian: *sciopero* (SHOW-per-o) and be prepared to do as the Romans do when you hear it—quiver with resignation. There's always a day or two's notice in advance, and usually strikes last only 12 or 24 hours—but long enough to throw a spanner in the works if you have to catch a plane. Keep your ears open.

By Train

Italy's national railway, the FS (*Ferrovie dello Stato*) is well run, inexpensive (though prices have recently risen, it is still cheap by British standards) and often a pleasure to ride. There are also several private rail lines around cities and in country districts. We have tried to list them all in this book. Some, you may find, won't accept Inter-Rail or EurRail passes. On the FS, some of the trains are sleek and high-tech, but much of the rolling stock hasn't been changed for fifty years. Possible FS unpleasantnesses you may encounter, besides a strike, are delays, crowding (especially at weekends and in the summer), and crime on overnight trains, where someone rifles your bags while you sleep. The crowding, at least, becomes much less of a problem if you reserve a seat in advance at the *Prenotazione* counter. The fee is small and can save you hours standing in some train corridor. On the upper echelon trains, reservations are mandatory. Do check when you purchase your ticket in advance that the date is correct; unlike in some countries, tickets are only valid the day they're purchased unless you specify otherwise. If you're coming back the same way in three days or less, save money with a *ritorno* (a one-way ticket is an *andata*). A number on your reservation slip will indicate in which car your seat is—find it before you board rather than after. The same goes for sleepers and couchettes on overnight trains, which must also be reserved in advance.

Tickets may be purchased not only in the stations, but at many travel agents in the city centres. The system is computerized and runs smoothly, at least until you try to get a reimbursement for an unused ticket (usually not worth the trouble). Be sure you ask which platform (*binario*) your train arrives at; the big permanent boards posted in the stations are not always correct. If you get on a train without a ticket you can buy one from the conductor, with an added 20 per cent penalty. You can also pay a conductor to move up to first class or get a couchette, if there are places available.

There is a fairly straightforward hierarchy of trains. At the bottom of the pyramid is the humble *Locale* (euphemistically known sometimes as an *Accelerato*), which often stops even where there's no station in sight; it can be excruciatingly slow. When you're checking the timetables, beware of what may look like the first train to your destination—if it's a *Locale*, it will be the last to arrive. A *Diretto* stops far less, an *Expresso* just at the main towns. *Rapido* trains whoosh between the big cities and rarely deign to stop. On some of these reservations are necessary, and on some there are only first-class coaches. On all of them, however, you'll be asked to pay a supplement—some 30 per cent more than a regular fare. The real lords of the rails are the TEE (Trans-Europe Express) *Super-Rapido Italiano* trains, kilometre-eaters that will speed you to your destination as fast as trains can go. Italy has three lines all to itself: the *Vesuvio* (Milan, Bologna, Florence, Rome, Naples), the *Adriatico* (Milan, Rimini, Pesaro, Ancona, Pescara, Foggia, Bari), and the *Colosseum/Ambrosiano* (Milan, Bologna, Florence, Rome). For these there is a more costly supplement and only first-class luxury cars. Of course there are others travelling between Italy and northern Europe; ask at any travel agent for details.

The FS offers several passes. One which you should ideally arrange at a CIT office before arriving in Italy, is the 'Travel-at-Will' ticket (*Biglietto turistico libera circolazione*), available only to foreigners. This is a good deal only if you mean to do some very serious train riding on consecutive days; it does, however, allow you to ride the *Rapidos* without paying the supplement. Tickets are sold for 8, 15, 21, or 30-day periods, first or second class, with 50 per cent reduction for children under 12. At the time of writing an eight-day second-class ticket is around £65, first-class £102. A more flexible option is the 'Flexi Card' which allows unlimited travel for either 4 days within a 9-day period (second class £48, first class £70), 8 days within 21 (second class £66, first class £100) or 12 days within 30 (second class £86, first class £128) and you don't have to pay any supplements. Another ticket, the *Kilometrico* gives you 3000 kilometres of travel, made on a maximum of 20 journeys and is valid for two months; one advantage is that it can be used by up to five people at the same time. However, supplements are payable on Intercity trains. Second-class tickets are currently £68, first-class £116. Other discounts, available only once you're in Italy, are 15 per cent on same-day return tickets and three-day returns (depending on the distance involved), and discounts for families of at least four travelling together. Senior citizens (men 65 and over, women 60) can also get a *Carta d'Argento* ('silver card') for L10 000 entitling them to a 30 per cent reduction in fares. For young people under 26 a *Carta Verde* entitles one to a 30 per cent discount (20 per cent in peak season—Easter and Christmas holidays and 25 June to 31 August).

Refreshments on routes of any great distance are provided by bar cars or trolleys; you can usually get sandwiches and coffee from vendors along the tracks at intermediary stops. Station bars often have a good variety of take-away travellers' fare; consider at least investing in a plastic bottle of mineral water, since there's no drinking water on the trains.

Besides trains and bars, Italy's stations offer other facilities. All have a *Deposito*, where you can leave your bags for hours or days for a small fee. The larger ones have porters (who charge L800–1000 per piece) and some even have luggage trolleys; major stations have an *Albergo Diurno* ('Day Hotel', where you can take a shower, get a shave and haircut, etc.), information offices, currency exchanges open at weekends (not at the most advantageous rates, however), hotel-finding and reservation services, kiosks with foreign papers, restaurants, etc. You can also arrange to have a rental car awaiting you at your destination—Avis, Hertz, Eurotrans, and Autoservizi Maggiore are the firms that provide this service.

Beyond that, some words need to be said about riding the rails on the most serendipitous national line in Europe. The FS may have its strikes and delays, its petty crime and bureaucratic inconveniences, but when you catch it on its better side it will treat you to a dose of the real Italy before you even reach your destination. If there's a choice, try for one of the older cars, depressingly grey outside but fitted with comfortably upholstered seats, Art Deco lamps, and old pictures of the towns and villages of the country. The washrooms are invariably clean and pleasant. Best of all, the FS is relatively reliable, and even if there has been some delay, you'll have an amenable station full of clocks to wait in; some of the station bars have astonishingly good food (some do not), but at any of them you may accept a well-brewed *cappuccino* and look blasé until the train comes in. Try to avoid travel on Friday evenings, when the major lines out of the big cities are packed. The FS is an honest crap shoot; you may have a train uncomfortably full of Italians (in which case stand by the doors, or impose on the salesmen and other parasites in first class, where the conductor will be happy to change your ticket). Now and then, you and your beloved will have a beautiful 1920s compartment all to yourselves for the night.

By Coach and Bus

Intercity bus travel is often quicker than train travel, but also a bit more expensive. The Italians aren't dumb; you will find regular bus connections only where there is no train to offer competition. Buses almost always depart from the vicinity of the train station, and tickets usually need to be purchased before you get on. In many regions they are the only means of public transport and are well used, with frequent schedules. If you can't get a ticket before the bus leaves, get on anyway and pretend you can't speak a word of Italian; the worst that can happen is that someone will make you pay for a ticket. Understand clearly that the base for all country bus lines will be the provincial capitals; we've done our best to explain the connections even for the most out-of-the-way routes.

City buses are the traveller's friend. Most cities label routes well; all charge flat fees for rides within the city limits and immediate suburbs, at the time of writing around L1000. Bus tickets must always be purchased before you get on, either at a tobacconist's, a newspaper kiosk, in many bars, or from ticket machines near the main stops. Once you get on, you must 'obliterate' your ticket in the machines in the front or back of the bus; controllers stage random checks to make sure you've punched your ticket. Fines for cheaters are about L20 000, and the odds are about 12 to 1 against a check, so you may take your chances against how lucky you feel. If you're good-hearted, you'll buy a ticket and help some overburdened municipal transit line meet its annual deficit.

By Taxi

Taxis are about the same price as in London. The average meter starts at L2500, and adds L600 per kilometre. There's an extra charge for luggage and for trips to the airport; and rates go up after 10 pm and on holidays.

By Car

The advantages of driving in Tuscany, Umbria, and the Marches generally outweigh the disadvantages. Before you bring your own car or hire one, consider the kind of holiday you're planning. If it's a tour of art cities, you'd be best off not driving at all: parking is impossible, traffic impossible, deciphering one-way streets, signals, and signs impossible. In nearly every other case, however, a car gives you the freedom and possibility of making your way through Italy's lovely countryside.

Be prepared, however, to face the highest fuel costs in Europe (when everyone else lowered theirs with slumping international prices, Italy raised them) and the Italians themselves behind the wheel, many of whom, from 21-year-old madcaps to elderly nuns, drive like idiots, taking particular delight in overtaking at blind curves on mountainous roads. No matter how fast you're going on the *autostrade* (Italy's toll motorways, official speed limit **130 km** per hour) someone will pass you going twice as fast. Americans in particular should be wary about driving in Italy. If you're accustomed to the generally civilized rules of motoring that obtain in North America, Italy will be a big surprise. Italians, and their northern visitors, do not seem to care if someone kills them or not. Especially in the cities, rules do not exist, and if you expect them to stop riding your tail you'll have a long time to wait. Even the most cultured Italians become aggressive, murderous humanoids behind the wheel, and if you value your peace of mind you'll stick with public transportation.

If you aren't intimidated, buy a good road map of Italy or a detailed one of the region you're travelling in (the Italian Touring Club produces excellent ones). If you've purchased petrol coupons (see 'Before you go'), you'll find the petrol stations that accept them put out signs. Many stations close for lunch in the afternoon, and few stay open late at night, though you may find a 'self-service' where you feed a machine nice smooth L10 000 notes. Petrol stations in the cities also sell the Discs you can put on your windscreen to park in the *Zona Disco* areas of a city. Autostrada tolls are high—to drive on the A1 from Milan to Rome will cost you around L40 000. The rest stops and petrol stations along the motorways are open 24 hours. Other roads—*superstrada* on down through the Italian grading system—are free of charge. The Italians are very good about signposting, and roads are almost all excellently maintained—some highways seem to be built of sheer bravura, suspended on cliffs, crossing valleys on enormous piers—feats of engineering that will remind you, more than almost anything else, that this is the land of the ancient Romans. Beware that you may be fined on the spot for speeding, a burnt-out headlamp, etc.; if you're especially unlucky you may be slapped with a *super multa*, a superfine, of L100 000 or more. You may even be fined for not having a portable triangle danger signal (pick one up at the frontier or from an ACI office for L1500).

The Automobile Club of Italy (ACI) is a good friend to the foreign motorist. Besides having bushels of useful information and tips, they offer a free breakdown service, and can be reached from anywhere by dialling 116—also use this number if you have an accident, need an ambulance, or simply have to find the nearest service station. If you need major repairs, the ACI can make sure the prices charged are according to their guidelines; if you have a Fuel Card (given when you purchase petrol coupons) you will, at least in theory if not always in reality, be given a car to use while your car is being repaired.

Italian Touring Club (ACI) addresses

Ancona: Corso Stamira 78, tel (071) 55 335
Arezzo: Viale Luca Signorelli 24a, tel (0575) 23 253
Ascoli Piceno: Viale Indipendenza 38a, tel (0736) 45 920
Florence: Viale Amendola 36, tel (055) 27 861
Grosseto: Via Mazzini 105, tel (0564) 21 071
Livorno: Via Verdi 32, tel (0586) 34 651

Lucca: Via Catalani 1, tel (0583) 582 626
Macerata: Via Roma 139, tel (0733) 31 141
Massa Carrara: Via Europa 9, tel (0585) 42 122
Perugia: Via M. Angeloni 1, tel (075) 71 941
Pesaro: Via S. Francesco 44, tel (0721) 33 368
Pisa: Via S. Martino 1, tel (050) 47 333
Pistoia: Via Racciardetto 2, tel (0573) 32 101
Siena: Viale Vittorio Veneto 47, tel (0577) 49 001
Terni: Viale C. Battisti 121/c, tel (0744) 400 239

Hiring a car is fairly simple if not particularly cheap. Italian car rental firms are called *Autonoleggi*. There are both large international firms through which you can reserve a car in advance, and local agencies, which often have lower prices. Air or train travellers should check out possible discount packages.

Most companies will require a deposit amounting to the estimated cost of the hire, and there is 18 per cent VAT added to the final cost. At the time of writing, a 5-seat Fiat Panda costs around L64 000 a day. Petrol is generally twice as expensive as in the UK. Rates become more advantageous if you take the car for a week with unlimited mileage. If you need a car for more than three weeks, leasing is a more economic alternative. The National Tourist Office has a list of firms in Italy that hire caravans (trailers) and campers.

By Motorbike or Bicycle

The means of transport of choice for many Italians, motorbikes, mopeds, and Vespas can be a delightful way to see the country. You should only consider it, however, if you've ridden them before—Italy's hills and aggravating traffic make it no place to learn. Italians are keen cyclists as well, racing drivers up the steepest hills; if you're not training for the Tour de France, consider the region's mountains and hills well before planning a bicycling tour—especially in the hot summer months. Bikes can be transported by train in Italy, either with you or within a couple of days—apply at the baggage office (*ufficio bagagli*). Renting either a motorbike or bicycle for long excursions is difficult though the main bike-rental shop in Florence, Ciao e Basta, tel (055) 263 985, offers cycling tours of Tuscany in 9 days in 50-km stages. Depending on how long you're staying, you may find it sensible (especially if you're coming from North America) to buy a second-hand bike in Italy when you arrive, either in a bike shop or through the classified ad papers put out in nearly every city and region. Alternatively, if you bring your own bike, do check the airlines to see what their policies are on transporting them.

Post Offices

The postal service in Italy is both the least efficient and the most expensive in Europe, and disgracefully slow; if you're sending postcards back home you can count on arriving there before they do. If it's important that it arrive in a week or so, send your letter *Espresso* (Swift Air Mail) or *Raccomandata* (registered delivery), for a L2000 supplement fee. Stamps (*francobolli*) may also be purchased at tobacconists (look for a big black T on the sign), but you're bound to get differing opinions on your exact postage. Mail to the

UK goes at the same rate as domestic Italian mail, but it's still twice as much to send a letter from Italy to Britain as vice versa. Air-mail letters to and from North America quite often take three or four weeks. This can be a nightmare if you're making hotel reservations and are sending a deposit—telex or telephoning ahead is far more secure if time is short.

Ask for mail to be sent to you in Italy either care of your hotel or addressed *Fermo Posta* (poste restante: general delivery) to a post office, or, if you're a card-holder, to an American Express Office. When you pick up your mail at the *Fermo Posta* window, bring your passport for identification. Make sure, in large cities, that your mail is sent to the proper post office; the **Posta Centrale** is often the easiest option.

The Italian postal code is most inscrutable in dealing with packages sent overseas. Packages have to be of a certain size, under a certain weight to be sent in certain ways, and must have a flap open for inspection or be sealed with string and lead. You're best off taking it to a stationer's shop (*cartolibreria*) and paying L800 for them to wrap it—they usually know what the postal people are going to require.

Telegrams (sent from post offices) are expensive but the surest way to get your message out of Italy. You can save money by sending it as a night letter (22 words or less).

Telephones

Like many things in Italy, telephoning can be unduly complicated and usually costs over the odds to boot. In many places you'll still find the old token *gettoni* telephones, in which you must insert a token (or better yet, several) before dialling. *Gettoni* cost L200 and are often available in machines next to the telephones, or from bars, news-stands, or *tabacchi*. If more *gettoni* are required while you are speaking, you'll hear a beep, which means put in more *gettoni* quickly or you'll be cut off. For long-distance calls (anyone in Italy with a different telephone code), put in as many as the telephone will take (about 10) and be ready to feed in more as you go along. Any unused *gettoni* will be refunded after your call if you push the return button. Other public phones will take either coins or *gettoni*.

For international calls, head either for a telephone office with booths (usually only in the larger cities and major train stations, operated by either SIP or ASST) or a bar with a telephone meter. If you want to reverse charges (call collect) you must do it from an office (tell them you want to telephone '*a erre*' and fill out the little card). Rates are lower if you call at a weekend (after 2:30 pm on Saturday until 8 am Monday morning—unfortunately just when many provincial telephone offices are closed). Phoning long-distance from your hotel can mean big surcharges.

Direct-dial codes are: USA and Canada 001, UK 0044 (leaving out the '0' before the British area code). If you're calling Italy from abroad, the country code is 39, followed by the area prefix—omitting the first '0'.

Official Holidays

The Italians have cut down somewhat on their official national holidays, but note that every town has one or two local holidays of its own—usually the feast day of its patron saint. Official holidays, on timetables for transportation and museum opening hours, etc. are treated the same as Sundays.

1 January (New Year's Day—*Capodanno*)
6 January (Epiphany, better known to Italians as the day of *La Beffana*—a kindly witch who brings the bambini the toys Santa Claus or *Babbo Natale* somehow forgot)
Easter Monday (usually pretty dull)
25 April (Liberation Day—even duller)
1 May (Labour Day—lots of parades, speeches, picnics, music and drinking)
15 August (Assumption, or *Ferragosto*—the biggest of them all—woe to the innocent traveller on the road or train!)
1 November (All Saints, or *Tutti Santi*—liveliest at the cemeteries)
8 December (Immaculate Conception of the Virgin Mary—a dull one)
Christmas and Boxing Day (*Santo Stefano*)

Opening Hours and Museums

Although it's beginning to change in the cities, most of Tuscany, Umbria, and the Marches closes down at 1 pm until 3 or 4 pm to eat and properly digest the main meal of the day. Afternoon hours are from 4–7, often from 5–8 in the hot summer months. Bars are often the only places open during the early afternoon. Shops of all kinds are usually closed on Saturday afternoons, Sunday, and Monday mornings as well—although grocery stores and supermarkets do open on Monday mornings (for bank opening hours see p. 8).

Churches have always been a prime target for art thieves and as a consequence are usually locked when there isn't a sacristan or caretaker to keep an eye on things. All churches, except for the really important cathedrals and basilicas, close in the afternoon at the same hours as the shops, and the little ones tend to stay closed. Always have a pocketful of L100 coins to batten the light machines in churches, or what you came to see is bound to be hidden in ecclesiastical shadows. Don't do your visiting during services, and don't come to see paintings and statues in churches the week preceding Easter—you will probably find them covered with mourning shrouds.

Many of Italy's museums are magnificent, many are run with shameful neglect, and many have been closed for years for 'restoration' with slim prospects of re-opening in the near future. With an estimated one work of art per inhabitant, Italy has a hard time financing the preservation of its national heritage; in the big cities you would do well to inquire at the tourist office to find out exactly what is open and what is 'temporarily' closed before setting out on a wild goose chase across town.

We have listed the hours of the important sights and museums. In general, Monday and Sunday afternoons are dead periods for the sightseer—you may want to make these your travelling day. Places without hours usually open on request—but it is best to go before 1 pm. We have also designated which attractions charge admission; unless labelled 'expensive' you'll have to pay between L500 and L3500 to get in. Expensive ones are more—up to L5000 for the Uffizi and other purveyors of big league culture. Citizens of Common Market countries under 18 and over 60 get in free.

Embassies and Consulates

If you're staying in Tuscany or the Marches, use the consulate in Florence; in Umbria, the one in Rome.

UK
Rome: Via XX Settembre 80a, tel (06) 475 5441
Florence: Lungarno Corsini 2, tel (055) 284 133

Ireland
Rome: Largo Nazareno 3, tel (06) 678 2541

USA
Rome: Via Vittorio Veneto 121, tel (06) 4674
Florence: Lungarno Amerigo Vespucci 46, tel (055) 298 276

Canada
Rome: Via Zara 30, tel (06) 854 825

Police Business

There is a fair amount of petty crime in the cities—purse snatchings, pickpocketing, minor thievery of the white collar kind (always check your change) and car break-ins and theft—but violent crime is rare. Nearly all mishaps can be avoided with adequate precautions. Scooter-borne purse-snatchers can be foiled if you stay on the inside of the pavement and keep a firm hold on your property; pickpockets most often strike in crowded street cars and gatherings; don't carry too much cash or keep some of it in another place. Be extra careful in train stations, don't leave valuables in hotel rooms, and always park your car in garages, guarded lots, or on well-lit streets, with temptations like radios, cassettes, etc., out of sight. Purchasing small quantities of reefer, hashish, cocaine, and LSD is legal although what a small quantity might be exactly is unspecified, so if the police don't like you to begin with, it will probably be enough to get you into big trouble.

Once the scourge of Italy, political terrorism has declined drastically in recent years, mainly thanks to special squads of the *Carabinieri*, the black-uniformed national police, technically part of the Italian army. Local matters are usually in the hands of the *Polizia Urbana*; the nattily dressed *Vigili Urbani* concern themselves with directing traffic and handing out parking fines. If you need to summon any of them, dial 113.

Photography

Film and developing are much more expensive than they are in the US or UK. You are not allowed to take pictures in most museums and in some churches. Most cities now offer one-hour processing if you need your pics in a hurry.

Lavatories

Frequent travellers have noted a steady improvement over the years in the cleanliness of Italy's public conveniences, although as ever you will only find them in places like train and bus stations and bars. Ask for the *bagno*, *toilette*, or *gabinetto*; in stations and the smarter bars and cafés, there are washroom attendants who expect a few hundred lire for keeping the place decent. You'll probably have to ask them for paper (*carta*). Don't confuse the Italian plurals: *Signori* (gents), *Signore* (ladies).

Women and Children

Italian men, with the heritage of Casanova, Don Giovanni, and Rudolph Valentino as their birthright, are very confident in their role as great Latin lovers, but the old horror stories of gangs following the innocent tourist maiden and pinching her behind are out of date. Most Italian men, especially in Tuscany and Umbria, are exquisitely polite and flirt on a much more sophisticated level. Still, women travelling alone may frequently receive undesired company, 'assistance', or whatever, from local swains (usually of the balding, middle-age-crisis variety): a firm 'no!' or '*Vai via!*' (Scram!), repeated as often as necessary, will generally solve the problem, which can be greatly reduced if you avoid lonely streets and train stations after dark. Travelling with a companion of either sex will buffer you considerably against such nuisances.

Even though a declining birthrate and the legalization of abortion may hint otherwise, children are still the royalty of Italy, and are pampered, often obscenely spoiled, probably more fashionably dressed than you are, and never allowed to get dirty. Yet most of them somehow manage to be well-mannered little charmers. If you're bringing your own *bambini* to Italy, they'll receive a warm welcome everywhere. Many hotels offer advantageous rates for children and have play areas, and most of the larger cities have permanent **Luna Parks**, or fun fairs. Other activities young children enjoy (besides the endless quantities of pizza, spaghetti, and ice cream) are the **Bomarzo Monster Park** in northern Lazio not far from the Umbrian border, **Pinocchio Park** in Collodi, near Pisa, **Città della Domenica** in Perugia, the **Pistoia Zoo**, the Nature Park in Cavriglia in the Valdarno. If a **circus** visits the town you're in, you're in for a treat; it will either be a sparkling showcase of daredevil skill or a poignant, family-run, modern version of Fellini's *La Strada*.

Sports and Activities

Tuscany, Umbria and the Marches offer quite a few recreational opportunities. The **sailing** is beautiful among the coves of the Tuscan archipelago and around the Argentario; if you want to learn how, there's a sailing school in Torre del Lago Puccini, tel (0584) 342 084. You can bring your boat to Italy for six months without any paperwork if you bring it by car; if you arrive by sea you must report to the Port Authority of your first port to show passports and receive your '*Constituto*' which identifies you and allows you to purchase fuel tax free. Boats with engines require a number plate, and if they're over 3 horsepower you need insurance. If you want to leave your boat in Italy for an extended period, you must have a Navigation Licence; after a year you have to start paying taxes on it. All yachts must pay a daily berthing fee in Italian ports. The National Tourist office has a list of ports that charter yachts in Tuscan ports.

The best (i.e. cleanest) **swimming** is to be found on the islands, especially on the beaches that look away from the mainland.

Rowing is the big sport at Umbria's Lake Piediluco, site of an international championship; when there's enough water, you can try your skills in the Arno (see Florence). There is also the annual rowing race between the four Old Maritime Republics of Venice, Amalfi, Genoa and Pisa, which alternates between the cities. Pisa will next host the race in 1991.

Riding is increasingly popular, and AGRITURIST (see Where to Stay, below) has a number of villa and riding holidays on offer in Tuscany. The National Association of Equestrian Tourism (ANTE) is probably more active here than anywhere in Italy, and stables are beginning to open up in Umbria as well; the region's riding centre is at Corciano, near Lake Trasimeno, with day and longer excursions available. For more information, write directly to the local Agriturist office. There are **race and trotting courses** in Florence and Montecatini Terme, but the real excitement takes place at the two annual *palios* in Siena and the one in Pesaro.

Other **ancient sports** are still popular, and not entirely as a tourist attraction; the rivalries between neighbourhoods and cities are intense. The Florentines play three games of Renaissance football a year (*calcio in costume*); Sansepolcro and Gubbio stage two crossbow matches a year against each other, while in Lucca the archers compete from different city quarters. Arezzo, Narni, Foligno, Pistoia and Ascoli Piceno have annual jousts; in Pisa it's medieval tug-of-war.

Hiking and signed trails are also far more developed in Tuscany; April–October is the best and safest time to go. There are several scenic routes through the mountains: the 4-day High Trail of the Apuan Alps, beginning from the Rifugio Carrara, above Carrara (for information tel (0585) 317 110, or the Italian Alpine Club (CAI) in Carrara, Via Giorgio, tel (0585) 76 782). A second trail, the Grand Apennine Excursion from Lake Scaffaiolo, goes along the mountain ridge that separates Tuscany from Emilia-Romagna, departing from Pracchia (tel (0573) 630 790 for information). There's a circular trail through the Garfagnana, starting from Castelnuovo di Garfagnana; contact the Comunità Montana Garfagnana, tel (0583) 63 306. In southern Tuscany, trails cover Monte Amiata from Abbadia San Salvatore (Comunità Montana dell'Amiata, tel (0564) 967 064). Other fine day trails are in the Casentino, from Badia Prataglia or Stia, or in the Nature Parks of Monti dell'Uccellina from Alberese or the Maremma. In Florence, you can get information from La Roncola, Via del Campuccio 98, tel (055) 229 8298. In Umbria, the local CAI offices can suggest routes: in Perugia, at Via della Gabbiaia 9; in Spoleto, Via Pianciani 4; in Terni, Via Roma 96.

Giglio and the other small islands, and the coastal parks near Argentario, are great places to go **bird watching**; ecologically hyper-aware Giglio offers nature appreciation and sketching classes for those who speak Italian, tel 809 034.

There are **golf courses** in Florence, Montecatini Terme, Punta Ala, Tirrenia, Orbetello, Portoferraio, and in Umbria, one near Lake Trasimeno at Ellera.

Tennis courts are nearly everywhere; each *comune* has at least one or two.

Gliding and **hang gliding** are big in Umbria, where the hills provide the proper updraughts; the centre for the sport is at Sigillo, near Gualdo Tadino, tel (015) 530 8703; the little airports at Foligno, tel (0742) 670 201, and Perugia, S. Egidio, tel (075) 692 9445, also offer gliding.

Potholers (Spelunkers) can find Tuscan caves to explore around Montecatini Alta, Monsummano, and Sarteano. Monte Cucco near Gualdo Tadino has the most important caves in Umbria; the Centro Nazionale di Speleologia Monte Cucco is in Costacciaro, tel (075) 917 0236.

Tuscany has major **ski resorts** at Abetone, north of Pistoia, and at Monte Amiata. In Umbria there's skiing in the Monti Sibillini, along the border of the Marches; many people also head south of the border into Lazio to the big ski complex at Terminillo, east of Rieti.

The most controversial sport in Italy is **hunting**, pitting avid enthusiasts against a burgeoning number of environmentalists who stage protests. The Apennines, especially in Umbria, are boar territory, and in autumn the woods are full of hunters. Pathetically tiny birds, as well as ducks and pigeons, are the other principal game.

Fishing in the sea is possible from the shore, boats, or under water (but not with an aqualung) without a permit, though it may not be especially fruitful; the Tyrhennian has been so thoroughly fished commercially that the government has begun to declare two- and three-month moratoria on all fishing to give the fish a break. Manmade lakes and streams are well stocked, however, and if you're more interested in the fresh fish than the sport, there are trout farms (especially in Umbria) where you can almost pick the fish out of the water with your hands. To fish in fresh water you need to purchase a year's membership card for L5000 from the Federazione Italiana della Pesca Sportiva which has an office in every province and can inform you about local conditions and restrictions. Bait and equipment are readily available.

Courses for Foreigners and Special Holidays

The Italian Institute, 39 Belgrave Square, London SW1X 8NX, tel (071) 235 1461 or 686 Park Avenue, New York, NY 10021, tel (212) 397 9300 is the main source of information on courses for foreigners in Italy. Graduate students should also contact their nearest Italian consulate to find out about scholarships—apparently many go unused each year because no one knows about them.

You can combine a stay in Tuscany, Umbria or the Marches with a course. One obvious choice, especially in this linguistically pure land of Dante, is **Italian language and culture**: there are special summer classes offered by the Scuola Lingua e Cultura per Stranieri of the University of Siena and the Università per Stranieri in Perugia, with special classes in August for teachers of Italian. Similar courses are held in Cortona, Viareggio (run by the University of Pisa), Urbino (at the University of Urbino, Via Saffi 2, Urbino), and, not surprisingly, Florence—sometimes there seem to be more American students than Florentines in the city; the following have courses all year round: the British Institute in Florence, Piazza Lanfredini, Lungarno Giucciardini 9, organizes language and cultural courses; the Centro di Cultura per Stranieri, Via Bolognese 52, offers history, literature, and art on both basic and advanced levels; the Scuola Lorenzo de' Medici has classes in language and art; the Centro Linguistico Italiano Dante Aligheri, Via de' Bardi 12, specializes in language courses.

Music courses complement the regions' numerous music festivals: in the summer Florence's Villa Schifanoia holds master classes for instrumentalists and singers; Certaldo's medieval music society, Ars Nova, sponsors a seminar in July. Siena's Accademia Musicale Chigiana, Via di Città offers master classes for instrumentalists and conductors; in July and August Barga holds an International Opera workshop.

Art lovers can take a course on medieval art in Spoleto in April, held by the Centro Italiano Studi di Alto Medioevo, in the Palazzo Ancaiani. Florence's Università Internazionale dell'Arte, in the Villa Tornabuoni, Via Incontri 3, offers courses October–April in history of art, restoration, and design, while the Istituto per l'Arte e il Restauro, in

Palazzo Spinelli, Borgo Santa Croce 10, holds workshops in art restoration. Perugia's Accademia delle Belle Arti Pietro Vanucci (Piazza San Francesco al Prato 5) offers painting and sculpture courses.

Special interest holidays and tours are increasingly popular. Agencies that offer them are:

UK

Across Trust (handicapped tours of Florence), Crown House, Morden, Surrey, tel (081) 540 3897

Alternative Travel Group (riding and walking holidays in Tuscany, walking holidays in Assisi), 3 George St, Oxford, tel (0865) 251 195

Art in Europe (art and architecture, wine and gastronomy tours in Tuscany), 78 Shaftesbury Way, Twickenham, Middx, tel (081) 898 9888

C.H.A. (Tuscan art tours), Birch Heys, Cromwell Range, Manchester, tel (061) 225 1000

Citalia (art tours in Tuscany and Umbria), Marco Polo House, 3–5 Lansdowne Rd, Croydon, Surrey, tel (081) 686 5533

Enterprise Holidays (singles holidays at Viareggio), Groundstar House, London Road, Crawley, tel (0293) 517 866

Inter-Church (Assisi, Florence, and Siena), 45 Berkeley St, London W1, tel (071) 734 0942

Island Sailing (flotilla holidays on Elba), The Post House, Port Solent, Portsmouth, Hants, tel (0705) 210 345

Italviaggi (walking and riding holidays in Tuscany) High Street, Gillingham, Dorset, tel (0747) 825 353

J.M.B. Travel Consultants (special events in Macerata, and Pesaro) Rushwick, Worcester, tel (0905) 425 628

Lirica-Pegasus Holidays (events in Macerata and Pesaro), 24A Earls Court Gardens, London SW5, tel (0273) 304 910

Magic of Italy (Umbria art tours, honeymoon holidays) 47 Shepherds Bush Green, London W12, tel (081) 743 9555

Magnum (senior citizens in Florence), 7 Westleigh Park, Blaby, Leicester, tel (0533) 777 123

Marina Holidays (riding tours at Montevarchi), 38 Endless St, Salisbury, Wilts, tel (0722) 332 121

Mosaic Elite (art in Urbino, Loreto, and Ancona), 73 South Audley St, London W1, tel (071) 493 3380

Nadfas (National Association of Decorative and Fine Arts Societies) (art tours of Florence, Tuscany, Pesaro, Urbino), Hermes House, 80–98 Beckenham Rd, Beckenham, Kent, tel (081) 658 2308, for members only

Prospect Art Tours (Florence and Umbria), 10 Barley Mow Passage, Chiswick, London, W4, tel (081) 995 2163

Quo Vadis (special events like Spoleto festival, Maggio Musicale in Florence, the Balestra in Gubbio and Sansepolcro, and the Palio in Siena), 243 Euston Road, London NW1, tel (071) 387 6122

Ramblers (walking tours in Siena and Perugia), Box 43, Welwyn Garden City, Herts, tel (0707) 331 133
SJA (art in Florence, Pisa, and Siena), 48 Cavendish Rd, London SW12, tel (071) 673 4849
Specialtours (Tuscan wine tours and art in Urbino), 2 Chester Row, London SW1, tel (071) 730 2297
Spes (Pilgrimages to Assisi, Siena, and Florence), Spes House, 18 Churton St, London SW1, tel (071) 821 5144
Voyages Jules Verne (painting holidays in Gubbio), 21 Dorset Square, London NW1, tel (071) 724 6624
Waymark (walking tours of San Gimignano and Tuscany), 295 Lillie Rd, London SW6, tel (071) 385 5015
World Wine Tours (Tuscan wine tours), 4 Dorchester Rd, Drayton St Leonard, Oxfordshire, tel (0865) 891 919

USA
Archaeological Tours, Inc. does tours of Etruscan sites in Tuscany and Umbria (30 East 42nd St, Suite 1202, New York, NY, tel (212) 986 3054)
NRCSA arranges language courses in Florence and Siena (823 North 22nd St, Milwaukee, WI, 53203, tel (414) 278 0631)
Abercrombie & Kent organizes walking tours of Tuscany (1420 Kensington Rd, Oak Brook, IL, 60521, tel (312) 954 2944)
Bicycle Italy offers a 'luxury bicycle tour' of Florence, Chianti, and Siena (2104 Glenarm Place, Denver, CO, 80205, tel (303) 296 6972)
The Bombard Society organizes balloon flights that take in Florence, Siena, San Gimignano, and Monte Oliveto Maggiore (6727 Curran St, McLean, VA, 22101, tel (703) 448 9407)
Travel Concepts, Inc. does an Italian and Tuscan cooking course at the Badia a Coltibuono (373 Commonwealth Ave, Suite 601, Boston, MA, 02115, tel (617) 536 1800
University Vacations offers a cultural programme for adult Americans in Cambridge and Florence (9602 NW 13th St, Miami, FL, 33172, tel (305) 591 1736)

Festivals

Although festivals in Tuscany, Umbria and the Marches are often more show than spirit (though there are several exceptions to the rule), they can add a note of pageantry or culture to your holiday. Some are great costume affairs, with roots dating back to the Middle Ages, and there are quite a few music festivals, antique fairs, and most of all, festivals devoted to food and drink. The following is a calendar of the major events.

January

1	Feast of the Gift, the mayor's donation of gold, frankincense, and myrhh at **Castiglione di Garfagnana**
24	Feast of San Feliciano, with a traditional fair, **Foligno**

27	Feast of Sant'Emiliano, with a procession of lights, **Trevi** (Perugia)
February	
	Carnival is celebrated in private parties nearly everywhere, and in **Viareggio** there's an enormous public one, with huge satirical floats, music, and parades. **Fano**, on the Adriatic, has a contemporary carnival with music, dancing, costume parades, etc., while more traditional Carnival celebrations take place in **Ascoli Piceno**. In **Bibbiena**, last day of Carnival is celebrated with a grand dance called the *Bello Ballo* and a huge bonfire, the *Bello Pomo*
5	Procession of Sant'Agata, **San Marino**, celebration of independence regained in 1740 after occupation began by Cardinal Alberoni.
	Olive and Bruschetta festival, **Spello** with a parade of olive pickers and garlic toast feast, all to traditional music
14	St Valentine's Day, with a fair, music, and fireworks, **Terni**
mid-Feb	Dog show and 'dog love' products trade fair, **Ancona**
March	
19	**Greve in Chianti** Pancake festival
	San Giuseppe, **Siena** (with rice fritters) and **Torrito di Siena**, with a donkey race and tournament
End of March-beginning April	International Assembly of Church Choirs, **Loreto**
April	
2	Palio of the Golden Frog, **Fermignano** (Pesaro), race, flag tossing, and parade in costume.
First 3 weeks	Huge Antiques Fair, **Todi**
Holy Week	Religious rites, torchlight processions, etc. in **Assisi**
Holy Thursday	Trial of Jesus and re-enactment of Passion of Christ on Good Friday, **Sigillo** (Perugia).
Good Friday	Way of the Cross candlelight procession, **Gràssina**, near Florence
	Evening procession of the Dead Christ, a 13th-century tradition accompanied by a haunting ancient penitential chant, **Gubbio**
	Procession of the Dead Christ, dating from the 16th century, in **Bevania** (Perugia)
Easter	Easter morning, *Scoppio del Carro*, expulsion of the cart in **Florence**
	Exposition of Mary's girdle from Donatello's pulpit, **Prato**
10	Liberty Festival, **Lucca**, honouring the former Republic of Lucca with a special mass, costumes, etc.

1st Sunday after Easter	National Kite Festival, **San Miniato**
2nd Sunday after Easter	Donkey Palio, in **Querceta** (Lucca)
30	*Cantamaggio*, parade of illuminated floats, **Terni**
30–5 May	Feast of San Pelligrino **Gualdo Tadino** (Perugia)
End of April–May	*Calendimaggio*, in **Assisi**; *Corso dell'Anello*, medieval Ring Tournament in **Narni**
April–June	Music festival, **Lucca**

May

All month	Iris Festivals, **Florence, San Polo Robbiana** (Chianti)
15	*Festa dei Ceri*, race of tower shrines in **Gubbio**
	Giostro della Quintana, medieval joust in **Foligno**
17–21	
Third week	Historical parade and crossbow tournament, **Massa Marittima**
	Sword derring do and Palio at **Camerino** (Macerata)
Ascension Day	Cricket Festival, with floats, and crickets sold in little cages, **Florence**
Last Sunday	Crossbow competition against Sansepolcro, in medieval costume, in **Gubbio**; Crossbow competition at **Montespertoli**, wine festival and cart processions
Pentecost (Whitsuntide)	Festival of the Piceni, celebrating the history of the Marches, at **Monterubbiano** (Ascoli Piceno)
May and June	*Maggio Musicale Fiorentino*, in **Florence**

June

Beginning of June	*Corpus Domini*, processions in **Orvieto**; flower carpets in the streets of **Spello**; procession on sawdust designs in the streets at **Camaiore** (Lucca); *Palio dei micci*, donkey race and historical re-enactments at **Querceta** (Lucca)
Mid-June–August	*Estate Fiesolana*—music, cinema, ballet, and theatre, in **Fiesole**
First Sunday	**Montecatini Terme**, garlic toast (*bruschetta*) festival
16–17	*Festa di San Ranieri*—lights festival and historic regatta in **Pisa**
18	*Festa del Barbarossa*, celebrating the meeting of the pope and emperor, with ballet, archery, snails, beans, and *pici* at **S. Quirico d'Orcia**
3 weekends	*Calcio in Costume*, Renaissance football game, in **Florence**
24	St John the Baptist's Day, with fireworks, in **Florence**
25	*Giocco del Ponte*, a traditional bridge tug-of-war game with a cart in the middle, **Pisa**

Last Sunday	**S. Donato in Poggio** (Florence province), *La Bruscellata*, a week of dancing, old love songs around a flowering tree
June–July	Festival of the Two Worlds, **Spoleto**
July	
Throughout month	**Perugia and Terni**, Umbria Jazz Festival
1	Versilian Historical Trophy, with a flag-throwing contest, **Querceta** (Lucca)
1–15	**Camaiore** (Lucca), Lyric season
2	*Palio*, in **Siena**
2nd Sunday	16th-century archery contest in **Fivizzano** (Massa) between court and country archers
3rd Sunday	Feast of San Paolino, **Lucca**, torchlight parade and crossbow contest
25	Joust of the Bear, a tournament dating back to the 1300s, **Pistoia**
Last week	Elban Wine Festival, **Le Ghiaie**
July–August	**S. Gimignano** concert and theatre festival
	Opera, ballet, and concerts at the Sferisterio, at **Macerata**
August	
All month	Outdoor Opera festival, **Torre del Lago Puccini**
	Folkloric and religious festivals, **Assisi**
August–September	Chamber music festival, **Città di Castello**
First weekend	*Torneo della Quintana*, a 15th-century pageant and joust in **Ascoli Piceno**
	Traditional thanksgiving festival in honour of S. Sisto, **Pisa**
2nd weekend	Battle for the Pail, **Sant'Elpidio a Mare** (Ascoli Piceno), four teams in medieval costume try to throw ball in well and keep others from doing so.
2nd Sunday	Regatta, **Porto Santo Stefano**; *Bruscello* stories, food and wine, in **Montepulciano**
	Crossbow tournament, **Massa Marittima**
14	*Palio dei quartieri*, flag tossing and crossbow contest, **Gubbio**
15	Beefsteak Festival, **Cortona**
	Palio dell'Assunta, at **Fermo** (Asoli Piceno), re-enactment of historical event of 1182, with a horse race
	Festa della Palombella, with a horse race, **Orvieto**
16	*Palio*, dating from 1147, in **Siena**
17	*Palio Marinaro*, neighbourhood boat races, in **Livorno**
15–30	International choir contest, **Arezzo**
Mid-Aug–Sept	Rossini Opera Festival, big name performers come to sing Rossini and much more at **Pesaro**
September	
First Sunday	**Arezzo**, Joust of the Saracen; **Cerreto Guidi**, *Palio dei Cerri* competition between neighbourhood groups and Renaissance processions; **Florence**, lantern festival

2nd Sunday	*Giostra della Quintana*, jousts in **Foligno**; crossbow contest with Gubbio in **Sansepolcro**; eating and dancing in **Greve in Chianti**
13	Holy Procession in honour of the *Volto Santo* by torchlight in **Lucca**
3rd Sunday	**Impruneta** wine festival; **Carmignano**, donkey race
22–24	Festival of the Portals, re-enactment in costume of historical events, **Gualdo Tadino** (Perugia)
Last week	*Sagra Musicale Umbra*, in **Perugia**

October

1	*Palio dei terzieri*, historical parade and cart race, **Trevi** (Perugia)
3–4	Feast of San Francesco, religious and civic rites in honour of Italy's patron saint, **Assisi**
	Wine festivals
Third week	National Esoterica Salon, **Ancona**

November

1–5	All Souls' Fair, **Perugia**
11	San Martino, with wine and chestnuts, **Sigillo** (Perugia)
22	Santa Cecilia, patroness of music, celebrated with concerts in **Siena**
24	Offering of candles, with processions in 14th-century costume, **Amelia** (near Terni)

December

8	Fair of the Immaculate Conception, **Bagni di Lucca**
9–10	Festa della Venuta, **Loreto**, celebrating the airborne arrival of the Holy House, with bonfires and religious ceremonies, and a procession of aviators bearing statue of the Madonna di Loreto, their patron saint.
13	Santa Lucia, celebrated with a pottery fair in **Siena**
24	Christmas cribs and Franciscan rites in **Assisi**; evergreen bonfire at **Camporgiano** (Lucca)
25–26	Display of the holy girdle and St Stephen's feast, **Prato**
	Exhibition

Shopping

'Made in Italy' of late has become a byword for style and quality, especially in fashion and leather, but also in home design, ceramics, kitchenware, jewellery, lace and linens, glassware and crystal, chocolates, hats, straw work, art books, engravings, handmade stationery, gold and silverware, a hundred kinds of liqueurs, wine, aperitifs, coffee machines, gastronomic specialities, antique reproductions, as well as the antiques themselves. If you are looking for the latter and are spending a lot of money, be sure to demand a certificate of authenticity—reproductions can be very, very good. To get your antique or modern art purchases home, you will have to apply to the Export Department of the Italian Ministry of Education—a possible hassle. You will have to pay an export tax as well; your seller should know the details.

Florence, which increasingly resembles a glittering medieval shopping mall, has the best variety of goods in the region. There are major monthly antique fairs in Arezzo (first Sunday), Gubbio and Pistoia (second Sunday), Lucca (third Sunday), and Florence (last Sunday). Ceramics are an old tradition in Montelupo, Gubbio, and Deruta; porcelain in Sesto Fiorentino; glassware in Empoli. Volterra is famous for its alabaster and alabaster art; Castelfidardo for its accordions; in Elba you can buy semi-precious stones and minerals, in the Mugello and Casentino wrought iron and copperware, straw goods in the lower Valdarno, and marble in Carrara, though taking it home may pose a bit of a problem. Wine and olive oil, bags of *porcini* mushrooms, jars of truffles, and other 'gastronomic' specialities are available everywhere.

Italy doesn't like department stores, but there are a few chains—*COIN* stores often have good buys on almost the latest fashions. *Standa* and *UPIM* are more like Woolworth's; they have a reasonable selection of clothes, houseware, etc., and often supermarkets in their basements. A few stay open throughout the day, but most take the same break as other Italian shops—from 1 pm to 3 or 4 pm. Be sure to save your receipts for Customs on the way home. Shipping goods is a risky business unless you do it through a very reputable shop. Note well that the attraction of shopping in Italy is strictly limited to luxury items; for less expensive clothes and household items you'll always, always do better in Britain or America. Prices for clothes, even in street markets, are often ridiculously high. Bargains of any kind are rare, and the cheaper goods are often very poor quality.

Italian clothes are lovely, but if you have a large-boned Anglo-American build, you may find it hard to get a good fit, especially on trousers or skirts (Italians are a long-waisted, slim-hipped bunch). Shoes are often narrower than the sizes at home.

Sizes

Women's Shirts/Dresses

UK	10	12	14	16	18
US	8	10	12	14	16
Italy	40	42	44	46	48

Sweaters

UK	10	12	14	16
US	8	10	12	14
Italy	46	48	50	52

Women's Shoes

UK	3	4	5	6	7	8
US	4	5	6	7	8	9
Italy	36	37	38	39	40	41

Men's Shirts

UK/US	14	14½	15	15½	16	16½	17	17½
Italy	36	37	38	39	40	41	42	43

Men's Suits

UK/US	36	38	40	42	44	46
Italy	46	48	50	52	54	56

Men's Shoes

UK	2	3	4	5	6	7	8	9	10	11	12
US	5	6	7	7½	8	9	10	10½	11	12	13
Italy	34	36	37	38	39	40	41	42	43	44	45

Weights and Measures

1 kilogramme (1000 g)—2.2 lb	1 lb—0.45 kg
1 etto (100 g)—¼ lb (approx)	
1 litre—1.76 pints	1 pint—0.568 litres
	1 quart—1.136 litres
	1 Imperial gallon—4.546 litres
	1 US gallon—3.785 litres
1 metre—39.37 inches	1 foot—0.3048 metres
1 kilometre—0.621 miles	1 mile—1.161 kilometres

Where to Stay

Hotels

Tuscany, Umbria and the Marches are endowed with hotels (*alberghi*) of every description, from the spectacular to the humble. These are rated by the government's tourism bureaucracy, from five stars at the luxurious top to one star at the bottom. The ratings take into account such things as a restaurant on the premises, plumbing, air conditioning, etc., but not character, style, or charm. Use the stars, which we include in this book, as a quick reference for prices and general amenities only. Another thing to remember about government ratings is that a hotel can stay at a lower rating than it has earned, so you may find a three-star hotel as comfortable as a four.

There's no inflation in Italy, if you believe the government; the prices simply keep increasing. With the vacation business booming, this curious paradox is well expressed in the prices of the country's hotels; every year costs rise by 6–8 per cent across the board, and are quickly catching up with northern Europe. The prices listed in this book are for double rooms only. For a single, count on paying two-thirds of a double; to add an extra bed in a double will add 35 per cent to the bill. Taxes and service charges are included in the given rate. Some establishments charge L10–25 000 for air conditioning. Also note that if rooms are listed without bath, it simply means the shower and lavatory are in the corridor. Prices are by law listed on the door of each room; any discrepancies could be reported to the local tourist office. Most rooms have two or three different rates, depending on the season. Costs are sometimes a third less if you travel in the district's low season. Some hotels, especially in resorts, close down altogether for several months of the year.

Breakfast is optional in most hotels, although in pensions it is mandatory. And you may as well expect to face half- (breakfast and lunch or dinner) or full-board requirements in the hotels that can get away with it—seaside, lake, or mountain resorts in season, spas and country villa hotels. Otherwise, meal arrangements are optional. Although eating in the hotel restaurant can be a genuine gourmet experience, in the majority of cases hotel food is mass-produced and bland, just as it is anywhere else.

Each province or region sets its own price guidelines for accommodation: a three-star hotel in Florence, for instance, will cost much more than a three-star hotel in the Umbrian countryside. In general, the further south you go, the cheaper the rates.

NOTE: **Throughout this book, prices listed are for a double room; it will be mentioned whether or not this includes a private bath.** Here is the range of prices you are likely to encounter for hotels in the various classifications in 1990/1991:

	High season	*Low season*	*Full pension (per person)*
*****	L360–775 000	L250–570 000	L280–500 000
****	L200–400 000	L150–270 000	L175–250 000
***	L130–220 000	L 90–180 000	L 90–185 000
**	L 65–90 000	L 50–75 000	L 65–11000
*	L 45–65 000	L 40–55 000	L 60–75 000

For rooms without bath, subtract 20–30 per cent. Many resort hotels in particular offer discounts for children and children's meals. A *camera matrimoniale* is a room with a double bed, a *camera doppia* has twin beds, a single is a *camera singola*. There are several hotel chains in Italy. CIGA (*Compagnia Grandi Alberghi*) has many of the most luxurious, many of them grand, turn-of-the-century establishments that have been exquisitely restored. Another plush chain, *Chateaux et Relais* specializes in equally comfortable, but more intimate accommodation, often in historical buildings. Both chains pride themselves on their gourmet restaurants. Even the once, fairly standard *Jolly Hotels*, Italy's oldest chain, are quickly up-grading. The petrol company AGIP operates most of the motels along the major motorways, and usually makes a decent effort to give them good restaurants. The National Tourist office has a complete list of these and booking information for both motels and five- and four-star hotels and chains. If you want to stay in a different kind of accommodation, you'll have to book ahead on your own. Outside the high season this is generally unnecessary; otherwise, and especially if you have a certain place in mind, it is essential to book several months in advance or even earlier if possible, considering the sorry state of the Italian post. (While you're at it, remember to request a room with a view, in places where that is the hotel's chief attraction.) If your Italian is nonexistent, the National Tourist Office's *Travellers' Handbook* has a sample letter and list of useful terms. Under Italian law, a booking is valid once a deposit has been paid. If you have to cancel your reservation, the hotel will keep the deposit unless another agreement has been reached. If you're coming in the summer without reservations, start calling around for a place in the morning.

One Italian institution, the *Albergo Diurno* (Day Hotel), may prove handy, though there seem to be fewer of them all the time. Located in the centre of the largest cities and at the railway stations, these are places where you can take a shower, a shave, have your hair done, etc. They are open 6 am–midnight.

Inexpensive Accommodation

Bargains are few and far between in Italy. The cheapest kind of hotel is called an inn, or *Locanda*; some provinces treat these as one-star hotels or list them separately (or not at all). The majority of inexpensive places will always be around the railway station, though in the large cities you'll often find it worth your while to seek out some more pleasant location in the historic centre. You're likely to find anything in a one-star Italian hotel. Often they will be practically perfect, sometimes almost luxurious; memorably bad experiences will be few, and largely limited to the major cities. In rural areas and islands that see some tourists, ask around for rooms in private homes.

Besides the youth hostels (see below), there are several city-run hostels, with dormitory-style rooms open to all. In cities like Assisi and Florence religious institutions often rent out extra rooms. Monasteries in the country sometimes take guests as well; if you seek that kind of quiet experience, bring a letter of introduction from your local priest, pastor, etc.

Youth and Student Hostels

You'll find youth hostels in Florence, Lucca, Perugia, Tavarnelle Val di Pesa, in Chianti, Abetone, Cortona, Foligno, Marina di Massa e Carrara, Ascoli Piceno, and Pesaro. The head organization in Italy is the Associazione Alberghi per la Gioventù, Via Cavour 44 (terzo piano), Roma, tel (06) 462 342. They can send you a list and map of all the hostels in Italy, which officially require an IYHF card. There are no age limits, and senior citizens are often given added discounts. Many youth hostels sell cards or you can pick up one in advance from:

UK: Youth Hostels Association, 14 Southampton St, London WC2
US: American Youth Hostels, 1332 Eye St NW, Suite 800, Washington, DC, 20005
Canada: Canadian Hostelling Association, Place Vanier, Tower A, 333 River Rd, Ottawa, Ontario, K1l 8H9

Accommodation—a bunk bed in single-sex room and breakfast—costs around L10 000 per day. There is often a curfew, and you usually can't check in before 5 or 6 pm. You can book in advance by sending your arrival and departure dates along with the number of guests (by sex) to the individual hostel, including international postal coupons for the return reply. The worst time to use the hostels is the spring, when noisy Italian school groups use them for field trips.

There are two other organizations to help students find lodgings in Italy—the Centro Turistico Studentesco e Giovanile (CTS), which has offices in every Italian city of any size and can book cheap accommodation for you, in their own town or at your next stop. The Associazione Italiana per il Turismo e gli Scambi Universitari can obtain rooms for foreign university students all year round in university towns. Write to them at Via Palestro 11, Rome 00185, tel 475 5265.

Facilities for the Handicapped

Hotel listings sometimes make a note of which establishments are suitable for the physically handicapped. There are also a number of tours that can make a holiday much smoother—a list is available from the National Tourist Office. RADAR publishes an extremely useful book, *Holidays and Travel Abroad—A Guide for Disable People*, available for £3.00 from their offices at 25 Mortimer St, London W1M 8AB, tel (071) 637 5400. Another useful book, *Access to the World: a Travel Guide for the Handicapped* by Louise Weiss, covers a wide range of topics with listings for individual countries. It's available for $14.95 from Facts on File, 460 Park Ave South, New York, NY, 10016.

Self-Catering Holidays: Villas, Farmhouses and Flats

Renting a villa, farmhouse, cottage, or flat has always been the choice way to visit Tuscany, and is becoming increasingly so in Umbria as well. If you're travelling with a family it is the most economic alternative—there are simple, economical cottages as well as the fabulous Renaissance villas furnished with antiques, gourmet meals, and swimming-pools. One place to look for holiday villas is in the Sunday paper; or, if you have your heart set on a particular area, write to its tourist office for a list of local rental agencies. These ought to provide photos of the accommodation to give you an idea of what to expect, and make sure all pertinent details are written down in your rental agreement to avoid misunderstandings later. In general minimum lets are for two weeks; rental prices usually include insurance, water, and electricity, and sometimes linens and maid service. Don't be surprised if upon arrival the owner 'denounces' (*denunziare*) you to the police; according to Italian law, all visitors must be registered upon arrival. Common problems are water shortages, unruly insects (see 'Flora and Fauna'), and low kilowatts (often you can't have your hot-water heater and oven on at the same time). Many of the companies listed below offer in addition to homes, savings on charter flights, ferry crossings or fly-drive schemes to sweeten the deal. Try to book as far in advance as possible for the summer season.

In the UK

Chapter Travel, 126 St John's Wood High Street, London NW8, tel (071) 586 9451 has the listings and handles bookings for the major Italian holiday home companies, largest of which is **Cuendet** which publishes an extensive illustrated catalogue of holiday villas, flats, and farmhouses in Umbria, Tuscany, and the Marches; their headquarters are at Il Cerreto, 53030 Strove, Siena, tel (0577) 301 013; they also have the listings of **Tuscan Enterprises**, a company headquartered in Castellina in Chianti, and their own listings called Italian Chapters.

Other worthy firms specializing in holiday rentals in Tuscany and Umbria are:

Vacanze in Italia, Bignor, Near Pulborough, West Sussex RH20 1QD, tel (07987) 362

Tuscany from Cottages to Castles, 54 Necton Rd, Wheathampstead, St Albans, Hertfordshire AL4 8AU, tel (058283) 4333

Lunigiana Holidays, 71 Busbridge Lane, Godalming, Surrey, tel (04868) 21 218

Tuscany Holidays, Glebe House Farm, St Andrew's Major, S. Glam, tel (0222) 513 824

Hoseasons Holidays, Sunway House, Lowestoft, Suffolk, tel (0502) 500 555

Other firms with listings in Tuscany, Umbria and the Marches include:

Bowhills Cottages, Swanmore, Southampton, tel (0489) 877 627

Bridgewater Villas, 37 King Street West, Manchester, tel (061) 832 6011

Citalia, Marco Polo House 3–5, Lansdowne Road, Croydon CR9 9EQ tel (081) 686 5336

Continental Villas, Eagle House, 58 Blythe Road, London, W14, tel (071) 371 1313

Interhome, 383 Richmond Rd, Twickenham, tel (081) 891 1294

Magic of Italy, 47 Shepherds Bush Green, London W12, tel (081) 743 9555

David Newman's European Collection, PO Box 733, 40 Upperton Rd, Eastbourne, tel (0323) 410 347

Pegasus, River House, Restmor Way, Hackbridge Rd, Wallington, Surrey, tel (081) 773 2323
Perrymead Properties Overseas, 55 Perrymead St, London SW6, tel (071) 736 4592
Pleasurewood Holidays, Somerset House, Gordon Road, Lowestoft, tel (0502) 517 271
Tourauto Holidays, Bridge House, Ware, Herts, tel (0920) 3050
Villas Italia (with a large number of listings on the Tuscan coast), 277 Shepherds Bush Rd, London W6, tel (081) 748 8668.

In the USA
Villas International, 71 W. 23 St, New York, NY, 10010, tel (800) 221 2260
CUENDET: Posarelli Vacations, 180 Kinderkamack Road, Park Ridge, NJ, 07656, tel (201) 573 9558 and Suzanne T. Pidduck, 1742 Calle Corva, Camarillo, CA, 93010, tel (805) 987 5278
Vacanze in Italia, 153 West 13th St, New York, NY, 10011, tel (212) 242 2145
At Home Abroad, 405 East 56th St, New York, NY, 10022, tel (212) 421 9165
Four Star Living, 964 Third Avenue, New York, NY, 10022, tel (212) 891 8199
Hideaways International, P.O. Box 1464, Littleton, MA, 01460, tel (617) 486 8955
Homeowners International, 1133 Broadway, New York, NY, 10010, tel (212) 691 2361 or (800) 367 4668
Italian Villa Rentals, 10604 N.E. 38th Place, Suite 222, Kirkland, Washington, 98033, tel (206) 827 3694
Overseas Connection, 70 West 71st St, Suite 1C, New York, NY, 10023, tel (212) 769 1170
Resort Villas International, 30 Spring St, Stamford, CT, 06901, tel (203) 965 0161
Rent in Italy, Elaine Muoio, 3801 Ingomar St N.W., Washington, DC, 20015, tel (202) 244 5345
RAVE (Rent-a-Vacation-Elsewhere), 328 East Main St, Suite 526, Rochester, NY, 14604, tel (716) 454 6440.

In Italy
The Best in Tuscany, Via Ugo Foscolo 72, Firenze, tel (055) 223 064, which specializes in posh villas with a domestic staff
Tuscan Enterprises, for houses in Chianti; write to Podere Casamonti, Castellina in Chianti, 53011 Siena
Toscanamare Villas, Via Donizetti 13, 55044 Marina di Pietrasante (LU), tel (0584) 23 844 (villas on the Versilia coast)
One Holidays, Piazza Arnolfo 5, 53034, Colle di Val d'Elsa, tel (0577) 922 619 (villas and flats)
Casaclub, Piazza del Sale 6, 53100, Siena, tel (0577) 44 041 (villas in Chianti)
Toscana Vacanze, Via XX Settembre 6, 52047 Marciano della Chiana, tel (0575) 845 348 (Villas in Chianti and environs)
Etruscan Itineraries, Box 167, 50013, Campi Bisenzio (FI), tel (055) 890 934 (villas in Tuscany and Umbria)

Farm holidays in Tuscany are organized by:
Associazione Regionale Agriturist, Piazza S. Firenze 3, 50122 Firenze, tel (055) 287 838

Turismo Verde, c/o Confcoltivatori, Piazza Indipendenza 10, 50129 Firenze, tel (055) 470 087
Associazione Regionale Terranostra, Via dei Magazzini 2, 50122 Firenze, tel (055) 214 430
Solemar Piazza Indipendenza 20, Firenze, tel (055) 473 488.
Or write directly to the provincial Agriturist office:

TUSCANY
Corso Italia 205, 52100 **Arezzo**, tel (0575) 22 280
Via D. Chiesa 4, 58100 **Grosseto**, tel (0564) 21 020
Via G. Marrado 14, 57126 **Livorno**, tel (0586) 812 7445
Vle. Barsanti e Matteucci, 55100 **Lucca**, tel (0583)332 044
Via Marina Vecchia (Pal. Standa), 54100 **Massa Carrara**, tel (0585) 40 701
Via B. Croce 62, 56100 **Pisa**, tel (050) 262 212
Via F. Pacini 45, 51100 **Pistoia**, tel (0573) 21 231
Piazza G. Matteotti 3, 53100 **Siena**, tel (0577) 46 194

UMBRIA
Piazza B. Michelotti 1, 06100 **Perugia**, tel (075) 61 481
Via di Piazza del Popolo 16, 05018 **Orvieto**, tel (0763) 42 820
UPA, Corso del Popolo 37, 05100 **Terni**, tel (0744) 43 448

MARCHES
Via Leopardi 2, 60100 **Ancona**, tel (071) 201 763
Via Trieste 52, 63100 **Ascoli Piceno**, tel (0736) 51 052
Corso Cavour 2, 62100 **Macerata**, tel (0733) 231 351
Piazzale Matteotti 28, 61100 **Pesaro**, tel (0721) 33 168

Alpine Refuges

The Club Alpino Italiano operates a large percentage of the *Rifugi Alpini*, or mountain huts in the Apennines. Facilities range from the basic to the grand; some are exclusively for hikers and mountain-climbers, while others may be reached by funivias, and are used by skiers in the winter and holidaymakers in the summer. Rates average L10 000 a night, but rise by 20 per cent between December and April. Write to the club at Via Foscolo 3, Milan, tel (02) 802 554 for a list of huts, their opening dates, and booking information.

Camping

Most of the official camp sites are near the sea, but there are also quite a few in the mountains and near the lakes, and usually one within commuting distance of major tourist centres. A complete list with full details for all of Italy is published annually in the Italian Touring Club's *Campeggi e Villaggi Turistici*, available in Italian bookshops for L22 000, or you can obtain an abbreviated list free from the Centro Internazionale Prenotazioni Federcampeggio, Casella Postale 23, 50042, Calenzano (Firenze); request their booking forms as well to reserve a place—essential in the summer months when the tents and caravans (campers) are packed cheek to cheek. Camping fees vary according to the camp ground's facilities, roughly L5000 per person (less for children); L5000–15 000 per tent or caravan; and L4000 per car. Camping outside official sites is kosher if you ask the landowner's permission first.

Caravans are available for hire at: GETUR, Via C. Liviero 2/h Città di Castello tel (075) 855 0200; INNOCENTI NOLEGGIO, Piazza Italia 25, Montecatini Terme, tel (0572) 78 873; ACI TOUR, Via Catalani 3, S. Lucia, Lucca, tel (0583) 588 181; CAMPERTOUR, Via S. Pietro a Quaracchi, Florence, tel (055) 372 336; FILCARAVAN, Via Concordia 12/14, Pierdiripa (PG), tel (0733) 292 467; LAIKA VIAGGI, Tavarnelle Val di Pesa, tel (055) 373 608.

Buying a House

Of all the regions in Italy Tuscany has the most foreigners with homes, so many, in fact, that prices have shot into the stratosphere in the most popular areas (especially around Florence and Siena, and in the Chianti). The more obscure areas of Tuscany as well as most of Umbria, on the other hand, still have a number of abandoned farmhouses just waiting for someone to renovate them; while the Marches has become the last frontier for bargains. Rural real estate is one of Italy's great buys, and the recommended way to do it is to buy a run-down property and restore it to your own needs and taste. But beware the pitfalls.

One agent we know is amazed that all English clients invariably express two major concerns about a property: drainage and the presence of a bidet in the bathroom, as if it were a tool of the devil! What they should be asking are questions about water supply (a major problem in Tuscany), electricity, and road access—often big problems for that isolated, romantic farmhouse that has caught your eye. Another thing to remember before purchasing a home or land is that you need permission from the local *comune* to make any changes or improvements, and it's no good buying anything unless you're pretty sure the *comune* will consent (for a sizeable fee, of course) to let you convert the old cellar or stable into a spare bedroom. A further point to remember is that though there are no annual rates (property tax) to pay, there is a 10 per cent IVA tax (VAT) to be paid on the purchase price for a house and 17 per cent on land, as well as hefty Capital Gains Tax on selling price and profit to be paid by the seller. Italians tend to get around this by selling at one price and writing down another on the contract. But remember if you sell you'll be in the same bind.

Once you've agreed to buy, you pay a deposit (usually 25–30 per cent) and sign a *compromesso*, a document that states that if you back out, you lose your deposit, and if the seller changes his mind, he forfeits double the deposit to you (be sure your *compromesso* includes this feature, called *caparra confirmatoria*). Always transfer payment from home through a bank, taking care to get and save a certificate of the transaction so you can take the sum back out of Italy when you sell. After the *compromesso*, your affairs will be handled by a *notaio*, the public servant in charge of registering documents and taxes who works for both buyer and seller. If you want to make sure your interests are not overlooked, you can hire a *commercialista* (lawyer-accountant) who will handle your affairs with the *notaio*, including the final transfer deed (*rogito*), which completes the purchase at the local Land Registry. Upon signing, the balance of the purchase price generally becomes payable within a year.

The next stage for most buyers, restoration, can be a nightmare if you aren't careful. Make sure the crew you hire is experienced and that you're pleased with the work elsewhere—don't hesitate to ask as many other people in your area as possible for advice.

Keep all receipts, and beware when builders and agents give you receipts for far less than their charges (or no receipts at all) to avoid taxes; you'll pay the difference in sales tax when you sell. Also expect to pay a lofty surcharge on electricity, water, and telephone bills unless you become an Italian resident and your Italian house is your primary residence. One book that offers some clues on the ins and outs of taxes, inheritance law, residency, gardening etc., is *Living in Italy*, published by Robert Hale, London 1987.

Eating Out

In Italy, the three Ms (the Madonna, Mamma, and Mangiare) are still a force to be reckoned with, and in a country where millions of otherwise sane people spend much of their waking hours worrying about their digestion, standards both at home and in the restaurants are understandably high. Everybody is a gourmet, or at least thinks they are, and food is not only something to eat, but a subject approaching the heights of philosophy—two Umbrian businessmen once overheard on a train heatedly discussed mushrooms for over four hours. Although ready-made pasta, tinned minestrone, and frozen pizza in the *supermercato* tempt the virtue of the Italian cook, few give in (although many a working mother wishes she could at times).

Regional traditions are strong in Italy, not only in dialect but in the kitchen. Tuscany, Umbria and the Marches are no exception and firmly maintain their distinctive cuisine even when you wish they wouldn't—especially in the case of Umbrian bread, described by astonished visitors as 'tasty as chewy water' and 'scarcely distinguishable from a cricket bat'. Although neither Tuscany nor Umbria ranks among the great culinary regions of Italy, both offer good, honest, traditional dishes, often humble, rarely elaborate. The Medici may have put on some magnificent feeds, but the modern Tuscan is known by his fellow Italians as a *mangiafagioli*, or bean eater. Some observers hold it as part of the austere Tuscan character, others as another sign of their famous alleged miserliness. Umbria, a historically poor area, never had a choice one way or the other.

The truth is, that although beans and tripe often appear on the menu, most people when dining out want to try something different, from other regions, perhaps, or the recent concoctions of Italian nouvelle cuisine, or *cucina nuova*, or perhaps a recipe from the Middle Ages or Renaissance. Some of the country's finest restaurants are in Tuscany and Umbria, including two generally ranked among the top five in all Italy; in practice, the diversity of dishes in Tuscany, from traditional to bizarre, is almost endless. Umbria is more conservative and not so sure about this newfangled *cucina nuova*. First, though, a few general comments on eating in Italy.

Breakfast (*colazione*) in Italy is no lingering affair, but an early morning wake-up shot to the brain: a *cappuccino* (espresso with hot foamy milk, often sprinkled with chocolate), a *caffè latte* (white coffee), or a *caffè lungo* (a generous portion of espresso), accompanied by a croissant-type roll, called a *cornetto* or *briosce*. This can be consumed in nearly any bar, and repeated during the morning as often as necessary, which is why breakfast in most Italian hotels is no big deal and seldom worth the price charged.

Lunch or *pranzo*, generally served around 1 pm, is the most important meal of the day for the Italians, with a minimum of a first course (*Primo piatto*—any kind of pasta dish, broth or soup, or rice dish or pizza), a second course (*Secondo piatto*—a meat dish, accompanied by a *contorno* or side dish—a vegetable, salad, or potatoes usually), followed by fruit or dessert and coffee. You can, however, begin with a platter of *antipasti*—the appetizers Italians do so brilliantly, ranging from warm seafood delicacies, to raw ham (*prosciutto crudo*), salami in a hundred varieties, lovely vegetables, savoury toasts, olives, paté, and many, many more. There are restaurants that specialize in antipasti, and they usually don't take it amiss if you decide to forget the pasta and meat and just nibble on these scrumptious hors d'oeuvres (though in the end it will probably cost as much as a full meal). Most Italians accompany their meal with wine and mineral water (*acqua minerale*, with or without bubbles *con* or *senza gas*, which supposedly aids digestion), concluding their meals with a *digestivo* liqueur.

Cena, the evening meal, is usually eaten at around 8 pm. This is much the same as pranzo although lighter, without the pasta; a pizza and beer, eggs, or a fish dish. In restaurants, however, Italians often order all the courses, so if you have only a sandwich for lunch you have a full meal in the evening.

In Italy the various types of restaurants—*ristorante, trattoria*, or *osteria*—have been confused. A trattoria or osteria can be just as elaborate as a restaurant, though rarely is a ristorante as informal as a traditional trattoria. Unfortunately the old habit of posting menus and prices in the windows has fallen from fashion, so it's often difficult to judge variety or prices. Invariably the least expensive restaurant-type place is the *vino e cucina*, simple places serving simple cuisine for simple everyday prices. It is essential to remember that the fancier the fittings, the fancier the bill, though neither of these points has anything at all to do with the quality of the food. If you're uncertain, do as you would at home—look for lots of locals. When you eat out, mentally add to the bill (*conto*) the bread and cover charge (*pane e coperto*, between L1500–2000), and a 15 per cent service charge. This is often included in the bill (*servizio compreso*); if not, it will say *servizio non compreso*, and you'll have to do your own arithmetic. Additional tipping is at your own discretion, but never do it in family-owned and -run places. Prices quoted for meals in this book are for an average complete meal, Italian-style with wine, for one person.

People who haven't visited Italy for years and have fond memories of eating full meals for under a pound will be amazed at how much prices have risen; though in some respects eating out in Italy is still a bargain, especially when you figure out how much all that wine would have cost you at home. In many places you'll often find restaurants offering a *menù turistico*—full, set meals of usually meagre inspiration for L15–20 000. Good, imaginative chefs often offer a *menù degustazione*—a set-price gourmet meal that allows you to taste their daily specialities and seasonal dishes. Both of these are cheaper than if you had ordered the same food à la carte. When you leave a restaurant you will be given a receipt (*ricevuto fiscale*) which according to Italian law you must take with you out of the door and carry for at least 300 metres. If you aren't given one, it means the restaurant is probably fudging on its taxes and thus offering you lower prices. There is a slim chance the tax police may have their eye on you and the restaurant, and if you don't have a receipt they could slap you with a heavy fine.

There are several alternatives to sit-down meals. The 'hot table' (*tavola calda*) is a stand-up buffet, where you can choose a simple prepared dish or a whole meal, depending on your appetite. The food in these can be truly impressive, though many offer only a few hot dishes, pizza and sandwiches. Little shops that sell pizza by the slice are common in city centres; some, called *gastronomia*, offer other take-out delicacies as well. At any delicatessen (*pizzicheria*), or grocer's (*alimentari*) or market (*mercato*) you can buy the materials for countryside or hotel-room picnics; some places in the smaller towns will make the sandwiches for you. For really elegant picnics, have a *tavola calda* pack up something nice for you. And if everywhere else is closed, there's always the railway station bars—these will at least have sandwiches and drinks, and perhaps some surprisingly good snacks you've never heard of before. Some of the station bars also prepare *cestini di viaggio*, full-course meals in a basket to help you through long train trips. Common snacks you'll encounter include *panini* of prosciutto, cheese and tomatoes, or other meats; *tramezzini*, little sandwiches on plain, square white bread that are always much better than they look; pizza, of course, or the traditional sandwich of Tuscany and Umbria, a hard roll filled with warm *porchetta* (roast whole pig stuffed with fennel and garlic).

Some Regional Specialities

The Tuscans will tell you the basic simplicity of their kitchen is calculated to bring out the glories of their wine, which may well be true, as it tends to be the perfect complement to a glass of Chianti or Vino Nobile. Nearly all are born of thrift, like *bruschetto*, a Tuscan and Umbrian favourite that takes sliced stale bread, toasted over the fire and rubbed with garlic. *Acqua cotta*, popular in southern Tuscany, is *bruschetto* with an egg; another version adds mashed tomatoes. The other traditional Tusco-Umbrian antipasto is *crostini*, thin slices of toast with a piquant paté spread of chicken livers, anchovies, capers, and lemons, or other variations (in Umbria it's often spleen). Umbrians also like platters of prosciutto, salami, sliced stuffed rabbit, and *capacolo*, which is better than it looks.

For *primo*, the traditional Tuscan relies mostly on soups. Perhaps most traditional is *ribollita* ('reboiled'), a hearty mushy vegetable soup with beans, cabbage, carrots and chunks of boiled bread. Another is *pappa col pomodoro*, which is basically *ribollita* with fresh tomatoes. *Panzanella*, or Tuscan *gazpacho* (a cold soup of tomatoes, cucumbers, onions, basil, olive oil and bread) can be a a godsend on a hot summer's day. The prince of Tuscan soups is Livorno's *cacciucco*, a heavenly fish soup that you have to go to Livorno to try. Other first courses you'll find are *fagioli ai fiasco* (beans with oil and black pepper simmered in an earthenware pot) or *fagioli all'uccelletto* (beans with garlic and tomatoes); the most Tuscan of pasta dishes is *pappardelle alla lepre* (wide noodles with a sauce of stewed hare). Umbrians are more fond of their pasta—*tagliatelle al funghi* (with mushrooms), or *al tartufi* (with truffles); *tortellini con panna* (with cream sauce); *cirioli* or *pici* or *stringozzi* (various names for rather fat, home-made spaghetti) with various sauces. The real test of an Umbrian chef is eggs with truffles, a difficult dish to time correctly but superb when successful.

Neither Tuscany nor Umbria offer exceptional *secondi*. Tuscany has its famous steak, *bistecca alla fiorentina* (cooked over coals, charred on the outside and pink in the middle, and seasoned with salt and pepper); otherwise, both the Tuscans and Umbrians are content with grilled chops—lamb, pork, or veal. *Fritto misto* is an interesting alternative, where lamb chops, liver, sweetbreads, artichokes, and courgettes (*zucchini*) are dipped in batter and deep fried. Otherwise look for *arista di maiale* (pork loin with rosemary and garlic), *francesina* (meat, onion, and tomato stew in Vernaccia di San Gimignano), *anatra* (duck, often served with truffles in Umbria), *piccione* (stuffed wild pigeon), *cinghiale* (boar), either roasted or in sausages or *stufato* (stewed). Both Tuscans and Umbrians are rather too fond of their *girarrosto*, a great spit of tiny birds and pork livers. In Tuscany it's fairly easy to find seafood as far inland as Florence—one traditional dish is *seppie in zimino*, or cuttlefish simmered with beets. In Umbria seafood is rare, though you can usually get trout. Hardy souls in Florence can try *cibreo* (cockscombs with chicken livers, beans, and egg yolks).

Tuscany's tastiest cheese is tangy *pecorino* made from ewe's milk; the best is made around Pienza. When it's aged it becomes quite sharp and is grated over pasta dishes. Umbria's best cheeses come from Norcia, so much so that most cheese shops are named after the town. Typical desserts, to be washed down with a glass of Vinsanto, include Siena's *panforte* (a rich, spicy dense cake full of nuts and candied fruit), *cenci*, a carnival sweet (deep fried strips of dough), *castagnaccio* (chestnut cake, with pine nuts, raisins, and rosemary), Florentine *zuccotto* (a cake of chocolate, nuts, and candied fruits), *biscottini di Prato* (almond biscuits softened in wine), *crostate* (fruit tarts) or perhaps a *gelato ai Baci* (made with Perugia's famous hazelnut chocolates).

In the Marches, seafood is the obvious speciality, especially in *brodetto*, a stew concocted of a dozen different types of fish, and *stoccafisso*, made of cod from the North Sea, dried on the Norwegian coast and served mixed with potatoes. Around Macerata look for *vincigrassi*, a kind of lasagne made with chicken giblets, fresh tomatoes, mozzarella and parmesan cheese.

Wine

Quaffing glass after glass of Chianti inspired Elizabeth Barrett Browning to write her best poetry, and the wines of Tuscany and Umbria may bring out the best in you as well. The first really to celebrate Tuscan wines was a naturalist by the name of Francesco Redi in the 1600s, who, like many of us today, made a wine tour of the region, then composed a dithyrambic eulogy called 'Bacchus in Tuscany'. Modern Bacchuses in Tuscany will find quite a few treats, some famous and some less well known, and plenty of cellars and *enacoteche* (wine bars) where you can do your own survey—there's a famous one in Siena with every wine produced in Tuscany, Umbria, the Marches and the rest of Italy as well.

Wine flasks

Most Italian wines are named after the grape and the district they come from. If the label says DOC (*Denominazione di Origine Controllata*) it means that the wine comes from a specially defined area and was produced according to a certain traditional method; DOCG (the G stands for *Garantita*) means that a high quality is also guaranteed, a badge worn only by the noblest wines. *Classico* means that a wine comes from the oldest part of the zone of production; besides the famous **Chianti Classico**, for instance, there are seven other DOC Chianti wines (Montalbano, Rufina, Colli Fiorentini, Colli Senesi, Colli Aretini, Colline Pisa and simple Chianti). Sangiovese is the chief grape of all Chianti as well as all the classified red wines of Tuscany. *Riserva*, or *superiore*, means a wine has been aged longer. Most Tuscan farmers also make a cask of **Vinsanto**, a dessert wine that can be sweet or almost dry, and which according to tradition is holy only because priests are so fond of it.

Tuscany produces 19 DOC and DOCG wines, including some of Italy's noblest reds: the dry, ruby red **Brunello di Montalcino** and the garnet **Vino Nobile di Montepulciano**, deep red with the fragrance of violets. Chianti may be drunk young or as a *Riserva*, especially the higher octane Chianti Classico. Lesser known DOC reds include dry, bright red **Rosso delle Colline Lucchesi**, from the hills north of Lucca; hearty **Pomino Rosso**, from a small area east of Rufina in the Mugello; **Carmignano**, a consistently fine ruby red that can take considerable aging, produced just west of Florence; and **Morellino di Scansano**, from the hills south of Grosseto, a dry red to be drunk young or old. The three other DOC reds from the coast are **Parrina Rosso**, from Parrina near Orbetello, **Montescudaio Rosso**, and **Elba Rosso**, a happy island wine, little of which makes it to the mainland. All three have good white versions as well.

Of the Tuscan whites, the most notable is **Vernaccia di S. Gimignano** (also a *Riserva*), dry and golden in colour, the perfect complement to seafood; delicious, but more difficult to find are dry, straw-coloured **Montecarlo** from the hills east of Lucca and **Candia dei Colli Apuani**, a light wine from mountains of marble near Carrara. From the coast comes **Bolgheri**, white or rosé, both fairly dry. Cortona and its valley produce **Bianco Vergine Valdichiana**, a fresh and lively wine; from the hills around Montecatini comes the golden, dry **Bianco della Valdinievole**. **Bianco di Pitigliano**, of a yellow straw colour, is a celebrated accompaniment to lobster.

The king of Umbrian vines produces the celebrated **Orvieto** and **Orvieto Classico**, a delicate wine, dry with a slightly bitter aftertaste; Orvieto Classico comes from the old *zona* around the Paglia river. The other DOC wines of Umbria are grown on the western hills of the region: the **Colli del Trasimeno**, from the hills around Umbria's largest lake (Rosso, a garnet, slightly tannic wine, Bianco, deep straw-coloured, dry and mellow); **Colli Perugini** from the hills of Perugia (dry ruby red, fruity, light white, and a dry, intense rosé); **Torgiano**, from a small zone near the village of that name (a dry, full-bodied Rosso (and a *Riserva*) and a light and lively Bianco); and **Colli Altotiberini** (a pleasant dry white and red, and a pale, fresh rosé). **Montefalco** produces three reds; a dry velvety Rosso, the dry, garnet Sagrantino, with the aroma of blackberries, and the sweetish Sagrantino Passito, made from raisins.

The rough and tumble slopes of the Marches conveniently produce a range of DOC white wines to go with the day's catch—wines still incognito outside Italy. The dry and delicate **Verdicchio** from the Jesi district and Matelica is the best known, and pale enough to mistake for water; as in Chianti, the oldest vineyards get to be called 'classic'

Verdicchio dei Castelli di Jesi Classico. Light golden **Falerio dei Colli Ascolani** is a dry wine consisting mainly of Trebbiano Toscano grapes, as is the pleasant **Bianco dei Colli Maceratesi**, from Macerata province and Loreto. Pinkish gold Biancame grapes are the base for **Bianchello del Metauro**, from the coast of Pesaro and hills along the Metauro river, a dry wine popular as an aperitif as well as a table wine. Red wines from the Marches are nearly all drunk young, like the sprightly, fruity ruby **Lacrima di Morro D'Alba**, the pomegranate-coloured **Sangiovese dei Colli Pesaresi**, and **Rosso Cònero** (made from Montepulciano grapes). The hills east of Ascoli Piceno produce **Rosso Piceno Superiore**, the one wine that is aged for any time. If you can find it, try **Vernaccia di Serrapetrona**, a naturally sparkling red wine, either dry or dessert, grown in a tiny area near Serrapetrona. The quality of the Marches' other sparkling wines has improved enough to win them the prestigious Torgiano award.

Itineraries

10 Days of Roman and Etruscan Sites

Day 1: **Florence** (Archaeology Museum; Etruscan tombs at Sesto Fiorentino) and **Fiesole** (Etruscan Walls, Roman theatre, and museum). Day 2: **Volterra** (museum, Etruscan arch, and Roman theatre). Days 3–4: The Etruscan cities of the coast: **Populonia, Vetulonia, Roselle** and **Ansedonia**, with stops at the Archaeology Museum in **Grosseto** and 'Frontone' (temple pediment) in **Orbetello**. Day 5: **Chiusi** (fine museum and only painted Etruscan tombs in Tuscany). Day 6: **Arezzo** (Roman amphitheatre and museum). Day 7: **Cortona** (Etruscan walls, gate, tombs, and museum). Day 8: **Perugia** (gates, tombs, and museum). Day 9: **Assisi** (Temple of Minerva—only complete Roman temple façade) and **Spello** (Roman Gates). Day 10: Roman ruins at **Carsulae** near San Gemini, and **Orvieto** (Etruscan tombs).

Early Medieval Art and Architecture, in Two Weeks

The best in Tuscany and Umbria, before 1200:

Day 1: **Florence** (Baptistry, S. Miniato). Day 2: **Pistoia** (Sant'Andrea, S. Giovanni Fuoracivitas). Day 3: the bizarre Pieve di Castelvecchio, near **Pescia**, and **Barga** cathedral. Day 4: **Lucca** (Cathedral and S. Michele). Day 5: **Pisa** (Field of Miracles, Museums, and S. Piero a Grado). Day 6: **Rosia, Sovicille** and the other churches just west of **Siena**. Day 7: S. Antimo, outside **Montalcino** and **Abbadia San Salvatore** (town and abbey). Day 8: the well-preserved medieval town of **Sovana**, near Pitigliano. Day 9: **Lugnano in Teverina** (S. Maria Assunta), **Terni**, S. Salvatore, and **Ferentillo** (S. Pietro in Valle). Days 10–11: **Spoleto** (S. Pietro, Cathedral, S. Salvatore); **Bevagna** (S. Salvatore and S. Michele); **Foligno** (Cathedral façade and S. Maria Infraportas), **Tempietto di Clitunno**; **Spello** (S. Claudio). Day 12: **Perugia** (S. Angelo) and **Arezzo** (S. Maria della Pieve). Day 13: **Gròpina**, near Loro Ciuffenna in the Valdarno, and **Poppi** (Castle). Day 14: **Stia** (San Pietro and Castello di Romena).

13-Day Tour of High Medieval Art and Architecture

Days 1–2: **Florence**: Orsanmichele, Bargello, Cathedral, Palazzo Vecchio, Palazzo Davanzati. Day 2: **Empoli** (Collegiata and museum) and **Certaldo** (Boccaccio's well-preserved home town). Day 3: **S. Gimignano** (Collegiata frescoes and the city itself—a genuine medieval monument). Day 4: **Volterra** (Civic buildings and art in Cathedral, S. Francesco). Day 5: **Massa Marittima** and **San Galgano**. Days 6–8: **Siena** (Palazzo Pubblico, Cathedral—and nearly everything else!). Day 9: Down highway to **Orvieto** (Cathedral and more). Day 10: **Todi** (Civic buildings and S. Fortunato). Day 11: **Perugia** (Palazzo dei Priori, Fontana Maggiore, many churches). Day 12: **Assisi** (great hoard of trecento frescoes in S. Francesco, many good churches); and lucky Day 13: the thoroughly medieval city of **Gubbio**.

Shooting a Renaissance Loop Outside Florence (13 Days)
Renaissance art somehow seems especially rarefied out in the provinces. Once you've paid your respects to Great Aunt Florence, visit Day 1: **Impruneta** (Collegiata), **Certosa di Galluzzo**, **Lastra a Signa** (Alberti's church) and **Poggio a Caiano**, the archetypal Renaissance villa. Day 2: **Prato** (S. Maria delle Carceri, Filippo Lippi's fresco cycle in the Cathedral, Donatello and Michelozzo's pulpit). Day 3: **Lucca**, for the sculpture of Matteo Civitali and Jacopo della Quercia. Day 4: **S. Gimignano**, which has much of the best painting outside Florence, by Gozzoli, Ghirlandaio, Sodoma, and more. Day 5: **Siena**, for the Sienese side of the Renaissance (Cathedral, especially pavements, tombs, and Piccolomini Library, and the Pinacoteca). Days 6–7: the exquisite monastic complex and frescoes at **Monte Oliveto Maggiore**, on the way to Pius II's planned city of **Pienza**; nearby **Montepulciano** for the best of classic Renaissance temples, Sangallo's S. Biagio, as well as other churches and palaces. Day 8: **Orvieto** (Cathedral frescoes by Angelico and Signorelli) and **Città della Pieve** (Perugino). Day 9: **Perugia** (Pinacoteca, S. Bernardino, and others). Day 10: **Cortona** (two Renaissance temples, Signorelli and Fra Angelico) and **Monte San Savino.** Day 11: **Arezzo** (Piero della Francesco's frescoes and S. Maria della Grazie). Day 12: more Pieros in **Monterchi** and **Sansepolcro.** Day 13: **La Verna** (Andrea della Robbia) and over the Passo di Consuma to Florence.

Villas and Gardens, in a week or so
A 'Two-Centre Holiday' as all are located near Florence and Lucca. Do check the opening hours and do the necessary telephoning before setting out. In **Florence** itself there are beautiful walks around the Boboli Gardens, the villas and gardens of **Arcetri**, the **Villa Stibbert and Garden**, and the villas and gardens in and around **Fiesole.** Then Day 1: **Medici villas and gardens** of La Petraia, Castello, and Careggi. Day 2: Into the Mugello: Gardens of **Pratolino**, and Medici Villas at **Cafaggiolo** and **Trebbio**. Day 3: More Medici villas and gardens: **Poggio a Caiano**, Villa Artimino and **Cerreto Guidi**. Days 4–5: Villas in Chianti: although only the **Castello di Brolio** and **Badia a Coltibuono** are open to the public, other striking estates include: Villa Tattali, Palazzo al Bosco, Villa Le Corti, Poggio Torselli, Vignamaggio, and the several around Castellina. From **Lucca** (Days 6–7): **Castello Garzoni**, with fabulous gardens, near Collodi, and the three villas northeast of Lucca itself: Villa Mansi, Villa Torrigiani, and Villa Pecci-Blunt. Other possibilities: the Medici Villa della Magia in **Quarrata**, southeast of Pistoia, and **Fosdinovo** castle up in the Lunigiana.

Nature and Scenery
For Tuscany and Umbria at their least civilised: starting with the grandest of all, Southern Umbria's **Piano Grande** around **Norcia**, in the shadow of the snow-capped

Monti Sibillini; also the **Cascata delle Marmore** and the **Valnerina** north of Arrone and any of the side roads through the mountains. Southern Tuscany's **Monte Amiata** is an isolated patch of lovely mountain forests. **Mediterranean Coastal Scenery**: maquis and pine forests, on **Monte Argentario**, with side trips to **Giglio** and the surrounding marshlands with wildlife reserves and exotic birds, like the **Monti dell'Uccellina**. Further north, there are ancient coastal forests around **Pietrasanta** and **San Rossore**. **Coastal Mountains**: the **Apuan Alps**, lush, streaked with marble, are located along the coast from Carrara down, while a bit further inland are the dense oak and chestnut forests of the **Garfagnana**. **Serious Apennines**: the entire ridge between Tuscany and Emilia-Romagna, around **Abetone**, **Firenzuola**, **Camaldoli** (with its ancient forest), **Pratomagno** (Monte Secchieta, and its panoramic roads), and the enchanting **Casentino**.

Two Weeks of Wine

For the best of Tuscan and Umbrian DOC wines, and some of the most ravishing scenery the two regions can offer: Day 1: Florence to **Carmignano**, **Cerruto Guidi**, and **Vinci** (wines: Carmignano and Chianti). Day 2: **Montecatini Alta**, **Collodi**, and **Montecarlo** (wines: Bianco della Valdinievole and Montecarlo). Day 3: south of the Arno to **S. Miniato** and environs, and **Certaldo** (wines: Bianco Pisano di S. Torpè and Chianti). Day 4: **S. Gimignano** and **Colle di Val d'Elsa** (wines: Vernaccia di S. Gimignano and Chianti Colli Senesi). Day 5: **Barberino Val d'Elsa** and **S. Casciano** to the Florence–Siena wine route, the Chiantigiana and **Greve in Chianti** (wines: Chianti, Chianti Colli Fiorentini, and Chianti Classico). Day 6: **Panzano** and **Radda in Chianti** (wine: Chianti Classico). Day 7: **Gaiole in Chianti**, **Castello di Brolio**, and **Siena**, with a stop at the Enoteca Nazionale (wines: Chianti Classico and Chianti Colli Senesi). Day 8: **Montalcino** (wine: Brunello). Day 9: **Montepulciano** (wine: Vino Nobile). Day 10: **Cortona** (wine: Bianco Vergine della Valdichiana). Day 11: **Tuoro** and **Passignano** on Lake Trasimeno, to **Perugia** (wines: Colli del Trasimeno and Colli Perugini). Day 12: **Torgiano** and its wine museum, **Bevagna**, and **Montefalco** (wines: Torgiana, Montefalco, and Sagrantino). Day 13: **Orvieto** (wine: Orvieto Classico). Day 14: **Sovana**, **Pitigliano**, **Saturnia** (wines: Morellino di Scansano and Bianco di Pitigliano). Day 15: check in at the spa at **Chianciano Terme** for liver repairs!

Ten Days of Curiosities

The unexpected, unique side of Tuscany and Umbria doesn't jump out at you; you'll have to look for it. In **Florence** you spend Days 1–3 seeing **Galileo's Forefinger** at the Museum of the History of Science; gruesomely realistic **Wax Anatomical models** at La Specola museum; a **151-kilo topaz** at the Museum of Mineralogy; a **16th-century Mexican Bishop's mitre** made out of feathers, in the Museo degli Argenti; **Islamic and Japanese armour** in the Villa Stibbert; or an ornate **Mozarabic Synagogue** or onion-domed **Russian Orthodox Church**. From there, head to Tuscany's northernmost town, **Pontrémoli** (Day 4) to see the mysterious **neolithic statue-steles,** and then down to **Carrara** for the eerie, almost black whiteness of the **marble quarries**. Day 5: **Pisa**—the **Leaning Tower** is only one of a score of oddities in the Field of Miracles; also take a look at the **Turkish war pennants** in S. Stefano. Day 6: **Volterra**, to see the *balze* and the unusual **Etruscan sculpture** in the Guarnacci Museum, on your way to the geothermal carnival of the **Metal Hills—geysers and sulphur lakes** around Larderello and Monterotondo. Day 7: detour to Elba for **Napoleon's Death Mask**, or even better, inland to **San Galgano**, with its ruined Gothic abbey and genuine **Sword-in-the-stone**. Day 8: if it's Saturday or Sunday, try the **Giardino dei Tarocchi** (at Capalbio, east of Orbetello), a bizarre collection of colossal modern sculptures, covered in bright ceramics and mirrors, dedicated to the 22 major arcana of the Tarot deck. Day 9: **Orvieto**, for one of the world's most remarkable wells, **Pozzo di S. Patrizio**, and a dip over the border into Lazio for the **Bomarzo Monster Park**, a Renaissance 'Sacred Wood' full of strange stone creatures. Day 10: if you're still game, **Terni** for the paintings of **Orneore Metelli**, a shoemaker who never learned the lessons of perspective, and **Ferentillo** up the Valnerina road for the **Chinese and Napoleonic mummies**.

Discover the Marches in 9 Days

Days 1–2: one day in **Urbino** to see the **Palazzo Ducale** and the town, another for excursions to outlying villages: **Urbania, Fermignano** or **San Leo**. Day 3: to **Fossombrone** with a look at the nearby **Gola del Furlo**. Day 4: a drive south through the mountains for a look at **Fabriano, Genga's** caves and Romanesque church, ending up in **Jesi**. Day 5: **Ancona** and a rest on the beaches around **Monte Conero**. Day 6: art at **Loreto** and, if time, accordions in **Castelfidardo**. Day 7: inland again for pretty towns and picture galleries: **Tolentino, Camerino** and **San Severino Marche**. Day 8: a scenic drive south along the flank of **Monti Sibillini**. Day 9: **Ascoli Piceno**.

Part II
TOPICS

Wild boars

Cittadini

Someone from Livorno, obviously, is a *Livornese*, and a Perugian, in his native language, would be a *Perugino* like his Renaissance fellow citizen who painted all those sweet Madonnas. However, knowing how to refer to a town's citizens in not always that easy. Italian libraries always have a fat reference book just for this purpose. Part of the confusion is due to the survival of ancient names, for example Neapolitans like to refer to themselves as *Parthenopeans* after the name of the original Greek settlement. Tuscany and Umbria have quite a few of these cases, but also quite a few others that are utterly inexplicable. Just for people who want to sharpen their Italian to a fine edge, here's a list of some of the most outlandish differences between *città* and *cittadini*:

Tuscany

Abbadia S. Salvatore	*abbadinghi*
Arezzo	*aretini*
Capolona (AR)	*pontesi*
Castelfiorentino	*castellani*
Castel S. Nicolò	*stradini*
Colle Val d'Elsa	*collegiani*
Montepulciano	*poliziani*
Sansepolcro	*biturgensi*

Umbria

Bevagna	*bevanati*

Città della Pieve	*pievesi*
Città di Castello	*tifernati*
Gubbio	*eugubini*
Norcia	*nursini*
Todi	*tudertini*

A Country Calendar

If there's a great sense of continuity in the land, it is the same with the rhythms of rural life in Tuscany and Umbria. Old traditions and seasonal changes are still of primary importance—Italians, for the most part, won't buy imported fruit or vegetables; even in the cities it's difficult to find a decent tomato in January. Even the chocolates disappear off the counter in July. Tuscany, like most of Italy, chooses to follow the calendar as a sort of sentimental journey through the rise and fall of the Year.

The traditional Florentine New Year was Annunciation Day in March, the time when the countryside really did seem to awaken—until the Medici Grand Dukes finally aligned Tuscany to the papal calendar in the 1500s. **January** still hibernates; if the ground is soft farmers may put in peas and garlic; roast chestnuts, polenta, *bruschetto* and game dishes are the highlights of the table. **February** is the month of pruning and planting garden vegetables in frames. Sticky sweet carnival pastries are unavoidable.

In **March** new fruit trees are planted and the vines are pruned; potatoes, fennel, spinach, carrots, parsley, and lettuce are planted directly in the garden. Blood oranges (from Sicily) and artichokes appear in the shops. The fruit trees burst into blossom, and continue through **April**, the time to plant sunflowers and corn, the other garden vegetables and most flowers. Lambs are slaughtered for Easter; young turkeys and pigs are purchased. The hunt for wild asparagus and salad greens is in full swing. Strawberries and medlars are the fruits of **May**, Tuscany's glory month, when the irises and roses bloom in profusion. *Fave* (broad beans) are the big treat, and in the mountains, in most years, you can stop lighting fires to stay warm in the evening. The first garlic, French beans, and potatoes are harvested in **June**, which is also the time to plant cabbage and cauliflowers. Cherries, apricots, plums, the first watermelons and fresh tomatoes appear; everyone's eating melon and prosciutto antipasti and dishes with courgette (zucchini) flowers. **July** brings an avalanche of zucchini and peaches. Country folk begin staying up past 10 pm, and scorpions come into your house to cool off.

In **August** an awful lot of chickens meet their maker, while the end of the month brings masses upon masses of tomatoes, which country families join together to conserve—a messy operation of steaming kettles and grinders that puts up a year's supply of tomato sauce. Apples, pears, and fresh figs are harvested in **September**, a golden, placid month when the village stationery shops begin stocking the schoolbooks for the new year. **October** is the *vendemmia*, or grape harvest, the highlight of the year for everyone outside the Umbrian Apennines; to make *vinsanto* it's essential to pick out very mature bunches and hang them up to dry. Hunting season opens, and folks begin to poke around for wild mushrooms. **November** is a busy month, the time to hunt for truffles, harvest olives, pomegranates, chestnuts, and take care of wine business. In **December** the family pig is slaughtered for next year's prosciutto and sausages. Orange persimmons hang like ornaments on the trees and plague the table—no one likes them, but everyone has plenty to give away; if they are indeed the apples of the Hesperides, as some scholars suggest, the afterlife must be a major disappointment. Much more delightful are the tiny tangerines from the south that flood the market. Christmas turkeys realize their time has come; and cakes are everywhere: dense confections of walnuts, raisins, and chocolate (*Panforte* of Siena or *Panpeppato* of Umbria) or tall, airy *Panettone* sold in cylindrical boxes.

Deluxe Virgins

Someday, on a trip to one of the fancier Italian food shops, you may pause near the section devoted to condiments and wonder at the beautiful display of bottles of unusually dark whiskies and wines, with corks and posh, elegant labels—why, some is even DOC, though much of it is far more costly than the usual DOC vintages. A closer look reveals these precious bottles are full of nothing but olive oil.

Admittedly *olio extra vergine di oliva* from Tuscany and Umbria makes a fine salad dressing—according to those in the know the oil of the Chianti brooks few rivals, Italian or otherwise. Its delicate, fruity fragrance derives from the excellent quality of the ripe olive and the low acidity extracted from the fruit without any refinements. The finest oil, Extra Virgin, must have less than 1 per cent acidity (the best has 0.5 per cent acidity). Other designations are Soprafino Virgin, Fine Virgin, and Virgin (each may have up to 4 per cent acidity) in descending order of quality. And as any Italian will tell you, it's good for you—and it had better be, because Tuscan or Umbrian chefs put it in nearly every dish, as they have for centuries. The only difference is that now it comes in a fancy package for a fancy price, a victim of the Italian designer label syndrome and (mostly) Tuscan preciosity. Not only does the olive oil have corks, but the trend in some of the smarter restaurants is to offer an olive oil list similar to a wine list—one restaurant in Tuscany even has an oil sommelier! DOC vinegar and sheep cheese are just around the corner.

The First Professional Philistine

Many who have seen Vasari's work in Florence will be wondering how such a mediocre painter should rate so much attention. Ingratiating companion of the rich and famous, workmanlike over-achiever and tireless self-promoter, Vasari was the perfect man for his time. Born in Arezzo, in 1511, a fortunate introduction to Cardinal Silvio Passerini gave him the chance of an education in Florence with the young Medici heirs, Ippolito and Alessandro. In his early years, he became a fast and reliable frescoist gaining a reputation for customer satisfaction—a real innovation in an age when artists were increasingly becoming eccentric prima donnas. In the 1530s, after travelling around Italy on various commissions, he returned to Florence just when Cosimo I was beginning his plans to remake the city in the image of the Medici. It was a marriage made in heaven. Vasari became Cosimo's court painter and architect, with a limitless budget and a large group of assistants, the most prolific fresco machine ever seen in Italy—painting over countless good frescoes of the 1300s along the way.

But more than for his paintings, Vasari lives on through his book, the *Lives of the Artists*, a series of exhaustive biographies of artists. Beginning with Cimabue, Vasari traces the rise of Art out of Byzantine and Gothic barbarism, through Giotto and his followers, towards an ever-improving naturalism, finally culminating in the great age of Leonardo, Raphael, and the divine Michelangelo, who not only mastered nature but outdid her. Leon Battista Alberti gets the credit for drafting the first principles of artistic criticism, but it was Vasari who first applied such ideas on a grand scale. His book, being the first of its kind, and containing a mine of valuable information on dozens of Renaissance artists, naturally has had a tremendous influence on all subsequent criticism. Art critics have never really been able to break out of the Vasarian straitjacket.

Much of Vasari's world seems quaint to us now: the idea of the artist as a kind of knight of the brush, striving for Virtue and Glory, the slavish worship of anything that survived from ancient Rome, artistic 'progress' and the conviction that art's purpose was to imitate nature. But many of Vasari's opinions have had a long and mischievous career in the world of ideas. His blind disparagement of everything medieval—really the prejudice of his entire generation—lived on until the 1800s. His dismissal of Sienese, Umbrian, and northern artists—of anyone who was not a Florentine—has not been entirely corrected even today. Vasari was the sort who founded academies, a cheerful conformist who believed in a nice, tidy art that went by the book. With his interior decorator's concept of Beauty, he created a style of criticism in which virtuosity, not imagination, became the standard by which art was to be judged. It is a lesson for us all; history offers few more instructive examples of the stamina and resilience of dubious ideas.

Flora and Fauna

No one would come to this part of Italy expecting to find an unspoiled wilderness. Most of Tuscany, in particular, has been cultivated so long and so intensively, that wildlife is completely pushed to the fringes. Nevertheless, there is a great variety of birds and beasts to complement the surprisingly wide range of landscapes. Cultivated Tuscany (see below, *landscapes*) is another world, the land of vineyards and olive groves, cypresses, poplars, and the occasional parasol pine. The rest of the territory divides neatly into three parts: the coastal zone, with its beaches and wetlands, the central hills, and the mountains.

For nature lovers, the coast will be by far the most interesting region; the malaria mosquito kept much of the southern Maremma undeveloped for centuries, leaving vast stretches of pine forest, along with cork oak and holm oak, a thriving wildlife (including even some wild horses) and marshlands that host a marvellous array of birds, from eagles to woodpeckers. Its protected nesting grounds (see the *Monti dell'Uccellina, Laguna di Orbetello* and *Lago di Burano*) are Italy's greatest stopover for migrating waterfowl—herons, cormorants, storks, kingfishers, osprey, and the only cranes left on the mainland. Deforested land beyond the marshes is covered with the characteristic Mediterranean scrub, or maquis (*macchia*, in Italian); either 'macchia alta' with shrub versions of pines (they harvest the pine nuts), oaks, beech, cypress, and laurel; or the 'macchia bassa' in drier regions, thick patches of broom, heather, lentisk, and other fragrant plants.

As for the animals, there are pretty much the same characters throughout Tuscany and Umbria, starting with those two regional totems, the viper and the boar. The bad old viper, the only really unpleasant thing you may meet out in the woods and fields, proliferates especially where farmlands have been abandoned; he's brownish-grey, about 2 feet long (never more than 3), and has a head vaguely diamond-shaped. Vipers are a nuisance only because there are so many of them, and because they object to being stepped on. If one bites you, you've got half an hour to find someone with the serum—or you can buy your own in any pharmacy. The boar, a shy, well-mannered creature, flourishes everywhere despite the Italians' best efforts to turn him into boar salami. In summer, you may hear them nosing around the villages at night looking for water.

Beyond these, there are plenty of hares and rabbits, foxes and weasels, also polecats, badgers, and porcupine in the wilder areas. Wolves, lynxes, and deer are extinct in most of Tuscany and Umbria, though a few of each survive in the higher reaches of the Apennines, and deer have been reintroduced in the Maremma coastal parks. There is a little isolated region in Tuscany, the Val di Farma north of Roccastrada, where you can find all of these, and even wildcats. The only mountain goats are found on the island of Montecristo.

Many writers on this part of Italy comment on the absence of birdsong. They're exaggerating. Italian hunters do shoot anything that flies, but there are still quite a few thrushes, starlings, wrens, and such, along with the white doves, ubiquitous in Umbria, that always make you think of Assisi and St Francis. Cuckoos unfailingly announce the spring, pheasants lay low during the hunting season, and an occasional owl can be heard in the country. Nightingales are rare, but there are supposed to be some around Lago di Massacuccioli and the northern coasts—in the evening you're far more likely to see little bats.

The insect world is well represented, and if you spend time in the country, you'll meet many of them: lovely butterflies and moths and delicate white creatures, with wings apparently made of feathers; rather forbidding black bullet bees and wasps that resemble vintage fighter planes. Beetles especially reach disproportionate sizes—if you're lucky you may see a *diavolo*, a large black or red beetle with long, gracefully curving antlers that sing when you trap them; Leonardo drew one in his notebooks. There are enough mosquitoes, midges, and little biting flies to be a nuisance in the summer, and perhaps most alarming at first sight, the shiny black scorpion, who may crawl inside through the window or up drains (you may want to keep the plugs in) or come in with the wood if you have a fire. Once inside they head for dark places like beds or shoes. One thwack with a shoe will do in even the largest scorpion (they're actually quite soft). If you happen to be stung, it may be painful but not deadly; the Italians recommend a trip to the doctor as a preventative against an infection or allergic reaction.

As for the forests, oaks, chestnuts, and beech predominate, along with tall, upright poplars ('Lombardy' poplars), pines, willows (not the weeping variety) and a few maples—with rounded leaves, not pointed as in northern Europe and America. Cypress trees are common. Incidentally the idea that there are erect, needle-like 'male' cypresses and blowsy 'female' ones is a misconception; the tidier ones have been planted, while shaggy cypresses are the wild variety. Parasol pines (really the *maritime pine*), that most characteristic Italian tree, make a grand sight isolated on a hill crest, or in large groves along the Maremma coast. At higher altitudes, there are large beech forests, along with pines and firs—some beautiful groves of silver firs grow around Monte Amiata, while in the Casentino near Camaldoli is a vast stretch of old, protected beech and pine forest; another, primarly chestnut forest, is contained in the Garfagnana's *Parco Naturale dell'Orecchiella*.

Wild Flowers: Though at first they may seem unfamiliar, many of the most common Italian wild flowers are close cousins to those seen in Northern Europe and America. There are a million varieties of buttercup, usually tiny ones like the *ranuncolo* and *bottoncini d'oro*, and of bluebell, often called *campanella* or *campanellina*. Many of the common five-petalled pink blossoms in spring fields are really small wild geraniums (*geranio*), with pointed leaves like the anemone, and you'll see quite a few varieties of violets (*violette*) with round or spade-shaped leaves (a few species are yellow). A daisy, in Italian, is a *margherita*, and they come in all sizes. Tiniest of all are the wild pink and blue forget-me-nots (*non ti scordar di me*); you'll have to look closely to see them in overgrown fields. Large swatches of lavender are one of the charms of the hills of Chianti.

The real star of Italian fields is the poppy, bright red and thriving everywhere. Dandelions and wild mustard are also plentiful, along with white, umbrella-like bunches of florets called *tragosellino* or *podragraria*, similar to what Americans call Queen Anne's Lace. More exotic flowers include wild orchids, some with small florets growing in spiky shoots, rhododendrons (in mountainous areas), five-petalled wild roses, and water lilies in the coastal Maremma.

There are other plants to look for; a dozen different kinds of greens the Italians gather for salads, anise, and fennel, wild hemp (only a fool would try to smoke it); mint, rosemary, and sage are common, and Italians beat the bushes with fervour every spring looking for wild asparagus. Also wild strawberries (*fragola del bosco*), raspberries (*lampone*), and blackberries (*rovo*).

A Florentine Puzzle

In a city as visually dry and restrained as Florence, every detail of decoration stands out. In the Middle Ages and Renaissance, Florentine builders combined their passion for geometry with their love of making a little go a long way; they evolved a habit of embellishing buildings with simple geometrical designs. Though nothing special in themselves—most are easily drawn with a compass and straight edge—in the context of Florence they stand out like mystic hieroglyphs, symbols upon which to meditate while contemplating old Florence's remarkable journey through the western mind.

The city is full of them, incorporated into façades and mosaics, windows and decorative friezes. Here are eight of them, a little exercise for the eye while tramping the hard pavements of Florence. Your job is to find them. Some are really obvious, others

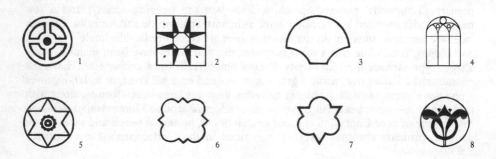

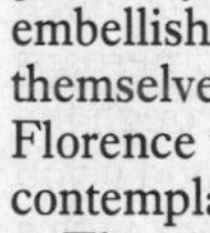
1

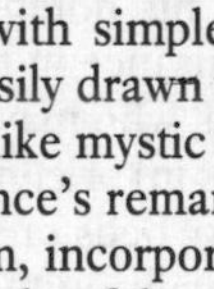
2

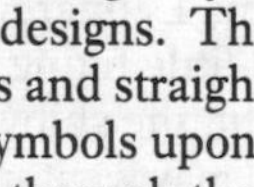
3

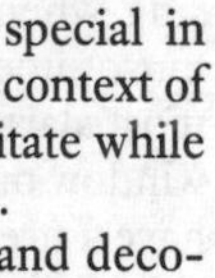
4

5

6

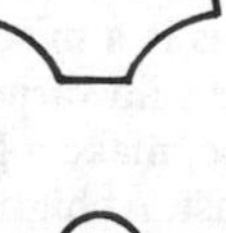
7

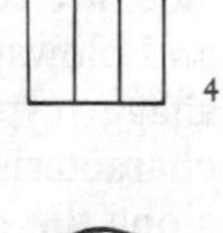
8

obscure. For no. 6 you should be able to find at least three examples (two across the street from each other) and if you're clever you'll find not only no. 5, a rather late addition to the cityscape, but also the medieval work that inspired it. Don't worry too much about the last one. But if you're an art historian or a Florentinophile, it's only fair that you seek out this hard one, too. Answers can be found on the last page of the book.

Guelphs and Ghibellines

One medieval Italian writer claimed that the great age of factional strife began with two brothers of Pistoia, named Guelf and Gibel. Like Cain and Abel, or Romulus and Remus, one murdered the other, starting the seemingly endless troubles that to many seemed a God-sent plague, meant to punish the proud and wealthy Italians for their sins. Medieval Italy may in fact have been guilty of every sort of jealousy, greed, and wrath, but most historians trace the beginnings of this party conflict to two great German houses, *Welf* and *Waiblingen*.

To the Italians, what those barbarians did across the Alps meant little; the chroniclers pinpoint the outbreak of the troubles to the year 1215, when a politically prominent Florentine noble named Buondelmonte del Buondelmonti was assassinated by his enemies while crossing the Ponte Vecchio. It was the tinder that ignited a smouldering quarrel all over Italy, particularly in Tuscany. The atmosphere of contentious city-states, each with its own internal struggles between nobles, the rich merchant class and the commons, crystallized rapidly into parties. In the beginning, at least, they stood for something. The Guelphs, largely a creation of the newly-wealthy bourgeois, were all for free trade and the rights of the free cities; the Ghibellines from the start were the party of the German emperors, nominal overlords of Italy who had been trying to assert their control ever since the days of Charlemagne. Naturally, the Guelphs found their protector in the emperors' bitter temporal rivals, the popes. This brought a religious angle into the story, especially with the advent of the heretical, Emperor Frederick II.

Everything about this convoluted history tends to confirm the worst suspicions of modern behavourist scientists. Before long, the labels Guelph and Ghibelline ceased to have any meaning at all. In the 13th and 14th centuries, the emperors and their Ghibelline allies helped the church root out heretical movements like the Patarenes, while the popes schemed to destroy the liberty of good Guelph cities, especially in Umbria, and incorporate them into the Papal State. In cities, like Florence, where the Guelphs won a final victory, they themselves split into parties, battling with the same barbaric gusto. Black was the Ghibelline colour, white the Guelph, and cities arranged themselves like squares on a chessboard. When one suffered a revolution and changed from Guelph to Ghibelline, or vice-versa, of course its nearest enemies would soon change the other way. Often the public buildings give us a clue as to the loyalties of a city in any given time. Simple, squared crenellations are Guelph (as in the Palazzo dei Priori in Perugia, or in a score of other town halls); ornate 'swallow-tail' crenellations (as in Frederick II's castle in Prato) are the mark of the Ghibelline. Siena was a generally Ghibelline city, but its great Palazzo Pubblico was built with square crenellations during a Guelph interlude under the rule of the Nine.

The English, like many uninvolved European nations, looked on all this with bewilderment. Edmund Spenser, in glosses to his *Shepheards' Calendar* (1579), wrote this fanciful etymology: 'when all Italy was distraicte into the Factions of the Guelfes and the Gibelins, being two famous houses in Florence, the name began through their great mischiefes and many outrages, to be so odious or rather dreadfull in the peoples eares, that if theyr children at any time were frowarde and wanton, they would say to them the Guelfe or the Gibeline came. Which words nowe from them (as may thinge els) be come into our vsage, and for Guelfes and Gibelines, we say *Elfes* and *Goblins*.'

Hermes Trismegistus

As you pass through the main portal of Siena cathedral, the figure before you on the famous marble pavement comes as a surprise—Hermes Trismegistus, someone rarely seen in art, though a mysterious protagonist in a great undercurrent of Renaissance thought. 'Thrice-great Hermes', mythical author of a series of mystic philosophical dialogues from the 2nd century AD, had a profound influence on Greek and Arabic thought, gradually becoming associated (correctly or not) with the Egyptian god Thoth, inventor of writing and father of a deep mystical tradition that continues to this day. In the 1400s, the Hermetic writings were introduced in the west, largely the work of Greek scholars fleeing the Ottoman conquest of Constantinople and Trebizond. They made quite a splash. Marsilio Ficino, the Florentine Humanist and friend of Cosimo de' Medici, completed the first Latin translation of the Hermetic books in 1471—Cosimo specifically asked him to put off his translations of Plato to get this more important work finished!

To the men of the Renaissance, Hermes was a real person, an Egyptian prophet, who lived in the time of Moses and was perhaps his teacher. They saw, revealed in the Hermetic books, an ancient, natural religion, prefiguring Christianity and complementary to it—and in fact much more fun than Christianity, for the magical elements in it were entirely to the taste of neo-Platonists like Ficino. From a contemporary point of view, the recovery of Hermes Trismegistus was one of the main intellectual events of the century, a century that witnessed a tremendous revival of natural magic, alchemy and astrology.

The memorable Hermes in Siena is surrounded by a bevy of ten Sybils: those of Cumae and Tivoli (the Italians), Delphi, Libya, the Hellespont, Phrygia and the rest. These ladies, part of a pan-Mediterranean religious tradition even older than Hermes Trismegistus, are far more common in Tuscan religious iconography (as in the Baptistry and S. Trínita in Florence, or most famously on Michelangelo's Sistine Chapel ceiling), for the belief that they all in some way foretold the birth of Christ.

Landscapes

Other regions in Italy are lusher, others have taller mountains and more fertile valleys, others support a far greater variety of flora and enjoy a more temperate climate. Yet when all is said and done, it is the landscapes of Tuscany and Umbria that exert the most lasting charm. In the painting of the Renaissance, the background of rolling hills, cypresses, poplars, and parasol pines, the vineyards and winding lanes are often more beautiful than the nominally religious subject in the foreground. Very early on, beginning with Giotto, artists took care to relate the figures in their composition to the architecture and the landscape, epitomized in the paintings of Leonardo da Vinci, where each tree and rock takes on an almost mystic significance.

Every Italian is born with an obsessive instinct to put in order, or '*sistemare*' things; with a history of wars, earthquakes, foreign rulers, and an age-old tendency to extremes of all descriptions, the race has had a bellyful of disorder and unpredictability. The tidy, ordered geometry and clipped hedges of an Italian garden are a perfect example of the urge to *sistemare* nature, and you'll find good examples of these in the Boboli, the Medici villas at Castello, and Collodi, the Tuscans, in the vanguard of Italy in so many ways, were the first to *sistemare* their entire territory. The vicious wars of the Middle Ages between cities and the Guelphs and Ghibellines devastated the countryside and much of the forests (as is visible in the harsh, barren brown and grey hills of trecento painting); the Black Death in the 1300s depopulated the cultivated areas, giving the Tuscans the unique opportunity to arrange things just so. Not entirely by coincidence, the late 14th century was the time when the elite, weary of the strife in the city, were discovering the joys of the country and building villas, playing the country squire and gentleman farmer whenever possible—already, in the *Decameron*, the nobles had estates in the environs of Florence. And they planted everything in its place according to elegance and discipline, each tree with its own purpose, a boundary marker, for shade, or to support a vine. Often cypresses and parasol pines stand strikingly along the crest of hills, not for aesthetics or a study in perspective, but for a windbreak. Strongest of all is the feeling that nothing has changed for centuries, that in the quattrocento Gozzoli and Fra Angelico painted the same scene you see today. Few landscapes anywhere are more ancient, or civilized.

The countryside of Umbria makes an interesting comparison to Tuscany. Its beauty is more dishevelled and rustic; its hills tend to be steeper, and its valleys narrower, planted with little of the precise elegance of Tuscany. It is celebrated for its green, the 'mystical' colour to suit its mystical, saintly nature; in the autumn and winter, mists swirl romantically through the mountains. One feature of the Umbrian landscape, however, is as artful as Tuscany—its tidy hill towns of pinkish grey stone. From some places you can see several at a time, like an archipelago of islands crowned with villages, one behind the other, vanishing into the bluish haze of the horizon.

Trends in Taste

> 'I took a quick walk through the city to see the Duomo and the Battistero. Once more, a completely new world opened up before me, but I did not wish to stay long. The location of the Boboli Gardens is marvellous. I hurried out of the city as quickly as I entered it.'
>
> —Goethe, on Florence in *Italian Journey*

Goethe, the father of the Italian Grand Tour, on his way from Venice to Rome, did not have much time for the city that likes to call itself 'The Capital of Culture'. Like nearly every traveller in the 18th and early 19th centuries, he knew nothing of Giotto, Masaccio, Botticelli, or Piero della Francesca; it was Roman statues that wowed him, the very same ones that the modern visitor passes in the corridors of the Uffizi without a second glance. Shelley managed to write pages on his visits to the museum without mentioning a single painting.

Some Tuscan attractions never change—the Leaning Tower, Michelangelo's *David*, the villas, the gardens and the cheap wine. Others have gone through an amazing rise or fall in popularity, thanks in part to John Ruskin, whose *Mornings in Florence* introduced the charms of the Romanesque architecture, Giotto, and the masters of the trecento; for him Orcagna was the master of them all (but in the 18th century, the Giottos in Santa Croce were whitewashed over, while many works of Orcagna had been destroyed earlier, by Vasari). Botticelli went from total obscurity in the 18th century to become the darling of the Victorians. Livorno and Viareggio on the coast, and Bagni di Lucca near the Garfagnana, used to have thriving English colonies—no more. But Tuscany itself used to be a very different place, where they used to play a betting game called *pallone*, somewhere between lawn tennis and jai alai; where in 1900 a herd of 150 camels, introduced by Grand Duke Ferdinand II in 1622, roamed the Pisan Park of San Rossore; where, as Robert and Elizabeth Browning found, the rent for a palazzo used to be laughably cheap.

But the story of the Venus de' Medici is perhaps the most instructive. The statue is a pleasant, if unremarkable Greek work of the 2nd century BC, but for two centuries it was Florence's chief attraction; the minute visitors arrived in Florence they would rush off to gaze upon her; those prone to write gushed rapturously of her perfect beauty. Napoleon kidnapped her for France, asking the great neo-classical sculptor Canova to sculpt a replacement; afterwards the Venus was one of the things Florence managed to get back, though her reign was soon to be undermined—Ruskin called her an 'uninteresting little person'. Since then she has stood forlornly in the Tribunale of the Uffizi, unnoticed and unloved.

Some things don't change. Over a hundred years after Goethe's blitz tour of Florence, Aldous Huxley had no time for the city, either: 'We came back through Florence and the spectacle of that second-rate provincial town with its repulsive Gothic architecture and its acres of Christmas card primitives made me almost sick. The only points about Florence are the country outside it, the Michelangelo tombs, Brunelleschi's dome, and a few rare pictures. The rest is simply dung when compared to Rome.'

Tuscany on Wheels

Tuscans always loved a parade, and to the casual reader of Renaissance history, it seems they're forever proceeding somewhere or another, even to their own detriment—during outbreaks of plague, holy companies would parade through an inflicted area, invoking divine mercy, while in effect aiding the spread of the pestilence. They also had a great weakness for allegorical parade floats. During the centuries of endless war each Tuscan city rolled out its war chariot or battle wagon, called the *Carroccio*, invented by a Milanese bishop in the 11th century. A *Carroccio*, drawn by six white oxen, was a kind of holy ship of state in a hay cart; a mast held up a crucifix while a battle standard flew from the yard arm, there was an altar for priests to say mass during the battle and a large bell to send signals over the din to the armies. The worst possible outcome of a battle was to lose one's *Carroccio* to the enemy, as Fiesole did to Florence. One is still in operation, in Siena, rumbling out twice a year for the Palio.

Medieval clerical processions, by the time of Dante, became melded with the idea of the Roman 'triumph' (*trionfo*); in Purgatory, the poet finds Beatrice triumphing with a cast of characters from the Apocalypse. Savonarola wrote of a *Triumph of the Cross*; Petrarch and Boccaccio wrote allegorical triumphs of virtues, love, and death. More interesting, however, are the secular Roman-style Triumphs staged by the Medici, especially at Carnival (the name of which, according to Burckhardt, comes from a cart, the pagan *carrus navalis*, the ship of Isis, launched every 5 March to symbolize the reopening of navigation). You can get a hint of their splendour from the frescoes at Poggio a Caiano; the best artists of the day would be commissioned to design the decorations—two particularly famous *trionfi* in Florence celebrated the election of Pope Leo X. The last relics of these parades are the huge satirical carnival floats at Viareggio.

Two lovely memories of Florence's processions remain. One is Gozzoli's fairy-tale frescoes in the chapel of the Medici palace, of the annual procession staged by the Compagnia de' Re Magi, the most splendid and aristocratic of pageants. The other comes from the Florentine Carnival, famous for its enormous floats, in which scenes from mythology were portrayed to songs and music. One year, for the masque of Bacchus and Ariadne, Lorenzo de' Medici composed the loveliest Italian poem to come out of the Renaissance, with the melancholy refrain:

Quanto è bella giovinezza,
Che si fugge tuttavia!
Chi vuol esser lieto, sia:
Di doman non c'è certezza.

Umbria's Totem Tubers

One of Umbria's most important cash crops has neither seeds nor a planting season, and adamantly refuses to grow in straight rows. Truffles they are, *tartufi*, and although they look a lot like granulated mud on your pasta, these earthy, aromatic, and aphrodisiac tubers are the most prized gourmet delicacy in Italy. Even in their natural state they aren't much to look at, bulbous lumps from the size of a pea to a baby's fist, and they're very picky about where they grow. The Apeninnes of Umbria are one of their favourite spots—here are the proper calcareous soils, oak trees, and exposures, especially in the eastern reaches around Norcia. This is the land of black truffle (*tuber melangosporum*), while in the hills around San Miniato in Tuscany, and in northeast Umbria, the more rare and costly white truffle (*tuber magnatum*) is found.

Gram per gram truffles are the most expensive comestible in the world; not only are they fairly rare, but they're hard to track down. An aura of mystery hangs over their birth; according to legend they are spawned by lightning bolts flickering among the oaks. Although high prices have of late led to serious experiments in truffle cultivation, the vast majority are still brought to market by truffle hunters and their keen-nosed, specially trained truffle hounds. Autumn is truffle season, during the night when the truffles smell the strongest, or perhaps because the best truffles are always on someone else's land. Fortunately, a little truffle goes a long way, and Italians will travel far to look, dreamy-eyed, at little glass jars of them at the truffle fairs in Città di Castello and San Miniato. Most supermarkets sell them as well—you can buy one the size of a marble for L30 000.

Part III

HISTORY & ART

Marzocco (Bargello, Florence)

Historical Outline

At times, the history of Tuscany and Umbria has been a small part of a bigger story—Rome's, or modern Italy's. However, the crucial eras of the Middle Ages and the Renaissance provided a tremendous chronicle of contending city states, each with a complex history of its own. For that reason, we have included detailed histories of the most important towns—Florence, Siena, Pisa, and Perugia, and covered the rest to a lesser extent. Here is a brief outline of the entire history for the region as a whole:

The Etruscans

Neolithic cultures seem to have occupied this part of Italy since about 4500 BC without distinguishing themselves artistically or politically. The dawn of history in these parts comes with the arrival of the **Etruscans**, though where they came from and precisely when they arrived remains one of the major mysteries of early Mediterranean history. According to their traditions, the Etruscans migrated from western Anatolia, *c.* 900 BC. Classical authors were divided on this point; some believed the migration theory, while others saw the Etruscans as the indigenous inhabitants of west-central Italy. Their language remains murky to modern scholars, but the discovery of Etruscan inscriptions on the Greek island of Lemnos, along with other clues, tends to support the Etruscan story.

Whatever, they were a talented people, and the great wealth they derived from an intensive agriculture, manufacturing, and above all mining (Elba and the Metal Hills) allowed these talents to blossom into opulence by the 7th century BC. Though they gave their name to modern Tuscany, the real centre of Etruscan civilization lay to the south; roughly the coast from Orbetello to Cervéteri (Caere) in Lazio and around Lakes Bolsena and Trasimeno. Never a unified nation, the Etruscans preferred the general Mediterranean model of the independent city state; the 12 greatest dominated central Italy in a federation called the **Dodecapolis**. Which cities were members is uncertain, but the 14 possible cities include *Veii*, *Cervéteri*, *Tarquinia* and *Vulci* (in Lazio), *Roselle*, *Vetulonia* and *Populonia* (on or near the Tuscan coast), *Volterra*, *Fiesole*, *Arezzo*, *Chiusi*, *Orvieto*, *Cortona* and *Perugia*.

Throughout their history, the Etruscans maintained extremely close trade and cultural ties with classical Greece. They sold Elban iron and bought Greek culture wholesale; the artistic thieving magpies of antiquity, they were able to take every style of Greek art, from the Minoan-style frescoes at Tarquinia to the classical bronzes now in the Florence Museum, and create something of their very own. In expressive portrait sculpture, though, they surpassed even the Greeks. A considerable mythology has grown up around the Etruscans. Some historians and poets celebrate them as a nation of free peoples, devoted to art, good food, and easy living. Less sentimental minds have tried to show the other side, a slave society run for the benefit of a military, aristocratic elite. Whichever, the art they left behind gives them a place as the most enigmatic, vivid and fascinating people of early Italy. It isn't difficult to see echoes of their culture in everything that has happened in this part of Italy for the last 2000 years.

Romans

Etruscan kings once ruled in Rome, but after the establishment of the Republic, this precocious city was to prove the end of the Etruscan world. All of southern Etruria was swallowed up by 358 BC, and internal divisions between the Etruscan cities allowed the Romans to push their conquest inevitably northwards. After the conquest of an Etruscan city, Roman policy was often diabolically clever; by establishing veterans' colonies in new towns nearby to draw off trade, Rome was able to ensure the withering of Etruscan culture and the slow extinction of many of Etruria's greatest cities.

Four other cultures from this time deserve a mention; first the **Umbrii**, a peaceful pastoral people indigenous to eastern Umbria and parts of the Marches. They adopted the Etruscan alphabet, but never had much to say in it—the only surviving inscription in Umbrian is in the museum of Gubbio. These earliest Umbrians had the good sense to avoid antagonizing Rome, and often allied themselves with the city in wars against other Italian tribes. The more warlike **Piceni**, most important of the tribes that occupied what is today the Marches, proved more antagonistic; in fact they played a leading role in the Social Wars of 92–89 BC, the last doomed attempt of the Italians to fight free of Roman imperialism. The wandering **Celts**, who occupied all northern Italy, often made themselves at home in the Apennines and northern Etruria; their influence on the region's culture is slight. And finally there was the unnamed culture of the rugged **Lunigiana**, around Pontrémoli, a people who carried their Neolithic customs and religion (see the statue-steles in the Pontrémoli museum) well into the modern era.

Under the empire, Etruria and Umbria were separate provinces, with the Tiber for a border. Both were relatively quiet, though the region experienced a north–south economic split to mirror the bigger one beginning across Italy. Southern Etruria, the old

Etruscan heartland, shrivelled and died under Roman misrule, never to recover. The north became more prosperous, and important new cities appeared: Lucca, Pisa, Florence, and to a lesser extent Assisi, Gubbio, and Siena.

The Dark Ages

Later Italians' willingness to create fanciful stories about the 'barbarian invasions' makes it hard to define what did happen in this troubled time. The first (5th-century) campaigns of the **Goths** in Italy did not seem to cause too much damage, but the curtain finally came down on Roman civilization with the Greek-Gothic wars of 536–563, when Eastern Emperor Justinian and his generals Belisarius and Narsus attempted to recapture Italy for Byzantium. The chronicles of many cities record the devastation of the Gothic King, Totila (the sack of Florence, and a seven-year siege of Perugia), though the Imperial aggressors were undoubtedly just as bad. In any case, the damage to an already weakened society was fatal, and the wars opened the way for the conquest of much of Italy by the terrible **Lombards** (568), who established the Duchy of Spoleto, with loose control over much of central Italy. Lucca, the late Roman and Gothic capital of Etruria, alone managed to keep the Lombards out. By this time, low-lying cities like Florence had practically disappeared, while the remnants of the other towns survived under the control of local barons, or occasionally under their bishops. Feudal warfare and marauding became endemic. In the 800s even a band of Arabs came looting and pillaging up the Valnerina, almost in the centre of the peninsula.

By the 9th century, things were looking up. Florence had re-established itself, and built its famous baptistry. The old counts of Lucca extended their power to become counts of Tuscany, under the Attoni family, lords of Canossa. As the leading power in the region, they made themselves a force in European affairs. In 1077, the great Countess Matilda, allied with the Pope, humbled Emperor Henry IV at Canossa—the famous 'penance in the snow' during the struggles over investiture. Perhaps most important of all was the growth of the maritime city of **Pisa** which gave Tuscany a new window on the world, building wealth through trade and inviting new cultural influences from France, Byzantium and the Muslim world.

Medieval Tuscany

By 1000, with the new millennium, all of northern Italy was poised to rebuild the civilization that had been lost centuries before. In Tuscany and Umbria, as elsewhere, increasing trade had created a rebirth of towns, each doing its best to establish its independence from local nobles or bishops, and to increase its influence at the expense of its neighbours. Thus a thousand minor squabbles were played out against the background of the major issues of the day; first the conflict over investiture in the 11th century, evolving into the endless factional struggles of **Guelphs** and **Ghibellines** after 1215 (see Topics, p. 49). Throughout, the cities were forced to choose sides between the partisans of the popes and those of the emperors. The Ghibellines' brightest hours came with the reigns of strong Hohenstaufen emperors **Frederick I Barbarossa** (1152–90) and his grandson **Frederick II** (1212–46), both of whom spent much time in Tuscany. An early Guelph wave came with the papacy of **Innocent III** (1198–1216), most powerful of the medieval pontiffs, and the Guelphs would come back to dominate Tuscany after the invasion of Charles of Anjou in 1261. Florence, Perugia, Arezzo, and

Lucca were the mainstays of the Guelphs, while Pisa, Pistoia, and Siena usually supported the Ghibellines.

In truth, it was every city for itself. By 1200, most towns had become free *comuni*; their imposing public buildings can be seen in almost every corner of Tuscany and Umbria. All the trouble they caused fighting each other (at first with citizen militias, later increasingly with the use of hired *condottieri*) never troubled the booming economy. Florence and Siena became bankers to all Europe, great building programmes went up, beginning with the Pisa cathedral complex in the 1100s, and the now tamed and urbanized nobles built fantastical skyscraper skylines of tower-fortresses in the towns. Above all, it was a great age for culture, the age of Dante (b. 1265) and Giotto (b. 1266). Another feature of the time was the 13th-century religious revival, dominated by the figure of **St Francis of Assisi**.

Background of the Renaissance

Florence, biggest and richest of the Tuscan cities, increased its influence all through the 1300s, gaining Prato and Pistoia, and finally winning a seaport with the capture of declining Pisa in 1406. This set the stage for the relative political equilibrium of Tuscany during the early Renaissance, the height of the region's wealth and artistic achievement. Many Umbrian cities, notably Perugia, participated in both, though Umbria as a whole could not keep up. The popes, newly established in Rome, sent Cardinal Albornoz across the territory in the 1360s with the aim of binding the region more closely to the Papal State; he built a score of fortresses across Umbria.

The **Wars of Italy**, beginning in 1494, put an end to Renaissance tranquillity. Florence was once more lost in its internal convolutions, twice expelling the **Medici**, while French and Imperial armies marched over the two regions. When the dust had cleared, the last of the free cities (with the exception of Lucca) had been extinguished, and most of Tuscany came under the rule of the Grand Duke **Cosimo I** (1537–74), the Medici propped on a newly-made throne by Emperor Charles V. Tuscany's economic and artistic decline was gentle compared with that of Umbria and the Marches; most of these two regions were incorporated into the Papal State during the 16th century.

The Modern Era

Though maintaining a relative independence, Tuscany had little to say in Italian affairs. After the Treaty of Câteau-Cambrésis in 1559, the Spaniards established a military enclave, called the Presidio, around Orbetello, precisely to keep an eye on central Italy. Cosimo I proved a vigorous ruler, though his successors gradually declined in ability. By 1600 it didn't matter. The total exhaustion of the Florentine economy kept pace with that of the Florentine imagination. By 1737, when the Medici dynasty became extinct, Tuscany was one of the torpid backwaters of Europe. It had no chance to decide its own destiny; the European powers agreed to bestow Tuscany on the House of Lorraine, cousins to the Austrian Habsburgs. Surprisingly enough, the Lorraines proved able and popular rulers, especially during the rule of the enlightened, progressive Peter Leopold (1765–90).

The languor of Lorraine and Papal rule was interrupted by Napoleon, who invaded central Italy twice and established a Kingdom of Etruria from 1801 to 1807. Austrian rule returned after 1815, continuing the series of well-meaning, intelligent Grand

Dukes. By now, however, the Tuscans and the rest of the Italians wanted something better. In the tumults of the Risorgimento, one of the greatest and kindest of the Lorraines, Leopold II, saw the writing on the wall and allowed himself to be overthrown in 1859. Tuscany was almost immediately annexed to the new Italian kingdom, which liberated Umbria in the same year.

Since then, the two regions have followed the history of modern Italy. The head start Tuscany gained under the Lorraine dukes allowed it to keep up economically with northern Italy, while Umbria had a hard job picking itself up off the floor. Florence had a brief moment of glory (1865–70) as capital of Italy, awaiting the capture of Rome. Since then, the biggest affair was World War II, with a long, tortuous campaign dragging across Tuscany and the Marches. The Germans based their Gothic Line on the Arno, blowing up all but one of Florence's bridges.

Art and Architecture in Tuscany and Umbria

Etruscans

Although we have no way of knowing what life was like for the average man in Camars or Velathrii, their tomb sculptures and paintings convince us that they were a talented, likeable people. Almost all of their art derives from the Greek; the Etruscans built classical temples (unfortunately of wood, with terracotta embellishments, so little survives), carved themselves sarcophagi decorated with scenes from Homer, and painted their pottery in red and black after the latest styles from Athens or Corinth. They excelled at portrait sculpture, and had a remarkable gift for capturing personality, sometimes seriously, though never heroically, often with an entirely intentional humour, and usually the serene smiles of people who truly enjoyed life.

Etruscan art in museums is often maddening; some of the works are among the finest productions of antiquity, while others—from the same time and city—are awkward and childish. Their talent for portraiture, among much else, was carried on by the Romans, and they bequeathed their love of fresco painting to the artists of the Middle Ages and Renaissance, who of course weren't even aware of the debt. After introducing yourself to the art of the Etruscans, it will be interesting to reconsider all that came later—in Tuscany, and indeed all Italy, you will find subtle reminders of this enigmatic people.

Romans and Dark Ages

After destroying the Etruscan nation, the Romans also began the extinction of its artistic tradition; by the Empire, there was almost nothing left that could be called distinctively Etruscan. All of Tuscany and Umbria contributed little under the Empire. In the chaos that followed, there was little room for art. What painting survived followed styles current in Byzantium.

Middle Ages

In both architecture and sculpture, the first influence came from the north. Lombard masons filled Tuscany and Umbria with simple Romanesque churches; the first (Spoleto, Bevagna, Gròpina, Abbadia S. Salvatore and in the Garfagnana, to name a few) follow the northern style, although it wasn't long before two distinctive Tuscan forms emerged: the Pisan style, characterized by blind rows of colonnades, black and white zebra stripes, and lozenge-shaped designs; and the 'Tuscan Romanesque' which developed around Florence, notable for its use of dark and light marble patterns and simple geometric patterns, often with intricate mosaic floors to match (the Baptistry and S. Miniato in Florence are the chief examples). In the cities in between—Lucca, Arezzo, and Pistoia—there are interesting variations on the two different styles, often carrying an element like stripes or arcades to remarkable extremes. The only real example of French Gothic in Tuscany is S. Galgano built by Cistercians in the 1200s, although the style never caught on here or anywhere else in Italy.

From the large pool of talent working on Pisa's great cathedral complex in the 13th century emerged Italy's first great sculptor, **Nicola Pisano**, whose Baptistry pulpit, with its realistic figures, derived from ancient reliefs. His even more remarkable son, **Giovanni Pisano**, prefigures Donatello in the expressiveness of his statues and the vigour of his pulpits; his façade of Siena cathedral, though altered, is a unique work of art. **Arnolfo di Cambio**, a student of Nicola Pisano, became chief sculptor-architect of Florence during its building boom in the 1290s, designing its cathedral and Palazzo Vecchio on a hitherto unheard-of scale and grandeur, before moving on to embellish Orvieto with statues and tombs. Orvieto, however, hired the more imaginative **Lorenzo Maitani** in the early 1300s to create a remarkable cathedral façade as individualistic as Siena's, a unique combination of reliefs and mosaics.

Painting at first lagged behind the new realism and more complex composition of sculpture. The first to depart from Byzantine stylization, at least according to the account in Vasari's *Lives of the Artists* (see Topics, p. 45), was **Cimabue**, in the late 1200s, who forsook Greek forms for a more 'Latin' or 'natural' way of painting. Cimabue found his greatest pupil, **Giotto**, as a young shepherd, chalk-sketching sheep on a piece of slate. Brought to Florence, Giotto soon eclipsed his master's fame (artistic celebrity being a recent Florentine invention) and achieved the greatest advances on the road to the new painting with a plain, rather severe approach that shunned Gothic prettiness while exploring new ideas in composition and expressing psychological depth in his subjects. Even more importantly, Giotto through his intuitive grasp of perspective was able to go further than any previous artist in representing his subjects as actual figures in space. In a sense Giotto actually invented space; it was this, despite his often awkward and graceless draughtsmanship, that so astounded his contemporaries. His followers, **Taddeo and Agnolo Gaddi** (father and son), **Giovanni da Milano**, and **Maso di Banco** filled Florence's churches with their own interpretations of the master's style. In the latter half of the 1300s, however, there also appeared the key figure of **Andrea Orcagna**, the most important Florentine sculptor, painter, and architect of his day. Inspired by the more elegant style of **Andrea Pisano's** Baptistry doors, Orcagna broke away from the simple Giottesque forms for a more elaborate, detailed style in his sculpture, while the fragments of his frescoes that survive have a vivid dramatic power which undoubtedly owe something to the time of the Black Death and social upheavals in which they were painted.

Siena never produced a Vasari to chronicle its accomplishments, though they were considerable; in the 13th and 14th centuries, Siena's Golden Age, the city's artists, like its soldiers, rivalled and often surpassed those of Florence. For whatever reason, it seemed purposefully to seek inspiration in different directions from Florence; at first from central Italian styles around Spoleto, then with prosperity and the advent of **Guido da Siena** in the early 1200s to the more elegant line and colour of Byzantium. Guido's work paved the way for the pivotal figure of **Duccio di Buoninsegna**, the catalyst who founded the essentials of Sienese art by uniting the beauty of Byzantine line and colour with the sweet finesse of western Gothic art. With Duccio's great followers **Pietro and Ambrogio Lorenzetti** and **Simone Martini**, the Sienese produced an increasingly elegant and rarefied art, almost oriental in its refined stylization. They were less innovative than the Florentines, though they brought the 'International Gothic' style—flowery and ornate, with all the bright tones of May—to its highest form in Italy. Simone Martini introduced the Sienese manner to Florence in the early 1400s, where it influenced most notably the work of **Lorenzo Monaco**, **Masolino**, and the young goldsmith and sculptor, **Ghiberti**. The Umbrian artists of the trecento, most of them anonymous, were also heavily influenced by the Sienese, and were just as colourful if less sophisticated.

The Renaissance

Under the assaults of historians and critics over the last two centuries, the term 'Renaissance' has become a vague and controversial word. Nevertheless, however you choose to interpret this rebirth of the arts, and whatever dates you assign to it, Florence inescapably takes the credit for it. This is no small claim. Combining art, science, and humanist scholarship into a visual revolution that often seemed pure sorcery to their contemporaries, a handful of Florentine geniuses taught the Western eye a new way of seeing. Perspective seems a simple enough trick to us now, but its discovery determined everything that followed, not only in art, but science and philosophy as well.

Leading what scholars used self-assuredly to call the 'Early Renaissance' is a triumvirate of three geniuses: Brunelleschi, Donatello, and Masaccio. **Brunelleschi**, neglecting his considerable talents in sculpture for architecture and science, not only built the majestic dome of Florence cathedral, but threw the Pandora's box of perspective wide open by mathematically codifying the principles of foreshortening. His good friend **Donatello**, the greatest sculptor since the ancient Greeks, inspired a new generation of both sculptors and painters to explore new horizons in portraiture and three-dimensional representation. The first painter to incorporate Brunelleschi and Donatello's lessons of spatiality, perspective, and expressiveness was the young prodigy **Masaccio**, who along with his master Masolino painted the famous Brancacci Chapel in the Carmine, studied by nearly every Florentine artist down to Michelangelo.

The new science of architecture, sculpture, and painting introduced by this triumvirate ignited an explosion of talent unequalled before or since—a score of masters, most of them Tuscan, each only following the dictates of his own genius to create a remarkable range of themes and styles. To mention only the most prominent: **Lorenzo Ghiberti**, who followed Donatello's advice on his second set of Baptistry doors to cause a Renaissance revolution; **Leon Battista Alberti**, who took Brunelleschi's ideas to their most classical extreme in architecture, creating new forms in the process; **Paolo Uccello**, one of the most provocative of artists, who according to Vasari drove himself bats with the study of perspective and the possibilities of illusionism; **Piero della Francesca** of Sansepolcro, who explored the limits of perspective and geometrical forms to create the most compelling, haunting images of the quattrocento;

Fra Angelico, who combined Masaccio's innovations and International Gothic colours and his own deep faith to create the most purely spiritual art of his time; **Andrea del Castagno**, who made use of perspective to create monumental, if often restless figures.

Some of Donatello's gifted followers were **Agostino di Duccio, Benedetto da Maiano, Desiderio da Settignano, Antonio and Bernardo Rossellino, Mino da Fiesole** and perhaps most famously, **Luca della Robbia**, who invented the coloured terracottas his family spread throughout Tuscany. And still more: **Benozzo Gozzoli,** whose enchanting springtime colours and delight in detail are a throwback to the International Gothic; **Antonio and Piero Pollaiuolo**, sons of a poultryman, whose new, dramatic use of line and form, often violent and writhing, would be echoed in Florentine Mannerism; **Fra Filippo Lippi**, a monk like Fra Angelico but far more earthly, the master of lovely Madonnas, teacher of his talented son **Filippino Lippi; Domenico Ghirlandaio**, whose gift of easy charm and flawless technique made him society's fresco painter; **Andrea del Verrocchio**, who could cast in bronze, paint, or carve with perfect detail; **Luca Signorelli**, who achieved apocalyptic grandeur in Orvieto Cathedral; **Perugino** (Pietro Vannucci) of Umbria, who painted the stillness of his native region into his landscapes and taught the young Raphael; and finally **Sandro Botticelli**, whose highly intellectual but lovely and melancholy, mythological paintings are in a class of their own.

The 'Early Renaissance' came to a close near the end of the 1400s with the advent of **Leonardo da Vinci**, whose unique talent in painting, only one of his hundred interests, challenged the certainty of naturalism with a subtlety and chiaroscuro that approaches magic. One passion, however, obsessed the other great figure of the 'High Renaissance', **Michelangelo Buonarroti**, whose consummate interest was the human body, at first graceful and serene as in most of his Florentine works, and later, contorted and anguished after he left for Rome.

Mannerism

Michelangelo left in Florence the seeds for the bold, neurotic avant-garde art that has come to be known as Mannerism. The first conscious 'movement' in Western art can be seen as a last fling amidst the growing intellectual and spiritual exhaustion of 1530s Florence, conquered once and for all by the Medici. The Mannerists' calculated exoticism and exaggerated, tortured poses, together with the brooding self-absorption of Michelangelo, are prelude to Florentine art's remarkably abrupt turn into decadence and prophesy its final extinction. Foremost among the Mannerist painters are two surpassingly strange characters, **Jacopo Pontormo** and **Rosso Fiorentino**, who were not in such great demand as the coldly classical **Andrea del Sarto** and **Bronzino**, consummate perfectionists of the brush, both much less intense and demanding. There were also charming reactionaries working at the time, especially **Il Sodoma** and **Pinturicchio**, both of whom left their best works in Siena. In sculpture **Giambologna** and to a lesser extent **Bartolommeo Ammannati** specialized in virtuoso controposto figures, each one more impossible than the last. With their contemporary, **Giorgio Vasari** himself, Florentine art lost almost all imaginative and intellectual content, and became a virtuoso style of interior decoration perfectly adaptable to saccharine holy pictures, portraits of newly enthroned dukes, or absurd mythological fountains and ballroom ceilings. In the cinquecento, with plenty of money to spend and a long Medici tradition of patronage to uphold, this tendency soon got out of hand. Under the reign of Cosimo I, indefatigable collector of *pietra dura* tables, silver and gold gimcracks, and exotic stuffed animals, Florence gave birth to the artistic phenomenon modern critics call kitsch.

The Rest Compressed

In the long, dark night of later Tuscan art a few artists stand out—the often whimsical architect and engineer, **Buontalenti**; **Pietro Tacca**, Giambologna's pupil with a taste for the grotesque; the charming Baroque fresco master **Pietro da Cortona**. Most of Tuscany, and particularly Florence, chose to sit out the Baroque—almost by choice, it seems, and we can race up to the 19th century for the often delightful 'Tuscan Impressionists' or *Macchiaioli* ('Splatterers'; best collection in Modern Art section of Pitti Palace), and in the 20th century, **Modigliani** of the oval faces (from Livorno); the Futurist **Gino Severini** (from Cortona); and **Ottoni Rosai**, the master of the quiet Florentine countryside.

Artists' Directory

This includes the principal architects, painters, and sculptors of Tuscany and Umbria. The works listed are far from exhaustive, bound to exasperate partisans of some artists and do scant justice to the rest, but we have tried to include only the best and most representative works that you'll find in our regions.

Agostino di Duccio (Florence, 1418–81). A precocious and talented sculptor, his best work is in the Malatesta Temple at Rimini. Sometimes seems a precursor of Art Deco (**Perugia**, S. Bernardino; **Florence**, Bargello; **Pontrémoli**, S. Francesco).

Alberti, Leon Battista (1404–72). Architect, theorist, and writer. His greatest contribution was recycling the classical orders and the principles of Vitruvius into Renaissance architecture. (**Florence**, Palazzo Rucellai, façade of S. Maria Novella, SS. Annunziata; **Lastra a Signa**, S. Martino).

L'Alunno (Niccolò di Liberatore, *c.* 1430–1502). Painter of Foligno; genuine Renaissance polish without much to challenge the imagination.

Allori, Alessandro (1535–1607). Florentine Mannerist painter, prolific follower of Michelangelo and Bronzino (**Florence**, SS. Annuziata, S. Spirito, Spedale degli Innocenti).

Ammannati, Bartolommeo (1511–92). Florentine architect and sculptor. Restrained, elegant in building (**Florence**, S. Trínita bridge, courtyard of Pitti Palace); neurotic, twisted Mannerist sculpture (**Florence**, Fountain of Neptune, Villa di Castello).

Andrea del Castagno (*c.* 1423–1457). Precise, dry Florentine painter, one of the first and greatest slaves of perspective (**Florence**, Uffizi, S. Apollonia, SS. Annunziata).

Angelico, Fra (or Beato) (Giovanni da Fiesole, *c.* 1387–1455). Monk first and painter second, but still one of the great visionary artists of the Renaissance (**Florence**, S. Marco—spectacular Annunciation and many more; **Cortona**, Cathedral Museum; **Fiesole**, S. Domenico).

Antonio da Fabriano (active *c.* 1450) one of the school of painters from the little Marches town of **Fabriano**; works there and in **Matelica**.

Arnolfo di Cambio (born in Colle di Val d'Elsa; *c.* 1245–1302). Architect and sculptor, pupil of Nicola Pisano and a key figure in his own right. Much of his best sculpture is in Rome, but he changed the face of Florence as main architect to the city's greatest building programme of the 1290s (**Florence**, Cathedral and Palazzo Vecchio; **Orvieto**, Museo Civico, S. Domenico).

Baldovinetti, Alesso (Florence, 1425–99). A delightful student of Fra Angelico who left few tracks; most famous for fresco work in **Florence** (SS. Annunziata, Uffizi, S. Niccolò sopr'Arno, S. Miniato).

Bandinelli, Baccio (1488–1559). Florence's comic relief of the late Renaissance; supremely serious, vain, and so awful it hurts—of course he was court sculptor to Cosimo I (**Florence**, Piazza della Signoria and SS. Annunziata).

Barocci, Federico (*c.* 1535–1612) intense proto-Baroque painter of Urbino, inexplicably influential and popular in his time (Palazzo Ducale and Duomo, **Urbino**).

Barna da Siena (active mid-1300s), one of the chief followers of Simone Martini, more dramatic and vigorous than the usual ethereal Sienese (Collegiata, **S. Gimignano**).

Bartolo di Fredi (Siena, active *c.* 1353–1410). Student of Ambrogio Lorenzetti, a genuine pre-Raphaelite soul, entirely at home in the Sienese trecento; employs colours never before seen on this planet (**Montepulciano**, Duomo; **S. Gimignano**, Collegiata).

Beccafumi, Domenico (*c.* 1486–1551). Sienese painter; odd mixture of Sienese conservatism and Florentine Mannerism (**Siena**, Pinacoteca).

Benedetto da Maiano (Florence, 1442–97). Sculptor, specialist in narrative reliefs (**Florence**, S. Croce, Strozzi Palace, Bargello; he also designed the brilliant loggia of S. Maria delle Grazie, **Arezzo**).

Berruguete, Pedro (*c.* 1450–1504). Great Spanish Renaissance painter who worked for the Duke of Urbino for many years and painted one of his most celebrated portraits (Ducal Palace, **Urbino**).

Bigarelli, Guido (13th century). Talented, travelling sculptor from Como, who excelled in elaborate and sometimes bizarre pulpits (**Barga**, **Pistoia** (S. Bartolomeo) and **Pisa Baptistry**).

Bonfigli, Benedetto (Perugia, *c.* 1420–1496). Umbrian painter, known for his painted banners in many Perugia churches.

Botticelli, Sandro (Florence, 1445–1510). Though technically excellent in every respect, and a master of both line and colour, there is more to Botticelli than this. Above every other quattrocento artist, his works reveal the imaginative soul of the Florentine Renaissance, particularly the great series of mythological paintings (**Florence**, Uffizi). Later, a little deranged and under the spell of Savonarola, he reverted to intense, though conventional religious paintings. Almost forgotten in the philistine 1500s and not rediscovered until the 19th century, many of his best works are probably lost (**Florence**, Accademia; **Montelupo**, S. Giovanni Evangelista).

Bronzino, Agnolo (1503–72). Virtuoso Florentine Mannerist with a cool, glossy hyper-elegant style, at best in portraiture; a close friend of Pontormo (**Florence**, Palazzo Vecchio, Uffizi; S. Lorenzo, SS. Annunziata).

Brunelleschi, Filippo (1377–1446). Florentine architect of genius, credited in his own time with restoring the ancient Roman manner of building—but really deserves more credit for developing a brilliant new approach of his own (**Florence**, Duomo cupola, Spedale degli Innocenti, S. Spirito, S. Croce's Pazzi Chapel, S. Lorenzo). Also one of the first theorists on perspective.

Buontalenti, Bernardo (1536–1608). Late Florentine Mannerist architect and planner of the new city of **Livorno**, better known for his Medici villas (**Artimino**, also the fascinating grotto in **Florence's** Boboli Gardens and Belvedere Fort, Uffizi Tribunale).

Cellini, Benvenuto (1500–71). Goldsmith and sculptor. Though a native of Florence, Cellini spent much of his time in Rome. In 1545 he came to work for Cosimo I and torment Bandinelli (*Perseus*, Loggia dei Lanzi; also works in the Bargello). As famed for his catty *Autobiography* as for his sculpture.

Cimabue (*c.* 1240–1302). Florentine painter credited by Vasari with initiating the 'rebirth of the arts'; one of the first painters to depart from the stylization of the Byzantine style (**Florence**, mosaics in Baptistry, Crucifix in Santa Croce; **Pisa**, cathedral mosaic; upper church of S. Francesco in **Assisi**).

Civitali, Matteo (Lucca, *c.* 1435–1501). Sweet yet imaginative, apparently self-taught. He would be much better known if all of his works weren't in Lucca (**Lucca**, Cathedral, Guinigi Museum).

Cola dell'Amatrice (1489–1559), architect and painter, a follower of Carlo Crivelli; worked mainly in **Ascoli Piceno** (Cathedral façade and town hall).

Coppo di Marcovaldo (Florence, active *c.* 1261–75). Another very early painter, as good as Cimabue if not as well known (**S. Gimignano**; **Pistoia**, cathedral).

Crivelli, Carlo (1430–95). A refugee from Venice who painted all over the Marches; obsessively precise and something of an eccentric—fond of painting fruit and cucumbers above some of the most spiritual Madonnas and saints ever created (**Corridonia, Ancona, Ascoli Piceno, Macerata**.

Daddi, Bernardo (active 1290–*c.* 1349). Master of delicate altarpieces (**Florence**, Orsanmichele, S. Maria Novella's Spanish chapel).

De Magistris, Simone (active 1560–1600). Little-known painter of the Marches, one of the last to keep up something of the style and individuality of the Renaissance (**Sarnano, San Ginesio, Camerino, Osimo, Ascoli Piceno**).

Desiderio da Settignano (Florence, 1428/31–61). Sculptor, follower of Donatello (**Florence**, S. Croce, Bargello, S. Lorenzo).

Dolci, Carlo (1616–86). Unsurpassed Baroque master of the 'whites of their eyes' school of religious art (**Florence**, Palazzo Corsini; **Prato**, Museo del Duomo).

Domenico di Bartolo (*c.* 1400–46). An interesting painter, well out of the Sienese mainstream; the unique naturalism of his art is a Florentine influence. His best work (not on view at present) are the frescoes of 15th-century hospital life in the Spedale di Santa Maria della Scala in **Siena**.

Domenico Veneziano (Florence 1404–61). Painter, teacher of Piero della Francesca; master of perspective with few surviving works (**Florence**, Uffizi).

Donatello (Florence, 1386–1466). The greatest Renaissance sculptor appeared as suddenly as a comet at the beginning of Florence's quattrocento. Never equalled in technical ability, expressiveness, or imaginative content, his works influenced Renaissance painters as much as sculptors. A prolific worker, and a quiet fellow who lived with his mum, Donatello was the perfect model of the early Renaissance artist—passionate about art, self-effacing, and a little eccentric (**Florence**, Bargello—the greatest works including the original St George from Orsanmichele, David, and Cupid-Atys, also at San Lorenzo, Palazzo Vecchio, and the Cathedral Museum; **Siena**, Cathedral).

Duccio di Buoninsegna (d. 1319). One of the first and greatest Sienese painters, Duccio was to Sienese art what Giotto was to Florence; ignored by Vasari, though his contributions to the new visual language of the Renaissance are comparable to Giotto's (**Siena**, parts of the great Maestà in the Cathedral Museum, also Pinacoteca; **Florence**, altarpiece in the Uffizi; **Castelfiorentino**, Pinacoteca).

Francesco di Giorgio Martini (Siena, 1439–1502). Architect—mostly of fortresses—sculptor and painter, his works are scattered all over Italy (**Cortona**, S. Maria di Calcinaio; elegant castles at **San Leo**, near Tavoleto, **Mondavio**, in the Marches).

Franciabigio (1482–1525). Most temperamental of Andrea del Sarto's pupils but only mildly Mannerist (**Florence**, Poggio a Caiano and SS. Annunziata).

Gaddi, Taddeo (*c.* 1300–*c.* 1366). Florentine; most important of the followers of Giotto. He and his son **Agnolo** (d. 1396) contributed some of the finest trecento fresco cycles (notably at S. Croce, and S. Ambrogio, **Florence**).

Gentile da Fabriano, Francesco di (*c.*1360–1427). Master nonpareil of the international gothic style. Best works in the Uffizi, **Florence**.

Ghiberti, Lorenzo (1378–1455). The first artist to write a biography was naturally a Florentine. He would probably be better known had he not spent most of his career working on the two sets of doors for the Florence Baptistry after winning the famous competition of 1401 (also **Florence**, statues at Orsanmichele; **Pistoia**).

Ghirlandaio, Domenico (Florence, *c.* 1448–94). The painter of the quattrocento establishment, master of elegant fresco cycles in which he painted all the Medici and Florence's banking elite. A great portraitist with a distinctive dry, restrained style (**Florence**, Ognissanti, S. Maria Novella, Spedale degli Innocenti; **San Gimignano**, Collegiata).

Giambologna (1529–1608). A Fleming, born Jean Boulogne; court sculptor to the Medici after 1567 and one of the masters of Mannerist virtuosity—also a man with a taste for the outlandish (**Florence**, Loggia dei Lanzi, Bargello, Villa della Petraia; **Pratolino**, the *Appennino*).

Giotto (*c.* 1266–1337). Shepherd boy of the Mugello, discovered by Cimabue, who became the first great Florentine painter—and recognized as such in his own time. Invented an essential and direct approach to portraying narrative fresco cycles, but is even more important for his revolutionary treatment of space and of the human figure. (**Florence**, S. Croce, Cathedral Campanile, Horne Museum, S. Maria Novella); **Assisi**, lower church frescoes at S. Francesco, attribution of the great upper church to him or his followers is the longest running battle in art history).

Giovanni da Milano (14th century). An innovative Lombard inspired by Giotto (**Florence**, S. Croce, **Prato**, Cathedral Museum).

Giovanni di Paolo (d. 1483). One of the best of the quattrocento Sienese painters; like most of them, a colourful reactionary still carrying on the traditions of the Sienese trecento (**Siena**, Pinacoteca).

Giovanni di San Giovanni (1592–1633). One of Tuscany's more prolific, but winning Baroque fresco painters (**Florence**, Pitti Palace, Villa della Petraia).

Girolamo di Giovanni (*c.* 1420–1473), refined painter from **Camerino** (in the Marches), little known because his best works are still there.

Giuliano da Rimini (active 1350s) recent studies attribute to this obscure figure the striking blue-green frescoes in the Basilica of San Nicola at **Tolentino**.

Gozzoli, Benozzo (Florence, d. 1497). Learned his trade from Fra Angelico, but few artists could have less in common. The most light-hearted and colourful of quattrocento artists, Gozzoli created enchanting frescoes at **Florence** (Medici chapel), **San Gimignano** (S. Agostino), **Pisa** (Camposanto), **Montefalco** (S. Francesco), and **Castelfiorentino** (Visitation Chapel).

Guido da Siena (active *c.* 1345–70). Interesting Sienese trecento painter; little is known about his life (**Grosseto** museum; **Perugia**, Pinacoteca).

Laurana, Luciano (*c.*1420–79), Dalmatian architect who worked for the court of **Urbino**, designing much of the Palazzo Ducale, one of the masterpieces of the Renaissance.

Leonardo da Vinci (1452–1519). We could grieve that Florence's 'universal genius' spent so much time on his scientific interests and building fortifications, and that his meagre artistic output was left unfinished or lost. All that is left in Tuscany is the *Annunciation* (**Florence**, Uffizi) and also models of all his gadgets at his birthplace, **Vinci**. As the pinnacle of the Renaissance marriage of science and art, Leonardo requires endless volumes of interpretation. As for his personal life, Vasari records him buying up caged birds in the market-place just to set them free.

Lippi, Filippino (Florence, 1457–1504). Son and artistic heir of Fra Filippo. Often seems a neurotic Gozzoli, or at least one of the most thoughtful and serious artists of the quattrocento (**Florence**, S. Maria Novella, Carmine, Badia, Uffizi).

Lippi, Fra Filippo (Florence, d. 1469). Never should have been a monk in the first place. A painter of exquisite, ethereal Madonnas, one of whom he ran off with (the model, at least, a brown-eyed nun named Lucrezia). The pope forgave them both. Lippi was a key figure in the increasingly complex, detailed painting of the middle 1400s (**Florence**, Uffizi; **Prato**, Cathedral and Civic Museum; **Spoleto**, Duomo).

Lorenzetti, Ambrogio (Siena, d. 1348). He could crank out golden Madonnas as well as any Sienese painter, but Lorenzetti was also a great innovator in subject matter and the treatment of landscapes. Created the first and greatest of secular frescoes, the *Allegories of Good and Bad Government* in **Siena's** Palazzo Pubblico, while his last known work, the 1344 *Annunciation* in Siena's Pinacoteca is one of the 14th century's most revolutionary treatments of perspective (also **Massa Marittima**, museum).

Lorenzetti, Pietro (Siena, d. 1348). Ambrogio's big brother, and also an innovator, standing square between Duccio di Buoninsegna and Giotto; one of the precursors of the Renaissance's new treatment of space (**Assisi**, S. Francesco; **Siena**, S. Spirito; **Arezzo**, Pieve di S. Maria; **Cortona**, Cathedral museum). Both Lorenzettis seem to have died in Siena during the Black Death.

Lorenzo di Credi (1439–1537). One of the most important followers of Leonardo da Vinci, always technically perfect if occasionally vacuous (**Florence**, Uffizi).

Lorenzo Monaco (Siena, 1370–1425). A monk at S. Maria degli Angeli in Florence and a brilliant colourist, Lorenzo forms an uncommon connection between the Gothic style of Sienese painting and the new developments in early Renaissance Florence (**Florence**, Uffizi, S. Trínita).

Lotto, Lorenzo (c. 1480–1556), Venetian, pupil of Giovanni Bellini, best known there as one of the first great portraitists. Spent his declining years in the Marches, where he left a considerable amount of uninspired religious work (**Jesi, Ancona, Recanati**).

Maitani, Lorenzo (d. 1330). Sienese sculptor and architect, his reputation rests almost entirely on the great façade of **Orvieto** Cathedral, where he spent most of his life as master of works.

Manetti, Rutilio (1571–1639). Quirky but somehow likeable Baroque painter, the last artist of any standing produced by Siena (**Massa Marittima**, cathedral).

Margarito d'Arezzo (13th century). A near contemporary of Giotto who stuck firmly to his Byzantine guns (**Arezzo**, museum).

Martini, Simone (Siena, d. 1344). Possibly a pupil of Giotto, Martini took the Sienese version of International Gothic to an almost metaphysical perfection, creating luminous, lyrical, and exquisitely drawn altarpieces and frescoes perhaps unsurpassed in the trecento (**Assisi**, S. Francesco; **Siena**, Palazzo Pubblico; **Pisa**, Museo S. Matteo; **Orvieto**, Museo Civico).

Masaccio (Florence, 1401–*c.* 1428). Though he died young and left few works behind, this precocious 'shabby Tom' gets credit for inaugurating the Renaissance in painting by translating Donatello and Brunelleschi's perspective onto a flat surface. Also revolutionary in his use of light and shadow, and in expressing emotion in his subjects' faces (**Florence**, S. Maria del Carmine, S. Maria Novella; **Pisa**, Museo S. Matteo).

Maso di Banco (Florence, active 1340s). One of the more colourful and original followers of Giotto (**Florence**, S. Croce).

Masolino (Florence, d. 1447). Perhaps 'little Tom' also deserves much of the credit, along with Masaccio, for the new advances in art at the Carmine in **Florence**; art historians dispute endlessly how to attribute the frescoes. It's hard to tell, for this brilliant painter left little other work behind to prove his case (**Empoli**, civic museum; **Todi**, S. Fortunato; also attributed Tau chapel, **Pistoia**).

Matteo da Gualdo (*c.* 1430–1503). Umbrian painter, perhaps more representative of the lot than Perugino. Created conventional, colourful works; probably never heard of Florence (works in his home town, **Gualdo Tadino**).

Matteo di Giovanni, (Siena, 1435–95). One Sienese quattrocento painter who could keep up with the Florentines; a contemporary described him as 'Simone Martini come to life again' (**Siena**, Pinacoteca, S. Agostino, S. Maria delle Neve).

Melozzo da Forli (1438–1494), famous for his perspectives and illusionism, but unfortunately little of his work survives; the best preserved (outside Rome) is the S. Marco sacristy in **Loreto** (also Ducal Palace, **Urbino**).

Memmi, Lippo (Siena, 1317–47). Brother-in-law and assistant of Simone Martini (**Siena**, S. Spirito; **S. Gimignano**, museum).

Michelangelo Buonarroti (Florence, 1475–1564). Born in Caprese (now Caprese Michelangelo) into a Florentine family of the minor nobility come down in the world, Michelangelo's early years and artistic training are obscure; he was apprenticed to Ghirlandaio, but showing a preference for sculpture was sent to the court of Lorenzo de' Medici. Nicknamed Il Divino in his lifetime, he was a complex, difficult character, who seldom got along with mere mortals, popes, or patrons. What he couldn't express by means of the male nude in paint or marble, he did in his beautiful but difficult sonnets. In many ways he was the first modern artist, unsurpassed in technique but also the first genius to go over the top. (**Florence**, Medici tombs and library in San Lorenzo, three works in the Bargello, the *Pietà* in the Museo del Duomo, the *David* in the Accademia, Casa Buonarroti, and his only oil painting, in the Uffizi).

Michelozzo di Bartolomeo (Florence, 1396–1472). Sculptor who worked with Donatello (**Prato**, pulpit of the Holy Girdle, and the tomb in **Florence's** Baptistry), he is better known as the classicizing architect favoured by the elder Cosimo de' Medici (**Florence**, Medici Palace, Chiostro of SS. Annunziata, convent of San Marco; Villas at **Trebbio** and **Cafaggiolo, Montepulciano**, S. Agostino; **Impruneta**, Tempietto).

Mino da Fiesole (Florence, 1429–84). Sculptor of portrait busts and tombs; like the della Robbias a representative of the Florentine 'sweet style' (**Fiesole**, cathedral; **Empoli**, museum; **Volterra**, cathedral; **Florence**, Badia, Sant'Ambrogio; **Prato**, cathedral).

Nanni di Banco (Florence, 1384–1421). Florentine sculptor influenced by the Gothic style (**Florence**, Orsanmichele, Porta del la Mandorla).

Nelli, Ottaviano (*c.* 1375–*c.* 1440). A typical, often charming representative of the early Umbrian school; most of his work is in his home town, **Gubbio**.

Orcagna, Andrea (Florence, d. 1368). Sculptor, painter and architect who dominated the middle 1300s in Florence, though greatly disparaged by Vasari, who destroyed much of his work. Many believe he is the mysterious 'Master of the Triumph of Death' of Pisa's Camposanto (**Florence**, Orsanmichele, S. Croce, S. Maria Novella, *Crucifixion* in refectory of S. Spirito, also often given credit for the Loggia dei Lanzi).

Perugino (Pietro Vannucci, Perugia, d. 1523). Perhaps the most distinctive of the Umbrian painters; created some works of genius, along with countless idyllic nativity scenes, each with its impeccably sweet Madonna and characteristic blue-green tinted background (**Città della Pieve**, S. Maria dei Bianchi; **Perugia**, Pinacoteca, Collegio del Cambio; **Trevi**, Madonna delle Lacrime; **Florence**, Uffizi, and S. Maddalena dei Pazzi and Cenacolo di Foligno).

Piero della Francesca (d. 1492). Painter, born at Sansepolcro, and one of the really unique quattrocento artists. Piero wrote two of the most important theoretical works on perspective, then illustrated them with a lifetime's work reducing painting to the bare essentials: mathematics, light, and colour. In his best work his reduction creates nothing dry or academic, but magic, almost eerie scenes similar to those of Uccello. And like Uccello or Botticelli, his subjects are often archetypes of immense psychological depth, not to be fully explained now or ever (**Arezzo**, S. Francesco and the Cathedral; **Urbino**, Palazzo Ducale; **Sansepolcro**, civic museum; **Monterchi**, cemetery church; **Florence**, Uffizi).

Piero di Cosimo (Florence, 1462–1521). Painter better known for his personal eccentricities than his art, which itself is pretty odd (**Florence**, Uffizi; **Fiesole**, S. Francesco).

Pierto da Cortona (1596–1699). Perhaps the most charming of Tuscan Baroque painters; his best is in Rome, but there are some florid ceilings in the Pitti Palace (**Florence**; also works in **Cortona**).

Pinturicchio (Perugia, 1454–1513). This painter got his name for his use of gold and rich colours. Never an innovator, but as an absolute virtuoso in colour, style, and grace no one could beat him. Another establishment artist, especially favoured by the popes, and like Perugino, he was slandered most vilely by Vasari (**Siena**, Piccolomini Library; **Spello**, S. Maria Maggiore; **Perugia**, Pinacoteca).

Pisano, Andrea (Pisa, d. 1348). Artistic heir of Giovanni and Nicola Pisano and teacher of Orcagna; probably a key figure in introducing new artistic ideas to **Florence** (Baptistry, south doors).

Pisano, Nicola (Pisa, active *c.* 1258–78). The first, great, medieval Tuscan sculptor created a little Renaissance all his own, when he adapted the figures and composition of ancient reliefs to make his wonderful pulpit reliefs in **Siena** and **Pisa Baptistry**. His son **Giovanni Pisano** (active *c.* 1265–1314) carried on the tradition, notably in the façade sculptures at **Siena** cathedral (also **Perugia**, S. Domenico, Fontana Maggiore, and great relief pulpits in **Pisa** cathedral and Sant'Andrea in **Pistoia**.

Pollaiuolo, Antonio (Florence, d. 1498). A sculptor, painter, and goldsmith whose fame rests on his brilliant, unmistakable line; he occasionally worked with his less gifted brother **Piero** (**Florence**, Uffizi and Bargello).

Pontormo, Jacopo (Florence, 1494–1556). You haven't seen pink and orange until you've seen the work of this determined Mannerist eccentric. After the initial shock, though, you'll meet an artist of real genius, one whose use of the human body as sole means for communicating ideas is equal to Michelangelo's (**Florence**, S. Felicità, his *Deposition* and Uffizi; **Poggio a Caiano**; **Carmignano**).

Quercia, Jacopo della (Siena, 1374–1438). Sculptor who learned his style from Pisano's cathedral pulpit; one of the unsuccessful contestants for the Florence baptistry doors. Maybe Siena's greatest sculptor, though his most celebrated work, that city's Fonte Gaia, is now ruined (**Lucca**, Cathedral *tomb of Ilaria del Carretto*; **San Gimignano**, Collegiata; **Siena**, Baptistry; **Volterra**, Cathedral).

Raphael (1483–1520). Born in Urbino in the Marches, Raphael spent time in Città di Castello, Perugia, and Florence before establishing himself in Rome. Only a few of the best works of this High Renaissance master remain in our area; those are in the Pitti Palace and Uffizi, **Florence**, and in **Perugia's** San Severo.

Robbia, Luca della (Florence, 1400–82). Greatest of the famous family of sculptors; he invented the coloured glaze for terracottas that we associate with the della Robbias, but was also a first-rate relief sculptor (the *cantorie* in **Florence's** Cathedral museum; **Impruneta**, Collegiata). His nephew Andrea (1435–1525) (best works in convent of **La Verna** and the Tempietto at **Montevarchi**) and Andrea's son Giovanni (1469–1529; best work, **Pistoia**, Ospedale del Ceppo) carried on the blue and white terracotta, sweet style in innumerable buildings across Tuscany.

Rosselli, Cosimo (1434–1507). Competent middle of the road Renaissance painter who occasionally excelled (**Florence**, S. Ambrogio).

Rossellino, Bernardo (1409–64). Florentine architect and sculptor best known as the planner and architect of the new town of **Pienza**. Also a sculptor (**Florence**, S. Croce, S. Miniato; **Empoli**, Pinacoteca). His brother **Antonio Rossellino** (1427–79) was also a talented sculptor (**Florence**, S. Croce).

Rossi, Vicenzo de' (1525–87). Florentine Mannerist sculptor of chunky male nudes (**Florence**, Palazzo Vecchio).

Rosso Fiorentino (Giovanni Battista di Jacopo, 1494–1540). Florentine Mannerist painter, perhaps very much underrated. He makes a fitting complement to Pontormo, both for his tortured soul and for the exaggerations of form and colour he used to create gripping, dramatic effects. Fled Italy after the Sack of Rome and worked for Francis I at Fontainebleau. (**Volterra** Pinacoteca has his masterpiece, the *Deposition*; **Florence**, Uffizi and S. Lorenzo; **Città di Castello**, Duomo).

Salimbeni, Iacopo (d. about 1427) and **Lorenzo** (d. 1420) Brothers from the Marches, charming masters of detail on the threshold of the Renaissance (**Urbino**, Oratorio di San Giovanni; **San Severino Marche**).

Salviati, Francesco (Florence, 1510–63). Friend of Vasari and a similar sort of painter—though much more talented. Odd perspectives and decoration, often bizarre imagery (**Florence**, Palazzo Vecchio and Uffizi).

Sangallo, Antonio da (brother of Giuliano, 1455–1537). Architect at his best in palaces and churches in the monumental style—notably at the great temple of S. Biagio, **Montepulciano**; the son, **Antonio da Sangallo the Younger**, also an architect, and the family's best, practised mainly at Rome.

Sangallo, Giuliano da (Florence, 1443–1516). Architect of humble origins who became the favourite of Lorenzo de' Medici. Often tripped up by an obsession, inherited from Alberti, with making architecture conform to philosophical principles (**Poggio a Caiano**; **Florence**, S. Maddalena dei Pazzi; **Prato**, S. Maria delle Carceri).

Il Sassetta (Stefano di Giovanni; active *c.* 1390–1450). One of the great Sienese quattrocento painters, though still working in a style the Florentines would have found hopelessly reactionary; an artist who studied Masaccio but preferred the Gothic elegance of Masolino. His masterpiece, the Borgo Sansepolcro polyptych, is dispersed through half the museums of Europe.

Signorelli, Luca (Cortona, d. 1523). A rarefied Umbrian painter and an important influence on Michelangelo. Imaginative, forceful compositions, combining geometrical rigour with a touch of unreality, much like his master Piero della Francesca (*The Last Judgement* in **Orvieto** cathedral; **Cortona**, civic and cathedral museums; **Monte Oliveto Maggiore**; **Sansepolcro**, museum).

Il Sodoma (Giovanni Antonio Bazzi, 1477–1549). Born in Piedmont, but a Sienese by choice, he was probably not the libertine his nickname, and Vasari's biography, suggest. An endearing, serene artist who usually eschewed Mannerist distortion; got rich through his work, then blew it all feeding his exotic menagerie and died in the poorhouse (**Monte Oliveto Maggiore**; **Siena**, Pinacoteca and S. Domenico).

Spinello, Aretino (late 14th century–1410). A link between Giotto and the International Gothic style; imaginative and colourful in his compositions (**Florence**, S. Miniato; **Arezzo**, museum). His son Parri di Spinello did many fine works, all around **Arezzo** (S. Maria delle Grazie).

Tacca, Pietro (1580–1640). Born in Carrara, pupil of Giambologna and one of the best, early Baroque sculptors (**Livorno**, *Quattro Mori*; **Florence**, Piazza SS. Annunziata fountain; **Prato**, Piazza del Comune).

Taddeo di Bartolo (1363–1422). The greatest Sienese painter of the late 1300s—also the least conventional; never a consummate stylist, he often shows a remarkable imagination in composition and treatment of subject matter (**Siena**, Palazzo Vecchio, S. Spirito; **Perugia**, Pinacoteca; **Colle di Val d'Elsa** museum and Collegiata; **Volterra**, Pinacoteca).

Talenti, Francesco (early 14th century). Chief architect of **Florence** cathedral and campanile after Arnolfo di Cambio and Giotto; his son **Simone** made the beautiful windows in **Orsanmichele** (and perhaps the Loggia dei Lanzi) in **Florence**.

Torrigiano, Pietro (1472–1528). Florentine portrait sculptor, famous for his work in Westminster Abbey and for breaking Michelangelo's nose.

Uccello, Paolo (1397–1475). No artist has ever been more obsessed with the possibilities of artificial perspective. Like Piero della Francesca, he used the new technique to create a magic world of his own; contemplation of it made him increasingly eccentric in his later years. Uccello's provocative, visionary subjects (*Noah* fresco in S. Maria Novella, and *Battle of San Romano* in the Uffizi, **Florence**) put him up with Piero della Francesca and Botticelli as the most intellectually stimulating of quattrocento artists (also attributed frescoes, **Prato** cathedral).

Vasari, Giorgio (Arezzo, 1511–74). Florentine sycophant, writer and artist; see p. 45. Also a pretty fair architect (**Florence**, Uffizi, Corridoio, and Fish Loggia).

Il Vecchietta (Lorenzo di Pietro, 1412–80). Sienese painter and sculptor, dry and linear, part Sienese Pollaiuolo and part Donatello (**Siena**, Loggia della Mercanzia, Baptistry).

Verrocchio, Andrea del (1435–88). Florentine sculptor who worked in bronze; spent his life trying to outdo Donatello. Mystic alchemist in his spare time, and interestingly enough the master of both Botticelli and Leonardo (Uffizi, S. Lorenzo, Orsanmichele, Palazzo Vecchio, and Bargello, **Florence**).

Masters and Students: the Progress of the Renaissance

The purpose of this chart is to show who learned from whom, an insight into some 300 years of artistic continuity. Solid lines represent a master–pupil relationship; dotted ones a strong influence or mutual influence.

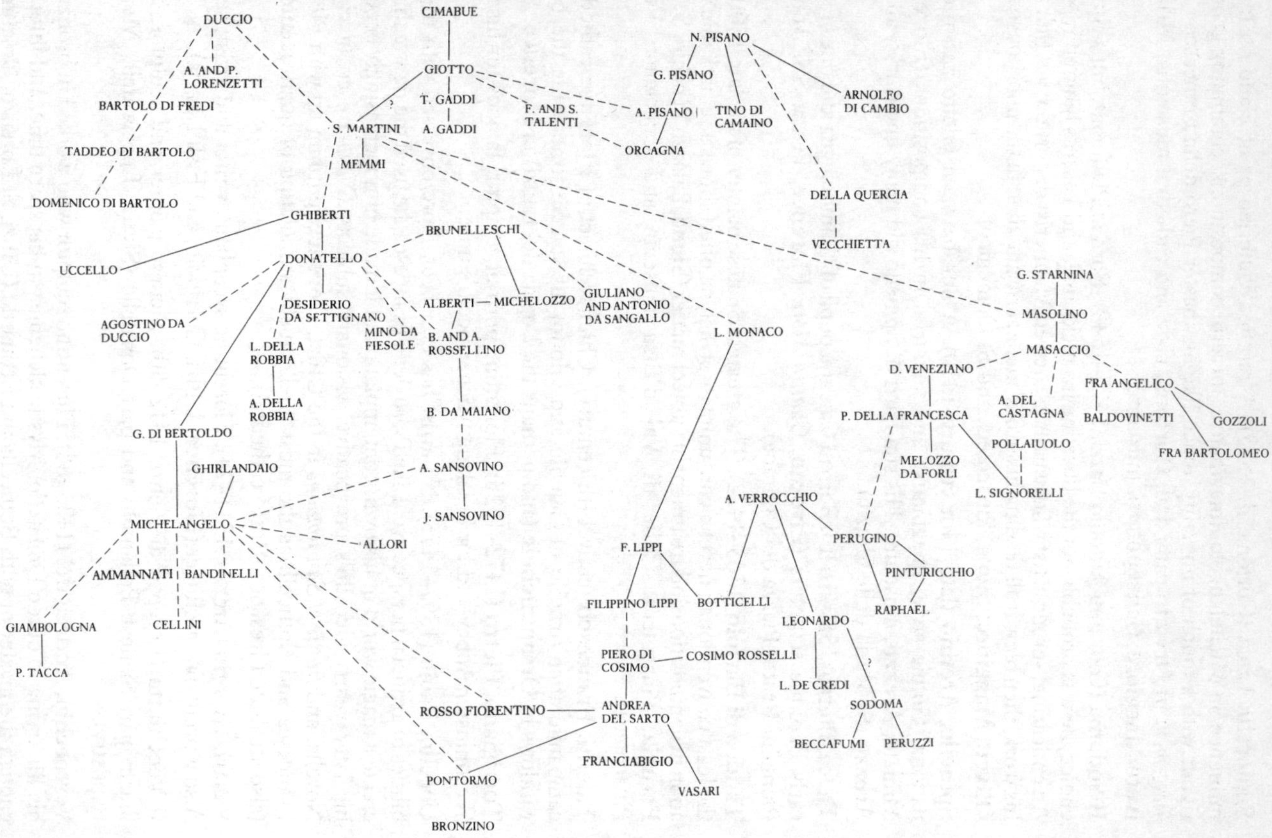

Part IV

FLORENCE

Chiesa di San Miniato

> 'Fine balm let Arno be;
> The walls of Florence all of silver rear'd,
> And crystal pavements in the public way...'
>
> —a 14th-century madrigal by Lapo Gianni

'Magari!'—If only!—the modern Florentine would add to this vision, to this city of art and birthplace of the Renaissance, built by bankers and merchants whose sole preoccupation was making more florins. The precocious capital of Tuscany began to slip into legend back in the 14th century, during the lifetime of Dante; it was noted as *different* even before the Renaissance, before Boccaccio, Masaccio, Brunelleschi, Donatello, Leonardo da Vinci, Botticelli, Michelangelo, Machiavelli, the Medici...

> 'This city of Florence is well populated, its good air a healthy tonic; its citizens are well dressed, and its women lovely and fashionable, its buildings are very beautiful, and every sort of useful craft is carried on in them, more so than any other Italian city. For this many come from distant lands to see her, not out of necessity, but for the quality of its manufactures and arts, and for the beauty and ornament of the city.'
>
> Dino Compagni in his *Chronicle* of 1312

According to the tourist office, 575 years after Dino, the first six months of 1987 saw 127,610 Americans, 77,606 Germans, 60,883 French, 36,069 Britons (the top four groups) as well as 786 Russians, 687 Venezuelans, and 344 Egyptians, among others, adding up to 567,619 foreigners and 374,426 Italians, for a grand total of 942,045 visitors who spent at least one night in a Florentine hotel. Some, perhaps, had orthodontist appointments. A large percentage of the others came to inhale the rarefied air of the cradle of Western civilization, to gaze at some of the loveliest things made by mortal hands and minds, to walk the streets of new Athens, the great humanist 'city built to the measure of man'. Calling Florence's visitors 'tourists', however, doesn't seem quite right; 'tourism' implies pleasure, a principle alien to this dour, intellectual, measured town; 'pilgrims' is perhaps the better word, cultural pilgrims who throng the Uffizi, the Accademia, the Bargello to gaze upon the holy mysteries of our secular society, to buy postcards and replicas, the holy cards of our day.

Someone wrote a warning on a wall near Brunelleschi's Santo Spirito, in the Oltrarno: '*Turista con mappa/ alla caccia di tesoro/ per finire davanti d'un piatto spaghetti al pomodoro*' (Tourist with a map, on a treasure hunt, only to end up in front of a plate of spaghetti with tomato sauce). Unless you come with the right attitude, Florence can be as disenchanting as cold spaghetti. It only blossoms if you apply your mind as well as your vision, if you go slowly and do not let the art bedazzle until your eyes glaze over in dizzy excess (a common complaint, known in medical circles as the Stendhal syndrome). Realize that loving and hating Florence at the same time may be the only rational response. It is the capital of contradiction; you begin to like it because it goes out of its way to annoy.

Florentine Schizophrenia

Dante's *Vita Nuova*, the autobiography of his young soul, was only the beginning of Florentine analysis; Petrarch, the introspective 'first modern man', was a Florentine born in exile; Ghiberti was the first artist to write an autobiography, Cellini wrote one of the most readable; Alberti invented art criticism; Vasari invented art history; Michelangelo's personality, in his letters and sonnets, looms as large as his art. In many ways Florence broke away from the medieval idea of community and invented the modern concept of the individual, most famously expressed by Lorenzo de' Medici's friend, Pico della Mirandola, whose *Oration on the dignity of man* tells us what the God on the Sistine Chapel ceiling was saying when He created Adam: '... And I have created you neither celestial nor terrestrial, neither mortal nor immortal, so that, like a free and able sculptor and painter of yourself, you may mould yourself entirely in the form of your choice.'

To attempt to understand Florence, remember one historical constant: no matter what the issue, the city always takes both sides, vehemently and often violently, especially in the Punch and Judy days of Guelphs and Ghibellines. In the 1300s this was explained by the fact that the city was founded under the sign of Mars, the war god; but in medieval astronomy Mars is also connected with Aries, another Florentine symbol and the time of spring blossoms. (The Annunciation, at the beginning of spring, was Florence's most important festival.) One of the city's oldest symbols is the lily (or iris), flying on its oldest gonfalons. Perhaps even older is its *marzocco*, originally an equestrian statue of Mars on Ponte Vecchio, later replaced by Donatello's grim lion.

Whatever dispute rocked the streets, Great Aunt Florence often expressed her schizophrenia in art, floral Florence versus stone Florence, epitomized by the irreconcilable differences between the two most famous works of art in the city: Botticelli's graceful, enigmatic *Primavera* and Michelangelo's cold perfect *David*. The 'city of flowers' seems a joke; it has nary a real flower, nor even a tree, in its stone streets, indeed, all effort has gone into keeping nature at bay, surpassing it with geometry and art. And yet the Florentines were perhaps the first since the Romans to discover the joys of the countryside. The rough, rusticated stone palaces, like fortresses or prisons, hide charms as delightful as Gozzoli's frescoes in the Palazzo Medici. Luca della Robbia's dancing children and floral wreaths are contemporary with the naked, violent warriors of the Pollaiuolo brothers; the writhing, quarrelsome statuary in the Piazza della Signoria is sheltered by the most delicate and beautiful loggia imaginable.

After 1500, all of the good, bad, and ugly symptoms of the Renaissance peaked in the mass fever of Mannerism. Then, drifting into a debilitating twilight of *pietra dura* tables, gold gimcracks, and interior decoration, Florence gave birth to the artistic phenomenon known as kitsch—the Medici Princes' Chapel is an early kitsch classic, still one of the heaviest baubles in the solar system. Since then, worn out perhaps, or embarrassed, this city built by merchants has kept its own counsel, expressing its argumentative soul in overblown controversies about traffic, art restoration, and the undesirability of fast-food counters and cheap pensions. We who find her fascinating hope she some day comes to remember her proper role, bearing the torch of culture instead of merely collecting tickets for the culture torture.

History

The identity of Florence's first inhabitants is a matter of dispute. There seems to have been some kind of settlement along the Arno long before the Roman era, perhaps as early as 1000 BC; the original founders may have been either native Italics or Etruscans. Throughout the period of Etruscan dominance, the village on the river lived in the shadow of *Faesulae*—Florence's present-day suburb of Fiesole was then an important city, the northernmost member of the Etruscan Dodecapolis. The Arno river cuts across central Italy like a wall. This narrow stretch of it, close to the mountain pass over to Emilia, was always the most logical place for a bridge.

Roman Florence can claim no less a figure than **Julius Caesar** for its founder. Like so many other Italian cities, the city began as a planned urban enterprise in an underdeveloped province; Caesar started it as a colony for his army veterans in 59 BC. The origin of the name—so suggestive of springtime and flowers—is another mystery. First it was *Florentia*, then *Fiorenza* in the Middle Ages, and finally *Firenze*. One guess is that its foundation took place in April, when the Romans were celebrating the games of the Floralia.

The original street plan of *Florentia* can be seen today in the neat rectangle of blocks between Via Tornabuoni and Via del Proconsolo, between the Duomo and Piazza della Signoria. Its Forum occupied roughly the site of the modern Piazza della Repubblica, and the outline of its amphitheatre can be traced in the oval of streets just west of Piazza Santa Croce. Roman *Florentia* never really imposed itself on the historian. One writer mentions it as a *municipia splendidissima*, a major town and river crossing along the Via Cassia, connected to Rome and the thriving new cities of northern Italy, such as Bononia and Mediolanum (Bologna and Milan). At the height of Empire, the municipal boundaries had expanded out to Via de' Fossi, Via S. Egidio, and Via de' Benci. Nevertheless, Florentia did not play a significant role either in the Empire's heyday or in its decline.

After the fall of Rome, Florence weathered its troubles comparatively well. We hear of it withstanding sieges by the Goths around the year 400, when it was defended by the famous imperial general Stilicho, and again in 541, during the campaigns of Totila and Belisarius; all through the Greek–Gothic wars Florence seems to have taken the side of Constantinople. The Lombards arrived around 570; under their rule Florence was the seat of a duchy subject to the then Tuscan capital of Lucca. The next mention in the chronicles refers to Charlemagne spending Christmas with the Florentines in the year 786. Like the rest of Italy, Florence had undoubtedly declined; a new set of walls went up under Carolingian rule, about 800, enclosing an area scarcely larger than the original Roman settlement of 59 BC. In such times Florence was lucky to be around at all; most likely throughout the Dark Ages the city was gradually increasing its relative importance and strength at the expense of its neighbours. The famous Baptistry, erected some time between the 6th and 9th centuries, is the only important building from that troubled age in all Tuscany.

By the 1100s, Florence was the leading city of the County of Tuscany. **Countess Matilda**, ally of Pope Gregory VII against the emperors, oversaw the construction of a new set of walls in 1078, this time coinciding with the widest Roman-era boundaries. Already the city had recovered all the ground lost during the Dark Ages, and the momentum of growth did not abate. New walls were needed again in the 1170s, to enclose what was becoming one of the largest cities in Europe. In this period, Florence owed its growth and prosperity largely to the textile industry—weaving and 'finishing' cloth not only from Tuscany but wool shipped from as far afield as Spain and England. The capital gain from this trade, managed by the *Calimala* and the *Arte della Lana*, Florence's richest guilds, led naturally to an even more profitable business—banking and finance.

The Florentine Republic Battles with the Barons

In 1125, Florence once and for all conquered its ancient rival Fiesole. Wealth and influence brought with them increasing political responsibilities. Externally the city often found itself at war with one or other of its neighbours. Since Countess Matilda's death in 1115, Florence had become a self-governing *comune*, largely independent of the emperor and local barons. The new city republic's hardest problems, however, were closer to home. The nobles of the county, encouraged in their anachronistic feudal behaviour by the representatives of the imperial government, proved irreconcilable enemies to the new merchant republic, and Florence spent most of the 12th century trying to keep them in line. Often the city actually declared war on a noble clan, as with the Alberti, or the Counts of Guidi, and razed their castles whenever they captured one. To complicate the situation, nobles attracted by the stimulation of urban life—not to mention the opportunities for making money there—often moved their entire families into Florence itself. They brought their country habits with them, a boyish eagerness to brawl with their neighbours on the slightest pretext, and a complete disregard for the laws of the *comune*. Naturally, they couldn't feel secure without a little urban castle of their own, and before long Florence, like any prosperous Italian city of the Middle Ages, featured a remarkable skyline of hundreds of tower-fortresses, built as much for status as for defence. Many were over 200 feet in height. It wasn't uncommon for the honest citizen to come home from a hard day's work at the bank, hoping for a little peace and quiet, only to find siege engines parked in front of the house and a company of bowmen commandeering the children's bedroom.

But just as Florence was able to break the power of the rural nobles, those in the town also eventually had to succumb. The last tower-fortresses were chopped down to size in the early 1300s. But even without the nobles, the Florentines found new ways to keep the pot boiling. The rich merchants who dominated the government, familiarly known as the *popolari grossi*, resorted to every sort of murder and mayhem to beat down the demands of the lesser guilds, the *popolari minuti*, for a fair share of the wealth; the two only managed to settle their differences when confronted by murmurs of discontent from what was then one of Europe's largest urban proletariats. But even beyond simple class issues, the city born under the sign of Mars always found a way to make trouble for itself. Not only did Florentines pursue the Guelph–Ghibelline conflict with greater zest than almost any Tuscan city; according to the chronicles of the time, they actually started it. In 1215, men of the Amidei family murdered a prominent citizen named Buondelmonte de' Buondelmonti over a broken engagement, the spark that touched off the factionalist struggles first in Florence, then quickly throughout Italy.

Guelphs and Ghibellines

In 13th-century Florence, there was never a dull moment. Guelphs and Ghibellines, often more involved with some feud between noble families than with real political issues, cast each other into exile and confiscated each other's property with every change of the wind. Religious strife occasionally pushed politics off the front page. In the 1240s, a curious foreshadowing of the Reformation saw Florence wrapped up in the **Patarene heresy**. This sect, closely related to the Albigensians of southern France, was as obsessed with the presence of Evil in the world as John Calvin—or Florence's own future fire-and-brimstone preacher, Savonarola. Exploiting a streak of religious eccentricity that has always seemed to be present in the Florentine psyche, the Patarenes thrived in the city, even electing their own bishop. The established Church was up to the challenge; St Peter Martyr, a bloodthirsty Dominican, led his armies of axe-wielding monks to the assault in 1244, exterminating almost the entire Patarene community.

In 1248, with help from Emperor Frederick II, Florence's Ghibellines booted out the Guelphs—once and for all, they thought, but two years later the Guelphs were back, and it was the Ghibellines' turn to pack their grips. The new Guelph regime, called the *primo popolo*, was for the first time completely in the control of the bankers and merchants. It passed the first measures to control the privileges of the turbulent, largely Ghibelline nobles, and forced them all to chop the tops off their tower-fortresses. The next decades witnessed a series of wars with the Ghibelline cities of Tuscany—Siena, Pisa and Pistoia, not just by coincidence Florence's habitual enemies. Usually the Florentines were the aggressors, and more often than not fortune favoured them. In 1260, however, the Sienese, reinforced by Ghibelline exiles from Florence and a few imperial cavalry, destroyed an invading Florentine army at the **Battle of Montaperti**. Florence was temporarily at the Ghibellines' mercy. Only the refusal of Farinata degli Uberti, leader of the exiles, to allow the city's destruction kept the Sienese from putting it to the torch—a famous episode recounted by Dante in the *Inferno*. (In a typical Florentine gesture of thanks, Dante found a home for Uberti in one of the lower circles of hell.)

In Florence, a Ghibelline regime under Count Guido Novello made life rough for the wealthy Guelph bourgeoisie. As luck would have it, though, only a few years later the Guelphs were back in power, and Florence was winning on the battlefield once again.

The new Guelph government, the *secondo popolo*, earned a brief respite from factional strife. In 1289, Florence won a great victory over another old rival, Arezzo. This was the **Battle of Campaldino**, where the Florentine citizen army included young Dante Alighieri. In 1282, and again in 1293, Florence tried to clean up an increasingly corrupt government with a series of reforms. The 1293 *Ordinamenti della Giustizia* once and for all excluded the nobles from important political offices. By now, however, the real threat to the Guelph merchants' rule came not so much from the nobility, which had been steadily falling behind in wealth and power for two centuries, but from the lesser guilds, which had been completely excluded from a share of power, and from the growing working class employed in the textile mills and foundries.

Despite all the troubles, the city's wealth and population grew tremendously throughout the 1200s. Its trade contacts spread across Europe, and crowned heads from London to Constantinople found Florentine bankers ready to float them a loan. About 1235 Florence minted modern Europe's first gold coin, the *florin*, which soon became a standard currency across the continent. By 1300 Florence counted over 100,000 souls—a little cramped, even inside the vast new circuit of walls built by the *comune* in the 1280s. It was not only one of the largest cities in Europe, but certainly one of the richest. Besides banking, the wool trade was also booming: by 1300 the wool guild, the *Arte della Lana*, had over 200 large workshops in the city alone.

Naturally, this new opulence created new possibilities for culture and art. Florence's golden age began perhaps in the 1290s, when the *comune* started its tremendous programme of public buildings—including the Palazzo della Signoria and the Cathedral; important religious structures, such as Santa Croce, were under way at the same time. Cimabue was the artist of the day; Giotto was just beginning, and his friend Dante was hard at work on the *Commedia*.

As in so many other Italian cities, Florence had been developing its republican institutions slowly and painfully. At the beginning of the *comune* in 1115, the leaders were a class called the *boni homines*, made up mostly of nobles. Only a few decades later, these were calling themselves *consules*, evoking a memory of the ancient Roman republic. When the Ghibellines took over, the leading official was a *podestà* appointed by the Emperor. Later, under the Guelphs, the *podestà* and a new officer called the *capitano del popolo* were both elected by the citizens. With the reforms of the 1290s Florence's republican constitution was perfected—if that is the proper word for an arrangement that satisfied few citizens and guaranteed lots of trouble for the future. Under the new dispensation, power was invested in the council of the richer guilds, the *signoria*; the new Palazzo della Signoria was designed expressly as a symbol of their authority, replacing the old Bargello, which had been the seat of the *podestà*. The most novel feature of the government, designed to overcome Florence's past incapacity to avoid violent factionalism, was the selection of officials by lot from among the guild members. In effect, politics was to be abolished.

Business as Usual: Riot, War, Plagues and Revolution

Despite the reforms of the *Ordinamenti*, Florence found little peace in the new century. As if following some strange and immutable law of city-state behaviour, no sooner had the Guelphs established total control than they themselves split into new factions. The radically anti-imperial **Blacks** and the more conciliatory **Whites** fought each other through the early 1300s with the same fervour they both had once exercised against the Ghibellines. The Whites, who included Dante among their partisans, came out losers when the Blacks conspired with the pope to bring Charles of Valois' French army into Florence; almost all of the losing faction were forced into exile in 1302. Some of them must have sneaked back, for the chronicles of 1304 record the Blacks trying to burn them out of their houses with incendiary bombs, resulting in a fire that consumed one fourth of the city.

Beginning in 1313, Florence was involved in an almost constant series of inconclusive wars with Pisa, Lucca, and Arezzo, among others. In 1325, the city was defeated and nearly destroyed by the great Lucchese general **Castruccio Castracani** (see Lucca). Castruccio died of a common cold while the siege was already under way, another example of Florence's famous good luck, but unfortunately one of the last. The factions may have been suppressed, but fate had found some more novel disasters for the city. One far-off monarch did more damage to Florence than its Italian enemies had ever managed—King Edward III of England, who in 1339 found it expedient to repudiate his foreign debts. Florence's two biggest banks, the Bardi and the Peruzzi, immediately went bust, and the city's standing as the centre of international finance was gravely damaged.

If anything was constant throughout the history of the republic, it was the oppression of the poor. The ruling bankers and merchants exploited their labour and gave only the bare minimum in return. In the 14th century, overcrowding, undernourishment and plenty of rats made Florence's poorer neighbourhoods a perfect breeding ground for epidemics. Famine, plagues and riots became common in the 1340s, causing a severe political crisis. At one point, in 1342, the Florentines gave over their government to a foreign dictator, Walter de Brienne, the French–Greek 'Duke of Athens'. He lasted only a year before a popular revolt ended the experiment. The **Black Death** of 1348, the background for Boccaccio's *Decameron*, carried off perhaps one half of the population. Coming on the heels of a serious depression, it was a blow from which Florence would never really recover.

In the coming two centuries, when the city was to be the great innovator in western culture, it was already in relative decline, a politically decadent republic with a stagnant economy, barely holding its own among the turbulent changes in trade and diplomacy. For the time being, though, things didn't look too bad. Florence found enough ready cash to buy control of Prato, in 1350, and was successful in a defensive war against expansionist Milan in 1351. Warfare was almost continuous for the last half of the century, a strain on the exchequer but not usually a threat to the city's survival; this was the heyday of the mercenary companies, led by famous *condottieri* like **Sir John Hawkwood** (Giovanni Acuto), immortalized by the equestrian 'statue' in Florence's cathedral. Before the Florentines made him a better offer, Hawkwood was often in the employ of their enemies.

Throughout the century, the Guelph Party had been steadily tightening its grip over the republic's affairs. Despite the selection of officials by lot, by the 1370s the party organization bore an uncanny resemblance to some of the big-city political machines common not so long ago in America. The merchants and the bankers who ran the party used it to turn the Florentine Republic into a profit-making business. With the increasingly limited opportunities for making money in trade and finance, the Guelph ruling class tried to make up the difference by soaking the poor. Wars and taxes stretched

Florentine tolerance to breaking point, and finally, in 1378, came revolution. The **Ciompi Revolt** (*ciompi*—wage labourers in the textile industries) began in July, when a mob of workers seized the Bargello. Under the leadership of a wool-carder named Michele di Lando, they executed a few of the Guelph bosses and announced a new, reformed constitution. They were also foolish enough to believe the Guelph magnates when they promised to abide by the new arrangement if only the *ciompi* would go home. Before long di Lando was in exile, and the ruling class firmly back in the seat of power, more than ever determined to eliminate the last vestiges of democracy from the republic.

The Rise of the Medici

In 1393, Florentines celebrated the 100th anniversary of the great reform of the *Ordinamenti*, while watching their republic descend irresistibly into oligarchy. In that year **Maso degli Albizzi** became *gonfaloniere* (the head of the *Signoria*) and served as virtual dictator for many years afterwards. The ruling class of merchants, more than a bit paranoid after the Ciompi revolt, were generally relieved to see power concentrated in strong hands; the ascendancy of the Albizzi family was to set the pattern for the rest of the republic's existence. In a poisoned atmosphere of repression and conspiracy, the spies of the Signoria's new secret police hunted down malcontents while whole legions of Florentine exiles plotted against the republic in foreign courts. Florence was almost constantly at war. In 1398 she defeated an attempt at conquest by Giangaleazzo Visconti of Milan. The imperialist policy of the Albizzi and their allies resulted in important territorial gains, including the conquest of Pisa in 1406, and the purchase of Livorno from the Genoese in 1421. Unsuccessful wars against Lucca finally disenchanted the Florentines with Albizzi rule. An emergency *parlamento* (the infrequent popular assemblies usually called when a coming change of rulers was obvious) in 1434 decreed the recall from exile of the head of the popular opposition, **Cosimo de' Medici**.

Perhaps it was something that could only have happened in Florence—the darling of the plebeians, the great hope for reform, happened to be the head of Florence's biggest bank. The Medici family had their roots in the Mugello region north of Florence. Their name seems to suggest they once were pharmacists (later enemies would jibe at the balls on the family arms as 'the pills'). For two centuries they had been active in Florentine politics; many had acquired reputations as troublemakers; their names turned up often in the lists of exiles and records of lawsuits. None of the Medici had ever been particularly rich until **Giovanni di Bicci de' Medici** (1360–1429) parlayed his wife's dowry into the founding of a bank. Good fortune—and a temporary monopoly on the handling of the pope's finances—made the Medici Bank Florence's biggest.

Giovanni had been content to stay on the fringe of politics; his son, Cosimo (known in Florentine history as 'il Vecchio', the 'old man') took good care of the bank's affairs but aimed his sights much higher. His strategy was as old as Julius Caesar—the patrician reformer, cultivating the best men, winning the favour of the poor with largesse and gradually, carefully forming a party under a system specifically designed to prevent such things. In 1433 Rinaldo degli Albizzi had him exiled, but too late; continuing discontent forced his return only a year later, and for the next 35 years Cosimo would be the unchallenged ruler of Florence. Throughout this period, Cosimo occasionally held public office—this was done by lottery, with the electoral lists manipulated to ensure a majority of Medici supporters at all times. Nevertheless, he received ambassadors at the new family palace (built in 1444), entertained visiting popes and emperors, and made all the important decisions. A canny political godfather and usually a gentleman, Cosimo also proved a useful patron to the great figures of the early Renaissance—Donatello and Brunelleschi, among others. His father had served as one of the judges in the famous competition for the baptistry doors, and Cosimo was a member of the commission that picked Brunelleschi to design the cathedral dome.

Cosimo did oversee some genuine reforms; under his leadership Florence began Europe's first progressive income tax, and a few years later the state invented the modern concept of the national debt—endlessly rolling over bonds to keep the republic afloat and the creditors happy. The poor, with fewer taxes to pay, were also happy, and the ruling classes, after some initial distaste, were positively delighted; never in Florence's history had any government so successfully muted class conflict and the desire for a genuine democracy. Wars were few, and the internal friction negligible. Cosimo died in August 1464; his tomb in San Lorenzo bears the inscription *Pater patriae,* and no dissent was registered when his 40-year-old son **Piero** took up the boss's role.

Lorenzo the Magnificent

Piero didn't quite have the touch of his masterful father, but he survived a stiff political crisis in 1466, outmanoeuvring a new faction led by wealthy banker Luca Pitti. In 1469 he succumbed to the Medici family disease, the gout, and his 20-year-old son **Lorenzo** succeeded him in an equally smooth transition. He was to last for 23 years. Not necessarily more 'magnificent' than other contemporary princes, or other Medici, Lorenzo's honorific reveals something of the myth that was to grow up around him in later centuries. His long reign corresponded to the height of the Florentine Renaissance. It was a relatively peaceful time, and in the light of the disasters that were to follow, Florentines could not help looking back on it as a golden age.

As a ruler, Lorenzo showed many virtues. Still keeping up the pretence of living as a private citizen, he lived relatively simply, always accessible to the voices and concerns of his fellow citizens, who would often see him walking the city streets. In the field of foreign policy he was indispensable to Florence and indeed all Italy; he did more than anyone to keep the precarious peninsular balance of power from disintegrating. The most dramatic affair of his reign was the **Pazzi conspiracy**, an attempt to assassinate Lorenzo plotted by Pope Sixtus IV and the wealthy Pazzi family, the pope's bankers and ancient rivals of the Medici. In 1478, two of the younger Pazzi attacked Lorenzo and his brother Giuliano during mass at the Cathedral. Giuliano was killed, but Lorenzo managed to escape into the sacristy. The botched murder aborted the planned revolt; Florentines showed little interest in the Pazzi's call to arms, and before nightfall most of the conspirators were dangling from the cornice of the Palazzo Vecchio.

Apparently, Lorenzo had angered the pope by starting a syndicate to mine for alum in Volterra, threatening the papal monopoly. Since Sixtus failed to murder Lorenzo, he had to settle for excommunicating him, and declaring war in alliance with King Ferrante of Naples. The war went badly for Florence and, in the most memorable act of his career, Lorenzo walked into the lion's cage, travelling to negotiate with the terrible Neapolitan, who had already murdered more than one important guest. As it turned out, Ferrante was only too happy to dump his papal entanglements; Florence found itself at peace once more, and Lorenzo returned home to a hero's welcome.

In other affairs, both foreign and domestic, Lorenzo was more a lucky ruler than a skilled one. Florence's economy was entering a long, slow decline, but for the moment the banks and mills were churning out just enough profit to keep up the accustomed level of opulence. The Medici Bank, unfortunately, was on the ropes. Partly because of Lorenzo's neglect, the bank came close to collapsing on several occasions—it seems Lorenzo made up the losses with public funds. Culturally, he was fortunate to be nabob of Florence at its most artistically creative period; future historians and Medici propagandists gave him a reputation as an art patron that is entirely undeserved. His own tastes tended towards bric-à-brac, jewellery, antique statues and vases; there is little evidence that he really understood or appreciated the scores of great artists around him. Perhaps because he was too nearsighted to see anything clearly, he never commissioned an important canvas or fresco in Florence (except for Luca Signorelli's mysterious *Pan*, lost in Berlin during the last war). His favourite architect was the hack Giuliano da Sangallo.

The Medici had taken great care with Lorenzo's education; he was brought up with some of the leading humanist scholars of Tuscany for tutors and his real interests were literary. His well-formed lyrics and winsome pastorals have earned him a place among Italy's greatest 15th-century poets; they neatly reflect the private side of Lorenzo, the retiring, scholarly family man who enjoyed life better on one of the many rural Medici estates than in the busy city. In this, he was perfectly in tune with his class and his age. Plenty of Florentine bankers were learning the joys of country life, reading Horace or Catullus in their geometrical gardens and pestering their tenant farmers with well-meant advice.

Back in town, they had thick new walls of rusticated sandstone between them and the bustle of the streets. The late 15th century was the great age of palace building in Florence. Following the example of Cosimo de' Medici, the bankers and merchants erected dozens of palaces (some of the best can be seen around Via Tornabuoni). Each one turns blank walls and iron-barred windows to the street. Historians always note one very pronounced phenomenon of this period—a turning inward, a 'privatization' of Florentine life. In a city that had become a republic only in name, civic interest and public life ceased to matter so much. The very rich began to assume the airs of an aristocracy, and did everything they could to distance themselves from their fellow citizens. Ironically, just at the time when Florence's artists were creating their greatest achievements, the republican ethos, the civic soul that had made Florence great, began to disintegrate.

Savonarola

Lorenzo's death, in 1492, was followed by another apparently smooth transition of power to his son Piero. But after 59 years of Medicean quiet and stability, the city was ready for a change. The opportunity for the malcontents came soon enough, when the timid and inept Piero allowed the invading King of France, **Charles VIII**, to occupy Pisa and the Tuscan coast. A spontaneous revolt chased Piero and the rest of the Medici into exile, while a mob sacked the family's palace. A new regime, hastily put together under Piero Capponi, dealt more sternly with the French (see p. 105) and tried to pump some new life into the long-dormant republican constitution.

The Florence that threw out the Medici was a city in the mood for some radical reform. Already, the dominating figure on the political stage was an intense Dominican friar from Ferrara named **Girolamo Savonarola**. Perhaps not surprisingly, this oversophisticated and overstimulated city was also in the mood to be told how wicked and decadent it was, and Savonarola was happy to oblige. A spellbinding revival preacher with a touch of erudition, Savonarola packed as many as 10,000 into the Duomo to hear his weekly sermons, laced with political sarcasm and social criticism. Though an insufferable prig, he was also a sincere democrat. There is a story that the dying Lorenzo called Savonarola to his bedside for the last rites, and that the friar refused him absolution unless he 'restored the liberty of the Florentines', a proposal that only made the dying despot sneer with contempt.

Savonarola also talked Charles VIII into leaving Florence in peace. Pisa, however, took advantage of the confusion to revolt, and the restored republic's attempts to recapture it were in vain. Things were going badly. Piero Capponi's death in 1496 left Florence without a really able leader, and Savonarolan extremists became ever more influential. The French invasion and the incessant wars that followed cost the city dearly in trade, while the Medici, now in Rome, intrigued endlessly to destroy the republic. Worst of all, Savonarola's attacks on clerical corruption made him another bitter enemy in Rome—none other than Pope Alexander VI himself, the most corrupt cleric who ever lived. The Borgia Pope scraped together a league of allies to make war on Florence in 1497.

This war proceeded without serious reverses for either side, but Savonarola was able to exploit it brilliantly, convincing the Florentines that they were on a moral crusade against the hated and dissolute Borgias, Medici, French, Venetians and Milanese. 1497 was undoubtedly the high point of Savonarola's career. The good friar's spies—mostly children—kept a close eye on any Florentines suspected of enjoying themselves, and collected books, fancy clothes and works of art for the famous **Bonfire of Vanities**. It was a climactic moment in the history of Florence's delicate psyche. Somehow the spell had been broken; like the deranged old Michelangelo, taking a hammer to his own work, the Florentines gathered the objects that had once been their greatest pride and put them to the torch. The bonfire was held in the centre of the Piazza della Signoria; a visiting Venetian offered to buy the whole lot, but the Florentines had someone hastily sketch his portrait and threw that on the flames, too.

One vanity the Florentines could not quite bring themselves to part with was their violent factionalism. On one side were the *Piagnoni* ('weepers') of Savonarola's party, on the other the party of the *Arrabbiati* ('the angry'), including the gangs of young delinquents who would demonstrate their opposition to piety and holiness by sneaking into the Cathedral and filling Savonarola's pulpit with cow dung. A Medicean party was also gathering strength, a sort of fifth column sowing discontent within the city and undermining the war effort. Three times, unsuccessfully, the exiled Medici attempted to seize the city with bands of mercenaries. The Pisan revolt continued, and Pope Alexander had excommunicated Savonarola and was threatening to place all Florence under an interdict. In the long hangover after the Bonfire of Vanities, the Florentines were growing weary of their preacher. When the *Arrabbiati* won the elections of 1498, his doom was sealed. A kangaroo court found the new scapegoat guilty of heresy and treason. After some gratuitous torture and public mockery, the very spot where the Bonfire of Vanities had been held now witnessed a bonfire of Savonarola.

Pope Alexander still wasn't happy. He sent an army under his son, Cesare Borgia, to menace the city. Florence weathered this threat, and the relatively democratic

'Savonarolan' constitution of 1494 seemed to be working out well. Under an innovative idea, borrowed from Venice and designed to circumvent party strife, a public spirited gentleman named **Piero Soderini** was elected *gonfaloniere* for life in 1502. With the help of his friend and adviser, **Niccolò Machiavelli**, Soderini kept the ship of state on an even keel. Pisa finally surrendered in 1509. Serious trouble returned in 1512, and once more the popes were behind it. As France's only ally in Italy, Florence ran foul of Julius II. Papal and Spanish armies invaded Florentine territory, and after their gruesome sack of Prato, designed specifically to overawe Florence, the frightened and politically apathetic city was ready to submit to the pope's conditions—the expulsion of Soderini, a change of alliance, and the return of the Medici.

The End of the Republic

At first, the understanding was that the Medici would live in Florence strictly as private citizens. But **Giuliano de' Medici**, son of Lorenzo and current leader of the clan, soon united the upper classes for a rolling back of Savonarolan democracy. With plenty of hired soldiers to intimidate the populace, a rigged *parlamento* on September 1512 restored Medici control. The democratic Grand Council was soon abolished; its new meeting hall in the Palazzo Vecchio (where Leonardo and Michelangelo were to have their 'Battle of the Frescoes') was broken up into apartments for soldiers. Soldiers were everywhere, and the Medicean restoration immediately took on the aspect of a police state. Hundreds of political prisoners spent time under torture in the Palazzo Vecchio's dungeons, among them Machiavelli.

Giuliano died in 1516, succeeded by his nephew **Lorenzo, Duke of Urbino**, a snotty young sport with a tyrant's bad manners. Nobody mourned much when syphilis carried him off in 1519, but the family paid Michelangelo to give both Lorenzo and Giuliano fancy tombs. Ever since Giuliano's death, however, the real Medici boss had been not Lorenzo, but his uncle Giovanni, who in that year became **Pope Leo X**. The Medici, original masters of nepotism, had been planning this for years. Back in the 1470s, Lorenzo il Magnifico realized that the surest way of maintaining the family fortunes would be to get a Medici on the papal throne. He had little Giovanni ordained at the age of 8, purchased him a cardinal's hat at 13, and used bribery and diplomacy to help him accumulate dozens of benefices all over France and Italy.

For his easygoing civility (as exemplified in his famous quote: 'God has given us the papacy so let us enjoy it'), and his patronage of scholars and artists, Leo became one of the best-remembered Renaissance popes. On the other side of the coin was his criminal mismanagement of the Church; having learned the advantages of parasitism, the Medici were eager to pass it on to their friends. Upper-class Florentines descended on Rome like a plague of locusts, occupying all the important sinecures and rapidly emptying the papal treasury. Their rapacity, plus the tremendous expenses involved in building the new St Peter's, caused Leo to step up the sale of indulgences all over Europe—disgusting reformers like Luther and greatly hastening the onset of the Reformation.

Back in Florence, Lorenzo Duke of Urbino and his successor Giulio, bastard son of Lorenzo's brother the murdered Giuliano, were little more than puppets; Leo always found enough time between banquets to manage the city's affairs. Giulio himself became pope in 1523, as **Clement VII**, thanks largely to the new financial interdependence between Florence and Rome, and now the Medici presence in their home city was reduced to two more unattractive young bastards, Ippolito and Alessandro, under the guardianship of Cardinal Silvio Passerini. As Leo had done, Clement attempted to run the city from Rome, but high taxes and the lack of a strong hand made the new Medici regime increasingly precarious; its end followed almost immediately upon the sack of Rome in 1527. With Clement a prisoner in the Vatican and unable to intervene, a delegation of Florentine notables discreetly informed Passerini and the Medicis that it was time to go. They took the hint, and for the third time in less than a century Florence had succeeded in getting rid of the Medici.

The new republic, though initiated by the disillusioned wealthy classes, soon found radical Savonarolan democrats gaining the upper hand. The Grand Council met once more, and extended the franchise to include most of the citizens. Vanities were cursed again, books were banned and carnival parades forbidden; the Council officially pronounced Jesus Christ 'King of the Florentines', just as it had done in the heyday of the Savonarolan camp meeting. In an intense atmosphere of republican virtue and pious crusade, Florence rushed headlong into the apocalyptic climax of its history.

This time, it did not take the Medici long to recover. In order to get Florence back, the witless Clement became allied to his former enemy, **Emperor Charles V**, a sordid deal that would eventually betray all Italy to Spanish control. Imperial troops were to help subdue Florence, and Clement's illegitimate son Alessandro was to wed Charles' illegitimate daughter. The bastards were closing in. Charles' troops put Florence under siege in December 1529. The city had few resources for the struggle, and no friends, but a heroic resistance kept the imperialists at bay all through the winter and spring. Citizens gave up their gold and silver to be minted into the republic's last coins. The councillors debated seizing little Catherine de' Medici, future Queen of France but then a prisoner of the republic, and dangling her from the walls to give the enemy a good target. Few artists were left in Florence, but Michelangelo stayed to help with his city's fortifications (by night he was working on the Medici tombs in San Lorenzo, surely one of the all-time astounding feats of fence-straddling in history; both sides gave him safe passage when he wanted to leave Florence, and again when he decided to come back).

In August of 1530, the Florentines' skilful commander, Francesco Ferruccio, was killed in a skirmish near Pistoia; at about the same time the republic realized that its mercenary captain within the walls, Malatesta Baglioni, had sold them out to the pope and emperor. When they tried to arrest him, Baglioni only laughed, and directed his men to turn their artillery on the city. The inevitable capitulation came on 12 August; after almost 400 years, the Florentine republic had breathed its last.

At first, this third Medici return seemed to be just another dreary round of history repeating itself. Again, a packed *parlamento* gutted the constitution and legitimized the Medici takeover. Again the family and its minions combed the city, confiscating back every penny's worth of property that had been confiscated from them. This time, however, was to be different. Florence had gone from being a large fish in a small Italian pond to a miniscule but hindersome nuisance in the pan-European world of papal and imperial politics. Charles V didn't much like republics, or disorderly politicking, or indeed anyone who might conceivably say no to him. The orders came down from the emperor in Brussels; it was to be Medici for ever.

Cosimo I: the Medici as Grand Dukes

At first little was changed, the shell of the republican constitution was maintained, but with the 20-year-old illegitimate Alessandro as 'Duke of the Florentine Republic'; the harsh reality was under construction on the height above the city's west end—the Fortezza da Basso, with its Spanish garrison, demanded by Charles V as insurance that Florence would never again be able to assert its independence. If any further symbolism was necessary, Alessandro ordered the great bell to be removed from the tower of the Palazzo Vecchio, the bell that had always summoned the citizens to political assemblies and the mustering of the army.

In 1537, Alessandro was treacherously murdered by his jealous cousin Lorenzino de' Medici. With no legitimate heirs in the direct line Florence was in danger of falling under direct imperial rule, as had happened to Milan two years earlier, upon the extinction of the Sforza dukes. The assassination was kept secret while the Medici and the diplomats angled for a solution. The only reasonable choice turned out to be 18-year-old **Cosimo de' Medici**, heir of the family's cadet branch. This son of a famous mercenary commander, Giovanni of the Black Bands, had grown up on a farm and had never been involved with Florentine affairs; both the elder statesmen of the family and the imperial representatives thought they would easily be able to manipulate him.

It soon became clear that they had picked the wrong boy. Right from the start, young Cosimo had a surprisingly complete idea of how he meant to rule Florence, and also the will and strength of personality to see his commands carried out. No one ever admitted liking him; his puritanical court dismayed even the old partisans of Savonarola, and Florentines always enjoyed grumbling over his high taxes, going to support 'colonels, spies, Spaniards, and women to serve Madame' (his Spanish consort Eleanor of Toledo).

More surprising still, in this pathetic age when bowing and scraping Italians were everywhere else losing both their liberty and their dignity, Cosimo held his own against both pope and Spaniard. To back up his growing independence, Cosimo put his domains on an almost permanent war footing. New fortresses were built, a big fleet begun, and a paid standing army took the place of mercenaries and citizen levies. The skeleton of the old republic was revamped into a modern, bureaucratic state, governed as scientifically and rationally as any in Europe. The new regime, well prepared as it was, never had a severe test. Early in his reign Cosimo defeated the last-ditch effort of the republican exiles, unreconstructed oligarchs led by the banker Filippo Strozzi, at the Battle of Montemurlo, the last threat ever to Medici rule. Cosimo's masterstroke came in 1557, when with the help of an Imperial army he was able to gobble up the entire Republic of Siena. Now the Medici rule extended over roughly the boundaries of modern Tuscany; Cosimo was able to cap off his reign in 1569 by purchasing from the Pope the title of Grand Duke of Tuscany.

Knick-knacks and Tedium: the Later Medici

For all Cosimo's efforts, Florence was a city entering a very evident decline. Banking and trade did well throughout the late 16th century, a prosperous time for almost all of Italy, but there were few opportunities for growth, and few Florentines interested in looking for it. More than ever, wealth was going into land, palaces and government bonds; the old tradition of mercantile venture among the Florentine elite was rapidly becoming a thing of the past. For culture and art, Cosimo's reign turned out to be a disaster. It wasn't what he intended; indeed the Duke brought to the field his accustomed energy and compulsion to improve and organize. Academies were founded, and research underwritten. Cosimo's big purse and his very modern concept of art as political propaganda helped change the Florentine artist from a slightly eccentric guild artisan to a flouncing courtier, ready to roll over at his master's command.

Michelangelo, despite frequent entreaties, always refused to work for Cosimo. Most of the other talented Florentines eventually found one excuse or another to bolt for Rome or even further afield, leaving lapdogs like **Giorgio Vasari** to carry on the grand traditions of Florentine art. Vasari, with help from such artists as Ammannati and Bandinelli, transformed much of the city—especially the interiors of its churches and public buildings. Florence began to fill up with equestrian statues of Medici, pageants and plaster triumphal arches displaying the triumphs of the Medici, sculptural allegories (like Cellini's *Perseus*) reminding us of the inevitability of the Medici, and best of all portraits of semi-divine Medici floating up in the clouds with little Cupids and Virtues.

It was all the same to Cosimo and his successors, whose personal tastes tended more to engraved jewels, exotic taxidermy and sculptures made of seashells. But it helped hasten the extinction of Florentine culture and the quiet transformation of the city into just another Mediterranean backwater. Cosimo himself grew ill in his later years, abdicating most responsibility to his son **Francesco** from 1564 to his death ten years later. Francesco, the genuine oddball among the Medici, was a moody, melancholic sort who cared little for government, preferring to lock himself up in the family palaces to pursue his passion for alchemy, as well as occasional researches into such subjects as perpetual motion and poisons—his agents around the Mediterranean had to ship him crates of scorpions every now and then. Despite his lack of interest, Francesco was a capable ruler, best known for his founding of the port city of Livorno.

Later Medici followed the general course established by other great families, such as the Habsburgs and Bourbons—each one was worse than the last. Francesco's death in 1587 gave the throne to his brother, **Ferdinando I**, founder of the Medici Chapels at San Lorenzo and another indefatigable collector of bric-à-brac. Next came **Cosimo II** (1609–21), a sickly nonentity who eventually succumbed to tuberculosis, and **Ferdinando II** (1621–70), whose long and uneventful reign oversaw the impoverishment of Florence and most of Tuscany. For this the Medici do not deserve much blame. A long string of bad harvests, beginning in the 1590s, plagues that recurred with terrible frequency as late as the 1630s, and general trade patterns that redistributed wealth and power from the Mediterranean to northern Europe, all set the stage for the collapse of the Florentine economy. The fatal blow came in the 1630s, when the long-deteriorating wool trade collapsed with sudden finality. Banking was going too, partly a victim of the age's continuing inflation, partly of high taxes and lack of worthwhile investments. Florence, by mid-century, found itself with no prospects at all, a pensioner city drawing a barely respectable income from its glorious past.

With **Cosimo III** (1670–1723), the line of the Medici crossed over into the realm of the ridiculous. A religious crank and anti-Semite, this Cosimo temporarily wiped out free thought in the universities, allowed Tuscany to fill up with nuns and Jesuits, and decreed fantastical laws like the one that forbade any man to enter a house where an unmarried woman lived. To support his lavish court and pay the big tributes demanded

Know your Medici!

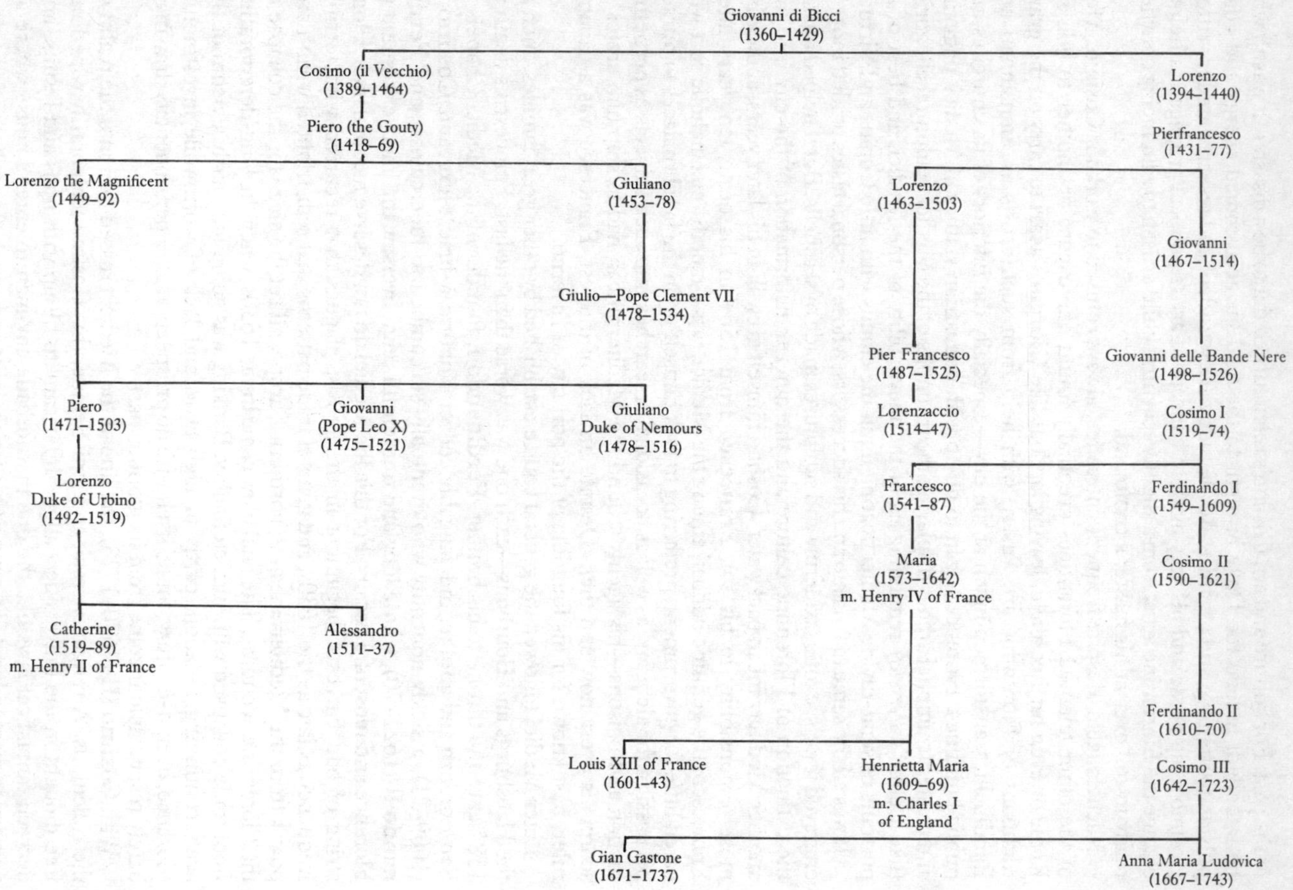
Giovanni di Bicci
(1360–1429)
Cosimo (il Vecchio)
(1389–1464)
Lorenzo
(1394–1440)
Piero (the Gouty)
(1418–69)
Pierfrancesco
(1431–77)
Lorenzo the Magnificent
(1449–92)
Giuliano
(1453–78)
Lorenzo
(1463–1503)
Giovanni
(1467–1514)
Giulio—Pope Clement VII
(1478–1534)
Pier Francesco
(1487–1525)
Giovanni delle Bande Nere
(1498–1526)
Piero
(1471–1503)
Giovanni
(Pope Leo X)
(1475–1521)
Giuliano
Duke of Nemours
(1478–1516)
Lorenzaccio
(1514–47)
Cosimo I
(1519–74)
Lorenzo
Duke of Urbino
(1492–1519)
Francesco
(1541–87)
Ferdinando I
(1549–1609)
Maria
(1573–1642)
m. Henry IV of France
Cosimo II
(1590–1621)
Catherine
(1519–89)
m. Henry II of France
Alessandro
(1511–37)
Ferdinando II
(1610–70)
Louis XIII of France
(1601–43)
Henrietta Maria
(1609–69)
m. Charles I
of England
Cosimo III
(1642–1723)
Gian Gastone
(1671–1737)
Anna Maria Ludovica
(1667–1743)

by Spain and Austria (something earlier Medici would have scorned) Cosimo taxed what was left of the Florentine economy into an early grave. His heir was the incredible **Gian Gastone** (1723–37). This last Medici, an obese, homosexual drunkard, senile and slobbering at the age of fifty, has been immortalized by the equally incredible bust in the Pitti Palace. Gian Gastone had to be carried up and down stairs on the rare occasions when he ever got out of bed (mainly to disprove rumours that he was dead); on the one occasion he appeared in public, the chronicles report him vomiting repeatedly out of the carriage window.

As a footnote on the Medici there is Gian Gastone's perfectly sensible sister, **Anna Maria Ludovica**. As the very last surviving Medici, it fell to her to dispose of the family's vast wealth and hoards of art. When she died, in 1743, her will revealed that the whole bundle was to become the property of the future rulers of Tuscany—whoever they should be—with the provision that not one bit of it should ever, ever be moved outside Florence. Without her, the great collections of the Uffizi and the Bargello might long ago have been packed away to Vienna or Paris.

Post-Medici Florence

When Gian Gastone died in 1737, Tuscany's fate had already been decided by the great powers of Europe. The Grand Duchy would fall to **Francis Stephen**, Duke of Lorraine and husband-to-be of the Austrian Empress Maria Theresa; the new duke's troops were already installed in the Fortezza da Basso a year before Gian Gastone died. For most of the next century, Florence slumbered peacefully under a benign Austrian rule. Already the first Grand Tourists were arriving on their way to Rome and Naples, sons of the Enlightenment like Goethe, who never imagined anything in Florence could possibly interest him and didn't stop, or relics like the Pretender Charles Edward Stuart, 'Bonnie Prince Charlie', Duke of Albany, who stayed two years. Napoleon's men occupied the city for most of two decades, without making much of an impression.

After the Napoleonic Wars, the Habsburg restoration brought back the Lorraine dynasty. From 1824 to 1859, Florence and Tuscany were ruled by Leopold II, that most useful and likeable of all Grand Dukes. This was the age when Florence first became popular among the northern Europeans—the time when the Brownings, Dostoevsky, Leigh Hunt and dozens of other artists and writers took up residence, rediscovering the glories of the city and of the early Renaissance. Grand Duke Leopold was decent enough to let himself be overthrown in 1859, during the tumults of the Risorgimento. In 1865, when only the Papal State remained to be incorporated into the Kingdom of Italy, Florence briefly became the new nation's capital. King Vittorio Emanuele moved into the Pitti Palace, and the Italian Parliament met in the great hall of the Palazzo Vecchio.

It was not meant to last. When the Italian troops entered Rome in 1870, Florence's brief hour as a major capital was at an end. Not, however, without giving the staid old city a memorable jolt towards the modern world. In an unusual flurry of exertion, Florence finally threw up a façade for its cathedral, and levelled the picturesque though squalid market area and Jewish ghetto to build the dolorous Piazza della Repubblica. Fortunately, the city regained its senses before too much damage was done. Throughout this century, Florence's role as a museum city has been confirmed with each passing year. The hiatus provided by World War II allowed the city to resume briefly its ancient delight in black-and-white political epic. In 1944–45, Florence offered some of the most outrageous spectacles of Fascist fanaticism, and also some of the most courageous stories of the Resistance—including that of the German consul Gerhard Wolf, who used his position to protect Florentines from the Nazi terror, often at great personal risk.

In August 1944, the Allied armies were poised to advance through northern Tuscany. For the Germans, the Arno made a convenient defensive line, requiring that all the bridges of Florence be demolished. All were, except for the Ponte Vecchio, saved in a last-minute deal, though the buildings on either side of it were destroyed to provide piles of rubble around the bridge approaches. After the war, all were repaired; the city had the Ponte della Trínita rebuilt stone by stone exactly as it was. No sooner was the war damage redeemed, however, than an even greater disaster attacked the Florentine past. The flood of 1966, when water reached as high as 21 feet, did more damage than Nazis or Napoleons; an international effort was raised to preserve and restore the city's monuments.

Careful planning has saved the best of the immediate countryside from a different sort of flood—postwar suburbanization—but much of the territory around the city has become covered by an atrocity of suburban sprawl, some of the most degraded landscapes in all of Italy. Today, Florentines worry most about creeping obsolescence and a lack of initiative. Business is slipping. Recently it was announced that the new high-speed Milan–Rome train will not even stop here. Increasingly, Florence is left with its memories and its tourists.

HIGHLIGHTS OF FLORENCE

Florence's museums, palaces, and churches contain more good art than perhaps any city in Europe, and to see it all without hardship to your eyes, feet, and sensibilities would take at least three weeks and some L100,000 in admissions. If you only have only a few days to spend, and if you might never come back again, the highlights will easily take up all of your time—the **Cathedral** and **Baptistry**, the paintings in the **Uffizi** (preferably not all in the same day) and the sculptures in the **Bargello**, which is more worthy of your brief time than the **Accademia**, where the rubbernecks pile in to see Michelangelo's *David*. Stop in for a look at the eccentric **Orsanmichele**, and see the Arno from the **Ponte Vecchio**, taking in some of the oldest streets in the city. If your heart leans towards the graceful lyricism of the 1400s, don't miss the **Cathedral Museum** and the Fra Angelicos in **San Marco**; if the lush virtuosity of the 1500s is your cup of tea, visit the **Pitti Palace**'s Galleria Pàlatina. Two churches on the edges of the centre, **S. Maria Novella** and **S. Croce** are galleries in themselves, containing some of the greatest Florentine art; **S. Maria del Carmine** has the recently restored frescoes of Masaccio and company. Devotees of the Michelangelo cult won't want to miss the Medici Chapels and library at **San Lorenzo**. When the stones begin to weary you, head for the green oasis of the **Boboli Gardens**. Finally, climb up to **San Miniato**, for the beautiful medieval church and the enchanting view over the city.

Florence's 'secondary' sights are just as interesting. You could spend a day walking around old **Fiesole**, or 15 minutes looking at Gozzoli's charming fresco in the **Palazzo Medici-Riccardi**. The **Palazzo Vecchio** has more, but less charming, Medici frescoes. You can see how a wealthy medieval Tuscan merchant lived at the **Palazzo Davanzati**, while the **Museum of the History of Science** will tell you about the scientific side of the Florentine Renaissance; **S. Trínita**, **S. Spirito**, **Ognissanti**, and the **Annunziata** all contain famous works from the Renaissance. The **Casa Buonarroti** has some early sculptures of Michelangelo; the **Archaeology Museum** has even earlier ones by the Etruscans, Greeks and Egyptians; the Pitti Palace's **Museo degli Argenti** overflows with Medicean jewellery and trinkets. Take a bus or car out to Lorenzo il Magnifico's **Villa at Poggio a Caiano**, or to the Medici's other garden villas: **La Petraia** and **Castello**, or **Pratolino**.

There are three museums with 19th- and 20th-century collections to bring you back to the present: the **Galleria d'Arte Moderna** in the Pitti Palace, the **Collezione della Ragione** and the **Photography Museum** in the Palazzo Rucellai. There are two museums founded by Englishmen: the **Horne Museum** with Renaissance art, and the eccentric **Stibbert Museum** with everything but the kitchen sink. Strangest of all are the museums in **La Specola**, featuring stuffed animals and anatomical wax figures.

GETTING TO AND AROUND

Florence is the central transport node for Tuscany and harder to avoid than to reach. It has only a dinky **civil airport**, Peretola, at Via del Termine 11, tel 317 123, with flight connections to Milan, Naples, Lugano, Rome, Nice, Munich, and Paris. Special train connections, however, link the city to the much larger international airport in Pisa (1 hr, L4900 one way, daily every 1–2 hrs). For flight information, ring 27 88. **Airline offices** in Florence are: Alitalia, Lungarno Acciaioli 10/12r, tel 263 208; British Airways, Via Vigna Nuova 36r, tel 218 655; Pan American, Lungarno Acciaioli 4, tel 263 804; TWA, Piazza Trínita 1r, tel 296 856.

By Train

Florence's central station is **Santa Maria Novella**, tel 278 785; there is another, **Campo di Marte**, located at the east end of town, mainly used for local lines and some trains to Rome. Bus 19 connects the two stations.

By Bus

It's possible to reach nearly every city, town, and village in Tuscany from Florence, which is wonderfully convenient—once you know which of several bus companies to patronize. The tourist office has a complete list of destinations, but here are some of the most popular:

SITA (near the station, Via S. Caterina da Siena 15, tel 211 487): towns in the Val d'Elsa, Chianti, Val di Pesa, Mugello, and Casentino; Arezzo, Bibbiena, Castelfiorentino, Certaldo, Consuma, Firenzuola, Marina di Grosseto, Montevarchi, Poggibonsi (for S. Gimignano and Volterra), Pontassieve, Poppi, Pratovecchio, Scarperia, Siena, Stia, Vallombrosa.

LAZZI (Piazza Stazione 4, tel 298 840): along the Arno to the coast, including Abetone, Calenzano, Cerreto Guidi, Empoli, Forte dei Marmi, Incisa Valdarno, Livorno, Lucca, Marina di Carrara, Marina di Massa, Montecatini Terme, Montelupo, Montevarchi, Pescia, Pisa, Pistoia, Pontassieve, Pontedera, Prato, Signa, Tirrenia, Torre del Lago, and Viareggio.

CLAP (Piazza Stazione 15r, tel 283 734): Lucca.

CAT (Via Fiume 2r, tel 283 400): Anghiari, Arezzo, Caprese, Città di Castello, Incisa Valdarno, Figline Valdarno, Sansepolcro.

CAP (Via Nazionale 13, tel 214 637): Borgo S. Lorenzo, Impruneta, Montepiano, Prato.

COPIT (Piazza S. Maria Novella, tel 215 451): Abetone, Pistoia, Poggio a Caiano, Vinci.
RAMA (Lazzi Station, tel 298 840): Grosseto.

Within Florence

Florence is at once one of the best and one of the worst cities to get around; best, because nearly everything you'll want to see is within easy walking distance; there are no hills to climb, and it's hard to lose your way for very long. Worst, because the walking itself will demonstrate that Dante didn't have to go far to find Purgatorio. Old Florence steadfastly refused to make any concessions to amenity. A rational, very businesslike town of dusty streets, though punctuated here and there by lovely buildings, it looks even worse with modern noise and dirt; the new streets are dull and anonymous; pavements are rare; and in the summer the hard, shadeless streets resemble ducts of a furnace going full blast.

The traffic problem is one of the grimmest and most carcinogenic in Italy. In 1988, with great fanfare and howls of protest, Florence attempted to do something about the cars that were choking it to death by greatly enlarging the limited access zone, the *zona a traffico limitato*, which the Florentines, with clenched teeth, somehow pronounce as ZTL. Within ZTL only buses, taxis, and cars belonging to residents are permitted; otherwise, you may pay to park in one of the city's car parks (the Fortezza da Basso is biggest and perhaps most convenient) or take your chances on a side street. Although this new regulation has been applauded by the privileged residents of the historic centre, merchants who have seen their business drop off considerably are furious, as are those who live along the outer avenues (at peak hours their streets turn into clogged car parks), nor has there been much improvement within ZTL; there are fewer cars, certainly, which allows the ones remaining to speed even faster down the medieval lanes...

Just to make life difficult, Florence has two sets of address numbers on every street—red ones for business, blue for residences; your hotel might be either one.

City buses (ATAF) can whizz or inch you across Florence, and are an excellent means of reaching sights on the periphery. Most lines begin at Santa Maria Novella station, and pass by Piazza del Duomo or Piazza San Marco. There's an information/ticket booth in the station, and at ATAF's central office in Piazza del Duomo 57. Tickets are good for 90 or 120 minutes after validation on the bus; 24-hour passes are available as well. The most useful buses for visitors are:

7: Station–Duomo–San Domenico–Fiesole
10: Station–Duomo–S. Marco–Ponte a Mensola–Settignano
11A: Viale Calatafimi–Duomo–Porta Romana–Poggio Imperiale
13: Station–Duomo–Piazzale Michelangelo
14: Rovezzano–Duomo–Station–Careggi
15: Fortezza da Basso car park–S. Marco–Via del Proconsolo–Ponte alle Grazie–Piazza Pitti–Piazza S. Spirito–Piazza del Carmine–Porta Romana–Via Maggio–Ponte S. Trínita–Via Tornabuoni–Via dei Servi–Fortezza da Basso
17B: Cascine–Station–Duomo–Via Lamarmora–Salviatino (for the youth hostel)
25/46: Station–S. Marco–Piazza Libertà–Via Bologna–Pratolino
28: Station–Via R. Giuliani–Castello–Sesto Fiorentino
31/32: Station–Via Vitt. Emanuele–Stibbert Museum
37: Station–Ponte alla Carraia–Porta Romana–Certosa di Galluzzo

38: Porta Romana–Pian dei Giullari

Taxis in Florence don't cruise; you'll find them in ranks at the station and in the major *piazze*, or else ring for a radio taxi: 4798 or 4390.

Bicycle, Scooter, and Car Hire

Hiring a bike can save you tramping time and angst, but watch out for cars and pedestrians. If you park your car at the car park at the Fortezza da Basso, you can have two bikes for two hours for free, between the hours of 8 am and 8 pm, on the presentation of your SCAF parking coupon at the Bici-Città booth, on the north side near the tour bus parking area. You can also hire a bike at **Ciao & Basta**, tel 293 357 or 263 985, located in Via Alamanni, down the steps from the station or at Costa dei Magnoli 24, or in spring and summer in Piazza Pitti. **Free Motor**, Via S. Monica 6/8r, near Piazza del Carmine, tel 295 102, hires out bikes and motorbikes and scooters; motorbikes are also available from **Eurodrive**, Via Alamanni 7/9r, tel 298 639; **Motorent**, Via S. Zanobi 9r, tel 490 113; **Sabra**, Via Artisti 8, tel 576 256; or **Program**, Borgo Ognissanti 96, tel 382 916.

When you can't take any more art, hire a car and escape into the ravishing countryside. Most firms are in easy walking distance from the station. Avis, Borgo Ognissanti 128r, tel 213 629; Europcar, Borgo Ognissanti 120r, tel 294 130; Hertz, Via M. Finiguerra 33, tel 282 260; Maggiore, Via M. Finiguerra 11, tel 294 578; InterRent, Via il Prato 1r, tel 218 665; Italy by Car, Borgo Ognissanti 113r, tel 293 021. Eurodrive, Via Alamanni 7/9r, tel 298 639, hires cars with drivers who speak English.

TOURIST INFORMATION

The head office is a bit out of the way, near Piazza Beccaria on Via Manzoni 16, tel 247 8141, open weekdays 8:30–1:30. Other information offices are at Via Tornabuoni 15, tel 217 459, open 8–2 and in Fiesole at Piazza Mino 5, tel 598 720, open 9–1 and 3–6. There's also a booth outside the station on the taxi side, near the underground passageway, that is open daily until 9 pm in summer and very genial.

There are no end of places to help you find a hotel (see 'Where to Stay') but these offices usually do not.

PRACTICAL INFORMATION

Central Post Office: Via Pellicceria, near Piazza della Repubblica, open 8 am–8 pm, Sat 8–1; telegram office open 24 hours, or tel 186.

Telephones: in the Central Post Office, 24 hours. Also in S. Maria Novella station, near platform 9.

Police: Emergency tel 113. The Ufficio Stranieri, in the Questura, Via Zara 2, tel 49 771, handles most foreigners' problems, and usually has someone around who speaks English. Go here for residents' permits, etc.

Medical: For an ambulance or first aid, Misericordia, Piazza del Duomo 20, tel 212 222. Doctor's night service, tel 477 891. General Hospital Santa Maria Nuova, in Piazza S. M. Nuova, tel 27 581, is the most convenient hospital. Tourist Medical Service, 24 hours a day, staffed by English and French speaking physicians at Via Lorenzo il Magnifico 59, ring first 475 411.

Pharmacies: open 24 hours every day in S. Maria Novella station, also Molteni, Via Calzaiuoli 7r and Taverna, Piazza S. Giovanni 20r, by the Baptistry.

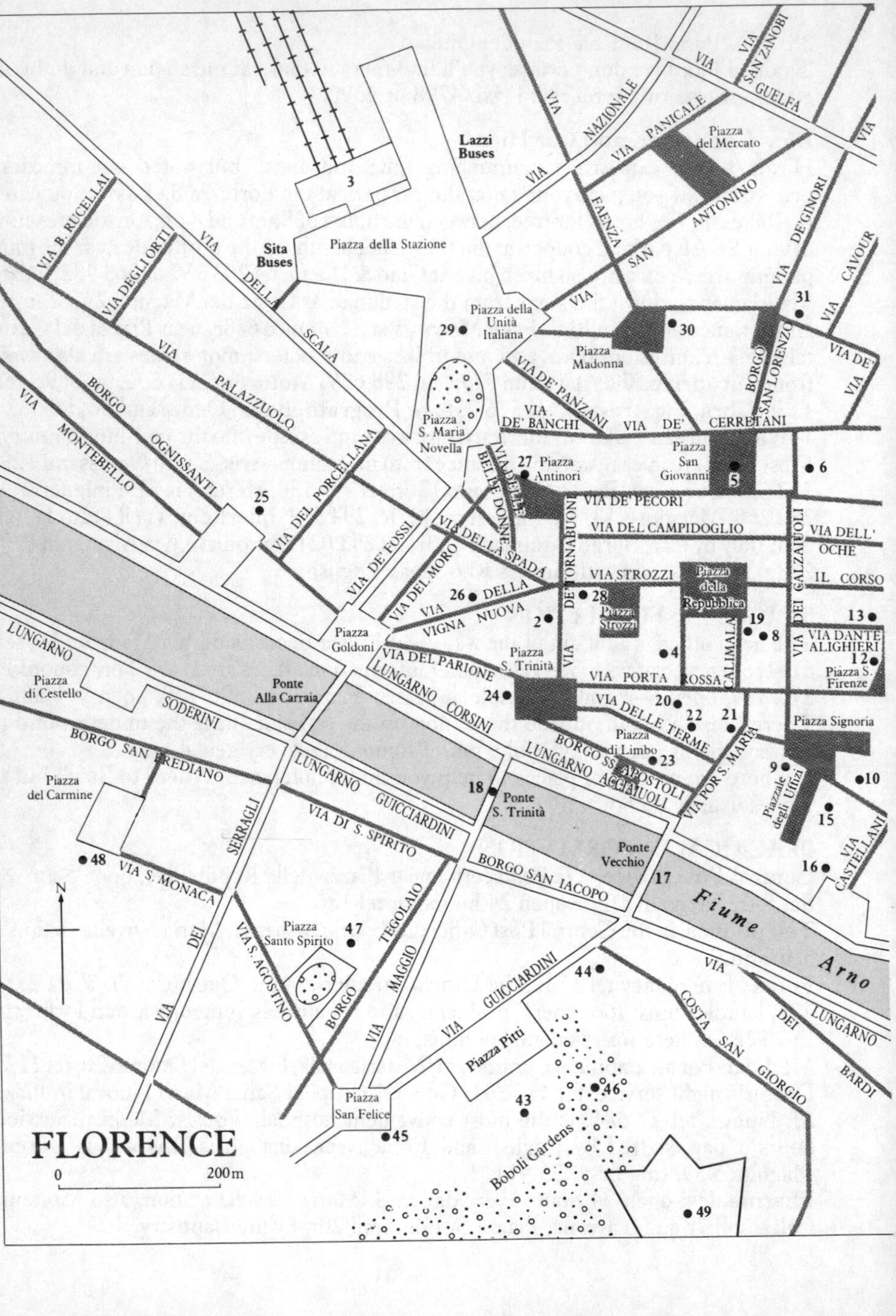

FLORENCE
0
200m
N
Lazzi Buses
Sita Buses
Piazza della Stazione
Piazza della Unità Italiana
Piazza S. Maria Novella
Piazza Madonna
Piazza del Mercato
Piazza San Giovanni
Piazza Antinori
Piazza della Repubblica
Piazza Strozzi
Piazza S. Trinità
Piazza Goldoni
Piazza di Cestello
Piazza del Carmine
Piazza di Limbo
Piazza Signoria
Piazzale degli Uffizi
Piazza S. Firenze
Piazza Santo Spirito
Piazza Pitti
Piazza San Felice
Ponte Alla Carraia
Ponte S. Trinità
Ponte Vecchio
Fiume Arno
Boboli Gardens
VIA B. RUCELLAI
VIA DEGLI ORTI
VIA DELLA SCALA
VIA PALAZZUOLO
BORGO OGNISSANTI
VIA MONTEBELLO
VIA DEL PORCELLANA
VIA DE' FOSSI
VIA DEL MORO
VIA DELLA SPADA
VIA DELLE BELLE DONNE
VIA DELLA VIGNA NUOVA
VIA DEL PARIONE
VIA DE' PANZANI
VIA DE' BANCHI
VIA DE' CERRETANI
VIA DE' PECORI
VIA DEL CAMPIDOGLIO
VIA STROZZI
VIA DE' TORNABUONI
VIA PORTA ROSSA
CALIMALA
VIA DEI CALZAIUOLI
VIA DELL' OCHE
IL CORSO
VIA DANTE ALIGHIERI
VIA DELLE TERME
BORGO SS. APOSTOLI
VIA POR S. MARIA
VIA CASTELLANI
VIA NAZIONALE
VIA FAENZA
VIA SAN ANTONINO
VIA PANICALE
VIA SAN ZANOBI
VIA GUELFA
VIA DE' GINORI
BORGO SAN LORENZO
VIA CAVOUR
VIA DE'
LUNGARNO SODERINI
BORGO SAN FREDIANO
LUNGARNO CORSINI
LUNGARNO ACCIAIUOLI
LUNGARNO GUICCIARDINI
VIA DI S. SPIRITO
BORGO SAN IACOPO
VIA S. MONACA
VIA DEI SERRAGLI
VIA S. AGOSTINO
BORGO TEGOLAIO
VIA MAGGIO
VIA GUICCIARDINI
VIA COSTA SAN GIORGIO
VIA DEI BARDI
LUNGARNO
2
3
4
5
6
8
9
10
12
13
15
16
17
18
19
20
21
22
23
24
25
26
27
28
29
30
31
43
44
45
46
47
48
49

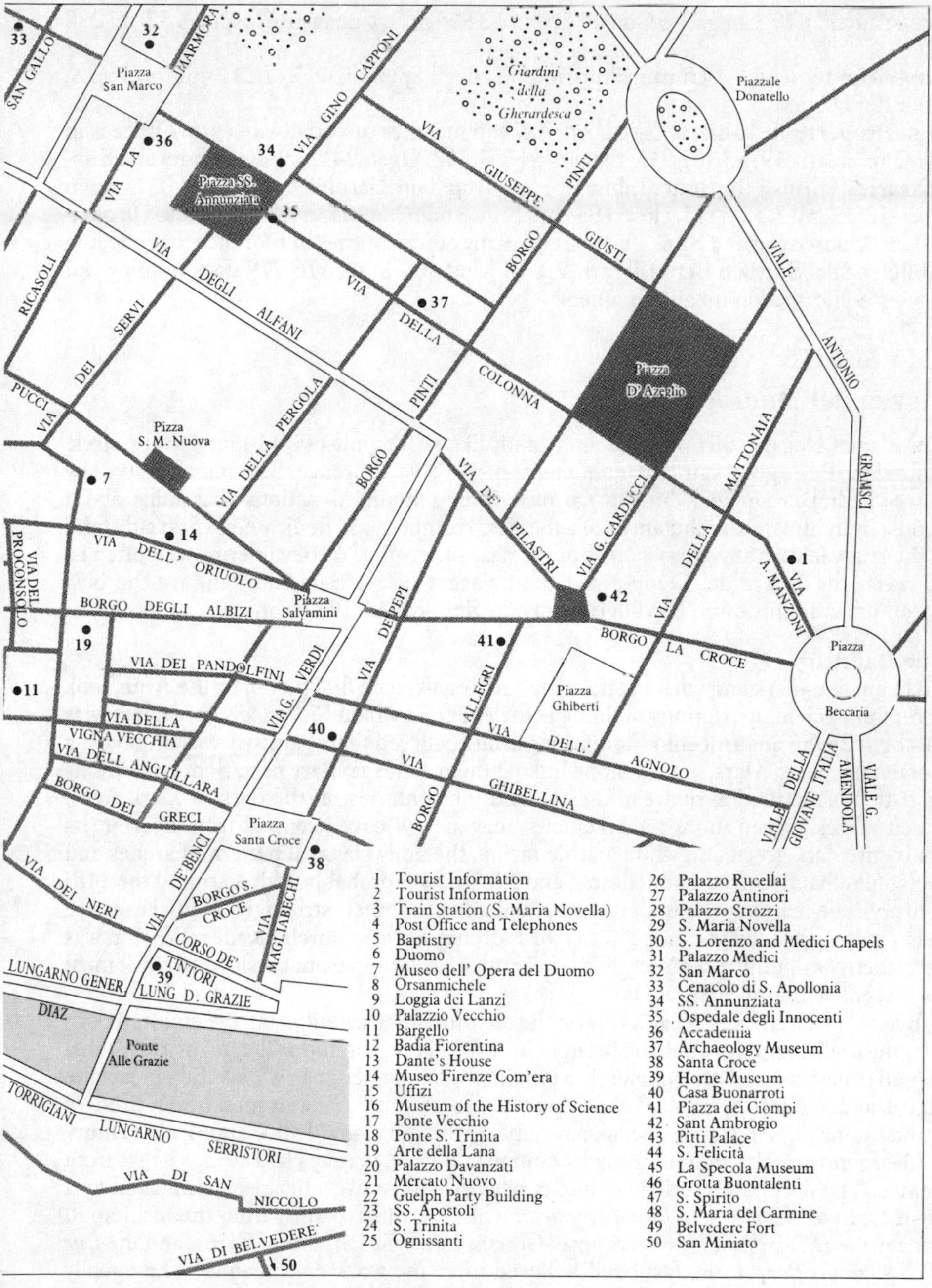

1 Tourist Information
2 Tourist Information
3 Train Station (S. Maria Novella)
4 Post Office and Telephones
5 Baptistry
6 Duomo
7 Museo dell' Opera del Duomo
8 Orsanmichele
9 Loggia dei Lanzi
10 Palazzio Vecchio
11 Bargello
12 Badia Fiorentina
13 Dante's House
14 Museo Firenze Com'era
15 Uffizi
16 Museum of the History of Science
17 Ponte Vecchio
18 Ponte S. Trinita
19 Arte della Lana
20 Palazzo Davanzati
21 Mercato Nuovo
22 Guelph Party Building
23 SS. Apostoli
24 S. Trinita
25 Ognissanti
26 Palazzo Rucellai
27 Palazzo Antinori
28 Palazzo Strozzi
29 S. Maria Novella
30 S. Lorenzo and Medici Chapels
31 Palazzo Medici
32 San Marco
33 Cenacolo di S. Apollonia
34 SS. Annunziata
35 Ospedale degli Innocenti
36 Accademia
37 Archaeology Museum
38 Santa Croce
39 Horne Museum
40 Casa Buonarroti
41 Piazza dei Ciompi
42 Sant Ambrogio
43 Pitti Palace
44 S. Felicità
45 La Specola Museum
46 Grotta Buontalenti
47 S. Spirito
48 S. Maria del Carmine
49 Belvedere Fort
50 San Miniato

Consulates: UK, Lungarno Corsini 2, tel 212 594. US, Lungarno Vespucci 38, tel 298 276.
American Express: at Universalturismo, Via degli Speziali, tel 217 241, just off Piazza della Repubblica.
Lost Property: in Italian is *Oggetti ritrovati* and includes **towed-away cars**. Office is in Via Circondaria 19, tel 367 943; for cars tel 351 562. Open 9–12, closed Thurs and Sun.
Libraries: British Institute Library, Lungarno Guicciardini 9, tel 284 031, open 9:45–12:45 and 3:15–7:15, closed Sat and Sun. American Library, Via S. Gallo 10, open 9–12:30, closed Sat and Sun. There are so many other libraries in Florence that one, the Biblioteca del Servizio Beni Librari, Via G. Modena 13, tel 576 779 does nothing but dispense information on all the others.

CITY SIGHTS

Piazza del Duomo

No, it's not elegant, this noisy urban island; like sharks, buses and tour groups circle around the three great spiritual monuments of medieval Florence. Saxophone players by the cathedral croon to a human carnival from a hundred nations that mills about good-naturedly while ambulances of a medieval brotherhood dedicated to first aid stand at the ready in case anyone swoons from ecstasy or art-glut. As bewildering as it often is, however, the Piazza del Duomo and the adjacent Piazza San Giovanni are the best introduction to this often bewildering city, beginning with the Baptistry...

The Baptistry

To begin to understand what magic made the Renaissance first bloom by the Arno, look here; this ancient, mysterious building is the egg from which Florence's golden age was hatched. By the quattrocento Florentines firmly believed their baptistry was originally a Roman temple to Mars, a touchstone linking them to a legendary past. Scholarship sets its date of construction between the 6th and 9th centuries, in the darkest Dark Ages, which makes it even more remarkable; it may as well have dropped from heaven. Its distinctive dark green and white marble facing, the tidily classical pattern of arches and rectangles that deceived Brunelleschi and Alberti, was probably added around the 11th century. The masters who built it remain unknown, but their strikingly original exercise in geometry provided the model for all of Florence's great church façades. When it was new, there was nothing remotely like it in Europe; to visitors from outside the city it must have seemed almost miraculous.

Every 21 March, New Year's Day on the old Florentine calendar, all the children born over the last 12 months would be brought here for a great communal baptism, a habit that helped make the baptistry not merely a religious monument but a civic symbol, in fact the oldest and fondest symbol of the republic. As such the Florentines never tired of embellishing it. Under the octagonal cupola, the glittering 13th- and 14th-century gold-ground mosaics show a strong Byzantine influence, perhaps laid by mosaicists from Venice. The decoration is divided into concentric strips: over the apse, dominated by a 28-ft figure of Christ, is a *Last Judgement*, while the other bands, from the inside out, portray the *Hierarchy of Heaven*, *Story of Genesis*, *Life of Joseph*, *Life of Christ*, and the *Life of St John the Baptist*, the last band believed to be the work of Cimabue. The equally beautiful mosaics over the altar and in the vault are the earliest, signed by a monk named Iacopo in the first decades of the 1200s.

To match the mosaics, there is an intricate tessellated marble floor, decorated with signs of the Zodiac; the blank, octagonal space in the centre was formerly occupied by the huge font. The green and white patterned walls of the interior, even more than the exterior, are remarkable, combining influences from the ancient world and modern inspiration for something entirely new, the perfect source that architects of the Middle Ages and Renaissance would ever strive to match. Much of the best design work is up in the **galleries**, not accessible, but partially visible from the floor.

The baptistry is hardly cluttered; besides a 13th-century Pisan style baptismal font, only the **Tomb of Anti-Pope John XXIII** by Donatello and Michelozzo stands out. This funerary monument, with scenographic marble draperies softening its classical lines, is one of the great prototypes of the early Renaissance. But how did this Anti-Pope John, deposed by the Council of Constance in 1415, earn the unique privilege of a fancy tomb in the baptistry? Why, it was thanks to him that Giovanni di Bicci de' Medici made the family fortune as head banker to the Curia.

THE GATES OF PARADISE

Historians used to pinpoint the beginning of the 'Renaissance' as the year 1401, when the merchants' guild, the Arte di Calimala, sponsored a competition for the baptistry's north doors. The **South Doors** (the main entrance into the baptistry) had already been completed by Andrea Pisano in 1330, and they give an excellent lesson on the style of the day. The doors are divided into 28 panels in quatrefoil frames with scenes from the life of St John the Baptist and the eight Cardinal and Theological Virtues, formal and elegant works in the best Gothic manner.

The celebrated competition of 1401—perhaps the first ever held in the annals of art—pitted the seven greatest sculptors of the day against one another. Judgement was based on trial panels on the subject of the *Sacrifice of Isaac*, and in a dead heat at the end of the day were the two by Brunelleschi and Lorenzo Ghiberti, now displayed in the Bargello. Ghiberti's more Classical-styled figures were eventually judged the better, and it was a serendipitous choice; he devoted nearly the rest of his life to creating the most beautiful bronze doors in the world while Brunelleschi, disgusted by his defeat, went on to build the most perfect dome. Ghiberti's first efforts, the **North Doors** (1403–24), are contained, like Pisano's, in 28 quatrefoil frames. In their scenes on the Life of Christ, the Evangelists, and the Doctors of the Church, you can trace Ghiberti's progress over the 20 years he worked in the increased depth of his compositions, not only visually but dramatically; classical backgrounds begin to fill up the frames, ready to break out of their Gothic confines. Ghiberti also designed the lovely floral frame of the doors; the three statues, of John the Baptist, the Levite and the Pharisee, by Francesco Rustici, were based on a design by Leonardo da Vinci and added in 1511.

Ghiberti's work pleased the Arte di Calimala, and they set him loose on another pair of portals, the **East Doors** (1425–52), his masterpiece and one of the most awesome achievements of the age. Here Ghiberti (perhaps under the guidance of Donatello) dispensed with the small Gothic frames and instead cast 10 large panels that depict the Old Testament in Renaissance high gear, reinterpreting the forms of antiquity with a depth and drama that have never been surpassed. Michelangelo declared them 'worthy to be the Gates of Paradise', and indeed it's hard to believe these are people, buildings, and trees of bronze and not creatures frozen in time by some celestial alchemy.

Ghiberti wasn't exactly slow to toot his own horn; according to himself, he personally planned and designed the Renaissance on his own. His unabashedly conceited *Commentarii* were the first attempt at art history and autobiography by an artist, and a work as revolutionary as his doors in its presentation of the creative God-like powers of the artist. It is also a typical exhibition of Florentine pride that he should put busts of his friends among the prophets and sibyls that adorn the frames of the East Doors. Near the centre, the balding figure with arched eyebrows and a little smile is Ghiberti himself.

The Duomo

For all its importance and prosperity, Florence was one of the last cities to plan a great cathedral. Work began in the 1290s, with the sculptor Arnolfo di Cambio in charge, and from the beginning the Florentines attempted to make up for their delay with sheer audacity. 'It will be so magnificent in size and beauty,' according to a decree of 1296, 'as to surpass anything built by the Greeks and Romans.' In response Arnolfo planned what in its day was the largest church in Catholicism; he confidently laid the foundations for an enormous octagonal crossing 44.5 m in diameter, then died before working out a way to cover it, leaving future architects the job of designing the biggest dome in the world.

Beyond its presumptuous size, the Cathedral of Santa Maria del Fiore shows little interest in contemporary innovations and styles; a visitor from France or England in the 1400s would certainly have found it somewhat drab and architecturally primitive. Visitors today often don't know what to make of it; they circle confusedly around its grimy, ponderous bulk (this is one of the very few cathedrals in Italy that you can walk completely around). Instead of the striped bravura of Siena or the elegant colonnades of Pisa, they behold an astonishingly eccentric green, white, and red pattern of marble rectangles and flowers—like Victorian wallpaper, or as one critic better expressed it, 'a cathedral wearing pyjamas'. On a sunny day, the cathedral under its sublime dome seems to sport festively above the dullish dun and ochre sea of Florence; in dismal weather it sprawls morosely across its piazza with all the qualities of a beached whale tarted up with a lace doily front.

The fondly foolish **façade** cannot be blamed on Arnolfo. His original design, only one-quarter completed, was taken down in a late 16th-century Medici rebuilding programme that never got off the ground. The Duomo turned a blank face to the world until the present neo-Gothic extravaganza was added in 1888. Walk around to the north side to see what many consider a more fitting door, the **Porta della Mandorla** crowned with an Assumption of the Virgin in an almond-shaped frame (hence 'Mandorla') made by Nanni di Banco in 1420.

BRUNELLESCHI'S DOME

Yet if this behemoth of a cathedral, this St Mary of the Floral Wallpaper, was created for no other reason than to serve as a base for its dome, it would be more than enough. Brunelleschi's dome, more than any landmark, makes Florence Florence. Many have noted how the dome repeats the rhythm of the surrounding hills, echoing them with its height and beauty; from those city streets fortunate enough to have a clear view, it rises among the clouds with all the confident mastery, proportions, and perfect form that characterize the highest aspirations of the Renaissance. But if it seems miraculous, it certainly isn't divine; unlike the dome of the Hagia Sophia, suspended from heaven by a golden chain, Florence's was made by man—one man, to be precise.

Losing the competition for the baptistry doors was a bitter disappointment to Filippo Brunelleschi. His reaction was typically Florentine; not content with being the second-best sculptor, he turned his talents to a field where he thought no one could beat him, launching himself in an intense study of architecture and engineering, visiting Rome and probably Ravenna to snatch secrets from the ancients. When proposals were solicited for the cathedral's dome in 1418, he was ready with a brilliant tour de force. Not only would he build the biggest dome of the time, and the most beautiful, but he would do it without any need for expensive supports while work was in progress, making use of a cantilevered system of bricks that could support itself while it ascended.

Brunelleschi studied, then surpassed the technique of the ancients with a system more simple than that of the Pantheon or Hagia Sophia. To the Florentines, a people who could have invented the slogan 'form follows function' for their own tastes in building, it must have come as a revelation; the most logical way of covering the space turned out to be a work of perfect beauty. Brunelleschi, in building this dome, put a crown on the achievements of Florence. After five hundred years it is still the city's pride and symbol.

The best way to appreciate Brunelleschi's genius is by touring inside the two concentric shells of the dome (see below), but before entering, note the eight marble ribs that define its octagonal shape; hidden inside are the three huge stone chains that bind them together. Work on the balcony around the base of the dome, designed by Giuliano da Sangallo, was halted in 1515 after Michelangelo commented that it resembled a cricket's cage. As for the **lantern**, the Florentines were famous for their fondness and admiration for Doubting Thomas, and here they showed why. Even though they marvelled at the dome, they still doubted that Brunelleschi could construct a proper lantern, and forced him to submit to yet another competition. He died before it was begun, and it was completed to his design by Michelozzo.

THE INTERIOR

After the façade, the austerity of the interior is almost startling. There is plenty of room; contemporary writers mention 10,000 souls packed inside to hear the brimstone and hell-fire sermons of Savonarola. Even with that in mind, the duomo hardly seems a religious building—more a *Florentine* building, with simple arches and counterpoint of grey stone and white plaster, full of old familiar Florentine things. Near the entrance, on the right-hand side, are busts of Brunelleschi and Giotto. On the left wall, posed inconspicuously, are the two most conspicuous monuments to private individuals ever erected by the Florentine Republic. The older one, on the right, is to **Sir John Hawkwood**, the famous English *condottiere* whose name the Italians mangled to Giovanni Acuto, a legendary commander who served Florence for many years and is perhaps best known to English speakers as the hero of *The White Company* by Arthur Conan Doyle. All along, Hawkwood had the promise of the Florentines to build him an equestrian statue after his death; it was a typical Florentine trick to pinch pennies and cheat a dead man—but they hired the greatest master of perspective, Paolo Uccello, to take a fresco that looked like a statue (1436). Twenty years later, they pulled the same trick again, commissioning another great illusionist, Andrea del Castagno, to paint the non-existent equestrian statue of another *condottiere*, Niccolò da Tolentino. A little further down, Florence commemorates its own secular scripture with Michelino's well-known fresco of Dante, a vision of the poet and his *Paradiso* outside the walls of Florence. Two singular icons of Florence's fascination with science stand at opposite ends of the building: behind the west front, a bizarre clock painted by Uccello, and in the pavement of the left apse, a gnomon fixed by the astronomer Toscanelli in 1475. A beam of sunlight strikes it every year on the day of the summer solstice.

For building the great dome, Brunelleschi was accorded a special honour—he is one of the few Florentines to be buried in the cathedral. His tomb may be seen in the **Excavations of Santa Reparata** (the stairway descending on the right of the nave; open 9:30–12 and 2:30–5; adm). Arnolfo di Cambio's cathedral was constructed on the ruins of the ancient church of Santa Reparata, which lay forgotten until 1965. Excavations have revealed not only the palaeo-Christian church and its several reconstructions, but also the remains of its Roman predecessor—a rather confusing muddle of walls that have been tidied up in an ambience that resembles an archaeological shopping centre. A coloured model helps explain what is what, and glass cases display items found in the dig, including the spurs of Giovanni de' Medici, who was buried here in 1351. In the ancient crypt of Santa Reparata are 13th-century tomb slabs, and in another section there's a fine pre-Romanesque mosaic pavement.

There is surprisingly little religious art—the Florentines for reasons of their own have carted most of it off into the Cathedral Museum (see below). Under the dome are the entrances to the two sacristies, with terracotta lunettes over the doors by Luca della Robbia; the scene of the *Resurrection* over the north sacristy is one of his earliest and best works. He also did the bronze doors beneath it, with tiny portraits on the handles of Lorenzo il Magnifico and his brother Giuliano de' Medici, targets of the Pazzi conspiracy in 1478. In the middle apse, there is a beautiful bronze urn by Ghiberti containing relics of the Florentine St Zenobius. The only really conventional religious decorations are the hack but scarcely visible frescoes high in the dome (some 90 m up), mostly the work of Vasari. As you stand there squinting at them, try not to think that the cupola weighs an estimated 25,000 tons.

A door on the left aisle near the Dante fresco leads up into the **dome** (daily 8:30–12:30 and 2:30–5:30, closed Sun; adm). The complicated network of stairs and walks between the inner and outer domes (not too difficult, if occasionally claustrophobic and vertiginous) was designed by Brunelleschi for the builders, and offers an insight on how thoroughly the architect thought out the problems of the dome's construction, even inserting hooks to hold up scaffolding for future cleaning or repairs; Brunelleschi installed restaurants to save workers the trouble of descending for meals. There is also no better place to get an idea of the dome's scale; the walls of the inner dome are 13 ft thick, and those of the outer dome 7 ft. These give the dome enough strength and support to preclude the need for further buttressing.

From the gallery of the drum you can get a good look at the lovely **stained glass** by Uccello, Donatello, Ghiberti and Castagno, in the seven circular windows, or *occhi*, made during the construction of the dome. Further up, the views through the small windows offer tantalizing hints of the breathtaking panorama of the city from the marble lantern at the top. The bronze ball at the very top was added by Verrocchio, and can hold almost a dozen people when it's open.

GIOTTO'S CAMPANILE

There's no doubt about it; the dome steals the show on Piazza del Duomo, putting one of Italy's most beautiful bell towers in the shade both figuratively and literally. The dome's great size—111.6 m to the bronze ball—makes the campanile look small, though 85.4 m is not exactly tiny. Giotto was made director of the cathedral works in 1334, and his basic design was completed after his death (1337) by Andrea Pisano and Francesco Talenti. It is difficult to say whether they were entirely faithful to the plan. Giotto was an artist, not an engineer. After he died, his successors realized the thing, then only 12 m high, was about to tumble over, a problem they overcame by doubling the thickness of the walls.

Besides its lovely form, the green, pink, and white campanile's major fame rests with Pisano and Talenti's **sculptural reliefs**—a veritable encyclopaedia of the medieval world view with prophets, saints and sibyls, allegories of the planets, virtues, and sacraments, the liberal arts and industries (the artist's craft is fittingly symbolized by a winged figure of Daedalus). All of these are copies of the originals now in the Cathedral Museum. If you can take another 400 steps or so, the terrace on top offers a slightly different view of Florence and of the cathedral itself (summer, daily 9–7:30, winter 9–5:30; adm).

Loggia del Bigallo

The most striking secular building on the Piazza del Duomo is the Loggia del Bigallo, south of the baptistry near the beginning of Via de Calzaiuoli. This 14th-century porch was built for one of Florence's great charitable confraternities, the Misericordia, which still has its headquarters across the street and operates the ambulances parked in front; in the 13th and 14th centuries members courageously nursed and buried victims of the plague. The Loggia itself originally served as a lost and found office, although instead of umbrellas it dealt in children; if unclaimed after three days they were sent to foster homes. In the 15th century the Misericordia merged with a similar charitable confraternity called the Bigallo, and works of art accumulated by both organizations over centuries are displayed in the diminutive but choice **Museo del Bigallo**, located next to the loggia at Piazza San Giovanni 1 (open only by request, tel 215 440). The most famous picture here is the fresco of *Madonna della Misericordia*, featuring the earliest known view of Florence (1342); other 14th-century works (by Bernardo Daddi, Niccolò di Pietro Gerini, and sculptor Alberto Arnoldi) portray the activities of the brotherhood, members of which may still be seen wearing the traditional black hoods that preserve their anonymity.

East of the Loggia del Bigallo, between Via dello Studio and Via del Proconsolo, is a stone bench labelled the 'Sasso di Dante'—**Dante's Seat**—where the poet would sit and take the air, observing his fellow citizens and watching the construction of the cathedral.

The Museo dell'Opera del Duomo

The Cathedral Museum (Piazza del Duomo 9, near the central apse; open Mon–Sat 9 am–8 pm and Sun 10–1; adm) is one of Florence's finest, and houses both relics from the actual construction of the cathedral and the masterpieces that once adorned it. The first room is devoted to the cathedral's sculptor-architect Arnolfo di Cambio and contains a drawing of his ornate, sculpture-filled façade that was but a quarter completed when the Medici had it removed in 1587. Here, too, are the statues he made to adorn it: the unusual Madonna with the glass eyes, Florence's old patron saints, Reparata and Zenobius, and nasty old Boniface VIII, who sits stiffly on his throne like an Egyptian god. There are the four Evangelists, including a St John by Donatello, and a small collection of ancient works—Roman sarcophagi and an Etruscan cippus carved with dancers. Two small rooms nearby contain materials from the construction of the dome—wooden models, tools, brick moulds, and instruments—as well as Brunelleschi's death mask. Also on the ground floor are several hack Mannerist models (one by dilettante Giovanni de' Medici) proposed in the 1580s for the cathedral—the façade could have been much, much worse. The Florentines were never enthusiastic about the worship of relics, and long ago they shipped San Girolamo's jawbone, John the Baptist's index finger and St Philip's arm across the street to this museum; note the 16th-century 'Libretto', a fold-out display case of saintly odds and ends, all neatly labelled.

On the landing of the stairs stands the *Pietà* that Michelangelo intended for his own tomb. The artist, increasingly cantankerous and full of *terribilità* in his old age, became exasperated with this complex work and took a hammer to the arm of the Christ—the first known instance of an artist vandalizing his own creation. His assistant repaired the damage and finished part of the figures of Mary Magdalene and Christ. According to Vasari, the hooded figure of Nicodemus is Michelangelo's self-portrait.

Upstairs, the first room is dominated by the two **Cantorie**, two marble choir balconies with exquisite low reliefs, made in the 1430s by Luca della Robbia and Donatello. Both works rank among the Renaissance's greatest productions. Della Robbia's delightful horde of laughing children dancing, singing, and playing instruments is a truly angelic choir, Apollonian in its calm and beauty, perhaps the most charming work ever to have been inspired by the forms of antiquity. Donatello's *putti*, by contrast, dance, or rather race, through their quattrocento decorative motifs with fiendish Dionysian frenzy. Even less serene is his statue of *Mary Magdalene*, surely one of the most jarring figures ever sculpted, ravaged by her own piety and penance, her sunken eyes fixed on a point beyond this vale of tears. Grey and weathered prophets by Donatello and others stand along the white walls. These originally adorned the façade of the campanile. According to Vasari, while carving the most famous bald one, *Habbakuk* (better known as '*lo zuccone*'), Donatello would mutter 'Speak, damn you. Speak!' The next room contains the original panels on the *Spiritual Progress of Man* from Giotto's campanile, made by Andrea Pisano.

The last room is dedicated to works removed from the baptistry, especially the lavish silver altar (14th–15th century), made by Florentine goldsmiths, portraying scenes from the life of the Baptist. Antonio Pollaiuolo used the same subject to design the 27 needlework panels that once were part of the priest's vestments. There are two 12th-century Byzantine mosaic miniatures, masterpieces of the intricate, and a *St Sebastian* triptych by Giovanni del Biondo that may well be the record for arrows; the poor saint looks like a hedgehog. Usually this room also contains a panel or two from Ghiberti's 'Gates of Paradise,' which are being restored one by one and make fascinating viewing close up.

Via Calzaiuoli and Piazza della Repubblica

Of all the streets that radiate from the Piazza del Duomo, most people almost intuitively turn down the straight, pedestrian-only Via Calzaiuoli, the Roman street that became the main thoroughfare of medieval Florence, linking the city's religious centre with the Piazza della Signoria. Widening of this 'Street of the Shoemakers' in the 1840s has destroyed much of its medieval character, and the only shoe shops to be seen are designer-label. Its fate seems benign, though, compared with what happened to the Mercato Vecchio, in the fit of post-Risorgimento 'progress' that converted it into the **Piazza della Repubblica**, a block to the right along Via Speziali.

On the map, it's easy to pick out the small rectangle of narrow, straight streets around Piazza della Repubblica; these remain unchanged from the little *castrum* of Roman days. At its centre, the old forum deteriorated through the Dark Ages into a shabby market square and the Jewish ghetto, a piquant, densely populated quarter known as the Mercato Vecchio, the epitome of the picturesque for 19th-century tourists but an eyesore for the movers and shakers of the new Italy, who tore down its alleys and miniature *piazze* to create a fit symbol of Florence's reawakening. They erected a triumphal arch to themselves and proudly blazoned it with the inscription: 'THE ANCIENT CITY CENTRE RESTORED TO NEW LIFE FROM THE SQUALOR OF CENTURIES'. The sad result of this well-intentioned urban renewal, the Piazza della Repubblica, is one of the most ghastly squares in Italy, a brash intrusion of ponderous 19th-century buildings and parked cars. Just the same it is popular with locals and tourists alike, full of outdoor cafés, something of an oasis among the narrow, stern streets of medieval Florence.

From Piazza della Repubblica the natural flow of street life will sweep you down to the **Mercato Nuovo**, the old Straw Market, bustling under a beautiful loggia built by Grand Duke Cosimo in the 1500s. Although you won't see more than a wisp of straw these days, vendors hawk purses, stationery, toys, clothes, umbrellas and knick-knacks. In medieval times this was the merchants' exchange, where any merchant who committed the crime of bankruptcy was publicly spanked before being carted off to prison; in times of peace it sheltered Florence's battle-stained *carroccio*. Florentines often call the market the 'Porcellino' (piglet) after the large bronze boar erected in 1612, a copy of the ancient statue in the Uffizi. The drool spilling from the side of its mouth reminds us that unlike Rome, Florence is no splashy city of springs and fountains. Rub the piglet's shiny snout, and supposedly destiny will one day bring you back to Florence. The pungent aroma of the tripe sandwiches sold nearby may give you second thoughts.

Orsanmichele

There is a wonderfully eccentric church on Via Calzaiuoli that looks like no other church in the world; Orsanmichele rises up in a tall, neat three-storey rectangle. It was built on the site of ancient San Michele ad Hortum (popularly reduced to 'Orsanmichele'), a 9th-century church located near a vegetable garden, which the *comune* destroyed in 1240 to erect a grain market; after a fire in 1337 the current market building (by Francesco Talenti and others) was erected, with a loggia on the ground floor and emergency storehouses on top where grain was kept against a siege.

The original market had a pilaster with a painting of the Virgin that became increasingly celebrated for performing miracles. The area around the Virgin became known as the Oratory, and when Talenti reconstructed the market, his intention was to combine both its secular and religious functions; each pilaster of the loggia was assigned to a guild to adorn with an image of its patron saint. In 1380, when the market was relocated, the entire ground floor was given over to the functions of the church, and Francesco Talenti's talented son Simone was given the task of closing in the arcades with lovely Gothic windows, later bricked in.

The church, however, is most famous as a showcase of 15th-century Florentine sculpture; there is no better place to get an idea of the stylistic innovations that succeeded one another throughout the decades. Each guild sought to outdo the others by commissioning the finest artists of the day to carve their patron saints and create elaborate canopied niches to hold them. The first statue to the left of the door is one of the oldest; Ghiberti's bronze *St John the Baptist*, erected in 1416 for the Arte di Calimala, was the first life-sized Renaissance statue cast in bronze. Continuing to the left on Via de' Lamberti you can compare it with Donatello's *St Mark*, patron of the linen dealers and used-cloth merchants. Finished in 1411, it is considered the first free-standing marble statue of the Renaissance.

The niches continue around Via dell'Arte della Lana, named after the Wool Merchants' Guild, the richest after that of the Bankers. Their headquarters, the **Palazzo dell'Arte della Lana** is linked by an overhead arch with Orsanmichele; built in 1308, it was restored in 1905 in a delightful William Morris style of medieval picturesque. The first statue on this façade of Orsanmichele is the Smiths' *St Eligio* by Nanni di Banco (1415), with a niche embellished with the guild's emblem (black pincers) and a bas relief below showing one of this rather obscure saint's miracles—apparently he shod a horse the hard way, by cutting off its hoof, shoeing it, then sticking it back on the leg. The other two statues on this street are bronzes by Ghiberti, the Wool Guild's *St Stephen* (1426) and the Exchange Guild's *St Matthew* (1422), the latter an especially fine work in a classical niche. On the Via Orsanmichele façade stands a copy of Donatello's famous *St George* (the original now in the Bargello) done in 1417 for the Armourers' Guild, with a dramatic predella of the saint slaying the dragon, also by Donatello, and believed to be one of the first examples of the use of perspective; next are the Stonecutters and Carpenters' Guild's *Four Crowned Saints* (1415, by Nanni di Banco), inspired by Roman statues. Nanni also contributed the Shoemakers' *St Philip* (1415), while the next figure, *St Peter* is commonly attributed to Donatello (1413). Around the corner on Via Calzaiuoli stands the bronze *St Luke*, patron of the Judges and Notaries, by Giambologna, a work of 1602 in a 15th-century niche, and the *Doubting of St Thomas* by Andrea del Verrocchio (1484), made not for a guild but the Tribunal of Merchandise, who like St Thomas wanted to be certain before making a judgement. In the rondels above some of the niches are terracottas of the guilds' symbols by Luca della Robbia.

Orsanmichele's dark **interior** is ornate and cosy, with more of the air of a guildhall than a church. It makes a picturebook medieval setting for one of the masterpieces of the trecento: Andrea Orcagna's beautiful Gothic **Tabernacle**, a large, exquisite work in marble, bronze, and coloured glass framing a contemporary painting of the Madonna (either by Bernardo Daddi or Orcagna himself), replacing the miraculous one, lost in a fire. The Tabernacle was commissioned by survivors of the 1348 Black Death. On the walls and pilasters are faded 14th-century frescoes of saints, placed as if members of the congregation; if you look at the pilasters across from the entrance and along the right wall you can see the old chutes used to transfer grain.

Piazza della Signoria

Italian city builders are renowned for effortlessly creating beautiful squares, but it's an art where the Florentines are generally all thumbs. Only here, in the city's civic stage do they achieve a grand, meaningful space, a much needed antidote to the stone gullies of the ancient centre, dominated by the sombre fortress and tower of the Palazzo Vecchio and a lively gathering of some of the best and worst of Florentine sculpture.

Although the Piazza della Signoria currently serves as Great Aunt Florence's drawing-room-cum-tourist-overflow-tank, in the old days it saw the public assemblies of the republic, which in Florence meant that the square often degenerated into a battleground for impossibly inscrutable internecine quarrels. These could be stirred up to mythic levels of violence; in the 14th century a man was eaten by a crowd maddened by a political speech. Such speeches were given from the *arringhiera*, or oration terrace in front of the Palazzo Vecchio, a word which gave us 'harangue'. It was in the Piazza della Signoria that Savonarola ignited his notorious Bonfire of Vanities in 1497, and here, too, the following year, the disillusioned Florentines ignited Savonarola himself. A small plaque in the pavement marks the exact spot, not far from Ammanati's fountain.

If, on the other hand, trouble came from without, the Florentines would toll the famous bell in the tower of the Palazzo Vecchio, and the square would rapidly fill with the gonfalons of the citizens' militia and the guilds. 'We will sound our trumpets!' threatened the French king Charles VIII, when the Florentines refused to shell out enough florins to make him and his army leave town. 'And we will ring our bell!' countered the courageous republican Piero Capponi—a threat that worked; Charles had to settle for a smaller sum. When Alessandro de' Medici was restored as duke of Tuscany three years later, one of his first acts was to smash the bell as a symbol of Florence's lost liberty.

Having a citizen's militia, as opposed to depending on foreign mercenaries, answered one of Machiavelli's requirements for a well-governed state. Training was taken fairly seriously; to build up their endurance, the republic's citizens played a ball game similar to rugby, believed to be descended from a Roman sport. Known these days as *Calcio in Costume*, it is played every June on a special ground of sand in the Piazza della Signoria, and it's good fun to watch the usually immaculate Florentines in their Renaissance duds mixing it up in the dirt (fighting is more than permitted, as long as it's one to one).

In the 1970s and '80s a different kind of battle has been waged in this piazza, spiced with good old-fashioned Florentine factionalism. At stake is the future of the Piazza della Signoria itself. In 1974, while searching for signs of the original paving stones, the Soprintendenza ai Beni Archeologici found, much to their surprise, an underground medieval casbah of narrow lanes, houses, and wells—the ruins of 12th-century Ghibelline Florence, built over the baths and other portions of Roman and Etruscan *Florentia*. The *comune* ordered the excavations filled in; from the city's point of view, the piazza, essential to the essential tourist trade, was untouchable. In the '80s, the communal government fell, and the excavations were reopened on the portion of the piazza near the loggia. There are proposals to excavate the rest of the square, much to the horror of the *comune*, and to create eventually an underground museum similar to the one in Assisi. Until the issue is decided, don't be surprised to find the piazza full of gaping holes.

The Loggia dei Lanzi

Generally of a lower key than a political harangue was the *parlamento*, a meeting of eligible male citizens to vote on an important issue (usually already decided by the bosses). On these occasions, the Florentines heard speeches from the platform of the graceful three-arched Loggia dei Lanzi, also known as the Loggia della Signoria or the Loggia dell'Orcagna, after Andrea Orcagna, the probable architect. Completed in 1382, when pointed Gothic was still the rage, the Loggia with its lofty round arches looks back to classical antiquity and looks forward to the Renaissance; it is the germ of Brunelleschi's revolutionary architecture. If the impenetrable, stone Palazzo Vecchio is a symbol of the republic's strength and authority, the Loggia dei Lanzi is a symbol of its capacity for beauty, a vote for the gentle, flora side of its personality.

The loggia received its name 'of the lances' after the Swiss lancers, the private bodyguard of Cosimo I, and it was the Grand Duke who in 1560 commissioned the most famous sculpture sheltered in the arcade, Cellini's bronze *Perseus*, a tour de force for its attention to detail and expressive composition, graceful and poised atop the gruesome bleeding trunk, eyes averted from the horrible head, capable of turning one into stone. The subject was a hint to the Florentines, to inspire their gratitude for Grand Ducal rule, which spared them from the monstrosity of their own unworkable republic. Nearby Giambologna's *Rape of the Sabines* (1583) is an essay in three-dimensional Mannerism. Its three figures of an old man, a young man, and a woman spiral upwards in a fluid contrapposto convulsion, one of the first sculptures designed to be seen from all sides. The loggia also shelters Giambologna's less successful *Hercules and Nessus*, a chorus line of six Roman vestal wallflowers, and several other works that contribute to the rather curious effect, especially at night, of people at a wild party frozen into stone by Medusa's magical gaze.

The first two statues placed in the square were carried there by republican enthusiasm. Donatello's *Judith and Holofernes* was hauled from the Medici palace and placed here in 1494 as a symbol of the defeat of tyranny. Michelangelo's *David* was equally seen as the embodiment of republican triumph (when it was finished in 1504, the Medici were in exile), though it is doubtful whether Michelangelo himself had such symbolism in mind, as the statue was intended to stand next to the cathedral, only to be shanghaied to the Piazza della Signoria by eager republican partisans. It was replaced by a copy in 1873 when the original was relocated with much pomp on a specially-built train to the Accademia. Later Florentine sculptors attempted to rival the *David*, especially the awful Baccio Bandinelli, who managed to get the commission to create a pendant to the statue and boasted that he could surpass Il Divino himself. The pathetic result, *Hercules and Cacus*, was completed in 1534; as a reward for his efforts, Bandinelli had to listen to his arch-enemy Cellini insult the statue in front of their patron, Cosimo I. An 'old sack full of melons' he called it, bestowing what has since become, for all practical purposes, the sculpture's alternative title.

Another overgrown victim of the chisel stands at the corner of the Palazzo Vecchio. Ammannati's **Neptune Fountain** (1575) was dubbed *Il Biancone* ('Big Whitey') almost as soon as it was unveiled; Michelangelo felt sorry for the huge block of marble Ammannati 'ruined' to produce Neptune, a lumpy, bloated symbol of Cosimo I's naval victories, who stands arrogantly over a low basin and a few half-hearted spurts of water, pulled along by four struggling sea steeds, mere hobby horses compared with Big Whitey himself.

The last colossus in the Piazza della Signoria is the *Equestrian Monument to Cosimo I* by Giambologna (1595), the only large-scale equestrian bronze of the late Renaissance. The scheme on the panels below the statue depicts scenes of Cosimo's brutal conquest of Siena, and of the 'Florentine Senate' and the Pope conferring the Grand Dukedom on Cosimo.

Directly behind Cosimo stands the **Tribunale di Mercanzia**, built in the 14th century as a commercial court for merchants of the guilds and adorned with heraldic arms. To the left of this (no. 7) is a fine, 16th-century contribution, the **Palazzo Uguccioni**, very much in the spirit of High Renaissance in Rome, and sometimes attributed to a design by Raphael.

Palazzo Vecchio

When Goethe made his blitz-tour of Florence, the Palazzo Vecchio (also called the Palazzo della Signoria) helped pull the wool over his eyes. 'Obviously,' thought the great poet, 'the people . . . enjoyed a lucky succession of good governments'—a remark which, as Mary McCarthy wrote, could make the angels in heaven weep. But none of Florence's chronic factionalism mars Arnolfo di Cambio's temple of civic aspirations, part council hall and part fortress. In many ways, the Palazzo Vecchio is the ideal of stone Florence: rugged and imposing, with a rusticated façade that was to inspire so many of the city's private palaces, yet designed according to the proportions of the Golden Section of the ancient Greeks. Its dominant feature, the 94-m tower, is a typical piece of Florentine bravado, for long the highest point in the city.

The Palazzo Vecchio occupies the site of the old Roman theatre and the medieval Palazzo dei Priori. In the 13th century this earlier palace was flattened along with the Ghibelline quarter interred under the piazza, and in 1299, the now ascendant Guelphs called upon Arnolfo di Cambio, master builder of the cathedral, to design the most impressive 'Palazzo del Popolo' (as the building was originally called) possible, with an

Palazzo Vecchio

eye to upstaging rival cities. The palace's unusual trapezoidal shape is often, but rather dubiously, explained as Guelph care not to have any of the building touch land once owned by Ghibellines. One doubts that even in the 13th century real estate realities allowed such delicacy of sentiments; nor does the theory explain why the tower has swallowtail Ghibelline crenellations, as opposed to the square Guelph ones on the palace itself. Later additions to the rear of the palace have obscured its shape even more, though the façade is essentially as Arnolfo built it, except for the bet-hedging monogram over the door hailing Christ the king of Florence, put up in the nervous days of 1529, when the imperial army of Charles V was on its way to destroy the last Florentine republic; the inscription replaces an earlier one left by Savonarola. The room at the top of the tower was used as prison for celebrities and dubbed the *alberghetto* ('the little hotel'); inmates included Cosimo il Vecchio before his brief exile, and Savonarola, who spent his last months, between torture sessions, enjoying a superb view of the city before his execution in the piazza below.

INSIDE THE PALAZZO VECCHIO

Today the Palazzo Vecchio serves as Florence's city hall, but nearly all of its historical rooms are open to the public (open 9 am–7 pm; holidays 8–1; closed Sat; adm, expensive, free on Sun). With few exceptions, the interior decorations date from the time of Cosimo I, when he moved his Grand Ducal self from the Medici palace in 1540. To politically 'correct' its acres of walls and ceilings in the shortest amount of time, he turned to his court artist Giorgio Vasari, famed more for the speed in which he could execute a commission than for its quality. On the ground floor of the palazzo, before you buy your ticket, you can take a gander at some of Vasari's more elaborate handiwork in the **Courtyard**, redone for the occasion of Francesco I's unhappy marriage to the plain and stupid Habsburg Joanna of Austria in 1565.

Vasari's suitably grand staircase ascends to the largest room in the palace, the vast **Salone dei Cinquecento**. The *salone* was added at the insistence of Savonarola for meetings of the 500-strong Consiglio Maggiore, the reformed republic's democratic assembly. Art's two reigning divinities, Leonardo da Vinci and Michelangelo, were commissioned in 1503 to paint the two long walls of the *salone* in a kind of Battle of the Brushes to which the city eagerly looked forward. Unfortunately, neither of the artists came near to completing the project; Leonardo managed to fresco a section of the wall, using the experimental techniques that were to prove the undoing of his *Last Supper* in Milan, while Michelangelo only completed the cartoons before being summoned to Rome by Julius II, who required the sculptor of the *David* to fulfil his own personal megalomania.

In the 1560s Vasari removed what was left of Leonardo's efforts and refrescoed the entire room as a celebration of Cosimo's military triumphs over Pisa and Siena, complete with an apotheosis of the Grand Duke on the ceiling. These wall scenes are inane, big and busy, crowded with men and horses who appear to have all the substance of overcooked pasta. The sculptural groups lining the walls of this almost uncomfortably large room (the Italian parliament sat here from 1865–1870 when Florence was the capital) are only slightly more stimulating; even Michelangelo's *Victory*, on the wall opposite the entrance, is more virtuosity than vision: a vacuous young idiot posing with one knee atop a defeated old man still half submerged in stone, said to be a self-portrait of the sculptor, which lends the work a certain bitter poignancy. The neighbouring work, a muscle-bound *Hercules and Diomedes* by Vicenzo de' Rossi, probably was inevitable in this city obsessed by the possibilities of the male nude.

Beyond the *salone*, behind a modern glass door, is a much smaller and much more intriguing room the size of a closet. This is the **Studiolo of Francesco I**, designed by Vasari in 1572 for Cosimo's melancholic and reclusive son, where he would escape to brood over his real interests in natural curiosities and alchemy. The little study, windowless and more than a little claustrophobic, has been restored to its original appearance, lined with allegorical paintings by Vasari, Bronzino and Allori, and bronze statuettes by Giambologna and Ammannati, their refined, polished, and erotic mythological subjects part of a carefully thought-out 16th-century programme on Man and Nature. The lower row of paintings conceals Francesco's secret cupboards where he kept his most precious belongings, his pearls and crystals and gold.

After the *salone* a certain fuzziness begins to set in. Cosimo I's propaganda machine in league with Vasari's fresco factory produced room after room of self-glorifying Medicean poofery. The first series of rooms, known as the **Quartiere di Leone X**, carry ancestor worship to extremes, each chamber dedicated to a different Medici: in the first Cosimo il Vecchio returns from exile amid tumultuous acclaim; in the second Lorenzo il Magnifico receives the ambassadors in the company of a dignified giraffe; the third and fourth are dedicated to the Medici popes, while the fifth, naturally, is for Cosimo I, who gets the most elaborate treatment of all.

Upstairs the next series of rooms is known as the **Quartiere degli Elementi**, with more works of Vasari and his studio, depicting allegories of the elements. Beyond these are several rooms currently used to display works pilfered by the Nazis during the war and since recovered. Many of the paintings were personally selected by Goering and Hitler, who were apparently quite fond of Leda and the Swan and other mild mythological erotica.

A balcony across the Salone dei Cinquecento leads to the **Quartiere di Eleonora di Toledo**, Mrs Cosimo I's private apartments. Of special note here is her chapel, one of the masterpieces of Bronzino, who seemed to relish the opportunity to paint something besides Medici portraits. The next room, the **Sala dell'Udienza**, has a magnificent quattrocento coffered ceiling by Benedetto and Giuliano da Maiano, and walls painted with a rather fine romp by Mannerist Francesco Salviati (1550–60).

The last room, the **Sala dei Gigli** ('of the lilies') boasts another fine ceiling by the da Maiano brothers; it contains Donatello's recently restored bronze *Judith and Holofernes*, a late and rather gruesome work of 1455; the warning to tyrants inscribed on its base was added when the statue was abducted from the Medici palace and placed in the Piazza della Signoria. Off the Sala dei Gigli are two small rooms of interest: the **Guardaroba**, or unique 'wardrobe' adorned with 57 maps painted by Fra Egnazio Danti in 1563, depicting all the world known at the time. The **Cancelleria** was Machiavelli's office from 1498–1512, when he served the republic as a secretary and diplomat. He is commemorated with a bust and a portrait; the original of Verrocchio's boy with the dolphin, from the courtyard fountain, is here as well. Poor Machiavelli died bitter and unaware of the notoriety that his works would one day bring him, and he would probably be amazed to learn that his very name had become synonymous with cunning, amoral intrigue. After losing his job upon the return of the Medici, and at one point tortured and imprisoned on a false suspicion of conspiracy, Machiavelli was forced into idleness in the country, where he wrote his political works and two fine plays, feverishly trying to return to favour, even dedicating his most famous book, *The Prince*, to the incompetent Lorenzo, Duke of Urbino (further glorified by Michelangelo's Medici tombs); his concern throughout was to advise realistically, without mincing words, the fractious and increasingly weak Italians on how to create strong states; his evil reputation came from openly stating what rulers do, rather than what they would like other people to think they do.

Two collections long housed in the Palazzo Vecchio, the excellent Collection of Old Musical Instruments, and the Collezione Loeser, a fine assortment of Renaissance art left to the city in 1928 by Charles Loeser, the Macy's department-store heir, have at the time of writing tumbled into Italian museum limbo. The violins and cellos (several by Cremona greats like Stradivarius and Guarneri) have been earmarked for a new destination; the tourist office can give you a status report.

Collezione della Ragione

After the pomposity of the Palazzo Vecchio and a Campari cure at the Piazza della Signoria's landmark **Café Rivoire**, you may be in the mood to reconsider the 20th century. The best place to do this in Florence is at its only museum of modern art, the Collezione della Ragione, located on the Piazza della Signoria, above the Cassa di Risparmio bank (open 9–2, holidays 8–1, closed Tues; adm). There are typical still lifes by De Pisis; equally still landscapes by Carlo Carra; mysterious baths by De Chirico; Tuscan landscapes by Mario Mafai, Antonio Donghi, and Ottone Rosai; a speedy Futurist horse by Fortunato Depero and a window with doves by Gino Severini; a number of richly coloured canvases by Renato Guttuso and paintings after Tintoretto by Emilio Vedova, and many others, surprises, perhaps, for those unfamiliar with living Italians as opposed to dead ones.

The Uffizi

Florence has the most fabulous art museum in Italy, and as usual we have the Medici to thank; for the building that holds these treasures, however, credit goes to Grand Duke Cosimo's much maligned court painter. Poor Giorgio Vasari! His roosterish boastfulness and the conviction that his was the best of all possible artistic worlds, set next to his very modest talents, have made him a comic figure in most art criticism. Even the Florentines don't like him. On one of the rare occasions when he tried his hand as an architect, though, he gave Florence something to be proud of. The Uffizi ('offices') were built as Cosimo's secretariat, incorporating the old mint (producer of the first gold florins in 1252), the archives, and the large church of San Pier Scheraggio, with plenty of room for the bureaucrats needed to run Cosimo's efficient, modern state. The matched pair of arcaded buildings have coldly elegant façades that conceal Vasari's surprising innovation: iron reinforcements that make the huge amount of window area possible and keep the building stable on the soft sandy ground. It was a trick that would be almost forgotten until the Crystal Palace and the first American skyscrapers.

Almost from the start the Medici began to store parts of their huge art collection in parts of the building. There are galleries in the world with more works of art—the Uffizi counts some 1800—but the Uffizi overwhelms by the fact that every one of its paintings is worth looking at. Queues in the summer are very common; try to arrive early (open daily except Monday, 9 am–7 pm, Sun 9–1; adm, expensive).

Near the ticket counter you can see what remains of the church of San Pier Scheraggio, now hung with Andrea Castagno's stately **Frescoes of Illustrious Men** (1450), including the Cumaean Sibyl(!) as well as Dante and Boccaccio, both of whom attended political debates in this very church. From here you can take the lift or sweeping grand stair up to the second floor, where the Medici once had a huge theatre, now home to the **Cabinet of Drawings and Prints**. Although the bulk of this extensive and renowned collection is only open to scholars with special permission, a roomful of tempting samples gives a hint what they have a chance to see.

Nowadays one thinks of the Uffizi as primarily a gallery of paintings, but for some hundred years after its opening, visitors came almost exclusively for the fine collection of Hellenistic and Roman marbles. Most of these were collected in Rome by Medici cardinals, and not a few were sources of Renaissance inspiration. The **Vestibule** at the top of the stair contains some of the best, together with Flemish and Tuscan tapestries made for Cosimo I and his successors. **Room 1**, if it has reopened, contains excellent early Roman sculpture.

ROOMS 2–6: 13TH AND 14TH CENTURIES

The Uffizi's paintings are arranged in chronological order, the better to educate its visitors on trends in Italian art. The roots of the Early Renaissance are most strikingly revealed in **Room 2**, dedicated to the three great **Maestà** altarpieces by the masters of the 13th century. All portray the same subject of the Madonna and Child enthroned with angels. The one on the right, by Cimabue, was painted around the year 1285 and represents a breaking away from the flat, styled Byzantine tradition. To the left is the so-called *Rucellai Madonna*, painted around the same period by the Sienese Duccio di Buoninsegna for S. Maria Novella. It resembles Cimabue's in many ways, but with a more advanced technique for creating depth, and the bright colouring that characterizes the Sienese school. Giotto's altarpiece, painted some 25 years later, takes a great leap forward, not only in his use of perspective, but in the arrangement of the angels, standing naturally, and in the portrayal of the Virgin, gently smiling, with real fingers and breasts.

To the left, **Room 3** contains representative Sienese works of the 14th century, with a beautiful Gothic *Annunciation* (1333) by Simone Martini and the brothers Pietro and Ambrogio Lorenzetti. **Room 4** is dedicated to 14th-century Florentines: Bernardo Daddi, Nardo di Cione, and the delicately coloured *San Remigio Pietà* by Giottino. **Rooms 5 and 6** portray Italian contributions to the International Gothic school, most dazzlingly Gentile da Fabriano's *Adoration of the Magi* (1423), two good works by Lorenzo Monaco, and the *Thebaid* of Gherardo Starnina, depicting the rather unusual activities of the 4th-century monks of St Pancratius of Thebes, in Egypt; a composition strikingly like Chinese scroll scenes of hermits.

ROOMS 7–9: EARLY RENAISSANCE

In the Uffizi, at least, it's but a few short steps from the superbly decorative International Gothic to the masters of the Early Renaissance. **Room 7** contains minor works by Fra Angelico, Masaccio and Masolino, and three masterpieces: Domenico Veneziano's pastel *Madonna and Child with Saints* (1448), one of the rare pictures by this Venetian master who died a pauper in Florence. It is a new departure not only for its soft colours (the hallmark of Venetian painting) but for the subject matter, unifying the enthroned Virgin and saints in one panel, in what is known as a *Sacra Conversazione*. Piero della Francesca's famous *Double Portrait of the Duke Federico da Montefeltro and his Duchess Battista Sforza of Urbino* (1465) depicts one of Italy's noblest Renaissance princes—and surely the one with the most distinctive nose. Piero's ability to create perfectly still, timeless worlds is even more evident in the allegorical 'Triumphs' of the Duke and Duchess painted on the back of their portraits. A similar stillness and fascination floats over into the surreal in Uccello's famous **Rout of San Romano** (1456), or at least the third of it still present (the other two panels are in the Louvre and London's National Gallery; all three once decorated the bedroom of Lorenzo il Magnifico in the Medici palace). Both Piero and Uccello were deep students of perspective, but Uccello went half-crazy; applying his principles to a violent battle scene has left us one of the most provocative works of all time—a vision of warfare in suspended animation, with pink, white, and blue toy horses, robot-like knights, and rabbits bouncing in the background.

Room 8 is devoted to the works of the rascally romantic Fra Filippo Lippi, whose ethereally lovely Madonnas were modelled after his brown-eyed nun. In his *Coronation of the Virgin* (1447) she kneels in the foreground with two children, while the artist, dressed in a brown habit, looks dreamily towards her; in his celebrated *Madonna and Child with Two Angels* (1445) she plays the lead before the kind of mysterious landscape Leonardo would later perfect. Lippi taught the art of enchanting Madonnas to his student Botticelli, who has some lovely works in this room and the next; Alesso Baldovinetti, a pupil of the far more holy Fra Angelico, painted the room's beautiful *Annunciation* (1447). **Room 9** has two small scenes from the *Labours of Hercules* (1470) by Antonio Pollaiuolo, whose interest in anatomy, muscular expressiveness and violence presages a strain in Florentine art that would culminate in the great Mannerists. He worked with his younger brother Piero on the refined, elegant *SS. Vincent, James, and Eustace*, transferred here from S. Miniato. This room also contains the Uffizi's best-known forgery: *The Young Man in a Red Hat* or self-portrait of Filippino Lippi, believed to have been the work of a clever 18th-century English art dealer who palmed it off on the Grand Dukes.

BOTTICELLI: ROOMS 10–14

To accommodate the bewitching art of 'Little Barrels' and his throngs of 20th-century admirers, the Uffizi converted four small rooms into one great Botticellian shrine. Although his masterpieces displayed here have become almost synonymous with the Florentine Renaissance at its most spring-like and charming, they were not publicly displayed until the beginning of the 19th century, nor given much consideration outside Florence until the turn of the century.

Botticelli's best works date from the days when he was a darling of the Medici—family members crop up most noticeably in the *Adoration of the Magi* (1476), where you can pick out Cosimo il Vecchio, Lorenzo il Magnifico, and Botticelli himself (in the right foreground, in a yellow robe, gazing at the spectator). His *Annunciation* is a graceful, cosmic dance between the Virgin and the Angel Gabriel. In the *Tondo of the Virgin of the Pomegranate* the lovely melancholy goddess who was to become his Venus makes her first appearance.

Botticelli is best known for his sublime mythological allegories, nearly all painted for the Medici and inspired by the Neoplatonic, humanistic and hermetic currents that pervaded the intelligentsia of the late 15th century. Perhaps no painting has been debated so fervently as *La Primavera* (1478). This was hung for years in the Medici Villa at Castello, and it is believed that the subject of the Allegory of Spring was suggested by Marsilio Ficino, one of the great natural magicians of the Renaissance, and that the figures represent the 'beneficial' planets able to dispel sadness. *Pallas and the Centaur* has been called another subtle allegory of Medici triumph—the rings of Athena's gown are supposedly a family symbol. Other interpretations see the taming of the sorrowful centaur as a melancholy comment on reason and civilization. Botticelli's last great mythological painting, *The Birth of Venus*, was commissioned by Lorenzo di Pierfrancesco and inspired by a poem by Poliziano, Lorenzo il Magnifico's Latin and Greek scholar, who described how Zephyr and Chloris blew the newborn goddess to shore on a scallop shell, while Hora hastened to robe her, a scene Botticelli portrays once again with dance-like rhythm and delicacy of line. Yet the goddess of love floats towards the spectator with an expression of wistfulness—perhaps reflecting the artist's own feelings of regret. For artistically, the poetic, decorative style he perfected in this painting would be disdained and forgotten in his own lifetime. Spiritually, Botticelli also turned a corner after creating this haunting, uncanny beauty—his, and Florence's farewell to a lovely road not taken. Although Vasari's biography of Botticelli portrays a prankster rather than a sensitive soul, the painter absorbed more than any other artist the *fin-de-siècle* neuroticism that beset the city with the rise of Savonarola. So thoroughly did he reject his Neoplatonism that he would only accept commissions of sacred subjects or supposedly edifying allegories like his *Calumny*, a small but disturbing work, and a fitting introduction to the dark side of the quattrocento psyche.

This large room also contains works by Botticelli's contemporaries. Two paintings on the *Adoration of the Magi*, one by Ghirlandaio and one by Filippino Lippi, show the influence of Leonardo's unfinished but radical work in pyramidal composition (in the next room); Leonardo himself got the idea from the large *Portinari Altarpiece* (1471) by Hugo Van der Goes in the middle of the room, a work brought back from Bruges by Medici agent Tommaso Portinari. Behind it hangs Lorenzo di Credi's *Venus*, a charmer inspired by Botticelli.

ROOMS 15–20: MORE RENAISSANCE

Room 15 is dedicated to the Florentine works of Leonardo da Vinci's early career. Here are works by his master Andrea Verrocchio, including the *Baptism of Christ*, in which the young Leonardo painted the angel on the left. Modern art critics believe the large *Annunciation* (1475) is almost entirely by Leonardo's hand—the soft faces, the botanical details, the misty, watery background would become the trademarks of his magical brush. Most influential, however, was his unfinished *Adoration of the Magi* (1481), a highly unconventional composition that Leonardo abandoned when he left Florence for Milan. Although at first glance it's hard to make out much more than a mass of reddish chiaroscuro, the longer you stare, the better you'll see the serene Madonna and Child surrounded by a crowd of anxious, troubled humanity, with an exotic background of ruins, trees, and horsemen, all charged with expressive energy. Other artists in Room 15 include Leonardo's peers: Lorenzo di Credi, whose religious works have eerie garden-like backgrounds, and the nutty Piero di Cosimo, whose dreamy *Perseus Liberating Andromeda* includes an endearing mongrel of a dragon that gives even the most reserved Japanese tourist fits of giggles. Tuscan maps adorn **Room 16**, as well as scenes by Hans Memling.

The octagonal **Tribuna** (Room 18) with its mother-of-pearl dome and *pietra dura* floor and table was built by Buontalenti in 1584 for Francesco I, and like the Studiolo in the Palazzo Vecchio, was designed to hold Medici treasures. For centuries the best-known of these was the *Venus de' Medici*, a 2nd-century BC Greek sculpture, farcically claimed as a copy of Praxiteles' celebrated Aphrodite of Cnidos, the most erotic statue in antiquity. In the 18th century, amazingly, this rather ordinary girl was considered the greatest sculpture in Florence; today most visitors walk right by without a second glance. Other antique works include the *Wrestlers* and the *Knife Grinder*, both copies of Pergamese originals, the *Dancing Faun*, the *Young Apollo*, and the *Sleeping Hermaphrodite* in the adjacent room, which sounds fascinating but is usually curtained off.

The real stars of the Tribuna are the Medici court portraits, many by Bronzino, who could not only catch the likeness of Cosimo I, Eleonora of Toledo and their children, but aptly portrayed the spirit of the day—these are people who took themselves very seriously indeed. They have for company Vasari's posthumous portrait of *Lorenzo il Magnifico* and Pontormo's *Cosimo il Vecchio*, Andrea del Sarto's *Girl with a Book by Petrarch*, and Rosso Fiorentino's *Angel Musician*, an enchanting work entirely out of place in this stodgy temple.

Two followers of Piero della Francesca, Perugino and Luca Signorelli, hold pride of place in **Room 19**; Perugino's *Portrait of a Young Man* is believed to be modelled on his pupil Raphael. Signorelli's *Tondo of the Holy Family* was to become the inspiration for Michelangelo's (see below). The Germans appear in **Room 20**, led by Dürer and his earliest known work, the *Portrait of his Father* (1490), done at age 19, and *The Adoration of the Magi* (1504), painted after his first trip to Italy. Also here are Lucas Cranach's Teutonic *Adam and Eve* and *Portrait of Martin Luther* (1543), not someone you'd expect to see in Florence. **Room 21** is dedicated to the great Venetians, most famously Bellini and his uncanny *Sacred Allegory* (1490s), the meaning of which has never been satisfactorily explained. There are two minor works by the elusive Giorgione, and typically weird *St Dominic* by Cosmè Tura. Later Flemish and German artists appear in **Room 22**, works by Gerard David and proto-Romantic Albrecht Altdorfer, and a portrait by Hans Holbein of *Sir Thomas More*. **Room 23** is dedicated to non-Tuscans Correggio of Parma and Mantegna of the Veneto, as well as Boltraffio's strange *Narcissus* with an eerie Leonardesque background.

ROOMS 25–27: MANNERISM

The window-filled South Corridor, with its views over the city and its fine display of antique sculpture, marks only the halfway point in the Uffizi but nearly the end of Florence's contribution. In the first three rooms, however, local talent rallies to produce a brilliantly coloured twilight in Florentine Mannerism. By most accounts, Michelangelo's only completed oil painting, the *Doni Tondo* (1506), was the spark that ignited Mannerism's flaming orange and turquoise hues. Michelangelo was 30 when he painted this unconventional work, in a medium he disliked (sculpture and fresco being the only fit occupations for a man, he believed). It's a typical Michelangelo story that when the purchaser complained the artist was asking too much for it, Michelangelo promptly doubled the price. As shocking as the colours are the spiralling poses of the Holy Family, sharply delineated against a background of five nude, slightly out-of-focus young men of uncertain purpose (are they pagans? angels? boyfriends? or just filler?)—an ambiguity that was to become a hallmark of Mannerism. In itself, the *Doni Tondo* is more provocative than immediately appealing; the violent canvas next to it, Rosso Fiorentino's *Moses Defending the Children of Jethro*, was painted some 20 years later and at least in its intention to shock the viewer puts a cap on what Michelangelo began.

Room 26 is dedicated to Raphael, who was in and out of Florence 1504–08. Never temperamental or eccentric like his contemporaries, Raphael was the sweetheart of the High Renaissance. His Madonnas, like *The Madonna of the Goldfinch*, a luminous work painted in Florence, have a tenderness that was soon to be over-popularized by others and turned into holy cards, a cloying sentimentality added like layers of varnish over the centuries. It's easier, perhaps, to see Raphael's genius in non-sacred subjects, like *Leo X with Two Cardinals*, a perceptive portrait study of the first Medici pope with his nephew Giulio de' Medici, later Clement VII. The same room contains Andrea del Sarto's most original work, the fluorescent *Madonna of the Harpies* (1517), named after the figures on the Virgin's pedestal. There are a couple of works by Pontormo here as well, but the best is in **Room 27**, *Supper at Emmaus* (1525), a strange canvas with peasant-faced monks emerging out of the darkness, brightly clad diners with dirty feet, and the Masonic symbol of the Eye of God hovering over Christ's head.

ROOMS 28–45

Although we now bid a fond farewell to the Florentines, the Uffizi fairly bristles with masterpieces from other parts of Italy and abroad. Titian's delicious nudes, especially the incomparably voluptuous *Venus of Urbino*, raise the temperature in **Room 28**; Parmigianino's hyper-elegant *Madonna with the Long Neck* (1536) in **Room 30** is a fascinating Mannerist evolutionary dead-end, possessing all the weird beauty of a foot-long dragonfly. Sebastiano del Piombo's recently restored *Death of Adonis* is notable for its melancholy, lagoony, autumn atmosphere and the annoyed look on Venus' face. **Room 34** holds Paolo Veronese's *Holy Family with St Barbara*, a late work bathed in a golden Venetian light, with a gorgeously opulent Barbara gazing on. In **Room 35** his contemporary Tintoretto is represented by a shadowy *Leda* languidly pretending to restrain the lusty swan; the Uffizi's El Greco is here as well, reminding us that this most Mannerist of Mannerists learned how to do it in Venice.

Room 41 is Flemish domain, with name-brand art by Rubens and Van Dyck; the former's *Baccanale* may be the most grotesque canvas in Florence. Struggle on gamely to **Room 43** to see three striking Caravaggios. His *Bacchus* and *The Head of Medusa* are believed to be self-portraits; in its day the fleshy, heavy-eyed Bacchus, half portrait and half still life, but lacking the usual mythological appurtenances, was considered highly iconoclastic. There are three portraits by Rembrandt in **Room 44**, including two of himself, young and old, and landscapes by Ruysdael. **Room 45** is given over to some fine 18th-century works, including two charming portraits of children by Chardin, and others by Goya and Longhi, and Venetian landscapes by Guardi and Canaletto. Even more welcome by this time is the bar at the end of the corridor, with a lovely summer terrace.

CORRIDOIO VASARIANO

In 1565, when Francesco I married Joanna of Austria, the Medici commissioned Vasari to link their new digs in the Pitti Palace with the Uffizi and the Palazzo Vecchio in such a manner that the Archdukes could make their rounds without rubbing elbows with their subjects. With a patina of 400 years, it seems that Florence wouldn't look quite right without this covered catwalk, leapfrogging on rounded arches from the back of the Uffizi, over the Ponte Vecchio, daintily skirting a medieval tower, and darting past the façade of S. Felicità to the Pitti Palace.

The Corridoio not only offers interesting views of Florence, but has been hung with a celebrated collection of artists' self-portraits, beginning with Vasari himself before continuing in chronological order, past the Gaddis and Raphael to Rembrandt, Van Dyck, Velazquez, Hogarth, Reynolds, Delacroix, Corot, and scores in between. Although at the time of writing undergoing restoration, the Corridoio is set to reopen in 1990 to small groups by appointment only; make one at the Uffizi ticket office.

The Ponte Vecchio and Ponte Santa Trínita

'Bent bridges seeming to strain like bows
And tremble with arrowy undertide...'
—Elizabeth Barrett Browning, *Casa Guidi Windows*

Often at sunset the Arno becomes a stream of molten gold, confined in its walls of stone and laced into its bed with the curving arches of its spans. That is, during those months when it has a respectable flow of water. But even in the torrid days of August, when the Arno shrivels into muck and spittle, its two famous bridges retain their distinctive beauty. The most famous of these, the Ponte Vecchio, the 'Old Bridge,' crosses the Arno at its narrowest point; the present bridge, with its three stone arches, was built in 1345, and replaces a wooden construction from the 970s, which in turn was the successor to a span that may well have dated back to the Romans.

On this bridge, at the foot of the *Marzocco*, or statue of Mars, Buondelmonte de' Buondelmonti was murdered in 1215, setting off the wars of the Guelphs and Ghibellines. The original Marzocco was washed away in a 14th-century flood, and Donatello's later version has been carted off to the Bargello.

Like old London Bridge, the Ponte Vecchio is covered with shops and houses. By the 1500s, for hygienic reasons, it had become the street of hogbutchers, though after Vasari built Cosimo's secret passage on top, the Grand Duke, for personal hygienic reasons, evicted the butchers and replaced them with goldsmiths. They have been there ever since, and shoppers from around the world descend on it each year to scrutinize the traditional Florentine talent for jewellery—not a few of the city's great artists began their careers as goldsmiths, beginning with Ghiberti and Donatello, and ending with Cellini, who never gave up the craft, and whose bust adorns the middle of the bridge. In the 1966 flood the shops did not prove as resilient as the Ponte Vecchio itself, and a fortune of gold was washed down the Arno. All has since been excellently restored.

In the summer of 1944, the river briefly became a German defensive line during the slow painful retreat across Italy. Before leaving Florence, the Nazis blew up every one of the city's bridges, saving only, on Hitler's special orders, the Ponte Vecchio, though they blasted a large number of ancient buildings on each side of the span to create piles of rubble to block the approaches. Florence's most beautiful span, the **Ponte S. Trínita,** had to go, however. Immediately after the war the Florentines set about replacing the bridges exactly as they were. In the case of S. Trínita it was quite a task. Old quarries had to be reopened to duplicate the stone, and old methods revived to cut it (modern power saws would have done it too cleanly). The graceful curve of the three arches was a problem; they could not be constructed geometrically, and considerable speculation went on over how the architect (Ammannati, in 1567) did it. Finally, recalling that Michelangelo had advised Ammanati on the project, someone noticed that the same form of arch could be seen on the decoration of the tombs in Michelangelo's Medici Chapel, constructed most likely by pure artistic imagination. Fortune lent a hand in the reconstruction; of the original statues of the 'Four Seasons', almost all the pieces were fished out of the Arno and rebuilt. Spring's head was eventually found by divers completely by accident in 1961.

The Museum of the History of Science

For all that Florence and Tuscany contributed to the birth of science, it is only fitting to have this museum in the centre of the city, behind the Uffizi in Piazza Giudici (Mon–Sat 9:30–1; Mon, Wed, and Fri also 2–5, closed Sun; adm, expensive). Much of the ground floor is devoted to instruments measuring time and distances that are often works of art in themselves: Arabian astrolabes and pocket sundials, Tuscan sundials in the shape of Platonic solids, enormous elaborate armillary spheres and a small reliquary holding the bone of Galileo's forefinger, erect, like a final gesture to the city that until 1737 denied him a Christian burial. Here, too, are two of his original telescopes and the lens with which he discovered the four moons of Jupiter. Other scientific instruments come from the Accademia del Cimento (of 'trial', or 'experiment'), founded in 1657 by Cardinal Leopoldo de' Medici, the world's first scientific organization, dedicated to Galileo's principle of inquiry and proof by experimentation; 'Try and try again' was its motto.

Upstairs, there's a large room filled with machines used to demonstrate principles of physics, which the ladies who run the museum will operate if you ask. Two unusual ones are the 18th-century automatic writer and the instrument of perpetual motion. The rooms devoted to medicine contain a collection of 18th-century wax anatomical models, designed to teach budding obstetricians about unfortunate foetal positions, as well as a fine display of surgical instruments from the period.

Dante's Florence and the Bargello

In 1265 Dante Alighieri was born in the quarter just to the north of the Piazza della Signoria; he was nine, attending a May Feast, 'when first the glorious Lady of my mind was made manifest to mine eyes; even she who was called Beatrice by many who know not wherefore'. Beatrice went on to wed another, and died suddenly in 1290; Dante tried to forget his disappointment and grief in battle, fighting in the wars against Arezzo and Pisa, then in writing his 'autopsychology' *La Vita Nuova*. In 1302, as a White Guelph, he was sent into exile. A friend just managed to rescue the manuscript of the *Inferno* from the crowds who came to sack and pillage his home. Dante died in Ravenna in 1321, and although he was never allowed to return home, the Florentines have belatedly tried to make amends to their poet. Yet the memorials fall curiously flat. His grand tomb in Santa Croce is empty and his huge statue in front of the church a glowering failure.

The best place to summon the shade of Italy's greatest poet is in the narrow medieval lanes of Florence, especially in his old haunts just to the north of Piazza della Signoria. Most scholars believe Dante was born on what is now Via Dante Alighieri. A modern bas-relief on one of the buildings shows the sights that would have been familiar to Dante, one of which would have been the sturdy well-preserved **Torre del Castagno** on Piazza San Martino, used as the residence of the *priori* before the construction of the Palazzo Vecchio. Here, too, is the tiny church of **San Martino del Vescovo**, Dante's parish church, founded in 986 but rebuilt in 1479 when it became the headquarters of the charitable Compagnia dei Buonuomini. The Compagnia commissioned a follower of Ghirlandaio to paint a series of colourful frescoes on the Life of St Martin and the Works of Charity, scenes acted out by quattrocento Florentines, in their own fashions on their own streets. The church also has a fine Byzantine Madonna, and one by Perugino (open 10–12 and 3–5, closed Sun).

Opposite the Piazza San Martino, an alley leads back to the **Casa di Dante**, traditionally considered the poet's birthplace. Now a museum dedicated to Dante (9:30–12:30 and 3–5, Sun 9:30–12:30, closed Wed; donation), it makes a game attempt to evoke Dante's life and times, in spite of neglect and stingy Florentine low-watt light bulbs. Near the entrance is an edition of *The Divine Comedy*, printed in tiny letters on a poster by a mad Milanese; of the manuscript reproductions, the most interesting is an illumination of the infamous murder of Buondelmonte de' Buondelmonti, with the Ponte Vecchio and a statue of Mars, the original *marzocco* in place. Upstairs there are copies of Botticelli's beautiful line illustrations for the *Commedia*.

From the house, Via S. Margherita continues to **Santa Margherita de' Cerchi**, where Dante married his second choice, Gemma Donati, whose family arms are among those adorning the 13th-century porch.

The Badia

Dante would also recognize the two great towers in Piazza San Firenze, the looming Bargello and the beautiful Romanesque campanile of the ancient Benedictine abbey, or Badia, which Dante cited in the *Paradiso*. The abbey was founded at the end of the 10th century by the widow of Umberto, the Margrave of Tuscany, and further endowed by their son Ugo, 'the Good Margrave'. Dante would come here to gaze upon his Beatrice, and some 50 years after the poet's death, Dante's first biographer, Boccaccio, used the Badia as his forum for innovative public lectures on the text of *The Divine Comedy*. Curiously, Boccaccio's (and later, the Renaissance's) principal criticism of the work is that Dante chose to write about lofty, sacred things in the vulgar tongue of Tuscany.

Except for the campanile, the Badia has become a hotchpotch from too many remodellings. Inside, however, are two beautiful things from the Renaissance: the *Tomb to Count Ugo* (1481) by Mino da Fiesole and the *Madonna Appearing to St Bernard* (1485), a large painting by Filippino Lippi. Through an unmarked door to the right of the choir, you can reach the upper loggia of the **Chiostro degli Aranci**, where the Benedictines grew oranges. Built in the 1430s, it is embellished with a fine contemporary series of frescoes on the life of St Bernard, painted by an unknown artist.

Museo Nazionale del Bargello

Across from the Badia looms the Bargello, a battlemented urban fortress, well proportioned yet of forbidding grace; for centuries it saw duty as Florence's prison. Today its only inmates are men of marble, gathered together to form Italy's finest collection of sculpture, a fitting complement to the paintings in the Uffizi. The Bargello is 'stone Florence' squared to the sixth degree, rugged and austere *pietra forte*, the model for the even grander Palazzo Vecchio. Even the treasures it houses are hard, definite, certain—and almost unremittingly masculine. The Bargello offers the best insight available into Florence's golden age, and it was a man's world indeed (open 9–2, Sun 9–1, closed Mon; adm).

Completed in 1255, the Bargello was originally intended as Florence's Palazzo del Popolo, though by 1271 it served instead as the residence of the foreign podestà, or chief magistrate, installed by Guelph leader Charles of Anjou. The Medici made it the headquarters of the captain of police (the *Bargello*), the city jail and torture chamber, a function it served until 1859. In the Renaissance it was the peculiar custom to paint portraits of the condemned on the exterior walls of the fortress; Andrea del Castagno was so good at it that he was nicknamed Andrea of the Hanged Men. All of these ghoulish souvenirs have long disappeared, as have the torture instruments—burned in 1786, when the death sentence was abolished. Today the **Gothic courtyard**, former site of the gallows and chopping block, is a delightful place, owing much to an imaginative restoration in the 1860s. The encrustation of centuries of podestà armorial devices and plaques in a wild vocabulary of symbols, the shadowy arcades and stately stairs combine to create one of Florence's most romantic corners.

THE MICHELANGELO ROOM

The main ground-floor gallery is dedicated to Michelangelo and his century, although it must be said that the Michelangelo of the Bargello somewhat lacks the accustomed angst and ecstasy. Especially irritating is his *Bacchus* (1496), a youthful work inspired by bad Roman sculpture, with all the personality of a cocktail party bore. Better to invite his noble *Brutus* (1540), even if he's just a bust—the only one the sculptor ever made, in a fit of republican fervour after the assassination of Duke Alessandro de' Medici. From Michelangelo's followers there's another tippling *Bacchus* by Sansovino, and Ammannati's *Leda and the Swan* (a work inspired by a famous but lost erotic drawing by Michelangelo).

The real star of the room is Benvenuto Cellini, who was, besides many other things, an exquisite craftsman and daring innovator. His large bust of *Cosimo I* (1548), with its fabulously detailed armour, was his first work cast in bronze; the unidealized features did not curry favour with the boss that poor Cellini worked so avidly to please. Here, too, is a preliminary model of the *Perseus*, as well as four small statuettes and the relief panel from the original in the Loggia dell'Orcagna.

The last great work in the room is by Medici court sculptor Giambologna, now again enjoying a measure of the fashionableness he possessed during his lifetime; art historians consider him the key Mannerist figure between Michelangelo and Bernini. Giambologna's most famous work, the bronze *Mercury* (1564), has certainly seeped into popular consciousness as the representation of the way the god should look. The stairway from the courtyard leads up to the shady **Loggia**, now converted into an aviary for Giambologna's charming bronze birds, made for the animal grotto at the Medici's Villa di Castello.

DONATELLO: THE SALONE DEL CONSIGLIO GENERALE

This magnificent hall, formerly the courtroom of the podestà, contains the greatest masterpieces of Early Renaissance sculpture. And when Michelangelo's maudlin self-absorption and the Mannerists' empty virtuosity begin to seem tiresome, a visit to this room, to the profound clarity of the greatest of Renaissance sculptors, will prove a welcome antidote. Donatello's originality and vision are strikingly modern—and mysterious. Unlike Michelangelo, who went so far as to commission his own biography when Vasari's didn't please him, Donatello left few traces, not only of his long life, but of what may have been the sources of inspiration behind his three celebrated works displayed here: the chivalric young *St George* (1416) from the façade of Orsanmichele, whose alert watchfulness, or *prontezza*, created new possibilities in expressing movement, emotion, and depth of character in stone. Note the accompanying bas-relief of the gallant saint slaying the dragon, a masterful work in perspective. Donatello's fascinatingly androgynous *David*, obviously from a different planet from Michelangelo's David, is cool and suave, and conquers his Goliath more by his charming enigmatic smile than muscles and virile arrogance. This was the first free-standing nude figure since antiquity, and one of the most erotic, exploring depths of the Florentine psyche that the Florentines probably didn't know they had. No one knows for whom Donatello cast it, or exactly when—around 1440, give or take ten years.

The same erotic energy and mystery surrounds the laughing, dangerous-looking, precocious boy Cupid, or *Atys Amor*; with its poppies, serpents, and winged sandals, it could easily be the ancient idol people mistook it for in the 1700s. Like Botticelli's mythological paintings, Cupid is part of the artistic and intellectual undercurrents of the period, full of pagan philosophy, a possibility rooted out in the terror of the Counter-Reformation and quite forgotten soon after.

Other Donatellos in the *salone* further display the sculptor's amazing diversity. The small marble *David* (1408) was his earliest important work. In the centre of the hall, his *Marzocco*, the symbol of Florence, long stood on the Ponte Vecchio. Although the two versions of Florence's patron saint, John the Baptist, are no longer attributed to Donatello, they show his influence in that they strive to express the saint's spiritual character physically rather than by merely adding his usual holy accessories. The *Dancing Putto* and two busts are Donatello's; his workshop produced the gilded bas-relief of the Crucifixion.

On the wall hang the two famous trial reliefs for the second set of baptistry doors, by Ghiberti and Brunelleschi, both depicting the Sacrifice of Isaac. Between the panels, the vigorous relief of a tumultuous *Battle Scene* is by the little-known Bertoldo di Giovanni, Donatello's pupil and Michelangelo's teacher. There are a number of other excellent reliefs and busts along the walls, by Agostino di Duccio, Desiderio da Settignano, and some of Luca della Robbia's sweet Madonnas. Currently this hall hosts celebrated busts including Verrocchio's lovely *Young Lady with Flowers*, with her hint of a smile and long, sensitive fingers.

DECORATIVE ARTS

The remainder of the first floor houses fascinating collections of decorative arts donated to the Bargello in the last century. The **Sala della Torre** is devoted to Islamic art. The **Salone del Podestà** contains splendiferous Byzantine and Renaissance jewellery, watches and clocks, and a Venetian astrolabe. Off this room is the **Cappella del Podestà** with its frescoes once attributed to Giotto.

Some of the most interesting items are in the next rooms, especially the works in the **ivory collection**—Carolingian and Byzantine diptychs, an 8th-century whalebone coffer from Northumbria adorned with runes, medieval French miniatures chronicling 'The Assault on the Castle of Love', 11th-century chess pieces, and more.

A stairway from the ivory collection leads up to the **Second Floor** (at the time of writing closed for rearrangement). It houses some of the finest enamelled terracottas of the della Robbia family workshop, a room of portrait busts, beautiful works by Antonio Pollaiuolo and Verrocchio, a collection of armour, and the most important collection of small Renaissance bronzes in Italy.

Piazza San Firenze to the Duomo

The strangely shaped square that both the Badia and the Bargello call home is named after the large church of **San Firenze**, an imposing ensemble, now partially used as Florence's law courts. At the corner of the square and Via Gondi, the **Palazzo Gondi** is a fine Renaissance palace built for a merchant by Giuliano da Sangallo in 1489 but completed only in 1884; it's not easy to pick out the discreet 19th-century additions. A block from the square on Via Ghibellina, the **Palazzo Borghese** (no. 110) is one of the finest Neoclassical buildings in the city, erected in 1822—for a party in honour of Habsburg Grand Duke Ferdinand III. The host of this famous affair was one of the wealthiest men of his day, the Roman prince Camillo Borghese, husband of the fascinating Pauline Bonaparte and the man responsible for shipping many of Italy's artistic treasures off to the Louvre.

From Piazza San Firenze, Via del Proconsolo leads straight to the Piazza del Duomo, passing by way of the **Palazzo Pazzi-Quaratesi** (no. 10), the 15th-century headquarters of the banking family that organized the conspiracy against Lorenzo and Giuliano de' Medici. At no. 12, the Palazzo Nonfinito—begun in 1593 but, as its name suggests, never completed—is now the home of the **Museo Nazionale di Antropologia ed Etnologia** (open only 1st and 3rd Sun of each month, 9–1), founded in 1869, the first ethnological museum in Italy, with an interesting collection of Peruvian mummies, musical instruments collected by Galileo Chini (who decorated the Liberty-style extravaganzas at Viareggio), some lovely and unusual items of Japan's Ainu and Pakistan's Kafiri, and a large number of skulls from all over the world.

Florence As It Was

Borgo degli Albizi, the fine old street passing in front of the Palazzo Nonfinito, was in ancient times the Via Cassia, linking Rome with Bologna, and it deserves a leisurely stroll for its palaces. If it, too, fails to answer to the Florence you've been seeking, take Via dell'Oriuolo (just to the left at Piazza del Duomo) for the **Museo di Firenze Com'Era** (Museum of Florence as It Was), located at no. 4 (9–2, Sun 8–1, closed Tues; adm). The jewel of this museum is right out in front, the nearly room-sized *Pianta della Catena*, most beautiful of the early views of Florence. It is a copy as the original, made in 1490 by an unknown artist—that handsome fellow pictured in the lower right-hand corner—was lost during the last war in a Berlin museum. This fascinating painting captures Florence at the height of the Renaissance, a city of buildings in bright white, pink and tan; the great churches are without their façades, the Uffizi and Medici chapels have not yet appeared, and the Medici and Pitti palaces are without their later extensions.

The museum is not large. At present it contains only a number of plans and maps, as well as a collection of amateurish watercolours of Florence's sights from the last century, and paintings of Florence's surroundings by Ottone Rosai, a local favourite who died in 1957. Today's Florentines seem much less interested in the Renaissance than in the city of their grandparents. For some further evidence, look around the corner of Via S. Egidio, where some recent remodelling has uncovered posters over the street from 1925, announcing plans for paying the war debt and a coming visit of the Folies Bergères. The Florentines have restored them and put them under glass.

From Via dell'Oriuolo, Via Folco Portinari will take you to Florence's main hospital, **Santa Maria Nuova**, founded in 1286 by the father of Dante's Beatrice, Folco Portinari. A tomb in the hospital's church, Sant'Egidio, is all that remains of the Portinari family. Readers of Iris Origo's *The Merchant of Prato* will recognize it as the workplace of the good notary, Ser Lapo Mazzei. The portico of the hospital, by Buontalenti, was finished in 1612.

Medieval Streets North of the Arno

Just west of Via Por S. Maria, the main street leading down to the Ponte Vecchio, you'll find some of the oldest and best-preserved lanes in Florence. Near the Mercato Nuovo at the top of the street (see p. 103) stands the **Palazzo di Parte Guelfa**, the 13th-century headquarters of the Guelph party, and often the real seat of power in the city, paid for by property confiscated from the Ghibellines; in the 15th century Brunelleschi added a hall on the top floor and an extension. Next door is the guildhall of the silk makers, the 14th-century **Palazzo dell'Arte della Seta** still bearing its bas-relief emblem, or 'stemma', of a closed door, the age-old guild symbol. It's worth continuing around the Guelph Palace to Via Pellicceria to see the fine ensemble of medieval buildings on the tiny square near Via delle Terme, named after the old Roman baths.

Palazzo Davanzati

To get an idea of what life was like inside these sombre palaces some 600 years ago, stroll over to nearby Via Porta Rossa, site of the elegant Palazzo Davanzati, now arranged as the **Museo della Casa Fiorentina Antica**, one of the city's most delightful museums, offering a chance to step back into domestic life of yore (9–1:15, Sun 9–12:15, closed Mon; adm). Originally built in the mid-14th century for the Davizzi family, the house was purchased by merchant Bernardo Davanzati in 1578 and stayed in the family until the 1900s. Restored by an antique collector in 1904, it is the best-preserved medieval-Renaissance house in Florence and has been furnished with period trappings and art.

The façade is basically as it was, except for a 16th-century addition of a fifth-floor loggia, replacing the battlements—in the rough-and-tumble urban 14th century, a man's home literally had to be a castle. But it was also a showroom for his prosperity, and by the standards of the day, the dwellers of this huge palace were multi-millionaires. From the grand loggia, used for sumptuous public entertainment, you enter the palace by way of a strikingly vertical **Courtyard**, which could be quickly cut off from the street in times of danger, as evidenced by the stout, iron-bolted door. Nor would any family feel safe without a year's store of grain and oil—against famine, siege, plagues, or inflation. One storeroom is now used for an audio-visual history of the house. The well in the corner served all the floors of the house, and there is a kind of medieval dumb waiter to transport the shopping up to the kitchen on the top floor.

Upstairs, past a 14th-century fresco of St Christopher on the landing, you arrive at the elegant **Sala Grande** used for formal gatherings, and again, for defence, when boiling oil and such could be dropped through the four hatches in the floor. The room contains a beautiful 16th-century table and cupboard, and luxuries like an automatic bellows and flues at the fireplace, glass windows, and a prettily painted ceiling. The bright and cosy dining room next door, the **Sala dei Pappagalli**, was named after the parrots that adorn the frescoes, cleverly painted complete with pretend hooks to resemble far more costly tapestries. Off the **Sala Piccola**, a child's bedroom, is one of the palace's bathrooms, which must have seemed almost decadently luxurious in the medieval city, where one of the laws declared that one had to shout three loud warnings before emptying a chamber pot into the street. The last room on the floor is an elegant bedroom called the **Sala dei Pavoni**, with an almost Moorish-style pattern painted on the walls with coats-of-arms, topped by a frieze of peacocks and other exotic birds playing among the trees. The bedspread is a rare 14th-century example from Sicily, portraying the story of Tristan and King Mark.

The same layout of rooms is repeated on the next floor. The **Salone** is adorned with 15th-century Flemish tapestries and a portrait of Giovanni di Bicci de' Medici. The dining room contains outlandish salt cellars (17th–18th centuries) and games chests. The **Sala Piccola** houses a fine collection of 15th-century *cassoni*, the elaborate wedding chests in which a bride stored her dowry of household linens, one of the main housewifely obsessions. They are especially interesting for the secular subjects chosen to adorn them, often depicted in contemporary dress. The bedroom, the **Camera della Castellana di Vergi**, is decorated with a lovely if slightly faded fresco from a medieval French romance. The 14th-century shoes displayed here were discovered in Boccaccio's house—high heels, at least, are certainly nothing new.

The **Kitchen**, as is usual in a medieval house, is located on the top floor in the hope that in case of fire, only that part would burn. Women would spend most of their day

Palazzo Davanzati

here, supervising the servants, sewing, and gossiping; as no servants' quarters existed in the palace, it is believed that the help sacked out on the floor.

Piazza Santa Trínita

Three old Roman roads—Via Porta Rossa, Via delle Terme and Borgo SS. Apostoli—lead into the irregularly-shaped Piazza S. Trínita. Borgo SS. Apostoli is named after one of Florence's oldest churches, the little Romanesque **Santi Apostoli** (11th-century), located in the sunken Piazzetta del Limbo, former cemetery of unbaptized babies.

Piazza S. Trínita itself boasts an exceptionally fine architectural ensemble, grouped around the 'Column of Justice' from the Roman Baths of Caracalla, given by Pius IV to Cosimo I, and later topped with a statue of Justice by Francesco del Tadda. Its pale granite is set off by the palaces of the piazza: the High Renaissance-Roman **Palazzo Bartolini-Salimbeni**, by Baccio d'Agnolo (1520), on the corner of Via Porta Rossa, formerly the fashionable Hôtel du Nord where Herman Melville stayed, and now the French Consulate; the medieval **Palazzo Buondelmonti**, between the two, with a 1530 façade by Baccio d'Agnolo, once home to the reading room and favourite haunt of such literati in Florence in the 19th century as Dumas, Browning, Manzoni, and Stendhal; and the magnificent curving **Palazzo Spini-Ferroni**, to the right of Borgo SS. Apostoli, built in 1289 and still retaining its original battlements. Directly across Via Tornabuoni, the British Consulate occupies the **Palazzo Masetti**, ironically once home to the flamboyant Countess of Albany, wife of Bonnie Prince Charlie who found happiness by leaving the Pretender for Italian dramatist Vittorio Alfieri, but insisted to the end that she was England's rightful Queen Louise.

Santa Trínita

The **Church of S. Trínita** has stood here, in one form or another, since the 12th century; its unusual accent on the first syllable (from the Latin *Trinitas*) is considered proof of its ancient foundation. Although the pedestrian façade added by Buontalenti in 1593 isn't especially welcoming, step into its shadowy 14th-century interior for several artistic treats, beginning with the **Bartolini-Salimbeni Chapel** (4th on the right), frescoed in 1422 by the Sienese Lorenzo Monaco; his marriage of the Virgin takes place in a Tuscan fantasy backdrop of pink towers. He also painted the chapel's graceful, ethereally coloured altarpiece of the *Annunciation*.

In the choir, the **Sassetti Chapel** is one of the masterpieces of Domenico Ghirlandaio, completed in 1495 for wealthy merchant Francesco Sassetti and dedicated to the *Life of St Francis*, but also to the life of Francesco Sassetti, the city and his Medici circle: the scene above the altar, of Francis receiving the Rule of the Order, is transferred to the Piazza della Signoria, watched by Sassetti (to the right, with the fat purse) and Lorenzo il Magnifico; on the steps stands the great Latinist Poliziano with Lorenzo's three sons. The *Death of St Francis* pays homage to Giotto's similar composition in S. Croce. The altarpiece, the *Adoration of the Shepherds* (1485), is one of Ghirlandaio's best-known works, often described as the archetypal Renaissance painting, a contrived but charming classical treatment; the Magi arrive through a triumphal arch, a Roman sarcophagus is used as manger and a ruined temple for a stable—all matched by the sibyls on the vault; the sibyl on the outer arch is the one who supposedly announced the birth of Christ to Augustus.

Santa Trínita is a Vallombrosan church and the first chapel to the right of the altar holds the Order's holy of holies, a painted crucifix formerly located up in San Miniato. The story goes that on a Good Friday, a young noble named Giovanni Gualberto was on his way to Mass when he happened upon the man who had recently murdered his brother. But rather than take his revenge, Gualberto pardoned the assassin in honour of the holy day. When he arrived at church to pray, this crucifix nodded in approval of his mercy. Giovanni was so impressed that he went on to found the Vallombrosan order in the Casentino.

The **Sanctuary** was frescoed by Alesso Baldovinetti, though only four Old Testament figures survive. In the second chapel to the left the marble *Tomb of Bishop Benozzo Federighi* (1454) is by Luca, the first and greatest of the della Robbias, and features his trademark, enamelled terracotta in a gold-ground mosaic. In the north side of the nave, in the fourth chapel, a detached fresco by Neri di Bicci portrays S. Giovanni Gualberto and his fellow Vallombrosan saints; over the arch you can see him forgiving the murderer of his brother.

Via Tornabuoni and the Palazzo Strozzi

The streets west of Piazza della Repubblica have always been the choicest district of Florence, and Via Tornabuoni the city's smartest shopping street. These days you won't find many innovations—Milan's current status as headquarters of Italy's fashion industry is a sore point with Florence, which used to be top dog and lost its position in the 1970s for the lack of an airport.

In the bright and ambitious 1400s, however, when Florence was the centre of European high finance, Via Tornabuoni and its environs was the area the new merchant elite chose for their palaces. Today's bankers build great skyscrapers for the firm and settle for modest mansions for themselves; in Florence's heyday, things were reversed. Bankers and wool tycoons really owned their businesses. While their places of work were quite simple, their homes were imposing city palaces, all built in the same conservative style and competing with each other in size like some Millionaires' Row in Victorian America.

The champion was the **Palazzo Strozzi**, a long block up Via Tornabuoni from Piazza Trínita. This rusticated stone cube of fearful dimensions squats in its piazza like the inscrutable monolith in *2001: A Space Odyssey*, radiating almost visible waves of megalomania. The palazzo was begun by Benedetto da Maiano in 1489 for the extraordinarily wealthy Filippo Strozzi, head of one of Florence's greatest banking clans and adviser to Lorenzo il Magnifico. When he died in 1491, the façade facing Piazza Strozzi was almost complete; future generations had neither the money nor the interest to finish the job. And one wonders whether his son, also called Filippo, ever took much pleasure in it; though at first a Medici ally like his father, and wed to Piero de' Medici's daughter, Filippo attempted to lead a band of anti-Medici exiles against Florence; captured and imprisoned in the Fortezza da Basso, he stabbed himself, while many other Strozzi went to Paris to become bankers and advisers to the king of France.

There are few architectural innovations in the Palazzo Strozzi, but here the typical Florentine palace is blown up to the level of the absurd: though three storeys like other palaces, each floor is as tall as three or four normal ones. Like Michelangelo's *David*, Florence's other beautiful monster, it emits the unpleasant sensation of what Mary

McCarthy called the 'giganticism of the human ego', the will to surpass not only antiquity but nature herself. Nowadays, at least, the Strozzi palace is moderately useful, as space to hold temporary exhibitions.

Palazzo Rucellai

There are two other exceptional palaces in the quarter. At the north end of Via Tornabuoni stands the beautiful golden **Palazzo Antinori** (1465, architect unknown), which has Florence's grandest Baroque temple, **San Gaetano** (1648, by Gherardo Silvani) as its equally golden companion. The second palace, Florence's most celebrated example of domestic architecture, is the **Palazzo Rucellai**, in Via della Vigna Nuova. Its original owner, Giovanni Rucellai, was a quattrocento tycoon like Filippo Strozzi, but an intellectual as well, whose *Zibaldone*, or 'commonplace book' is one of the best sources available on the life and tastes of the educated Renaissance merchant. In 1446 Rucellai chose his favourite architect, Leon Battista Alberti, to design his palace. Actually built by Bernardo Rossellino, it follows Alberti's precepts and theories in its use of the three classical orders; instead of the usual rusticated stone, the façade has a far more delicate decoration of incised irregular blocks and a frieze, elements influential in subsequent Italian architecture—though far more noticeably in Rome than Florence itself. Originally the palace was only five bays wide, and when another two bays were added later the edge was left ragged, unfinished, a nice touch, as if the builders could return at any moment and pick up where they left off. The frieze, like that on S. Maria Novella, portrays the devices of the Medici and Rucellai families (Giovanni's son married another daughter of Piero de' Medici), a wedding believed to have been fêted in the **Loggia dei Rucellai** across the street, also designed by Alberti.

Since 1987, the Palazzo Rucellai has housed Florence's new museum, the **Museo di Storia della Fotografia Fratelli Alinari** (9–1 and 2:30–7:30; Sat and Sun 9–1 and 4–7:30; on Tues, Fri, and Sat, until 10:30 pm; adm) devoted to the history of photography. Exhibits come from the fascinating archives of the Alinari brothers, who founded the world's first photography society in 1852. Keep an eye out for posters concerning special shows.

Behind the Rucellai palace (on Via della Spada) lies the ancient church of **San Pancrazio**, with an antique-style porch by Alberti; at one point in its up-and-down career the church served as a tobacco factory. The reason for visiting, however, is the **Rucellai Chapel**, designed in 1467 by Alberti (entrance at no. 18, at erratic hours), built to house the unique model of the Sanctuary of the Holy Sepulchre in Jerusalem that is Giovanni Rucellai's funerary monument.

Ognissanti

Before taking leave of old Florence's west end, head back to the Arno and **Piazza Goldoni**, named after the great comic playwright from Venice. The bridge here, the **Ponte alla Carraia**, is new and nondescript, but its 1304 version played a leading role in that year's most memorable disaster: a company staging a water pageant of the Inferno, complete with monsters, devils, and tortured souls, attracted such a large crowd that the bridge collapsed under the weight, and all were drowned. Later it was drily commented that all the Florentines who went to see Hell that day found what they were looking for.

The most important building on the piazza, the **Palazzo Ricasoli**, was built in the 15th century but bears the name of one of unified Italy's first Prime Ministers, Bettino 'Iron Baron' Ricasoli. Just to the west, on Lungarno Corsini, looms the enormous **Palazzo Corsini**, the city's most prominent piece of Roman Baroque extravagance, begun in 1650 and crowned with a bevy of statues. The Corsini, the most prominent family of 17th- and 18th-century Florence, were reputedly so wealthy that they could ride from Florence to Rome entirely on their own property. The **Galleria Corsini** is considered the finest private gallery in the city (adm by appointment only, tel 283 044; enter from Via Parione), with paintings by Giovanni Bellini, Signorelli, Filippino Lippi, and Pontormo, and *Muses* from the ducal palace of Urbino, painted by Raphael's first master, Timoteo Viti. Further east on Lungarno Corsini stood the Libreria Orioli, which published the first edition of *Lady Chatterley's Lover* in 1927.

To the west of Piazza Goldoni lies the old neighbourhood of the only Florentine to have a continent named after him: Amerigo Vespucci (1451–1512) was a Medici agent in Seville, and made two voyages from there to America, on the heels of Columbus. His parish church, **Ognissanti** (All Saints'), is set back from the river behind a Baroque façade, on property given in 1256 by the Umiliati, a religious order that specialized in wool-working. The Vespucci family tomb is below the second altar to the right, and little Amerigo himself is said to be pictured next to the Madonna in the fresco of the Madonna della Misericordia—probably another Florentine tall story. Also buried in Ognissanti was the Filipepi family (one of whom was Botticelli).

The best art is in the **Convent**, just to the left of the church at no. 42 (open Sat, Mon and Tues, 9–12; you may have to ring). Frescoed in the Refectory is the great Last Supper, or *Cenacolo*, painted by Domenico Ghirlandaio in 1480. It's hard to think of a more serene and elegant Last Supper, almost like a garden party with its background of fruit trees and exotic birds; a peacock sits in the window, cherries and peaches litter the lovely tablecloth. On either side of the fresco are two scholarly saints moved here from the church itself: Ghirlandaio's *St Jerome* and on the right, young Botticelli's *St Augustine.*

Santa Maria Novella

As in Venice and so many other Italian cities, the two churches of the preaching orders—the Dominicans' S. Maria Novella and the Franciscans' S. Croce—became the largest and most prestigious in the city, where wealthy families vied to create the most beautiful chapels and tombs. In Florence, by some twitch of city planning, both of these sacred art galleries dominate broad, stale squares that do not invite you to linger; in the irregular **Piazza Santa Maria** you may find yourself looking over your shoulder for the ghosts of the carriages that once raced madly around the two stout obelisks set on turtles, just as in a Roman circus, in the fashionable carriage races of the 1700s. The arcade on the south side, the **Loggia di San Paolo**, is very much like Brunelleschi's Spedale degli Innocenti, although it suffers somewhat from its use as a busy bus shelter; the lunette over the door, by Andrea della Robbia, shows the *Meeting of SS. Francis and Dominic.*

S. Maria Novella redeems the anomie of its square with its stupendous black and white marble **façade**, the finest in Florence. The lower part, with its looping arcades, is Romanesque work in the typical Tuscan mode, finished before 1360. In 1456 Giovanni Rucellai commissioned Alberti to complete it, a remarkably fortunate choice. Alberti's half not only perfectly harmonizes with the original, but perfects it with geometrical harmonies to create what appears to be a kind of Renaissance Sun Temple. The original builders started it off by orienting the church to the south instead of west, so that at noon the sun streams through the 14th-century rose window. The only symbol Alberti put on the façade is a blazing sun; the unusual sundials, over the arches on the extreme right and left, were added by Cosimo I's court astronomer Egnazio Danti. Note how the base of the façade is also the base of an equilateral triangle, with Alberti's sun at the apex.

The beautiful frieze depicts the Rucellai emblem (a billowing sail), as on the Palazzo Rucellai. The wall of Gothic recesses to the right, enclosing the old cemetery, are *avelli*, or family tombs.

The **interior** is vast, lofty, and more 'Gothic' in feel than any other church in Florence—no thanks to Vasari, who was set loose to remodel the church to 16th-century taste, painting over the original frescoes, removing the rood screen and Dominicans' choir from the nave, and remodelling the altars; in the 1800s restorers did their best to de-Vasari S. Maria with Neo-Gothic details. Neither party, however, could touch two of the interior's most distinctive features—the striking stone vaulting of the nave and the perspective created by the columns marching down the aisles, each pair placed a little closer together as they approach the altar.

Over the portal at the entrance is a fresco lunette by Botticelli that has recently been restored. One of S. Maria Novella's best-known pictures is at the second altar on the left: Masaccio's *Trinity*, painted around 1425, and one of the revolutionary works of the Renaissance. Masaccio's use of architectural elements and perspective gives his composition both physical and intellectual depth. The flat wall becomes a deeply recessed Brunelleschian chapel, calm and classical, enclosed in a coffered barrel vault; at the foot of the fresco a bleak skeleton decays in its tomb, bearing a favourite Tuscan reminder: 'I was that which you are, you will be that which I am.' Above this morbid suggestion of physical death kneel the two donors; within the celestially rational inner sanctum the Virgin and St John stand at the foot of the Cross, humanity's link with the mystery of the Trinity. In the nearby Brunelleschi-designed pulpit Galileo was first denounced by the Inquisition for presuming to believe that the earth went around the sun.

There is little else to detain you in the aisles, but the first chapel in the left transept, the **Cappella Strozzi**, is one of the most evocative corners of 14th-century Florence, frescoed entirely by Nardo di Cione and his brother, Andrea Orcagna; on the vault pictures of St Thomas Aquinas and the Virtues are echoed in Andrea's lovely altarpiece of *The Redeemer donating the Keys to St Peter and the Book of Wisdom to St Thomas Aquinas*; on the left wall there's a crowded scene of Paradise, with the righteous lined up in a medieval class photograph. On the right, Nardo painted a striking view of Dante's Inferno, with all of a Tuscan's special attention to precise map-like detail.

In the richly decorated **Sacristy** hangs Giotto's recently restored *Crucifix* (*c.* 1300), one of the artist's first works. In the **Gondi Chapel** hangs another famous Crucifix, carved in wood by Brunelleschi, which, according to Vasari, so astonished his friend Donatello that he dropped the eggs he was carrying in his apron when he first saw it.

The charming fresco cycle in the **Sanctuary** (1485–90), painted by Domenico Ghirlandaio, portrays the *Lives of the Virgin, St John the Baptist and the Dominican Saints* in magnificent architectural settings; little Michelangelo was among the students who helped him complete it. Nearly all of the bystanders are portraits of Florentine quattrocento VIPs, including the artist himself (in the red hat, in the scene of the *Expulsion of St Joachim from the Temple*) but most prominent are the ladies and gents of the Tornabuoni house. More excellent frescoes adorn the **Filippo Strozzi Chapel**, the finest work ever to come from the brush of Filippino Lippi, painted in 1502 near the end of his life; the exaggerated, dark and violent scenes portray the lives of St Philip (his crucifixion and his subduing of the dragon before the Temple of Mars, which creates such a stench it kills the heathen prince) and of St John the Evangelist (raising Drusiana from the dead and being martyred in boiling oil). The chapel's beautifully carved tomb of Filippo Strozzi is by Benedetto da Maiano. The **Rucellai Chapel** contains a marble statue of the Madonna and Bambino by Nino Pisano and a fine bronze tomb by Ghiberti, which makes an interesting comparison with the three Gothic tombs nearby in the right transept. One of these contains the remains of the Patriarch of Constantinople, who died in here after the failure of the Council of Florence, in 1439, to reunite the Western and Eastern Churches.

THE GREEN CLOISTER AND SPANISH CHAPEL

More great frescoes await in S. Maria Novella's Cloisters, all recently restored and open as a city museum (entrance just to the left of the church; open 8–1, closed Fri; weekends 9–2; adm; free Sun). The first cloister, the so-called Green Cloister, one of the masterpieces of Paolo Uccello and his assistants, is so named after the *terraverde* or green

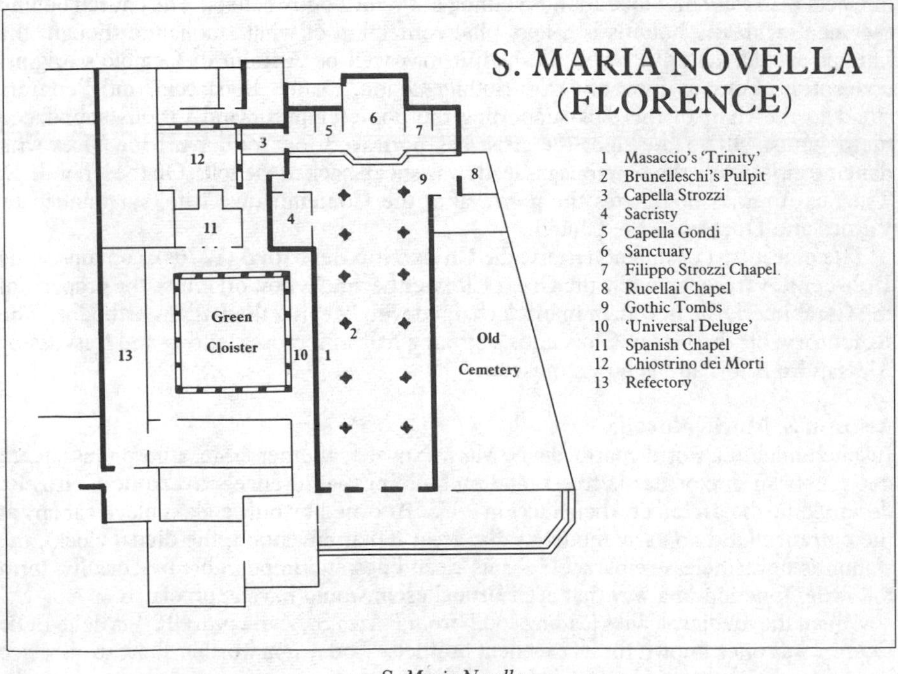

S. Maria Novella

earth pigment used by the artist, which lends the scenes from Genesis their eerie, ghostly quality. Much damaged by time and neglect, they are nevertheless striking for their two Uccellian obsessions—perspective and animals, the latter especially notable in the scene of the Creation. Best known, and in better condition than the others, is Uccello's surreal *Universal Deluge*, a composition framed by the steep walls of two arks, before and after views, which have the uncanny effect of making the scene seem to come racing out of its own vanishing point, a vanishing point touched by divine wrath in a searing bolt of lightning. In between the claustrophobic walls the flood rises, tossing up a desperate ensemble of humanity, waterlogged bodies, naked men bearing clubs, crowded in a jam of flotsam and jetsam and islets rapidly receding in the dark waters. In the right front, amidst the panic, stands a tall robed man, seemingly a visionary, perhaps even Noah himself, looking heavenward while a flood victim seizes him by the ankles. Some of Uccello's favourite perspective studies were headgear, especially the wooden hoops called *mazzocchi* which he puts around the neck and on the head of his figures.

The **Spanish Chapel** opens up at the far end of the cloisters, taking its name from the Spanish court followers of Eleonora di Toledo who worshipped here; the Inquisition had earlier made the chapel its headquarters in Florence. The chapel is, again, famous for its frescoes, the masterpiece of a little-known 14th-century artist named Andrea di Buonaiuto, whose subject was the Dominican cosmology, perhaps not something we have much empathy for these days, but here beautifully portrayed, so that even the 'Hounds of the Lord' (a pun on the Order's name, the 'Domini canes') on the right wall, seem more like pets than militant bloodhounds sniffing out unorthodox beliefs. The church behind the scene with the hounds is a fairy pink confection of what Buonaiuto thought the Duomo would look like when finished; it may well be Arnolfo di Cambio's original conception. Famous Florentines, including Giotto, Dante, Boccaccio, and Petrarch, stand to the right of the dais supporting the pope, emperor and various sour-faced hierophants. Off to the right the artist has portrayed four rather urbane Vices with dancing girls, while the Dominicans lead stray sheep back to the fold. On the left wall, St Thomas Aquinas dominates the portrayal of the Contemplative Life, surrounded by Virtues and Doctors of the Church.

The oldest part of the monastery, the **Chiostrino dei Morti** (1270s), contains some 14th-century frescoes, while the **Great Cloister** beyond is now off limits, the property of the Carabinieri, the new men in black charged with keeping the Italians orthodox. The **Refectory**, off the Green Cloister, is a striking hall with cross vaulting and frescoes by Alessandro Allori and is now a museum.

Around S. Maria Novella

Just behind, but a world apart from S. Maria Novella, another large, amorphous square detracts from one of Italy's finest modern buildings—Florence's **Stazione Centrale**, designed by the architect Michelucci in 1935. Adorned by only a glass block canopy at the entrance (and an early model of that great Italian invention, the digital clock), the station is nevertheless remarkable for its clean lines and impeccable practicality; form following function in a way that even Brunelleschi would have appreciated.

One of the medieval lanes leading south from Piazza S. Maria Novella, Via delle Belle Donne, was once known for its excellent brothels. Today it is worth a short stroll to see one of the very few crossroads in Italy marked by a cross, a Celtic custom that never really caught on here—Italians are far more fond of corner shrines to the Madonna or some lucky saint. According to legend, **Croce del Trebbio** (from a corruption of 'trivium') marks the spot of a massacre of Patarene heretics in the 1240s, after the masses had been excited by a sermon given by the fire-eating Inquisitor St Peter Martyr from the pulpit of S. Maria Novella.

San Lorenzo

The lively quarter just east of S. Maria Novella has been associated with the Medici ever since Giovanni di Bicci de' Medici commissioned Brunelleschi to rebuild the ancient church of San Lorenzo in 1420; subsequent members of the dynasty lavished bushels of florins on its decoration and Medici pantheon, and on several projects commissioned from Michelangelo. The mixed result of all their efforts could be held up as an archetype of the Renaissance, and one which Walter Pater described as 'great rather by what it designed or aspired to do, than by what it actually achieved'. One can begin with the façade of corrugated brick, the most *nonfinito* of all of Michelangelo's unfinished projects; commissioned by Medici Pope Leo X in 1516, the project never got further than Michelangelo's scale model, which may be seen in the Casa Buonarroti. To complete the church's dingy aspect, the piazza in front contains a universally detested 19th-century statue of Cosimo I's dashing father, Giovanni delle Bande Nere, who died at age 28 of wounds received fighting against Emperor Charles V.

The **interior**, although completed after Brunelleschi's death, is true to his design, classically calm in good grey *pietra serena*. The artistic treasures it contains are few but choice, beginning with the second chapel on the right, housing *The Marriage of the Virgin*, a 1523 work by the Mannerist Rosso Fiorentino. Joseph, usually portrayed as an old man, according to Rosso is a Greek god with golden curls in a flowing scene of hot reds and oranges—a powerful contrast to the chapel's haunting, hollow-eyed tomb slab of the Ray Charles of the Renaissance, Francesco Landini (died 1397), the blind organist whose madrigals were immensely popular and influential in Italian music. At the end of the right aisle, there's a lovely, delicately worked tabernacle by Desiderio da Settignano.

Most riveting of all, however, are **Donatello's pulpits**, the sculptor's last works, completed by his pupils after his death in 1466. Cast in bronze, the pulpits were commissioned by Donatello's friend and patron Cosimo il Vecchio, some think to keep the sculptor busy in his old age. Little in Donatello's previous work prepares the viewer for these scenes of Christ's passion and Resurrection, with their rough and impressionistic details, their unbalanced and overcrowded compositions, more reminiscent of Rodin than anything Florentine. Unfortunately they were set up on columns in the 17th century, just above eye level, like so many things in Florence. Nearby, directly beneath the dome, lies buried Donatello's patron and Florence's original godfather, Cosimo il Vecchio; the grille over his grave bears the Medici arms and the simple inscription, 'Pater Patriae'.

It was the godfather's father, Giovanni di Bicci de' Medici, who in 1420 commissioned Brunelleschi to build the **Old Sacristy**, off the left transept. Often cited as one of the first and finest works of the early Renaissance, Brunelleschi designed this cube of a sacristy according to carefully calculated mathematical proportions, emphasized with a colour scheme of white walls, articulated in soft grey *pietra serena* pilasters and cornices; a dignified decoration that would become his trademark, something

Florentine architects would borrow for centuries. Donatello contributed the terracotta tondoes and lunettes, as well as the bronze doors, embellished with lively Apostles. The Sacristy was built to hold the sarcophagi of Giovanni di Bicci de' Medici and his wife, in the centre of the room; in 1472 Lorenzo il Magnifico and his brother Giuliano had Verrocchio design the beautiful bronze and red porphyry wall tomb for their father Piero the Gouty and their uncle Giovanni. Unfortunately Verrocchio saw fit to place this in front of Brunelleschi's original door, upsetting the careful balance.

The chapel across the transept from the entrance to the Old Sacristy holds a 19th-century monument to Donatello, who is buried here, at his request, near Cosimo il Vecchio. The lovely *Annunciation* is by Filippo Lippi; the large, colourful fresco of the *Martyrdom of St Lawrence* around the corner in the aisle is by Bronzino and has just been restored.

Just beyond the Bronzino a door leads into the 15th-century **Cloister**, and from there a stair leads up to Michelangelo's celebrated **Biblioteca Laurentiana** (Tues–Sat, 8–2). If Brunelleschi's Old Sacristy heralded the Renaissance, Michelangelo's library, and especially its vestibule, is Mannerism's prototype, or Brunelleschi gone haywire, no longer serene and mathematically perfect, but complicated and restless, the architectural elements stuck on with an eye for effect rather than for any structural purpose. The vestibule barely contains the remarkable stair, flowing down from the library like a stone cascade, built by Vasari after a drawing by Michelangelo.

Now you have to ask to delve into a collection that ranges from a very rare 5th-century Virgil and other Greek and Latin codices, beautifully illuminated manuscripts, and the original manuscript of Cellini's autobiography.

THE MEDICI CHAPELS

San Lorenzo is most famous, however, for the Medici Chapels, which lie outside and behind the church (open 9–2, Sun 9–1, closed Mon; adm, expensive). The entrance leads through the crypt, a dark and austere place where many of the Medici are actually buried. Their main monument, the family obsession, is just up the steps, and has long been known as the **Chapel of the Princes**, a stupefying, fabulously costly octagon of death that, as much as the Grand Dukes fussed over it, lends their memory an unpleasant aftertaste of cancerous bric-à-brac that grew and grew. Perhaps one would have to be a genuine Medici to love its insane, trashy opulence; all of Grand Duke Cosimo's descendants, down to the last, Anna Maria Ludovica, worked like beavers to finish it according to the plans left by Cosimo's illegitimate son, dilettante architect Giovanni de' Medici. Yet even today it is only partially completed, the *pietre dure* extending only part of the way up the walls. The 19th-century frescoes in the cupola are a poor substitute for the originally planned 'Apotheosis of the Medici' in lapis lazuli, and the two statues in gilded bronze in the niches over the sarcophagi (each niche large enough to hold a hippopotamus) are nothing like the intended figures to be carved in semi-precious stone. The most interesting feature is the inlaid *pietra dura* arms of Tuscan towns and the large Medici arms above, with their familiar six red boluses blown up as big as beachballs.

A passageway leads to Michelangelo's **New Sacristy**, commissioned by Leo X to occupy an unfinished room originally built to balance Brunelleschi's Old Sacristy. Michelangelo's first idea was to turn it into a new version of his unfinished, overly ambitious Pope Julius Tomb, an idea quickly quashed by his patrons, who requested instead four wall tombs. Michelangelo only worked on two of the monuments, but managed to finish the New Sacristy itself, creating a silent and gloomy mausoleum, closed-in and grey, a chilly introspective cocoon calculated to depress even the most chatty tour groups.

Nor are the famous tombs guaranteed to cheer. Both honour nonentities: that of *Night and Day* belongs to Giuliano de' Medici, son of Lorenzo il Magnifico and Duke of Nemours, and symbolizes the Active Life, while the *Dawn and Dusk* is of Lorenzo de' Medici, Duke of Urbino and nephew of Giuliano (and dedicatee of *The Prince*) who symbolizes the Contemplative Life (true to life in one respect—Lorenzo was a disappointment to Machiavelli and everyone else, passively obeying the dictates of his uncle Pope Leo X). Idealized statues of the two men, in Roman patrician gear, represent these states of mind, while draped on their sarcophagi are Michelangelo's four allegorical figures of the Times of Day, so heavy with weariness and grief they seem ready to slide off on to the floor. The most finished figure, *Night*, has always impressed the critics; she is almost a personification of despair, the mouthpiece of Michelangelo's most bitter verse:

> 'Sweet to me is sleep, and even more to be like stone
> While wrong and shame endure;
> Not to see, nor to feel, is my good fortune.
> Therefore, do not wake me; speak softly here.'

Both statues of the dukes look towards the back wall, where a large double tomb for Lorenzo il Magnifico and his brother Giuliano was originally planned, to be decorated with river gods. The only part of this tomb ever completed is the statue of the *Madonna and Child* now in place, accompanied by the Medici patron saints, *Cosmas and Damian*.

In 1975, charcoal drawings were discovered on the walls of the little room off the altar, attributed to Michelangelo, who may have hidden here in 1530, when the Medici had regained Florence and apparently would only forgive the artist for aiding the republican defence if he would finish their tombs. But Michelangelo had had enough of their ducal pretences and went off to Rome, never to return to Florence.

Mercato Centrale and Perugino

What makes the neighbourhood around San Lorenzo so lively is its street market, which the Florentines run with an almost Neapolitan flamboyance every day except Sunday and Monday. Stalls selling clothes and leather extend from the square up Via dell'Ariento and vicinity (nicknamed 'Shanghai') towards the **Mercato Centrale**, Florence's main food market, a cast-iron and glass confection of the 1870s, brimful of fresh fruit and vegetables, leering boars' heads and mounds of tripe (open Mon–Sat 7–1, also Sat 4:30–7:30).

Beyond the market, at Via Faenza 42, is the entrance to Perugino's **Cenacolo di Foligno** fresco, housed in the ex-convent of the Tertiary Franciscans of Foligno (Sun and holidays 9–12). This 1490s Umbrian version of the Last Supper was discovered in the 1850s and has recently been restored—and closed off again. For its current status check at the tourist office.

Palazzo Medici-Riccardi

A block from San Lorenzo and the Piazza del Duomo stands the palace that once held Florence's unofficial court, where ambassadors would call, kings would lodge, and important decisions would be made. Built in 1444 by Michelozzo for Cosimo il Vecchio, it was the principal address of the Medici for a hundred years, until Cosimo I abandoned it for larger quarters in the Palazzo Vecchio and the Pitti Palace. In 1659 the Riccardi purchased the palace, added to it and did everything to keep it glittering until Napoleon and his debts drove them to bankruptcy in 1809. The palace is now used as the city's prefecture.

In its day, though, it was the largest private address in the city, where the family lived with the likes of Donatello's *David* and *Judith and Holofernes*, Uccello's *Battle of S. Romano* and other masterpieces now in the Uffizi and Bargello. Frescoes are much harder to move, however, and the Palazzo Medici is worth visiting to see the most charming ones in Italy, Benozzo Gozzoli's 1459 *Procession of the Magi*, located in the **Medici Chapel** upstairs (open 9–12:30 and 3–5; Sun 9–12, closed Wed).

Painted in a delightful, decorative manner more reminiscent of International Gothic than the awakening Renaissance style of his contemporaries, Gozzoli took a religious subject and turned it into a merry, brilliantly coloured pageant of beautifully dressed kings, knights, and pages, accompanied by greyhounds and a giraffe, who travel through a springtime landscape of jewel-like trees and castles. This is a largely secular painting, representing less the original Three Kings than the annual pageant of the *Compagnia dei Magi*, Florence's richest confraternity. The scene is wrapped around three walls of the small chapel—you feel as if you had walked straight into a glowing fairytale world. Most of the faces are those of the Medici and other local celebrities; Gozzoli certainly had no qualms about putting himself in the scene, in the crowd of figures on the right wall, with his name written on his red cap. In the foreground, note the black man carrying a bow. Blacks, as well as Turks, Circassians, Tartars and others, were common enough in Renaissance Florence, originally brought as slaves. By the 1400s, however, contemporary writers mention them as artisans, fencing masters, soldiers, and one famous archery instructor, who may be the man pictured here.

The altarpiece, an ethereal *Madonna* by Filippo Lippi (or an imitator), has been moved into the other room of the palace opened to visitors, the **Gallery**, up the second flight of stairs on the right, from the courtyard. It's hard to imagine a more striking contrast than that between Gozzoli and the Neapolitan, Luca Giordano (nicknamed 'Luca fa presto' or 'Luke Does-it-fast'), who painted this hilarious ceiling for the Riccardi in 1683, as a left-handed compliment to the Medici for selling them the palace. No longer mere players in a religious pageant, the Medici, or at least the overstuffed Grand Duke Cosimo III and his unspeakable heir Gian Gastone, take the leading roles, defying the laws of gravity and good taste in an apotheosis of marshmallow clouds.

San Marco

From the Medici palace, Via Cavour heads north for Piazza San Marco, a lively square full of art students from the nearby Accademia. The north side of the square is occupied by the **Church and Dominican Convent of San Marco**. The Convent was Cosimo il Vecchio's favourite pious project; in 1437 he commissioned Michelozzo to enlarge and rebuild it, and to add to it Europe's first public library, where Florentine scholars and humanists rediscovered the ancient classics that Cosimo's agents collected for him (now in the Laurentian Library). A later prior of San Marco, Savonarola, had little use for the

Medici, though he owed his position to the influence of Lorenzo the Magnificent in 1491.

San Marco is best known for the works of the other-worldly Fra Angelico, in residence here between 1436 and 1447, and in charge of decorating the new convent constructed by Cosimo. His paintings and frescoes in San Marco, itself unchanged from the 1400s, offer a unique opportunity to see his works in the peaceful, contemplative environment in which they were meant to be seen (open 9–2, Sun 9–1, closed Mon; adm).

Every painter in the 15th century earned his living painting sacred subjects, but none painted them with the deep conviction and faith of the 'Blessed' Angelico, who communicated his Biblical visions in soft angelic pastels, bright playroom colours and an ethereal blondness, so clear and limpid that they just had to be true. 'Immured in his quiet convent,' wrote Henry James, 'he apparently never received an intelligible impression of evil; and his conception of human life was a perpetual sense of sacredly loving and being loved.' Yet the gentle friar was certainly not artistically naive, and adopted many of his contemporaries' innovations, especially artificial perspective, in his technique.

A visit to S. Marco begins with Michelozzo's harmonious **Cloister of S. Antonio** in which Fra Angelico painted the frescoes in the corners. Just off the cloister, the **Pilgrim's Hospice**, also by Michelozzo, has been arranged as a gallery of Fra Angelico's paintings, gathered from all over Florence. Here you'll find his great *Last Judgement* altarpiece (1430), a serenely confident work in which all the saved are well-dressed Italians, holding hands, led by an angel in a celestial dance. They are allowed to keep their beautiful clothes in heaven, while the bad (mostly princes and prelates) are stripped to receive their interesting tortures.

One of the most charming works is the *35 scenes from the Life of Christ*, acted out before strikingly bare, brown Tuscan backgrounds, painted as cupboard doors for SS. Annunziata. Three of the scenes are by Fra Angelico's talented apprentice, Alesso Baldovinetti. The noble, gracefully lamenting figures in the magnificent *Deposition altarpiece* from S. Trínita stand before an elegant townscape dominated by Fra Angelico's ziggurat-style concept of the Temple in Jerusalem. Other masterpieces include the **Tabernacle of the Linaioli** (the flax-workers), with a beautiful predella. The same holds true for the *Pala di San Marco*, the predella picturing SS. Cosmas and Damian, patrons of medicine and the Medici, in the act of performing history's first leg transplant.

Other rooms off the cloister contain works by Fra Bartolomeo, another resident of the convent, whose portraits capture some of the most sincere spirituality of the late 15th century. The **Chapter House** contains Fra Angelico's over-restored fresco of *Crucifixion and Saints*, a painting that lacks his accustomed grace; in the **Refectory** there's a more pleasing *Last Supper* by the down-to-earth Domenico Ghirlandaio.

Stairs lead up to Michelozzo's beautiful **Convent**, where at the top your eyes meet the Angelic Friar's masterpiece, a miraculous *Annunciation* that one can't help but think earned him his beatification. The subject was a favourite with Florentine artists, not only because it was a severe test—expressing a divine revelation with a composition of strict economy—but because the Annunciation, falling near the spring equinox, was New Year's Day for Florence until the Medici adopted the pope's calendar in the 1600s.

The monks of San Marco each had a small white cell with a window and a fresco to serve as a focal point for their meditations. Fra Angelico and his assistants painted 44 of these; those believed to have been done by the master are along the outer wall (cells 1–9, the *Noli me Tangere*, another *Annunciation*, a *Transfiguration*, a *Harrowing of Hell*, a *Coronation of the Virgin*, and others). He also painted the scene in the large cell used occasionally by Cosimo il Vecchio and other visiting celebrities. One corridor is entirely painted with scenes of the Crucifixion, all the same but for some slight difference in the pose of the Dominican monk at the foot of the Cross; walking past and glancing in the cells successively gives the impression of an animated cartoon. The **Prior's cell** at the end belonged to Savonarola; it has simple furniture of the period and a portrait of Savonarola in the guise of St Peter Martyr (with an axe in his brain) by his friend Fra Bartolomeo. In a nearby corridor hangs a copy of the anonymous painting in the Corsini Gallery, of Savonarola and two of his followers being burned at the stake in the Piazza della Signoria. The **Library**, entered off the corridor, is as light and airy as the cloisters below, and contains a collection of beautiful choir books. Architecturally the library was one of Michelozzo's greatest works, radiating a wonderful spirit of serenity, church-like with its vaulted nave and aisles.

The **Church of San Marco** was rebuilt, along with the convent, in the 15th century, though the interior was rearranged by Giambologna and the Baroque façade added in 1780. The right aisle has an altar topped by an 8th-century mosaic from Constantinople, reminiscent of works from Ravenna. There's a painting by Fra Bartolomeo nearby of a *Madonna and six saints*.

University Museums and the Botanical Garden

Near San Marco, at Via La Pira 4, the University of Florence runs several small museums; nearly all the collections were begun by the indefatigable Medici. The **Geology and Palaeontology Museum** has one of Italy's best collections of fossils, many uncovered in Tuscany, including antiquated elephants from the Valdarno (Mon 2–6; Tues, Wed, Thurs, and Sat 9–1). The **Mineralogy and Lithology Museum** houses strange and beautiful rocks, especially from Elba, the treasure island of minerals; there's a topaz weighing in at 151 kg, meteorites, and a bright collection of Medici trinkets, worked from stones in rainbow hues (weekdays 9–1, Wed also 3–6). The **Botanical Museum** is of less interest to the casual visitor, though it houses one of the most extensive herbariums in the world; most impressive here are the exquisite wax models of plants made in the early 1800s (open Mon, Wed, and Fri 9–12). Also on Via La Pira is the entrance to the University's **Giardino dei Semplici**, the botanical garden created for Cosimo I. The garden maintains its original layout, with medicinal herbs, Tuscan plants, flowers, and tropical plants in its greenhouses.

Sant'Apollonia and the Scalzo

Cenacoli, or frescoes of the Last Supper, became almost *de rigueur* in monastic refectories; in several of these the Last Supper is all that remains of a convent.

Until 1860, the Renaissance convent of **Sant'Apollonia** (off Piazza S. Marco, at Via XXVII Aprile 1) was the abode of cloistered nuns, and the fresco of the Last Supper in their refectory was a secret. When the convent was suppressed, and the painting discovered under the whitewash, the critics believed it to be the work of Paolo Uccello, but lately have unanimously attributed it to Andrea del Castagno, painted around 1440. The other walls have sinopie of the Crucifixion, Entombment, and Resurrection by Castagno; in the vestibule there are good works by Neri di Bicci and Paolo Schiavo (9–2, Sun 9–1, closed Mon).

Not far away you can enter a radically different artistic world in the **Chiostro dello Scalzo**, again off Piazza S. Marco at Via Cavour 69. Formerly part of the Confraternity of San Giovanni Battista, all that has survived is this cloister, frescoed (1514–24) with scenes of the life of St John the Baptist by Andrea del Sarto and his pupil Franciabigio. Del Sarto, Browning's 'perfect painter', painted these in monochrome grisaille, and while the scene of the *Baptism of Christ* is a beautiful work, some of the other panels are the most unintentionally funny things in Florence—the scene of Herod's banquet is reduced to a meagre breakfast where the king and queen look up indignantly at the man bringing in the platter of the Baptist's head as if he were a waiter who had made a mistake with their order.

The Galleria dell'Accademia

From Piazza San Marco, Via Ricasoli makes a beeline for the Duomo, but on most days (open 9–2, Sun 9–1, closed Mon; adm, expensive) the view is obstructed by the crowds milling around no. 60; in the summer the queues are as long as those at the Uffizi, all anxious to get a look at Michelangelo's *David*. Just over a hundred years ago Florence decided to take this precocious symbol of republican liberty out of the rain and install it, with much pomp, in a specially-built classical exedra in this gallery.

Michelangelo completed the *David* for the city in 1504, when he was 29, and it was the work that established the overwhelming reputation he had in his own time. The monstrous block of marble—17 ft high but unusually shallow—had been quarried 40 years earlier by the Cathedral Works and spoiled by other hands. The block was offered around to other artists, including Leonardo da Vinci, before young Michelangelo decided to take up the challenge of carving the largest statue since Roman times. And it is the dimensions of the *David* that remain the biggest surprise in these days of endless reproductions. Certainly as a political symbol of the Republic, he is excessive—the irony of a David the size of a Goliath is disconcerting—but as a symbol of the artistic and intellectual aspirations of the Renaissance he is unsurpassed.

And it's hard to deny, after gazing at this enormous nude, that these same Renaissance aspirations, by the 1500s, began snuggling uncomfortably close to the frontiers of kitsch. Disproportionate size, according to kitsch authorities, is one symptom; the calculated intention to excite a strong emotional response is another. In the *David*, virtuosity eclipses vision, and commits the even deadlier kitsch sin of seeking the sterile Empyrean of perfect beauty—most would argue that Michelangelo here achieves it, perhaps capturing his own feelings about the work in the *David*'s chillingly vain, self-satisfied expression. This is also one of the few statues to have actually killed someone. During a political disturbance in the Piazza della Signoria, its arm broke off and fell on a farmer.

In the Galleria next to the *David* are Michelangelo's famous *nonfiniti*, the four *Prisoners* or Slaves, worked on between 1519 and 1536, sculpted for Pope Julius' tomb and left in various stages of completion, although it is endlessly argued whether this is by design or through lack of time. Whatever the case, they illustrate Michelangelo's view of sculpture as a prisoner in stone just as the soul is a prisoner of the body.

The Gallery was founded by Grand Duke Pietro Leopold in 1784 to provide students with examples of art from every period. The big, busy Mannerist paintings around the *David* are by Michelangelo's contemporaries, among them Pontormo's *Venus and Cupid*, with a Michelangelesque Venus among theatre masks. Other rooms contain a good selection of quattrocento painting, including the *Madonna del Mare* by Botticelli, a damaged Baldovinetti, the *Thebaid*, by a follower of Uccello, and Perugino's *Deposition*. The painted frontal of the **Adimari chest** shows a delightful wedding scene of the 1450s, with the Baptistry in the background, that has been reproduced in half the books ever written about the Renaissance.

The hall off to the left of the *David* was formerly the women's ward of a hospital, depicted in a greenish painting by Pontormo. Now it is used as a gallery of plaster models by 19th-century members of the Accademia, a surreal, bright white Neoclassical crowd.

Opificio delle Pietre Dure

Around the corner from the Accademia, in Via degli Alfani 78, is the workshop of *pietre dure*, inlaid 'hard stones' or semi-precious stones (9–1, closed Sun; adm). Cosimo I was the first to actively promote what was to become Florence's special craft, and it was Ferdinando I who founded the Opificio in 1588, as a centre for craftsmen.

Still on Via degli Alfani, across Via dei Servi, stands the **Rotonda di Santa Maria degli Angeli**, an octagonal building begun by Brunelleschi in 1434, one of his last works and one of the first centralized buildings of the Renaissance.

Piazza Santissima Annunziata

This lovely square, really the only Renaissance attempt at a unified ensemble in Florence, is surrounded on three sides by arcades. In its centre, gazing down the splendid vista of Via dei Servi towards the Duomo, stands the *equestrian statue of Ferdinand I* (1607), by Giambologna and his pupil Pietro Tacca, made of bronze from Turkish cannons captured during the Battle of Lepanto. More fascinating than Ferdinand are the pair of bizarre Baroque fountains, also by Tacca, that share the square. Though possessed of a nominally marine theme, they resemble tureens of bouillabaisse that any ogre would be proud to serve.

Filippo Brunelleschi, in the 1420s, struck the first blow for classical calm in this piazza when he built the celebrated **Spedale degli Innocenti** and its famous portico—an architectural landmark, but also a monument to Renaissance Italy's long, hard and ultimately unsuccessful struggle towards some kind of social consciousness. Even in the best of times, Florence's poor were treated like dirt; if any enlightened soul had been so bold as to propose even a modern conservative 'trickle down' theory to the Medici and the banking elite, their first thought would have been how to stop the leaks. Babies, at least, were treated a little better. The Spedale degli Innocenti was the first hospital for foundlings in Italy and the world, and still serves as an orphanage today, as well as the local nursery school.

The Spedale was Brunelleschi's first completed work and demonstrates his use of geometrical proportions adapted to traditional Tuscan Romanesque architecture. His lovely portico is adorned with the famous blue and white tondoes of infants in swaddling clothes by Andrea della Robbia, added as an appeal to charity in the 1480s after several children died of malnutrition. Brunelleschi also designed the two beautiful cloisters of the convent; the **Chiostro delle Donne**, reserved for the hospital's nurses, is especially fine. Upstairs, the **Museo dello Spedale** (9–2, Sun 8–1, closed Wed; adm) contains a number of detached frescoes from Ognissanti and other churches, among them an unusual series of red and orange prophets by Alessandro Allori; other works include a *Madonna and Saints* by Piero di Cosimo, a *Madonna and Child* by Luca della Robbia, and the brilliant *Adoration of the Magi* (1488) painted by Domenico Ghirlandaio for the hospital's church, a crowded, colourful composition featuring portraits of members of the Arte della Lana, who funded the Spedale.

Santissima Annunziata

The second portico on the piazza was built in 1600 in front of Florence's high society church, Santissima Annunziata. Founded in 1250, the church was rebuilt by Michelozzo beginning in 1444 and funded by the Medici, who saw the need for a bigger, grander church to house the pilgrims attracted by a miraculous image of the Virgin. As a shelter for the crowds, Michelozzo designed the **Chiostrino dei Voti**, an atrium in front of the church. Most of the Chiostrino's frescoes are by Andrea del Sarto and his students but the most enchanting work is Alesso Baldovinetti's *Nativity* (1462)—unfortunately faded, though you can make out the ghost of a transcendent landscape. Also present are two youthful works: Pontormo's *Visitation* and Rosso Fiorentino's more Mannerist *Assumption*.

The interior is the most gaudy, lush Baroque creation in the city, the only one the Florentines ever spent much money on during the Counter-Reformation. Michelozzo's design includes an unusual polygonal Tribune around the sanctuary, derived from antique buildings and entered by way of a triumphal arch designed by Alberti. Directly to the left as you enter is Michelozzo's marble **Tempietto**, hung with lamps and candles, built to house the miraculous *Annunciation*, painted by a monk, with the help of an angel who painted the Virgin's face. Its construction was funded by the Medici, who couldn't resist adding an inscription on the floor that 'The marble alone cost 4000 florins!' The ornate canopy over the *tempietto* was added in the 17th century.

The next two chapels on the left side contain frescoes by Andrea del Castagno, painted in the 1450s but whitewashed over by the Church when it read Vasari's phoney story that Castagno murdered his fellow painter Domenico Veneziano—a difficult feat, since Veneziano outlived his supposed murderer by several years. Rediscovered in 1864, Castagno's fresco of *St Julian and the Saviour* in the first chapel has some strange Baroque bedfellows by Giambattista Foggini; the next chapel contains his highly unusual *Holy Trinity with St Jerome*. The right aisle's fifth chapel contains a fine example of an early Renaissance tomb, that of the obscure Orlando de' Medici by Bernardo Rossellino. The neighbouring chapel in the transept contains a painted crucifix by Baldovinetti, while the next one has a *Pietà*, the funerary monument of Cosimo I's court sculptor and Cellini's arch-rival Baccio Bandinelli; in this *Pietà* he put his own features on Nicodemus, as Michelangelo did in the *Pietà* in the Museo del Duomo. Bandinelli's most lasting contribution (or piece of mischief) was his establishing of the first 'Accademia' of art in 1531, which eventually did away with the old artist-pupil relationship for the more impersonal approach of the art school.

Nine semicircular chapels radiate from the Tribune. The one in the rear contains the *sarcophagus of Giambologna*, a far more successful follower of Michelangelo; his pupil Pietro Tacca is buried with him, in this chapel designed by Giambologna before his death. The next chapel to the left contains a *Resurrection* by Bronzino, one of his finest religious paintings. On the left side of Alberti's triumphal arch, under a statue of St Peter, is the grave of Andrea del Sarto; next to it is the *Tomb of Bishop Angelo Marzi Medici* (1546), one of Florence's loudest Counter-Reformation blasts.

A door from the left transept leads into the **Chiostro dei Morti**, most notable for Andrea del Sarto's highly original *Madonna del Sacco* (1525), named after the sacks of grain on which St Joseph leans. The **Cappella di San Luca**, located off the cloister (but rarely open), belongs to Florence's Academy of Design and contains the graves of Cellini, Pontormo, Franciabigio and other artists.

Archaeology Museum

From Piazza SS. Annunziata, Via della Colonna leads to Florence's **Museo Archeologico** (9–2, Sun 9–1, closed Mon; adm), housed in the 17th-century Palazzo della Crocetta, originally built for Grand Duchess Maria Maddalena of Austria. Like nearly every other museum in Florence, this impressive collection was begun by the Medici, beginning with Cosimo il Vecchio and accelerating with the insatiable Cosimo I and his heirs. The Medici were especially fond of Etruscan things, while the impressive Egyptian collection was begun by Leopold II in the 1830s. At the time of writing the museum is undergoing rearrangement, but with a little luck you'll be able to find your way around.

The ground floor is devoted to Greek and Etruscan art, including the famous bronze *Chimera*, a remarkable beast with the three heads of a lion, goat and snake. This Etruscan work of the 5th century BC, dug up near Arezzo in 1555 and immediately snatched by Cosimo I, had a great influence on Mannerist artists. There is no Mannerist fancy about its origins, though; like all such composite monsters, it is a religious icon, a calendar beast symbolizing the three seasons of the ancient Mediterranean agricultural year. In the same hall stands the *Arringatore*, or Orator, a monumental bronze of the Hellenistic period, a civic-minded and civilized-looking gentleman, dedicated to Aulus Metellus.

Among the beautiful, often strange Etruscan urns and alabaster sarcophagi, mirrors and small bronzes, there is plenty of Greek art; Etruscan noble families were wont to buy up all they could afford. The beautiful Hellenistic horse's head once adorned the Palazzo Medici-Riccardi. The *Idolino*, a bronze of a young athlete, is believed to be a Roman copy of a 5th-century BC Greek original. There is an excellent *Kouros*, a young man in the archaic style from 6th-century BC Sicily, and some beautiful vases. An unusual, recent find, the silver *Baratti Amphora*, was made in the 4th century BC in Antioch and covered with scores of small medallions showing mythological figures. Scholars believe that the images and their arrangement may encode an entire system of belief, the secret teaching of one of the mystic-philosophical cults common in Hellenistic times, and they hope some day to decipher it.

The Egyptian collection has recently been modernized; there are some interesting small statuettes, mummies, canopic vases, and a unique wood-and-bone chariot, nearly completely preserved, found in a 14th-century BC tomb in Thebes. Out in the garden are several reconstructed Etruscan tombs (usually closed). A magnificent collection of precious stones and cameos, coins, and sculpture is kept under wraps and may only be visited by scholars with special permission.

Santa Maria Maddalena dei Pazzi and the Synagogue

East of the Archaeological Museum, Via della Colonna becomes one of Florence's typical straight, boring Renaissance streets. It's worth detouring down Borgo Pinti, to no. 58, to visit one of the city's least known but most intriguing churches, **Santa Maria Maddalena dei Pazzi**, a fine example of architectural syncretism (open 9–12 and 5–7).

The church itself was founded in the 13th century, rebuilt in classically Renaissance style by Giuliano da Sangallo, then given a full dose of Baroque when the church was rededicated to the Counter-Reformation saint of the Pazzi family. Inside it's all high theatre, with a gaudy *trompe l'oeil* ceiling, paintings by Luca Giordano, florid chapels, and a wild marble chancel. From the Sacristy a door leads down into a crypt full of mouldering ecclesiastics to the Chapter House, which contains a fresco of the *Crucifixion* (1496), one of Perugino's masterpieces. Despite the symmetry and quiet, contemplative grief of the five figures at the foot of the Cross and the magic stillness of the luminous Tuscan-Umbrian landscape, the fresco has a powerful impact, giving the viewer the uncanny sensation of being able to walk right into the scene.

Nearby, on Via Farina, stands Florence's tall and charming **Synagogue** (1874–82), done in a sort of Mozarabic Pre-Raphaelite architecture inspired by the Hagia Sophia and the Transito Synagogue of Toledo. Florence's Jewish community, although today only 1200 strong, has long been one of the most important in Italy, invited to Florence by the Republic in 1430, but repeatedly exiled and readmitted after that.

Florence's Ghetto, begun by Cosimo I in 1551, was opened in 1848, and demolished soon after, creating the need for a new synagogue. Although seriously damaged by the Nazis in August 1944—and later by the Arno in 1966—it has been lovingly restored. Security is tight, but the synagogue may be toured Mon, Tues, and Thurs 2–5:30 and Sun 9:30–12:30 and 2–5:30 (men must cover their heads). There's a small **Jewish Museum** upstairs, with a documentary history of Florentine Jews as well as ritual and ceremonial items from the synagogue's treasure (open May–Sept on Sun, Mon and Wed 9–6, Tues and Thurs 9–1; in April and Oct, Sun and Thurs 9–1).

From the synagogue it's a long two blocks north to Piazza Donatello. Donatello's name deserves better than this traffic conundrum, a swollen artery in Florence's busy system of *viali* that take traffic around the centre. Pity Elizabeth Barrett Browning (1809–61) and the other expatriates buried in the piazza's **English Cemetery**; they deserve better than to spend eternity in a traffic island.

Sant'Ambrogio and the Flea Market

The streets of Sant'Ambrogio, south of the synagogue, are among the most dusty and piquant in the centre city, a place where tourists seldom tread. Life revolves around **Sant'Ambrogio** and its neighbouring food market, made of cast iron in 1873; the church (rebuilt in the 13th century, 19th-century façade) is of interest for its artwork: the second chapel on the right has a lovely fresco of the *Madonna enthroned with saints* by Orcagna (or his school) and the **Cappella del Miracolo**, just left of the high altar, contains Mino da Fiesole's celebrated marble *Tabernacle* (1481) and his own tomb. The chapel has a fresco of a procession by Cosimo Rosselli, especially interesting for its depiction of 15th-century costume and its contemporary portraits. Andrea Verrocchio is buried in the fourth chapel on the left; on the wall by the second altar, there's a *Nativity* by Baldovinetti. The fresco of an atypical *St Sebastian* on the entrance wall is by Agnolo Gaddi.

From Sant'Ambrogio take Via Pietrapiana to the bustling **Piazza dei Ciompi**, named after the wool-workers' revolt of 1378. In the morning, Florence's flea market or **Mercatino** takes place here, the best place in town to buy that 1940s radio or outdated ball gown you've always wanted. One side of the square is graced with the **Loggia del**

Pesce, built by Vasari in 1568 for the fishmongers of the Mercato Vecchio; when that was demolished the loggia was salvaged and re-erected here.

Casa Buonarroti

Michelangelo never lived in this house, at Via Ghibellina 70, though he purchased it in 1508. That wasn't the point, especially to an artist who had no thought for his own personal comfort, or anyone else's—he never washed, and never took off his boots, even in bed. Real estate was an obsession of his, always working to restore the status of the semi-noble but impoverished Buonarroti family. His nephew Leonardo inherited the house and several works of art in 1564; later he bought the two houses next door to make the house a memorial to his uncle, hiring artists to paint scenes from Michelangelo's life. In the mid-19th century, the house was opened to the public as a Michelangelo museum (9–2, Sun 9–1, closed Tues; adm).

The ground floor is dedicated to mostly imaginary portraits of the artist, and works of art collected by his nephew's descendants, including an eclectic Etruscan and Roman collection and a lovely predella of the *Life of St Nicolas of Bari* by Giovanni di Francesco. The main attractions, however, are upstairs, beginning with Michelangelo's earliest known work, the beautiful bas-relief of *The Madonna of the Steps* (1490–1), the precocious work of a 16-year-old influenced by Donatello and studying in the household of Lorenzo the Magnificent; the relief of a *Battle Scene*, inspired by classical models, dates from the same period. Small models and drawings of potential projects line the walls; there's the wooden model for the façade of San Lorenzo, with designs for some of the statuary Michelangelo intended to fill in its austere blank spaces—as was often the case, his ideas were far too grand for his patron's purse and patience.

The next four rooms were painted in the 17th century to illustrate Michelangelo's life, virtues, and apotheosis, depicting a polite, deferential, and pleasant Michelangelo hobnobbing with popes. Those who know the artist best from *The Agony and the Ecstasy* may think they painted the wrong man by mistake. One of the best sections is a frieze of famous Florentines in the library. Other exhibits include a painted wooden *Crucifix* discovered in S. Spirito in 1963 and believed by most scholars to be a documented one by Michelangelo, long thought to be lost; the contrapposto position of the slender body, and the fact that only Michelangelo would carve a nude Christ weigh in favour of the attribution.

Santa Croce

No place in Florence so feeds the urge to dispute as the church of Santa Croce, Tuscany's 'Westminster Abbey', the largest Franciscan basilica in Italy, a must-see for every tour group. It was here that Stendhal gushed: 'I had attained to that supreme degree of sensibility where the divine intimations of art merge with the impassioned sensuality of emotion. As I emerged from the port of Santa Croce, I was seized with a fierce palpitation of the heart; I walked in constant fear of falling to the ground.' But don't be put off; most people manage to emerge from a visit without tripping over themselves.

The contradictions begin in the **Piazza Santa Croce**, which has its interesting points—the row of medieval houses with projecting upper storeys, supported by stone brackets; the faded bloom of dancing nymphs on the **Palazzo dell'Antella**; the curious

SANTA CROCE, FLORENCE

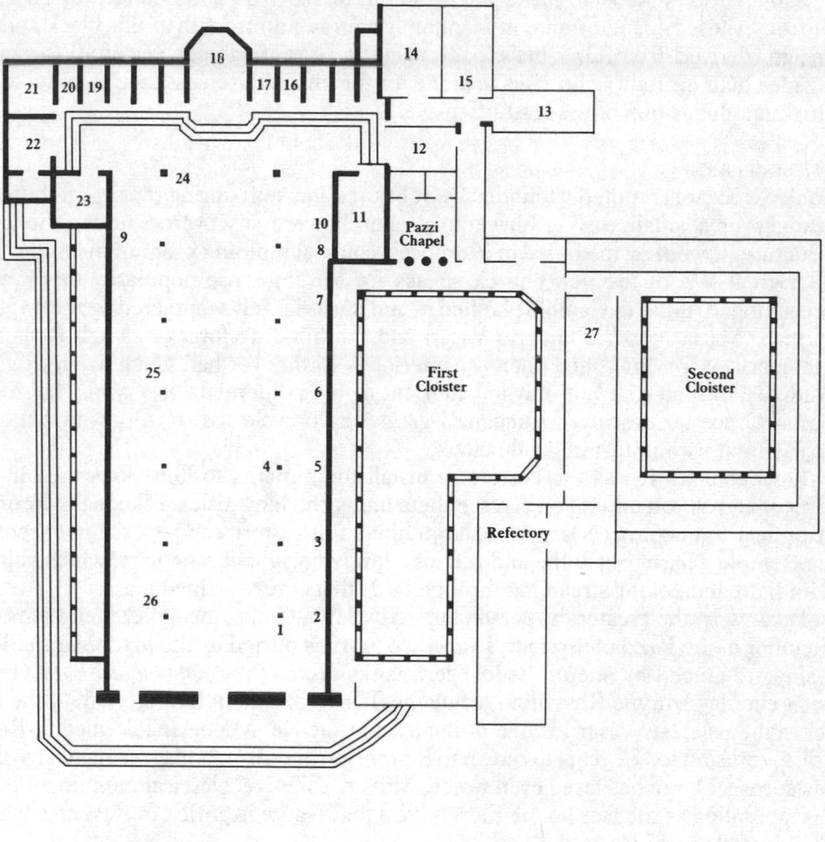

1 Madonna de Latte
2 Tomb Of Michelangelo
3 Monument To Dante
4 Benedetto da Maiano's Pulpit
5 Vittorio Alfieri's Tomb
6 Tomb Of Machiavelli
7 Donatello's 'Annunciation'
8 Tomb of Leonardo Bruni
9 Tomb Of Carlo Marsuppini
10 Tomb of Rossini
11 Castellani Chapel
12 Baroncelli Chapel
13 Medici Chapel
14 Sacristy
15 Rinnuccini Chapel
16 Peruzzi Chapel
17 Bardi Chapel
18 Sanctuary
19 Bardi di Libertà Chapel
20 Bardi di Vernio Chapel
21 Niccolini Chapel
22 Bardi Chapel
23 Salviati Chapel
24 Monument To Alberti
25 Tomb Of Lorenzo Ghiberti
26 Galileo's Tomb
27 Museo dell' Opera di S. Croce

14th-century **Palazzo Serristori-Cocchi**, opposite the church; a grim 19th-century statue of Dante (if Dante really looked like that, it's no wonder Beatrice married someone else). Because this piazza is the lowest-lying in the city, it suffered the worst in the 1966 flood, when 18 feet of oily water poured in.

Santa Croce's Neo-Gothic façade was built in 1857–63 and financed by Sir Francis Sloane, whose Sloane Square in London has more admirers than this black and white design, derived from Orcagna's Tabernacle in Orsanmichele. Yet of all the modern façades built on Italy's churches to atone for the chronic Renaissance inability to finish anything, this is one of the least offensive.

THE INTERIOR

Santa Croce was reputedly founded by St Francis himself; during repairs after the flood, vestiges of a small early 13th-century church were discovered under the present structure. It went by the board in Florence's colossal building programme of the 1290s. The great size of the new church speaks for the immense popularity of Franciscan preaching. Arnolfo di Cambio planned it, and it was largely completed by the 1450s, but as in S. Maria Novella, Giorgio Vasari and the blinding forces of High Renaissance mediocrity were unleashed upon the interior. Vasari never had much use for the art of Andrea Orcagna—he not only left him out of his influential *Lives of the Artists* but in Santa Croce he destroyed Orcagna's great fresco cycle that once covered the nave, replacing it with uninspired side altars.

For centuries it was the custom to install monuments to illustrious men in Santa Croce, and as you enter, you can see them lining the long aisles. Like many Franciscan churches, Santa Croce's large size, its architectural austerity and open timber roof make it resemble a barn, but at the end there's a lovely polygonal sanctuary, which shimmers with light and colour streaming through its 14th-century stained glass.

Perversely, the greater the person buried in Santa Croce, the uglier their memorial. A member of the Pazzi conspiracy, Francesco Nori, is buried by the first pillar in the right aisle, and graced by one of the loveliest works of art, the *Madonna del Latte* (1478), a bas-relief by Antonio Rossellino, while the **Tomb of Michelangelo** (1570, the first in the right aisle), by Vasari, is one of the least attractive. Michelangelo died in Rome in 1564, refusing for 35 years to return to Florence while alive, but agreeing to give the city his corpse. Dante has fared even worse, with an 1829 Neoclassical monument that's as disappointing as the fact (to the Florentines) that Dante is buried in Ravenna, where he died in exile in 1321.

Facing the nave, Benedetto da Maiano's **marble pulpit** (1476) is one of the most beautiful the Renaissance ever produced. Behind it, the **Vittorio Alfieri Monument** (1809) was sculpted by Neoclassical master Antonio Canova and paid for by his lover, the Countess of Albany. Next is the nondescript 18th-century **Monument of Niccolò Machiavelli**, and then Donatello's **Annunciation** (1430s?), a tabernacle in gilded limestone, the angel wearing a remarkably sweet expression as he gently breaks the news to a grave, thoughtful Madonna. Bernardo Rossellino's **Tomb of Leonardo Bruni** (1447), another masterpiece of the Renaissance, is perhaps the one monument that best fits the man it honours. Bruni was a Greek scholar, a humanist, and the author of the first major historical work of the period, *The History of Florence*, a copy of which his tranquil effigy holds. The tomb, with its Brunelleschian architectural setting, proved a great inspiration to other artists, most obviously Desiderio da Settignano and his equally beautiful **Tomb of Carlo Marsuppini** (1453) directly across the nave, and the less inspired, more imitative **Monument to Rossini** crowded in to the left. The last tomb in the aisle belongs to poet and patriot Ugo Foscolo.

Santa Croce is especially rich in trecento frescoes, providing a unique opportunity to compare the work of Giotto with his followers. The south transept's **Castellani Chapel** has some of the later, more decorative compositions, by Agnolo Gaddi (*Scenes from the Lives of Saints*, 1380s). The beautiful **Baroncelli Chapel** was painted with *Scenes from the Life of the Virgin* by Agnolo's father Taddeo, Giotto's assistant, in the 1330s, and includes a bright, gilded altarpiece, the *Coronation of the Virgin* by Giotto and his workshop.

The next portal gives on to a **Corridor** and the **Medici Chapel**, both designed by Michelozzo, containing one of Andrea della Robbia's finest altarpieces and a 19th-century fake Donatello, a relief of the *Madonna and Child* that fooled the experts for decades. From the corridor a door leads to the **Sacristy**, its walls frescoed by Taddeo Gaddi (*The Crucifixion*), Spinello Aretino, and Niccolò di Pietro Gerini. Behind the 14th-century grille, the **Rinuccini Chapel** was frescoed by one of Giotto's most talented followers, the Lombard Giovanni da Milano, in the 1360s.

GIOTTO'S CHAPELS

The frescoes in the two chapels to the right of the sanctuary, the **Peruzzi Chapel** and the **Bardi Chapel**, were painted by the legendary Giotto in the 1330s, towards the end of his life, when the artist returned from Padua and his work in the Arena chapel. The frescoes have not fared well during the subsequent 650 years; Giotto, to begin with, painted large parts of the walls *a secco* (on dry plaster) instead of *affresco* (on wet plaster), presenting the same kind of preservation problems that bedevil Leonardo's *Last Supper*; secondly, the 18th century thought so little of the frescoes that they were whitewashed over as eyesores. Rediscovered some 150 years later and finally restored in 1959, the frescoes now, even though fragmentary, may be seen more or less as Giotto painted them. The Peruzzi Chapel contains scenes from the *Lives of St John the Evangelist and the Baptist*. In the Bardi Chapel the subject is the *Life of St Francis*, which makes an interesting comparison with the frescoes in Assisi. The contrast between Giotto's frescoes and the chapel's 13th-century altarpiece, also showing scenes of the *Life of St Francis*, is a fair yardstick for measuring the breadth of the Giottesque revolution.

Agnolo Gaddi designed the stained glass around the **Sanctuary**, as well as the fascinating series of frescoes on the *Legend of the True Cross*—how Seth received a branch from St Michael and planted it over Adam's grave, how the tree that grew from it was shaped into a beam for a bridge, then buried by Solomon when his guest the Queen of Sheba prophesied that it would some day bring about the end of the Jews. The beam was dug up and made into Christ's Cross. It made a miraculous reappearance in Emperor Constantine's dream, before the Battle of Milvian Bridge, when he heard a voice saying that under this sign he should conquer. His mother, St Helen, went to the Holy Land and found the Cross, but it was stolen by a Persian king and eventually recovered by Emperor Heraclius.

Further to the left are two more chapels frescoed by followers of Giotto: the fourth, the **Bardi di Libertà Chapel**, by Bernardo Daddi and the last, the **Bardi di Vernio**

Chapel, by Maso di Banco, one of the most innovative and mysterious artists of the trecento. The frescoes illustrate the little-known *Life of St Sylvester*—his baptism of Emperor Constantine, the resurrection of the bull, the closing of the dragon's mouth and resurrection of two sorcerers; on the other wall of the chapel are a *Dream of Constantine* and *Vision of SS. Peter and Paul*. In the corner of the transept, the richly marbled **Niccolini Chapel** offers a Mannerist-Baroque change of pace, built by Antonio Dossi in 1584, and decorated with paintings by Allori. Next, the second **Bardi Chapel** houses the famous Crucifix by Donatello that Brunelleschi called 'a peasant on the Cross'. The last of the funeral monuments, near the door, are those of Lorenzo Ghiberti and Galileo, the latter an 18th-century work. For running afoul of the Inquisition, Galileo was not permitted a Christian burial until 1737.

THE PAZZI CHAPEL

One of Santa Croce's chapels carries an entrance fee, but it's well worth it (9–12:30, 3–5, until 6:30 in the summer, closed Wed; adm). Brunelleschi, who could excel on the monumental scale of the cathedral dome, saved some of his best work for small places. Without knowing the architect, and something about the austere religious tendencies of the Florentines, the Pazzi Chapel is inexplicable, a Protestant reformation in architecture, unlike anything ever built before. The 'vocabulary' is essential Brunelleschi, the geometric forms emphasized by the simplicity of the decoration: *pietra serena* pilasters and rosettes on white walls, arches, 12 terracotta tondoes of the Apostles by Luca della Robbia, coloured rondels of the Evangelists in the pendentives by Donatello, and a small stained-glass window by Baldovinetti. Even so, that is enough. The contemplative repetition of elements makes for an aesthetic that posed a direct challenge to the International Gothic of the time.

Leaving the Pazzi Chapel (notice Luca della Robbia's terracotta decorations on the portico), a doorway on the left of the cloister leads to another work of Brunelleschi, the **Second Cloister**, with the same subtlety, one of the quietest spots in Florence.

The old monastic buildings off the first cloister now house the **Museo dell'Opera di Santa Croce**, where you can see Cimabue's celebrated *Crucifix*, devastated by the flood, and partly restored after one of Florence's perennial restoration controversies. The refectory wall has another fine fresco by Taddeo Gaddi, of the *Tree of the Cross and the Last Supper*; fragments of Orcagna's frescoes salvaged from Vasari's obliteration squads offer powerful, nightmarish vignettes of The Triumph of Death and Hell. Donatello's huge gilded bronze statue of *St Louis of Toulouse* (1423)—a flawed work representing a flawed character, according to Donatello—was made for the façade of Orsanmichele. The museum also contains works by Andrea della Robbia, and a painting of Mayor Bargellini with a melancholy Santa Croce submerged in the 1966 flood for a backdrop; under the colonnade there's a statue of Florence Nightingale, born in and named after the city in 1820.

Around Santa Croce: the Horne Museum

The east end of Florence, a rambling district packed with artisans and small manufacturers, traditionally served as the artists' quarter in Renaissance times. Still one of the livelier neighbourhoods, with a few lingering artists lodged in the upper storeys, hoping to breathe inspiration from the very stones where Michelangelo walked, it is a good place to observe the workaday Florence behind the glossy façade. Just west of Piazza Santa Croce is a series of streets—Via Bentacorti, Via Torta, and Piazza Peruzzi—which make an almost complete ellipse. These mark the course of the inner arcade of the Roman amphitheatre, some stones of which can still be seen among the foundations of the old palaces.

From Santa Croce, the pretty Borgo S. Croce leads towards the Arno and the delightful **Horne Museum**, housed in a Renaissance palace. Herbert Percy Horne (1844–1916) was an English art historian, biographer of Botticelli, and Florentinophile, who bequeathed his collection to the nation (Via de' Benci 6, open 9–1, 3 mornings a week; adm). A large *Deposition*, the last work of Gozzoli, sadly darkened with age, a painting by the great Sienese Pietro Lorenzetti, and a tondo by Piero di Cosimo hang on the first floor. The next room contains Horne's prize, Giotto's golden painting of young *St Stephen*, also Signorelli's *Redeemer*, a beardless, girlish youth, Beccafumi's *Decalione e Pirra*, and a saccharine *St Sebastian* by Carlo Dolci. Room 3 has a rousing quattrocento battle scene, taken from a marriage chest, good 15th-century wood inlays, and a relief of the head of *St John the Baptist* by Desiderio da Settignano. Upstairs a diptych attributed to Barna da Siena holds pride of place, together with an impressive array of Renaissance furniture and housewares.

North Bank Peripheral Attractions: the Cascine

The newer sections of the city are irredeemably dull. Much of Florence's traffic problem is channelled through its ring of avenues, or *viali*, laid out in the 1860s by Giuseppe Poggi to replace the demolished walls. On and along them are scattered points of interest, including some of the old city gates; the distances involved and danger of carbon monoxide poisoning on the *viali* make the idea of walking insane.

Bus 17C from the station or Duomo will take you through the congestion to the **Cascine**, the long (3.5 km), narrow public park lining this bank of the Arno, originally used as the Medici's dairy farm, or *cascina*, and later as a Grand Ducal hunting park and theatre for public spectacles. A windy autumn day here in 1819 inspired Shelley to compose the *Ode to the West Wind*. Three years later Shelley's drowned body was burnt on a pyre in Viareggio, by his friend Trelawny; curiously, a similar incineration took place in the Cascine in 1870 when the Maharajah of Kohlapur died in Florence. According to ritual his body had to be burned near the confluence of two rivers, in this case, the Arno and Mugnone at the far end of the park, on a spot now marked by the Maharajah's equestrian statue. Florentines come to the Cascine to play; it contains a riding school, race tracks, a small amusement park and zoo for the children, tennis courts, and a swimming-pool.

Beyond the train station, cars and buses hurtle around and around the **Fortezza da Basso**, an enormous bulk built by Antonio da Sangallo on orders from Alessandro de' Medici in 1534. It immediately became the most hated symbol of Medici tyranny. Ironically, the duke who built the the Fortezza da Basso was one of very few to meet his end within its ramparts—stabbed by his relative and bosom companion 'Lorenzaccio' de' Medici. As a fortress, the place never saw any action as thrilling or vicious as the Pitti fashion shows that take place behind the walls in its 1978 aluminium exhibition hall.

Just east of the Fortezza, at the corner of Via Leone X and Viale Milton, there's an unexpected sight rising above the sleepy residential neighbourhood—the five graceful onion domes of the **Russian Church**, made even more exotic by the palm tree tickling its side. In the 19th century, Florence was a popular winter retreat for Russians who could afford it, among them Dostoevsky and Maxim Gorky. Completed by Russian architects in 1904, it is a pretty jewel box of brick and majolica decoration, open on the third Sunday of the month, when morning services are held in Russian.

Stibbert Museum

From Piazza della Libertà, dull Via Vittorio Emanuele heads a kilometre north to Via Stibbert and the Stibbert Museum (alternatively, take bus 31 or 32 from the station). Those who make the journey to see the lifetime's accumulations of Frederick Stibbert (1838–1906), who fought with Garibaldi and hobnobbed with Queen Victoria, can savour Florence's most bizarre museum, and one of the city's most pleasant small parks, laid out by Stibbert with a mouldering Egyptian temple sinking in a pond (open for tours on the hour, 9–1, Sun 9–12:30—when you may wander at will—closed Thurs; adm; and just try to obey the sign on the door: 'Comply with the Forbidden Admittances!').

Stibbert's Italian mother left him a 14th-century house, which he enlarged, joining it to another house to create a sumptuous Victorian's version of what a medieval Florentine house should have looked like—64 rooms to contain a packrat's treasure hoard of all things brilliant and useless, from an attributed Botticelli to snuff boxes, to what a local guide intriguingly describes as 'brass and silver basins, used daily by Stibbert'. Stibbert's serious passion, however, was armour, and he amassed a magnificent collection from all times and places. The best pieces are not arranged in dusty cases, but with a touch of Hollywood, on grim knightly mannequins ranked ready for battle.

The Oltrarno

Once over the Ponte Vecchio, a different Florence reveals itself: greener, quieter, and less burdened with traffic. The Oltrarno is not a large district. A chain of hills squeezes it against the river, and their summits afford some of the best views over the city. Once across the Arno, the Medici's catwalk becomes part of the upper façade of **Santa Felicità**, one of Florence's most ancient churches, believed to have been founded by the Syrian Greek traders who introduced Christianity to the city, and established the first Christian cemetery in the small square in front of the church. Rebuilt in the 18th century, there is one compelling reason to enter, for here, in the first chapel on the right, is the *ne plus ultra* of Mannerism: Pontormo's weirdly luminous *Deposition* (1528), painted in jarring pinks, oranges, and blues that cut through the darkness of the little chapel. The composition itself is highly unconventional, with an effect that derives entirely from the use of figures in unusual, exaggerated poses; there is no sign of a cross, the only background is a single cloud. Sharing the chapel is Pontormo's *Annunciation* fresco, a less idiosyncratic work, as well as four tondoes of the Evangelists in the cupola, partly the work of Pontormo's pupil and adopted son, Bronzino.

The Pitti Palace

As the Medici consolidated their power in Florence, they made a point of buying up the most important properties of their former rivals, especially their proud family palaces.

The most spectacular example of this ducal eminent domain was Cosimo I's acquisition of the Pitti Palace, built in 1457 by a powerful banker named Luca Pitti who seems to have had vague ambitions of toppling the Medici and becoming the big boss himself. The palace, with its extensive grounds, now the Boboli Gardens, was much more pleasant than the medieval Palazzo Vecchio, and in the 1540s Cosimo I and his wife Eleanor of Toledo moved in for good. The palace remained the residence of the Medici, and later the House of Lorraine, until 1868. The original building, said to have been designed by Brunelleschi, was only as wide as the seven central windows of the façade. Succeeding generations found it too small for their burgeoning hoards of bric-à-brac, and added several stages of symmetrical additions, resulting in a long bulky profile, resembling a rusticated Stalinist ministry on its bleak asphalt piazza.

There are eight separate museums in the Pitti, including collections dedicated to clothes, ceramics, and carriages—a tribute to Medici acquisitiveness in the centuries of decadence, a period from which, in the words of Mary McCarthy, 'flowed a torrent of bad taste that has not yet dried up . . . if there had been Toby jugs and Swiss weather clocks available, the Grand Dukes would certainly have collected them.' For the diligent visitor who wants to see everything, the Pitti is pitiless; it is impossible to see all in one day.

GALLERIA PALATINA

The Pitti museum most people see is the Galleria Palatina, containing the Grand Dukes' famous collection of 16th–18th-century paintings, stacked on the walls in enormous gilt frames under the berserk opulence of frescoed ceilings celebrating planets, mythology, and of course, the Medici. The gallery is on the first floor of the right half of the palace (ticket office on the ground floor, off Ammannati's exaggerated rustic courtyard, a Mannerist masterpiece; open 9–2, Sun 9–1, closed Mon; adm, expensive).

The entrance to the Galleria is through the Neoclassical **Sala Castagnoli**, with the *Tavola delle Muse* in its centre, itself an excellent introduction to the Florentine 'decorative arts'; the table, a paragon of the intricate art of *pietra dura*, was made in the 1870s. The Galleria's best paintings are in the five former reception rooms off to the left, with colourful ceilings painted in the 1640s by Pietro da Cortona, one of the most interesting Italian Baroque artists. The first is the **Sala di Venere**, with several works by Titian, including his early *Concert*, believed to have been partly painted by Giorgione; a powerful *Portrait of Pietro Aretino*, his close and caustic friend, who complained to the artist that it was all too accurate and gave it to Cosimo I. There are two beautiful, optimistic landscapes by Rubens, painted at the end of his life, and an uncanny self-portrait, *La Menzogna* (the Falsehood) by Neapolitan Salvator Rosa. The centrepiece statue, the *Venus Italica*, was commissioned by Napoleon from Neoclassical master Antonio Canova in 1812 to replace the Venus de' Medici which he 'centralized' off to Paris—a rare case of the itchy-fingered Corsican trying to pay for something he took.

In the **Sala di Apollo** there's more Titian—his *Portrait of a Grey-eyed Gentleman*, evoking the perfect 16th-century English gentleman, a romantic character with an intense gaze, and his more sensuous than penitent *Mary Magdalene*—as well as works by Andrea del Sarto and Van Dyck.

The **Sala di Marte** has two works of Rubens, *The Four Philosophers*, and the *Consequences of War*, as well as some excellent portraits by Tintoretto and Van Dyck (*Cardinal*

Bentivoglio), and Titian's rather dashing *Cardinal Ippolito de' Medici* in Hungarian costume. Ippolito, despite being destined for the Church, was one of the more high-spirited Medici, and helped defend Vienna from the Ottomans before being poisoned at the age of 24.

The **Sala di Giove**, used as the Medici throne room, contains one of Raphael's best-known portraits, the lovely and serene *Donna Velata* (1516). The small painting of *The Three Ages of Man* is usually attributed to Giorgione. Salviati, Perugino, Fra Bartolomeo, and Andrea del Sarto are also represented; in the **Sala di Saturno** Raphael dominates, with several paintings from his Florence days: *Maddalena and Agnolo Doni* (1506) and the *Madonna 'del Granduca'*, influenced by the paintings of Leonardo. Some 10 years later, Raphael had found his own style, beautifully evident in his famous *Madonna della Seggiola* ('of the chair'), perhaps the most popular work he ever painted, and one that is far more complex and subtle than it appears. The rounded, intertwining figures of the Madonna and Child are seen as if through a slightly convex mirror, bulging out—one of the first examples of conscious illusionism in the Renaissance.

The last of the reception rooms, the **Sala dell'Iliade** (frescoed in the 19th century), has some fine portraits by the Medici court painter and Rubens' friend, Justus Sustermans. Two *Assumptions* by Andrea del Sarto, *Philip II* by Titian, and a Velazquez equestrian portrait of Philip IV share the room with one of the most unusual residents of the gallery, *Queen Elizabeth*, who seems uncomfortable in such company. Just off this room lies the pretty **Sala della Stufa**, frescoed with the *Four Ages of the World* by Pietro da Cortona. Caravaggio's *Sleeping Cupid* is in the next room, the **Sala dell'Educazione di Giove**. A couple of rooms down you can peek into the Empire bathroom of Elisa Baciocchi, Napoleon's sister, who ruled the Département de l'Arno between 1809 and 1814, and seemingly spent much of those years redecorating the Pitti.

Some of the more interesting paintings to ferret out in the remainder of the gallery include Filippino Lippi's *Death of Lucrezia* and Raphael's *Madonna dell'Impannata*, both in the **Sala di Ulisse**. In the adjacent **Sala di Prometeo** don't miss Filippo Lippi's lovely *Tondo of the Madonna and Child*, Rubens' *Three Graces*, and Baldassare Peruzzi's unusual *Dance of Apollo*.

THE STATE APARTMENTS

The right half of the Pitti also contains the State Apartments (same hours as the Galleria Palatina, though at the time of writing closed for restoration). These were last redone in the 19th century by the Dukes of Lorraine, with touches by the Kings of Savoy, who occupied them during Florence's interlude as national capital. Among the garish furnishings, there is a fine series of Gobelin tapestries ordered from Paris by Elisa Baciocchi.

GALLERIA D'ARTE MODERNA

On the second floor above the Galleria Palatina has been installed Florence's modern—read late 18th- and 19th-century—art museum (tickets in the courtyard, same hours as the Galleria Palatina; adm, expensive). Though the monumental stair may leave you breathless (the Medici negotiated it with sedan chairs and strong-shouldered servants), consider a visit for some sunny painting of the Italy of your great-grandparents and some amazing, kitsch statuary, obsessed with death and beauty. The underrated 'Splatterers' or *Macchiaioli* (Tuscan Impressionists) illuminate room 16 and the rest of the museum, forming an excellent introduction to the works by Silvestro Lega, Giovanni Fattori, Nicolo Cannicci, Francesco Gioli, Federigo Zandomeneghi, and Telemaco Signorini, with an interval dedicated to the Risorgimento battle scenes. While the canvases radiate light, the morbid statues become more frequent and stupefying: don't miss the *Pregnant Nun* and the *Suicide*, by Antonio Ciseri in Room 19.

MUSEO DEGLI ARGENTI

The ground floor on the left side of the Pitti was used as the Medici summer apartments and now contains the family's remarkable collection of jewellery, vases, trinkets, and pricey curiosities (9–2, Sun 9–1, closed Mon; adm valid for Costume and Porcelain museums). The Grand Duke's guests would be received in four of the most delightfully frescoed rooms in Florence, beginning with the **Sala di Giovanni di San Giovanni**, named after the artist who painted it in the 1630s. The theme is the usual Medicean self-glorification—but nowhere does such dubious material achieve such flamboyant treatment. Here the Muses, chased from Paradise, find refuge with Lorenzo il Magnifico; Lorenzo smiles as he studies a bust of Pan by Michelangelo. His real passion, a collection of antique vases carved of semi-precious stones or crystal, is displayed in a room off to the left; the vases were dispersed with the rise of Savonarola, but Lorenzo's nephew Cardinal Giulio had no trouble in relocating them, as Lorenzo had his initials LAUR.MED. deeply incised into each. The three **Reception rooms** were painted in shadowy blue *trompe l'oeil* by two masterful Bolognese illusionists, Agostino Michele and Angelo Colonna.

The Grand Dukes' treasure hoard is up on the mezzanine. These golden toys are only a fraction of what the Medici had accumulated; despite the terms of Anna Maria's will, leaving everything to Florence, the Lorraines sold off the most valuable pieces and jewels to finance Austria's wars. Among the leftovers here, however, is a veritable apoplexy of fantastical bric-à-brac: jewelled bugs, cameos, sea monster pendants, interlaced ivory cubes, carved cherry pits, gilt nautilus shells, chalices made of ostrich eggs, enough ceramic plates to serve an army, a Mexican mitre made of feathers, intricate paper cutouts, cups carved from buffalo horns, and 17th-century busts and figurines made of seashells that would not shame the souvenir stand of any seaside resort.

MORE PITTI MUSEUMS

The **Museum of Costumes** (same hours as the Argenti) is housed in the Meridiana pavilion, the south extension of the Pitti, a dull addition added by the Lorraines; its prize exhibit is the reconstructed dress that Eleanor of Toledo was buried in—the same one that she wears in Bronzino's famous portrait. The **Porcelain Museum** (open Tues, Thurs, and Sat 9–2) is housed in the airy casino of Cosimo III, out in the Giardino del Cavaliere in the Boboli Gardens (follow the signs). The **Museo delle Carrozze**, with a collection of Medici and Lorraine carriages and sedan chairs, has been closed for years.

Finally, the hardest part of the Pitti to get into may be worth the trouble if you're fond of Spanish painting. Until it finds a permanent home, the **Contini Bonacossi Collection** resides in the Meridiana pavilion. This recent bequest includes works of Cimabue, Duccio, and Giovanni Bellini, some sculpture and china, and also paintings by El Greco, Goya, and Velasquez—the last represented by an exceptional work, *The Water Carrier of*

Seville (open for tours at 10 am, Tues, Thurs, and Sat—you must make an appointment with the secretary of the Uffizi Gallery).

Boboli Gardens

Stretching back invitingly from the Pitti, the shady green of the Boboli Gardens, Florence's largest (and only) central public garden, is an irresistible oasis in the middle of a stone-hard city. Originally laid out by Buontalenti, the Boboli reigns as queen of all formal Tuscan gardens, the most elaborate and theatrical, a Mannerist–Baroque co-production of Nature and Artifice laid out over a steep hill, full of shady nooks and pretty walks and beautifully kept. The park is guarded by a platoon of statuary, many of them Roman works, while others are absurd Mannerist pieces like Cosimo I's court dwarf posing as a chubby Bacchus astride a turtle (near the left-hand entrance, next to Vasari's Corridor).

Just beyond this lies the remarkable **Grotta di Buontalenti**, one of the architect's most imaginative works, anticipating Gaudì with his dripping, stalactite-like stone, from which fantastic limestone animals struggle to emerge. Casts of Michelangelo's *nonfiniti* slaves stand in the corners, replacing the originals put there by the Medici, while back in the shadowy depths stands a luscious statue of Venus coming from her bath by Giambologna. For all that, the grotto is not a favourite with the Florentines and is usually locked up.

The **Amphitheatre**, ascending in regular tiers from the palace, was designed like a small Roman circus to hold Medici court spectacles. It has a genuine obelisk, of Rameses II from Heliopolis, snatched by the ancient Romans and shipped here by the Medici branch in Rome. The granite basin, large enough to submerge an elephant, came from the Roman Baths of Caracalla. Straight up the terrace is the **Neptune Fountain**; a signposted path leads from there to the pretty **Kaffeehaus**, a boat-like pavilion with a prow and deck offering a fine view of Florence and drinks in the summer. From here the path continues up to the **Belvedere Fort** (see p. 155). Other signs from the Neptune Fountain point the way up to the secluded **Giardino del Cavaliere**, located on a bastion on Michelangelo's fortifications (open same hours as the Porcelain Museum). Cosimo III built the casino here to escape the heat in the Pitti Palace; the view over the ancient villas, vineyards, and olives is pure Tuscan enchantment.

Casa Guidi

In the old days the neighbourhood around the Pitti was a fashionable address, but in the 19th century rents for a furnished palace were incredibly low. Shortly after their secret marriage, the Brownings found one of these, the **Casa Guidi** at Piazza S. Felice 8, the perfect place to settle; during their 13 years here they wrote their most famous poetry. Now owned by the Browning Institute, you can visit it weekdays 3–6. Dostoevsky wrote *The Idiot* while living nearby, at no. 21 Piazza Pitti.

Stuffed Animals and Wax Cadavers

Past the Pitti on Via Romana 17, are two of Florence's great oddball attractions, both part of the **La Specola** museum. The Zoological Section (Tues 9–12:30, Sun 9–12) has a charmingly old-fashioned collection of nearly everything that walks, flies, or swims, from the humble sea worm to the rare Madagascar Aye-Aye or the swordfish, with an accessory case of different blades. Some trophies bagged by the hunt-crazy House of Savoy are displayed, and near the end come small wax models of human and animal anatomy, wax eggs, a wax peeled chicken and wax skinned cat. The real horror show stuff, however, is kept hidden away in the **Museum of Waxes** (Sat 2–5, 3–6 June–Sept). Dotty, prudish old Cosimo III was a hypochondriac and morbidly obsessed with diseases, which his favourite artist, a Sicilian priest named Gaetano Zumbo, was able to portray with revolting realism. His macabre anatomical models were one of the main sights for Grand Tourists in the 18th century.

Santo Spirito

Piazza Santo Spirito, the centre of the Oltrarno, usually has a few market stalls under the plane trees as well as a quiet café or two; on one side, a plain 18th-century façade hides Brunelleschi's last, and perhaps greatest church. He designed Santo Spirito in 1440 and lived only to see one column erected, but subsequent architects were faithful to his elegant plan for the interior. This is done in the architect's favourite pale grey and *pietra serena* articulation, a rhythmic forest of columns with semicircular chapels gracefully recessed into the transepts and the three arms of the crossing. The effect is somewhat spoiled by the ornate 17th-century *baldacchino*, which sits in this enchanted garden of architecture like a 19th-century bandstand.

The art in the chapels is meagre, as most of the good paintings were sold off over the years. The best include Filippino Lippi's beautiful *Madonna and Saints* in the right transept, Verrocchio's jewel-like *St Monica and Nuns*, an unusual composition and certainly one of the blackest paintings of the Renaissance, pervaded with a dusky, mysterious quality; Verrocchio, who taught both Leonardo and Botticelli, was a hermetic alchemist on the side. The fine marble altarpiece and decoration in the next chapel is by Sansovino; the elaborate barrel-vaulted **Vestibule** and octagonal **Sacristy**, entered from the left aisle, are by Giuliano da Sangallo, inspired by Brunelleschi.

To the left of the church, in the refectory of the vanished 14th-century convent are the scanty remains of a *Last Supper* and well-preserved, highly dramatic *Crucifixion* by Andrea Orcagna, in which Christ is seen alone against an enormous dark sky, with humanity ranged below and angels like white swallows swirling around in a cosmic whirlwind. The refectory also contains an interesting collection of Romanesque odds and ends, including 13th-century stone sea lions from Naples (open 9–1, Sun 8–1, closed Mon; adm).

Santa Maria del Carmine

There is little to say about the surroundings, the piazza, the rough stone façade, or the interior of the Oltrarno's other great church, Santa Maria del Carmine, which burned in 1771 and was reconstructed shortly after. Miraculously, the **Brancacci Chapel**, one of the landmarks in Florentine art, survived both the flames and attempts by the authorities to replace it with something more fashionable. Three artists worked on the Brancacci's frescoes: Masolino, who began them in 1425, and who designed the cycle, his pupil Masaccio, who worked on them alone for a year before following his master to Rome, where he died at the age of 27, and Filippino Lippi, who finished them 50 years later. Filippino took care to imitate Masaccio as closely as possible, and the frescoes have an appearance of stylistic unity. Between 1981 and 1988 they were subject to one of Italy's most publicized restorations, cleansed of 550 years of dirt and overpainting, enabling us to see what so thrilled the painters of the Renaissance.

Masaccio in his day was a revolution and a revelation in his solid, convincing naturalism; his figures stand in space, without any fussy ornamentation or Gothic grace, very much inspired by Donatello's sculptures. Masaccio conveyed emotion with broad, quick brush strokes and with his use of light, most obvious in his almost Impressionistic scene of the *Expulsion of Adam and Eve*, one of the most memorable and harrowing images created in the Renaissance. In the *Tribute Money*, the young artist displays his mastery of Brunelleschian artificial perspective and light effects. The three episodes in the fresco show an official demanding tribute from the city, St Peter fetching it, on Christ's direction, from the mouth of a fish, and lastly, his handing over of the money to the official. Other works by 'Shabby Tom' include *St Peter Baptising* on the upper register, and *St Peter Healing with his Shadow* and *St Peter Enthroned and Resurrecting the Son of the King of Antioch*, the right half of which was finished by Fra Filippino Lippi. The more elegant and unearthly Masolino is responsible for the remainder, except for the lower register's *Release of St Peter from Prison*, *St Peter Crucified* and *St Paul Visiting St Peter in Prison*, all by Filippino Lippi, based on Masaccio's sketches (open 7–12 and 3:30–7).

Among the detached frescoes displayed in the cloister and refectory is a good one by Fra Filippo Lippi, who was born nearby in Via dell'Ardiglione.

Around the Oltrarno

Those with the time or inclination to stroll the streets of the Oltrarno can discover one of the city's last real residential neighbourhoods, the streets lined with bakeries and barbershops instead of boutiques and restaurants. The westernmost quarter within the medieval walls, Borgo San Frediano, is known for its workshops and unpretentious antique dealers. The **Porta San Frediano**, its tall tower guarding the Pisa road, has its old wooden door and locks still in place. The domed 17th-century church of **San Frediano in Cestello**, with its blank poker face, is the landmark along this stretch of the Arno.

The neighbourhoods get trendier as you head east, especially along busy Borgo Santo Spirito, its extension Borgo S. Jacopo, and wide Via Maggio, leading inland from the Ponte S. Trínita. All have fine palaces and medieval towers pruned by the Republic. Many great medieval bankers also erected their palaces in the Oltrarno. Several may still be seen along Via de' Bardi, east of the Ponte Vecchio, especially the 13th–14th-century **Palazzo dei Mozzi** in the piazza of the same name. Across the piazza is the **Museo Bardini/Galleria Corsi** (open 9–2, Sun 8–1, closed Wed; adm), an eclectic collection of art and architectural fragments left to the city in 1922 by art dealer Stefano Bardini. Bardini built this rather lugubrious palace to incorporate the doorways, ceilings, and stairs that he salvaged from the demolition of the Mercato Vecchio and other buildings in central Florence; he even installed a mock crypt to display his tombs and funereal altarpieces (there's an especially fine one by Andrea della Robbia). Also outstanding are Tino da Camaino's trecento *Charity*, a *Madonna* attributed to Donatello, a panel painting of *St Michael* by Antonio Pollaiuolo, and a magnificent set of Persian carpets, old musical instruments, furniture, and armour. Near the museum, the nondescript postwar **Ponte**

alle Grazie replaced a famous medieval bridge with seven chapels on it, home to seven nuns, who one imagines spent much of their time praying that the Arno wouldn't flood.

Further east, narrow Via di S. Niccolò leads to **San Niccolò sopr'Arno**, a church rebuilt in the 14th century, with a lovely fresco in the sacristy of the *Madonna della Cintola* ('of the girdle') by Baldovinetti. The street ends with a bang at **Porta San Niccolò**, an impressively looming gate of 1340 that has recently been restored. A smaller gate just to the south, the **Porta S. Miniato**, stands near the walkway up to San Miniato (see below).

A City with a View

Great Aunt Florence, with her dour complexion and severe, lined face, never was much of a looker from street level, but improves with a bit of distance, either mental or from one of her hilltop balconies: the Belvedere Fort, San Miniato, Piazzale Michelangelo, Bellosguardo, Fiesole, or Settignano. Few cities are so endowed with stunning vistas; and when you look down upon Florence's palaces and towers, her loping bridges and red tile roofs and famous churches, Brunelleschi's incomparable dome seems even more remarkable, hovering like a benediction over the city.

Belvedere Fort and Arcetri

One of Florence's best and closest balconies is the **Belvedere Fort**, a graceful six-point star designed by Buontalenti and built 1590–95, not so much for the sake of defence but to remind any remaining Florentine republicans who was boss. Since 1958, it has been used for special exhibitions, and one can always enjoy the unforgettable views of Florence and countryside from its ramparts, daily between 8am and 8pm. It can be reached from the Boboli Gardens, or by ascending one of Florence's prettiest streets, **Costa San Giorgio**, which begins in Piazza S. Felicità, just beyond the Ponte Vecchio. Costa San Giorgio winds up the hill, lined with old villas and walled gardens. The villa at no. 19 was, from 1610 to 1631, the home of Galileo. At the top of the street stands the arch of the **Porta San Giorgio**, guarded by a 13th-century relief of St George and the dragon.

In this part of Florence, the countryside begins right at the city wall, a rolling landscape of villas and gardens. Via San Leonardo winds its way out towards Arcetri; a 10-minute walk will take you to the 11th-century **San Leonardo in Arcetri** (usually open Sunday mornings). There is a wonderful 13th-century pulpit, originally built for San Pier Scheraggio, and a small rose window, made according to legend from a wheel of Fiesole's *carroccio*, captured by Florence in 1125. A half kilometre further on, past the Viale Galileo crossroads, Via San Leonardo changes its name to Via Viviani, where it passes the **Astrophysical Observatory** and the **Torre del Gallo**, a reconstruction of a 14th-century tower by art dealer Stefano Bardini. Another kilometre further on Via Viviani reaches the settlement of Pian de' Giullari, where Galileo spent the last years of his life, in the 16th-century **Villa il Gioiello**, virtually under house arrest after his encounter with the Inquisition in 1631, and where Milton is believed to have visited him.

San Miniato

From Porta San Miniato you can walk up to San Miniato church on the stepped Via di San Salvatore al Monte, complete with the Stations of the Cross, or take the less pious

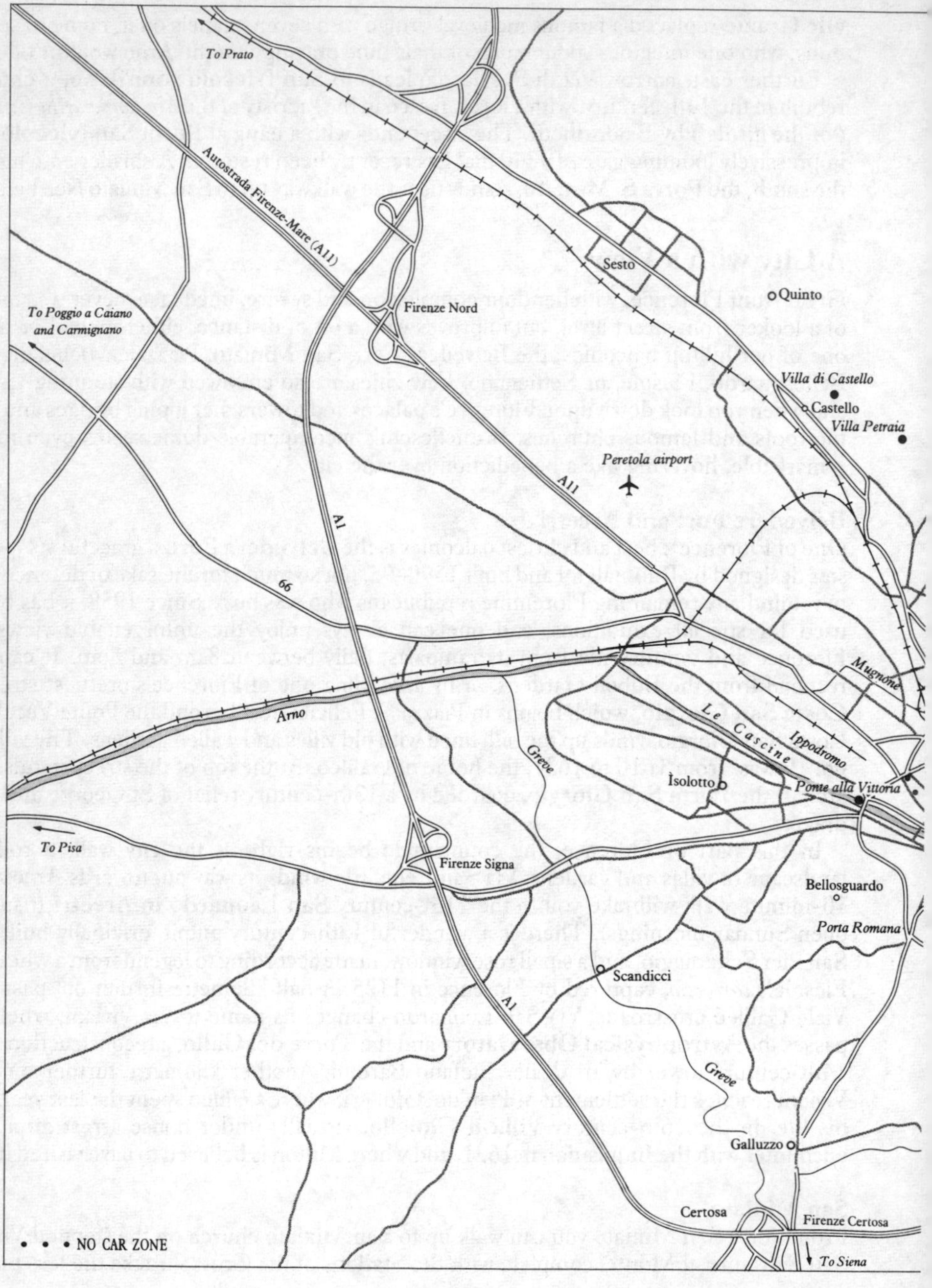
To Prato
Autostrada Firenze-Mare (A11)
Sesto
Quinto
Firenze Nord
To Poggio a Caiano and Carmignano
Villa di Castello
Castello
Villa Petraia
Peretola airport
A11
A1
66
Mugnone
Arno
Le Cascine
Ippodromo
Greve
Isolotto
Ponte alla Vittoria
To Pisa
Firenze Signa
Bellosguardo
Porta Romana
Scandicci
A1
Greve
Galluzzo
Certosa
Firenze Certosa
To Siena
• • • NO CAR ZONE

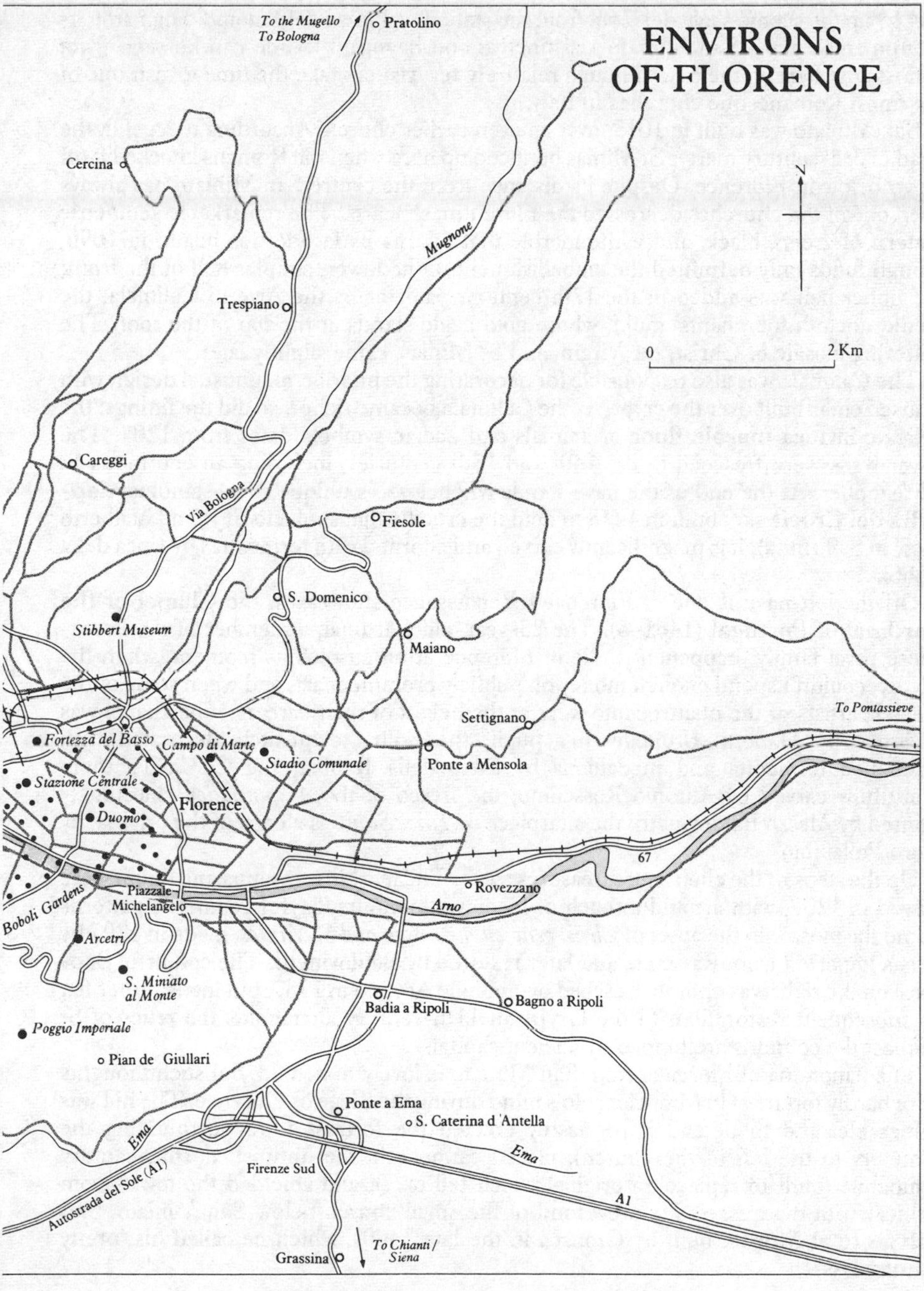
ENVIRONS OF FLORENCE
To the Mugello
To Bologna
Pratolino
Cercina
Mugnone
Trespiano
0
2 Km
N
Careggi
Via Bologna
Fiesole
S. Domenico
Stibbert Museum
Maiano
Settignano
To Pontassieve
Fortezza del Basso
Campo di Marte
Stadio Comunale
Ponte a Mensola
Stazione Centrale
Florence
Duomo
67
Rovezzano
Piazzale
Michelangelo
Arno
Boboli Gardens
Arcetri
S. Miniato
al Monte
Badia a Ripoli
Bagno a Ripoli
Poggio Imperiale
Pian de Giullari
Ponte a Ema
S. Caterina d'Antella
Ema
Ema
Firenze Sud
Autostrada del Sole (A1)
A1
Grassina
To Chianti /
Siena

bus 13 up the scenic Viale dei Colli from the station or Piazza del Duomo. High atop its monumental steps, San Miniato's distinctive and beautiful façade can be seen from almost anywhere in the city, although relatively few visitors take the time to visit one of the finest Romanesque churches in Italy.

San Miniato was built in 1015, over an even earlier church. According to legend, the head of 3rd-century martyr St Minias bounced up here when the Romans knocked it off down below in Florence. Despite its distance from the centre San Miniato has always been one of the churches dearest to the Florentines' hearts. The remarkable geometric pattern of green, black, and white marble that adorns its façade was begun in 1090, though funds only permitted the embellishment of the lower, simpler half of the front; the upper half was added in the 12th century, paid for by the Arte di Calimala, the medieval cloth merchants' guild, whose gold eagle stands at the top of the roof. The glittering mosaic of Christ, the Virgin, and St Minias, came slightly later.

The Calimala was also responsible for decorating the interior, an unusual design with a raised choir built over the crypt. As the Calimala became richer, so did the fittings; the delicate intarsia **marble floor** of animals and zodiac symbols dates from 1207. The lower walls were frescoed in the 14th and 15th centuries, including an enormous St Christopher. At the end of the nave stands Michelozzo's unique, free-standing **Cappella del Crocifisso**, built in 1448 to hold the crucifix that spoke to St John Gualberto (now in S. Trínita); it is magnificently carved and adorned with terracottas by Luca della Robbia.

Off the left nave is one of Florence's Renaissance showcases, the **Chapel of the Cardinal of Portugal** (1461–6). The 25-year-old Cardinal, a member of the Portuguese royal family, happened to die in Florence at an auspicious moment, when the Medici couldn't spend enough money on publicly prominent art, and when some of the greatest artists of the quattrocento were at the height of their careers. The chapel was designed by Manetti, Brunelleschi's pupil; the ceiling exquisitely decorated with enamelled terracotta and medallions by Luca della Robbia; the Cardinal's tomb beautifully carved by Antonio Rossellino; the fresco of the *Annunciation* charmingly painted by Alesso Baldovinetti; the altarpiece of *Three Saints* is a copy of the original by Piero Pollaiuolo.

Up the steps of the choir more treasures await. The marble transenna and pulpit were carved in 1207, with art and a touch of medieval humour. Playful geometric patterns frame the mosaic in the apse, of *Christ between the Virgin and St Minias*, made in 1297 by artists imported from Ravenna, and later restored by Baldovinetti. The colourful **Sacristy** on the right was entirely frescoed by Spinello Aretino in 1387, but made rather flat by subsequent restoration. In the **Crypt** an 11th-century altar holds the relics of St Minias; the columns are topped by ancient capitals.

The panorama of Florence from San Miniato is lovely to behold, but such thoughts were hardly foremost in Michelangelo's mind during the Siege of Florence. The hill was vulnerable, and to defend it he hastily erected the fortress (now surrounding the cemetery to the left of the church), placed cannons in the unfinished 16th-century campanile (built to replace an original which fell over), and shielded the tower from artillery with mattresses. He grew fond of the small church below San Miniato, **San Salvatore al Monte**, built by Cronaca in the late 1400s, which he called his 'pretty country lass'.

With these associations in mind, perhaps, the city named the vast, square terrace car park below **Piazzale Michelangelo**, the most popular viewpoint only because it is the only one capable of accommodating an unlimited number of tour buses. Besides another copy of the *David* and a fun, tacky carnival atmosphere rampant with souvenirs, balloons, and ice cream, the Piazzale offers views that can reach as far as Pistoia on a clear day.

Bellosguardo

Many would argue that the finest of all views over Florence is to be had from Bellosguardo, located almost straight up from Porta Romana at the end of the Boboli Gardens or Piazza Torquato Tasso. Non-mountaineers may want to take a taxi; the famous viewpoint, from where you can see every church façade in the city, is just before Piazza Bellosguardo.

Fiesole

Florence liked to look at itself as the daughter of Rome, and in its fractious heyday explained its quarrelsome nature by the fact that its population from the beginning was of mixed race, of Romans and 'that ungrateful and malignant people who of old came down from Fiesole', according to Dante. First settled in the 2nd millennium BC, it became the most important Etruscan city in the region. Yet from the start Etruscan *Faesulae*'s relationship with Rome was rocky, especially after sheltering Catiline and his conspirators in 65 BC. Because of its lofty position, Fiesole was too difficult to capture, so the Romans built a camp below on the Arno to cut off its supplies. Eventually Fiesole was taken, and it dwindled as the Roman camp below grew into the city of Florence, growth the Romans encouraged to spite the old Etruscans on their hill. This easily defended hill, however, ensured Fiesole's survival in the Dark Ages. When times became safer, families began to move back down to the Arno to rebuild Florence. They returned to smash up most of Fiesole after defeating it in 1125; since then the little town has remained aloof, letting Florence dominate and choke in its own juices far, far below.

But ever since the days of the *Decameron*, whose storytellers retreated to its garden villas to escape the plague, Fiesole has played the role of Florence's aristocratic suburb; its cool breezes, beautiful landscapes, and belvedere views make it the perfect refuge from the torrid Florentine summers. There's no escaping the tourists, however; we foreigners have been tramping up and down Fiesole's hill since the days of Shelley. A day trip has become an obligatory part of a stay in Florence, and although Fiesole has proudly retained its status as an independent *comune*, you can make the 20-minute trip up on Florence city bus 7 from the station or Piazza S. Marco. If you have the time, walk up (or perhaps better, down) the old, hilly, villa- and garden-bordered lanes to absorb some of the world's most civilized scenery.

Around Piazza Mino

The long sloping stage of Piazza Mino is Fiesole's centre, with the bus stop, the local tourist office, the cafés, and the **Palazzo Pretorio**, its loggia and façade emblazoned with coats-of-arms. The square is named after a favourite son, the quattrocento sculptor Mino da Fiesole, whom Ruskin preferred to all others. An example of his work may be seen in the **Duomo**, whose plain façade dominates the north side of the piazza. Built in

1028, it was the only building spared by the vindictive Florentines in 1125. It was subsequently enlarged and given a scouring 19th-century restoration, leaving the tall, crenellated campanile as its sole distinguishing feature. Still, the interior has an austere charm, with a raised choir over the crypt similar to San Miniato. Up the steps to the right are two beautiful works by Mino da Fiesole: the *Tomb of Bishop Leonardo Salutati* and an altar front. The main altarpiece in the choir, of the Madonna and saints, is by Lorenzo di Bicci, from 1440. Note the two saints frescoed on the columns; it was a north Italian custom to paint holy people as if they were members of the congregation. The crypt, holding the remains of Fiesole's patron, St Romulus, is supported by ancient columns bearing doves, spirals, and other early Christian symbols.

Behind the Cathedral, on Via Dupré, the **Bandini Museum** contains more sacred works, including numerous della Robbia terracottas, some good trecento paintings by Lorenzo Monaco, Neri di Bicci, and Taddeo Gaddi (daily, except Sun, 10–12 and 3–7; in winter 9:30–12:30 and 2:30–5; adm).

Archaeological Zone

Behind the cathedral and museum is the entrance to what remains of *Faesulae*. Because Fiesole avoided trouble in the Dark Ages, its Roman monuments have survived in much better shape than those of Florence; although hardly spectacular the ruins are made charming by the olive groves and cypresses that surround them. The small **Roman Theatre** has survived well enough to host plays and concerts in the summer; Fiesole would like to remind you that in the ancient times it had the theatre and plays while Florence had the amphitheatre and wild beast shows. Close by are the rather confusing remains of two superimposed temples, the baths, and an impressive stretch of Etruscan walls (best seen from Via delle Mura Etrusche, below) that proved their worth against Hannibal's siege. The **Archaeology Museum** is housed in a small 20th-century Ionic temple, displaying some very early small bronze figurines with flapper wing arms, Etruscan funerary urns and stelae, including the interesting 'stele Fiesolana' with a banquet scene.

Walking Around Fiesole

From Piazza Mino, Via S. Francesco ascends steeply (at first) to the hill that served as the Etruscan and Roman acropolis. Halfway up is a terrace with extraordinary views of Florence and the Arno sprawl, with a monument to the three *carabinieri* who gave themselves up to be shot by the Nazis in 1944 to prevent them from taking civilian reprisals. The church nearby, the **Basilica di Sant' Alessandro**, was constructed over an Etruscan/Roman temple in the 6th century, re-using its lovely *cipollino* (onion marble) columns and Ionic capitals, one still inscribed with an invocation to Venus. At the top of the hill, square on the ancient acropolis, stands the monastery of **San Francesco**, its church containing a famous early cinquecento *Annunciation* by Raffaellino del Garbo and an *Immaculate Conception* by Piero di Cosimo. A grab bag of odds and ends collected from the four corners of the world, especially Egypt and China, is displayed in the quaint **Franciscan Missionary Museum** in the cloister; it also has an Etruscan collection (10–12, 3–5).

There are much longer walks along the hill behind the Palazzo Pretorio. The panoramic Via Belvedere leads back to Via Adriano Mari, and in a couple of kilometres to the bucolic **Montecéceri**, a wooded park where Leonardo da Vinci performed his flight experiments, and where Florentine architects once quarried their dark *pietra serena*, quarries now abandoned but open for exploration. In Borgunto, as this part of Fiesole is called, there are two 3rd-century BC **Etruscan tombs** on Via Bargellino; east of Borgunto scenic Via Francesco Ferrucci and Via di Vincigliata pass by Fiesole's castles, the **Castel di Poggio**, site of summer concerts, and the **Castel di Vincigliata**, dating back to 1031, while further down is American critic Bernard Berenson's famous **Villa I Tatti**, which he left, along with a distinguished collection of Florentine art, to Harvard University as the Centre of Italian Renaissance Studies. The road continues down towards Ponte a Mensola (6 km from Fiesole; see below) and Settignano, with buses back to Florence.

San Domenico di Fiesole

Between Fiesole and Florence, you can reach San Domenico most pleasantly on foot, leaving Fiesole's Piazza Mino on Via Vecchia Fiesolana, the steep and narrow old road that passes, on the left, the **Villa Medici**, built by Michelozzo for Cosimo il Vecchio; in its lovely garden on the hillside, Lorenzo and his friends of the Platonic Academy would come to get away from the world; it was also the lucky Iris Origo's childhood home (no adm). San Domenico, at the bottom of the lane, is best known as the church and convent where Fra Angelico first entered his monkish world. The 15th-century church of **San Domenico** contains his lovely *Madonna with Angels and Saints*, in the first chapel on the left, as well as a photograph of his *Coronation of the Virgin*, which the French snapped up in 1809 and sent to the Louvre. Across the nave there's a *Crucifixion* by the school of Botticelli, an unusual composition of verticals highlighted by the cypresses in the background. In the chapterhouse of the monastery (ring the bell at no. 4) Fra Angelico left a fine fresco of the *Crucifixion* before moving down to Florence and San Marco.

Badia Fiesolana

The lane in front of San Domenico leads down in five minutes to the Badia Fiesolana, the ancient cathedral of Fiesole, built in the 9th century by Fiesole's bishop, an Irishman named Donatus, with a fine view over the rolling countryside, with Florence in the background. Though later enlarged, perhaps by Brunelleschi, it has preserved the elegant façade of the older church, a charming example of the geometric black and white marble inlay decoration that characterizes Tuscan Romanesque churches. The interior, open only on Sunday mornings, is adorned with *pietra serena* very much in the style of Brunelleschi. The convent buildings next door are now the home of the European University Institute.

Settignano

The least touristic hill above Florence sits under the village of Settignano (bus 10 from the station or Piazza S. Marco). The road passes by way of **Ponte a Mensola**, where Boccaccio spent his childhood, and where it is believed he set the first scenes of the *Decameron*, at the Villa Poggio Gherardo. A Scottish Benedictine named Andrew founded its church of **San Martino a Mensola** in the 9th century and was later canonized. Rebuilt in the 1400s, it has three good trecento works: Taddeo Gaddi's

Triptych, his son Agnolo's panel paintings on St Andrew's casket, and another triptych, on the high altar, by the school of Orcagna; from the quattrocento there's a *Madonna and Saints* by Neri di Bicci and an *Annunciation* by a follower of Fra Angelico.

Settignano is one of Tuscany's great cradles of sculptors, producing Desiderio da Settignano, and brothers Antonio and Bernardo Rossellino; Michelangelo spent his childhood here as well, in the Villa Buonarroti. Strangely enough, not one left any work as a reminder here; the good art in the central church of **Santa Maria** is by Andrea della Robbia (an enamelled terracotta of the Madonna and Child) and Buontalenti (the pulpit). There are, however, more splendid views of Florence from Piazza Desiderio, and a couple of places to quaff a leisurely glass of Chianti.

Medici Villas

Like their Bourbon cousins in France, the Medici dukes liked to pass the time acquiring new palaces for themselves. In their case, however, the reason was less self-exaltation than simple property speculation; the Medici always thought several generations ahead. As a result the countryside is littered with Medici villas, most of them now privately owned, though some are at least partly open to the public.

Villa Careggi

Perhaps the best-known of all is Careggi (Viale Pieraccini 17, bus 14C from the station), a villa that began as a fortified farmhouse and was enlarged for Cosimo il Vecchio by Michelozzo in 1434. In the 1460s the villa at Careggi became synonymous with the birth of humanism. The greatest Latin and Greek scholars of the day, Ficino, Poliziano, Pico della Mirandola, and Argyropoulos, would meet here with Lorenzo il Magnifico and hold philosophical discussions in imitation of a Platonic symposium, calling their informal society the Platonic Academy. It fizzled out when Lorenzo died. Cosimo il Vecchio and Piero had both died at Careggi, and when he felt the end was near, Lorenzo had himself carried out to the villa, with Poliziano and Pico della Mirandola to bear him company. After Lorenzo died, the villa was burned by Florentine republicans, though Cosimo I later had it rebuilt, and Francis Sloane had it restored. It is now used as a nursing home, and can only be visited by request (ask inside at the office of the Unità Operativa Affari Generali of USL), but you can stroll through its gardens and woods for free.

Villa della Petraia

Further east, amid the almost continuous conurbation of power lines and industrial landscapes that blight the Prato road, the Villa della Petraia manages to remain Arcadian on its steeply sloping hill (very hard to reach on your own; take a taxi or, if you are adventurous, bus 28 from the station, and get off after the wastelands, by Via Reginaldo Giuliano). La Petraia was purchased by Grand Duke Ferdinando I in 1557 and rebuilt by Buontalenti, keeping the tower of the original country castle intact. Unfortunately Vittorio Emanuele II liked it as much as the Medici, and redesigned it to suit his relentlessly bad taste. Still, a tour of the villa's interior (9–4, 9–1 winter; adm) is worth while for the ornate Baroque court, frescoed with a pastel history of the Medici by 17th-century masters Volterrano and Giovanni di San Giovanni; Vittorio Emanuele II added the glass roof so that he could use the space as a ballroom. Of the remainder of the palace, you're likely to remember best the Chinese painting of Canton and the games room, with billiard tables as large as football fields and perhaps the world's first pinball machine, made of wood. A small room contains one of Giambologna's most endearing statues, *Venus Wringing Water from Her Hair*. La Petraia's beautiful garden and park, shaded by ancient cypresses, is open throughout the afternoon.

Villa di Castello

One of Tuscany's most famous gardens is just down the hill from La Petraia, at Villa di Castello (turn right at Via di Castello and walk 500 yards). The villa was bought in 1477 by Lorenzo di Pierfrancesco and Giovanni de' Medici, cousins of Lorenzo il Magnifico who were Botticelli's best patrons, and they hung the walls of this villa with his great mythological paintings now in the Uffizi. The villa was sacked in the 1530 siege, restored by Cosimo I, and today is the headquarters of the Accademia della Crusca, founded in 1582 and dedicated to the study of the Italian language (no adm). The **Garden** (open 9–6:30 in the summer, till 4:30 in winter, closed Mon) was laid out for Cosimo I by Tribolo, who also designed the fountain in the centre, with a statue of *Hercules and Antenaeus* by Ammannati. Straight back from the fountain is the garden's main attraction, a fascinating example of the Medici penchant for the offbeat and excessive, an artificial cavern known as the **Grotto degli Animali**, filled by Ammanati and Giambologna with marvellous, true-to-life statues of every animal, fish, and bird known to man (some copies of Giambologna's originals in the Bargello), and lined with mosaics of pebbles and seashells. The shady terrace above offers the best view over the geometric patterns of the garden below; a large statue by Ammanati of January, or *Gennaio*, emerges shivering from a pool of water among the trees.

A 20-minute walk north from Villa di Castello to Quinto Fiorentino will take you to two unusual 7th-century BC **Etruscan Tombs**. Neither has any art, but the chambers under their 8-metre artificial hills bear an odd relationship to ancient cultures elsewhere in the Mediterranean—domed tholos tombs as in Mycenaean Greece, corbelled passages like the *navetas* of Mallorca, and entrances that look like the sacred wells of Sardinia. **La Montagnola**, Via Filli. Rosselli 95, is open Sat and Sun 10–1, also in summer Tues and Thurs 10–1, and Sat and Sun afternoons 5–7; **La Mula**, Via della Mula 2, is open Sat 10–12, also in summer Tues 10–12 and Sat 3–6:30.

Sesto Fiorentino

You can change gears again by heading out a little further in the sprawl to Sesto Fiorentino, a suburb that since 1954 has been home to the famous Richard-Ginori china and porcelain firm. Founded in Doccia in 1735, the firm has opened the **Doccia Museum** on Via Pratese 31 (signposted) to display a neat chronology of its production of Doccia ware, including many Medici commissions (a ceramic Venus de' Medici), fine painted porcelain, and some pretty Art Nouveau works (Tues–Sat, 9:30–1 and 3:30–6:30; adm).

Villa Demidoff at Pratolino

The village of Pratolino lies 12 km north of Florence along Via Bolognese and was the site of Duke Francesco I's favourite villa in the 1570s, later demolished. Its enormous park, however, has survived and has recently been opened to the public. For its design, Francesco commissioned Buontalenti—artist, architect, and hydraulics engineer, nicknamed 'delle Girandole' for the wind-up toys he made—and he made Pratolino the marvel of its day, full of water tricks, ingenious automata, and a famous menagerie. Sadly, none of Buontalenti's tricks has survived, but the largest ever example of this play between art and the environment has (perhaps because it is impossible to move)—Giambologna's massive *Appennino*, a giant rising from stone, part stalactite, part fountain himself. The rest of the park is an invitingly cool refuge from a Florentine summer afternoon.

Poggio a Caiano

Of all the Medici villas, Poggio a Caiano is the most evocative of the country idylls so delightfully described in the verses of Lorenzo il Magnifico; this was his favourite retreat (COPIT buses go past every half hour, departing from the loggia in Piazza S. Maria Novella). Originally a farmhouse purchased by Lorenzo in 1480, he had it rebuilt by Giuliano da Sangallo in a classical style that presages Palladio. It was Lorenzo's sole architectural commission, and its classicism matched the mythological nature poems he composed here, most famously *L'Ambra*, inspired by the stream Ombrone that flows nearby.

Sangallo designed the villa according to Alberti's description of the perfect country house, and added a classical frieze on the façade, sculpted with the assistance of Andrea Sansovino (now replaced with a copy). Some of the other features—the clock, the curved stair, and central loggia—were later additions. In the **interior** (open 9–1:30, Sun 9–12:30, closed Mon) Sangallo designed an airy, two-storey **Salone**, which the two Medici popes had frescoed by 16th-century masters Pontormo, Andrea del Sarto, Franciabigio, and Allori. The subject, as usual, is Medici self-glorification, and depicts family members dressed as Romans in historical scenes that parallel events in their lives. In the right lunette, around a large circular window, Pontormo painted the lovely *Vertumnus and Pomona* (1521), a languid summer scene under a willow tree, beautifully coloured. The pleasant **grounds** (open 9–6:30, till 4:30 in winter; 9–12:30 Sun) contain many fine old trees and a 19th-century statue celebrating Lorenzo's *L'Ambra*.

Carmignano and Villa Artimino

A local bus continues 5 km southwest of Poggia a Caiano to the village of **Carmignano**, famous for possessing, in its church of San Michele, Pontormo's uncanny painting of *The Visitation* (1530s), one of the masterpieces of Florentine Mannerism. There are no concessions to naturalism here—the four soulful, ethereal women, draped in Pontormo's accustomed startling colours, barely touch the ground, standing before a scene as substantial as a stage backdrop. The result, however, is one of the most unforgettable images produced in the 16th century.

Also south of Poggio a Caiano, at **Comeana** (3 km, signposted) is the well-preserved Etruscan **Tomba di Montefortini**, a 7th-century BC burial mound, 11 m high and 80 m in diameter, covering two burial chambers. A long hall leads down to the vestibule and rectangular tomb chamber, both carefully covered with false vaulting, the latter preserving a wide shelf, believed to have been used for gifts for the afterlife. An equally impressive tomb nearby, the **Tomba dei Boschetti**, was seriously damaged over the centuries by local farmers (Montefortini open 9–1, closed Mon, Boschetti always open).

The Etruscan city of Artimino, 4 km west, was destroyed by the Romans and is now occupied by a small town and another Medici property, the **Villa Artimino** ('La Ferdinanda'), built as hunting lodge for Ferdinando I by Buontalenti. Buontalenti gave it a semi-fortified air with buttresses to fit its sporting purpose, but the total effect is simple and charming, the long roofline punctuated by innumerable chimneys; the graceful stair was added in the last century, from a drawing by the architect in the Uffizi. An **Etruscan Archaeological Museum** has been installed in the basement, containing items found in the tombs; among them a unique censer with two basins and a boat, bronze vases, and a red figured krater painted with initiation scenes, found in a 3rd-century tomb (villa open Tues 9–12:30 and 3–6, winter 8:30–12 and 2–4; museum open Sat 3:30–6:30, Sun 9–12, and Mon 9–12 and 3–6; adm). There's a convenient place for lunch in the grounds. Also in Artimino is an attractive Romanesque church, **San Leonardo**, built of stones salvaged from earlier buildings.

Poggio Imperiale and the Certosa del Galluzzo

One last villa open for visits, the **Villa di Poggio Imperiale**, lies south of Florence, at the summit of Viale del Poggio Imperiale, which leaves Porta Romana with a stately escort of cypress sentinels. Cosimo I grabbed this huge villa from the Salviati family in 1565, and it remained a ducal property until there were no longer any dukes to duke. Its Neoclassical façade was added in 1808, and the audience chamber was decorated in the 17th century by Rutilio Manetti and others. Much of the villa is now used as a girls' school (open Tues, 10–12 by request, tel 451 208).

The **Certosa del Galluzzo** (also known as the Certosa di Firenze) lies further south, scenically located on a hill off the Siena road (take bus 36 or 37 from the station). Founded as a Carthusian monastery by 14th-century tycoon Niccolò Acciaiuoli, the monastery has been inhabited since 1958 by Cistercians, one of whom takes visitors around (9–12 and 4–7 in summer, 9–12 and 3–5 winter). The Certosa has a fine 16th-century courtyard and an uninteresting church, though the crypt-chapel of the lay choir contains some impressive tombs. The **Chiostro Grande**, surrounded by the monks' cells, is decorated with 66 majolica tondoes of prophets and saints by Giovanni della Robbia and assistants; one cell is opened for visits, and it seems almost cosy. The Gothic **Palazzo degli Studi**, intended by the founder as a school, contains five lunettes by Pontormo, painted while he and his pupil Bronzino hid out here from the plague in 1522.

FESTIVALS AND ANNUAL EVENTS

Traditional festivals in Florence date back centuries. Easter Sunday's *Scioppio del Carro*, or 'Explosion of the Cart', commemorates Florentine participation in the First Crusade in 1096. The Florentines were led by Pazzino de' Pazzi, who upon returning home, received the special custody of the flame of Holy Saturday, with which the Florentines traditionally relit their family hearths. To make the event more colourful, the Pazzi constructed a decorated wooden ox cart to carry the flame. They lost the job after the Pazzi conspiracy in 1478, and since then the city has taken over the responsibility. In the morning, a fireworks-filled wooden float is pulled by white oxen from the Porta a Prato to the Cathedral, where, at noon, during the singing of the Gloria, it is ignited by a 'dove' that descends on a wire from the high altar.

On Ascension Day (in May), there's the *Festa del Grillo* (cricket festival) in the Cascine; Michelangelo was thinking of its little wooden cricket cages when he mocked Ammanati's gallery on the cathedral dome. June is the time of the three matches of *Calcio Storico in Costume* (historical football in 16th-century costume) in the Piazza della Signoria, played by 27-men teams from Florence's four quarters, in memory of a defiant football match played in Piazza S. Croce in 1530, during the siege by Charles V. Flag throwing and a parade in historical costume are part of the pre-game ceremonies. The *Festa delle Rificolone* on 7 September is one of Florence's more lively festivals, with a parade of floats followed by a party in the streets. The best fireworks are reserved for the day of Florence's patron, St John (24 June).

Florentines adore cultural events. The big summer festival is the *Estate Fiesolana*: from late June–August the old Roman theatre is the site of concerts, ballet, theatre, and films, for reasonable prices. The *Maggio Musicale Fiorentino*, the city's big music festival, spans from late April to the beginning of July and brings in big-name concert stars. Events take place in the Teatro Comunale, Corso Italia 16 (just off Lungarno Vespucci, tel 216 253 or 277 9236 for ticket information). There's usually some kind of music in the Piazza della Signoria on Thursday nights during the summer, and the summer season of the **Teatro Comunale** (opera, concerts, and ballet) which take place in the Boboli Gardens, the Teatro Comunale, and the Teatro della Pergola (Via della Pergola 18, tel 247 9651). From April to June you can see the offerings of independent film makers at the **Florence Festival** in the Palazzo dei Congressi, tel 294 353. In May, don't miss the **Iris Festival** up at Piazzale Michelangelo.

SHOPPING

Although central Florence sometimes seems like one solid boutique, the city is no longer the queen of Italian fashion—the lack of an airport, more than anything else, has sent most of the big designers to Milan. Many of the big **fashion** names of the 60s and 70s, the international chain stores of the 80s, are represented in smart Via Tornabuoni, Via Calzaiuoli, and in the streets around the Duomo. **Leather** is something Florence is still known for, and you'll see plenty of it in the centre, around Via della Vigna Nuova and Via del Parione, and less expensively at an unusual institution called the **Leather School**, which occupies part of S. Croce's cloister (entrance at Piazza S. Croce 16 or Via S. Giuseppe 5r). Florence is also famous for its **jewellery**, and the shops on and around the Ponte Vecchio are forced by the nature of their location into wide-open competition, and good prices for Florentine brushed gold (although much of it is made in Arezzo these days) and antique jewellery are more common than you may think.

Florence is also one of the few places in the world to make **marbled paper**, an art brought over from the Orient by Venice in the 12th century. Each sheet is hand dipped in a bath of colours to create a delicate, lightly coloured clouded design; no two sheets are alike. Marbled-paper-covered stationery items or just sheets of marbled paper are available at **Giulio Giannini e Figlio**, Piazza Pitti 37r, the oldest manufacturer; at **Il Papiro**, with three shops (Via Cavour 55r, Piazza del Duomo 24r, and Lungarno Acciaiuoli 42r); **La Bottega Artigiana del Libro**, Lungarno Corsini 40r; and **Il Torchio**, Via de' Bardi 17. These shops (and many others) also carry Florentine paper with its colourful Gothic patterns.

Bookworms do better in Florence than most Italian cities, although the prices of **books** in English will make you weep. The **Paperback Exchange**, Via Fiesolana 31r or **Seeber**, Via Tornabuoni 68r, have the widest selections in English, with many books about Florence. **Feltrinelli**, Via Cavour 2, has books in English and an excellent selection of art books; ditto for the **BM Bookshop** at Borgo Ognissanti 4r. **Franco Maria Ricci**, Via delle Belle Donne 41r, has a fabulous collection of art books.

Borgo Ognissanti and the various Lungarni are the place to look for **antiques** and **art galleries** like **P. Bazzanti e Figli**, Lungarno Corsini 40, where you can pick up an exact replica of the bronze pig in the Mercato Nuovo. An Italian carnival mask is much easier to carry and can be found at **Atelier Alice**, Via Faenza 12 or at **I Mascheroni Atelier**, Via dei Tavolini 13r. The **Casa dei Tessuti**, Via de' Pecori 20–24r keeps Florence's ancient **cloth** trade alive with lovely linens, silks, and woollens. For **silver**, **crystal** and **porcelain** from Florence's own Richard-Ginori, **A. Poggi**, Via Calzaiuoli 105r and 116r, has one of the city's widest selections. Fashionable **towels** and **bed linens** are available from **Ghezzi**, Via Calzaiuoli 110r. **Città del Sole**, on Borgo Ognissanti, near Piazza Goldoni, is the best **toy** shop in Florence, and if you happen to have or know the kind of little girls who can wear white, **Caponi**, Borgo Ognissanti 12r has a fairytale selection of **dresses**.

Serious collectors may want to check Florence's busy **auction houses**: **Palazzo Internazionale delle Aste ed Esposizioni**, Via Maggio 11, tel 293 000; **Sotheby's Italia**, Via G. Capponi 26, tel 247 9021; **Casa d'Aste Pitti**, Via Maggio 15, tel 296 382; and **Casa d'Aste Pandolfini**, Borgo degli Albizi 26, tel 234 0888.

There are a number of speciality **food** shops around the Mercato Centrale, or you can pick up items like truffle cream at **Allrientar Gastronomia**, in Borgo SS. Apostoli; for **wines** and **liquors** try **Biagini**, Via dei Banchi 57, off Piazza S. Maria Novella; the biggest selection of natural, organic and **vegetarian** foods is at **Sugar Blues**, Via XXVII Aprile 16/48r. **Medieval cures** and **Dominican remedies** are still sold in the **Farmaceutica di Santa Maria Novella**, Via della Scala 16n, which hasn't changed much since 1612.

Florence's lively **street markets** offer good bargains, fake designer clothing and even some authentic labels. The huge **San Lorenzo market** is the largest and most boisterous, where many Florentines buy their clothes; the **Mercato Nuovo** or Straw Market is the most touristic, but not flagrantly so. There's an extensive clothes and shoes market every Tuesday morning in the Cascine, but perhaps the most fun is the **Flea Market** in Piazza dei Ciompi, offering all kinds of desirable junk.

SPORTS

The one activity many summertime visitors begin to crave after tramping through the sights is a dip in a **pool**. The prettiest one is the Piscina le Pavoniere, in the Cascine, open June–Sept 10–6:30; others are Bellariva, up the Arno at Lungarno Colombo 2, open June–Sept 11–5. There are two covered, year-round pools: Amici del Nuoto, Via del Romito 38, tel 483 951 and Costoli, Via Paoli, near Campo di Marte, tel 675 744. If there's enough water in the Arno, you can try **rowing** or canoeing; contact the Società Canottieri Comunali, Lungarno Ferrucci 6, tel 681 2151, or the Società Canottieri Firenze, Lungarno dei Medici 8, tel 282 130. The Cascine has Florence's **race course**

(Ippodromo Le Cascine, tel 353 394) and **trotting course** (Ippodromo delle Mulina, tel 411 130); the nearest place to go riding in the Tuscan hills is the Country Riding Club, Via di Grioli, at Badia a Settimo in Scandicci, 6 km southwest of Florence, tel 790 277. The nearest **golf course**, the 18-hole Golf Club Ugolino, is in Gràssina, 7 km southeast of Florence, on the Chiantigiana-Impruneta, tel 205 1009, a lovely course laid out among olives and cypresses. For **tennis**, try the Circolo Tennis alle Cascine, tel 356 651.

ENTERTAINMENT

Nightlife with Great Aunt Florence is still awaiting its Renaissance; according to the Florentines themselves she's conservative, somewhat deaf, and retires early—1 am is very, very late in this city. However, there are plenty of people who wish it weren't so, and slowly, slowly, Florence by night is beginning to mean more than the old *passeggiata* over the Ponte Vecchio and an ice cream, and perhaps a late trip up to Fiesole to contemplate the lights. Look for listings of concerts and events in Florence's daily, *La Nazione*; the tourist office's free *Florence Today* contains bilingual monthly information and calendar, as does a booklet called *Florence Concierge Information*, available in hotels and tourist offices; the monthly *Firenze Spettacolo*, sold in news-stands, is only in Italian but fills you in on ecology and trekking activities, film societies, bar music, and the latest New Age mumbo jumbo to rock Florence. For a listing of all current films being shown in Florence (Italian and dubbed in Italian), tel 198.

Opera and concert season runs from Nov–April at the **Teatro Comunale**. Big-name jazz performers, classical artists, and others are brought to Florence by **Musicus Concentus**, Piazza del Carmine 14, tel 287 347, while rock and jazz tours that stop in Florence happen in the big Palasport, at Campo di Marte, in Viale Paoli. Films in English are shown daily at the **Cinema Astro**, Piazza San Simone near Santa Croce (no tel; closed Mon and July).

If you want to join Florence's swells, put on the dog and head out to elegant **Caffedecò**, Piazza della Libertà 45–46r, done in tasteful art deco, with live jazz (closed Mon); **Dolce Vita**, Piazza del Carmine, is one of the most popular places in the '80s in the Oltrarno, a bar to see and be seen in; the older pub/wine bar **Rifrullo**, Via S. Niccolò 55r, is probably the most popular of all and one of the first to attract people to the Oltrarno; there's no word for 'cosy' in Italian, but the Rifrullo does the best it can. Alternative-minded Florentines for the past 10 years have frequented the **Caffè Voltaire**, Via della Scala 9r (Piazza S. Maria Novella), where on any given evening you may find a poetry reading, salsa, reggae, jazz, samba, blues, or *cucina nuova*; if you're going to live in Florence for a while, consider becoming a member of its club (closed Sun). Italian craziness and banana splits are on tap at the **Kiwi Videobar**, Via F. Bronzetti 12 (closed Mon); **Saxbar**, Viale dei Mille 83/84r has one of the city's widest selections of foreign beers to wash down its fancy cold or hot sandwiches and jazz on Thurs and Sun (closed Wed). **Riflessi d'Epoca**, Via dei Renai 13r, frequently has live jazz in a smoky ambience. It stays open later than the average club (i.e. after 1 am) as does **Stonehenge**, Via dell'Amorino 16r, near S. Lorenzo, with rock and cocktails from 10 pm on. Another good bet for jazz is the **Jazz Club**, Via Nuova de Caccini (closed Mon).

Among the discos **Tenax**, out near the airport in Via Pratese 47, Peretola (bus 29/30) and the new post-disco **Paramatta** at Poggetto are perhaps the most fashionable, but close down in the summer; the latter offers live music on Fridays and a trip into the new Florentine psyche. Two old standbys see most of the Florentine/foreigners disco action, with the provocative names of **Space Electronic Disco**, Via Palazzuolo 37, a high-tech noise box and **Yab Yum**, Via dei Sassetti 5, with summer action in Central Park, in the Cascine, except on Monday. For something out of the ordinary, head out on a Friday night at 10 pm to **Tangenziale Est**, Via Soffici 65 at Poggio a Caiano, tel 877 202 for the latest in Eastern European New Wave, Heavy Metal, and rock.

CAFES AND GELATERIE

Many of Florence's grand old cafés were born in the last century, although the oldest, **Gilli**, Piazza della Repubblica 13–14r dates back to 1733, when the Mercato Vecchio still occupied this area; its two panelled back rooms are especially pleasant in the winter. Another famous café in Piazza della Repubblica is the **Giubbe Rosse**, rendezvous of Florence's literati at the turn of the century; the chandelier-lit interior has changed little since. Florence's most elegant and classy watering hole, however, is the **Rivoire**, in the Piazza della Signoria 5r, with a marble detailed interior as lovely as the piazza itself. **Giacosa**, Via Tornabuoni 83, has a certain sparkle, good sandwiches and ice cream, and a reputation for having invented the Negroni (gin, Campari, and vermouth). Coffee connoisseurs claim the best cup served in Florence is at none of the above but at the less elegant **Robiglio**, Via dei Servi 112.

Florence lays some claim to being the ice-cream capital of the world, a reputation that owes much to the decadently delicious confections and rich *semifreddi* served at **Vivoli**, Via Isola delle Stinche 7r (between the Bargello and S. Croce), closed Mon. It has plenty of challengers for the *gelato* throne; try **Ricchi Alfredo**, Piazza S. Spirito 9r, in the Oltrarno, and **Perché no?**, Via Tavolini 194, near Via Calzaiuoli.

WHERE TO STAY (tel prefix 055)

Florence has some exceptionally lovely hotels, and not all of them at Grand Ducal prices, although basc rates here are the highest in Tuscany. In this town historic old palace-hotels are the rule rather than the exception; those listed below are some of the more atmospheric and charming, but to be honest, few are secrets, so reserve as far in advance as possible. There are almost 400 hotels in Florence, not enough for anyone who arrives in July and August without a reservation. But don't despair; there are several hotel consortia that can help you find a room in nearly any price range for a small commission. If you're arriving by car or train, the most useful will be ITA:

ITA: in Santa Maria Novella station, tel 282 893, open 9am–8:30 pm; in the AGIP service station at Peretola, to the west of Florence on A11 (tel 440 790). Between March and Nov there's an office in the Chianti-Est service plaza on the A1, and another in the Fortezza da Basso (tel 471 960)
Florence Promhotels: Viale A. Volta 72 (tel 570 481)
Toscana Hotels 80: Viale Gramsci 9 (tel 247 8543). These last two take bookings by 'phone or mail.

Nearly every hotel in Florence with a restaurant will require half board, and many will try and lay down a heavy breakfast charge as well that is supposed to be optional.

Expensive

In the city the luxury leader is the *****__Excelsior__, Piazza Ognissanti 3, tel 264 201, former Florentine address of Napoleon's sister Carolina. Lots of marble, neoclassically plush, lush and green with plants, immaculately staffed, smart roof garden with views down the Arno, and decadently luxurious bedrooms; not even Gian Gastone de' Medici had heated towel racks. The bar and restaurant are added amenities (L350–600 000). In a more tranquil spot, on Florence's plane-tree shaded 'London square', there's the *****__Regency Umbria__, Piazza d'Azeglio 3, tel 245 247, charming and intimate with only 29 air-conditioned rooms; between the two wings there's an elegant town garden. The public rooms are beautifully panelled, and the fare in the dining room superb; there's a private garage for your car (L360–560 000).

A Renaissance palace now owned by the descendants of sculptor Giovanni Dupre, the ****__Mona Lisa__, Borgo Pinti 27, tel 247 9751 is one of the most charming small hotels in Florence, hiding behind its stern façade. The *palazzo* is well preserved, the furnishings are family heirlooms, as are the many works of art. Try to reserve one of the tranquil rooms that overlook the garden; all are air-conditioned and have frigo-bars. The Mona Lisa has no restaurant, though breakfast is available; it also has private parking (L130–250 000). The Tuscan-Edwardian ****__Villa Carlotta__, Via Michele di Lando 3, tel 220 530, is in a quiet residential district in the upper Oltrarno, close to the Porta Romana. The 26 sophisticated rooms have recently been tastefully refurnished and have every luxury; there's a garden and glassed-in veranda, where the large breakfasts are served; a private garage offers safe parking (L180–260 000).

Among the many hotels along the Arno, one of the most pleasant is the ****__Principe__, Lungarno Vespucci 34, tel 284 848, a small comfortable hotel, centrally air-conditioned and sound-proofed, with a little garden at the back; the nicer rooms have terraces over the Arno (L240 000). Near the train station one of the most attractive hotels is the ****__Atlantic Palace__, Via Nazionale 12, tel 213 031, with large, striking bedrooms built in the framework of a 17th-century convent, luxuriously furnished and air-conditioned (L250 000). A large, but attractive hotel in an older palace, the ****__Anglo-American__, near the Cascine on Via Garibaldi 9, tel 282 114, is decorated in a light, airy, garden style that makes a pleasant retreat after pounding the pavements; the rooms are air-conditioned and there's parking nearby (L200–280 000).

Moderate

The most delightful choice in this category (moderate, by Florentine standards) was designed for the Servite fathers by Antonio da Sangallo the Elder, who added a loggia to match Brunelleschi's Spedale degli Innocenti across the square. The ***__Loggiato dei Serviti__, Piazza SS. Annunziata 3, tel 263 592, has since been redone with the best of Florentine taste and refinement, with Italian and English antiques; all rooms have mini-bars, and air conditioning and colour TVs are available as well; parking is possible in a nearby garage. The lovely garden is a blessing in the middle of Florence (L130 000, including breakfast). Another excellent small hotel, the ***__Beacci Tornabuoni__, Via Tornabuoni 3, tel 212 645, puts you in the centre of fashionable Florence, on the top three floors of an elegant Renaissance palace. The rooms are comfortable, air-conditioned and equipped with mini-bars, though it's more fun to sit over your drink on the panoramic roof terrace (half board, L140–170 000, depending on the plumbing).

A 15th-century palace in the Oltrarno, the ***Annalena**, Via Romana 34, tel 222 402, is a grand and famous old *pensione*, with high ceilings, antiques, and art, its rooms large and comfortable, all with private baths, the atmosphere friendly. The large garden at the back is a blessing (L130 000). ***Aprile**, Via della Scala 6, tel 216 237, is near the station but miles away in atmosphere. Housed in a 15th-century Medici palace, it is still decorated with frescoes and paintings, and there's a small courtyard for sitting outside (L120 000, all with bath). One of the best places to stay in the very heart of Florence is the popular ***Hermitage**, very near the Ponte Vecchio in Vicolo Marzio 1, tel 287 216. Reserve well in advance to get one of its 14 cosy old rooms, even further in advance to get one overlooking the Arno; the views from the roof garden while sipping your morning coffee make it worth the trouble (L80 000 without bath, L125 000 with). ***La Residenza**, on top of a Renaissance palace at Via Tornabuoni 8, tel 284 197 has the overgrown Palazzo Strozzi for a neighbour, and you can gaze down Florence's version of Fifth Avenue from the roof garden. The decor is pretty and welcoming, the elevator a well-maintained antique (L85 000 without bath, L120 000 with). Right in the middle of Florence, on a narrow lane off Piazza della Signoria, there's the noisy, ageing, dimly lit ***Porta Rossa** at Via Porta Rossa 19, tel 287 551. It isn't for everyone, but there are plenty of visitors to Florence who swear they wouldn't stay anywhere else. The Porta Rossa, which traces its origins back to the Middle Ages, has character, with its frayed 19th-century grandeur and a difficult, classically Florentine staff, who have plenty of tales to tell from the hotel's long history (L70–85 000 without bath, L90–120 000 with).

Inexpensive

The obvious place to look is the seedy, crowded tourist-student inferno that surrounds the central station, especially in Via Nazionale, Via Fiume, Via Guelfa, and Via Faenza down to Piazza Indipendenza. Many of the cheapest places post minions in the station to snatch up weary back-packers. Although convenient if you arrive by train, few of these hotels will brighten your stay in Florence; grouchy owners who lock the door at midnight seem to be the rule. There are a couple of noteworthy exceptions: ****Splendor**, Via San Gallo 30 (off Via Guelfa), tel 483 427, is on the fringe of the zone, near Piazza S. Marco; its old frescoes and antiques hint of past splendour, and some of the bedrooms are almost palatial; others aren't, but there's an attractive terrace (L75 000). Another solid recommendation in the area, ***Tony's Inn**, Via Faenza 77, tel 217 975, is run by a friendly Italian-Canadian couple; rooms are pleasant, most have private baths (L50 000). Near S. Maria Novella, also in spitting distance of the station, ***La Mia Casa**, Piazza S. Maria Novella 23, tel 213 061, offers simple rooms, inexpensive breakfasts, free showers and a free film in English every night (L48 000).

The old town has a number of inexpensive hotels, less touristic than those by the station. Just off Via Calzaiuoli, ***Maxim**, Via de' Medici 4, tel 217 474, has nice, quiet rooms that go for L50 000 . Up two flights of stairs in the heart of medieval Florence ***Cestelli**, Borgo SS. Apostoli 25, tel 214 213 has only seven rooms, but they're gems and lovingly maintained, and a bargain at L50 000, without bath. You can sleep in the palace of Dante's in-laws at the ***Orchidea**, Borgo degli Albizi 11, tel 248 0346, a charming old place, but no private baths or breakfast (L42 000). In the same vicinity, ***Brunori**, Via del Proconsolo 5, tel 263 648, is a small, friendly place (L52 000). Near Ponte alle Grazie, ****Rigatti**, Lungarno Diaz 2, tel 213 022, is the classiest inexpensive hotel in Florence, well worth paying a bit more for style and the pretty garden, although it's only enjoyed by those who reserve well ahead of time (L75 000).

Not many people travelling on the cheap make it over to the Oltrarno, making it less frenetic. An excellent choice, if you can get a room, is the genteel ***Bandini**, Piazza S. Spirito 9, tel 215 308, located on a quiet square far from tourist Florence. Recently endowed with a lift, guests are rewarded with a beautiful Tuscan loggia; this palace was one of the innovators of that delightful architectural feature (L55 000). ****La Scaletta**, Via Guicciardini 13, tel 283 028 has a more central, busy location, near the Ponte Vecchio, offering good rooms and a great roof terrace (L70 000).

Besides hotels, a number of institutions and private homes let rooms—there's a complete list in the back of the annual provincial hotel book. Many take women only, and fill up with students in the spring when Italian schools make their annual field trips. There are two youth hostels to choose from in Florence: **Ostello Europa Villa Camerata**, Viale A. Righe 2/4 (bus 17B from the station), tel 601 451, has 500 beds for people with IYHF cards. Located in an old *palazzo* with gardens, it is a popular place, and you'd be wise to show up at 2 pm to get a spot in the summer; maximum stay 3 days. **Ostello Santa Monaca**, Via S. Monaca 6, tel 268 338, has 111 beds near the Carmine church; sign up for a place in the morning.

In Fiesole

Many frequent visitors to Florence wouldn't stay anywhere else: it's cooler, quieter, and at night the capital far below twinkles as if made of fairy lights. If money is no object, the superb choice is the ********Villa San Michele**, in a breathtaking location just below Fiesole on Via Doccia 4, tel 59 451, with a façade and loggia reputedly designed by Michelangelo himself. Originally a monastery in the 14th century, it has been carefully reconstructed after bomb damage in World War II to create one of the most beautiful hotels in Italy, set in a lovely Tuscan garden, complete with a pool. Each of its 29 rooms is richly and elegantly furnished and air-conditioned; the more plush suites have jacuzzis. The food is delicious, and the reasons to go down to Florence begin to seem insignificant; a stay here is complete in itself. Paradise, however, comes at a price: L425–700 000 per person on half-board terms, closed mid-Nov–mid-March. Even if you aren't driving, you can reach ****Pensione Bencista,** Via B. da Maiano 4, in S. Domenico di Fiesole, tel 59 163, by bus 7. The pension is located in a sprawling villa dating back to the 14th century, added to over the centuries. Many of the rooms are furnished with antiques, and while not plush and full of amenities, there's a garden and view that make up for the lack of posh plumbing (L75 000). Right in the centre of Fiesole, on Piazza Mino, the *******Aurora,** tel 59 100 has air-conditioned rooms in a totally modernized, very elegant 19th-century building (L100–125 000).

Villa Hotels in the Florentine Hills

If you're driving, you may be inspired to lodge outside of central Florence, where you can park without hassles or paying a fortune for the privilege. A luxurious choice near Piazzale Michelangelo, is the opulent *******Grand Hotel Villa Cora,** Viale Machiavelli 18–20, tel 229 8451, a 19th-century mansion set in a beautiful formal garden overlooking the Oltrarno. Built by the Baron Oppenheim, it later served as the residence of the wife of Napoleon III, Empress Eugenie. Its conversion to a hotel has dimmed little of its splendour; some of the bedrooms have frescoed ceilings and lavish 19th-century furnishings—all are air-conditioned and have frigo-bars, and there's a pretty pool. In the summer meals are served in the garden, and there's a fine view of Florence from the roof terrace (L280–480 000). In the same area there's the far less pretentious ***Villa **Liberty**, a 14-room charmer, with a garden and air-conditioned rooms on Viale Michelangelo 40, tel 683 819 (L85–130 000).

In the 12th century a tower was built at Bellosguardo, enjoying one of the most breathtaking views over the city. It was later purchased by the Cavalcanti, friends of Dante, and a villa was added below the tower; Cosimo I confiscated it; the Michelozzi purchased it from the Medici; Elizabeth Barrett Browning wrote about it. In 1988 it opened its doors as a small hotel, the ****Torre di Bellosguardo**, Via Roti Michelozzi 2, tel 229 8145. Frescoes by Baroque master Poccetti adorn the entrance hall, fine antiques adorn the rooms, each unique, and fitted out with modern baths. The large and beautiful terraced garden has a pool; for a splurge reserve the two-level tower suite, with fabulous views in four directions (L220–300 000). Another lovely choice, the *****Villa La Massa**, Via La Massa 6, tel 630 051, is located up the Arno, some 6 km from Florence at Candeli. The former 15th-century villa of Count Giraldi, the hotel retains the old dungeon (now one of two restaurants), the family chapel (now a bar), and other early Renaissance amenities, combined with 20th-century features like tennis courts, a pool, air conditioning. The furnishings are fit for a Renaissance princeling, there's dining and dancing on the Arno in the summer, a shady garden, and a hotel bus to whizz you into the city (L275–420 000). In the other direction, at Colonnata di Sesto Fiorentino, the ****Villa Villoresi**, Via Ciampi 2, tel 448 9032, is a lovely oasis on a hill above one of Florence's more unbecoming tentacles. One of its charms is that it hasn't been too pristinely redone, and has kept much of its slightly faded appeal as well as its frescoed ceilings, antiques, chandeliers, and hospitable Contessa. There's a garden and pool—a great place to bring the children, and not bad value for L150 000. There are two former residences north of the centre: ***Villa le Rondini**, Via Bolognese Vecchia 224, tel 400 081, with a number of separate villas in a large park, a heated pool, and tennis (L120 000, with bath), and the far simpler ***Villa Natalia**, Via Bolognese 106, tel 490 773, with a garden and quiet rooms (L50 000 with bath).

Further afield, near Poggio a Caiano, the ***Hermitage**, Via Gineparia 112 at Bonistallo, tel 877 244, is a fine affordable choice for families; there's a pool in the grounds, air-conditioned rooms, not to mention gallons of fresh air and quiet (L100 000, all with bath). Near Carmignano you can play the Medici in the refurbished outbuildings of Grand Duke Ferdinand's Villa at Artimino in the ****Paggeria Medicea**, Viale Papa Giovanni XXIII 3, tel 871 8081. It has some unusual amenities—a hunting reserve and a lake stocked with fish, also a pool and tennis court, and pleasant modern rooms, many with balconies, all air-conditioned (L125–175 000).

EATING OUT

For better or worse, the real Florentine specialities rarely turn up on many restaurant menus, and you'll probably finish your stay without ever learning what a Florentine cook can do with cocks' combs, calves' foot, and tripe. Florence in its loftier moods likes to call itself the 'birthplace of international haute cuisine', a claim that has very much to do with Catherine de' Medici, a renowned trencherwoman, who brought a brigade of Florentine chefs with her to Paris and taught the Frenchies how to eat artichokes, but has little to do with the city's contribution to the Italian kitchen; everyone knows its only really popular dish, *bistecca alla Fiorentina*—thick grilled steaks seasoned with salt and pepper. Nevertheless, like any sophisticated city with lots of visitors, Florence has plenty of fine restaurants; even in the cheaper places, standards are high, and if you don't care for anything fancier, there will be lots of good red Chianti to wash down your meal. Please note that many of the best places are likely to close for all of August; you would also be wise to call ahead and reserve, even a day or two in advance.

Expensive

Florence is blessed with one of the finest gourmet restaurants in Italy, the **Enoteca Pinchiorri**, Via Ghibellina 87, near the Casa Buonarroti, tel 242 777. The owners inherited the building, a wine shop, some 10 years ago, and have converted it into a beautifully appointed restaurant, with meals served in a garden court in the summer; they've also increased what was already in the cellars to an astonishing collection of some 80,000 bottles of the best Italy and France have to offer. The cooking, a mixture of *nouvelle cuisine* and traditional Tuscan recipes, wins prizes every year. You may leave behind as much as L100 000 here—much more if you order a prestigious wine or champagne (closed Sun and Mon lunch, and Aug). **Relais le Jardin**, the restaurant in the Regency Umbria hotel in Piazza d'Azeglio 5, tel 245 247, is rapidly establishing itself as one of Florence's best; the setting is lovely and refined, and dishes like delicate crêpes filled with zucchini blossoms, artichoke hearts, or asparagus and medallions of veal with rhubarb are bringing Florentines and visitors back for more (L80 000; closed Sun). For a special romantic evening, Florence offers—what else but Dante by Candlelight or **Dante al Lume di Candela**, in the heart of the historic centre, Via delle Terme 23r, tel 294 566, where you can go ethnic with bean and tripe specialities, or test the famous aphrodisiac qualities of truffles, oysters, and champagne (L65 000; closed Sun).

Moderate

One of the most Florentine of Florentine restaurants, **Cibreo** overlooks the market of Sant'Ambrogio on Via dei Macci 118/r, tel 234 1100. The decor is simple—food is the main concern here, and all of it is market fresh. You can go native here and order tripe antipasto, pumpkin soup, and cocks' combs and kidneys, or play it safe with prosciutto from the Casentino, a fragrant soup (no pasta here) of tomatoes, mussels, or bell pepper, leg of lamb stuffed with artichokes or duck stuffed with sultanas and pine nuts. Top it off with a delicious lemon *crostata* or cheese cake; accompany it with an excellent choice of Italian or French wines, or a prized bottle of Bass Armagnac (L60 000; closed Sun and Mon, Easter, mid-July–mid-Sept). **Buca Lapi**, Via del Trebbio 1/r, tel 213 768, is another traditional Florentine restaurant, located since 1800 in the old wine cellar of the lovely Palazzo Antinori. Experiment with *pappardelle al cinghiale* (wide pasta with boar), which tastes better than it sounds; the *bistecca fiorentina* here is hard to beat, downed with many different Tuscan wines (L50 000). In the Oltrarno, **Il Barone di Porta Romana**, Via Romana 123, tel 220 585 is one of the least typical Florentine restaurants, with dining out in a large garden and fresh fish dishes the speciality (try the spaghetti with crabmeat); in the winter operations move indoors and heartier meat dishes reign, served with plenty of *porcini* mushrooms and truffles (L55–65 000; closed Sun).

Sabatini, Via Panzani 41, behind S. Maria Novella, tel 282 802, the only Florentine restaurant with a branch in Tokyo, has been a favourite with tourists and locals for decades. It's a little old-fashioned, but you may find the sober elegance the perfect setting for enjoying their big Florentine steaks, the flamboyant *spaghetti alla lampada* and homemade pasta, herbed leg of lamb, and a decadent *semifreddo* with hot chocolate sauce (L55–65 000; closed Mon and first 2 weeks July). If *cucina nuova fiorentina* sounds intriguing, try the fare at **Caffè Concerto**, Lungarno Colombo 7, tel 677 377, served on a fine veranda overlooking the Arno; unlike most restaurants it remains open late for light midnight suppers (L45–55 000; closed Sun and 3 weeks in Aug). **Le Fonticine**, Via Nazionale 79, tel 282 106, surrounded by the tourist madness near the railway station, has not let its considerable success ruin it; fine homemade pasta cooked in the style of Italy's culinary capital, Bologna, and the thickest *bistecca* in Florence, and lots of truffles, served in a cosy atmosphere with beamed ceiling and walls covered with Tuscan paintings (L45 000; closed Sat and Sun, Aug).

Inexpensive

In the Oltrarno you can descend into a subterranean wine cellar; **Il Cantinone**, Via S. Spirito 5, tel 218 898, specializes in Chianti Classico and country cooking—*pappa al pomodoro* (thick tomato soup), polenta with boar, beans and sausage; one room is devoted to wine tasting and antipasti (L25–30 000). Near the Piazza dei Ciompi, **La Vie en Rose**, Borgo Allegri 68, tel 245 860, is a popular place serving delights like fresh green pasta with clams and saffron, and duck with prunes for around L35 000. For a change of pace, **Il Cuscussù**, Via Farini 2a, tel 241 890, offers imaginative kosher meals—couscous, goulash, and near-eastern favourites, served with Chianti or Israeli wines (L30 000). Next to S. Croce, **Il Carretto**, Via San Giuseppe 22, tel 241 773 is a pleasant little place with a big menu, tasty pizzas baked in a traditional wood-burning oven (L28 000). Nearby, at Via San Giuseppe 26, **Trattoria del Francescano**, tel 241 605, offers tempting competition followed by delicious desserts (L40 000; closed Wed and 2 weeks in Aug). **Garga**, Via del Moro 40, tel 298 898 is a charming if slightly cramped place run by a Florentine and his Canadian wife, serving mouthwatering homemade pasta, and delicately prepared meat and fish dishes (L40 000; closed Mon). On Via Ghibellina 51, **Ristorante Dino**, tel 241 452, has excellent seasonal dishes and a famous *filettino di maiale al cartoccio* (pork fillets baked in paper) and a wide selection of wines (L40 000; closed Sun evening and Mon). And finally, for the cheapest meal in Florence, there's the lunch counter in the Sant'Ambrogio Market; no tables, no courtesies, and plenty of butchers and grocers to rub elbows with, but two courses of home cooking for L9000.

Central Florence, by popular demand, is full of *tavole calde*, pizzerias, cafeterias, and snack bars, where you can grab a sandwich or a salad instead of a full sit-down meal (one of the best piazza-by-the-slice places is just across from the Medici Chapels). This may change. Lately the city has been trying to banish 'fast food' from the centre, in a bizarre attempt to upscale its tourism—they would prefer that we bought fewer hamburgers and more jewellery.

Restaurants Around Florence

In Fiesole there are plenty of mediocre overpriced restaurants and one where the food is excellent: **Cave da Maiano**, Via delle Cave 16, tel 59 133, at Maiano. On its beautiful garden terrace are served delights like green tortellini, filled with veal and chicken, or an excellent risotto; roast pigeon, *involtini* of veal and mushrooms, followed by excellent desserts (L40 000). In Artimino, near Carmignano, **Da Delfina**, Via della Chiesa, tel 871 8074 is worth the drive out for its enchanting surroundings, lovely views, the charming atmosphere, and sublime cooking—homemade tagliatelle with a sauce made from greens, risotto with garden vegetables, wild asparagus, succulent kid and lamb dishes—at equally lovely prices (L35–45 000). Near the Medici villa in Artimino **Biagio Pignatta**, tel 871 8080, has an excellent *ribollita*, crêpes alla Catherine de' Medici and more for around L35 000.

Part V

CHIANTI AND THE MUGELLO

Villa Cafaggiolo

These two regions, Chianti to the south and the Mugello to the north of Florence, one world-famous and one obscure, are delightfully rural and endowed with every Tuscan charm. No Brunelleschi could have designed the grand stone farmhouses that crown every hill, built with an intuitive aesthetic that rarely fails, each different, offering endless variations of arches, loggias, and towers, set in an equally endless variety of rolling hills, vineyards, olives, and cypresses. Towns are few, monuments scattered and of minor interest, paintings and sculpture very rare. But you'll find few places more enchanting to explore—by car, by bicycle, by foot—in a day or a lifetime.

Chianti

> From good Chianti, an aged wine, majestic and
> imperious, that passes through my heart and chases
> away without trouble every worry and grief...
>
> —Francesco Redi, *Bacchus in Tuscany*

In the 17th century, naturalist and poet Francesco Redi was the first to note the virtues of 'Florentine red' from Chianti, but since then the Italians have invested a lot of worry and grief into defining exactly what 'Chianti' means. The name apparently derives from an Etruscan family named Clanti; geographically it refers, roughly, to the hilly region between Florence and Siena, between the Florence-Siena Superstrada del Palio and the

A1 between Florence and Arezzo. The part of this region in Siena province is known as *Chianti Storico* or Chianti Geografico, once the territories of the Lega del Chianti, a consortium of barons formed in 1385 to protect their interests (and their wine), who adopted a black cockerel as their emblem.

But Chianti is an oenological name as well as a geographical one, and as such first became official in 1716, when Grand Duke Cosimo III defined which parts of Tuscany could call their vintage Chianti, in effect making wine history—it was the first time that a wine had its production area delimited. The Lorraine grand dukes promoted advances in winemaking techniques and the export of Chianti. Yet the Chianti as we know it had yet to be developed, and it was largely the creation of one man—the 'Iron Baron', Bettino Ricasoli, briefly the second prime minister of unified Italy. The baron was very wealthy but not very good looking, and Luigi Barzini, in *The Italians*, recounts how jealous he became when a young man asked his new bride to dance at a ball in Florence. Ricasoli at once ordered her into their carriage and gave the driver the address of the ancient family seat at Brolio in the Monti del Chianti—an isolated castle that the poor woman rarely left ever after.

To pass the time the baron began to experiment with different vines and processes, eventually hitting upon a pleasing mix of red Sangiovese and Canaiolo grapes, with a touch of white Malvasia, twice fermented in the old Tuscan manner. At the same time the famous dark green flask was invented, the *strapeso*, with its straw liner woven by the local women. The end product took the Paris Exhibition of 1878 by storm; imitators soon appeared, and in 1924, the boundaries of Chianti Storico were slightly more than doubled to create *Chianti Classico*, drawn by local producers to protect the wine's name, adopting the now familiar black cockerel of the Lega del Chianti as its symbol. In 1967 Chianti Classico, along with Tuscany's six other Chianti vinicultural zones, was given its *denominazione di origine* status, and production soared, but quality and sales declined. To improve the wine, the Chianti Classico Consortium upscaled to a DOCG rating to guarantee all wines bearing the black cockerel would be tested and approved by a panel of judges.

But it was tales of Elizabeth Barrett Browning quaffing Chianti and finding her inspiration in its ruby splendour, as well as the sunny rural elegance of the region, that attracted first the English and Dutch, the Swiss, Americans, French and Germans, especially in the 1960s and 70s, who form one of Italy's densest foreign colonies, wrily nicknamed 'Chianti-shire'. They brought into the region more money than Chianti's mouldering barons and contessas had seen since the Renaissance; real property prices shot to the moon. But the presence of so much money has begun to cast a shadow over the heart of this ancient, enchanting region; snobbery and pretensions threaten to poison the pleasurable plonk of yesteryear; limited edition numbered bottles, offered by some vintners, are a bit too much; designer-label Chianti is just around the corner. The old vines, following the contours of the hills, are being pulled out for specialized vines in geometric straight lines. And as any old timer will tell you, the modern DOCG Chianti Classico sniffed and gurgled by wine professionals isn't anything like the joyous, spontaneous wine that made Chianti famous in the first place.

Some 800 farms and estates (only a selection of the most historic are listed in the text below) produce wine in the mere 70,000 hectares in the Chianti Classico zone, and one of the chief pleasures in visiting is trying as many labels as possible—with the different mixtures of grapes, different soils, and bottling methods, each should be, or at least strives to be, individual. Nor do the estates limit themselves to Chianti; many produce Vinsanto, a white wine called Bianca della Lega, and many reds, as well as Chianti's other speciality, an especially delicate *extra-vergine* olive oil. Before setting out, ring in advance to check hours.

GETTING AROUND

The two main north–south routes through Chianti, the old Roman Via Cassia (N. 2) and the Chiantigiana (N. 222) rival one another in beauty; an ideal motoring wine tour would take in the east–west N. 429 between the Badia a Coltibuono and Castellina. Distances aren't great, though the single-lane winding routes make for leisurely travel.

Public transportation is fairly easy in Chianti and all by bus, though you may not always find connections between two towns very commodious; from Florence SITA buses will take you to Greve (25 km/45 min), Gaiole (55 km/1½ hrs), Castellina in Chianti (44 km/1 hr), Mercatale, S. Casciano in Val di Pesa (17 km/25 min) Tavernelle Val di Pesa (29 km/40 min), Panzano, Strada, and Radda (42 km/1 hr); CAP buses run frequently from Florence to Impruneta (14 km/20 min). From Siena TRA-IN buses go to Castellina (20 km/25 min), Radda (30 km/40 min), Tavernelle (38 km/50 min) and S. Casciano (49 km/1¼hrs), Tavarnuzze and Strada.

Western Chianti: Florence to Tavernelle Val di Pesa

Chianti begins 10 km south of Florence, but on the way you may want to follow the sign west off N. 222 just past the autostrada, for **Ponte a Ema** and the prettily sited 14th-century chapel of the Alberti, **Santa Caterina dell'Antella**, with contemporary frescoes on St Catherine's life, one of Spinello Aretino's greatest works (closed Sun). Further along, at Grassina, there's a turn off to **Impruneta**, a large town on a plateau noted for its terracotta tiles (including those on Brunelleschi's dome) and pottery, very much on sale, especially during the enormous **St Luke's Horse and Mule Fair** in October. The fair takes place in the main piazza, in the shadow of Impruneta's pride and joy, the ancient **Collegiata**, built to house a miraculous icon of the Madonna and Child attributed to St Luke, dug up by a team of oxen in the 10th century. Bombed during the last war, restorers took the opportunity to bring the Collegiata back to its appearance in the Renaissance, to match its two beautiful chapels, one housing the icon and the other a piece of the True Cross, both designed by Michelozzo and richly decorated with enamel terracottas by Luca della Robbia. In an adjacent chapel there's a marble relief of the *Finding of the Icon* by the school of Donatello; the bronze crucifix in the nave is attributed to Giambologna. The campanile survives from the 13th century, and the fine portico was built in 1634.

Machiavelli in Exile

From the N. 222 south of Florence, a by-road leads west from Tavarnuzze (8 km) for **Sant'Andrea in Percussina**, long the country fief of the Machiavelli. Here Niccolò spent his tedious exile, which he described in a letter as whiling away the day in the tavern

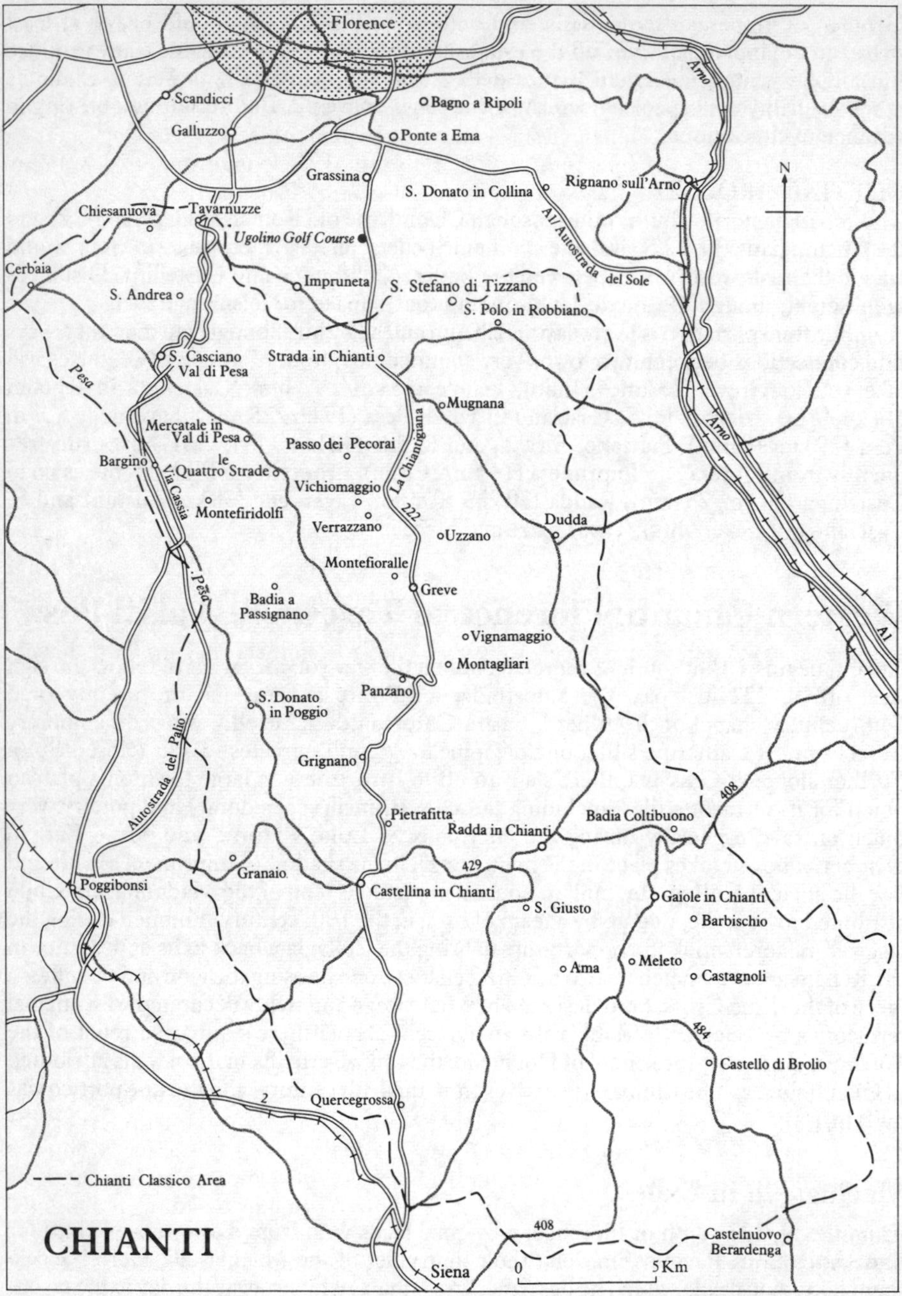

Florence
Arno
Scandicci
Bagno a Ripoli
Galluzzo
Ponte a Ema
Grassina
Rignano sull'Arno
N
S. Donato in Collina
Chiesanuova
Tavarnuzze
A1/Autostrada del Sole
Ugolino Golf Course
Cerbaia
Impruneta
S. Stefano di Tizzano
S. Andrea
S. Polo in Robbiano
S. Casciano Val di Pesa
Strada in Chianti
Pesa
Mugnana
Mercatale in Val di Pesa
Passo dei Pecorai
Bargino
le Quattro Strade
Via Cassia
La Chiantigiana
222
Vichiomaggio
Montefiridolfi
Verrazzano
Dudda
Uzzano
Montefioralle
Greve
Badia a Passignano
Vignamaggio
A1
Montagliari
Panzano
S. Donato in Poggio
Autostrada del Palio
Grignano
408
Pietrafitta
Badia Coltibuono
Radda in Chianti
429
Granaio
Poggibonsi
Castellina in Chianti
S. Giusto
Gaiole in Chianti
Barbischio
Ama
Meleto
Castagnoli
484
Castello di Brolio
2
Quercegrossa
Chianti Classico Area
408
Castelnuovo Berardenga
CHIANTI
Siena
0
5 Km

'playing at *cricca* and tric-trac, and this gave rise to a thousand arguments and endless exchanges of insults, most of the time there is a fight over a penny . . . and so surrounded by these lice, I blow the cobwebs from my brain and relieve the unkindness of my fate.' In the evening he would retire to work on *The Prince*. His old tavern is still a tavern and his home, the **Albergaccio**, contains a small museum devoted to his life. Near Chiesanuova, to the north, there's the fine 16th-century **Palazzo al Bosco**, attributed by some to Michelangelo, an interesting villa built atop a 13th-century structure (tel 824 2212; tours of the cellars, tastings and sales of Chianti and Rosso di San Valentino, and olive oil available). The stately, theatrical 15th-century **Villa Tattoli** to the west (on the Chiesanuova-Cerbaia road) features two levels of arcades (tel 827 042, offering tours of the cellars, Chianti and olive oil). Near Cerbaia itself, 5 km from S. Casciano, **Villa Talente**, former property of the artists who built Orsanmichele in Florence, tel 826 388, offers Chianti, white wine, and olive oil.

WHERE TO STAY AND EAT (tel prefix 055)

In this section of Chianti, hotels tend to be small and usually annexed to restaurants, though note that many of the larger wine estates have a few rooms or apartments to let; call ahead to see what's available. At Bagno a Ripoli, near Ponte a Ema, *****__Villa La Massa__, Via La Massa 6, tel 630 051, will indulge you in luxury and Tuscan tranquillity—hopefully not spoilt when you get the bill—L350 000. Bagno a Ripoli's **Centanni**, Via Centanni 7, tel 630 122 is an exceptionally pleasant restaurant among the olive groves, where you can dine on a delicious array of antipasti, and Renaissance recipes like *brasata dei Medici*, a sweet and sour, braised beef dish dating from the 17th century (L40 000; closed Sat lunch & Sun).

Impruneta has little in the way of hotels, but ***__La Vallombrosina__, Via Montebuoni 95, tel 202 0491 will provide a comfortable roof over your head (L95 000, with bath). **I Falciani**, Via Cassia 245, tel 202 0091 is a rustic place full of locals, where you may dine with the TV for company or not on tasty *crostini, ribollita*, and in the fall, hunters' roast meat platter or Tuscan fried chicken (L25–30 000). Machiavelli's ancient tavern in Sant'Andrea in Percussina is now owned by the Conti Serristori Wine Company and called the **Osteria di Machiavelli**, tel 828 471, serving simple Tuscan meals—in summer, be sure to order the refreshing *panzanella* for starters—and fine wines from the estate (L40 000); you can also buy bottles to take home.

Along the Via Cassia (N. 2)

Up-to-date **San Casciano in Val di Pesa**, 17 km south of Florence, is the largest and busiest town in Chianti. Long an outpost of Florence, it suffered numerous vicissitudes until its **walls** were begun by the ill-fated Duke of Athens in 1342. Within these, near the gateway, the church of **Santa Maria del Prato** (1335) has retained its trecento interior and trecento art: a fine pulpit by Giovanni Balducci da Pisa, a pupil of Andrea Pisano, a crucifix attributed to Simone Martini, a triptych by Ugolino di Neri, and framed paintings on the pilasters of Giotto's pupil, Taddeo Gaddi. In the vicinity of San Casciano Florentine merchants and noblemen dotted the countryside with villas: the late Renaissance **Villa Le Corti**, 2 km east on the Mercatale road, owned by the princely

Corsini family for the past six centuries (tel 820 123, with the estate's Chianti on sale); the 17th-century **Poggio Torselli**, just off N. 2, approached through a long avenue of cypresses and surrounded by a lovely garden (tel 820 214, offering its own Chianti label).

Mercatale, Bargino, and Barberino Val d'Elsa

Mercatale, 5 km east of S. Casciano, grew up around its *mercato*, or market, protected in the old days by the **Castle of the Florentine Bishops**, now a ruin fit only to protect the odd lizard. A far more muscular castle, just to the east on the road to Passo dei Pecorai is the **Castello di Gabbiano**, bound by four round towers. The Bardi put it up in the 11th century, before they moved to Florence and founded the greatest pre-Medici bank (tel 821 053, it offers tastings and lunches with advance notice, on sale are its own brand of Chianti, Vinsanto, grappa, and olive oil). Other villas worth visiting near Mercatale are: **Villa Caserotta**, former property of the Strozzi, and the fortified **Villa Palagio**, on the Mercatale–Campoli–Montefiridolfi road, adapted from a 14th-century castle. A narrow lane by-way the Mercatale-Panzano road will bring you to **La Torre a Luciana**, an unspoiled medieval hamlet once belonging to the Pitti family.

The Via Cassia, between San Casciano and Bargino, passes by the ancient **Castle of Bibbione**, once residence of the Buondelmonte family, who owned much of the surrounding territory in the days when they were throwing fat on the Guelph and Ghibbeline fires in Florence. Near **Bargino**, in the same bellicose spirit, is the impressive fortified hamlet of **Montefiridolfi**, just east of the Via Cassia. This road, meanwhile, rolls south through some lovely hills towards **Tavarnelle Val di Pesa**, a town of mostly 19th-century origin, and the medieval **Barberino Val d'Elsa**, with some Etruscan finds in the town hall and a good Romanesque church, the **Pieve di Sant'Appiano**, built in the 10th century. From here the Via Cassia continues to **Poggibonsi** (see p. 316), with a possible detour to **La Paneretta**, a sturdy 15th-century fort amid the olive groves, with Baroque frescoes inside.

WHERE TO STAY AND EATING OUT (tel prefix 055)

Most of the district's lodgings are here, as well as some of Chianti's best restaurants, among them **La Tenda Rossa**, located to the north in Cerbaia, in Piazza del Monumento 9, tel 826 132. This is a family-run abode of haute cuisine: pumpkin-filled tortellini, or perhaps lettuce crêpes filled with artichoke hearts for starters, followed by chicken breasts with grated *porcini* mushrooms, or duck's breast in balsam vinegar. The challenge is trying to save room for one of the Red Tent's excellent, innovative desserts, all prepared with the lightest of touches (L70 000, but worth it). ***L'Antica Posta**, in S. Casciano's Piazza Zannoni 1 (tel 820 116), has 10 comfortable rooms, all with bath (L75–110 000), as well as a restaurant to rival the Tenda Rossa, but with more Persian rugs and silver decorations; among the offerings are a risotto with artichokes and crayfish, *taglierini* with razor clams and asparagus, breast of pheasant flavoured with thyme, or rabbit in a sauce of creamed mussels; the wine list is superb. Reservations are obligatory (L75 000+ à la carte, but around L55 000 for a *menu degustazione* with wine). Fresh, fresh fish is on the menu at **Nello**, Via IV Novembre 64, in S. Casciano, tel 820 163, and you can start with something you don't find every day in Tuscany—*pesto alla genovese*; the wines include most Chianti labels (L35–40 000). Other places to sleep in the area are all small: ****Mini Soggiorno**, Via Leonardo da Vinci 5, tel 820 732 in

Bardella has simple rooms for L48 000, all with bath; ***Bargino**, Via Cassia 122, tel 820 732, in Bargino has seven rooms in a garden along the old Roman road, all with bath (L42–50 000).

In Mercatale, **La Biscondola**, Via Grevigiana, tel 821 381 enjoys a fine sunny and protected location where you can linger over traditional dishes like *pappa al pomodoro*, rabbit in mushrooms and white wine (a Chianti speciality) or a superb *bistecca alla fiorentina* (L40 000); and you can spend the night in the little ***Soggiorno Paradiso**, Piazza V. Veneto 28, tel 821 327, for L48 000, with bath. In Tavarelle try **La Fattoria**, Via del Cerro 11, tel 807 000, a typical Chianti farmhouse converted into an attractive restaurant that offers ravioli filled with truffles, and a succulent suckling pig roasted in a wood oven (L40 000). Tavarnelle has Chianti's pleasant **Youth Hostel**, on Via Roma 137, tel 807 7009, open year round, with 59 beds.

Central Chianti: Along the Chiantigiana

From Florence the scenic Chiantigiana, or N. 222 passes the Ugolino Golf Course (see Florence: Sports) and offers its first tempting detour at Petigliolo: turn left after 4 km for the ivy-covered **Santo Stefano a Tizzano**, a Romanesque church built by the Buondelmonti, not far from an 11th-century castle-villa, the **Castello di Tizzano** (tel 640 026, offering Chianti Riserva, Vinsanto Naturale, and prize-winning olive oil). The same road continues for 2 km to **San Polo in Robbiana**, the centre of Tuscany's iris industry, celebrated in an **Iris Festival** in May. On a hill from San Polo you can see a lonely building once belonging to the Knights Templar; an equally ancient church, **San Miniato in Robbiana** was reconsecrated in 1077 by the Bishop of Fiesole, according to a still legible inscription. San Polo's **Antico Toscano**, tel 855 110 is a wine shop with offerings from all over the region.

Strada, a village 14 km from Florence along the Chiantigiana, is believed to have received its odd name from an old Roman road. Just to the south the road towards the Valdarno was protected in the Middle Ages by the **Castello di Mugano**, one of the best-preserved in the region and polished up by a recent restoration. The rolling countryside is the dominant feature along the Chiantigiana until **Vicchiomaggio** with a distinctive castle that once hosted Leonardo da Vinci. This is now the British-run **Fattoria Castello di Vicchiomaggio**, tel 853 003, offering its own label of Chianti, Vinsanto, olive oil, and honey. Nearby **Verrazzano** is a name that New Yorkers will recognize at once; in the castle was born Giovanni da Verrazzano, not the usual Chianti landlubber but a captain who, in the service of Francis I of France, discovered New York Harbour in 1524 and Manhattan island as well. He disappeared on his second voyage to Brazil, but surely smiles down from heaven on the enormous bridge named in his honour, so many miles away from Chianti. His birthplace, the **Castello di Verrazzano**, tel 853 949, offers a variety of wines and olive oils, and tastings with 3 days' notice. Just east of the Chiantigiana, 1.5 km north of Greve stands the fine **Castello di Uzzano**, built by the bishop of Florence in the 13th century and since then gradually converted into one of Chianti's most impressive villa estates (tastings on a day's notice, tel 853 032).

Greve and Environs

The biggest **wine fair** in Chianti occurs every September in the medieval townlet of Greve (pop. 10,800), and as such it is looked upon as the capital of Chianti. Located on the banks of the river Greve, it is celebrated for its charming, arcaded, funnel-shaped **Piazza del Mercatale**, with a statue of Verrazzano in its centre. And that's about all—its castle was burned in 1387, and its Franciscan monastery converted to a prison in the last century! However, in the parish church of **Santa Croce** there's a triptych by Lorenzo di Bicci and a painting by the 'Master of Greve'.

Greve is awash in wine. Seek out specialized wine shops like the **Bottega del Chianti Classico**, Via Cesare Battisti 6, and the **Enoteca di Gallo Nero**, Piazzetta S. Croce 8, or the **Castello di Querceto** just outside of town on the Figline Val d'Arno road (tel 856 979), a lovely place offering a wide variety of wines, including Sangiovese aged in wooden *barriques* and olive oil; tastings with 5 days' notice. On the Chiantigiana, near Sant'Eufrosino, **Fontodi**, tel 852 005, also has wine aged in *barriques*, Chianti, Bianco della Lega and olive oil; tastings with 3 days' notice.

A kilometre to the west of Greve is the ancient village and castle of **Montefioralle**, where the people of Greve lived in the bad old days. Recently restored, it is an interesting place to poke around in, with its octagonal walls intact, its old tower houses, and two Romanesque churches, **S. Stefano**, housing early Florentine paintings, and the porticoed **Pieve di San Cresci a Montefioralle**, just outside the walls. A minor road west of Montefioralle passes in a kilometre the ruined castle of **Montefili**, built in the 900s as the eastern outpost of one of Chianti's most powerful religious institutions, the **Badia a Passignano**, a fortified complex of ancient foundation, since converted into a villa. The old abbey church, **San Michele**, can be visited, and contains paintings by Ghirlandaio, Alessandro Allori, and Domenico Cresti (better known as Passignano) and a bust of San Giovanni Gualberto, founder of the Vallombrosan Order, who arrived here preaching reform in the mid-11th century. Most of the buildings you see date from the 14th century, with a few remodellings in the 17th and 19th centuries.

Just east of Greve, **Vignamaggio** is the site of a beautiful old villa built by the Gherardini family, the most famous member of whom, Lisa, was born here, and later married Francesco del Giocondo before going on to pose for the world's most famous portrait. **Panzano**, an important agricultural centre 6 km south of Greve on the Chiantigiana, played an important role in the Florence–Siena squabbles, but retains only part of its medieval castle. Today it is best known for its embroidery, and visited for the **Pieve di San Leolino**, 1 km south, with its pretty 16th-century portico on a 12th-century Romanesque structure; inside there's a triptych by Mariotto di Nardo. Another Romanesque church south of Panzano, **Sant'Eufrosino**, just off N. 222, is especially worth visiting for its fine views. Near Panzano, the **Fattoria Montagliari** sells a wide variety of its own wines, grappa, olive oil, cheese, salame, honey, etc. **Pietrafitta**, 9 km further south and 4 km from Castellina, is a lovely old hamlet hidden in the woods.

Castellina in Chianti

One of Chianti's most charming hilltop villages, Castellina (pop. 2700) was fortified by Florence as an outpost against Siena, and its fortunes for centuries depended on who was momentarily on top in their bitter, stupid, endless war. Most grievous to the

Florentines was its loss to a combined Sienese-Aragonese siege in 1478, though after the fall of Siena itself in 1555, both cities lost interest in Castellina, and today it looks much as it did in the quattrocento: the old circuit of **walls** is almost intact, complete with houses built into and on top of them; the **Rocca**, or fortress, in the centre, its mighty donjon now home of the mayor; and the covered walkway, or **Via delle Volte**, part of the 15th-century defensive works. Less historic but just as worth visiting is the **Bottega del Vino Gallo Nero,** Via della Rocca 10 with a vast assortment of wines and olive oils. A kilometre from the centre, you can explore the **Ipogeo Etrusco di Montecalvario**, a 6th-century BC Etruscan tomb that has recently been restored. West of Castellina on N. 429, **Granaio** is synonymous with one of Chianti's most renowned wineries, the **Melini Wine House**, established in 1705 and one of the big innovators in Chianti technology.

There are many splendid old farmhouses and villas around Castellina, nearly all formerly fortifications along Chianti's medieval Maginot line, like the **Villa La Leccia** just southwest of Castellina, and the **Castello di Campalli** near **Fonterutoli**, an ancient hamlet south on the Chiantigiana. In the 13th century Florence and Siena often met here trying to work out peace settlements, none of which endured very long. Peace, however, is the rule at the **Fattoria di Fonterutoli**, in the family since 1435, tel (0577) 740 476, producing wine in traditional oaken casks, Chianti, Bianco della Lega, and other wines, honey, products made from lavender, and an *extra-vergine* that many consider Tuscany's finest. In the vicinity, another old castle with two towers, the **Villa Cerna**, tel (0577) 743 020, now sells Chianti, Vinsanto, and many other wines and olive oil; tastings with a week's notice.

Further south, **Quercegrossa**, 10 km from Siena, is practically a suburb of that city, and was the birthplace of the great quattrocento sculptor Jacopo della Quercia. A by-road forks northeast of here for Vagliagli, site of the medieval **Fattoria della Aiola**, tel (0577) 322 615, with wines, grappa, olive oil, honey, and vinegar.

WHERE TO STAY

Greve (tel prefix 055): Near the centre there's the pleasant and recently refurbished *****Del Chianti**, Piazza Matteotti 86, tel 853 763, with comfortable, stylish air-conditioned rooms, and a pool and garden in the back (L85–110 000). *****Da Verrazzano**, Piazza Matteotti 28, tel 853 189, has rather pricey but elegant 11 rooms in the middle of Greve (L80–100 000 depending on the plumbing). Just south, *****Villa le Barone** in Panzano, Via S. Leolino 19, tel 852 215, is the 16th-century villa of the della Robbia family, who still own it and run it as a lovely, intimate hotel, a great base for visiting the region, or for just lounging around in the pretty garden by the pool; a good place to bring the children. Naturally many of the rooms are decorated in della Robbia blue and white. Minimum stay 3 nights (L125 000).

Castellina (tel prefix 0577): ******Tenuta di Ricavo**, 3 km north of Castellina, tel 740 221, is more than a hotel—it's an entire medieval hamlet of stone houses, wonderfully isolated in the pines and a large garden with a swimming pool. Many of the rooms are in the old houses, ideal for families; open June–Sept (L150–240 000 per person half board). ******Villa Casalecchi**, set among the trees and vineyards on a slope, tel 740 240, is a comfortable old house, with some elegant rooms full of antiques and some not so elegant, but a big swimming pool and enchanting views over the hills; open April–Oct (L170 000). Two old farmhouses have recently been combined to create the smart new

***Salivolpi, just outside Castellina on Via Salivolpi, tel 740 484; a garden and pool are added attractions (L55–65 000).

EATING OUT

In San Polo, or rather out in the open countryside, **Trattoria Merendero** in Via S. Lavagnini 14, tel (055) 855 019, offers some tasty un-Tuscan surprises: fried stuffed olives (a speciality of the Marches) and *spaghetti al pesto*, as well as the region's old standbys (L30 000). In and around Greve there are plenty of choices; one of the most charming is right in the centre: **Giovanni da Verrazzano** (see the hotel above) furnished with 19th-century antiques, and with a lovely terrace for summer dining, overlooking the piazza. The main meat dishes are especially good here—*nana in sugo* (duck in wine sauce), turkey with olives, and a greatly varied mixed grill (L40 000). Nearby in Montefioralle, the **Taverna del Guerrino**, Via di Montefioralle 39, tel 853 106, is a fine, rustic place surrounded by a panoramic garden, offering good Tuscan home cooking, including Tuscan gazpacho—*panzanella*—stuffed tomatoes, sausage and beans *all'uccelletto* and wines from the local fattoria (L25–30 000). **La Cantinetta**, on the Chiantigiana 93, in Spedaluzzo (near Greve), tel 857 2000, has good homemade pasta and country specialities like stuffed rabbit, pigeon, stuffed artichokes, and grilled meats (L40 000). To the south in Panzano, **Montagliari**, Via di Montagliari 27, tel 852 184, is decorated in the style of an old Tuscan farmhouse, with tables out in the panoramic garden. First courses include ravioli filled with walnuts or penne with raw tomatoes and basil; for seconds try the boar *alla cacciatora* or the *pollastro Montagliari al vino bianco* (chicken with white wine and black olives); reservations obligatory; L60 000. In Castellina, **Antica Trattoria La Torre**, Piazza Umberto 1, tel (0577) 740 236, is a popular, family-run place, with a cosy atmosphere and tasty dishes like risotto with mushrooms and an exceptional *Fagiano alla Torre*, prepared to an ancient Chianti recipe (L40 000). There's another good restaurant near Castellina towards Poggibonsi, at S. Antonio al Ponte: **Pestello**, tel (0577) 740 215, in an old stone building tastefully redone, specializing in *pappardelle sul coniglio* (though you've really got to be a pro to tell rabbit sauce from the usual hare); also roast meats, game, and local wine, L35 000.

Monti del Chianti: Radda and Gaiole

East of Castellina lies the steeper, more rugged region of the Monti del Chianti. One of the higher hills supports the ancient capital of the Lega del Chianti, **Radda** (pop. 1650) where the streets have kept their medieval plan, radiating from the central piazza and its stately **Palazzo Comunale**, encrusted with coats-of-arms and a 15th-century fresco in the atrium of the Madonna, the Baptist, and St Christopher. Just outside of town is a pretty porticoed Franciscan church, called the **Monastero**, dating from the 15th century. There are two resolutely medieval villages nearby: **Ama**, with its castle 8 km to the south, near the attractive Romanesque church of **S. Giusto**; and **Volpaia**, 7 km to the north, with another ancient castle and walls, and an unexpected 'Brunelleschian' church, called La Commenda, in a doll-sized piazza. Also near Radda, the **Fattoria Vigna Vecchia**, tel 738 090, offers Chianti, grappa, Vinsanto, olive oil, and tastings with 3 days' notice.

Gaiole, 10 km east of Radda, is reached by way of the ancient **Badia a Coltibuono,** one of the gems of Chianti, a singular place set among centuries-old trees and gardens. The abbey is believed to have been founded in 770, but passed over to the Vallombrosan Order in the 12th century. The Romanesque church of **San Lorenzo** dates from 1049, while the monastery was converted into a splendid villa, owned in the 19th century by the Poniatowski, one of Poland's greatest noble families, and now occupied by a wine estate (P. Stucchi Prinetti, tel 749 498) and restaurant (see p. 188).

Gaiole (pop. 4780) was an ancient market town and these days is basically a modern one; the **Agricoltori Chianti Geografico**, Via Mulinaccio 10, tel (0577) 749 489, is the headquarters of local cooperative where you can purchase Chianti, Vernaccia di S. Gimignano, Vinsanto and olive oil; the **Enoteca Montagnani**, Via B. Bandinelli 9, specializes in Chianti Classico. Beside wine tasting Gaiole has little to offer, but serves as a starting point for visiting the impressive castles in this strategic area between the Arno and Siena. Just to the west are the walls and imposing donjon of the **Castello di Vertine,** a well-preserved slice of the 13th-century and one of the most striking sights in all Chianti. To the east of Gaiole stands the ancient fortified village of **Barbischio**, and just 3 km south on N. 408 is the impressive medieval **Castello di Meleto** with its sturdy cylindrical towers still intact. From here the road continues another 4.5 km up to the mighty **Castello di Castagnoli**, guarding a fascinating little medieval town in a commanding position.

Most majestic of all is the Iron Baron's celebrated isolated **Castello di Brolio**, some 10 km south of Gaiole along N. 484, high on its own hill with views for miles around. First mentioned in 1009, when Matilda of Tuscany's father Bonifacio donated it to the monks of the Badia in Florence, it came into the possession of the Ricasoli in 1167. The castle was bombarded for weeks in 1478 by the Aragonese and Sienese, who later had it demolished, so the 'the walls levelled with the earth'. After the war, Florence rebuilt it, and in the mid-19th century Baron Ricasoli converted it into the splendid fortified residence while experimenting on the modern formula for Chianti (open daily 9–12 and 3 to sunset); the **Barone Ricasoli Wine House**, tel (0577) 747 104, offers its famous wines, olive oil, and more. At Madonna del Brolio, 10 km to the south, you can also visit the **Cantine Barone Ricasoli** by phoning ahead, tel (0577) 311 961. The **Fattoria dei Pagliaresi**, tel (0577) 359 070 is located near Castelnuovo Berardenga, between S. Gusmé and Pianella and offers older wines as well as new, and olive oil. There are riding stables 5 km east at the **Fattoria San Giusto**, at Monti, tel (0577) 363 011. To the south, **Castelnuovo Berardenga** is an agricultural centre with the remains of a 14th-century castle, and from here it's 16 km to **Montaperti**, where Florence almost went down the tubes (to continue south, see p. 337).

WHERE TO STAY (tel prefix 0577)

Radda: ****Villa Miranda** (or Minucci) is located in Villa a Radda, tel 738 021, a small inn founded in 1842, an old posthouse, though now there's a swimming pool instead of a stable. There's a good restaurant, featuring good homecooking and a dish called *coniglio ubriaco al Chianti* (rabbit drunk on Chianti). Rooms L70 000 with bath, L55 000 without, meals L35 000. The ******Fattoria Vignale**, Via Pianigiani 15, tel 738 300, has 12 rooms available from April–Oct, in a charming old house, with fine views over the pool and countryside, (L150–200 000, with breakfast). Much simpler are the nine rooms annexed to a very popular restaurant, ***Il Girarrosto**, in the village centre at Via Roma 41, tel 738 010 (L35 000 without bath, L42 000 with).

Gaiole: ****Park Hotel Cavarchione** on the Vertine road, tel 749 550, is an imaginatively renovated farmhouse with only 11 rooms, run by Germans, with lovely views, pool, and garden (open mid-March–Oct, L175–190 000). ***Foresteria di Spaltenna**, in Spaltenna, a hill just above Gaiole, tel 749 483, is beautifully located in a proper old fortified monastery; with some theatrical medieval touches; and few creature comforts, but what do you expect in a monastery? Closed Nov–Mar; seven antique furnished rooms L130 000 with bath. There are three large apartments available in the famous **Castello di Brolio**; write (Castello di Brolio, Gaiole in Chianti, Siena), or call (0566) 747 104 far in advance.

EATING OUT

In Radda, **Petroio**, Via XX Settembre 23, tel (0577) 738 094, is a good, family-run place belonging to the Fattoria Vignale featuring Tuscan home cooking, very popular locally (L35 000); if you're in the mood for a roast meat and wine debauch, try **Il Girarrosto** (L30 000; see hotels, above). **Badia a Coltibuono**, located next to the old abbey of the same name between Radda and Gaiole, tel (0577)749 424, offers delicious tortelloni 'dalla zia Carla', meats roasted on a spit, and tempting desserts (L40–50 000). An old mill converted into a restaurant, **Il Molino** along the Via Chiantigiana 31, at Le Bagnaie-Monti, near Gaiole, tel (0577) 747 062, where the menu features a nourishing minestrone and well-prepared marinated loin of pork with rice (L25–30 000). In Brolio, **Da Gino**, tel (0577) 747 194, is operated by the castle and serves good, if not wildly imaginative, Tuscan cuisine with Castello di Brolio wines, not surprisingly (L25 000).

The Mugello

Over the years, as their ambitions became less discreet, the Medici concocted a pretty story of how they descended from knights of Charlemagne. In truth they came down to Florence from the Mugello, the hilly region just to the north—as did Giotto and Fra Angelico. As far back as Boccaccio's time, the Mugello was considered the loveliest region of the Florentine *contada*, and its bluish green hills are dotted with elegant weekend and summer retreats, rather smarter than the typical stone *fattorie* of the Chianti. The Florentines come here whenever they can, and if you find yourself stewing with them in the traffic gridlocks approaching Piazza della Libertà, know that all you have to do is turn up Via Bologna and in 10 minutes you'll be in a cool, enchanting world immersed in green.

The Mugello is to the north of Florence, where altitudes rise appreciably towards the central Apennine spine that divides Tuscany from Emilia-Romagna. Tucked in these hills lies the Mugello basin, a broad valley along the river Sieve and its tributaries, which, in the Miocene era, held a lake. Most of the towns of the Mugello are here, surrounded by a sea of vines; olives cover the slopes, but soon give way to deep forests of pines, chestnuts, and oaks, cool and refreshing, dotted with small resorts. And like any fashion-conscious Florentine, the Mugello changes colours with the seasons, and is strikingly beautiful any time of year, a place to return to, again and again.

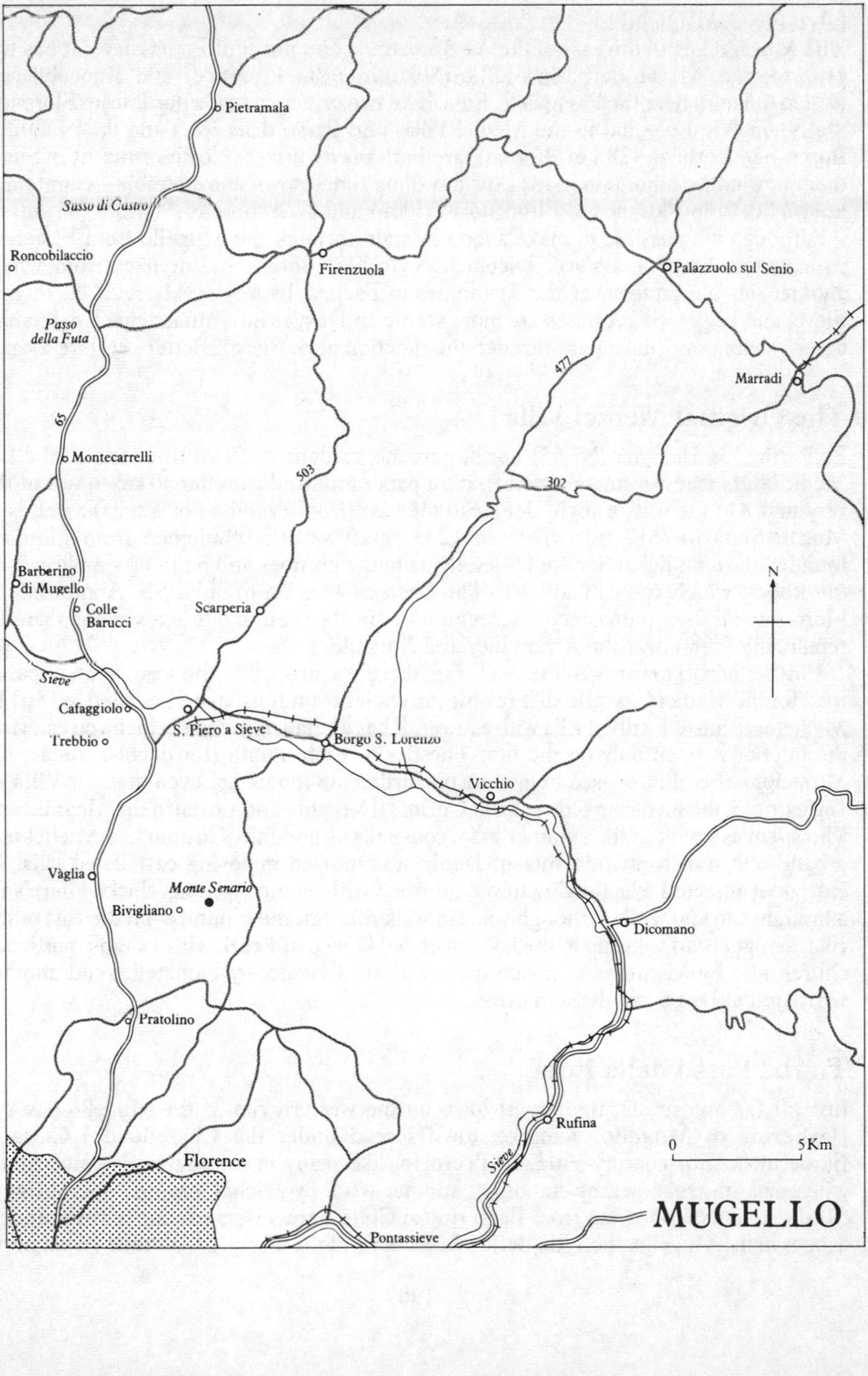
Pietramala
Sasso di Castro
Roncobilaccio
Firenzuola
Palazzuolo sul Senio
Passo della Futa
477
Marradi
65
503
302
Montecarrelli
Barberino di Mugello
Colle Barucci
Scarperia
N
Sieve
Cafaggiolo
S. Piero a Sieve
Trebbio
Borgo S. Lorenzo
Vicchio
Vàglia
Monte Senario
Bivigliano
Dicomano
Pratolino
Rufina
0
5 Km
Sieve
Florence
Pontassieve
MUGELLO

GETTING AROUND

The Mugello lies to the east of the A1 Autostrada and north of Pontassieve. It has two exits off the A1: at Barberino (28 km/20 min from Florence) and Roncobilaccio (47 km/35 min) near the Passo della Futa. The two principal roads north from Florence, the N. 65 (Via Bologna) to the Medici Villas and Passo della Futa and the N. 302 to Borgo San Lorenzo (28 km/40 min), are both pretty drives. North of the river Sieve, though, winding mountain roads slow travelling times down considerably—count on at least 2 hrs from Florence to Firenzuola (51 km) and even more to Marradi (64 km).

Although it's possible to make a loop by train through the Mugello from Florence, passing through Pontassieve, Dicomano, Vicchio, Borgo S. Lorenzo (from where another line continues over the Apennines to Faenza, by way of Marradi), S. Piero a Sieve, and Vàglia, SITA buses are more scenic and just as infrequent; check timetables before setting out (most pass through the junction at S. Piero). Better yet, hire a car.

The Original Medici Villa

Following Via Bologna (N. 65) north, past the gardens of **Pratolino**, one of the last Medici villas (see Around Florence), it's a panoramic and winding 30 km to two of the very first. On the way, a slight detour to the east (from Pratolino or Vàglia) ascends to **Monte Senario** (817 m), where in 1233 seven wealthy noblemen from Florence founded the mendicant Servite Order, living in the grottoes and building simple cells in the woods, which you can still see. The Servites went on to build SS. Annunziata in Florence, but their monastery here, rebuilt in the 16th century, is less striking than the remarkable views over the Arno valley and Mugello.

Further north, towards S. Piero a Sieve, there's a turn-off to the west on an unpaved road for the Medici **Castello di Trebbio**, an ancient family estate remodelled in 1461 by Michelozzo into a fortified villa with a tower. It has an Italian garden, which you can visit; the interior is open only on the first Tuesday of each month (for details, contact the Municipio of S. Piero—see below). A bit further up looms the even grander **Villa of Cafaggiolo**, the favourite old estate of Cosimo il Vecchio and Lorenzo the Magnificent, who spent as much of the summer in its cool halls as possible. Cosimo had Michelozzo expand and transform this ancient family seat into an imposing castellated villa, its entrance protected by a bulging tower, adorned with an incongruous clock. There's no admittance to Cafaggiolo, though you can walk through the grounds. To the east of the villa, a minor road leads up to the lovely wooded **Bosco ai Frati**, with a simple porticoed church also by Michelozzo; inside there's a fine Crucifix by Donatello, and another attributed to Desiderio da Settignano.

To the Passo della Futa

Just off the autostrada, the largest town on the western rim of the Mugello basin is **Barberino di Mugello**, a market town spread under the **Castello dei Cattani**. Barberino's 15th-century **Palazzo Pretorio**, like many in the region, is emblazoned with coats-of-arms; nearby stands yet another work by Michelozzo, the open **Loggie Medicee**. On N. 65, 5 km from Barberino at Colle Barucci, stands one of the grandest estates in the Mugello, the **Villa delle Maschere** ('of the masks'). Continue 14 km north for the breathtaking views from the **Passo della Futa** (903 m), a pass on the principal Apennine watershed; from here, the whole of the Mugello is spread out below like a relief map. Not surprisingly, in 1944 the Passo della Futa was the Germans' strong point on the Gothic Line—until the allies rendered it useless by capturing Firenzuola to the north. Beyond the pass the road passes under the craggy **Sasso di Castro** (1276 m); at La Casetta you can turn off for Firenzuola (see below) or hot foot it over the mountains in time for dinner in Bologna, the culinary capital of Italy.

Scarperia

Standing at the major crossroads of the N. 65 north and the N. 551 along the Sieve, **S. Piero a Sieve** is a busy little town defended by a mighty Medici citadel, the **Fortezza di San Martino**, designed by Buontalenti in 1571. Its Romanesque parish church, with a façade of 1776, contains a remarkable octagonal baptismal font in polychrome terracotta, by Luca della Robbia. From here's it's 4 km (30 km from Florence) to **Scarperia**, the most charming little town in the Mugello, built high up on a shelf over the valley. Florence fortified it in 1306, and laid out its simple rectangular plan, with one long main street. Scarperia's landmark is **Palazzo Pretorio** (1306), so heavily coated with stone and ceramic coats-of-arms that it resembles a page from a postage stamp album; its atrium and upper halls have 14th- and 15th-century frescoes, the earliest ones by the school of Giotto. The oratory of the **Madonna di Piazza** has an attractive Renaissance front and a cinquecento fresco of the Madonna and Child, attributed to Iacopo del Casentino; another church in Scarperia is dedicated to Our Lady of the Earthquakes(!) with a fresco attributed by some to Filippo Lippi.

From the 16th century, Scarperia had the monopoly on the manufacture of cutlery in Tuscany, and supplied the duchy not only with knives, forks, and scissors, but daggers and swords. At the turn of the century there were 46 thriving firms, though machine-made competition has since reduced this to a mere six who make shepherds' knives and other specialized tools—efforts are now being made to revive the old craft. Scarperia is better known these days for the **Autodromo Internazionale del Mugello**, a 5-km track built by Florence's Auto Club in 1976, which sounds ghastly but is fairly well hidden in the hills east of town. Four km north of Scarperia you can visit the Mugello's most fascinating historical relic, the parish church of **Sant'Agata a Fagna**, constructed at the turn of the millennium and restored after an earthquake in 1919, with an unusual apse and a magnificent pulpit from 1175, decorated with white and green marble intarsia designs and animals.

Refreshingly cool even in August, **Firenzuola** is 22 km north of Scarperia. A small holiday resort, it was devastated in World War II and rebuilt along the lines of the original street plan, between the Porta di Bologna and the Porta di Firenze. West 4 km in **Cornachiaia** there's a church believed to date back to Carolingian times.

WHERE TO STAY AND EAT (tel prefix 055)

The Mugello has quite a few hotels, most fairly pricey and nearly all located in the countryside, where you'll need a car to reach them. The most comfortable, in the resort of Bivigliano near Monte Senario, is the ****__Giotto Park Hotel__, Via Roma 11, tel 406 608, a small, newish but restful villa, set in a garden with a tennis court. Prices depend on the season: L140–175 000; there are cheaper rooms, some without bath in the annex. Between Barberino and the Passo della Futa, at Montecarelli, there's the ***Pallereto**, Via Astroni 67, tel 842 3081, a fine little resort hotel with a garden, pool, and tennis; L85 000, all with bath. In Barberino itself, ****Il Cavallo**, Via della Repubblica 7, tel 841 039, is a posthouse dating from the early 19th century (L65 000, less without bath). Il Cavallo also has a good restaurant, with fresh seafood specialities including pasta with scampi and a delicious surf and turf (seafood and beef) grill (L45 000). In S. Piero a Sieve, ***Ebe**, Via Provinciale, tel 848 019, has 10 simple but pleasant rooms, none with bath (L38 000), attached to a fine restaurant that serves delicacies from nearby Emilia-Romagna like tortellini with orange filling and other delicious pasta dishes, as well as tender grilled meats (L30–40 000). In Scarperia, the ****Scarperia Ristora**, Via Kennedy 17, tel 843 0452, is a tidy little hotel overlooking a shady garden (L48–70 000, all with bath). In the mountains north of Firenzuola, at Pietramala, the *****Antica Casa Gualtieri**, Via Nazionale 81, tel 813 418, is a charming place to help you beat the heat (L65–75 000, all with bath).

Borgo S. Lorenzo and Vìcchio

Borgo S. Lorenzo (pop. 14,900) on the river Sieve, is the boom town of the Mugello, surrounded by new residential neighbourhoods with gardens full of little chameleons; and indeed they are fond of animals here, as evidenced by the **Statue of Fido** in honour of man's best friend, in Piazza Dante. Otherwise, the main 'sights' here are two fine Romanesque churches: **S. Lorenzo**, with an unusual hexagonal campanile built in 1263, and 3 km north, the parish church of **S. Giovanni Maggiore**, where the bell tower is square at the base and ends up octagonal on top; here, too, there is another lovely 12th-century pulpit in marble intarsia. To the north the road divides into N. 477 to **Palazzuolo sul Senio** and N. 302 to **Marradi**, both small resorts as well; in Palazzuolo you can visit a small **Ethnographic Museum** in the 14th-century Palazzo dei Capitani (July–Aug 5–7, winter Sun only 2–6).

Vìcchio, east of S. Lorenzo, is a sleepy little town that gave birth to the Blessed Fra Angelico (Giovanni da Fiesole, 1387–1455) and was often home away from home for Benvenuto Cellini. The Palazzo Pretorio contains the **Museo Comunale Beato Angelico** (Sun 10–12, other times by request), with detached frescoes, Etruscan finds from nearby Poggio alla Colla, and a 13th-century holy water stoup. Not to be outdone, the nearby, and even more minute hamlet of **Vespignano** was the birthplace of Giotto di Bondone (1267–1337). The presumed, simple, stone cottage where the father of Renaissance painting first saw the light of day has been carefully restored as the **Casa di Giotto** (Tues, Thurs 10–12 and 4–7:30, Sat–Sun 10–12 and 3–7). According to tradition, Cimabue first discovered Giotto near the old (but also restored) bridge over the torrent Enza, where the young shepherd was sketching his sheep on a stone.

The Valdisieve

The lower Sieve valley is mostly industrial: **Dicomano** can boast of an interesting fresco by the school of Piero della Francesca but little else besides the junction for N.67, which climbs east into a pretty range of mountains called the Alpe di San Benedetto.

S. Godenzo, 10 km up N. 67, is the largest village here, site of an 11th-century **Benedictine abbey**; its plain church has a raised presbytery and a polyptych by the school of Giotto. From S. Godenzo a road continues up to the birthplace of Andrea del Castagno, now called **Castagno d'Andrea** (727 m), a small holiday village that translates as 'Andrew's chestnut', or you can continue winding 18 km into the mountains to **S. Benedetto in Alpe**, with a 9th-century Benedictine abbey that sheltered Dante (*Inferno*, Canto XVI, 94–105), where horses may be hired to visit the enchanting Valle dell'Arquacheta with its pretty waterfall. In the old town of **Portico di Romagna** 11 km further north, the Portinari family, including the beautiful Beatrice, spent their summers—their house still stands in the main street. Deeper into Romagna lie the fascinating medieval town of **Brisighella**, the ceramic city of **Faenza**, and **Ravenna**, not only filled with ravishing Byzantine mosaics from the time of Justinian but also the site of Dante's real tomb.

There is little along the lower Sieve, though **Rufina**, 10 km south of Dicomano, is dominated by the 16th-century **Villa Poggio Reale**, of interest to wine lovers for its production of *Chianti Putto* and *Pomino* wines. In Poggio Reale there's a small wine museum (call ahead, tel 839 003). From **Pontassieve**, a large town at the confluence of the Sieve and the Arno, scenic N. 70 leads up to the dramatic **Passo della Consuma** (1023 m) before descending into the Casentino (see p. 362).

PRATO, PISTOIA, AND THE VALDARNO

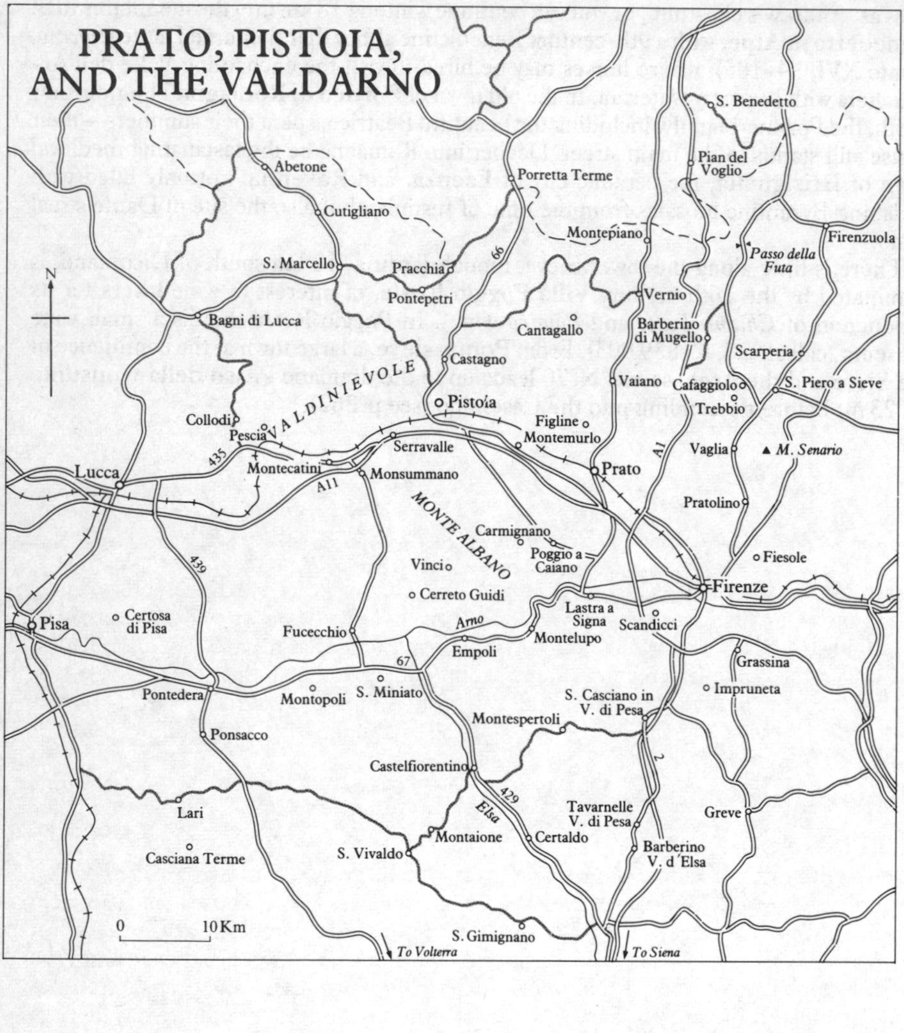

Part VI
THE VALDARNO, PRATO AND PISTOIA

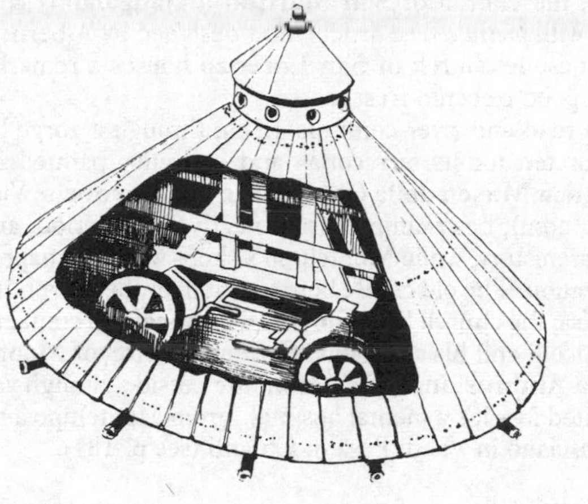

Leonardo's Tank

There are two routes between Florencc and Pisa, whether you travel by car, bus or train. The route along the Arno, often hemmed in by the hills, has always been historically and economically the least important and carries less traffic; the large cities of Prato, Pistoia, and Lucca grew up in an arc north of the Monte Albano hills, where there's more fertile land and room to grow. The first route described, along the Arno, takes in nearby Florentine towns of Vinci, Castelfiorentino, and Certaldo.

Down the Arno to Pisa

GETTING AROUND

If you're driving, persist: the Florentine sprawl finally gives way at Signa and after that the Arno road (N. 67) becomes even scenic in stretches. LAZZI buses take the main route to Pisa; SITA goes directly from Florence to Castelfiorentino or Certaldo; for Vinci, COPIT. Trains at least once an hour follow the Arno between Florence and Pisa, and at Empoli turn off for Castelfiorentino, Certaldo, Poggibonsi, and Siena. Note that San Miniato and Fucecchio share a railway station; local buses commute from there to both centres.

Florence to Empoli

The old Florentine satellite town of **Scandicci** (6 km west), once in the business of renting villas to foreigners like Dylan Thomas and D.H. Lawrence (who finished *Lady*

Chatterley's Lover here), has since the war found more profit in industry. Most of the towns along the Arno specialize in certain products; in **Lastra a Signa** it's straw goods, sold in many village shops. Lastra retains its 14th-century walls and the **Loggia di Sant'Antonio**, all that survives of the hospital founded by Florence's Silk Guild and built in 1411; many believe Brunelleschi was the architect, and that the work was a prototype of Florence's Spedale degli Innocenti, which the same guild also funded. Just outside of Lastra, the church of **San Martino a Gangalandi** contains a beautiful, semicircular apse with *pietra serena* articulation designed by Alberti. In **Signa**, the next village, the Romanesque church of **San Lorenzo** houses a remarkable 12th-century marble pulpit and good trecento frescoes.

After Signa the road and river continue 12 km through a gorge before **Montelupo Fiorentino**, celebrated for its terracottas and delicately painted ceramics since the Renaissance. The new **Museo della Ceramico e del Territorio**, Via Baccio Sinaldi 45 (3–8, closed Mon, adm), has examples from nearly every period, and a display on the lower Valdarno's prehistory, while Montelupo's shops would be happy to sell you a more recent ceramic creation. The old **castle** here was built by the Florentines in 1203, during the wars against Pisa; the church **San Giovanni Evangelista** contains a lovely *Madonna and Saints* by Botticelli and his assistants. On the outskirts of Montelupo, you can see Buontalenti's **Villa Ambrosiana** (1587) from the outside, though you'll probably want to avoid being invited in—it's a mental hospital. From Montelupo a road leads in 20 km southeast to S. Casciano in Val di Pesa in Chianti (see p. 181).

Empoli

TOURIST INFORMATION

Empoli: Piazza Farinata degli Uberti 8/9, tel (0571) 76 115.

The modern market town of Empoli, 32 km from Florence, was witness to one of the turning points in Tuscan history: in 1260, the Ghibellines of Siena, fresh from their great victory over Florence at Montaperti, held a parliament in Empoli to decide the fate of their arch enemy. All were for razing Florence to the ground, once and for all, and waited for the approval of their leader, Farinata degli Uberti. The Uberti were Florentine gangster nobles famous for their hatred of their fellow citizens, but Farinata surprised all when he stood up and announced that, even if he had to stand alone, he would defend Florence for as long as he lived. The Sienese let their captain have his way, and lost their chance of ever becoming *numero uno* in Tuscany. The prosperous new Empoli (pop. 45,000), produces green glass and raincoats; little in it recalls the days of Farinata, until you reach the piazza named after him: here is the palace where the parliament convened, across from Empoli's gem of a Romanesque church, the **Collegiata Sant'Andrea**, with its green and white marble geometric façade in the style of Florence's San Miniato. The lower portion dates from 1093; the upper had to wait until the 18th century, but it harmonizes extremely well.

The Pinacoteca

Empoli has its share of 13th- and 14th-century Florentine art as well, much of it now in the small but choice **Pinacoteca** in the Collegiata's cloister (10–12, closed Mon, adm; if no one's there, ask at the Libreria S. Paolo). The most celebrated work is Masolino's

Pietà fresco, with its poignant faces; upstairs there's an elegant relief of the *Madonna and Child* by Mino da Fiesole, a marble *Annunciation* group by Bernardo Rossellino, and a painted tabernacle of *S. Sebastian* by his brother Antonio. Lorenzo Monaco contributes a long-eyed *Madonna and Saints*; in Lorenzo di Bicci's scene of S. Nicola da Tolentino shielding Empoli from a rain of plague arrows is a quattrocento view of the city. There are a rare series of frescoes by Masolino's master, Starnina, two saints by Pontormo, who was born nearby, and the fine *Tabernacle of the Holy Sacrament* by Francesco Botticini and his son Raffaello, with a good predella. The upper Loggia has works by Andrea della Robbia, and the suspended wooden wings of the donkey that is made to fly down on a wire from the church tower on *Corpus Domine* (although a papier mâché donkey has of late replaced the real one). Empoli's **Santo Stefano** church has another beautiful fresco by Masolino, but it's only open Saturday evenings for mass.

Cerreto Guidi and Vinci

Northwest of Empoli, in the Monte Albano, lies the old hill townlet of **Cerreto Guidi** (COPIT buses from Piazza Vittoria), former property of the Counts of Guidi and taken over by Florence in 1237. It is known these days for its *Chianti Putto*, and for the **Villa Medicea**, rebuilt by Cosimo I, a relatively simple cottage as Medici villas go, but approached by a grandiose double ramp of bricks called the 'Medici bridges', built by Buontalenti. The grand dukes came here often until 1576, when Cosimo I's daughter Isabella was murdered here by her husband Paolo Orsini for her infidelities; if you look carefully you can find the unhappy couple among the scores of Medici portraits that form the villa's chief decoration (9–5, Sun 9–1, closed Mon). From the terrace there are fine views of the Monte Albano, almost treeless here.

From Cerreto it's 5 km to **Vinci**, a tiny town set among hills of olives and vines. It is, of course, most famous as the home of Leonardo, who was born in a humble house in Archiano on 15 April, 1452, the illegitimate son of the local notary and a peasant girl. In his honour, the town's landmark, Conti Guidi Castle, has been converted into the **Museo Leonardiano** (daily 9:30–12 and 2:30–6; adm), packed full of models of inventions he designed in his *Codex Atlanticus* notebooks, most of which this supreme 'Renaissance man' never had the time or attention span to build. The museum has kindly added descriptions in English of the nearly 100 machines, including some inspired by those invented by Brunelleschi to build Florence's cathedral dome, a flying machine, paddle boat, spring-driven mechanical car, an almost perfect modern bicycle, diving gear, a parachute, and a device to walk on water.

Also present are Leonardo's famous tank, machine gun and helicopter. 'I'll do anything for money', this otherwise gentle fellow once said, surely one of the most startling quotes of the Renaissance. But nothing could be more typical of the age than brilliance combined with utter immorality; while he often neglected his art, Leonardo was always happy to help the bellicose princes who employed him with their military problems. We should probably be thankful that these gadgets never escaped from his notebook. Leonardo was baptized in the font in **Santa Croce**, next door to the museum.

From Vinci it's a 3-km walk (or drive) southeast to **Archiano**, where the simple stone house where Leonardo was born has been restored (9:30–12 and 2:30–6, closed Wed). There are plans to restore the beautiful landscape between Vinci and Archiano to its 16th-century appearance.

San Miniato

Just southwest of Empoli, the river Elsa flows into the Arno near **San Miniato** (pop. 23,000), a refined old hill town that grew up at the crossroads of the Via Francigena (the main pilgrimage route from France to Rome) and the Florence-Pisa road; on a clear day the view takes in everything from Fiesole to the sea. Its defensibility and strategic location made it the Tuscan residence of the Emperors, from Otto IV to Frederick II; Matilda of Tuscany was born here in 1046, and in the 12th century it was an important imperial fortress, protecting the crossroads and levying tolls on travellers and merchandise. Of the citadel, only two towers survive: the present campanile of the cathedral and the taller 'Torrione', in the shady Prato del Duomo that crowns San Miniato, with peculiar chimney-like structures on top. It was from the top of this tower that Frederick II's secretary and court poet Pier della Vigna, falsely accused of treason, leapt to his death, to be discovered by Dante in the forest of suicides (*Inferno* XIII). Also in the Prato del Duomo stands the 12th-century **Palazzo dei Vicari dell'Imperatore** and the **Duomo** itself, with a Romanesque brick façade, incorporating pieces of sculpted marbles and 13th-century majolica that catch the light as the sun sets. Most of the art in the interior is Baroque, except for a fine 13th-century holy water stoup, while most of the earlier artworks from the region have been placed in the **Diocesan Museum**, to the left of the cathedral (open usually 10–12:30 and 4–7, closed Mon). Among the prizes is the fresco of the *Maestà* by the Sienese 'Maestro degli Ordini', a bust of Christ attributed to Verrocchio, and Neri di Bicci's *Madonna*. Since 1968, the Prato del Duomo has been the site of the **National Kite Flying Contest** every first Sunday after Easter.

More art awaits in the Piazza del Popolo's 14th-century church of **San Domenico**—minor works by Masolino, Pisanello, the della Robbias, and Bernardo Rossellino, who carved the fine *tomb of Giovanni Chiellini*, the Florentine founder of San Miniato's Hospital of Poor Pilgrim Priests in the 15th century; the tomb is modelled after Rossellino's famous tomb of Leonardo Bruni in Florence's Santa Croce.

Kite contests aren't the only sidelight to San Miniato—there's a visit paid by Napoleon in 1797, not to glory in this old seat of emperors but to visit his relatives in the **Palazzo Bonaparte**. In the surrounding countryside are rich caches of white truffles, hunted fervently in the autumn for the large market on the last Sunday in November; and many of what appear to be plain-looking Romanesque churches around San Miniato are actually tobacco-curing barns from the 1900s.

Castelfiorentino and San Vivaldo

Some 12 km south along the Valdelsa from San Miniato, **Castelfiorentino** (pop. 18,000) is another old hill town, though much rebuilt after damage in World War II. Castelfiorentino's church of **Santa Verdiana** dates from the 18th century and houses the local **Pinacoteca** (open on request), with some excellent trecento paintings, including a lovely Sienese *Madonna*, attributed to Duccio da Boninsegna, another one by Francesco Granacci, and a triptych by Taddeo Gaddi. The **Cappella della Visitazione** (Via Gozzoli 55) is covered with frescoes by the charming Benozzo Gozzoli and his school (at the time of writing being restored).

One of the more unusual sights in Tuscany, the **Monastery of San Vivaldo**, lies in the rather empty zone to the southwest of Castelfiorentino, beyond the old village of

Montaione. Vivaldo was a hermit of San Gimignano who lived in a hollow chestnut tree and was found dead there in 1301, still in the attitude of prayer. A Franciscan community grew up in his footsteps, and in 1500, when the monastery was being rebuilt, one member, Fra Tommaso da Firenze, had the idea of taking advantage of the monastery's wooded hills to build a 'New Jerusalem', constructing 34 chapels replicating the sites of Christ's Passion. To make the symbolic journey seem even more real to pilgrims, the 34 chapels combined polychrome terracottas by Giovanni della Robbia and others, set in frescoes—Pope Leo X immediately granted a fat indulgence to anyone who did the whole route. Today only 17 of the chapels survive, in a lovely wooded setting.

Certaldo

Certaldo (pop. 16,000), former seat of Florence's deputy, or Vicarate of the Valdelsa, is synonymous with Giovanni Boccaccio, who spent the last 13 years of his life up in the lovely old town, known as Castello, which could be a set for the *Decameron* itself. Everything here is of good, honest brick, from the pavements to the *palazzi*, of which the most striking is the 14th-century castellated **Palazzo Pretorio**, studded with the arms of the former Vicars. Inside it has a beautiful courtyard and museum (9–12 and 3–6, summer 4–7, closed Mon) containing Etruscan artefacts, detached frescoes, and in the annexed church and cloister, Gozzoli's *Tabernacle of the Punished*, not one of his more cheerful works. In the old jail the walls still bear the forlorn *graffiti* of past prisoners.

The house traditionally associated with Certaldo's great author, the **Casa di Boccaccio**, Via Boccaccio 18, has been restored and is now the seat of the International Centre of Boccaccio Studies. Boccaccio died here in 1375 and lies buried in **SS. Michele ed Iacopo**, under an epitaph he penned himself; a 16th-century monument erected in his honour was destroyed by prudes in 1783. Boccaccio himself in his later years regretted the racy frivolity of his most famous book, wishing he had spent his time on serious Latin works—not a regret too many people have ever shared. From Certaldo a pretty road leads 13 km south to **San Gimignano** (p. 320).

WHERE TO STAY AND EAT

The lower Arno Valley isn't exactly awash in pleasure domes, but neither will you have to sleep in the car or starve. If it's time to eat just as you're leaving or approaching Florence, consider a stop at **Fiore**, Via di Marciola 112, in S.Maria a Marciola, near Scandicci, tel (055) 768 678, not only for its delicious crêpes and *fritto misto* of meats and greens, but for its lovely garden setting and pine-clad slopes (L45 000). Further along in Montelupo, *****Tonio**, Via 1 Maggio 23, tel (0571) 541 444, is a pleasant place to relax, with a large garden and nice, cool rooms in the summer (L90 000). Vinci has the flagrantly touristy **Da Pippo** near the Leonardo museum, Via della Torre 19, tel 56 100; the fare is undistinguished, but there's a pretty view from the terrace (L35 000).

In San Miniato, you can sleep near the top of the town at *****Miravalle**, Piazza Castello 3, tel (0571) 418 075, located in Frederick II's 12th-century imperial palace. Beautiful views, especially from the restaurant (all rooms with bath, L85 000). **Il Canapone**, Piazza Bonaparte 5, tel (0571) 418 121, is a simple place where you can try the local truffles on spaghetti, in risotto, or with veal scallopine; in the spring there's rice with asparagus (L40 000). Certaldo has three small hotels, of which the most interesting is ****Il Castello**, Via della Rena 6, tel (0571) 668 250, all rooms with bath (L75 000).

Empoli to Pisa

There is no compelling reason to stop in the lower Valdarno unless you're running low on petrol. If you're spending more time here, consider a visit to **Fucecchio**, most notable for its panoramic views, or **Montòpoli in Val d'Arno**, a tiny medieval town dating from the 11th century on the south bank. Further down river lies industrial **Pontedera**, where the Piaggio Company produces most of Italy's motorscooters. Here you may consider heading south on N. 439 to Volterra (see p. 325), by way of **Ponsacco** and the four-towered **Villa di Camugliano**, built by Alessandro and Cosimo I, an example of far-flung Medici real estate speculation. Between here and Volterra roll the Pisan Hills, some of the quietest, more rural countryside in Tuscany; the main attraction here may be precisely its lack of art and history. Alternatively, from Ponsacco, you can head southwest to tiny **Lari**, with the remains of a Medici fortress, and if your rheumatism is acting up, to **Casciano Terme**, famous for its cures in Roman times, and rebuilt by the Pisans in the 14th century. **Rivalto**, a hamlet 6 km south of the spa, has almost perfectly preserved its medieval character.

Vicopisano, north of the Arno, defended the eastern frontier of Pisa from the ambitions of Lucca, and its impressive *castello* was remodelled by Brunelleschi after the Florentine conquest of Pisa; now vineyards surround its mighty walls and towers. Across the bridge, **Cascina** still has most of its medieval walls and Roman grid plan from its days as a military camp. There are three churches worth visiting: **San Casciano**, an unusual 12th-century Romanesque church, with blind arches and some fine sculptural details; Romanesque **San Benedetto a Settimo**, adorned with a 14th-century alabaster altarpiece of Irish make; and **San Giovanni Evangelista**, built by the Knights of St John, with trecento Sienese frescoes, recently restored after the church was used as a barn for several centuries. Further west lies the Certosa of Pisa (8 km) and Pisa itself (14 km; see p. 250).

WHERE TO STAY AND EATING OUT

One of interior Tuscany's finest seafood restaurants is in Fucecchio: **Le Vedute**, Via Romana-Lucchese 121, tel (0571) 297 201, a pleasant country place, where in summer you can linger on the veranda over your favourite denizen of the deep—good meats as well, especially in autumn (L45–50 000). Across the Arno, in little Montòpoli in Val d'Arno, the old town hall has been converted into an inn, ****Quattro Gigli**, Piazza Michele 2, tel (0571) 466 940. Its 20 rooms vary in quality (L45–50 000 without bath, L50–65 000 with); the restaurant, beyond the permanent display of Montòpoli's painted ceramics, features an imaginative menu, based on Tuscan dishes, with plenty of mushrooms, vegetables, and greens depending on the season, and an Italian rarity—roast potatoes. The duck and game dishes are excellent (L40 000). If you feel irresistibly drawn to the solitude of the Pisan hills, there are plenty of rooms in Casciana Terme, and a good restaurant in Perignano, near Lari, **Lido**, Via Livornese 322, tel (0587) 616 020, featuring warm seafood antipasti for starters and sea bass (L35–45 000).

Prato

Prato is only 18 km from Florence but a world away in atmosphere; this is a city that works for its living, where the population has doubled since World War II to 145,000, the third in Tuscany after Florence and Livorno. And a vibrantly, joyously proletarian city it is, fond of Henry Moore and comic books and avant garde theatre and Heavy Metal bars, full of people wanting you to sign petitions or buy encyclopaedias who are proud to live in 'the Manchester of Tuscany'. Living in Florence's shadow for the past thousand years has not dampened Prato's spirits as much as one might suppose; as in the days of the famous Merchant of Prato, this city still makes its living from the manufacture of textiles, and especially the recycling of old wool and rags. And in the Renaissance Prato made enough profit from these rags to hire the greatest artists of the day to embellish its churches and palaces.

History

Prato made its historical debut in the 9th century, under the name of Borgo al Cornio; outside the town was a meadow, or *prato*, site of the market and fortifications, which gradually became so important that the whole town took the name. It was first ruled by the Alberti, one of the region's more ambitious feudal families, who conquered lands from the Maremma to the Mugello. In 1107 Countess Matilda personally led a combined Tuscan army against Prato to humble the Alberti; in 1140 the Pratesi humbled their counts even more by taking away most of their power and running their city as a free *comune*. In 1193, at the height of its power, it even managed to snatch some of Florence's own *contado*. By this time Prato was one of Europe's most important manufacturers of woollens, so wealthy that the University of Paris even had a special college for students from Prato. Florence, however, could not countenance so near and ambitious a rival, and in 1350, on the charges of fomenting rebellion in the Valdelsa, Florence besieged Prato, and an honourable peace was made; the next year Florence cemented its hold over its neighbour by *purchasing* it for 17,500 florins from its nominal overlord, the Angevin Queen of Naples.

Despite the ignominy of being bought, Prato functioned more as Florence's ally than its possession, retaining a certain amount of local autonomy. The late 14th century was the day of Francesco di Marco Datini, the Merchant of Prato, one of the richest men in the world and history's first recorded workaholic businessman. Yet although he built his palace in his hometown of Prato, the big profits were in Florence, and Datini spent most of his time there. Under the influence of Savonarola's preaching, Prato joined Florence in rebelling against Medici rule, but was soon to play the unfortunate role of whipping boy, when the Spaniards, at the instigation of the Medici Pope Leo X, besieged and sacked the city with an unheard-of brutality. Since that dark day, Prato's history has followed that of its imperious neighbour.

GETTING AROUND

Prato is easily reached by train from Florence (18 km/25 min), Pistoia (17 km/25 min) or Bologna, and has two stations, the **Stazione Centrale**, facing a pretty green square just on the other bank of Prato's river, the Bisenzio; and the **Stazione Porta Serraglio**, just north of the walls and closer to the centre, on the Florence–Pistoia line. This was one of Italy's first railways, built in 1848 for the Lorraine grand dukes by an Englishman named Ralph Bonfield, who so pleased the grand duke that he was made the Count of St George of Prato. These days, the Prato tourist office is searching for his descendants, to claim

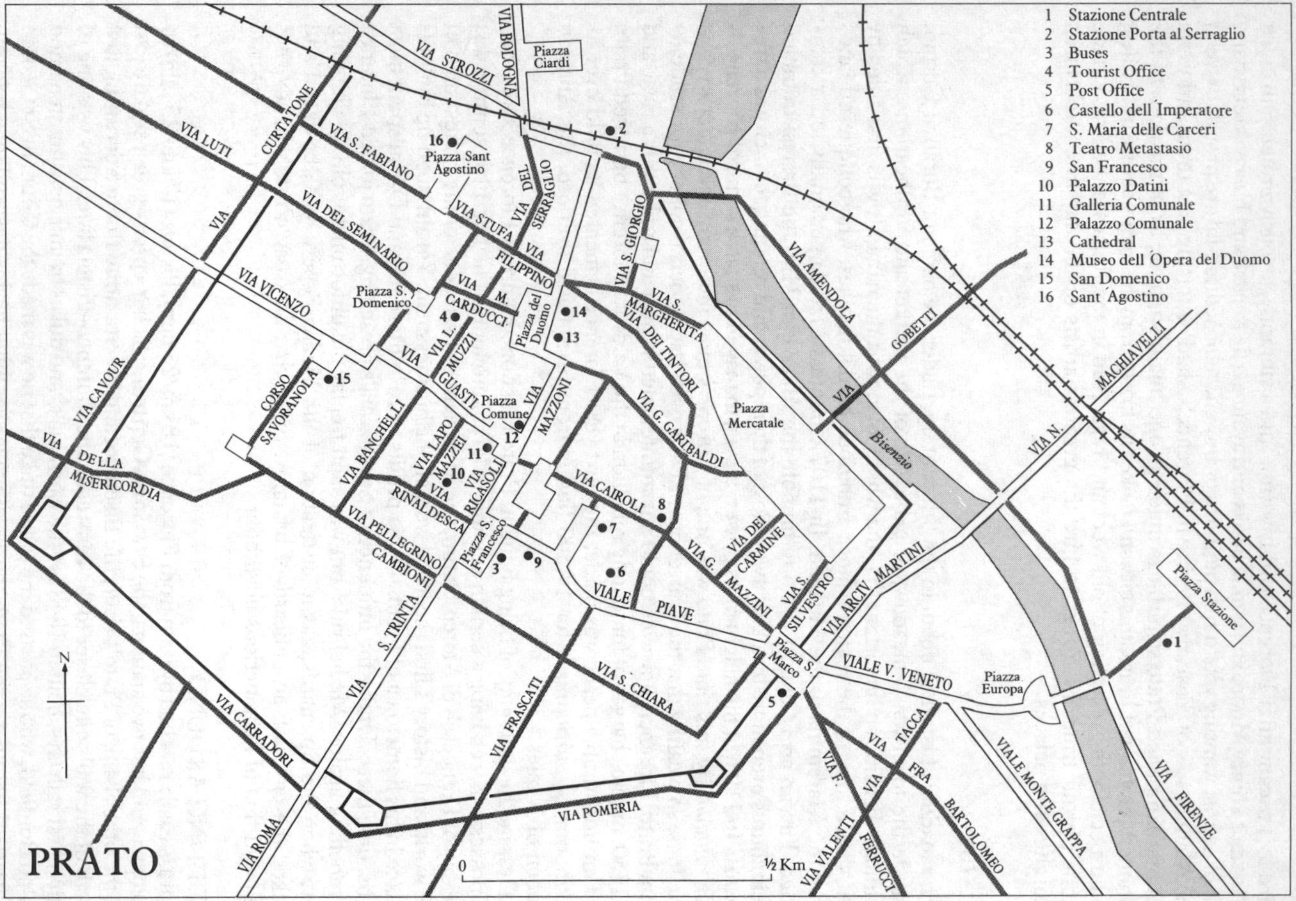
PRATO
1 Stazione Centrale
2 Stazione Porta al Serraglio
3 Buses
4 Tourist Office
5 Post Office
6 Castello dell´Imperatore
7 S. Maria delle Carceri
8 Teatro Metastasio
9 San Francesco
10 Palazzo Datini
11 Galleria Comunale
12 Palazzo Comunale
13 Cathedral
14 Museo dell´Opera del Duomo
15 San Domenico
16 Sant´Agostino
VIA STROZZI
VIA BOLOGNA
Piazza Ciardi
VIA LUTI
CURTATONE
VIA S. FABIANO
Piazza Sant Agostino
VIA DEL SERRAGLIO
VIA STUFA
VIA FILIPPINO
VIA DEL SEMINARIO
VIA S. GIORGIO
VIA AMENDOLA
VIA GOBETTI
VIA N. MACHIAVELLI
VIA VICENZO
Piazza S. Domenico
VIA M. CARDUCCI
Piazza del Duomo
VIA S. MARGHERITA
VIA DEI TINTORI
VIA L. MUZZI
VIA GUASTI
Piazza Comune
VIA MAZZONI
VIA G. GARIBALDI
Piazza Mercatale
Bisenzio
VIA CAVOUR
CORSO SAVORANOLA
VIA BANCHELLI
VIA LAPO MAZZEI
VIA RICASOLI
VIA DELLA MISERICORDIA
RINALDESCA
VIA PELLEGRINO
CAMBIONI
Piazza S. Francesco
VIA CAIROLI
VIA DEI CARMINE
VIA G. MAZZINI
VIA S. SILVESTRO
VIA ARCIV MARTINI
VIALE PIAVE
Piazza Stazione
VIA S. TRINTA
VIA S. CHIARA
Piazza S. Marco
VIALE V. VENETO
Piazza Europa
VIA CARRADORI
VIA FRASCATI
VIA TACCA
VIA FRA BARTOLOMEO
VIALE MONTE GRAPPA
VIA FIRENZE
VIA F. FERRUCCI
VIA VALENTI
VIA POMERIA
VIA ROMA
0
½ Km
N

the title and supply a likeness of Bonfield so they can erect a proper monument in his honour. All Bonfields take note! **Buses** from Prato depart from the Piazza del Duomo (CAP buses, every half hour to Florence and Mugello) and Piazza San Francesco (LAZZI buses, to Florence, Pistoia, Montecatini, Lucca, Pisa and Viareggio). Prato has an exit on the autostrada A11 between Florence and Pisa (from Florence get on it at Peretola). Note that the centre is closed to traffic; Piazza Mercatale is a convenient place to park.

TOURIST INFORMATION

Via L. Muzzi 51, near the Duomo, tel (0574) 35 141; Piazza S. Maria Carceri 15, tel 24 112.

Frederick's Castle

Most people, whether arriving by car, bus, or at the Stazione Centrale, approach the walled core of Prato through the Piazza San Marco, embellished with a white puffy sculpture by Henry Moore from 1970. Viale Piave continues to the defiantly Ghibelline swallowtail crenellations of the **Castello dell'Imperatore**. This marks a strange interlude in Prato's past, built in 1237 by Frederick II, Holy Roman Emperor, Swabian and Hohenstaufen heir to the Normans in Southern Italy and Sicily. Frederick, unlike his grandfather Frederick Barbarossa, never spent much time in Tuscany, preferring his more civilized dominions in Apulia and Sicily, where he could discuss poetry, philosophy and falconry (in Arabic or Latin) with his court scholars. When he did come, it was in magnificent progresses featuring dancing girls, elephants and the Muslim imperial bodyguard. His Tuscan taxpayers were not impressed; neither did they much appreciate Frederick's tolerant, syncretistic approach to religion. The popes excommunicated him twice. He built this castle here because he had to, not so much to defend Prato, but to defend his imperial *podestà* from the Pratesi, and perhaps to impress the locals with its design—its clean lines must have seemed very sharp and modern in the 13th century. There is nothing in it any more, though the city often uses the space for special exhibitions. Usually it's possible to walk up along its walls for a bird's-eye view of Prato (9–12 and 4–7, closed Wed).

Next to the castle stands the unfinished black and white marble face of **Santa Maria delle Carceri**, begun in 1485 by Giuliano da Sangallo. Brunelleschian architecture was always a fragile blossom, as is shown clearly by the failure of this sole serious attempt to transplant it outside the walls of Florence. Santa Maria always merits a mention in architectural histories. It was an audacious enterprise; Sangallo, a furiously diligent student of Vitruvius and Alberti, attempted a building based entirely on philosophical principles. Order, simplicity, and correct proportion, as in Brunelleschi's churches, were to be manifest, with no frills allowed. Sangallo, the favourite of Lorenzo the Magnificent, proved unfortunately a better theorist than architect. Santa Maria turned out tedious and clumsy, a tombstone for the theoretical architecture that was a fad in the 1400s, more often expressed in paintings than actual buildings. The interior is better than the exterior, a plain Greek cross very much in the Brunelleschian manner with a decorative frieze and tondos of the four Evangelists by Andrea della Robbia. The name of the church—*carceri* means prisons—refers to a miracle, a speaking image of the Virgin painted on a nearby prison wall, that occasioned the building of the church. Behind the church is Prato's celebrated theatre, the **Teatro Metastasio**, one of the most acclaimed and innovative in Italy.

Piazza San Francesco and Datini

From Santa Maria delle Carceri you can see the apse of Prato's huge brick **Church of San Francesco**, dating from the end of the 13th century, and embellished in front with white and green marble stripes. Inside, on the left wall is the *Tomb of Gemignano Inghirami*, one of Europe's crack lawyers of the quattrocento; the design is attributed to Bernardo Rossellino (1460s); while near the altar is the *tomb slab of Francesco di Marco Datini* (1330–1410) by Niccolò di Piero Lamberti. Off the elegant Renaissance cloister you'll find the entrance to the **Cappella Migliorati**, beautifully frescoed in 1395 by Niccolò di Pietro Gerini, one of the period's finest draughtsmen; here he depicts the *Lives of SS. Anthony Abbot and Matthew*.

Niccolò also frescoed the **Palazzo Datini** (nearby on Via Rinaldesca), the showplace palace built in the 1390s by the Merchant of Prato. If there were an Accountants' Hall of Fame, Francesco di Marco Datini would surely be in it; he helped invent that dismal science. Nor did he ever let anyone throw anything away, leaving to posterity 150,000 documents, ledgers (all inscribed: 'For God and Profit') and private letters that are stored in the archives in this palace; these formed the basis for Iris Origo's fascinating account of his life and times, *The Merchant of Prato*. Datini left nearly all of his indecent fortune to the Ceppo, a Pratese charity he founded in 1410 and which now has its headquarters on the first floor of this palace; in gratitude the city had the façade frescoed with scenes of his life, unfortunately now much faded.

Galleria Comunale

Just north lies Prato's charming civic centre, the **Piazza del Comune**, decorated with a 19th-century **statue of Datini** with bronze reliefs of the merchant's life, and a pretty fountain by Tacca nicknamed 'Il Bacchino', or Little Bacchus (1659). The city's **Palazzo Comunale**, behind the portico, retains only traces of its medieval heritage; drop in to see its **Sala di Consiglio** with its coffered ceiling, two quattrocento frescoes and portraits of the grand dukes. The rugged **Palazzo Pretorio** is nothing but medieval, a relic of the days when Prato governed itself without any help from the Medici; the stair on the façade leads up to the **Galleria Comunale** (9–1, 3–7, closed Sun, adm) with a good collection of mostly Florentine art: there's a tabernacle by Filippino Lippi, which he painted for his mother and which was later restored after damage in the war; up in the grand **Salone Udienza** with the fine wood ceiling is Bernardo Daddi's *Story of the Holy Girdle*, a predella telling the tale of Prato's most famous relic, the Virgin Mary's belt. According to tradition she gave it to Doubting Thomas, from whom it was passed down until it became part of the dowry of a woman who married Michele, a knight from Prato during the First Crusade. Michele returned to Prato and hid the precious relic under his mattress; angels lifted him off, and the girdle was given into the care of the cathedral. In the same hall are fine 14th-century works by Giovanni di Milano, Michele di Firenze, Lorenzo Monaco, and a tondo attributed to Luca Signorelli. Filippo Lippi painted the *Madonna del Ceppo* for the Ceppo offices in the Palazzo Datini; it portrays the tycoon himself, with four fellow donors, who contributed less and thus get portrayed as midgets. In an adjoining room, the most curious work is by Battistello, a follower of Caravaggio, whose unique *Noli me tangere* portrays Christ wearing a fedora at a rakish angle, doing a quick dance step to evade the Magdalene's touch.

Cathedral of Santo Stefano

In the centre of Prato rises its cathedral, like a faded beauty that never recovered from the blow of a broken engagement. It was begun with great promise in the 13th century, and added to off and on for the next 200 years, with ever dwindling passion and money. Its best features are an exotic, almost Moorish campanile, an Andrea della Robbia lunette of the Madonna and St Stephen over the door, a big clock on the half-striped façade that makes you smile when you notice it sitting where the rose window ought to be, and above all, the circular **Pulpit of the Sacred Girdle**, projecting from the corner of the façade. Perhaps no other church in Italy has such a perfectly felicitous ornament, something beautiful and special that the Pratesi look at every day as they walk through the piazza. Michelozzo designed it (1428) and Donatello added the delightful reliefs of dancing children and *putti* (replaced by casts), along the lines of his *cantoria* in Florence's cathedral museum. The Holy Girdle is publicly displayed from here five times a year: Easter Day, 1 May, 15 August, 8 September and Christmas Day.

The Duomo's interior continues the motif of green and white stripes in its Romanesque arcades and ribs of the vaulting. The **Chapel of the Sacred Girdle**, just to the left as you enter, is protected by a screen, and within is covered with frescoes by Agnolo Gaddi on the legend of the Girdle (see above), and adorned with a beautiful marble statue of the *Madonna and Child* by Giovanni Pisano. In the left aisle there's a masterful **pulpit** carved by Mino da Fiesole and Antonio Rossellino, with harpies around the base. Bring L500 to illuminate Filippo Lippi's celebrated frescoes in the choir, on the *Lives of SS John the Baptist and Stephen*, the merry monk's first major work (1452–66); while painting these scenes, Lippi fell in love with a brown-eyed novice, Lucrezia Buti, who according to tradition posed for his beautiful version of Herod's Banquet, either as the melancholy Salome herself or as the figure in the long white dress, second from the right;

Pulpit of the Sacred Girdle

Fra Filippo placed himself among the mourners for St Stephen, third from the right, in a red hat. The less lyrical frescoes in the next chapel (lit along with the choir) are by Uccello and Andrea di Giusto. There's a lovely, almost Art Nouveau candelabra on the high altar by Maso di Bartolomeo (1440s); a close relative to Maso's work in Pistoia cathedral.

The **Museo dell'Opera del Duomo** (9:30–12:30, 3–6:30, Sun 9:30–12:30, closed Tues, adm) is located next door, in the cloister, one side of which retains its 12th-century geometric marble decorations and rambunctuous capitals. The rather tragic star of the museum is the original pulpit of the Sacred Girdle, Donatello's merrily dancing *putti* made lepers by car exhaust. Lippi's recently restored *Death of San Girolamo* was painted to prove to the bishop that he was the man to fresco the cathedral choir. Other works include his son Filippino's *St Lucy* with her lamp, blissfully ignoring the knife in her throat, and another full-length portrait, of *Fra Jacopone di Todi*, believed to be an early work of Uccello. More dancing *putti* adorn the *Reliquary of the Sacred Girdle* (1446) by Maso di Bartolomeo, stolen but recently recovered at the Todi antique fair. Other works include the saccharine *Guardian Angel* by Carlo Dolci, a sophisticated Madonna with saints by the quattrocento 'Master of the Nativity of Castello', and a strange reliquary that resembles a mushroom.

Walking though Prato

Most of Prato's old streets are anonymous, self-effacing Tuscan. Some areas suffered bomb damage in the war, notably the great pear-shaped **Piazza Mercatale**, on the banks of the Bisenzio. This was long the working core of the city, surrounded entirely by porticoes and workshops; it was and is the site of Prato's big market and fairs. A few faded peeling, porticoed buildings remain, overlooking the river that has laundered Prato's principal industry for eight centuries.

If it's Sunday, it's a good day to visit the sturdy brick **San Domenico** on the west side of town, a large Gothic church begun in 1283 and completed by Giovanni Pisano, one side of it lined with arcades. There's not much to see inside, but in the adjacent convent, the painter Fra Bartolomeo's home and Pratese address of Savonarola, there's the **Museum of Mural Painting** (Sun 9:30–12:30, or tel 460 392), which despite the bravura of its name is only a collection of detached frescoes from surrounding churches, but worth a look for the charming quattrocento *graffiti* court scenes from the Palazzo Vaj, a sinopia from the cathedral attributed to Uccello, and Niccolò di Piero Gerini's *Tabernacle of the Ceppo*. Just north of San Domenico, **San Fabiano**, Via del Seminario 30, has an enchanting pre-Romanesque mosaic pavement, depicting mermaids, birds and dragons biting their own tails (see Pienza, p. 342, for some idle speculation about these); north of San Fabiano 15th-century **Sant'Agostino** contains Prato's most ridiculous painting, the *Madonna della Consolazione* (attributed, naturally, to Vasari), who does her consoling by distributing belts from heaven. South of the city walls on Viale della Repubblica 9 (which begins at a bridge over the Bisenzio), one of Prato's textile institutes has a unique collection of fabrics and looms dating back to the 5th century AD in the **Museo del Tessuto** (open 9–12, closed Sun).

WHERE TO STAY (tel prefix 0574)

Prato's hotels are mostly of the businessman variety, but can be a good bet in the summer when Florence is packed to the gills. Convenient if you're arriving by train, *****San**

Marco, between the Stazione Centrale and the Castello, Piazza San Marco 48, tel 21 321, is a pleasant place (L65–75 000 without bath, L90–110 000 with). Over the river and in the hills to the east the relaxing ***Villa S. Cristina**, Via Poggio Secco 58, tel 595 951, has a garden, pool, and most other comforts for L125 000. For modernity and air-conditioning, try ***Flora**, Via Cairoli 31, near S. Maria dei Carceri, tel 20 021 (L95–120 000, all with bath). The **Stella d'Italia** is Prato's old-fashioned once grand hotel, looking on to the cathedral in Piazza Duomo 8, tel 27 910, with slightly faded rooms for L48–54 000 without bath, L70–80 000 with. On a quiet square just on the far side of the Stazione Porta al Serraglio, the *Toscana**, Piazza Ciardi 3, tel 28 098, is the best of the budget choice; some rooms are air-conditioned (L36 000, all without bath).

EATING OUT

One reason for staying in Prato is the restaurants, especially if you like fish, the speciality of **Il Pirana**, Via Valentini 110 (south of Viale Veneto, the main street between the central station and Piazza San Marco), tel 25 746. The Pirana has an entirely justifiable reputation as one of the best seafood restaurants in inland Tuscany; try the scampi (L60 000). Opposite the Metastasio theatre, **Trattoria Bruno**, Via Verdi 12, tel 23 810, is an unpretentious, small establishment with an innovative chef who turns out dishes like tagliatelle with artichokes and veal *scaloppa* with truffles or stuffed celery, and more traditional Tuscan favourites like brains and kidneys; L40 000 or so, closed Sun and Thurs eve. Less expensively, **Trattoria Lapo**, Piazza Mercatale 141, tel 23 745, is unspectacular but usually crowded (L18–25 000). For a light meal, a pizza, or a quick beer and sandwich, the Pratesi head over to **Brunch One**, Via F. Ferrucci 43/a; in the evening they drift over to Piazza S. Agostino for tasty sandwiches, chips, and one of 250 different labels of beer available. Homesick Brits and anglophiles in Prato meet at the **Nelson Pub**, Via S. Trinita 117.

North of Prato: the Val di Bisenzio

Prato's river begins some 40 km up in the Apennines, and along its valley runs N. 325, a secondary highway towards Bologna. This valley was long the fief of the Alberti counts, whose fortifications dot its steep sides. **Vaiano**, the first town on the main route, has a Romanesque abbey church and green striped campanile as its landmark; just beyond are the impressive ruins of the Alberti's **Rocca di Cerbaia** (12th century). The highway continues to **San Quirico di Vernio**, with another ruined Alberti castle up above. From S. Quirico's neighbour to the west, **Cantagallo** ('Cock's crow'), a lovely walking path leads up to the **Piano della Rasa** in little over an hour, a panoramic valley with an alpine refuge open between April and October. Further north on N. 325, at the small resort of **Montepiano**, the waters destined for the Tyrrhenian and Adriatic split and go their own ways. There is another ancient abbey here, the Vallombrosan **Badia di Santa Maria**, with good 13th- and 14th-century frescoes. From the abbey begins another fine walking path up to **Alpe di Cavarzano** (1008 m), and from there, in another hour, up to the highest peak in the region, **Monte La Scoperta** (1278 m).

Figline and Montemurlo

The old road between Prato and Pistoia passes near **Figline di Prato**, a medieval village known for its terracotta vases. Figline has a good 14th-century parish church with contemporary mural paintings, including a primitive *Last Supper* and a *St Michael* with a finely detailed background; a small parish museum contains other 'primitives'. **Montemurlo**, on its hill over the plain of Prato, is another medieval town, formerly the castle of the Guidi counts that in 1537 was the Alamo for the anti-Medici republican oligarchs of Florence, led by Filippo Strozzi, defeated here once and for all by the troops of Cosimo I. The old walled town of Montemurlo is interesting to explore, with an impressive and rather stylish **Rocca** for its crown, approached these days by a Mannerist ramp. The Romanesque church of 'Beheaded John' (**San Giovanni Decollato**) has a pretty campanile and some good art in its Baroqued interior, including a miraculous Byzantine crucifix and a 16th-century painting by Giovanni da Prato illustrating its story.

Pistoia

You know Pistoia (pop. 94,500) is near when the road plunges into a Lilliputian forest of miniature parasol pines and cypresses, all in tidy rows. These are Italy's most extensive ornamental nurseries, a gentle craft that thrives in the rich soil at the foot of the Apennines. But Pistoia wasn't always content to cultivate its own garden; this is the place, after all, that gave us the word 'pistol'—originally surgical knives made in the city, and later coming to mean daggers and guns. Today it specializes in light rail trains (the Breda works built the cars for the Washington D. C. metro), also mattresses, cymbals and baby trees; its notorious, dark past lingers only in Florentine histories; modern Pistoiese laugh it off, and if you find the ghosts of its intrigues haunting the often grim, ancient lanes, there are plenty of lovely old churches where you can exorcize them. The historic centre of Pistoia is almost perfectly intact, and there is some fine art to be seen behind its medieval walls, part Pisan, part Florentine, reflecting its position between the two great rivals, but all seldom sampled by the movable feast of tourism.

History

> ... Proud you are, envious, enemies of heaven,
> Friends to your own harm and, to your own neighbour,
> The simplest charity you find a labour.
>
> —*Invective against the People of Pistoia*, a sonnet by Michelangelo

Pistoia's fellow Tuscans have long looked askance at her, ever since Roman times, when the city was called *Pistoria* and saw the death struggle of the Catiline conspiracy, the famous attempted coup against the Roman Republic in 62 BC, which ended when the legions tracked down the escaped Catiline and his henchmen near Pistoia. Its position on the Via Cassia helped it prosper under the Lombards, who elevated it to a royal city. In 1158 Pistoia became a *comune*, and enough of a threat that Florence and Lucca ganged up against it twice. In the 13th century Pistoia's evil reputation gave it credit for having begun the bitter controversy between Black and White Guelphs that so obsessed Florence; Dante, himself a victim of that feud, never let a chance go by in the *Divina Commedia* to curse and condemn the fateful city. In 1306 Florence exacted revenge by capturing Pistoia, and as usual adapted its politics to the nature of its conquests: Prato she made an ally, Pisa she held with fortresses, but Pistoia she controlled with factions. The only interlude came between 1315–28, when Lucca's Castruccio Castracani held Pistoia as part of his short-lived empire, though after his fall the Florentines soon returned. The city, preoccupied with its own quarrels, carried on happily ever after, living well off its old speciality, iron working. It supplied the conspirators of Europe with fine daggers, and later, keeping up with technology, with pistols.

GETTING AROUND

Pistoia lies along the A11, and at the foot of two important routes north over the Apennines, the N. 64 towards Bologna and N. 633 to Abetone. From the station, just south of the city walls at the end of Via XX Settembre, there are frequent trains along the main Florence–Lucca line. COPIT buses for Vinci and Empoli (37 km/2 hrs—a beautiful, twisting road over the Monte Albano), Cutigliano (37 km/1 hr 45 min), Abetone (50 km/2 1/2 hrs), the zoo, Montecatini (16 km/30 min), and other destinations in Pistoia's little province depart from Piazza San Francesco. LAZZI buses depart for Florence (35 km/1 hr), Prato, Lucca (43 km/1 1/2 hrs), Montecatini, Viareggio and Pisa (65 km/2 hrs) from Viale Vittorio Veneto, near the train station. Cars are banned from the city centre, but there's plenty of parking around the Fortezza S. Barbara in the southeast corner of the walls.

TOURIST INFORMATION

Piazza Duomo, in the Bishop's palace, tel (0573) 21 622. Also in Corso Gramsci 110, tel 34 326.

Post Office: Via Roma 5.

Telephones: Corso A. Gramsci 96.

Piazza del Duomo

Pistol-Pistoia no longer packs any heat, but it packs in the heart of its 16th-century diamond-shaped walls one of the finest squares in Italy, a lesson in the subtle medieval aesthetic of urban design, an art lost with the endless theorizing and compulsive regularity of the Renaissance. The arrangement of the buildings around the L-shaped **Piazza del Duomo** seems haphazard at first. The design is meant to be experienced from street level; try walking into the piazza from a few of its surrounding streets, and you'll see how from each approach the monuments reveal themselves in a different order and pattern, like the shaking of a kaleidoscope; the windows of the Palazzo del Comune echo those on the Palazzo del Podestà, and the striped decoration of the baptistry is recalled in the campanile and Duomo. Much of old Pistoia is like this, shaped by centuries of anonymous builders into a work of art, one that appeals not only to the eye but the brain. Once you learn how to see it, you may find the rigid symmetry of Renaissance and Baroque design looking a little wearisome.

The piazza provides the perfect setting for Pistoia's great annual party, the colourful *Giostra dell'Orso*, the 'Joust of the Bear', which takes place 25 July, after a month of concerts, fairs, and exhibits. The Joust began in the 14th century, pitting twelve knights against a bear dressed in a checked cloak. The bear has been replaced by two wooden dummies, but the pageantry remains the same.

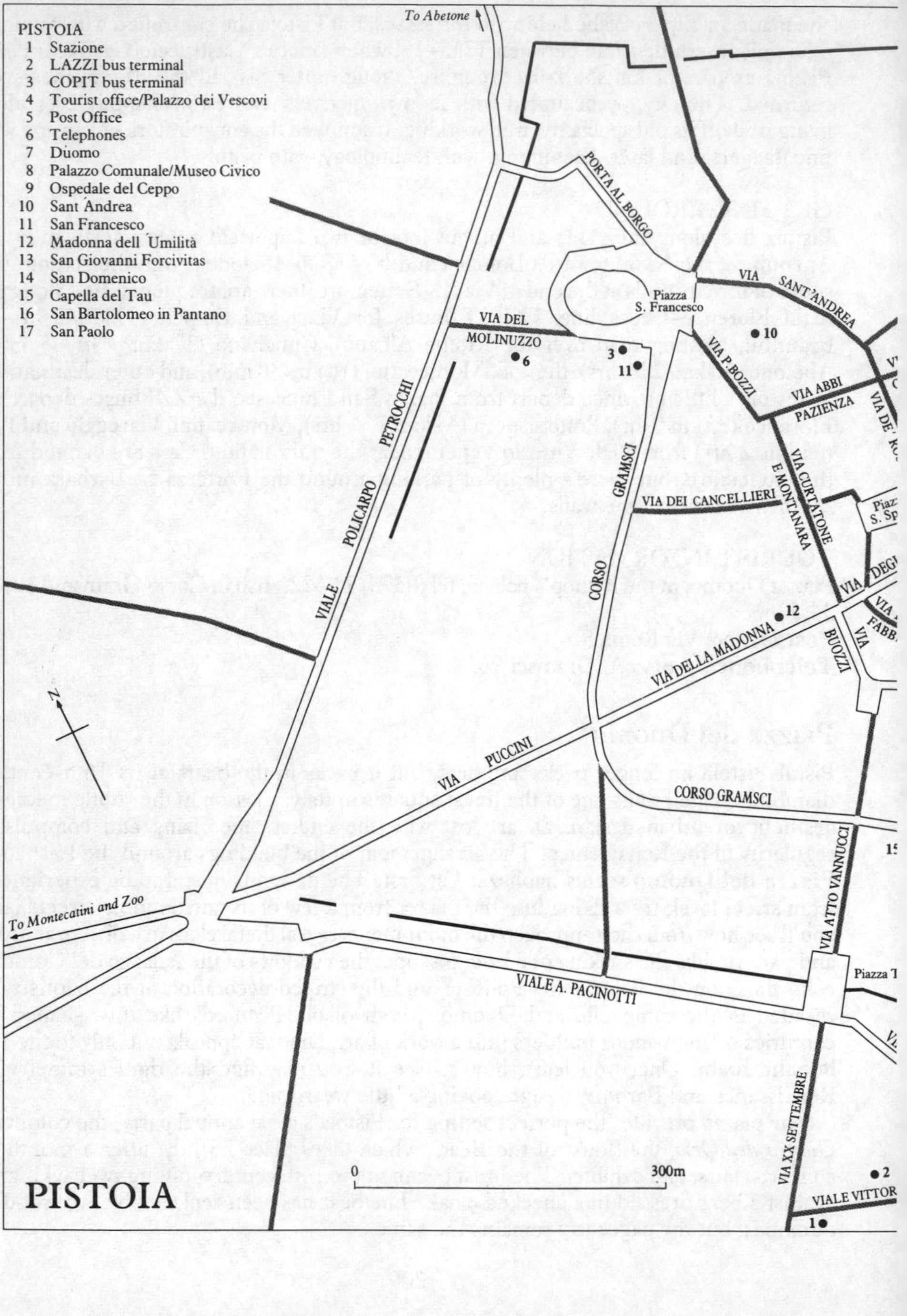
PISTOIA
1 Stazione
2 LAZZI bus terminal
3 COPIT bus terminal
4 Tourist office/Palazzo dei Vescovi
5 Post Office
6 Telephones
7 Duomo
8 Palazzo Comunale/Museo Civico
9 Ospedale del Ceppo
10 Sant´Andrea
11 San Francesco
12 Madonna dell´Umilità
13 San Giovanni Forcivitas
14 San Domenico
15 Capella del Tau
16 San Bartolomeo in Pantano
17 San Paolo
To Abetone
PORTA AL BORGO
VIA SANT'ANDREA
Piazza S. Francesco
VIA DEL MOLINUZZO
VIA P. BOZZI
VIA ABBI PAZIENZA
VIALE POLICARPO PETROCCHI
CORSO GRAMSCI
VIA CURTATONE E MONTANARA
VIA DEI CANCELLIERI
VIA DELLA MADONNA
VIA BUOZZI
VIA PUCCINI
CORSO GRAMSCI
VIA ATTO VANNUCCI
To Montecatini and Zoo
VIALE A. PACINOTTI
VIA XX SETTEMBRE
0 300m
PISTOIA

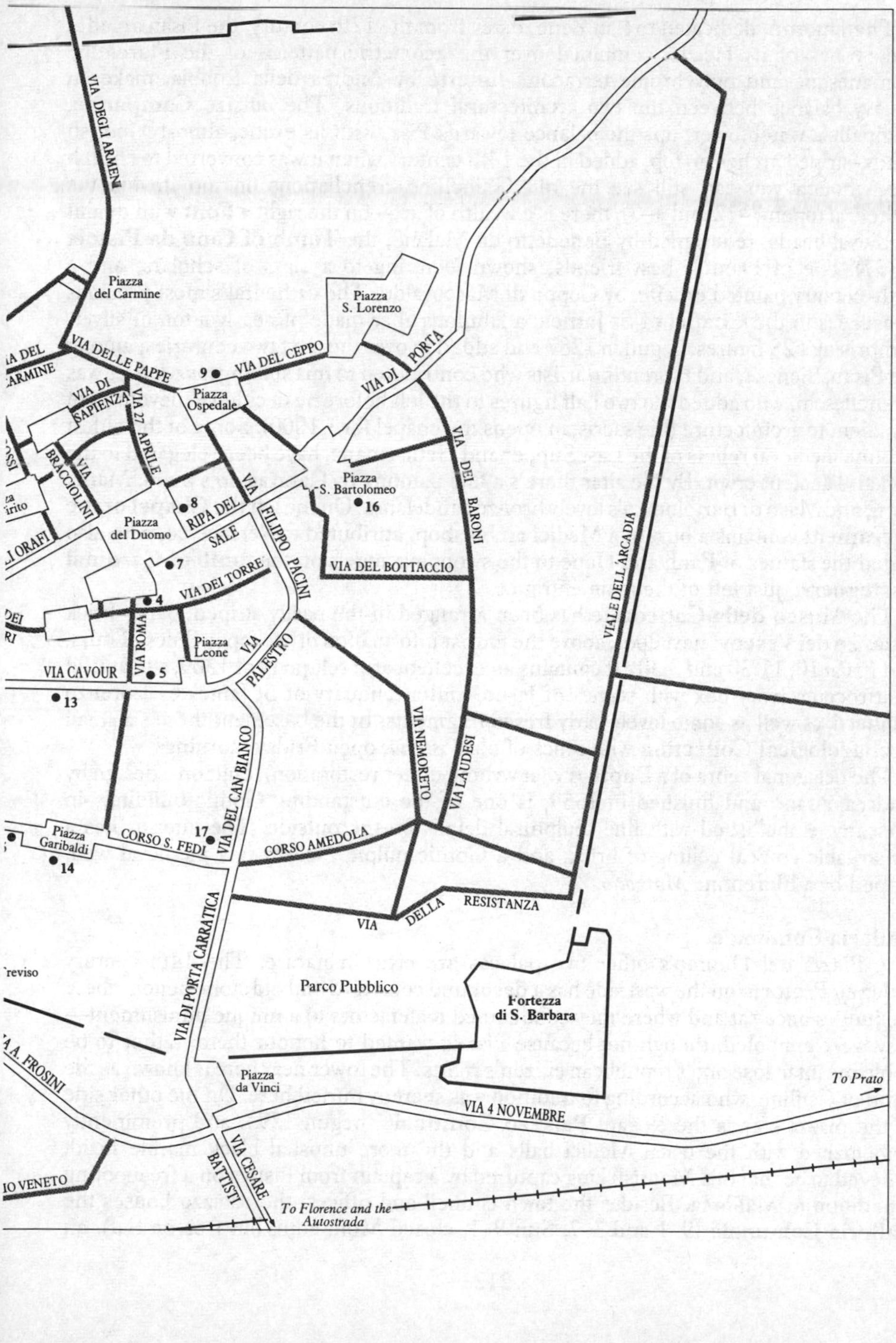
Piazza del Carmine
Piazza S. Lorenzo
VIA DELLE PAPPE
VIA DEL CEPPO
VIA DI PORTA
9
Piazza Ospedale
VIA DI SAPIENZA
VIA 27 APRILE
VIA BRACCIOLINI
VIA DEL BARONI
Piazza S. Bartolomeo
16
8
RIPA DEL SALE
VIA FILIPPO PACINI
Piazza del Duomo
7
VIA DEL BOTTACCIO
VIA DEI TORRE
4
VIA ROMA
Piazza Leone
VIA PALESTRO
VIA CAVOUR
5
13
VIALE DELL'ARCADIA
VIA NEMORETO
VIA LAUDESI
VIA DEL CAN BIANCO
17
Piazza Garibaldi
CORSO S. FEDI
14
CORSO AMEDOLA
VIA DELLA RESISTANZA
VIA DI PORTA CARRATICA
Parco Pubblico
Fortezza di S. Barbara
Piazza da Vinci
VIA 4 NOVEMBRE
To Prato
VIA CESARE BATTISTI
To Florence and the Autostrada

The **Duomo**, dedicated to San Zeno, dates from the 12th century; the Pisan arcades and stripes of its façade, combined over the geometric patterns of the Florentine Romanesque and polychrome terracotta **lunette** by Andrea della Robbia, make an uneasy balance between the two architectural traditions. The outsize **Campanile**, originally a watchtower, tips the balance towards Pisa, with its exotic, almost Moorish candy-striped arches on top, added in the 14th century when it was converted to church use—though you can still see the old Ghibelline crenellations on top. Inside the cathedral (open 7–12 and 4–7), there is a wealth of art—on the right a **Font** with quaint medieval heads, redesigned by Benedetto da Maiano, the **Tomb of Cino da Pistoia** (1337), one of Dante's best friends, shown lecturing to a class of scholars, and a 13th-century painted crucifix by Coppo di Marcovaldo. The cathedral's most precious treasure is in the **Chapel of St James**: a fabulous altar made of nearly a ton of silver, comprising 628 figures, begun in 1287 and added to over the next two centuries; among the Pisan, Sienese, and Florentine artists who contributed to this shining *tour de force* was Brunelleschi, who added the two half figures to the left before he decided to devote all of his talent to architecture (the sacristan opens the chapel for L1000). Some of the oldest art, fine medieval reliefs of the Last Supper and Gethsemane, have been relegated to the dim and ancient crypt. By the altar there's a fine painting by Caravaggio's pupil, Mattia Preti, and Maso di Bartolomeo's lovely bronze candelabra. On the left the **Chapel of the Sacrament** contains a bust of a Medici archbishop, attributed to Verrocchio, who also added the statues of Faith and Hope to the swooping angels on the **tomb of Cardinal Forteguerri**, just left of the main entrance.

The **Museo della Cattedrale** has been arranged in the partly striped, partly brick **Palazzo dei Vescovi** next door, above the tourist information office (open Tues, Thurs, and Fri at 10, 11:30 and 3:30); it contains an excellent arm reliquary of 1369, a beautiful quattrocento ivory box with scenes of Jason, and a reliquary of St James by Lorenzo Ghiberti, as well as some lovely early fresco fragments. In the basement there's a small **Archaeological Collection** with relics of old *Pistoria*, open Friday mornings.

The octagonal zebra of a **Baptistry** (at writing under restoration), built on a design by Andrea Pisano and finished in 1359, is one of the outstanding Gothic buildings in Tuscany, embellished with fine sculptural details on the outside. The interior has a remarkable conical ceiling of brick, and a Gothic pulpit. Nearby is a medieval well, topped by a Florentine *Marzocco*.

Galleria Comunale

The Piazza del Duomo's other two palaces are civic in nature. The 14th-century **Palazzo Pretorio** on the west side has a decorated courtyard and old stone bench where the judges once sat and where they condemned malefactors to a unique punishment—they were ennobled, though not because Pistoia wanted to honour them; rather to be noble meant to lose one's republican citizen's rights. The tower near here is known as the tomb of Catiline, who according to tradition was secretly buried here. On the other side of the piazza stands the elegant **Palazzo Comunale**, begun 1294, and prominently embellished with the usual Medici balls and the more unusual black marble head, believed to be that of a Moorish king captured by a captain from Pistoia on a freebooting expedition to Mallorca. Besides the town council and offices, the palazzo houses the **Galleria Comunale** (9–1 and 3–7, Sun 9–1, closed Mon; adm, but free on Sat), an excellent collection of great and odd paintings to suit even the most jaded of palettes. Pistoiese patrons were uncommonly fond of 'Sacred Conversations'—group portraits of saints around the Madonna, and there are good ones by Mariotto de Nardo, Beccafumi, Lorenzo di Credi and Pistoia's own Gerino Gerini (1480–1529), a follower of Raphael. From the 15th-century 'Maestro delle Madonne di Marmo' there's a sweetly smiling marble relief of the Madonna and child; then two fancy St Sebastians with flowing curls, who precede *The Madonna della Pergola*, by local painter Bernardino di Antonio Detti (1498–1554), whose flacid charwoman of a Madonna holds a child with a large housefly on his chubby arm before a crazy quilt of confusing iconography—children playing dolls, the Judgement of Solomon, a child with a fruitbowl, a floor littered with flowers, amulets, spoons, and rags.

Plod up two more flights of stairs for some screamingly lurid paintings from the 17th–19th centuries, with plenty of historical canvases of murder and mayhem that suggest the local taste for violence lingered at least in art. There are two eerie mythological paintings swathed in Caravaggesque darkness by Cecco Bravo; a 17th-century *Young Woman with a Flower*, bathed in a ghostly light; a sensuous, pouting St Sebastian, disdainfully plucking arrows from his chest; a ridiculous allegory of Medici rule in Pistoia, with *putti* scattering the family's lily symbol like flowers over the city; a Magdalene fondly patting a skull; two nightmarish, imaginary battle scenes by a 17th-century Neapolitan named Francesco Graziani. Two contemporary Pistoiese have their say here as well, Marino Marini (on the ground floor) and Giovanni Michelucci (on the mezzanine).

Ospedale del Ceppo and Sant'Andrea

In medieval Tuscany, it was the custom to collect alms in a hollowed-out log (or *ceppo*) left in a public place, to be gathered and distributed to the poor at Christmastime. *Ceppo* became synonymous with the word charity, as in Datini's famous foundation in Prato, and even earlier here in Pistoia, when the **Ospedale del Ceppo** was founded in the 13th century. Still in use at the same address (walk down Via Pacini from the Palazzo Comunale), this was given a fine arcaded porch in the 1500s, in the style of famous Spedale degli Innocenti in Florence. And as in Florence, the della Robbias were called upon to provide the decoration, in this case the usually insipid Giovanni, who with the help of his workshop and other artists, created not only the typical della Robbian tondoes, but a unique terracotta frieze that spans the entire loggia in resplendent Renaissance technicolor, with scenes of the acts of mercy and theological virtues. Inside there's a small museum dedicated to Pistoia's old iron industry, especially surgical knives, open upon request (tel 367 821, ext 13)

A short walk west of the hospital on Via S. Andrea is the 12th-century **Sant'Andrea**, with a Pisan façade and over the door, a charming bas-relief of the Journey of the Magi, dated 1166, and a pair of ghastly, leering lions. The real jewel, however, is inside: Giovanni Pisano's hexagonal **pulpit** (1297), exquisitely carved in stirring high relief with scenes of the Nativity, Massacre of the Innocents, Adoration of the Magi, Crucifixion, and Last Judgement, with Sibyls in the corners and pedestals in the forms of the four Evangelists—one of the masterpieces of Italian Gothic. Sant'Andrea contains three other crucifixions: Giovanni Pisano's wood crucifix in the right aisle, a medieval version over the main altar, portraying Christ crowned and dressed in a kingly robe, and in the right nave, a large, rather mysterious painting of a saint crucified on a tree (8–12:30 and 3–6).

San Francesco and the Madonna dell'Umilità

Pretty striped churches circle the centre of Pistoia like zebras on a merry-go-round. The two plain ponies in the lot are to the west. The large **San Francesco al Prato** in Piazza S. Francesco, plain and Gothic like most Franciscan churches, has some notable 14th-century frescoes, especially in the chapel to the left of the altar, with Sienese scenes portraying the Triumph of St Augustine. On the side of the church there's an ancient olive tree and a memorial to assassinated prime minister Aldo Moro, a stark contrast with the heroic Fascist-era war monument in the piazza itself. South on Corso Gramsci is Pistoia's main theatre, the 1694 **Teatro Manzoni**; further south, on Via della Madonna, towers Pistoia's experiment in High Renaissance geometry, the octagonal, unstriped **Basilica della Madonna dell'Umilità** begun in 1518 by local architect and pupil of Bramante, Ventura Vitoni, who graced it with an imposing barrel-vaulted vestibule. In the 1560s Giorgio Vasari was called upon to crown Vitoni's fine start; not content to limit his mischief to Florence, he added a dome so heavy that the basilica has been threatening to collapse ever since. More work to shore it up is currently underway.

San Giovanni Fuoricivitas and San Domenico

South of the Piazza del Duomo (Via Roma to Via Cavour) lies the tiny **Piazza San Leone**, the ancient Lombard centre of Pistoia; its stubby tower once belonged to the nastiest Pistoian of them all, a 13th-century noble thug and church robber named Vanni Fucci whom Dante found in one of the lower circles of Hell, entwined in a serpent, cursing and making obscene gestures up at God. Around the corner of Via Cavour, the 12th-century **San Giovanni Fuoricivitas** claims the honour of being the most striped church in all Christendom, its green and white flank an abstract pattern of lozenges and blind arches that out-Pisas anything in Pisa. In the dark, gloomy interior, only four things are lit: the dramatic pulpit (1270) by Fra Gugliemo da Pisa, a pupil of Nicola Pisano, a holy water stoup supported by caryatids by Giovanni Pisano, a polyptych by Taddeo Gaddi, and a white, glazed terracotta group of the *Visitation* by Luca or Andrea della Robbia.

Little Piazza Garibaldi to the south is adorned with a good equestrian statue of Garibaldi, some florid street lamps, and **San Domenico**, begun in the late 13th century. In its spacious, airy interior, there's a splendid Baroque organ from 1617 and two Renaissance tombs: that of Filippo Lazzari, by the Rossellino brothers, portraying the deceased lecturing to his pupils (one of whom can't help yawning), and the other of Lorenzo da Ripafratta, with a fine effigy. In 1497, Benozzo Gozzoli died of the plague in Pistoia and is buried somewhere in the cloister of San Domenico; you can see a fresco he began of the Journey of the Magi nearby. Although the monastery is still in use, you can ring to see the frescoes in the chapter house, among them good Sienese works and a crucifixion with its sinopia, dating back to the mid-13th century. Even more interesting are the frescoes across the street in the little **Cappella del Tau** (so-named after the blue T its priests wore on their vestments)—vividly coloured scenes of Adam and Eve and assorted saints, attributed in part to Masolino. Next to it, at no. 72, note the coat-of-arms over the pretty window of two dancing bears, recalling the Giostra dell'Orso. There's another good Gothic façade on **San Paolo**, a block to the east, with broader stripes and a statue of St James on the very top, attributed to Orcagna.

There are more old churches in central Pistoia, but only one other worth going out of your way to visit: **San Bartolomeo in Pantano** ('St Bart in the Bog'), on the east side of town, built on marshy land in the 8th century and sinking gently into the ground ever since. It has an attractive, partially completed façade, and inside, a carved marble lectern of 1250 by Guido da Como.

The Zoo, the Medici, and some Iron

Of all the stripes in Pistoia, the best may well be on the zebras in the **Pistoia Zoo**, 4 km northwest of the city in Via Pieve a Celle. Though the Medici always kept big menageries, modern Italians usually don't care for zoos; this is one of the best in the country, even though it's only 20 years old. Polar bears, kangaroos, giant turtles, reptiles, and all the other zoo favourites are in attendance (9–5 in the winter, 9–7 summer, adm expensive). Southeast 13 km off Alt. N. 66 is yet another Medici villa, the **Villa della Magia in Quarrata**, begun in 1318, and in 1536 the meeting place of Charles V and Alessandro de' Medici. Its grand hall has 18th-century frescoes, and according to rumour visitors are allowed in twice a week (ask at the Pistoia tourist office). In Pistoia itself you can visit one of the city's wrought-iron 'laboratories', Bartoletti, in Via Sestini 110, tel 452 318, open Mon–Sat.

WHERE TO STAY (tel prefix 0573)

Pistoia is more used to lodging and feeding business rather than pleasure travellers. The one exception is ***__Il Convento__**, Via S. Quirico 33, tel 452 651, 5 km east of the centre at Pontenuovo; as its name implies, it is a former convent, preserving its exterior if not all of its interior. The setting is quiet with views over Pistoia; there's a pool and one of the city's better restaurants as well (L85–95 000, all with bath). In the city itself, there's the older, comfortable ***__Leon Bianco__**, Via Panciatichi 2, tel 26 275, with views over the campanile (L80 000), or the newer ***__Piccolo Ritz__**, Via Vannucci 67, tel 26 775 near the station, with a bit of a garden and a garage (L55 000 without bath, L85 000 with). The **__Appenino__**, also near the station in Via XX Settembre 21, tel 32 243, has simple but adequate rooms, most with bath (L65 000, a few cheaper without bath). For something less expensive, try *__Firenze__**, a skip away from Piazza del Duomo at Via Curtatone e Montanara 42, tel 23 141, with clean and quiet rooms for L38 000, L45 000 with bath.

EATING OUT

Pistoia is known, not for its good restaurants, but for its lack of them. In the city itelf there are mostly simple trattorias and pizzas; on Via Panchiatichi 4, **Cucciolo della Montagna**, tel 29 733, is the best in town, with good Tuscan cooking (L30 000). Pistoia's other dining worthies are outside of town: **Rafanelli**, at S. Agostino (Via Sant'Agostino 47, tel 23 046), where Tuscan homecooking (*maccheroni* with duck, game dishes, lamb) is served in a pretty country villa setting (L25–35 000; closed Sun eve, Mon & Aug). **La Cugna**, Via Bolognese 238, in La Cugna, tel 475 000, is a simple, mountain-style restaurant, offering tasty tagliatelle with ham, *porcini* mushrooms and cream, and grilled steaks (L30 000).

The Mountains of Pistoia

North of Pistoia rise a fairly unspoiled stretch of the central Apennines, luxuriantly forested and endowed with some lovely mountain escape routes, deep green in the summer and ski white in the winter. Main routes include the beautiful Bologna road (N. 64) known as the 'Porrettana' which follows the Bologna-Pistoia railway through the sparsely settled mountains, and the equally beautiful, parallel N. 632, less encumbered with traffic. The main mountain resorts up to Abetone are along the N. 66 and N. 12, as easily reached from Lucca as from Pistoia.

TOURIST INFORMATION

San Marcello Pistoiese: Via Marconi, tel (0573) 630 145.
Cutigliano: Via Tigri, tel (0573) 68 029.
Abetone: Piazzale Piramidi, tel (0573) 60 231.

Due north of Pistoia, 10 km along a by-road towards Piteccio, is the ancient hamlet of **Castagno**, converted into a unique open-air art gallery. Its lanes are embellished with 20th-century frescoes on the twelve months; modern statues pose in the nooks and crannies; and Castagno's ancient church and oratory dedicated to St Francis, both with interesting frescoes, have recently been restored. A 4 km backtrack will take you to the main N. 66; at Pontepetri (20 km) N. 632 veers north to the formerly popular little mountain resort of **Pracchia**.

Most visitors these days continue along N. 66 for the newer summer-winter resorts by way of the lovely state forest of Teso, at the fine old villages of **Maresca** and **Gavinana**. The latter is notorious in the annals of Florentine history for the defeat of its army by the imperial forces of Charles V, a battle that cost the lives of both commanders. The Florentine leader, Francesco Ferrucci, was knifed in the back, and is remembered with his own little museum in the main piazza. N. 66 continues to **San Marcello Pistoiese**, 29 km from Pistoia, the 'capital' of the mountains, in a lovely setting, where since 1854 the inhabitants have launched a hot-air balloon every 8 September as a farewell to summer. All year round, however, you can walk over the 220-metre **suspension bridge of Mammiano**, which would perhaps look more at home in the Andes. **Cutigliano**, 7 km north, is a growing winter resort with 27 km of ski trails and a cable car up to its highest peak, Doganaccia (1175 m). In the village the **Palazzo Pretorio** fairly bristles with the coats-of-arms of its former governors.

Near the northern border of Tuscany, through a lush and ancient forest, lies **Abetone** (1400 m), one of the most famous resorts in the central Apennines. Named after a huge fir tree, the town grew up in the late 18th century, when Grand Duke Pietro Leopoldo built the road to the Duchy of Modena, a road specially designed not to pass through the detested Papal States (the modern province of Bologna). Two milestones at Abetone mark the old boundary. The closest major ski resort to Florence, it is highly developed, with 30 km of trails, four cable cars and other chairlifts; in the summer its cool altitudes, swimming pools, and other recreational facilities make it almost as popular, especially as a weekend retreat. At other seasons, rain is not exactly unknown.

WHERE TO STAY (tel prefix 0573)

In the mountains, many hotels are open only during the ski season and in July and August. A pleasant hotel open all year in San Marcello Pistoiese is *****Il Cacciatore**, Via

Marconi 87, tel 630 533, nothing fancy, but green and quiet (L75 000). Cutigliano is a few degrees smarter, with big resort hotels like ***Piandinovello**, Via Sestaione 131, tel 673 076, with a swimming pool and tennis courts (L78 000, all with bath, open 20 Dec–20 April and July–Aug), or near the centre of the village, ***Rondò Priscilla**, tel 68 148, a small hotel with a garden and pool, open all year (L70–85 000, all with bath). Up in Abetone there's the elegant ****Palazzaccio** in Piazza Piramidi, tel 60 067, open July–Aug and Dec–April (L110 000), or the ***Regina**, on quieter Via Uccelliera 9, tel 60 007, July to mid-Sept and Dec–April (L80 000, all with bath). Abetone also has a youth hostel, the **Ostello della Neve**, at Cosuma, tel 60 117, with room for 92 people, open Dec–March and July–Aug). There are quite a few economical holiday villas near the towns and alpine refuges in the surrounding mountains; the Pistoia tourist office has a complete list.

EATING OUT

In Cutigliano, **Fagiolino**, Via Carega 1, tel 68 014, offers traditional Tuscan-mountain cuisine (*risotto ai funghi*, roast kid, raspberry torte) served on a panoramic veranda (L30–40 000). In Abetone, **La Capannina**, Via Brennero 256, tel 60 562, has a rustic décor and rustic but excellently prepared dishes, with lots of *porcini* mushrooms, or ravioli with walnut sauce, trout, pigeon, with wild berries for dessert, all accompanied by a wide selection of wines (L35 000).

Montecatini Terme

West of Pistoia lies the Valdinievole, the 'Valley of Mists', a land obsessed with water, though mostly of the subterranean, curative variety, available in Italy's most glamorous thermal spa, Montecatini. Leonardo da Vinci's first known drawing was of a view towards Montecatini from Lamporecchio, near his hometown of Vinci (see p. 197), and it is believed that his lifetime fascination with canals and locks and currents and dams and the misty, watery backgrounds of his most famous paintings come from a childhood spent in the Valdinievole. He even designed a fountain for the baths of Montecatini in one of his notebooks, which after 380 years is currently being built of Carrara marble as his monument.

Even in these days of holistic medicine, preventive medicine, herbal cures, and pharmaceutical paranoia, it is the despair of the Montecatini tourist board that Anglo-Saxons from both sides of the Atlantic refuse to believe that soaking in or drinking mere water can do anything as beneficial for them as imbibing a pitcher of Chianti. Unlike continental enthusiasts, we defy the wisdom of the ancients—especially the Romans, who spent the plunder accumulated from conquering the world on ever more fabulous baths. But it is sometimes forgotten that taking the waters, no matter how hot, radio-active, or chock full of minerals, is only half of the cure; the other is simply to relax, to stroll through gardens, listen to a little music, linger in a café, to indulge in a bit of the old *dolce far niente*. And in Montecatini (pop. 21,500) you can do just that without touching a blessed, unfermented drop, surrounded by Belle Epoque nostalgia from the days when the spa seethed with dukes, politicians, literati, and actresses; you may recognize it as one of the locations in Nikita Mikhalhov's recent film, *Oci Ciornie*, starring Marcello Mastroianni.

Tettuccio, Montecatini Terme

GETTING AROUND

Montecatini is easily reached by train from Florence (51 km/1 ½ hrs), Pistoia (16 km/25 min) and Lucca (27 km/45 min). The station (tel 78 551) is on Via Toti, as is the LAZZI bus terminal (tel 71 181), with connections to Pescia (8 km), Monsummano (2 km), Lamporecchio, Serravalle (6 km), Collodi (13 km), as well as Florence, Pistoia, Pisa, Livorno, Viareggio, Prato, Carrara, and Lucca.

TOURIST INFORMATION

Via Verdi 66, tel (0572) 772 244.

Parco delle Terme

A short stroll up from the station, past Montecatini's trendy boutiques, cafés, cinemas and some of its 200 hotels to Via Verdi, will take you into Montecatini's mineral water Elysium, the immaculately groomed **Parco delle Terme**, where the high temples of the cult dot the shaded lawn. The Lorraine grand dukes, spa soaks like their Habsburg cousins, were behind the initial development of Montecatini's springs, and many of the baths, or *Terme*, are Neoclassical pavilions—monumental, classical, and floral architecture that lent itself nicely to the later Liberty-style embellishments of the 1920s. You can take in some of these Art Nouveau fancies in Montecatini's **Municipio**, on Via Verdi opposite the park, or in the most sumptuous and ancient of its nine major bathing establishments, **Tettuccio**. In the 1370s a group of Florentines attempted to extract mineral salts from the spring and built a little roof (or *Tettuccio*) over it; and although they failed it was soon discovered that the water had a good effect on rotten livers—one of the first to come here was Francesco Datini, the Merchant of Prato, in 1401. By the 18th century, Tettuccio was in a state of a ruin, and Grand Duke Leopold I had it splendidly rebuilt. His façade remains, while the interior was redone by Montecatini's greatest architect, Ugo Giovanozzi, in the 1920s, embellished with paintings by Italy's Art Nouveau master Galileo Chini and ceramic pictures by Cascella in the drinking gallery;

there's an elegant café, fountains, a reflecting pool and rotunda, writing hall, music rooms, a little city within a city—all adorned with scenes from an aquatic Golden Age of languid nymphs—the perfect place to sip your morning glass of liver-flushing water.

Other establishments, each with their special virtues, are nearby—the Palladian-style arcade of the **Regina** spring; the **Terme Leopoldine**, another grand ducal establishment, with mud baths housed in a temple-like building dedicated to Aesculapius, the god of health; the half-neo-Renaissance, half-modern **New Excelsior baths**; the pretty Tuscan rustic **Tamerici**, in its lush garden; the **Torretta**, with its phony medieval tower and afternoon concerts in the loggia. Note that the baths are open May–October, except for the Excelsior, which stays open all year. Tickets for a day or subscriptions are available from the central office in Via Verdi 41 (tel 75 851) and prices aren't exactly healthy for your wallet: a morning visit to Tettuccio is L14 000 in the high season.

During Digestion

While the water works its way through your system, you can work your way through Montecatini's diversions. There's the **Art Academy**, consisting solely of donations from Montecatini's admirers—the piano Verdi used during his annual stays in the Locanda Maggiore, where he composed *Otello*, and art by Salvador Dali, Galileo Chini, Fattori, and many others. There's another, wooded park to explore, just behind the Parco delle Terme, called **Le Panteraie** (with a swimming pool), where deer roam freely; you can sip an elegant coffee at the **Gran Caffè Gambrinus**, or perhaps play a round at the beautiful **Montecatini Golf Course**, set among olive groves and cypresses (tel 628 714), or a game of tennis at the courts in Via dei Bari (tel 767 587); or try to win back your hotel bill at the trotting races at the **Ippodromo**. The **Circolo dei forestieri** (foreigners' club) and the **Kursaal** (with cinema, night club, games) are popular meeting places. One of the prettiest excursions is to take the funicular up to **Montecatini Alto,** the original old hilltown, with breathtaking views over the Valley of Mists and a charming little piazza with a charming little theatre; nearby you can visit the stalactites in the **Grotta Maona** (April-Oct).

WHERE TO STAY (tel prefix 0572)

Even if you don't care to take the waters, Montecatini's scores of hotels ensure that you can find a room in a pinch. Italy's choicest spa has no fewer than six hotels that claim the title of 'Grand' and a half-dozen others that only decline to for discretion's sake. **Full board** is the rule here.

Of the grandest, the *******Grand Hotel Bellavista**, Viale Fedeli, tel 580 395, offers golf, tennis, indoor pool, luxurious rooms, sauna, health club, and an infinite number of opportunities for self-indulgence (L360 000). But for genuine Belle Epoque charm, the *******Grand Hotel & La Pace**, Viale della Torretta 1, tel 75 801, is renowned throughout Europe, with a similarly impressive array of luxuries (around L430 000, open April–Oct). At the ******Grand Hotel Plaza e Locanda Maggiore**, in Piazza del Popolo 7, tel 75 831, you can check into Verdi's favourite hotel, open year round, with a pool and air-conditioned rooms (L175 000). One of the more charming 'moderate' choices is the *****Belvedere**, next to the Parco delle Terme, Viale Fedeli 10, tel 70 251, with an indoor pool, tennis, and friendly service (L95 000, open April–Oct). On a quiet side street near the park, *****Corallo**, Viale Cavallotti 116, tel 78 288, is small but refined and open all year, with a pool and garden (L40–60 000 without bath, L75–95 000 with). Up in Montecatini Alto, ***Bellosguardo**, Via Mura Grocco 11, tel 78 637, has a garden and views (L36–50 000, all with bath).

EATING OUT

Although most guests dine in their hotels in Montecatini, it's worth breaking loose at least once to try the imaginative fare at the **Enoteca da Giovanni**, Via Garibaldi 25, tel 71 695, a unique and much honoured place where game dishes—hare, venison, wild duck—turn into impeccably *haute cuisine* surprises at the hands of a genuine master chef; you won't even miss the L40–55 000 price. If you're feeling romantic, **Gourmet**, Via Amendola 6, tel 771 012, offers elegant dinners by candlelight, with piano music to set the mood, for around L40 000. Up in Montecatini Alto, just above the funicular station, **Lido's**, Via Fratelli Guermani 2, tel 766 378, has an elegant dining room with panoramic views, where you can ruin your waistline with cannelloni filled with truffles, or rich lasagne, or pheasant cooked with cream, ham and truffles, and sinful desserts (L50–75 000). When you get tired of being healthy, dip into the vintages at the enoteca at Via Forini 13, or the Antinori 'Degustazione Vini' on Via Verdi 35.

Monsummano and Serravalle

Lovely narrow lanes crisscross the Valdinievole landscape, offering tempting excursions further afield. Five km east of Montecatini is its sister spa, **Monsummano Terme**, offering vapour baths in natural grottoes. The first of these strange caves was discovered by accident in 1849, when the Giusti family moved a boulder and found the entrance to a stalactite cave, the **Grotta Giusti**, 100 m deep, with three small lakes fed by hot springs (open April-Nov); a second steamy cave, the **Grotta Parlanti** (May–Oct), is used for serious treatments. Monsummano, however, hasn't rested on its vapours, but has transformed itself into one of Italy's biggest shoe-making towns; like Montecatini it has an old antecedent atop a hill, **Monsummano Alto**, all but abandoned these days, but with a pretty Romanesque church, a romantically ruined castle, and splendid views. Another panoramic view may be had from **Montevettolini**, 4 km from Monsummano, site of a villa built by Ferdinando I in 1597.

If you prefer your castles more intact, continue east to the old fortress at **Serravalle Pistoiese**, which, as its name translates, 'locks the valley' between the Apennines and Monte Albano. Its old Lombard tower and 14th-century additions saw considerable action in Tuscany's days of inter-urban hooliganism.

Pescia

To the west of Montecatini, there's another attractive old hilltown, **Buggiano Castello**, and for those who imagine that fresco went out of fashion years ago, there's San Michele in nearby **Ponte Buggianese**, freshly frescoed in stark colours by Pietro Annigoni. The colours are even more dazzling in **Pescia** (pop. 20,000), Italy's capital of flowers, a title this little city with a green thumb has snatched from Sanremo on the Riviera. Some 3 million cut flowers are sent off every day in the summer from Pescia's giant market; besides carnations, lilies, and gladioli, it is celebrated by gourmets for its tender asparagus and its white beans.

Pescia has a number of interesting monuments, beginning with a 14th-century church of **San Francesco**, containing a portrait of St Francis with scenes from his life, painted in 1235 by Bonaventura Berlinghieri and considered to be one of the most authentic likenesses of the saint; also be sure to take a look at the Crucifixion by Puccio Capanna in the sacristy. The **Duomo** was rebuilt in the 1600s, but has a fine Romanesque campanile wearing its little cupola like a beanie, and a late terracotta triptych by Luca della Robbia. On the long, narrow Piazza Mazzini stands the imposing **Palazzo del Vicario**, with the usual mishmash of stone escutcheons; in nearby **Sant'Antonio**, built in the 1360s, look up the 'Ugly Saints', a 13th-century wood Deposition from the Cross.

The green, hilly region of prosperous villages north of Pescia in the upper Valdinievole is fondly known as its 'Little Switzerland'. In its cheerful core, some 12 km from Pescia, stands one of Italy's most bizarre churches, the 12th-century **Pieve di Castelvecchio**, decorated with frightening stone masks, grinning and grimacing, that would look more at home in the Heart of Darkness.

Collodi and Pinocchio

Just west of Pescia is the little old town of Collodi, often visited as a child by Florentine writer Carlo Lorenzo (1826–90), whose uncle was a factor at the local castle; Lorenzo was so fond of it that he took its name as his own when he published his *Adventures of Pinocchio*, Italy's greatest contribution to children's literature. In honour of the creator of the naughty wooden puppet, Collodi has built the **Parco di Pinocchio** (8:30–sunset, adm), with a bronze statue of the puppet by Emilio Greco and a piazza of mosaics with scenes from the book by Venturino Venturi, as well as other figures, all very much in the angular style of the late 1950s and early '60s; a lawn maze, a museum dedicated to the book, a playground and other amusements for the kids. Adults, meanwhile, can try to work their way through a much older labyrinth in the magnificent hillside gardens of the **Castello Garzoni**, designed in the 17th century by Ottaviano Diodati of Lucca,and considered one of the finest late Italian gardens, ornate with fountains and statuary. The castle itself 'of a hundred windows' has a few grand rooms, and the kitchen where young Carlo sat and dreamed up Pinocchio (gardens open 8–1 and 2:30–4:30, summer 8–sunset; castle open daily May–Oct, in winter Sat afternoon and Sun only, adm.)

WHERE TO STAY AND EATING OUT (tel prefix 0572)

In Monsummano, near the vaporous grottoes, the villa of the family of the poet Giuseppe Giusti has been converted into the charming *****Grotto Giusti**, Via Grotta Giusti 171, tel 51 165, with frescoed ceilings and antiques (April–Oct, L80–150 000). Up above Monsummano in Montevettolini, **San Michele**, Piazza Bargellini 80, tel 62 447, is a café-bar-enoteca-pizzeria-restaurant where the menu tempts with a tasty array of antipasti (smoked Canadian salmon, caviar, *carpaccio* with truffles), followed by spaghetti with lobster, perhaps, and prawns (L50 000).

Just outside Pescia, the large *****Villa delle Rose**, Via del Castellare, tel 451 301, has a pleasant garden and pool and comfortable, modern rooms (L85 000). In Pescia you can dine very well at **Cecco**, Via Forti 84, tel 477 955, featuring seasonal dishes starring

Pescia's famous asparagus, or wild mushrooms or truffles or zucchini flowers; among the desserts, there's *torta di Cecco*, prepared according to an ancient recipe (L35 000). **La Buca**, in Pescia's Piazza Mazzini, tel 477 339, serves traditional Tuscan favourites like *pappa al pomodoro, panzanella* and fish grilled over coals (L25 000).

Part VII

LUCCA, THE GARFAGNANA, AND LUNIGIANA

Church of San Michele, Lucca

LUCCA

Nowhere in Lucca will you see the
face of a Philistine.

—Heine, *Travels in Lucca*

Of all Tuscany's great cities, Lucca (pop. 92,500) is the most cosy, sane, and domestic, a tidy gem of a town encased within its famous walls. Yet even these hardly seem formidable, more like garden walls than something that would keep the Florentines at bay. The old ramparts and surrounding areas, once the outworks of the fortifications, are now full of lawns and trees, forming a miniature green belt; on the walls, where the little city's soldiers once patrolled, citizens ride their bicycles and walk their dogs, and often stop to admire the view.

Like paradise, Lucca is entered by way of St Peter's Gate. Once in you'll find tidy, well-preserved Romanesque churches and medieval towers that destroyed Ruskin's romantic notion that a medieval building had to be half ruined to be beautiful, a revelation that initiated his study of architecture. Nor do Lucca's numerous Liberty-style shop signs show any sign of rust; even the mandatory, peeling ochre paint and green shutters of the houses seem part of some great municipal housekeeping plan. Bicycles have largely replaced cars within the walls. At first glance it seems too bijou, a good burgher's daydream. But after its long and brave history it has certainly earned the right to a little quiet. The annual hordes of Tuscan tourists leave Lucca alone for the most part, though there seems to be a small number of discreet visitors, many of them German and Swedish, who come back every year. They don't spread the word, apparently trying to keep one of Italy's most beautiful cities to themselves.

History

Lucca's rigid grid of streets betrays its Roman origins; it was founded as a colony in 180 BC as *Luca*, and in 56 BC entered the annals of history when Caesar, Pompey, and Crassus met here to form the ill-fated First Triumvirate. It was converted to Christianity early on, by St Peter's disciple Paulinus, who became first bishop of Lucca. The city did especially well in the Dark Ages; in late Roman times it was the administrative capital of Tuscany, and under the Goths managed to repulse the murderous Lombards; its extensive archives were begun in the 8th century, and many of its churches were founded shortly after. By the 11th and 12th centuries Lucca emerged as one of the leading trading towns of Tuscany, specializing in the production of silk, sold by colonies of merchants in the East and West, who earned enough to make sizeable loans to Mediterranean potentates. A Lucchese school of painting developed, such as it is, and beautiful Romanesque churches were erected, influenced by nearby Pisa. Ghibellines and Guelphs, and then Black and White Guelphs made nuisances of themselves as they did everywhere else, and Lucca often found itself pressed to maintain its independence from Pisa and Florence.

In 1314, at the height of the city's wealth and power, the Pisans and Ghibellines finally managed to seize Lucca. But Lucca had a trump card up a secret sleeve: a remarkable adventurer named Castruccio Castracani. Castracani, an ambitious noble who for years had lived in exile—part of it in England—heard the bad news and at once set forth to rescue his hometown. Within a year he had chased the Pisans out and seized power for himself, leading Lucca into its most heroic age, capturing most of Western Tuscany to form a little Luccan empire, subjugating even big fish like Pisa and Pistoia. After routing the Florentines at Altopascio in 1325, Castracani was planning to snatch Florence, too, but died of malaria just before the siege was to begin—another example of Florence's famous good luck. Internal bickering between the powerful families soon put an end to Lucca's glory days, though in 1369 the city managed to convince Emperor Charles IV to grant it independence as a republic, albeit a republic ruled by oligarchs like Paolo Guinigi, the sole big boss between 1400–30.

But Lucca continued somehow to escape being gobbled up by its voracious neighbours, functioning with enough tact and tenacity to survive even after the arrival of the Spaniards—a fact one can attribute not so much to its great walls as to its relative insignificance. After the Treaty of Câteau-Cambresis, Lucca amazingly found itself standing together with Venice as the only truly independent states in Italy. And like Venice, the city was an island of relative tolerance and enlightenment during the Counter-Reformation, its garden walls in this case proving stout enough to deflect the viperous Inquisition. In 1805 Lucca's independence ended when Napoleon gave the republic to his sister Elisa Baciocchi, who ruled as its princess; it was given later to Marie Louise, Napoleon's widow, who governed well enough to become Lucca's favourite

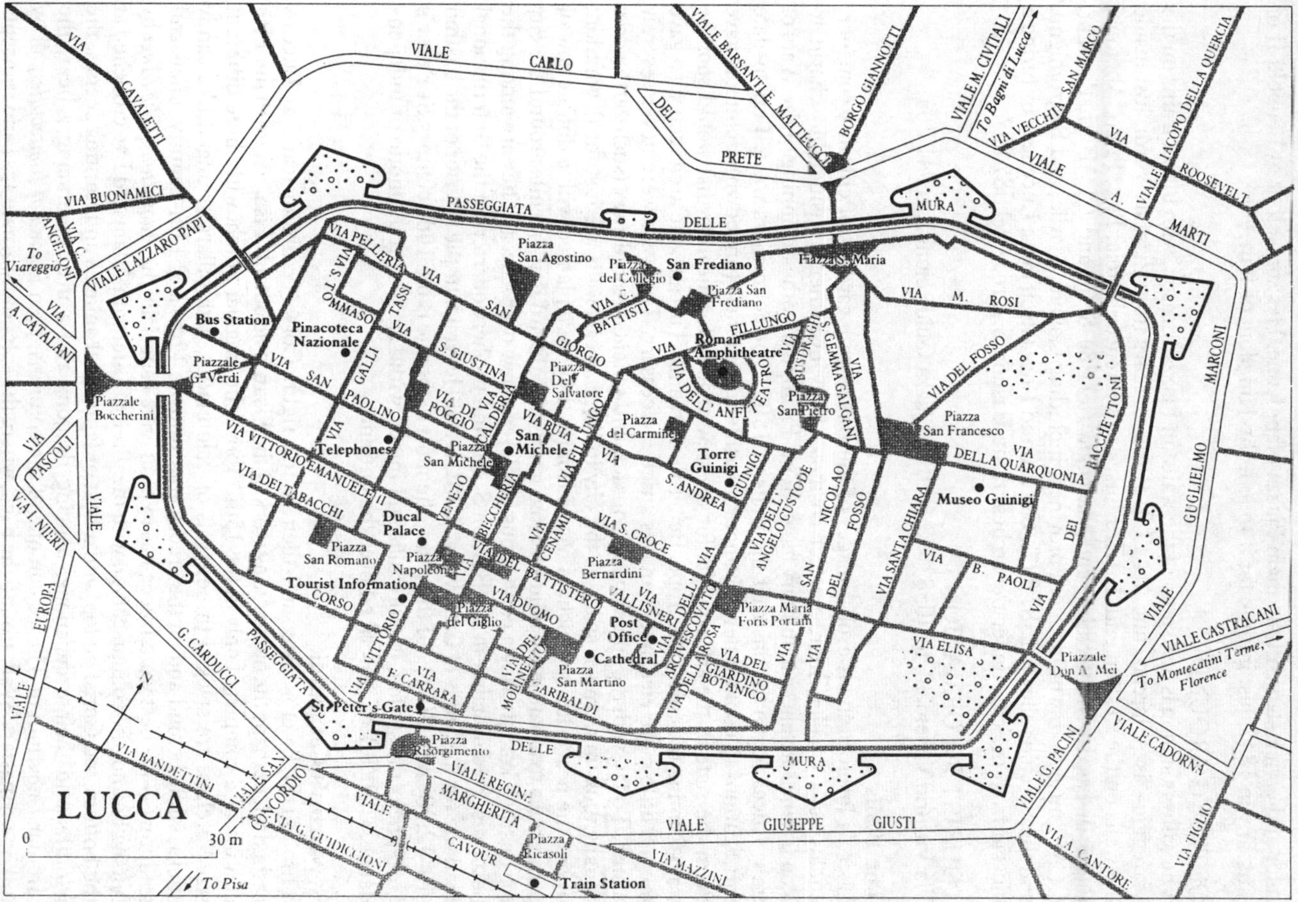
LUCCA
0
30 m
N
To Viareggio
To Pisa
To Bagni di Lucca
To Montecatini Terme, Florence
Bus Station
Pinacoteca Nazionale
Telephones
Ducal Palace
Tourist Information
St Peter's Gate
Train Station
San Michele
San Frediano
Roman Amphitheatre
Torre Guinigi
Museo Guinigi
Post Office
Cathedral
Piazzale Boccherini
Piazzale G. Verdi
Piazza San Agostino
Piazza del Collegio
Piazza San Frediano
Piazza S. Maria
Piazza Del Salvatore
Piazza del Carmine
Piazza San Pietro
Piazza San Francesco
Piazza San Michele
Piazza San Romano
Piazza Napoleone
Piazza del Giglio
Piazza Bernardini
Piazza Maria Foris Portam
Piazza San Martino
Piazza Risorgimento
Piazza Ricasoli
Piazzale Don A. Mei
PASSEGGIATA DELLE MURA
VIALE CARLO DEL PRETE
VIALE BARSANTI E. MATTEUCCI
BORGO GIANNOTTI
VIALE M. CIVITALI
VIA VECCHIA SAN MARCO
VIA IACOPO DELLA QUERCIA
VIALE A. MARTI
VIA ROOSEVELT
VIALE GUGLIELMO MARCONI
VIALE CASTRACANI
VIALE CADORNA
VIA TIGLIO
VIALE G. PACINI
VIA A. CANTORE
VIALE GIUSEPPE GIUSTI
VIA MAZZINI
VIALE REGINA MARGHERITA
VIALE CAVOUR
VIA G. GUIDICCIONI
VIALE SAN CONCORDIO
VIA BANDETTINI
VIALE EUROPA
VIA I. NIERI
VIA PASCOLI
VIALE G. CARDUCCI
VIA A. CATALANI
VIA C. ANGELONI
VIALE LAZZARO PAPI
VIA BUONAMICI
VIA CAVALETTI
VIA PELLERIA
VIA S. TOMMASO
VIA TASSI
VIA GALLI
VIA SAN PAOLINO
VIA S. GIUSTINA
VIA SAN GIORGIO
VIA C. BATTISTI
VIA FILLUNGO
VIA DELL' ANFITEATRO
VIA BUSDRAGHI
VIA S. GEMMA GALGANI
VIA M. ROSI
VIA DEL FOSSO
VIA BACCHETTONI
VIA DELLA QUARQUONIA
VIA DI POGGIO
VIA CALDERIA
VIA BUIA
VIA S. ANDREA
VIA GUINIGI
VIA DELL' ANGELO CUSTODE
VIA SAN NICOLAO
VIA DEL FOSSO
VIA SANTA CHIARA
VIA DEI BACCHETTONI
VIA B. PAOLI
VIA ELISA
VIA VITTORIO EMANUELE II
VIA DEI TABACCHI
VIA VENETO
VIA BECCHERIA
VIA CENAMI
VIA S. CROCE
VIA DEL BATTISTERO
VIA DUOMO
VIA PALLISNERI
VIA DELL' ARCIVESCOVATO
VIA DELLA ROSA
VIA DEL GIARDINO BOTANICO
CORSO VITTORIO
VIA F. CARRARA
VIA DEL MOLINETTO
VIA GARIBALDI

ruler and earn a statue in the main Piazza Napoleone. Her son sold it to Leopold II of Tuscany in 1847, just in time for it to join the Kingdom of Italy.

GETTING AROUND

The railway station is just south of the walls on Piazza Ricasoli, with lots of trains on the Viareggio-Pisa-Florence line (tel 47 013). Buses leave from Piazzale Verdi, just inside the walls on the western end: LAZZI buses to Florence, Pistoia, Pisa, Prato, Abetone, Bagni di Lucca, Montecatini, and Viareggio (tel 584 876), and CLAP (that's right, CLAP) buses to towns in Lucca province, including Collodi, Marlia, and Segromigno, and the Serchio valley (tel 587 897). Get around Lucca itself like a Lucchese by hiring a bicycle from the city, under the arches of the Bastion S. Croce, tel 587 857.

TOURIST INFORMATION

Via Vittorio Veneto 40, tel (0583) 43 639, or Piazza Guidiccioni 2, tel 41 205.

The Walls

Lucca's lovely bastions evoke images of the walled rose gardens of chivalric romance, enclosing a smaller, more perfect cosmos. They owe their considerable charm to Renaissance advances in military technology. Prompted by the beginning of the Wars of Italy, Lucca began to construct the walls in 1500. The councillors wanted up-to-date fortifications to counter new advances in artillery, and their (unknown) architects gave them the state of the art, a model for the new style of fortification that would soon be transforming the cities of Europe. Being Renaissance Tuscans, the architects also gave them a little more elegance than was strictly necessary. The walls were never severely tested. Today, with the outer ravelins, fosses, and salients cleared away (such earthworks usually took up as much space as the city itself), Lucca's walls are just for decoration; under the peace-loving Duchess Marie Louise they were planted with a double row of plane trees to create a splendid elevated garden boulevard that extends around the city for nearly 4 km, offering a continuous bird's-eye view over Lucca. They are among the best preserved in Italy—in the Bastion S. Paolino the headquarters of the 'International Institute for the Study of City Walls' (CISCU) will let you tour the interior of the bastion (10–12:30 and 3:30–6). Of the gates, the most elaborate is the 16th-century **St Peter's Gate**, near the station, its portcullis still intact, with Lucca's proud motto of independence, LIBERTAS, inscribed over the entrance.

St Martin's Cathedral

Through St Peter's Gate, and then to the right, Corso Garibaldi leads to Lucca's cathedral, perhaps the outstanding work of the Pisan style outside Pisa, begun in the 11th century and completed only in the 15th. Above the singular porch, with three different sized arches, are stacked three levels of colonnades, with pillars arranged like candy sticks, while behind and on the arches are exquisite 12th- and 13th-century reliefs and sculpture—the best work Lucca has to offer. See especially the *Adoration of the Magi* by Nicola Pisano, the column carved with the Tree of Life, with Adam and Eve crouched at the bottom and Christ on top, and a host of fantastical animals and hunting scenes, the Months and their occupations, dancing dragons and a man embracing a bear, the circular Labyrinth of Theseus on one of the columns, even *Roland at Roncevalles*, all by unknown masters. Walk around the back, where the splendidly ornate apse and transepts are set off by the green lawn. The **Campanile**, crenellated like a battle tower, dates from 1060 and 1261.

The dark interior offers an excellent introduction to the works of Lucca's one and only great artist, **Matteo Civitali** (1435–1501), who worked as a barber until his mid 30s, when he decided he'd much rather be a sculptor. He deserves to be better known—only everything he made is still in Lucca. His most famous work, perhaps, is the octagonal **Tempietto** (1484), a marble tabernacle in the middle of the left aisle, containing Lucca's most precious holy relic, the world-weary *Volto Santo* ('Holy Image'), a cedar wood crucifix said to be a true portrait of Jesus, sculpted by Nicodemus, an eyewitness to the crucifixion. Saved from the Iconoclasts, it was set adrift in an empty boat and floated to Luni, where the bishop was instructed by an angel to place it in a cart drawn by two white oxen, and where the oxen should halt, there too should the image remain. They made a lumbering beeline for Lucca, where the *Volto Santo* has remained ever since. Its likeness appeared on the republic's coins, and there was a devoted cult of the image in medieval England; Lucca's merchant colony in London cared for a replica of the *Volto Santo* in old St Thomas, and according to William of Malmesbury, King William Rufus always swore by it, '*per sanctum vultum de Lucca*.' Long an object of pilgrimage, the image goes out for a night on the town in a candlelight procession each 13 September.

Further up the left aisle a chapel contains Fra Bartolomeo's *Virgin and Child Enthroned*, and in the transept, the remarkable **Tomb of Ilaria del Carretto** (1408), perhaps Jacopo della Quercia's most beautiful work, a tender, tranquil effigy of the young bride of boss Paolo Guinigi, complete with the family dog, waiting for his mistress to awaken. Here, too, is della Quercia's *St John the Evangelist* and an altar by Giambologna, of *Christ with SS. Peter and Paul*. Civitali carved the cathedral's high altar, and also two expressive tombs in the south transept. A door from the right aisle leads to the Sacristy, with a good *Madonna Enthroned with Saints* by Domenico Ghirlandaio; a side altar near here has a typically strange composition from the Venetian Tintoretto, a *Last Supper* with a nursing mother in the foreground and cherubs floating around Christ. In the centre, roped off, is a particularly fine section of the inlaid marble floor; on the entrance wall, a 13th-century sculpture of St Martin has been brought in from the façade. An **Antique Market** takes place in the cathedral's Piazza di San Martino the third Saturday and Sunday of each month.

Piazza Napoleone and Piazza San Michele

The pious Lucchesi once required 70 churches to minister to their spiritual needs. Fewer are necessary these days, and even fewer stay open during the day, but their fine medieval façades constitute some of Lucca's chief ornaments. One of these, **San Giovanni** with an 1187 portal, lies on the Via del Duomo between Piazza San Martino and the shady twin squares in Lucca's centre, **Piazza del Giglio** and **Piazza Napoleone**, the focus of the Lucchesi's evening *passeggiata*. The architectural hodgepodge of a palace on Piazza Napoleone, formerly the seat of the republican council, has been called the **Palazzo Ducale** ever since it was used by Lucca's queen for a day, Elisa Bonaparte Baciocchi. In the 16th century, Ammannati had a go at it, and the courtyard, at least, still preserves signs of his Mannerist handiwork. One of Matteo Civitali's most beautiful works, the tomb of San Romano, is in the rarely-opened church of **San Romano**, behind the Palazzo Ducale.

Via Vittorio Veneto leads from Piazza Napoleone into Piazza San Michele, with a church many people mistake for Lucca's cathedral. Built about the same time, and with a similar Pisan façade, it is a building almost as impressive. The full name, **San Michele in Foro**, comes from its location on what was Roman Lucca's forum. The ambitious façade rises high above the level of the roof, to make the building look even grander. Every column in the Pisan arcading is different; some doubled, some twisted like corkscrews, inlaid with mosaic Cosmati work, or carved into medieval monsters. The whole is crowned by a giant statue of the Archangel, and on the corner of the façade is a Madonna by Civitali; the graceful, rectangular campanile is Lucca's tallest and loveliest. Inside, there's a glazed terracotta *Madonna and Child* attributed to Luca della Robbia and a painting of plague saints by Filippino Lippi. Giacomo Puccini began his musical career as a choirboy in San Michele (his father and grandfather had been organists in the cathedral)—he didn't have far to go, as he was born in Via di Poggio 30, just across the street from the façade. The house is now a little **Puccini Museum**, with manuscripts, letters, mementoes, the overcoat and odds and ends of the great composer, as well as the piano he used to compose *Turandot* (10–12 and 4–6, closed Sun).

Pinacoteca Nazionale

The quarter west of San Michele is perfumed by the big state tobacco factory, a fine aroma that hides the fact that it produces Toscanelli cigars, the world's vilest smokes. Via Paolina (the Roman *decumanus major*) leads shortly to the church of **San Paolino** where little Puccini played the organ to earn some pin money. It contains two beautiful works: a 13th-century French *Madonna and Child* brought back by Lucchese merchants of Paris, and an anonymous quattrocento Florentine *Coronation of the Virgin*, with Mary hovering over a city of pink towers; she is crowned by God the Father instead of Christ, who usually does the honours.

The **Pinacoteca Nazionale** is housed in the 17th-century Palazzo Mansi, just off Via Paolina (open 9–7; Sun and Mon 2–7; adm). Most of the art, as well as the rich furnishings in several of the rooms, dates from the 17th century; the few paintings which might be interesting, portraits by Pontormo and Bronzino, are all indefinitely at the restorer's. In the study hangs a dark and damaged Veronese, and Tintoretto's *Miracle of St Mark freeing the slave*, showing, with typical Tintorettian flamboyance, Venice's patron saint dive-bombing from heaven to save the day. The 1600s frescoes are more fun than the paintings, especially the *Judgement of Paris*, which Venus wins by showing a little leg. And one can't help but wonder what Rococo dreams tickled the fancy sleep of the occupants of the amazing bedroom.

San Frediano and the Amphitheatre

East of San Michele, medieval **Via Fillungo** and its surrounding lanes make up the busy shopping district, a tidy nest of straight and narrow alleys where the contented cheerfulness that distinguishes Lucca from many of its neighbours seems somehow magnified. Along Via Fillungo you can trace the old loggias of 14th-century palaces, now bricked in, and the ancient **Torre delle Ore** (tower of hours) which since 1471 has striven to keep the Lucchesi on time, and perhaps now suggests that it's time for a coffee in Lucca's historic **Caffè di Simo** at Via Fillungo 58. At Via Fillungo's northern end stands the tall church and taller campanile of **San Frediano**, built in the early 1100s, and shimmering with the colours of the large mosaic on its upper façade, showing Christ and the Apostles in an elegant flowing style. The palatial interior houses Tuscany's most remarkable baptismal font, the 12th-century *Fontana lustrale* carved with reliefs, and behind it, an equally beautiful lunette of the *Annunciation* by Andrea della Robbia. In the last chapel on the left are an altarpiece and two tomb slabs by Jacopo della Quercia and his assistants. The bedecked mummy is of St Zita, patroness of maids and ladies-in-waiting; even in England maids traditionally belonged to the Guild of St Zita. The Lucchesi are very fond of her, and on 26 April they bring her incorrupt body out to caress. If the sacristan's about, ask to see the 12th-century bronze Arabian falcon in the **museo**.

Next to San Frediano, on Via Battisti, the **Palazzo Pfanner** has a pretty 18th-century garden, a fine stair, a collection of silks made in Lucca, and 17th–19th-century costumes (9:30–1:30, summer also 3–7). In the other direction, skirting Via Fillungo, narrow arches lead into something most visitors miss, the **Roman Amphitheatre**. Only outlines of its arches are still traceable in the outer walls, while within the inner ring only the form remains—the marble was probably carted off to build San Michele and the cathedral—but Lucca is a city that changes so gradually and organically that the outline has been perfectly preserved. The foundations of the grandstands now support a perfect ellipse of medieval houses. Duchess Marie Louise cleared out the old buildings in the former arena, and now, where gladiators once slugged it out, there is a wonderfully atmospheric piazza, where the boys play football and the less active sit musing in the one sleepy café.

The streets in this part of Lucca have scarcely changed in the past 500 years. Along Via S. Andrea and narrow Via Guinigi, you'll pass a number of resolutely medieval palaces, including that of the Guinigi family. Their lofty stronghold, the **Torre Guinigi**, stands next to their palace and is one of Lucca's landmarks; like the walls, it has trees sprouting out of its top—the best example of that quaint Italian fancy (another is in Arrone, in Umbria's Valnerina). One of the most elaborate of medieval family fortresses, the tower has recently been restored; it's worth the stiff climb up for the view over the city and the Apuan Alps (April–Sept 9–7, Oct–Mar 10–5; adm).

The East Side

Roman Lucca ended near the Guinigi palace, and when a new church was built in the early 12th century it was outside the gate, hence **Santa Maria Forisportam** ('outside of the gate') in Via Santa Croce, a pretty church in the Pisan style with blind arcades. Inside, it not only looks but smells terribly old, and contains two paintings by the often-esoteric Guercino. Beyond the church is the best-preserved gate of 1260, the **Porta San Gervasio** giving on to the former moat, now a picturesque little canal running along Via del Fosso. Just across the canal from the gate is **S. Trinità**, home of Civitali's *Madonna della Tosse* (Our Lady of the Cough), a bit too syrupy sweet, but perhaps that helped the cure (if closed, ask for the key in the convent next door). Nearby on Via Elisa is the entrance to the **Villa Bottini gardens** (9–1:30, summer till 7), one of the few green oases inside the city walls.

At the northern end of Via del Fosso stands a 17th-century column dedicated to another Madonna, and to the east, the church of **San Francesco**, a typical 13th-century Franciscan preaching church with the tombs of Castracani and Lucchese composer

Luigi Boccherini (he of the famous *minuet*, d. 1805), and some fine detached frescoes of the Florentine school. Beyond San Francesco stands the palatial brick Villa Guinigi, built in 1418 by the big boss Paolo Guinigi in his glory days. Now the **Museo Nazionale Guinigi** (9–6:30, Mon 9–2; adm), its ground floor houses an interesting collection of Romanesque reliefs, capitals, and transennas, some of which are charmingly primitive—St Michael slaying the dragon, Samson killing the lion, a 9th-century transenna with birds and beasts, spirals and daggers. Room IV has a lovely *Annunciation* by Civitali, and beyond, a set of Neoclassical reliefs from the Palazzo Ducale of the *Triumphs of Duchess Maria Luisa*. The painting gallery upstairs contains intarsia panels from the cathedral, each with scenes of Lucca as seen from town windows, some trecento works by the Lucca school and a charming quattrocento *Madonna and Child* by the 'Maestro della Vita di Maria'. Other rooms contain a miasma of oversize 16th-century canvases, some by Vasari.

Villas around Lucca

In 16th-century Lucca, as elsewhere in Italy, trade began to flounder, and once-plucky, daring merchants, or at least those sufficiently well-upholstered, turned to the more certain joys of real estate, where they could genteelly decline in a little country palace and garden. For the Lucchesi, the favourite area to construct such pleasure domes was in the soft, rolling countryside to the north and northeast of the city. Three of these villas or their grounds are open for visits. In Segromigno, 10 km from Lucca in the direction of Pescia, there's the charming, mid-16th-century but often modified **Villa Mansi**, embellished with a lovely half Italian (i.e. geometric) and half English (i.e. not geometric) garden laid out by the great Sicilian architect Juvarra (10–12:30 and 3–6, park only; adm). Nearby in Camigliano, the even more elaborate **Villa Torrigiani**, also begun in the 16th century, was long celebrated for its fabulous parties and entertainments. Set in a lush park of pools and trees, it is furnished with 16th–18th-century furnishings (villa open April–Oct, 9–12 and 2–6:30, park open same hours all year; adm expensive). Elisa Bonaparte Baciocchi combined a villa and a summer palace to make her country retreat, now called the **Villa Pecci-Blunt ex-Villa Reale** in Marlia. Only the park and the Giardino Orsetti are open, but they are lovely, and used as the site of Lucca's **summer music festival**, which not surprisingly features more than a pinch of Puccini (guided tours, Oct–June daily except Mon at 10, 11, 3, 4, 5, and 6. In July and Aug, Tues–Thurs and Sun only at 10, 11, 4, 5, and 6; adm).

The Lucchese Plain

East and west of Lucca, what was swampland in the Middle Ages has been reclaimed to form a rich agricultural plain. One of its features are its 'courts'—farm hamlets not constructed around a central piazza, but with houses in neat rows. At one time there were 1100 such 'courts' on the plain. Among the highlights of the area is curious **Castello di Nozzano** just to the west, built by Matilda of Tuscany on its hill, its pretty tower now incongruously topped by a large clock. To the east, one of the first villages, **Capannori** is the head town of several 'courts' and has a couple of interesting Romanesque churches, especially the 13th-century **Pieve San Paolo**, around which a small village incorporated itself, using the campanile for defence. The most imposing monument near Capannori is the 19th-century **Acquedotto del Nottolini**, which is also visible from the autostrada. Just south is the pretty hilltop village of **Castelvecchio**, its tall houses forming an effective circular wall. **Altopàscio**, on the Lucca–Empoli road, was built around an 11th-century hospice run by an obscure chivalric order called the Hospitaller Knights of the Order of Altopàscio, who originally occupied themselves with rescuing travellers from the swamps. Only the campanile of their church remains in the village today. **Montecarlo** gives its name to a very good dry white wine produced in the immediate area.

WHERE TO STAY (tel prefix 0583)

Lucca can be less than charm city if you arrive without booking ahead; there simply aren't enough rooms (especially inexpensive ones) to meet demand, and the Lucchesi aren't in any hurry to do anything about it. Outside of the city, at Massa Pisana (on Via Nuova per Pisa 1616, tel 590 068), you can bed down in Castruccio Castracani's own palace, built for the great Lucchese warlord in 1321. The ****__Villa Principessa__, often rebuilt since, currently wears the façade of a stately Rococo mansion, surrounded by acres of 18th-century gardens and a pool. Thoroughly modern inside, amenities include air conditioning, TVs, and minibars in the rooms (L200–360 000, depending on season; open Mar–Nov). Inside the walls, in central Piazza Puccini, you cannot do better than the slightly frayed, green-shuttered and thoroughly delightful ***__Universo__, tel 43 678; Ruskin and nearly everyone else who followed him to Lucca slept here (L90 000, some rooms nicer than others). **__La Luna__, in a quiet part of the centre at Corte Compagni 12, tel 43 634, is a cosy place, with a private garage for your car (L70 000 without bath, L85 000 with). **__Ilaria__, Via del Fosso 20, tel 47 558, offers 14 sparkling rooms on Lucca's baby canal (L68 000, all with bath). **__Villa Casanova__, in Via Casanova, just outside of the city at Balbano (city bus 5), tel 548 429, has simple rooms but a pleasant garden, tennis, and a swimming pool to lounge by (L48 000 without bath, L65 000 with). Friendly, well-run *__Diana__ near the cathedral on Via del Molinetto 11, tel 42 202, has some of the nicest L45–70 000 rooms in Tuscany, some with bath. Last and least, near San Michele, *__La Pace__, Corte Portici 2, tel 44 981, has quiet, old-fashioned rooms for L30–42 000 without bath. The modern, comfortable, and rarely crowded **Youth Hostel** is 2 km north of town on Via del Brennero, in Salicchi (bus 7 from the station), tel 953 686, open 15 Mar–15 Oct.

EATING OUT

Within the walls: **Il Buca di Sant'Antonio**, Via della Cervia 3, tel 55 881, has been an inn since 1782, offering old recipes like smoked herring and kid on a spit, and newer dishes like ravioli with ricotta and sage (L30–40 000). Opposite the Hotel Universo on Piazza del Giglio, **Il Giglio**, tel 44 058, is Lucca's best seafood palace—river trout is a speciality as well—for around L35 000. For something less expensive, seek out Via San Tommaso, in the northwest corner within the walls, where you can enjoy some surprising dishes at rock-bottom prices at **Da Giulio**, tel 55 948; get there early to find a table (L20 000 at the most). For simpler fare, there's a good **Tavola Calda** in Via S. Croce 46, or the **Birreria Le Bistrot** on Via della Fratta 22, tel 47 421, with sandwiches and beer, a garden and a genuine Wurlitzer spinning out the tunes.

LUCCA, GARFAGNANA, AND LUNIGIANA

Outside the town: Lucca does especially well at table if you have the horsepower to reach its immediate surroundings. Duck with truffles, wild boar, and grilled seafood are a few of the treats on the extensive menu at **Solferino**, run by the same family for four generations and famous throughout Tuscany for almost as long. Simple Tuscan country specialities are also in evidence but this is one place where you might want to splurge (up to L60 000; situated 6 km west of Lucca in San Macario, on the Viareggio road, tel 59 118). Another good choice, north of town in Ponte a Moriano, **La Mora**, Via Sesto 104, tel 57 109, located in an old posthouse with four cosy rooms inside and dining under the pergola in summer, serving, according to season, delicious ravioli with asparagus or truffles, or gourmet roast lamb (L40–45 000). **Vipore**, in nearby Pieve S. Stefano, tel 59 245, is located in a 200-year-old farmhouse, with views over the fertile plain of Lucca. First quality prime ingredients go into fresh pasta and meat dishes (L40 000). In Montecarlo try a bottle of local wine, an excellent accompaniment to dishes like truffle crêpes, at **Forassiepi** at Porta Belvedere, tel 59 005, located in a former oil press; from the terrace you can see as far as Collodi and the Valdinievole (L35 000).

The Garfagnana and Lunigiana

The rugged northern finger of Tuscany encompasses the region's 'Alps', the tall and jagged **Alpi Apuane**, which like the real Alps wear brilliant white crowns, though not made of snow—that's marble up there, the 'tears of the stars', the purest and whitest in Italy. Historically the land divided into two mini-regions: along the bank of the Serchio river, between the Apuan Alps and the Apennines is the **Garfagnana**; while the region north of the village of Piazza al Serchio is the **Lunigiana**, former hinterland of the ancient Roman port of Luni.

The Garfagnana and Lunigiana are fairly undiscovered, and threaten to dispel many people's typical image of Tuscany; the mountains are too high, the valleys too narrow, and pine forests are more in evidence than vineyards and olive groves. Yet a spell in this striking mountain scenery can be just the ticket when the thought of another cathedral or picture gallery begins to pall.

The Garfagnana

For many years the chief export of the Garfagnana has been Italians; the green hills and mountains, the narrow valley of the Serchio, between the Apennines and the Apuan Alps, the stone villages perched on slopes that look so picturesque on postcards were simply never generous enough to provide a sufficient livelihood for their inhabitants. The chief staple of the district until recently was flour made from chestnuts, and chestnut groves still cover much of the region.

GETTING AROUND

LAZZI buses from Lucca connect the city to Bagni di Lucca (27 km/40 min), Barga (37 km/1 hr), and Castelnuovo di Garfagnana (50 km/1 ½ hrs); trains on the scenic

Lucca–Aulla line go up the Serchio valley, though beware that the stations for Bagni di Lucca and Barga are quite a distance from their centres and don't always have connecting buses; you'd be better off taking the bus to begin with. If you're driving from the south, most convenient way into these mountains begins at Lucca; the N. 12 and N. 445 routes follow the river Serchio.

TOURIST INFORMATION
Bagni di Lucca: Viale Umberto I 139, tel (0583) 87 946.
Barga: Piazza Angelico, tel (0583) 73 499, summer only.
Castelnuovo di Garfagnana: in the Rocca, tel (0583) 62 268.

Lucca to Bagni di Lucca

North of Lucca, the first tempting detour off N. 12 is to one of the many Romanesque churches in the region, **San Giorgio di Brancoli**, near Vinchiana, as notable for its lovely setting as for its 12th-century pulpit. **Diécimo**, back on the N. 12, has a name that survives from Roman times—it lies 10 Roman miles (18 km) from Lucca. The landmark here is the mighty Romanesque campanile of the 13th-century church of S. Maria, standing out starkly against the surrounding hills. **Borgo a Mozzano**, 4 km upstream, is famous for its beautiful little hog-back bridge, with arches in five different shapes and sizes, dedicated to the Magdalene, or to the Devil, who according to legend built it one dark and stormy night in exchange for the first soul to cross. The clever villagers outwitted him (as they invariably do in such stories) by sending a dog over in the morning. The real builder in this case was the less lethal 11th-century Countess Matilda who, besides the bridge, endowed the villages around Borgo with a set of solid Romanesque parish churches; in Borgo's church there's a wooden *San Bernardino* by Civitali.

To the north, just above the confluence of the Serchio river and the Torrente Lima lie the long and narrow riverside hamlets that make up **Bagni di Lucca**, Lucca's once grand old spa, first mentioned in the days of Countess Matilda. In the early 1800s, under the patronage of Elisa Bonaparte Baciocchi, it enjoyed a moment in high society's favour—long enough to build one of Europe's first official gambling casinos (1837; roulette was invented here), an Anglican church in an exotic Gothic Alhambra style, and an unusual 1840 suspension bridge (the **Ponte alle Catene**)—before sinking into obscurity. In Bagni's heyday, though, Montaigne, Byron, Browning, Shelley and Heine came to take the sulphur and saline waters, and perspire in a natural vapour bath. Heine was particularly enthusiastic: 'A true and proper sylvan paradise. I have never found a valley more enchanting,' he wrote; even the mountains are 'nobly formed' and not 'bizarre and Gothic like those in Germany'. Little has changed since, and these days Bagni di Lucca is a sleepy but charming little place, with some pretty villas, elegant thermal establishments that spring into action every summer, a miniature pantheon, and a fancy Circolo dei Forestieri, or foreigners' club (now a restaurant), on the riverfront.

Up the Lima Valley

From Bagni di Lucca, the N. 12 leads towards S. Marcello Pistoiese and the ski resort of Abetone (see p. 208), following the lovely valley of the Lima. A by-road beginning at

Bagni leads to picturesque, rugged, stone hamlets like **Pieve di Controne** and **Montefegatesi** which only appear on the most detailed maps; from Montefegatesi, an unpaved road continues to the dramatic gorge of **Orrido di Botri** at the foot of the Alpe Tre Potenze (1940 m). As the by-road winds back towards N. 12 at Scesta, it passes **San Cassiano**, site of a fine 13th-century Pisan-style church with a delicately carved façade; in its isolated setting few people ever see it. Other by-roads from the N. 12 lead to fine, tiny hamlets like **Vico Pancellorum** to the north and **Lucchio** to the south.

To Barga and the Cave of the Wind

The Garfagnana proper begins where the Lima flows into the river Serchio at Fornoli. In the 14th century this area was ruled by the kinsmen of Castruccio Castracani; one of their prettiest mountain hamlets is **Tereglio**, along the scenic northeast road to the **Alpe Tre Potenze**, before it meanders on to Abetone. The Castracani had their base up at **Coreglia Antelminelli**, high above the Serchio and the main N. 445 (turn off at Piano di Coreglia). Coreglia's parish church contains a magnificent 15th-century processional cross, and there's a **Museo della Figurina** devoted to the Garfagnana's traditional manufacture of plaster figures (open summer 4–7, winter 10–12).

To the north, the lovely hill town of **Barga** (pop. 11,000) stands above its modern offspring, Fornaci di Barga on the main N. 445. Barga was astute enough to maintain its independence until 1341, when it decided to link its fortunes with Florence. At the very top of town stands Barga's chief monument, its celebrated **Cathedral**, begun in the year 1000 on a terrace, with a panoramic view over the rooftops and of surrounding hills apparently clad in green velvet, and bare mountains scoured with white marble. Built of a blond stone called *alberese di Barga*, its square façade is discreetly decorated with a shallow pattern, charming reliefs and two leering lions; on the side the campanile is incorporated into the church; over the portal, there's a relief of a feast scene with a king and dwarfs. There's yet another dwarf inside, supporting one of the red marble pillars of the **pulpit** by the idiosyncratic 13th-century Como sculptor, Guido Bigarelli. The other pillars required a pair of lions, one grinning over a conquered dragon, one being both stroked and stabbed by a man. Less mysterious are the naive reliefs around the pulpit itself, startlingly sophisticated versions of familiar scriptural scenes. In the choir note the venerable polychrome wood statue of St Christopher (early 1100s) and a choir screen with more strange medieval carvings, including a mystic mermaid (see Pienza, p. xxx). Around the back, the cathedral's garden has a magnificent Lebanon cedar. Next to the cathedral stands the **Palazzo Pretorio** and 14th-century **Loggetta del Podestà**; if you go down the stairs towards the dungeon you can see Barga's old corn measures—a medieval Bureau of Standards.

The rest of Barga is a photogenic ensemble of archways and little *palazzi* piled on top of each other, with walls, gates, and a ravine planted with kitchen gardens. Things get lively in July and August with the classes and performances of **Opera Barga** in the old Dei Differenti Theatre, founded in 1600. Between Barga and Fornaci di Barga, you can measure the showy success of the city's emigrants who returned to build modern palaces in the suburb of Giardino.

From Barga you can take a 17-km potholing detour to Fornovalasco in the Apuan Alps to see Tuscany's best cave, the **Grotto del Vento**, a long cavern of fat stalactites, bottomless pits and abysses, and subterranean lakes and streams, set in a barren, eerie landscape (open April–Sept, at other times Sun and holidays only. Guided tours of one or two hours, from 10–12 and 3–6, and at 10 and 2, three-hour tours for real cave fiends; adm expensive. Try to come in the morning when it's less crowded; for information, tel 763 084).

Castelnuovo di Garfagnana

Hanging over the Serchio, 11 km north of Barga, is the lively little town of **Castelnuovo di Garfagnana**, the region's 'capital', guarded by the **Rocca**, a fine castle decorated in the best 14th-century manner. Its most famous commander was poet Ludovico Ariosto, author of that great Renaissance epic poem of chivalry and fantasy, *Orlando Furioso*. Ariosto, in the employ of the Este Dukes of Ferrara, competently chased bandits and collected tolls here from 1522–1525, but didn't enjoy the job. 'I'm not a man to govern other men,' he wrote to his lover in Ferrara. 'I have too much pity, and can't deny the things they require me to deny.'

Castelnuovo makes an excellent base for excursions into its often wild surroundings. To the northeast, past the small resort of **Castiglione di Garfagnana** a tortuous mountain road continues through 16 km of magnificent scenery to the **Foce delle Radici** (the pass into Emilia-Romagna) and **S. Pelligrino in Alpe**, with magnificent views and an ancient monastery, and a good little ethnographic museum, the **Museo della Campagna** (July–Sept, 8:30–1 and 3–8; at other times tel 68 180). West of Castelnuovo a truly scenic road leads over the Apuan Alps to Carrara and the coast, through the desolate valley of the Turrite Secca, its sombre features relieved by the romantic little oasis of **Isola Santa** (13 km)—a tiny village in the trees on its own tiny lake, once a hideout for medieval renegades; now it is abandoned, save for a few old folks and the sheep who lives behind the altar of the church.

North of Castelnuovo the road enters Garfagnana Alta, one of the least-known corners of Tuscany, where Donatello and Piero della Francesca seem far away indeed. Just north of Castelnuovo, explorers can take a winding by-road to the unspoiled **Parco dell'Orecchiella**, with eagles, mouflons, deer, and a botanical garden, its mountains crisscrossed by paths; pick up a map at the park's visitor centre in Orecchiella. At Poggio, back on the Serchio, there's a turn off for **Careggine**, a lofty old hamlet with commanding views, and the artificial **Lago di Vagli**. Creating this lake submerged the medieval village of Fabbriche, of which the top of the campanile may still be seen sticking stubbornly out of the water. Above, there are more stunning views from **Vagli di Sopra**, village of old marble quarries and an 18th-century road, deteriorated into a footpath, which leads into the comely Valle di Arnetola. Towering over all is **Mt Pisanino** (1945 m), the tallest of the Apuan Alps; the road approaching the summit and the alpine refuge of Donegani, by way of the lakelet of Gramolazzo, begins at **Piazza al Serchio**, where you leave both the Serchio and the Garfagnana behind.

WHERE TO STAY AND EATING OUT (tel prefix 0583)

There's nothing exceptional in the Garfagnana, but the Italians, at least, firmly believe the further north in Tuscany you go, the better the cooking, graced by the kindly influences of Liguria and Emilia-Romagna; the pasta dishes in the region are especially good. Specialities include *torte di erbe* (vegetable pies), chestnut puddings and *pattona* (chestnut biscuits). Bagni di Lucca has some quiet, modest old hotels like ***__Silvania__, at Lugliano, tel 87 586, very tranquil and nice rooms, all with bath (L60 000), or the ** **Svizzero**, ineffably Tuscan, a delightful place where the clock is stopped at about 1840 (Via Casalini 30, tel 87 114; L48 000). Toscanini stayed in the small *__Roma__, Via Umberto I 110, tel 87 278, with a shady little garden in back (L48 000 with bath, some cheaper without). These two are in the pretty suburb of Villa di Bagni, a couple of kilometres up the river; in the medieval part of Bagni, there's the **__Bridge__, Piazza Ponte a Serraglio 5A, tel 87 147. The best places to eat are the **Ruota**, 3 km at Fornoli, Via Giovanni XXIII 29/A, tel 86 071, with good Tuscan cooking for L30 000; and **Da Vinicio**, a block west of Bagni's bridge; chaotic and popular pizzeria, also good roast pigeon and seafood (L 25 000).

Outside Barga, there's a huge 234-room resort hotel ****__Il Ciocco__ in Castelvecchio, 6 km north at Pascoli, tel 7191, indoor pool, tennis, air conditioning, in short, the works for L170–220 000. **__Villa Libano__, Via del Sasso 6, tel 73 059, is a lovely place in a courtyard, set next to Barga's city park; there's a restaurant with tables out in the garden. (L45 000 without bath, L50 000). Again, the best restaurant is out of town, at Albiano 5 km north, **Terrazza**, tel 766 141, featuring the half-crazy specialities of the Maremma, around L20 000. In Castelnuovo di Garfagnana, dear old **__Da Carlino__, Via Garibaldi 15, tel 62 045, is the traveller's choice, offering rooms for L50 000 without bath, L70 000 with. If you take the route over the Apuan Alps, stop for lunch at Isola Santa. **Da Giacco** is a downright quaint sort of roadside inn, with a dog sleeping by the wood stove and an owner who remembers a little tortuous English from his days in New Jersey. Roast trout, polenta with mushrooms, and a terrace overlooking the lake (L35 000).

The Lunigiana

Even less populous and less visited than the Garfagnana, the Lunigiana, separating Liguria and Emilia-Romagna from the rest of Tuscany, has traditionally been a tough nut for its would-be governors to crack. The Romans of Luni (founded in 180 BC to contain the fearsome Ligurians) found it a wild place; even in the 7th century, missionaries were still bashing revered ancient idols. This rugged territory of chestnut forests is crowded with the castles of would-be rulers and other toll-collecting gangsters. In the early 1900s the Lunigiana was a stronghold of rural anarchism, and in 1944 its partisans made it one of the bigger free zones in the north. Since then life has been fairly tranquil in the Lunigiana; rocky, forested landscapes, ruined castles (many were bombed in the last war), and simple Romanesque churches form the main attractions.

GETTING AROUND

If you're approaching from the north, trains and autostrade from Genoa (A12) and Parma (A15) merge near Aulla. From here there are frequent trains to Massa-Carrara, Viareggio and Pisa, Pontrémoli or Lucca. Bus service in the Lunigiana is provided by CAT, with Aulla as the main depot; there are services to Massa and Carrara, and to Bagnone, Filattiera, Fivizzano, Fosdinovo, Licciana Nardi, Pontrémoli and Villafranca. Train times from Lucca are Aulla (85 km/2 hrs) and Pontrémoli (108 km/2½ hrs).

Country bridge, Lunigiana

TOURIST INFORMATION
Pontrémoli: Piazza Municipio, tel (0187) 831 180.

Piazza al Serchio to Aulla

Beyond Piazza al Serchio, the first town of consequence along the N. 445 is fortified **Casola in Lunigiana** (20 km); just beyond it a road veers south for the tiny spa of **Equi Terme** in the mountains above. Equi is less visited these days for its waters than for its cave, charmingly called **La Buca del Cane** (Dog's Hole) after its relics of prehistoric man's best friend. Our ancestors also apparently socialized with bears (or ate them), judging by the bones found here (9–12 and 2–5, summer 9–12 and 4–7; adm). **Fivizzano** to the north (on N. 63 or by road from Casola) belonged to the Malaspina of Massa until the Medici snatched it and fortified it as a grand ducal outpost. The main square, **Piazza Medicea**, has a grand fountain paid for by Cosimo III, a few Florentine-style palaces, and the 13th-century parish church. There are two interesting Romanesque chapels in the vicinity, **S. Maria Assunta**, 3 km towards Pognana, in a lovely isolated setting, and 12th-century **San Paolo a Vendaso** with carved capitals inside, on N. 63 towards the Passo di Cerreto. From Ceserano, on N. 445, N. 446 heads southwest over the mountains to Sarzana, passing by way of **Fosdinovo**, the Malaspina castle that hosted Dante in 1306, one of the most beautiful and majestic in the Lunigiana. Inside there's an interesting collection of arms and ornaments found in tombs (daily 10–12, 4–7 pm, in winter 9–12, 3–6).

Aulla

Aulla grew up at the Lunigiana's hotly-contested crossroads, guarding access into the Magra valley. The powerful, foursquare 16th-century **Fortezza della Brunella** (open 9–12 and 2–5) was built by the Genoese, who bought Aulla in 1543; Napoleon handed it over to his sister Elisa in Lucca. Nearby are the citadels of two other rivals who long fought for the town—the Bishop of Luni's **Caprigliola**, a fortified village still inaccessible to motor traffic (6 km southwest on N. 62), the Malaspina's fortified hamlet of **Bibola** and their romantically ruined **Ponzanello**, both due south of Aulla. The Malaspina also fortified the strategic road to the pass, at **Licciana Nardi** and especially at **Bastia**, 4 km further on.

From Aulla you may want to tuck down into Liguria and the **Italian Riviera** to visit the 'Gulf of the Poets' (or more prosaically, the Gulf of La Spezia), named after Byron (who swam across it) and Shelley, whose last home was in San Terenzo near the old Pisan town of **Lerici**. On the western shore of the Gulf (in Liguria) lies the enchanting old Genoese town of Portovenere, named after the goddess of love herself. The excavations of ancient Luni are near Carrara (see p. 245).

North of Aulla, **Villafranca in Lunigiana** takes its name from its location on a branch of the Via Francigena, the pilgrimage route from France; it offers the visitor the 16th-century church of **San Francesco** and, in an old mill, an **Ethnographic Museum** devoted to rural life in the Lunigiana, especially the chestnut industry (9–1 and 3–6, closed Mon; adm). From Villafranca yet another mighty castle beckons up at **Bagnone**, 5 km east.

Pontrémoli

Long, low-key, stretched out lazily along the shallow river Magra and the Torrente Verdi, Pontrémoli (pop. 10,200) is chief town of the Lunigiana and the northernmost in Tuscany. It wasn't always so peaceful: in the old days the quarrels between local Guelphs and Ghibellines led Castruccio Castracani to build a fortress in 1322, called *Cacciaguerra* ('Drive-away war') in the town centre to keep the two parties apart until they made peace. Of this noble effort only the **Torre del Campanone** and what is now the campanile of the **Duomo** survive. The Duomo itself has a fine, ballroom interior, unusual for Tuscany. Over the Torrente Verdi, the church of **San Francesco**, with a Baroque entrance, contains a lovely polychrome relief of the Madonna and Bimbo attributed to Agostino di Duccio. Between the centre and the station the oval 18th-century church of **Nostra Donna** is a rare example of Rococo in Tuscany.

Behind all these baubles, this hidden corner of Italy holds a genuine prehistoric mystery. To learn about it, climb up the narrow medieval lanes above Pontrémoli to the gloomy, 14th-century **Castello del Piagnaro** and its archaeology museum (Oct–May 9–12 and 2–5, summer 9–12 and 4–7, closed Mon; adm). It holds over a score of large, carved statue-steles of an unknown culture that flourished in the Lunigiana between 3rd millennium BC and the 2nd century BC. The steles, a sort of menhirs with personality, include stylized warriors with daggers or axes, and women with little knobby breasts. The oldest (3000–2000 BC) have a U for a face and a head hardly distinguishable from the trunk; the middle period (2000–8th century BC) sport anvil heads and eyes; the last group (7th–2nd century BC) are mostly warriors, with a weapon in each hand, just as Virgil described the Gauls who invaded Lazio. Often discovered near sources of water, some scholars think they may have symbolized the heavens (the head), the earth (the arms and weapons) and the underworld (the lower third, buried in the ground). Similar statue-steles turn up in southern Corsica and other places around the Mediterranean.

Statue-steles, Pontrémoli

Some of the steles had their heads knocked off, a sure sign that the pope's missionaries in the 8th century were doing their job. Curiously, in the nearby hamlet of Vignola, a folk memory survives of the destruction of idols; during the patron saint's festival they make little wooden idols strangely similar to Pontrémoli's statue-steles and burn them to celebrate the triumph over the pagans.

In 1471 the Virgin made an appearance a mile south of Pontrémoli, and to honour the spot the **Church of SS. Annunziata** was built with a lovely marble **Tempietto** by Jacopo Sansovino, a quattrocento fresco of the Annunciation by Luca Cambiaso, an elegant triptych of uncertain hand or date, and some fun *trompe l'oeil* frescoes by a Baroque painter from Cremona named Natali.

WHERE TO STAY AND EATING OUT

Pioneers in the Lunigiana will find a comfortable bed and a tasty meal at Equi Terme's **La Posta** in Piazza delle Terme, tel (0585) 97 937 (rooms, all with bath, L36 000; delicious antipasti, lasagne and more for around L30 000). A good central base in the region, the old-fashioned ***Alpi Apuane**, is in a former posthouse at Pallerone near Aulla, tel 418 045, although rooms (L28 000) are only a sideline to the fine restaurant, cosy in the winter with its fireplace. Specialities here include wildfowl excellently prepared—pheasant, duck, and pigeon, and for big appetites, kid with polenta (L30 000). Up in fortified Bagnone, **I Fondi**, Via della Repubblica 22, tel (0187) 496 086, offers good, solid country cooking—trout, mushroom dishes, rabbit, stuffed cabbage, venison with polenta—amid Italian rustic elegance (L35 000). In Fivizzano, ****Il Giardinetto**, Via Roma 151, tel (0585) 92 060, is a delightful place to sleep and eat overlooking the Piazza Medicea. The rooms are comfortable, and as the name implies, there's a little garden to lounge in (L38 000, all with bath). The hot and cold antipasti are especially tempting, as well as the pasta and game dishes, and a flan with spinach and cheese, made from a Renaissance recipe (L35 000). In Tresana, north of Aulla, **Da**

Fabio is a popular trattoria in a rustic 17th-century building, that people drive out of their way to visit; the specialities are rustic, and prices at L30 000 are pleasant, too.

Pontrémoli is rich in good restaurants, and has two smart hotels, the new *****Golf Hotel**, outside of town in a pine wood, Via Pineta, tel (0187) 831 573, offering 90 very comfortable rooms, all with bath and TV (L70–85 000), and the *****Hotel Napoleon**, Piazza Italia 2B, tel 830 544, with garage, and modern rooms (L90 000). There is another very inexpensive *locanda*, ***Bonzani**, near the station in Via Malaspina 64, tel 830 011, which is the kind of place that if you wiggle the night table the overhead light bulb goes out, but deserves a mention for the lovely gentleman who runs it, 'Bonus Zanum', the self-proclaimed last Indo-European and surely the only hotelkeeper in Italy who not only speaks English but has taught himself Sanskrit, Latin, Aramaic, Greek, French, and a little Russian, too (L32 000). When it's time to eat, there's the age-old **Da Bussé**, Piazza del Duomo 9, tel 831 371, featuring Pontrémoli's special pasta *testaroli*, roast meats, stuffed vegetables and other local dishes (L30 000). **Bacciotini**, Via Ricci Armani 4, tel 830 120, offers *testaroli* with pesto from nearby Liguria, and dishes with wild mushrooms, the local passion (L30 000). Another good bet in the centre, **Da Fernando**, Via San Gemignano 52, tel 830 653, is a little bistro in a 17th-century building, where you can dine on *testaroli* with pesto or boar *alla cacciatora*, L25 000.

Part VIII

THE TUSCAN COAST

Castello Malaspina, Massa

The Etruscan Riviera, the Tyrrhenian shore, Tuscany by the sea—call it what you will, most of it is flat, straight, dull, and endowed with wide sandy beaches that are usually crowded. The sea isn't quite as clean as it might be, and the closer you get to the mouth of the Arno and Livorno, the less savoury it becomes. If you're intent on a spell on the beach, you may well find Tuscany's archipelago of seven islands more congenial—the sea is cleaner and the coast and beaches prettier. But what is harder to escape, unless you go to the smallest islands, is Italian beach culture. Much of the shore is privately owned and you must pay for access to a veritable wall of lounge chairs and beach umbrellas, packed as densely as possible; behind this there's inevitably a busy road, where the traffic is mainly vans with loudspeakers and motorcycles; behind the busy road is another wall of hotels, and perhaps a few pine woods.

The most beautiful and fashionable section of the Tuscan coast is the Argentario, around Porto Santo Stefano, but it's also the most expensive. Elba, the largest island, is rugged and beautiful, but very busy as a Euro-holiday beacharama. Other places are an acquired taste like, Viareggio, with more character than most and a Puccini opera festival, or Livorno, one of Italy's largest ports, famous for its seafood restaurants. The mellow old city of Pisa, an ancient maritime republic long ago silted up by the Arno, needs no introduction. In Carrara you can learn about marble in the Apuan Alps, in the Maremma you can learn about Italian cowboys and discover the lovely old town of Massa Marittima.

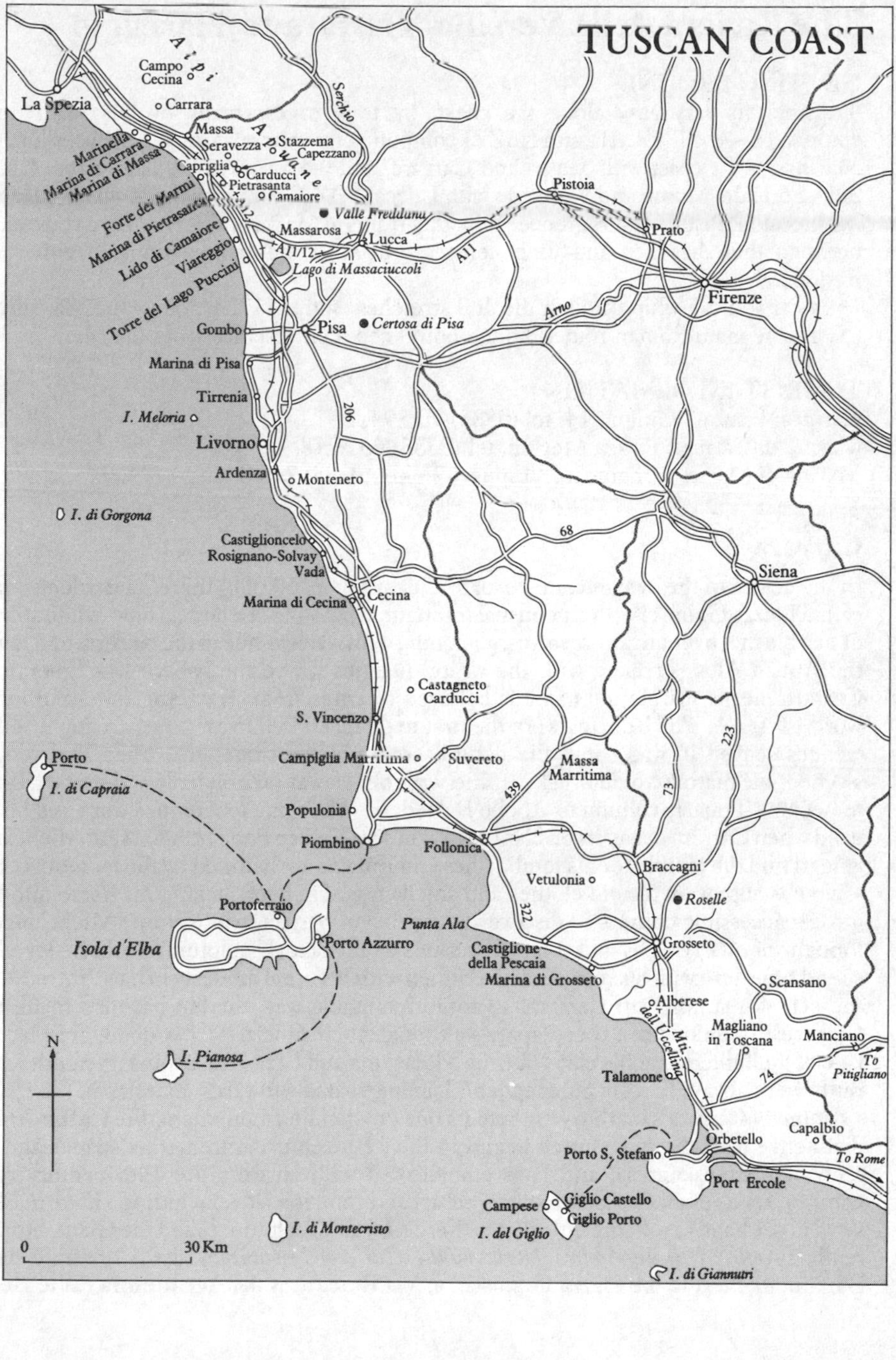
TUSCAN COAST
Alpi Apuane
Campo Cecina
La Spezia
Carrara
Massa
Marinella
Marina di Carrara
Marina di Massa
Seravezza
Stazzema
Capezzano
Capriglia
Carducci
Pietrasanta
Camaiore
Forte dei Marmi
Marina di Pietrasanta
Lido di Camaiore
Viareggio
Torre del Lago Puccini
Serchio
Valle Freddana
Massarosa
Lucca
A11/12
A11
A12
Lago di Massaciuccoli
Pistoia
Prato
Firenze
Arno
Pisa
Certosa di Pisa
Gombo
Marina di Pisa
Tirrenia
I. Meloria
Livorno
Ardenza
Montenero
206
I. di Gorgona
Castiglioncelo
Rosignano-Solvay
Vada
Marina di Cecina
Cecina
68
Siena
Castagneto Carducci
S. Vincenzo
Campiglia Marittima
Suvereto
Massa Marittima
Porto
I. di Capraia
Populonia
Piombino
Follonica
439
73
223
Braccagni
Vetulonia
Roselle
322
Portoferraio
Isola d'Elba
Porto Azzurro
Punta Ala
Castiglione della Pescaia
Grosseto
Marina di Grosseto
Scansano
Alberese
Mti. dell'Uccellina
Magliano in Toscana
Manciano
To Pitigliano
74
N
I. Pianosa
Talamone
Capalbio
Orbetello
Porto S. Stefano
To Rome
Port Ercole
Giglio Castello
Campese
Giglio Porto
I. di Montecristo
I. del Giglio
0
30 Km
I. di Giannutri

The Riviera della Versilia: Carrara to Viareggio

GETTING AROUND

Transport is very easy along the coast, by train or especially by bus, with three companies—CAT, CLAP, and LAZZI competing for your custom. CAT buses link the Marinas of the coast with Massa and Carrara, and the towns of the Lunigiana. CLAP links Forte dei Marmi and Viareggio with Lucca; LAZZI connects the coast with Lucca, Montecatini, Pistoia and Florence. Note that trains to Massa or Carrara leave you exactly between their beaches and their centres, but CAT bus connections to either are frequent.

By car you can whip through the dull stretches on the A12, or follow the Via Aurelia (N. 1), the main Roman route, though both keep their distance from the sea.

TOURIST INFORMATION

Carrara: Piazza 2 Giugno 14, tel (0585) 70 894.
Marina di Carrara: Piazza Meconi, tel (0585) 632 218.
Marina di Massa: Lungomare Vespucci 24, tel (0585) 240 046.

Carrara

In the centre of the dynamic, up-to-date Carrara (pop. 69,000) there's a garden square called Piazza Gramsci with an unusual fountain, consisting of a large, snow-white sphere of marble that hypnotically revolves, glistening with water, while in the background tower the Apuan Alps, streaked with the white quarries where the sphere was 'liberated'. Carrara means marble; its name is believed to come from 'Kar', the Indo-European word for stone. The Romans were the first to extract it 2000 years ago, driving wooden wedges soaked in water into the natural cracks in the stone, and when the wedges swelled, the marble would break off, and was rolled away on iron balls and sent to Rome to become Trajan's column or Apollo Belvedere. The same techniques were still being used when Carrara began its brilliant revival in 1502, when Pope Julius II sent Michelangelo to find the marble for his tomb. These mountains are haunted by the memory of the 'divine' sculptor, in his old clothes and smelly goatskin boots, taking his horse into the most inaccessible corners to discover new veins of perfect, white stone. Michelangelo thought of quarrying as an art just as serious as the actual sculptural work; he loved to spend time here with his rock, and he claimed with his usual modesty to have 'introduced the art of quarrying' to Carrara. In some intangible way, marble has also made the Carraresi traditionally a breed apart—although their official past is dominated by the rule of godfatherish noble clans like the Malaspina and Cybo-Malaspina, the undercurrents were always fiercely independent, leaning strongly towards anarchism.

Some of Carrara's marble went into its one outstanding monument, the **Cathedral**, a distinctive Romanesque church begun in the 11th century with marble stripes and an arch of marble animals, and later embellished with an exquisite 14th-century rose window, made of marble lace, and marble art and statues inside, including a huge marble bowl in the baptistry. In the little piazza there's a bulky sculpture called the Giant, but it is really supposed to be *Andrea Doria in the Guise of Neptune* by the Florentine hack Bandinelli. Next to the Piazza Gramsci, on Via Roma 1, is the **Accademia delle Belle**

Arti, in a medieval castle converted into a palace in the 16th century by Alberico Cybo-Malaspina, the great Marchese di Massa, whose descendants ruled Massa and Carrara until dying out in 1829, when the little state joined the Duchy of Modena until unification. The Accademia's courtyard contains sculptures from ancient Luni and the *Edicola dei Fantescritti*, a Roman tabernacle found in the Fantescritti quarry, with bas-reliefs of Jove, Hercules, and Bacchus, arm in arm like old chums, surrounded by graffiti by Giambologna and other sculptors who visited the quarries.

Marble Quarries and Roman Ruins

Even though Carrara exports half a million tons of different marbles a year, there is little danger of it running out soon; one wonders if they're joking when they gravely mention that there are only a few cubic kilometres of good stone left. Visiting one of the **quarries** surrounding Carrara is an unforgettable sight; usually they extend straight up to the sky, a blinding white scar down the mountain with a narrow access road zigzagging perpendicularly to the top. Signs from the centre of Carrara direct you to the quarries, or *Cave di Marmo*—**Colonnata** (8 km, founded as colony of Roman slaves), **Fantiscritti** (a Roman quarry still in use) and **Ravaccione** (with fine views over the mountains). Before heading out stop by the **Museo del Marmo**, on Viale XX Settembre (the main road between Carrara and the train station; open May–Sept 10–1 and 3:30–6:30, in June from 5–8 pm) which takes you through the wonderful world of marble with remarkable photographs of the marble workers of a hundred years ago and the surreal world of the quarries; halls of polished slabs introduce the amazing variety of marbles and travertines from the area, and then from around the world; and there's marble art and a room of mod marble to prove it's no fuddy-duddy stone limited to churches and public buildings.

The proximity of the Apuan Alps, only a few kilometres from the sea, gives this stretch of coast a certain majesty. The beach at **Marina di Carrara** is divided in two by the marble port, from which the big blocks are sent all over the world; in July and August the port-resort puts on a big show of marble arts and crafts. Just to the north, on the border of Liguria near Marinella, you can visit the site of Roman **Luni**, a colony built as a bulwark against the fierce Ligurians. The city survived until the Middle Ages; the power-hungry Bishop of Luni survived even longer, until 1929, when the bishopric was combined with that of La Spezia. Excavations have brought to light a sizeable amphitheatre, forum, houses, temples, etc.; on the site is the **Museo Nazionale di Luni** (9–12 and 4–7, 2–5 winter, closed Mon; adm), with an interesting collection of marble statuary, coins, jewellery, portraits, etc., as well as a display of modern archaeological techniques used in excavating the site, which can be toured with a guide. To the east off N. 446, 20 km up in the mountains above Carrara, there is an extraordinary panoramic view over the marble quarries from **Campo Cecina**. The city of Carrara has an alpine refuge here, which can be a base for exploring some of the Apuan Alps' network of trails (the tourist office has a map).

Massa

Massa (pop. 66,200), nearly the same size as Carrara and co-capital of the province, was the principal seat of the Cybo-Malaspina dukes. They were never great builders or patrons, except when it came to their own digs—their polychrome 17th-century **Palazzo Cybo-Malaspina**, on central Piazza degli Aranci, with its orange trees and obelisk, and their **Castello Malaspina** up the hill on Via della Rocca, an 11th-century castle with Renaissance additions, including a beautiful, ornate courtyard, loggias, and frescoed rooms (9–12 and 4–7, winter 2–5, closed Mon; adm). From Massa there are other marble quarries to visit, by **Pasquilio** 11 km east, a balcony with views over the Gulf of La Spezia; in the same area, the **Pian della Fioba** has a botanical garden planted with the flora of the Apuan mountains, more stunning views, and another alpine refuge open all year round.

Marina di Massa, on a marsh drained in the last century, is a lively proletarian resort with lots of pine trees; its neighbour, **Cinquale**, the 'Marina' of the old hill town of Montignoso, is smaller and prettier, and between it and Forte dei Marmi there's a long stretch of free beach. Near Montignoso stand the picturesque ruins of the **Castle of Aghinolfi**, a Lombard outpost built in 600 by King Agilufo.

Around Forte dei Marmi

Forte dei Marmi is one of the larger and, for the past decade or so, one of the trendier resorts on the coast. Founded in 1788, when Grand Duke Leopoldo constructed the fortress and seaport to serve the marble quarried from Seravezza, its old loading pier is now used as a promenade. In the 1860s the first holiday villas were built, and today it still has a residential, garden air and a popular white sandy beach. **Marina di Pietrasanta** is about the same, but has in its **Parco della Versiliana** that last section of the primordial coastal forest, lush with parasol pines, holm oaks, and myrtles. This was a favourite haunt of Gabriele D'Annunzio, and in the summer there are concerts, plays, and ballets in its small outdoor theatre. **Lido di Camaiore**, the last resort before Viareggio, caters mainly to families, and differs from its neighbours for its elevated garden terrace along the beach front.

Inland from Forte dei Marmi is the important marble town of **Seravezza**, where Michelangelo lived in 1517 during one of his marble pilgrimages, this time to Monte Altissimo, rich in statue stone. Not long afterwards, Duke Cosimo I commissioned Ammannati to build the **Villa Medicea** with its good Mannerist courtyard. The **Cathedral** contains works by Florentine goldsmiths, including a crucifix attributed to one of the Pollaiuolo brothers; 5 km away the beautifully situated **Pieve alla Cappella** has a fine rose window nicknamed the 'Eye of Michelangelo.' Another pretty place to visit in these mountains of quarries and chestnut forests is **Stazzema**, with a Romanesque church and more stunning views. The quarries near Stazzema produce a blue and white streaked marble called 'flowered' that found its way into the Medici's Princes' Chapel. Among the mountains in the area is the curious Monte Forata (1223 m) with a hole near its summit.

Pietrasanta

Pietrasanta, near the coast, is a mellow old town rich in marbly traditions. Its walls date from 1255, though its regular quadrangle of streets suggests a Roman origin. Life centres around the large central Piazza del Duomo, with its Florentine Marzocco on a pillar (1514) and the **Duomo di San Martino**, begun in 1256 and restored in 1630 and 1824, with a rose window carved of a single block of marble and more marble inside as well as a bronze crucifix by Tacca and a 13th-century fresco by the school of Giotto. Its Renaissance campanile looks half finished. It shares the piazza with the **Palazzo Pretorio** and **Sant'Agostino** (14th century) with an attractive minimalist Pisan façade. From here a road leads up to the citadel, or **Rocca Arrighina**, built in the 1300s by Castruccio Castracani and illuminated at night; it often hosted emperors on their way to Rome but all they left behind is the view. You can see what contemporary would-be Michelangelos are up to at the 'Mostra dell'Artigianato' on Viale Marconi 5 (Mon–Fri 9:30–12:30 and 3–6:30, summer 4–8), or turn right from the main gate for the central market building, its parking adorned with the world's most erotic market statue, of a woman *en déshabillé* pulling a young bull after her.

The Mountains beyond Pietrasanta

From Pietrasanta a road heads inland towards **Valdicastello Carducci** (birthplace of the poet Giosue Carducci) passing by way of the 9th-century **Pieve di SS. Giovanni and Felicità**, the oldest church in the Versilia, with 14th-century frescoes. There are lovely views stretching from La Spezia to Pisa from **Capezzano** and **Capriglia**, on the same winding further up in the mountains. **Camaiore** (from the Roman *Campus Major*, pop. 31,000) is an industrial town on the road to Lucca, of interest for its Romanesque churches—the **Collegiata, SS. Giovanni e Stefano** (with a stately bell tower and Roman sarcophagus for a font), and the 8th-century **Badia dei Santi Benedettini**, remodelled in the 11th century and adorned with a lovely portal. In Piazza Diaz, the little **Museo d'Arte Sacra** contains some lovely Flemish tapestries (open only Sat 10–12, summer Tues and Sat 4–6). A panoramic road from Camaiore leads up to **Monteggiori**, with more fine views. Other destinations around Camaiore include the beautiful **Valle Freddana** and Monte Magno; **Pieve a Elici**, near Massarosa, with another excellent Romanesque church, 11th-century **San Pantaleone**. From here a minor road continues up through majestic chestnut groves to **Montigiano**, one of the finest balconies in the Apuans.

WHERE TO STAY AND EATING OUT (tel prefix 0585)

Carrara: the best hotel is called, naturally, ***__Michelangelo__, Corso F.illi Rosselli 3, tel 70 861, with modern rooms and a parking garage (L60–75 000 all with bath). There's a youth hostel at Marina di Massa e Carrara, if you're game, called **Ostello Apuano**, Viale delle Pinete 89, tel 780 034, open mid-march to Sept and charging 11 000 a head, including breakfast. There are quite a few good restaurants—if you're lucky you may find a bottle of Candia, the white wine eked from Carrara's mountain terraces. Try **Soldani**, Via Mazzini 11, tel 71 459, which offers simple dishes from other Italian regions, exquisitely prepared (L40 000). Among the quarries in Colonnata, at **Da Venanzio**, tel 799 220, you can try the local speciality, a delicate bacon, or crêpes, delicious tortelli, pigeon in balsam vinegar or even roast beef (L30 000).

Forte dei Marmi: Hotels here are more modern than in Viareggio, and the cruel rule of fashion is making prices higher all the time. Try ****__Raffaeli Park__, Via Mazzini 37, tel 81 494 (L120–220 000) or its less expensive companion, ***__Raffaeli Villa Angelo__,

Via Mazzini 64, tel 80 652 (L75 000 without bath, L85 000 with). Both have their stretch of private beach, a pool, tennis and air-conditioned rooms. Less expensive places go for the same rates as in Viareggio, but there are considerably fewer of these. Dining is a delight at the Versilia's finest restaurant, **Lorenzo**, Via Carducci 61, tel 84 030, where seafood beautifully and imaginatively prepared is a winning trump card. Be sure to reserve (L55–60 000). Another good seafood restaurant, **Tre Stelle**, Via Montauti 6, tel 80 220, offers more traditional Italian dishes (L40 000).

Viareggio

TOURIST INFORMATION
Viale Carducci 10, tel (0584) 962 233.

Up until the 1820s Viareggio (pop. 59,000), Tuscany's biggest seaside resort, was little more than a fishing village, named after the medieval royal road, the 'Via Regia' that connected Migliarino and Pietrasanta. After the 14th-century battles with Pisa, Genoa, and Florence, this little village was the republic of Lucca's sole access to the sea. Fortifications were built—Forte del Motrone (which it lost in 1441) and the Torre del Mare and **Torre Matilde**, near the canal (Thurs–Sat 3–5:30, summer 4–7) which the Lucchesi managed to hold on to until the 19th century, although it was too marshy to do them much good. It was Lucca's beloved Duchess Maria Luisa who drained the swamps, developed the shipyards and fishing and resort industries, and laid out the near grid of streets; by the 1860s the first cabanas and beach umbrellas made their début.

By the turn of the century Viareggio was booming, embellished with playful, intricate, wooden Art Nouveau buildings that lined its celebrated seaside boardwalk, the Passeggiata Viale Regina Margherita. In 1917 a massive fire destroyed nearly all of this, and when it was rebuilt in the 1920s, its most important buildings were designed by Galileo Chini and the eclectic Alfredo Belluomini. Chini (1873–1956) was one of the founders of Italian Art Nouveau, or the Liberty Style, which first caught the public's fancy in the 1902 Esposizione Internazionale di Arti Decorative in Turin. Chini was especially well known for florid ceramics, but he also designed stage sets for the New York Metropolitan Opera's premieres of his friend Puccini's operas: *Turandot*, *Manon Lescaut*, and *Gianni Scicchi*, as well as the throne room of the King of Siam (1911–14). In Viareggio he worked with Belluomini to produce what has become the symbol of Viareggio, the colourful, twin-towered **Gran Caffè Margherita**, in a kind of Liberty-Mannerism; as well as the **Bagna Balena** and what is now the Supercinema, all on the Passeggiata. You can compare their work with the 1900 **Negozio Martini**, the only wooden building to survive the 1917 fire. Chini and Belluomini also designed a number of hotels (see p. 249) as well as Puccini's villa on Piazza Puccini, and the buildings at Piazza D'Azeglio 15 and Viale Manin 20.

Even more colourful are the floats used in Viareggio's famous **Carnival**. It was begun in the 1890s but has grown to rival the much older carnivals of Rome and Venice, and in pure frivolity has surpassed them all. In the centre of the action are large, usually very satirical papier-mâché floats; if you can't return on Shrove Tuesday to join the massive parade, you can see them being created in the huge **float hangars** along Viale Marco Polo. At the Società Ippica Viareggina, Via Comparini 8, tel 391 176, you can hire a horse to explore the pine woods just south of Viareggio.

Torre del Lago and Puccini

Puccini spent most of his later years in his villa at **Torre del Lago**, 6 km south of Viareggio along Via dei Tigli (buses from Piazza D'Azeglio), a lovely road passing through an extensive pine wood. His villa is on the banks of shallow **Lake Massaciuccoli**, where he could practise 'my second favourite instrument, my rifle' on passing coots. The villa contains its original furnishings, old photos, the piano on which Puccini composed many of his operas, his rifles, and other mementoes. The maestro and his wife and son are buried in the adjacent chapel (open April-Sept 9–12 and 3–7, Oct–Mar 9–12 and 2:30–5; adm). In August Torre del Lago holds a **popular opera festival** in its outdoor theatre, presenting famous and obscure works by the great composer; for a schedule and tickets contact the Festival Pucciniano, Piazzale Belvedere Puccini, Torre del Lago, tel (0584) 343 322.

Most of Lake Massaciuccoli and the marshlands, the *macchia*, and beaches to the south are part of the **Parco Naturale Migliarino S. Rossore Massaciuccoli**. Boats from Torre del Lago explore some of these wetlands, or you can go by car to the tiny village of Massaciuccoli. The wild beaches between Viareggio and Torre del Lago, with their low dunes and scrubby pine forest, are free and undeveloped. The forest of San Rossore, in existence since Roman times, is nowadays threatened by the spray from the polluted sea, which is unfortunately killing the pines (San Rossore is open Sundays and holidays only, 8:30–5:30 winter, till 7:30 summmer; to visit on weekdays tel (050)27 272).

WHERE TO STAY (tel prefix 0584)

If you're Viareggio bound, why not stay in a Chini-Belluomini confection for the total experience? One of their most extravagant is the ******Excelsior**, built in 1923; the original decor of the public rooms is well preserved (Viale Carducci 88, tel 50 726, open May–15 Oct, L120–200 000, all rooms with TV and bath). Belluomini on his own built the ******Grand Hotel & Royal**, Viale Carducci 44, tel 45 151, in a kind of neo-Renaissance eclectic style, with an impressive lobby (May-Sept, with an indoor pool and parking, L155–200 000). Another aging queen by both men is the *****Hotel Liberty**, Lungomare Manin 18, tel 46 247 (open April-Oct, all rooms with bath, L50–85 000). They also designed the ****Villa Argentina**, Via Fratti 400, tel 962 474, in 1926, the only one that stays open all year (L46–52 000 without bath, L50–60 000 with). There are scores of other hotels along the beach front, especially less expensive ones in the L35–50 000 range.

EATING OUT

One might suspect that the hordes of Italians who descend on Viareggio every summer do so mainly to eat; the resort has a disproportionate number of good restaurants. Heading the list, the **L'Oca Bianca** on Via Aurelia north of the centre, tel 64 191, is the place to go for Mediterranean lobster (aragosta), all kinds of fish, and elaborately prepared and served gourmet concoctions. Try the *menu degustazione* for L55–60 000—you could spend considerably more à la carte. **Barrasca**, Via Garibaldi 122, tel 31 402, offers a real surprise—Sardinian dishes, not often seen outside of the island; not only *mallorredus* (nasty-looking Sard pasta), but great seafood antipasti and stews (L45 000 and maybe more). Also very good and creative, and very popular, is **Romano**, Via

Mazzini 122, tel 31 382, elegant, with a dining room and interior garden, and delicious seafood *à la Toscana*; reserve a table L45–50 000 or **Margherita**, Via Regina Margherita 30, tel 962 553, with a sommelier not of wine but olive oil! The seafood is delicious and varied, though, and there's a good wine list, too (L40 000). For seafood with less pretensions and lower prices, try **Trattoria Giorgio**, Via Zanardelli 71, tel 44 493, about L30–35 000. A good place to go wine tasting is **Il Puntodivino**, Via Mazzini 229, tel 43 357; the wines and champagnes come from all over Italy and France, even if the food is local—try the prawns with prosciutto, or if you're in a wild mood, anchovies with fennel (L30 000).

PISA

Pisa (pop. 104,000) is at once the best known and the most mysterious of Tuscan cities. Its most celebrated attraction has become, along with the Colosseum, gondolas, and spaghetti a symbol for the entire Italian republic; even the most illiterate recognize at least the 'Leaning Tower of Pizza' even if they've never heard of Florence or Siena. Tour buses disgorge thousands every day into the Field of Miracles, who spend a couple of hours and leave again for places more tangible, like Florence, Elba or Rome. At night even the Pisani make a mass exodus into the suburbs, as if they sense that the city was too big for them, not physically, but in terms of unfulfilled ambitions, of past greatness nipped in the bud.

Yet go back to about 1100, when according to the chroniclers, precocious Pisa was 'the city of marvels', the 'city of ten thousand towers', with a population of 300,000—or so it seemed to the awed writers of that century, who, at least outside Venice, had never before seen such an enormous, cosmopolitan and exotic city in Christian Europe since the fall of Rome. Pisan merchants made themselves at home all over the Mediterranean, bringing back new ideas and new styles in art in addition to their fat bags of profit, contributing as much to the rebirth of Western culture as any city. Pisan Romanesque, with its stripes and blind arcades, which had such a wide influence in Tuscany, was inspired by the great Moorish architecture of Andalucia; Nicola Pisano, first of a long line of great sculptors, is as important to the renaissance of sculpture as Giotto is to painting.

Like a Middle Eastern city, Pisa has put all of its effort into one fabulous spiritual monument, while the rest of the city wears a decidedly undemonstrative, almost anonymous face, a little run down. It is a subtle place, a little sad perhaps, but strangely seductive if you give it a chance. After all, one can't create a Field of Miracles in a void.

History

In the Middle Ages, Pisa liked to claim that it began as a Greek city, founded by colonists from Elis. Most historians, however, won't give them credit for anything earlier than 100 BC or so, when a Roman veterans' colony was settled there. Records on what followed are scarce, but Pisa, like Amalfi and Venice, must have had an early start in building a navy and establishing trade connections. By the 11th century, the effort had blossomed into opulence; Pisa had built itself a small empire, including Corsica, Sardinia, and for a while the Balearics. Around 1060, work was begun on the great cathedral complex and many other buildings, inaugurating the Pisan Romanesque.

In 1135 Pisa captured and sacked its greatest rival in the Western Mediterranean, Amalfi. The First Crusade, when Pisa's archbishop led the entire fleet in support of the Christian knights, turned out to be an economic windfall for the city. Unlike Amalfi, from the start Pisa had adopted a course of combat with the states of the Moslem world, less from religious bigotry than a clear eye on the main chance. When the Pisans weren't battling the Moslems of Spain and Africa, they were learning from them. A steady exchange of ideas brought much of medieval Arab science, philosophy and architecture into Europe through Pisa's port. Pisa's architecture, the highest development of the Romanesque in Italy, saw its influence spread from Sardinia to Apulia in southern Italy; when Gothic arrived in Italy Pisa was one of the few cities to take it seriously, and the city's accomplishments in that style rank with Siena's. In science, Pisa contributed a great though shadowy figure, that most excellent mathematician Nicolo Fibonacci, who either rediscovered the principle of the Golden Section or learned it from the Arabs, and also introduced Arabic numerals to Europe. Pisa's scholarly traditions over the centuries would be crowned in the 1600s by its most famous son, Galileo Galilei.

Pisa was always a Ghibelline city, the greatest ally of the emperors in Tuscany if only for expediency's sake. When a real threat came, however, it was not from Florence or any of the other Tuscan cities, but from the rising mercantile port of Genoa. After years of constant warfare, the Genoese devastated the Pisan navy at the Battle of Meloria (an islet off Livorno) in 1284. It meant the end of Pisan supremacy, but all chance of recovery was quashed by an even more implacable enemy: the Arno. Pisa's port was gradually silting up, and when the cost of dredging became greater than the traffic could bear, the city's fate was sealed. The Visconti of Milan seized the economically enfeebled city in 1396, and nine years late Florence snatched it from them. Excepting the period 1494–1505, when the city rebelled and kept the Florentines out despite an almost constant siege of 15 years, Pisa's history was ended. The Medici dukes did the city one big favour, supporting the university and even removing Florence's own university to Pisa. In the last 500 years of Pisa's long, pleasant twilight, this institution has helped the city stay alive and vital, and in touch with the modern world; one of its students was Enrico Fermi.

GETTING AROUND

By Air

Pisa has Tuscany's international airport, Galileo Galilei, in the suburb of San Giusto, 3 km south of the city; tel 28 088 for general information, or British Airways, tel 501 838, or Alitalia, tel 48 025. Most of the big car rental firms are there, ready to outfit you with wheels (Hertz, tel 444 26; Avis tel 42 028; Maggiore tel 42 574; Budget tel 45 490).

By Train

The airport is linked to Pisa by train or city bus no. 5, departing from Piazza Stazione, in front of the main station, which lies south of the Arno (tel 28 546). Many trains (Florence-Pisa or Genoa-Rome lines) also stop at Stazione San Rossore; if you're making Pisa a day trip you may want to get off there, as it's only a few blocks from the cathedral and Leaning Tower—or else bus no. 1 will take you there from the central station.

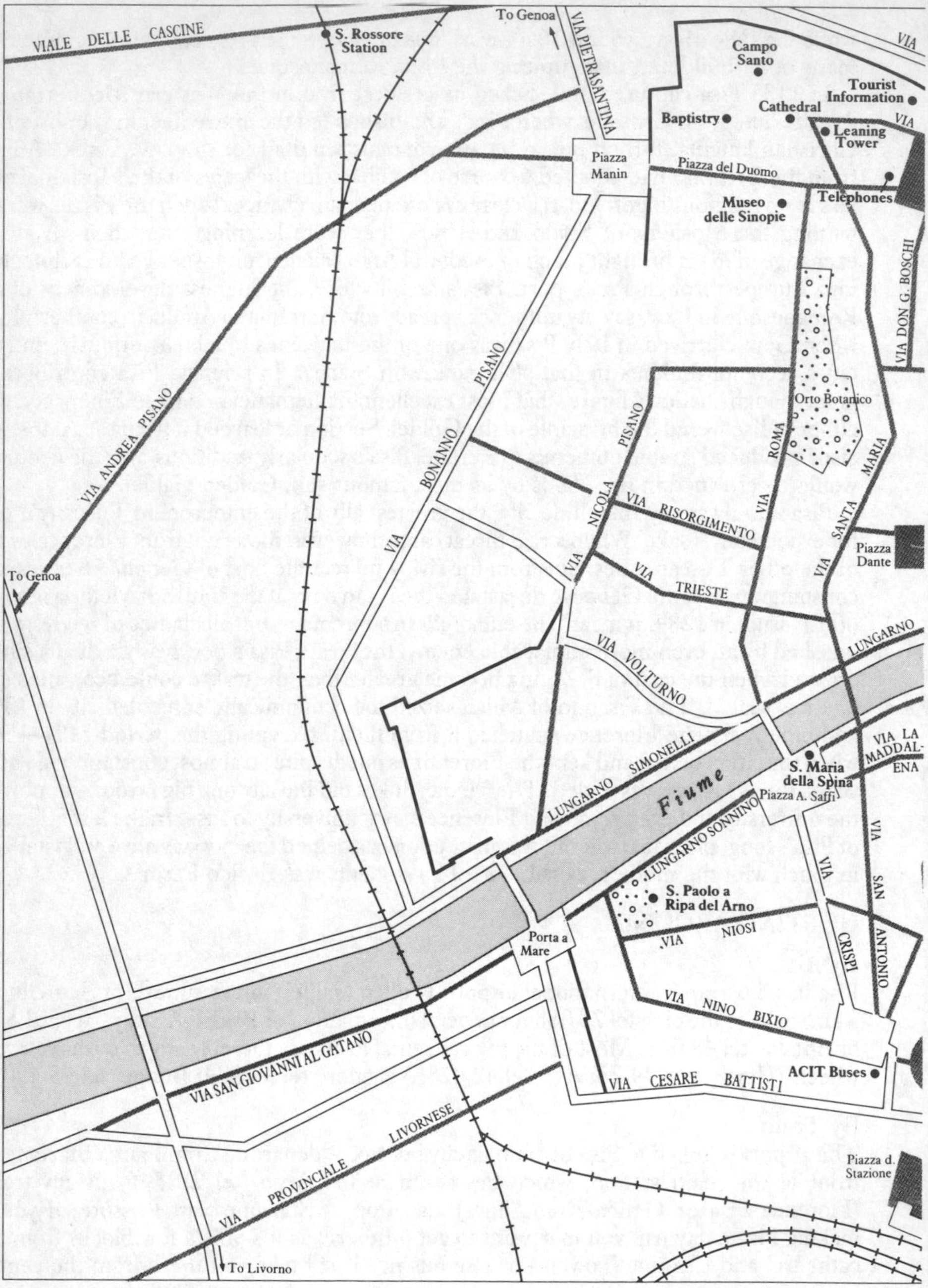
VIALE DELLE CASCINE
S. Rossore Station
To Genoa
VIA PIETRASANTINA
Campo Santo
Tourist Information
Cathedral
Baptistry
Leaning Tower
Piazza Manin
Piazza del Duomo
Telephones
Museo delle Sinopie
VIA DON G. BOSCHI
VIA ANDREA PISANO
VIA BONANNO PISANO
VIA NICOLA PISANO
VIA ROMA
Orto Botanico
VIA SANTA MARIA
VIA RISORGIMENTO
Piazza Dante
To Genoa
VIA TRIESTE
VIA VOLTURNO
LUNGARNO
VIA LA MADDALENA
LUNGARNO SIMONELLI
Fiume
S. Maria della Spina
Piazza A. Saffi
LUNGARNO SONNINO
S. Paolo a Ripa del Arno
VIA NIOSI
VIA CRISPI
VIA SAN ANTONIO
Porta a Mare
VIA NINO BIXIO
VIA SAN GIOVANNI AL GATANO
ACIT Buses
VIA CESARE BATTISTI
VIA PROVINCIALE LIVORNESE
Piazza d. Stazione
To Livorno

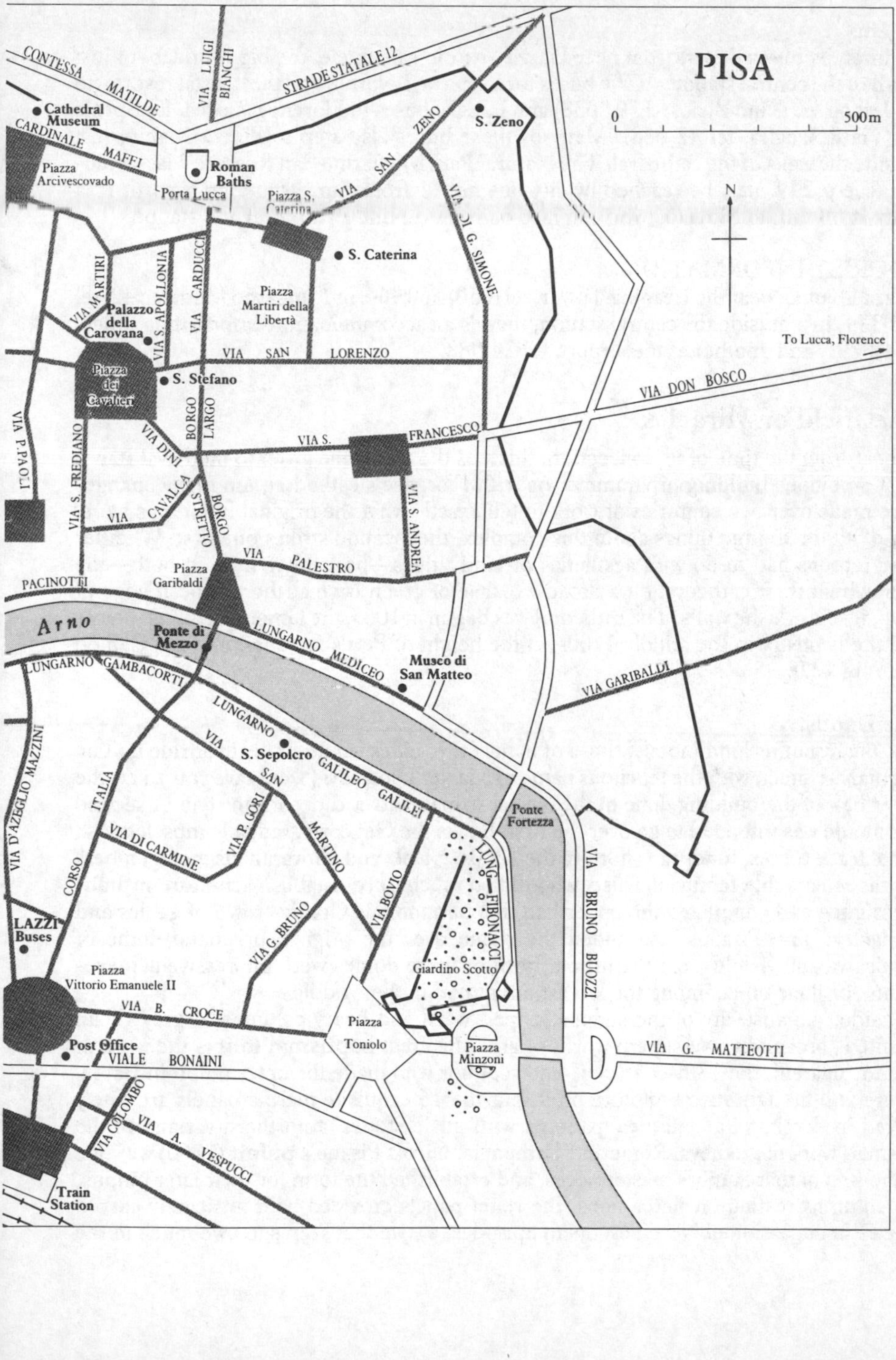
PISA
0
500m
N
To Lucca, Florence
CONTESSA
MATILDE
STRADE STATALE 12
VIA LUIGI BIANCHI
Cathedral Museum
CARDINALE
MAFFI
Piazza Arcivescovado
Roman Baths
Porta Lucca
S. Zeno
VIA SAN ZENO
Piazza S. Caterina
S. Caterina
VIA G. SIMONE
VIA MARTIRI
VIA S. APOLLONIA
VIA CARDUCCI
Piazza Martiri della Libertà
Palazzo della Carovana
Piazza dei Cavalieri
S. Stefano
VIA SAN LORENZO
VIA DON BOSCO
VIA P. PAOLI
VIA S. FREDIANO
VIA DINI
BORGO LARGO
VIA S. FRANCESCO
VIA CAVALCA
BORGO STRETTO
VIA S. ANDREA
Piazza Garibaldi
VIA PALESTRO
PACINOTTI
Arno
Ponte di Mezzo
LUNGARNO MEDICEO
Musco di San Matteo
LUNGARNO GAMBACORTI
VIA GARIBALDI
LUNGARNO GALILEO GALILEI
VIA SAN MARTINO
S. Sepolcro
VIA D'AZEGLIO MAZZINI
CORSO ITALIA
VIA DI CARMINE
VIA P. GORI
Ponte Fortezza
LUNG—FIBONACCI
VIA BOVIO
VIA BRUNO BUOZZI
VIA G. BRUNO
LAZZI Buses
Giardino Scotto
Piazza Vittorio Emanuele II
VIA B. CROCE
Piazza Toniolo
Piazza Minzoni
VIA G. MATTEOTTI
Post Office
VIALE BONAINI
VIA COLOMBO
VIA A. VESPUCCI
Train Station

By Bus

All intercity buses depart from near Piazza Vittorio Emanuele, the big roundabout just north of the central station: ACIT buses for Volterra, Livorno, and the coastal resorts (to the left on Via Nino Bixio, tel 501 038) and LAZZI buses to Florence, Lucca, La Spezia (on Via d'Azeglio, tel 42 688). Many of these buses also stop at Piazza Manin, just outside the walls of the cathedral. The Natural Park Migliarino San Rossore Massaciuccoli (see p. 249) may be reached by city bus no. 11 from Lungarno Gambacorti. Pisa lends itself well to **bicycles**; you can hire one at Via Nino Bixio, near the station.

TOURIST INFORMATION

Piazza Duomo, near the Leaning Tower, tel (050) 560 464, or Lungarno Mediceo 42, tel 542 344. Just outside the central station, there's an accommodation/information office, tel 42 291, and another at the airport, tel 28 088.

The Field of Miracles

Almost from the time of its conception, this was the nickname given to medieval Italy's most ambitious building programme. As with Florence's cathedral, too many changes were made over two centuries of work to tell exactly what the original intentions were. But of all the unique things about this complex, the location strikes one first. Whether their reasons had to do with aesthetics or land values—probably a little of both—the Pisans built their cathedral on a broad expanse of green lawn at the northern edge of town, just inside the walls. The cathedral was begun in 1063, the famous Leaning Tower and the baptistry in the middle 1100s, at the height of Pisa's fortunes, and the Campo Santo in 1278.

The Baptistry

The biggest of its kind in Italy; those of many other cities would fit neatly inside it. The original architect, with the felicitous name of Master Diotisalvi ('God save you'), saw the lower half of the building done in the typical stripes-and-arcades Pisan style. A second colonnade was intended to go over the first, but as the Genoese gradually muscled Pisa out of trade routes, funds ran short. In the 1260s, Nicola and Giovanni Pisano, members of that remarkable family of artists who did so much to re-establish sculpture in Italy, redesigned and completed the upper half in a harmonious Gothic crown of gables and pinnacles. The Pisanos also added the dome over the original prismatic dome of Diotisalvi, still visible from the inside. Both of these domes were impressive achievements for their time, among the largest attempted in the Middle Ages.

Inside, the austerity of the simple, striped walls and heavy columns of grey Elban granite is broken by two superb works of art. The great **baptismal font** is the work of Guido Bigarelli, the 13th-century Como sculptor who made the crazy pulpit in Barga. There is little figurative sculpture on it, but the 16 exquisite marble panels are finely carved in floral and geometrical patterns with inlaid stones, a northern variant on the Cosmati work of medieval Rome and Campania. Nicola Pisano's **pulpit** (1260) was one of the first of that family's masterpieces, and established the form for their later pulpits, the columns resting on fierce lions, the relief panels crowded with intricately carved figures in impassioned New Testament episodes, a style that seems to owe much to the reliefs on old Roman triumphal arches and columns. The baptistry is famous for its uncanny acoustics; if you have the place to yourself, try singing a few notes from the centre of the floor. If there's a crowd the guards will be just waiting for someone to bribe them to do it.

The Cathedral

One of the first and finest works of the Pisan Romanesque, the cathedral façade, with four levels of colonnades, turned out to be a little more ornate than Buscheto, the architect, had planned back in 1063. These columns, with similar colonnades around the apse and the Gothic frills later added around the unique elliptical dome, are the only showy features on the calm, restrained exterior. On the south transept, the late 12th-century **Porte San Ranieri** has a fine pair of bronze doors by Bonanno, one of the architects of the Leaning Tower. The Biblical scenes are enacted among real palms and acacia trees; naturally, the well-travelled Pisans would have known what such things looked like.

On the inside, little of the original art survived a fire in 1595. The roof went, as well as the Cosmati pavement, of which only a few patches still remain. A coffered Baroque ceiling and lots of bad painting were contributed during the reconstruction, but some fine work survives. The great mosaic of Christ Pantocrator in the apse is a work of Cimabue, and there are portraits of the saints by Andrea del Sarto in the choir. The **pulpit** (*c.* 1300), by Giovanni Pisano, is the acknowledged masterpiece of the family. The men of 1595 used the fire as an opportunity to get rid of this nasty old medieval relic, and the greatest achievement of Pisan sculpture sat disassembled in crates, quite forgotten until this century. Works of genuine inspiration often prove profoundly disturbing to ages of certainty and good taste. Pisano's pulpit is startling, mixing classical and Christian elements with a fluency never seen before his time. St Michael, as a *telamone*, shares the honour of supporting the pulpit with Hercules and the Fates, while prophets, saints, and sibyls look on from their appointed places. The relief panels, jammed with expressive faces, diffuse an electric immediacy equal to the best work of the Renaissance. Notice particularly the *Nativity*, the *Massacre of the Innocents*, the *Flight into Egypt*, and the *Last Judgement*.

The Leaning Tower

The stories claiming the tilt was accidental were most likely pure fabrications, desperate tales woven by the Pisans to account for what, before mass tourism, must have seemed a great civic embarassment. The argument isn't very convincing. It seems hard to believe that the tower would start to lean when only 10 m tall; half the weight would still be in the foundations. The argument then insists that the Pisans doggedly kept building it after the lean commenced. The architects who measured the stones in the last century to get to the bottom of the mystery concluded that the tower's odd state was absolutely intentional from the day it was begun in 1173. Mention this to a Pisan, and he will be as offended as if you had suggested lunacy is a problem in his family.

But the leaning campanile is hardly the only strange thing in the Field of Miracles. The more time you spend here, the more you will notice: little monster-griffins, dragons and such, peeking out of every corner of the oldest sculptural work, skilfully hidden where you have to look twice to see them, or the big bronze griffin sitting on a column atop the cathedral apse (a copy) and a rhinoceros by the door, Moslem arabesques in the Campo Santo, perfectly classical Corinthian capitals in the cathedral nave and pagan images in the pulpit. The elliptical cathedral dome, in its time the only one in Europe, shows that the Pisans had not only the audacity but the mathematical skills to back it up. You may have noticed that the baptistry too is leaning—about 1.5 m, in the opposite direction. And the cathedral façade leans outwards about 40 cm, hard to notice but disconcerting if you see it from the right angle. This could hardly be accidental. So much in the Field of Miracles gives evidence of a very sophisticated, strangely modern taste for the outlandish. Perhaps the medieval master masons in charge here simply thought that plain perpendicular buildings were becoming just a little trite.

Whatever, the campanile is a beautiful building and something unique in the world—also a very expensive bit of whimsy, with some 190 marble and granite columns. At the moment, it's also proving expensive to the local and national governments as they try to decide how best to shore up the tower. Only relatively recently, the tilt has been increasing and it's bound to come crashing down in 200 years or so unless something is done. Various proposals have been made to stabilize the monument; none has yet won a consensus of opinion, though a number of experts would like to lighten the tower by knocking off the top bell chamber, added in the 1300s. Whatever plan is adopted in the end will set Italy back some tens of billions of lire. Late in 1989, the diligent doctors of the campanile finally decided it had become a little too precarious for traffic. It has been closed indefinitely.

The Campo Santo

If one more marvel in the Campo dei Miracoli is not excessive, there is this remarkable cloister, as unique in its way as the Leaning Tower (Oct–Mar 9–5; April-Sept 9–7; adm). Basically, the cemetery is a rectangle of gleaming white marble, unadorned save for the blind arcading around the façade and the beautiful Gothic tabernacle of the enthroned Virgin Mary over the entrance. With its uncluttered, simple lines, the Campo Santo seems more like a work of our own century that the 1300s.

The cemetery began, according to legend, when the battling Archbishop Lanfranchi, who led the Pisan fleet into the Crusades, came back with boatloads of soil from the Holy Land for extra-blessed burials. Over the centuries an exceptional hoard of frescoes and sculpture accumulated here. Much of it went up in flames on a terrible night in July 1944, when an Allied incendiary bomb hit the roof and set it on fire. Many priceless works of art were destroyed and others, including most of the frescoes, damaged beyond hope of ever being perfectly restored. The biggest loss, perhaps, was the set of frescoes by Benozzo Gozzoli—the *Tower of Babylon, Solomon and Sheba, Life of Moses* and the *Grape Harvest* and others; in their original state they must have been as fresh and colourful as his famous frescoes in Florence's Medici Palace. Even better known, and better preserved, are two 14th-century frescoes of the *Triumph of Death* and the *Last Judgement* by an unknown artist (perhaps Andrea Orcagna of Florence) whose failure to sign the work unfortunately put him down to posterity as the 'Master of the Triumph of Death'. In this memento of the century of plagues and trouble, Death (in Italian, feminine, *La Morte*) swoops down on frolicking nobles, while in the *Last Judgement* (which has very little heaven, but plenty of hell) the damned are variously cooked, wrapped up in snakes, poked, disembowelled, banged up and chewed on; still, they are some of the best paintings of the trecento, and somchow seem less gruesome and paranoid than similar works of centuries to come (though good enough to have inspired that pop classic, Lizst's *Totentanz.*)

For another curiosity, there's the *Theological Cosmography* of Piero di Puccio, a vertiginous diagram of 22 spheres of the planets and stars, angels, archangels, thrones and dominations, cherubim and seraphim, etc.; in the centre, the small circle trisected by a T-shape was a common medieval map pattern for the known earth. The three sides represent Asia, Europe, and Africa, and the three lines the Mediterranean, the Black Sea, and the Nile. Among the sculpture in the Campo Santo, there are sarcophagi and Roman bath tubs, and in the gallery of pre-war photographs of the lost frescoes, a famous Hellenistic marble vase with bas-reliefs.

The Museo delle Sinopie and Museo del Duomo

There are two museums surrounding the Campo dei Miracoli: opposite the cathedral, the **Museo delle Sinopie** (9:30–12:20 and 3–4:30 or later; adm) contains the pre-painting sketches in plaster of the frescoes lost in the Campo Santo fire. Many of these are works of art in their own right, which, though faint, help give an idea how the frescoes once looked.

The **Museo del Duomo**, near the Leaning Tower in Piazza Arcivescovado (9–5, summer 8–8; adm expensive), has been newly arranged in the old Chapter House, with descriptions in English available for each room. The first rooms contain the oldest works—beautiful fragments from the cathedral façade and altar; two Islamic works, the very strange, original **Griffin** from the top of the cathedral, believed to have come from Egypt in the 11th century, and a basin with an intricate decoration. Statues by the Pisanos from the baptistry were brought in from the elements too late; worn and bleached, they resemble a convention of mummies. Other sculptures in the next room survived better: Giovanni Pisano's grotesque faces, his gaunt but noble *St John the Baptist* and the lovely *Madonna del Colloquio*, who speaks to her child with her eyes; and fine works by Tino di Camaino, including the tomb of S. Ranieri and his sculptures from the tomb of Emperor Henry VII, sitting among his court like some exotic oriental potentate. In Room 9, in the Cathedral Treasure, Giovanni Pisano's lovely ivory *Madonna and Child* steal the show, curving to the shape of the elephant's tusk; there's an ivory coffer and the cross that led the Pisans on the First Crusade. Upstairs are two rare illuminated 12th- and 13th-century scrolls (called exultet rolls), perhaps the original visual aids; the deacon would unroll them from the pulpit as he read so the congregation could follow the story with the pictures. There are also some extremely big angels used as candle sticks, intarsia, Etruscan and Roman odds and ends (including a good bust of Caesar) and prints and engravings of the original Campo Santo frescoes made in the 19th century. The courtyard has a unique view of the Leaning Tower, which seems to be bending over to spy inside.

North Pisa

With the cathedral on the very edge of town, Pisa has no real centre. Still, the Pisans are very conscious of the division made by the Arno; every year in June the two sides fight it out on the Ponte di Mezzo in the *Gioco del Ponte*, a sort of medieval tug-of-war where the opponents try to push a big decorated cart over each other.

From the Field of Miracles, Via Cardinale Maffi leads east to the ruins of some **Roman Baths** near the Lucca Gate; two interesting churches in the neighbourhood are **San Zeno**, in a corner of the walls, with some parts as old as the 5th century, and **Santa Caterina**, a Dominican church with a beautiful, typically Pisan façade. Inside there is an *Annunciation* and a sculpted tomb by Nino Pisano, and a large painting from the 1340s of the *Apotheosis of St Thomas Aquinas*, with Plato and Aristotle in attendance and defeated infidel philosopher Averroes below.

One long street near the Campo dei Miracoli begins as Via Carducci, becoming the old, arcaded **Borgo Largo** and **Borgo Stretto**. The twisting alleys of the lively market area are just off to the west, along with the **University**, still one of Italy's most important, and the **Piazza dei Cavalieri**. Duke Cosimo I started what was probably the last crusading order of knights, the Cavalieri di Santo Stefano, in 1562. The crusading urge had ended long before, but the duke found this a useful tool for placating the anachronistic fantasies of the Tuscan nobility—most of them newly titled bankers—and for licensing out freebooting expeditions against the Turks. Cosimo had Vasari build the **Palazzo della Carovana** for the order, conveniently demolishing the old Palazzo del Popolo, the symbol of Pisa's lost independence. Vasari gave the palace an outlandishly ornate *graffito* façade; the building now holds a college of the university founded by Napoleon. Next door, **Santo Stefano**, the order's church, is also by Vasari, though the façade was designed by a young Medici dilettante; inside are some long fantastical war pennants the order's pirates captured from the Moslems in North Africa. Also on the piazza, the **Palazzo dell'Orologio** was built around the 'Hunger Tower' (left of the big clock), famous from Dante's story in the *Inferno* of Ugolino della Gherardesca, the Pisan commander who was walled in here with his sons and grandsons after his fickle city began to suspect him of intrigues with the Genoese.

From the piazza, Via Dini and Via S. Francesco lead to the church of **San Francesco**: Gothic, with a plain marble façade, but containing some good paintings—a polyptych over the altar by Tommaso Pisano, frescoes by Taddeo Gaddi, Niccolò di Pietro Gerini (in the Chapter House) and in the sacristy, by Taddeo di Bartolo (*Stories of the Virgin*, 1397). The unfortunate Count Ugo and sons are buried in a chapel near the altar.

Museo di San Matteo

On the Lungarno Mediceo, an old convent which also served as a prison now immures much of the best Pisan art from the Middle Ages and Renaissance (8:30–7:30, Sun 8:30–1:30, closed Mon; adm). It has works by Giunta Pisano, believed to be the first artist to ever sign his work (early 1200s), and an excellent and well arranged collection of 1300s paintings by Pisans and other schools gathered from the city's churches; a polyptych by Simone Martini, paintings by Francesco Traini, Taddeo di Bartolo, Agnolo Gaddi, Antonio Veneziano, and Turino Vanni; some sculptures by the Pisanos (especially the *Madonna del Latte* by Andrea and Nino); medieval ceramics from the Middle East, brought home by old Pisan sea dogs. In Room 7, after all the trecento works, the early Renaissance comes as a startling revelation, as it must have been for the people of the 15th century: here is Neri di Bicci's wonderfully festive *Coronation of the Virgin*, bright with ribbons, a *Madonna* from the decorative Gentile da Fabriano, a sorrowful *St Paul* by Masaccio, whose features and draperies are softly moulded, an anonymous *Madonna with Angel Musicians*, and a beautifully coloured *Crucifixion* by Gozzoli that looks more like a party than an execution. The last great work is Donatello's gilded bronze reliquary bust of *San Lussorio*, who could pass for Don Quixote. Someday the museum's collection of Mannerists and other later artists will be arranged downstairs.

South of the Arno

After the Campo dei Miracoli, the thing that has most impressed Pisa's visitors is its languidly curving stretch of the Arno, an exercise in Tuscan gravity, the river lined with two mirror image lines of blank-faced yellow and tan buildings, all the same height, with no remarkable bridges or any of the picturesque quality of Florence. Its uncanny monotony is broken by only one landmark, but it is something special. Near the Solferino Bridge, **Santa Maria della Spina** sits on the bank like a precious Gothic jewel box. Though one of the few outstanding achievements of Italian Gothic, originally it wasn't Gothic at all. Partially rebuilt in 1323, its new architect—perhaps one of the Pisanos—turned it into an extravaganza of pointed gables and blooming pinnacles. All of the sculptural work is first class, especially the figures of Christ and the Apostles in the 13 niches facing the streets. The chapel takes its name from a thorn of Christ's crown of thorns, a relic brought back from the Crusades.

Only a few blocks west, near the walls where the famous 'Golden Gate'—medieval Pisa's door to the sea—once stood, remains of the old Citadel and Arsenal are still visible across the river. On the southern side, **San Paolo a Ripa del Arno** has an interesting 12th-century façade similar to that of the cathedral. San Paolo stands in a small park, and interestingly it is believed to have been built over the site of Pisa's original cathedral; perhaps building cathedrals in open fields was an old custom. Behind it the unusual and very small 12th-century chapel of **Sant'Agata** has eight sides and an eight-sided prismatic roof like an Ottoman tomb. Just across Ponte Solferino, behind the Palazzo Reale, is the large church of **San Nicola**, with a fine painting of the *Madonna* by Traini, and a sculpture of the same by Nino Pisano, and a painting of St Nicolas of Toletino shielding Pisa from the plague. Ask the sacristan to show you the famous spiral stair in the 13th-century campanile.

Down the Arno, the monotony is briefly broken again by the arches of 17th-century **Logge di Banchi**, the old silk and wool market, at the Ponte di Mezzo and at the head of Pisa's main shopping street, Corso Italia. A bit further down is another octagonal church, **San Sepolcro** built originally for the Knights Templar by Diotisalvi. **Palazzo Lanfranchi** further down is used for exhibitions. There's a small but shady park in the former Bastion Sangallo.

SHOPPING AND ACTIVITIES

Pisa is the best place in Tuscany to purchase bizarre and tacky **souvenirs**, and the best selection is crowded around the Campo dei Miracoli. Light-up Leaning Towers in pink and yellow come in all sizes and are an amazing good buy; some have pen and pencil set attached for the scholar, or grinning plastic kittens for the kids' room, or naked ladies for your favourite uncle. The other specialities are **medieval weapons**: crossbows, cudgels, maces, whips, plastic skulls, reptiles, and insects. If you'd prefer a **book** in English to these delights, try Feltrinelli at Corso Italia 117. You can go **riding** at the Cooperativa Agrituristica in Via Tre Colli, in Calci, or **swim** in the pool in Via Andrea Pisano, or have a **drink** in Pisa's oldest coffeehouse, the Antico Caffè dell'Ussero, at Lungarno Pacinotti 27.

FESTIVALS

In June there's the *Gioco del Ponte* and historic procession (see p. 257) as well as the historic **regatta and lights festival of San Ranieri**, when the banks of the Arno glimmer with tens of thousands of bulbs. Folklore displays are on top for San Sisto (6 August). Every four years Pisa is the site of the Old Maritime Republics boat race (next 1991), a race between old sea rivals Pisa, Venice, Genoa, and Amalfi.

WHERE TO STAY (tel prefix 050)

Capital of day trippers, Pisa isn't known for fine hotels, but there's usually enough room for the relatively few visitors who elect to stay overnight. The best, very close to the Campo dei Miracoli, is the ****__Grand Hotel Duomo__, Via S. Maria 96, tel 561 894, a modern though richly-appointed luxury hotel with a roof garden and a garage; all the rooms are air-conditioned (L85–170 000). Right in the centre of Lungarno Pacinotti, the royal ***__Royal Victoria__, tel 23 381, is a tasteful and modern establishment. Its best features are rooms overlooking the Arno and its own garage; parking can be a problem in Pisa (L25–44 000 without bath, L45–80 000 with). Many of the middle-range hotels are on the streets around the train station, south of the Arno, like the ***__Terminus & Plaza__, Via Colombo 45, tel 45 043 (L45–85 000 depending on the plumbing). If you're driving you may want to stay just outside of the city on N. 1 (Via Aurelia) in Madonna dell'Acqua, tel 890 726, a large hotel with a park and a pool, open April–15 Nov (L90–130 000).

Inexpensive places are spread throughout town, and most of them are often full of students; it's always best to call first, or else go up to the Campo dei Miracoli and try the *__Gronchi__, Piazza Arcivesovado 1, tel 561 823 (L36–39 000); the *__Helvetia__, Via Don Boschi 31, tel 41 232 (L30–35 000, some higher with bath); or *__Di Stefano__ at Via Sant'Apollonia 35, tel 26 359 (L34–38 000). All are relatively convivial places within a few blocks of the cathedral.

EATING OUT

In Pisa, walks on the wild side of the Tuscan kitchen seem more common than in other towns—eels and squid, *baccalà*, tripe, wild mushrooms, 'twice-boiled soup' and some dishes that cannot be found in the fattest dictionaries, and that waiters cannot satisfactorily explain. Don't be intimidated; there's always more common fare present on the menu, and occasionally the more outlandish items turn into surprisingly refined treats—especially so at **Ristorante Sergio**, a highly regarded temple of Pisan cuisine, in a medieval setting on the Lungarno Pacinotti near the Royal Victoria, tel 48 245. The menu changes according to what's available and fresh, but whatever they find you are assured of one of the finest dining experiences in this corner of Italy. There's a *menu degustazione* for L70 000, where you can sample the best dishes of the day; à la carte may be considerably less. A less expensive gourmet stronghold in Pisa, the **Ristoro dei Vecchi Macelli**, Via Volturno 49 on the north bank of the Arno, by Ponte Solferino, tel 20 424, with highly imaginative dishes based on coastal Tuscan traditions (L40–55 000).

Those eels from Lake Massaciuccoli and other fresh seafood delicacies hold pride of place at **Lo Schiaccianoci** east of the station at Via Vespucci 102, tel 21 024 (L30–40 000). **Da Bruno**, Via Luigi Bianchi, tel 550 964, outside the walls a few blocks east of the Campo dei Miracoli, is another place to see how well you like simple Pisan cooking—things like polenta with mushrooms and *baccalà* (dried codfish) (L35 000). Pisa is well endowed with unpretentious trattorias, many of them near the centre around the university. On Piazza S. Frediano, **Turiddu** has *baccalà* too, and very good rabbit,and even a Tuscan version of *saltimbocca* for about L25 000. Near the station in Piazza Vittorio Emanuele 22, **Centrale**, tel 23 335, has a large menu of old favourites for L20 000; **Da Gino** next door has slightly cheaper prices and simple 'tratt' decor. If you just want a snack, try the offerings at the **Tavola Calda** in Via del Borghetto 39, just beyond the San Matteo museum.

Around Pisa

A couple of kilometres up river to the east, stands 'Pisa's second leaning tower', the campanile of the Romanesque **San Michele dei Scalzi**. **Calci**, under the slopes of Monte Pisano, has a good 11th-century church and an eroded giant of a campanile; 11 km from Calci, in a prominent site overlooking the Arno, is the ornate **Certosa di Pisa**, founded in 1366, but completely Baroqued in the 18th century, in a kind of 1920s Spanish-California exhibition style with three fine cloisters. There are lavish pastel frescoes by Florentine Baroque artist Bernardo Poccetti and his school, and a giraffe skeleton, stuffed penguins, Tuscan minerals, wax intestines—all part of the university's **Natural History Collections**, founded by the Medici, housed in the Certosa since 1981 (guided visits, May–Oct 9–7, Nov–April 9–4, Sun 9–12, closed Mon; adm; for the natural history, by appointment tel 937 092).

Towards the coast, 6 km from Pisa, is the beautifully isolated basilica of **San Piero a Grado**. According to tradition it was founded in the first century by St Peter himself, and in the Middle Ages was a popular pilgrimage destination. Although first documented in the 8th century, the current buildings are 11th century, embellished with blind arcades and ceramic tondoes. Like many early churches and basilicas, it has an apse on either end, though in different sizes; the columns were brought in from a variety of ancient buildings. The altar stone, believed to have been set there by Peter himself, was found in recent excavations that uncovered the remains of several previous churches. Frescoes in the nave by a 14th-century Lucchese, Deodato Orlandi, tell the *Story of St Peter* with effigies of the popes up to the millennium (John XVIII) and a view of heaven.

In 1822, a strange ceremony took place on the wide, sandy beach of **Gombo**, near the mouth of the Arno, described in morbid detail by Edward Trelawny: 'the brains literally seethed, bubbled, and boiled as in a cauldron, for a very long time. Byron could not face this scene, he withdrew to the beach and swam off to the *Bolivar*.' Such was Shelley's fiery end, after he drowned sailing from Livorno. Gombo, and Pisa's other beaches, the **Marina di Pisa** and **Tirrenia** are often plagued by pollution, although Marina di Pisa makes a pretty place to stroll, with its Liberty-style homes and pine forests.

LIVORNO

> ... There is plenty of space; it is a fully registered cemetery with an attendant keeper. So, if any of you have the intention of retiring to this very interesting part of Tuscany you will be well taken care of!
>
> Horace A. Hayward, on the British Cemetery in Livorno

Right from its founding in 1577, the English spent so much time in this city and grew so fond of it, that they decided to rename it. It's time that the bizarre anglicization of *Leghorn* be put to sleep. The city that Duke Cosimo founded to replace Pisa's silted-up harbour is named *Livorno*. It hasn't much in common with the other Tuscan cities—full of sailors and African pedlars, blissfully unafflicted with architecture and art, as picturesque and romantic as Buffalo, New York. Instead of frescoes, Livorno has perhaps the best seafood on the Tyrrhenian coast. Instead of rusticated *palazzi* and marble temples, it has canals, docks, and a very lively citizenry famous for free thinking and tolerance. And instead of winding country lanes, there are big white ferries to carry you off to the Tuscan Islands, Corsica, or Sardinia.

History

The site had always been a safe harbour, and in the Middle Ages there was a small fortress to watch over it. It's odd no one thought of making a port here long before Cosimo. The Pisani considered it briefly in the 1300s, when it was becoming clear that Pisa's own port would eventually fill up with the sands of the Arno. Eventually the fortress fell into the grasp of the Genoese, who sold it to Florence in 1421. Cosimo I, in his attempts to build Tuscany into a modern state, first saw the advantage of having a good port to avoid trading at the mercy of the Spaniards and Genoese. Cosimo expanded the fortress, but it was not until the reign of his successors, Francesco and Ferdinando, that Livorno got off the ground. The first stone was laid on 28 March 1577, and a regular gridiron city soon appeared, designed by Buontalenti, and surrounded by fortresses and canals. Almost from the beginning there was an English connection. Sir Robert Dudley, illegitimate son of the earl of Leicester—Queen Elizabeth's favourite—left England in 1605 after failing to prove his legitimacy in the Star Chamber court. (Perhaps he had other reasons; immediately upon arrival he converted to Catholicism and obtained a papal divorce from the wife he had abandoned back home.) Dudley built warships for the grand dukes, fortified the port of Livorno, and drained the coastal swamps, making the region healthy and inhabitable for the first time.

In 1618, Livorno was declared a free port, free not only for trade but for the practice of any faith and for men of whatever nationality. It was a brilliant stroke, designed to fill out the population of this very rough and dangerous new town, and it goes to the eternal credit of the Medici dukes, an act of tolerance almost unthinkable in the Catholic Mediterranean of the 1600s. Before long, Livorno was full of persecuted Jews, Greeks, English Catholics, Spanish Moslems, and loose ends from around Europe. As the only safe trading port in a sea full of Spaniards, the port acquired thriving communities of English and Dutch merchants. In the 1700s progressive, tolerant Livorno was a substantial city, a breath of fresh air in the decadent Mediterranean and a home away from home for British travellers. Shelley wrote *The Cenci* here, as well as *To a Skylark*; he bought his fatal sailboat in Livorno's port.

Livorno declined a little when the same low tariffs and trading advantages became available in other Mediterranean ports. The Austrian dukes, especially Leopold II, helped keep Livorno ahead of its rivals; nevertheless, true to its traditions the city contributed greatly to the mid-century revolutionary movements and the wars of the Risorgimento. After unification it was still a lively place, full of men of many nations; also it began to make its first cultural contributions to the new Italy—the operatic composer Mascagni, the painter Modigliani, and several other artists of the Macchiaioli school. World War II and its bombers hit Livorno harder than anywhere in Tuscany, but the city rebuilt quickly. Long before other ports, Livorno realized the importance of container shipping. As the Mediterranean's first big container port, Livorno today has become the second city of Tuscany, and Italy's second largest port (after Genoa).

GETTING AROUND

Livorno's train station is on the edge of the city, with plenty of trains to Pisa, Florence, and any point along the Tyrrhenian coast. Some trains to Pisa go on to Lucca-Pistoia-Florence. There are some connections to Volterra, with a change down the coast at Cecina. The station is well over a mile from the city centre; take the no. 1 bus (most other city buses also pass through the centre, though as one old Livornese put it, they make 'vicious circles' before getting there). Buses for all villages in Livorno province (the strip of coast down as far as Follonica) leave from Piazza Grande. LAZZI buses for Florence depart from Via Saffi, on the Fosse Reale, just off Piazza Cavour.

Ferries: Livorno is the main port for ferries to Corsica, with daily departures (NAVARMA line) from late March to early November; it's a 4-hour trip to Bastia, one very pleasant town (US citizens will need a visa; there's a French consulate at Via Montegrappa 6, tel 896 368). NAVARMA has daily ferries as well to Olbia in Sardinia (a nasty town on a wonderful island) from late June through September; there are other departures on the Sardinia Ferries line (prettier boats, higher fares). For the Tuscan Islands, services are handled by TOREMAR, a daily trip to Capraia (once a week, continuing to Elba), and a daily afternoon run to Portoferraio, Elba, from 16 June to 30 September. All ticket offices are in the port area.

TOURIST INFORMATION

Piazza Cavour 6 (3rd floor), tel (0586) 898 111; in summer a booth in the port, on the Molo Mediceo.

Four Moors, Inigo Jones, and the American Market

There isn't a lot to see in Livorno. You may enjoy the place and stay for a day or two, or you may be ready to bolt after five minutes. Though the streets are usually brimming, a combination of the prevailing north Tuscan austerity and an excess of dreary architecture make Livorno a disconcertingly anonymous city. It would have been a perfect setting for a German expressionist film of the 20s; unfortunately, its cinematic possibilities have not yet been exploited. There's nothing disconcerting about the **port**, a busy, fascinating jumble of boats, cranes, docks, and canals. Close to the port entrance on Piazza Micheli,

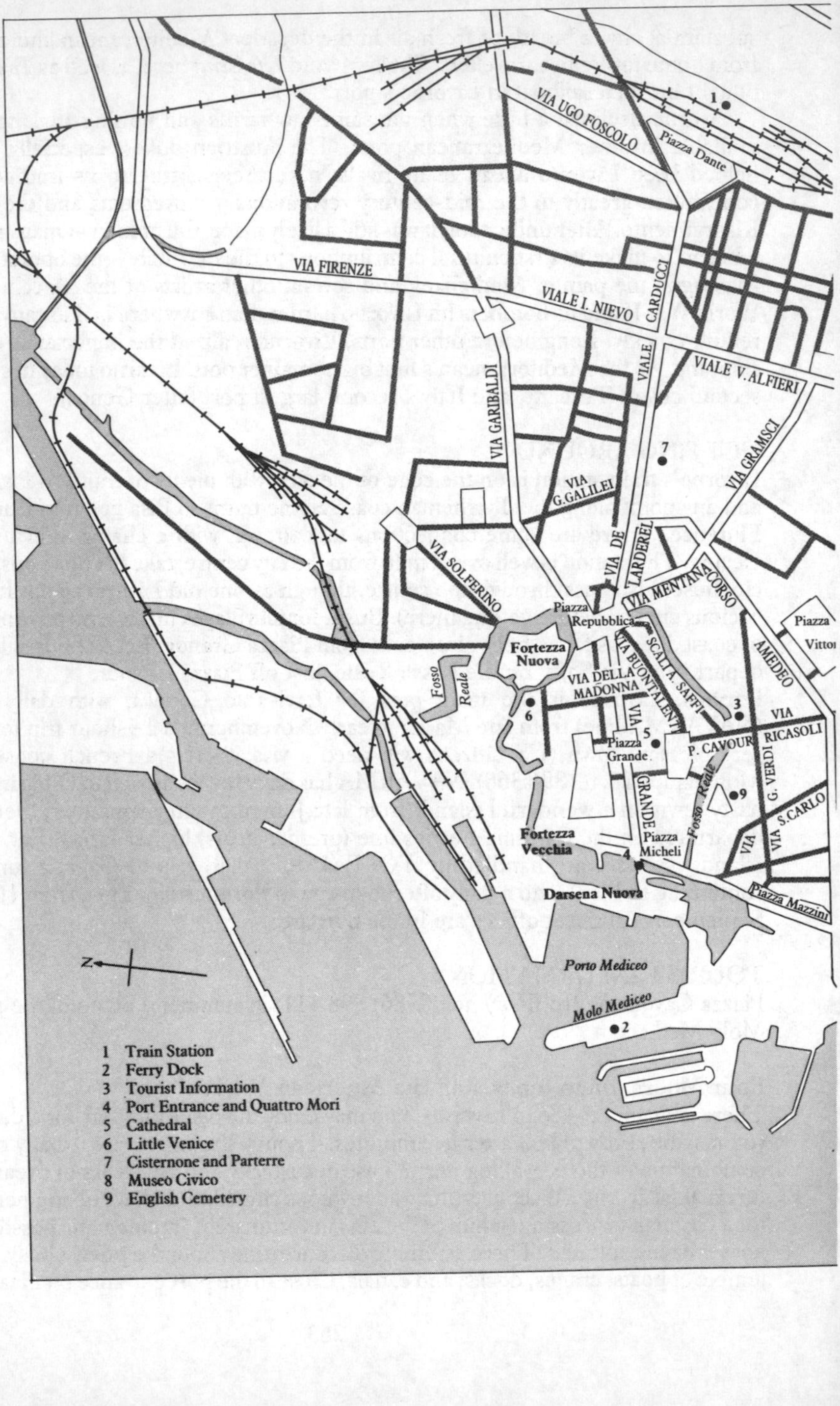
VIA UGO FOSCOLO
Piazza Dante
VIA FIRENZE
VIALE I. NIEVO
VIALE CARDUCCI
VIALE V. ALFIERI
VIA GARIBALDI
VIA GRAMSCI
VIA G.GALILEI
VIA DE LARDEREL
VIA SOLFERINO
VIA MENTANA
CORSO AMEDEO
Piazza Repubblica
Piazza Vittor
Fortezza Nuova
Fosso Reale
VIA DELLA MADONNA
SCALI A. SAFFI
VIA BUONTALENTI
VIA GRANDE
Piazza Grande
P. CAVOUR
VIA RICASOLI
VIA G. VERDI
VIA S.CARLO
Fortezza Vecchia
Piazza Micheli
Darsena Nuova
Piazza Mazzini
Porto Mediceo
Molo Mediceo
N
1 Train Station
2 Ferry Dock
3 Tourist Information
4 Port Entrance and Quattro Mori
5 Cathedral
6 Little Venice
7 Cisternone and Parterre
8 Museo Civico
9 English Cemetery

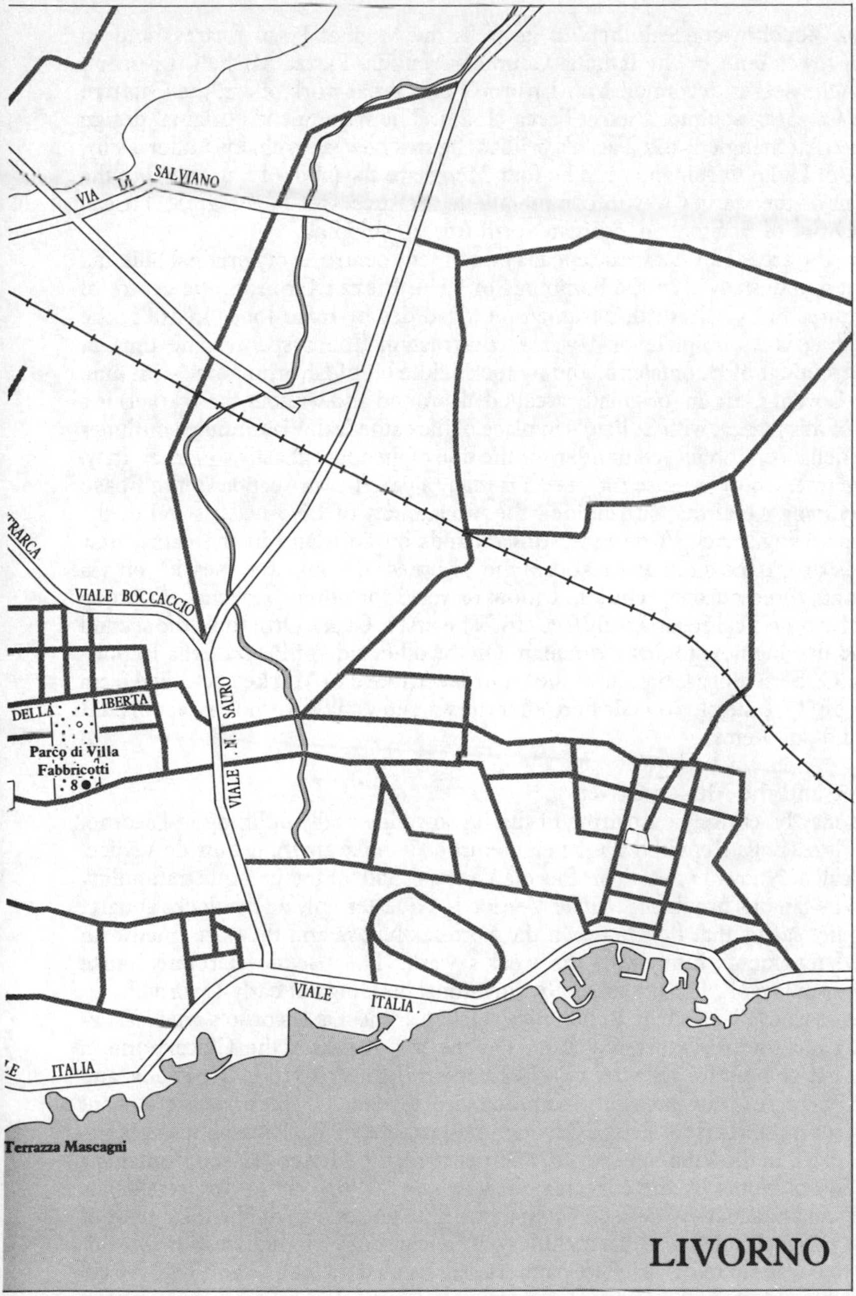
VIA DI SALVIANO
TRARCA
VIALE BOCCACCIO
DELLA LIBERTA
Parco di Villa Fabbricotti
8
VIALE N. SAURO
VIALE ITALIA
LE ITALIA
Terrazza Mascagni
LIVORNO

the **Fortezza Vecchia** conceals behind its walls the original Pisan fortress and an 11th-century tower built by the famous Countess Matilda. Piazza Micheli, Livorno's front door to the sea, is decorated with Livorno's only great work of art, the **Quattro Mori** of the Carraran sculptor Pietro Tacca (1623). The monument's original design became somewhat mangled, and Tacca's brilliant figures now sit in chains under a silly, earlier statue of Duke Ferdinando I. The four Moors are a symbol of Sardinia, but the original intent of the statues was to commemorate the successes of the great Tuscan pirates, the Order of St Stephen, against North African shipping.

From here, the arcaded **Via Grande** leads into the city centre; every original building on this street was destroyed in the bombings of 1944. **Piazza Grande**, the centre of Livorno, features the **Cathedral**, designed on a bad day by Inigo Jones in 1605; the present building is a complete post-war reconstruction. Jones spent some time in Tuscany as a student of Buontalenti, and he took a little bit of Livorno home with him. His plan for Covent Garden (originally arcaded all around and without the market) is a simple copy of this piazza, with St Paul's in place of the cathedral. Via Grande continues on to Piazza della Repubblica, contender for the title of the most ghastly square in Italy. There are no trees on it, because the piazza is really a paved-over section of the **Fosso Reale**, the curving canal that surrounded the original city of Livorno. Just off to the north, the sprawling, brick **Fortezza Nuova** stands on an island in the canal, now landscaped as a park and a popular resort of the Livornese on Sundays. Nearby, on Via della Madonna, three adjacent churches (now recycled for other uses) make a fitting memorial of Livorno's career as a truly free city. The first is Greek Orthodox, the second Catholic, and the one next to that Armenian. On the other side of Piazza della Repubblica, Piazza XX Settembre is the site of the Saturday **American Market**, so called from the vast stores of G. I. surplus on sale here after the war, now still Livorno's street market for clothes and odd items.

Little Venice and the Museo Civico

By now, you may be entirely despairing of finding anything really uplifting in Livorno. But just off Piazza della Repubblica is a neighbourhood unlike anything outside Venice. In fact, they call it 'Nuova Venezia', or 'Piccola Venezia', and for picturesque tranquillity it may outdo its famous precursor. **Little Venice** is a quarter only a few blocks square, laced with quiet canals that flow between the Fortezza Nuova and the port, lined with sun-bleached tenements hung with the week's wash. The pseudo-Baroque **Santa Caterina** church is typical of the ungainly, functional buildings of early Livorno.

Leading east from Piazza della Repubblica, Viale Carducci is Livorno's *grand boulevard*, heading out towards the rail station. On the way it passes the **Cisternone**, a Neoclassical palace built for the water works Leopold II constructed in the 1830s, and next to it the **Parterre**, a city park with a sad zoological garden. The other main route out of Livorno's centre starts from Piazza Cavour, and leads down Via Ricasoli towards the southern suburbs. In the Villa Fabbricotti, another park, the **Museo Civico**, contains a good collection of works by the Macchiaioli, Italy's late 19th-century Impressionists (10–1, Thurs and Sat also 4–7, closed Mon; adm). The museum is on the third floor of the city library, a small collection that includes only one work by Modigliani, but a wealth of paintings that lead up to his art. The painters represented include Ulivi Liegi, Mario Puccini, that rare blossom Lodovico Tommasi and Livorno's own Giovanni Fattori.

Little Venice

Together, they make a natural progression from the Biedermeier art of the 1860s—stirring scenes of Italian volunteers leaving for the front—to the sweet haziness of the Belle Epoque 1890s.

Along the coast, Viale Italia leads past the **Terrazza Mascagni**, a grandiose overlook on the sea, past the Italian Naval Academy, and then through some neighbourhoods of surprisingly blatant neo-Gothic and Art Nouveau villas of the 1890s, on the way to **Ardenza**, with its seafront park and marina.

The English Cemetery and Montenero

For a sentimental journey into Livorno's cosmopolitan past, pay a visit to the **English Cemetery** on Via Adua, next to the Anglican Church. Crotchety old Tobias Smollett, who never stopped crabbing about Italy and never got to leave it, is interred here, along with many members of the British trading community and quite a few Americans. Many of the tombs are truly monumental, some with inscriptions from Scripture or Shakespeare, some charmingly original. Many among the British community, including Byron and Shelley, chose to spend their time not in Livorno itself, but up on the suburban hill of **Montenero** to the south. A charming, old-fashioned funicular railway takes you to the top, a sanctuary and pilgrimage site since an apparition of the Virgin Mary in the 1300s. The present church, full of ex-votos, is the work of an 18th-century architect named Giovanni del Fantasia; there's also a small museum, an ancient pharmacy, and a number of caves, the Grotte del Montenero.

WHERE TO STAY (tel prefix 0586)

Some of the rooms at the ***__Gran Duca__**, Livorno's most interesting hotel, look out over the Quattro Mori and the busy port; though modern inside, the Gran Duca is built into a surviving section of the walls right on Piazza Micheli 16, tel 891 024, at the entrance to the harbour area (L100 000, some rooms with TV). Another possibility (especially if you have a car) is the ***__Gennarino__**, a converted turn-of-the-century neo-Gothic palace on the shore road,Viale Italia 301, tel 803 109 (L78 000). Being a port town, there's an abundance of less expensive hotels. Many, though none especially distinguished, can be found across the wide piazza from the train station. Dozens more crowd the centre around the port and Via Grande. Some of them are screaming dives, though Corso Mazzini, a few blocks south of the Fosso Reale, has some nice ones, especially the old-fashioned ***Corsica** at no. 148, tel 882 103 (L38–45 000 depending on the plumbing). Right in the centre, a block off Via Grande at Via dell'Angiolo 23, tel 888 581, the ***Europa** has clean, remodelled rooms—but singles only—for L27–35 000.

EATING OUT

The main purpose of a trip to Livorno is to eat seafood. The Livornese have their own ways of preparing it, now much copied throughout Tuscany, and restaurants usually prove easier on your budget than elsewhere. Besides lobster and grilled fish, pasta dishes with seafood figure on all the local menus, as does *the* Livornese dish, *cacciucco*, the famous fish stew that is to Livorno what the Leaning Tower is to Pisa. Try them at **L'Antico Moro**, on a narrow street near the city market, Via di Franco 59, tel 884 659, a bargain at L30–35 000. At Viale Carducci 63 towards the train station, **La Barcarola**, tel 402 367, is a very big and very noisy place, where *zuppa di pesce, penne* with scampi, and everything else good from the Tyrrhenian is cooked in the good old Livornese style (L40–50 000; closed Sun & Aug). At Borgo dei Cappuccini 5, near the mouth of the Fosso Reale, **Osteria del Mare**, tel 881 027, is a little place serving grilled fish, lobster and spaghetti *alle vongole* for around L35 000. One of the best inexpensive places is **L'Attias**, Via Ricasoli 127, tel 899 441, a popular neighbourhood place with *cacciucco*, though you may want to take a taxi; it's hard to reach by car (L45 000). Another popular spot is **Trattoria Galileo**, Via delle Campana, tel 889 009, two blocks north of Piazza Repubblica (L18–22 000, with some seafood). Some of the best restaurants are to the south in the seaside suburb of Ardenza. **Da Oscar**, Via Franchini 78, tel 501 258, has been a favourite for decades; there is a good selection of wines to go with the linguine and clams, excellent risottos and grilled *triglie* and *orate* (L35–40 000; closed Mon).

Tuscan Islands: Gorgona and Capraia

The Tuscan Archipelago is a broad arch of islets, stretching from Livorno to Monte Argentario and enclosing Elba, the only large and heavily populated member of the group. Fate has usually not been kind to these islands; after deforestation, Saracen and Turkish pirates, and finally the Italian government, not much is left. Two of the islands are still prison camps, one a nature preserve where no one is allowed to stay overnight. The others will be dealt with later (Elba is most conveniently reached from Piombino, Giglio and Giannutri from Porto S. Stefano); **Gorgona** and **Capraia** get a daily boat from Livorno—and are in fact administratively part of Livorno.

To see **Gorgona**, 37 km from Livorno, you'll either have to get permission from the Ministero di Grazia e Giustizia in Rome (quite difficult) or else punch a *carabiniere*. Gorgona, a hilly, rectangular square mile, was first used as a prison by Pope Gregory the Great. A Carthusian monastery lasted until the new Italian state expropriated the entire island in 1869; in the beginning, it was to be a 'model prison' with workshops and vineyards, but it wasn't long before it deteriorated into just another lock-up. There's nothing to see on Gorgona, except maquis and a handful of olive trees, and you'll have to be content with the view from the boat, which stops daily on the way to Capraia to drop off new cons and supplies. Ambitious plans are afoot to close the prison and turn Gorgona into a wildlife preserve, but so far nothing has been decided.

Capraia

Capraia, 65 km from Livorno, is the third largest of the islands, after Elba and Giglio. It measures about 10 km by 5, and has some 400 inhabitants. Like Elba, it is mountainous, but has fewer trees; most of the island is covered with scrubby *macchia*.

History

In Roman times Capraia seems to have been a private estate, and the ruins of an extensive villa can be seen. In the days of the Empire, the island was occupied by a colony of Christian monks. Such an island was perfect for the Christian ideal of withdrawal and contemplation, but it also prevented the Church authorities from keeping a close watch on the colony, and the monks slipped into unorthodoxy and loose behaviour; an armed mission from Pope Gregory the Great was needed to force them back in line in the late 6th century.

When Saracen pirates began to infest the Tyrrhenian Sea, Capraia, like most of the group, became deserted. The Pisans thought it important enough to repopulate and fortify in the 11th century. Genoa eventually gained control, as she did in Corsica only 32 km away. The proximity gave Capraia its one big moment in history; in 1767 the revolutionary forces of the Corsican nationalist leader, Pasquale Paoli, and the weakness of the Genoese, resulted in, of all things, an independent Capraia, which soon learned to support itself by piracy. French occupation put an end to that four years later.

WHAT TO SEE

Seven years ago tourist accommodation on Capraia consisted of one hotel and two tiny pensions. Today, by a miracle of 20th-century Eurotourism, these have all grown into three-star hotels, and two more have sprouted to join them. It helps that Capraia is an island, and a pretty one, but its real attraction is its natural setting, its deep-sea diving and marine grottoes. In the last century the northern quarter of the island was put to use as an agricultural penal colony, which is what it still is today. The civilian population is almost entirely concentrated in the port and only town, **Capraia Isola**. The port is actually half a kilometre away from the town, connected by the island's only paved road. In the town are the Baroque church and convent of **Sant'Antonio**. Used as a barracks in the last century, it is now crumbling and abandoned. On the outskirts are the ruins of the **Roman villa**, apocryphally the abode of Augustus' profligate daughter Julia, and an 11th-century Pisan chapel dedicated to the **Vergine Assunta**. Overlooking it all is the large and impressive fortress of **San Giorgio**, begun by the Pisans and completed by the Genoese. The well-preserved **watchtower** at the port was built by the Genoese Bank of St George.

On the eastern side of town there is a beach under the cliffs with an interesting tower, built by the Pisans, and connected to the cliff by a natural bridge. A visiting Californian at the turn of the century was so struck by it that he built a copy of it on a beach near San Diego.

From Capraia Isola a road leads southwest across the island, passing another Pisan church, that of **Santo Stefano**, built on the ruins of a 5th-century church used by the early monks, destroyed by the Saracen pirates. Near Monte Pontica is a cave, the **Grotta di Parino**, a sacred spot used as a place of meditation by the monks. The road ends at a lighthouse on the western coast. Just south of here is a sea cave, the **Grotta della Foca**, where some Mediterranean seals are still reported to live. At the southern tip of the island is another Genoese watchtower, the **Torre dello Zenobito.**

Livorno's Coast

Livorno's clever tourist office has taken to calling this shore the 'Etruscan Riviera', conjuring up the irresistible idea of Etruscans lounging in beach chairs the way they do on their funerary urns. Beyond Antignano, the shoreline becomes jagged and twisting, dotted with beaches that are usually more than well exploited. **Castiglioncello** is a pretty corner of the coast, but the beaches are narrow and packed with Italians throughout the summer. Nearby **Rosignano** is a similar resort, graced with a gargantuan chemical plant. **Vada** and **Cecina Mare** are a little better; at least both have stretches of free beach. Cecina Mare, 36 km from Livorno, is a suburb of Tuscany's newest city, **Cecina**, founded only a century ago, now an unkempt town populated by dissipated factory hands and motorcycle-heads. **San Vicenzo** is a booming, awful resort, but it has miles of good beaches on either side, perhaps your best chance on this strip of coast for a little seaside peace and quiet.

Next is the half-moon **Golfo di Baratti**, with more tranquil beaches and some Etruscan tombs from the once mighty town of **Populonia**. Modern Populonia has a small archaeological museum (ask there about visits to the ruins of the Etruscan city and tombs, which include a so-called 'arsenal' where the Etruscans turned Elban iron into armaments). Populonia also has an impressive medieval castle. **Piombino**, at the tip of this stubby peninsula, is Tuscany's Steel City, mercilessly flattened during the war, and mercilessly rebuilt afterwards. The government might close the obsolete steel works at any time, but Piombino will at least remain the major port for Elba. The towns up in the hills of interest include: **Bolgheri**, near Cecina, centre of a DOC wine area (Bolgheri is a little-known, dry white wine), **Castagneto Carducci**, a pretty town where strawberries are grown, and finally **Suvereto**, a pretty, seldom-visited medieval village with an arcaded Palazzo Comunale and the 12th-century Pisan church of San Giusto.

EATING OUT

If the vast beaches of San Vicenzo fail to tempt, its seafood restaurants might, most tantalizingly **Gambero Rosso**, Piazza della Vittoria 13, tel (0565) 701 021, where the devilishly perfect and delicate crustaceans, pasta, pheasant and pigeon dishes, and fish so fresh and good is matched only by an equally devilishly thorough wine list. Take the easy way out and order the menu degustazione (L90 000; slightly more à la carte). If your pockets aren't that deep, the nearby **Il Bucaniere**, Via Marconi 8, tel (0565) 703 387 is under the same management, occupying the beach, cabins, and a bathing establishment from the '50s; and delicious seafood and more for L45 000.

Elba

When the government closed the steel mills on Elba after the war, the national and local governments sought to make up the lost income by promoting tourism on the island. They have been singularly successful; Elba has become one of Europe's holiday playgrounds, and with tourists approaching some two million every year, prosperity has returned to its 30,000 inhabitants.

Tourist Elba, however, is no glamour puss. It is a comfortable place that attracts mainly families. Germans in particular are fond of the island; they have bought up most of the southern coast, and many of them come back every year. There is no single, big, crowded, tourist ghetto, as is true on some other Mediterranean islands, but plenty of quiet, small resorts all around the coast. The lives of the Elbans themselves have adjusted to the cyclical rhythms of tourist migrations. In winter the island seems empty; much of the population stays only to work during the season. Other activities do exist to supplement tourism, such as fishing and mining, but the old iron mines, after thousands of years, have finally given out. The last of them closed in 1984.

In an unspectacular way, Elba is beautiful. Pink and green predominate—pink for the granite outcrops and houses, green because the island is heavily forested. Like its neighbour Corsica, it is a chain of mountains rising out of the sea, the tallest of which are to the west, grouped around Monte Capanne (1000 m). For a mineralogist, Elba is a holiday dream—besides iron ore, dozens of common and rare minerals are found there, everything from andalusite to zircon. For most people, however, Elba's greatest attraction is its wealth of beaches. The coastline, all bays and peninsulas, is over 150 km in length, and there are beaches everywhere, large and small, sand or pebbles. Even in the crush of August, there's plenty of Elba-room for all, and if you look carefully, you just might find a beach that's not too crowded.

History

Able was I ere I saw Elba
—the Napoleonic palindrome

Elba is close enough to the Italian mainland to have been inhabited from the earliest times. When Neanderthal Man was tramping through the neighbourhood about 50,000 years ago, Elba may have still been linked to the peninsula. Later peoples, a seemingly unending parade of them, colonized the island after 3000 BC, drawn by Elba's treasure hoard of metals. In the Copper Age they mined its copper; in the Bronze Age they alloyed the copper into bronze. The copper gave out just in time for the Iron Age, and Elba, conveniently, had vast deposits of this also. Competition was fierce: Etruscans and Greeks fought over the island and established colonies of miners, but neither left any permanent settlements.

For Rome, expanding across the Italian peninsula in the 4th century BC, Elba was an important prize. After its conquest at the end of the century, the Romans founded towns to consolidate their hold; thenceforth, whenever the Roman legions ran their swords through Teutons, Persians, Gauls, Carthaginians, or each other, they usually did it with Elban iron. The mines and forges, then as now, were concentrated on the eastern third of the island; the remainder became a holiday spot for the wealthy, as witnessed by the remains of large villas discovered near Portoferraio.

The fall of Rome brought invasions, disorder, depopulation, and pirates to Elba; the Lombards in the 6th century, under the murderous Gummarith, subjugated the island with their usual bloodshed; Saracens and adventurous barons from Italy fought for the scraps. By the 11th century Pisa, as the island lay across its most important trade route, had assumed complete control. It held the island for almost 500 years, constructing fortresses at Luceri and Volterraio and exploiting the mineral resources. At the time the capital was called *Ferraia*, of which the modern capital of Portoferraio was only the port. Not a trace remains of the medieval city, and archaeologists are still trying to discover its site.

From the 13th century on, Genoa contested Pisa's possession of the island. In the 16th century, Duke Cosimo I saw his opportunity and seized it for Florence. He built Portoferraio and the walls around it, but soon had to contend with the growing power of Spain in the western Mediterranean, and after some inconclusive skirmishes, Elba was partitioned between Tuscany and Spain. Spain built the town and fortress of Porto Azzurro as a counter to Portoferraio, an arrangement that lasted throughout the 18th century, despite French efforts to grab the island.

NAPOLEON

During the Napoleonic wars, Elba was occupied for a time by the English, and Portoferraio was unsuccessfully besieged for over a year by Napoleon's troops in 1799. Napoleon finally annexed it in 1802, probably with no premonitions that the 1814 Treaty of Fontainebleau would put a temporary end to the First Empire and send him to Elba. After all these centuries, Elba suddenly found itself on the centre stage of world history.

Napoleon himself chose Elba, from the variety of small Mediterranean outposts offered him, for 'the gentleness of its climate and its inhabitants'. Also, perhaps because on clear days he could see his own island of Corsica. No one, however, seems to have consulted the Elbans themselves on the matter, and they can be excused for the cold indifference with which they received their new ruler. On 4 May 1814, he arrived at Portoferraio with some 500 of his most loyal officers and soldiers and a British Commissioner charged with keeping an eye on him. But Napoleon soon won over the hearts of the Elbans by being the best governor they ever had. New systems of law and education were established, the last vestiges of feudalism abolished, and what would today be called economic planning was begun; he reorganized the iron mines and started Elba's modern network of roads.

Not that Napoleon ever really took his stewardship seriously. Remaking nations and institutions was a reflex by then, after doing it all across Europe for 20 years. It was the return to France that occupied his attention. The atmosphere was thick with intrigues and rumours, and secret communications flowed incessantly between Napoleon and his partisans on the Continent. On 20 February 1815, just nine months after his arrival, the Elbans and the embarrassed British watchdog awakened to find the emperor missing. The 'Hundred Days' had begun. Later, after Waterloo, a smaller, gloomier, and more distant island would be found to keep Napoleon out of trouble.

Elba was returned to Tuscany, and soon after joined the new Kingdom of Italy. World War II hit Elba hard; Portoferraio and environs were bombed in 1943–44, first by the Allies, and then by the Germans. In 1944, in one of the more disgraceful episodes of the war, Elba was 'liberated' by Free French and African troops, with more murder, pillage, and rape than had been seen in the Mediterranean since the days of the pirates.

GETTING TO AND AROUND

You'll never have to wait long for a ferry to Elba, especially during the summer. Gritty Piombino is the major point of departure. Any train going down the Tyrrhenian coast will take you as far as the station called Campiglia Marittima; from there the FS operates a regular shuttle train to Piombino (don't get off at the central station; the train has a short stop there and continues to the port). Two companies run services to Elba, TOREMAR (head office: Scali del Corso 5, Livorno, tel (0586) 22 772) and NAVARMA (head office: Piazzale Premuda 13, Piombino, tel (0565) 33 032). The most frequent passage is the 1-hour Piombino–Cavo–Portoferraio trip, and there are also TOREMAR ferries that go from Piombino to Rio Marina and then to Porto Azzurro (2 hours). Services to Elba can be as frequent as every half-hour in July, down to two or three in winter. TOREMAR also has a daily Livorno-Portoferraio run (5 hours) by way of Gorgona and Capraia. Note that the NAVARMA service is really a part of the ferry trip from Piombino to Bastia, in Corsica. To keep up with demand in the summer, TOREMAR also runs hydrofoils on the Piombino-Portoferraio run; these only take 30–40 minutes, but are more expensive.

Elba has an efficient bus service to all corners of the island, and buses depart with some frequency. The hub of the system is Portoferraio, with buses leaving and returning to the terminal by the Grattacielo, facing the harbour. There are a couple of **car hire** agencies on the island: Maggiore, Calata Italia 8, Portoferraio, tel 915 368; or Avis, Via IV Novembre, in Porto Azzurro, tel 95 000.

TOURIST INFORMATION

The office for the island is the Grattacielo, Calata Italia 26 in Portoferraio, just across from the ferry dock, tel (0565) 916 350; also in Piazza Virgilio, tel (0565) 914 671. In the summer the Livorno EPT runs a booth in Piombino, just across from the ferry dock, tel (0565) 36 432.

Portoferraio

Portoferraio, with 11,000 souls, is the capital and only city of Elba. The massive walls built by Duke Cosimo remain, though Portoferraio has spilled out westwards along the bay. Here the ferries dock at the Calata Italia, where the visitor's introduction to Elba is the **Gratticielo** ('skyscraper'), a 10-storey pile of peeling paint built in the 1950s that is one of the most endearingly hideous buildings in the Mediterranean. It is also the most important building for tourists, since it contains the tourist information office, most of the ferryboat offices, and the Portoferraio bus terminal at the back, with connections to all of Elba's towns and resorts.

Follow Calata Italia and its various pseudonyms under the walls, next the old U-shaped harbour. On the far side rises the **Torre del Martello**, from which in the old days a chain was stretched across the harbour in times of danger. The main gate of the city is the **Porta a Mare** at the base of the U, over which can be seen the inscription of Duke Cosimo reminding us with the accustomed Medicean vanity how he built the whole town 'from the foundations upwards'; the new town had originally been dubbed Cosmopolis.

Directly inside the Porta a Mare is **Piazza Cavour**. Portoferraio is a big natural amphitheatre; from the piazza the town slopes upwards in all directions towards the walls on the high cliffs. North of the Piazza, Via Garibaldi leads up to the main attraction, Napoleon's house, the **Palazzo dei Mulini** (9–2, Sun 9–1, closed Mon; adm). Napoleon had the house built according to his own simple tastes; inside can be seen his furnishings, books and other paraphernalia, including the flag with three golden bees that he bestowed on the Elbans. It's worth the trip just to see the contemporary political cartoons mocking the emperor. The gardens around the house offer fine views over the city walls. On either side you can see the two Medici fortresses dominating the highest points in the city: **Forte Falcone** to the west and **Forte Stella** to the east, the former still used by the Italian navy, the latter used as housing.

On the way down Via Garibaldi, you may want to stop at one of the parish churches, the **Misericordia** or the **Holy Sacrament**, both of which have copies of Napoleon's death mask; on 5 May the Misericordia holds a procession with a replica of Napoleon's coffin to commemorate his death. The **Town Hall**, originally a bakery for Cosimo's troops, was the boyhood home of Victor Hugo, whose father was the French military commander in Elba. There's a Roman altar displayed in the courtyard, and inside, the **Biblioteca Foresiana** has a collection of books about Elba and a small picture collection. Two blocks west is the **Teatro dei Vigilanti**, built by Napoleon around an abandoned church, while east of Via Garibaldi lies the **Piazza della Repubblica**, the throbbing heart of Portoferraio, with its crowded cafés, 18th-century **Cathedral**, not really a cathedral at all these days, and the nearby market.

Around Portoferraio

Most of Portoferraio's hotels and restaurants are in the modern extension outside the city walls. There's a pebble beach, **Le Ghiaie** on the north side, and another called **Le Viste** under the walls near Forte Falcone. Two roads lead from the capital, one along the northern coast to the small resorts of **Acquaviva** and **Viticcio**, and to **Capo d'Enfola**, a lovely headland rising sheer out of the sea, barely connected to the rest of the island.

The second road runs south to the junction of **Bivio Boni**, where it branches to the east and west. Nearby there is the thermal spa at **San Giovanni**, and the ruins of a Roman villa at **Le Grotte**, on the south shore of the Gulf of Portoferraio, more interesting for the view than the little that remains. There are beaches here at Ottone, Magazzini, and **Bagnaia**, the latter the site of the simple, beautiful 12th-century **Church of Santo Stefano**, the best Pisan monument in the archipelago. At **Acquabona** you can shoot some bogies at Elba's only golf course (9 holes), or continue west from Bivio Boni to the resort at **Biodola Bay** and the **Villa Napoleonica di San Martino**. The emperor soon tired of life in Portoferraio and built this house as his country retreat. In later years the husband of his niece (daughter of Jèrome) purchased the place and added a pretentious Neoclassical façade with big Ns pasted everywhere; it's now another Napoleonic museum (9–2, Sun 9–1, closed Mon).

Eastern Elba

Rio nell'Elba is the old mining centre, though it's not at all what one would expect a mining town to look like—it's as pleasant and pastel as any other Elban town, set in the hills overlooking the eastern coast. Archaeological sites, the scanty remains of mines and Etruscan mining camps dot the neighbourhood. There are many undeveloped beaches on the western side of Rio's peninsula, including Nisporto and Nisportino. The road between Portoferraio and Rio passes the steep hill of **Volterraio**, where you can make the long climb to the 11th-century Pisan castle on the summit.

Rio Marina, as its name implies, is the port for Rio nell'Elba. Here, the **Mineralogical Museum** (open Sat mornings, call ahead tel 962 001) in the Palazzo Comunale has displays of all the island's unusual rocks and minerals. Rio Marina has a busy harbour, its many small fishing boats under the vigilant eye of an octagonal Pisan watchtower. The eastern side of this peninsula, like the western side, has some fine beaches where you can sometimes escape the crowds—Ortano, Porticciolo, Barbarossa, and many others. On the northern tip stands **Cavo**, an older resort town on a tiny port.

Porto Azzurro and Capoliveri

South of Rio, the road passes through some difficult terrain towards **Porto Azzurro**, built by the Spaniards and now a large holiday town. Until 1947 it was called *Porto Longone*. The fortress, built in 1603 to withstand the Austrians and French, was later converted into a famous Italian calaboose that hosted many political prisoners and criminal celebrities. Besides the town beach, there are several others nearby, including a bizarre one at **Terrenere**, where a yellow-green sulphurous pond festers near the blue sea in a landscape of pebble beach and ancient mine debris—for those jaded travellers seeking something beyond Elba's mass tourism. During the season, day excursions run from Porto Azzurro to the island of Montecristo.

Just north of Porto Azzurro is the **Sanctuary of Monserrato**, a famous shrine with an icon known as the 'Black Madonna'. The Spanish governor built this here in 1606 because the mountain (Monte Castello) reminded him of the peculiar mountain of Monserrat near Barcelona. Similar Black Madonnas are revered from Portugal to Poland; over the centuries the oxidation of yellow paint has darkened them (just as it threatens Van Gogh's *Sunflowers*). South of Porto Azzurro is another Spanish fortress at **Capo Focardo**, on a large oval-shaped peninsula consisting of Monte Calamita and the rough hill country around it.

On this peninsula is **Capoliveri**, one of the oldest inhabited sites on the island. The town takes its name from the Roman *Caput Liberi*, which may refer either to the worship of Liber, an Italian equivalent of Dionysus (this has always been a wine-growing area) or to the free men (*liberi*) who lived there. In Roman times Capoliveri was an 'Alsatia', a refuge for any man who could escape to it. It has had a reputation for independence ever since, giving a bad time to the Pisans, the Spanish, and even Napoleon. Today it is a peaceful place, with fine views from its hilltop over the surrounding countryside and sea. Although Capoliveri is very scenic and surrounded by beaches, much of its coast is privately owned. South of Capoliveri, near the coast, is the **Sanctuary of the Madonna delle Grazie**, with a painting of the Madonna and Child by the school of Raphael, miraculously saved from a shipwreck. The coast west of Capoliveri is marked by two lovely broad gulfs, **Golfo Stella** and **Golfo della Lacona**, separated by a steep, narrow tongue of land. Both are developed resort areas, with centres at Lacona and Lido Margidore.

Western Elba

Beyond Biodola, the scenic corniche road west from Portoferraio passes through the adjacent resort towns of **Procchio** and **Campo all'Aia**, the former larger and one of the more expensive resorts on Elba. Seven km west is **Marciana Marina**, another popular resort, with a 15th-century Pisan watchtower, the **Torre Saracena**. This is the port for Marciana, the oldest continuously inhabited town on Elba.

In the 14th and 15th centuries, when life near the coast wasn't safe, Marciana was the 'capital' of the feudal Appiani barons, the most powerful family on the island. Today, high in the mountain forests on the slopes of Monte Capanne, it is a surprisingly beautiful town of narrow streets, stone stairs, archways, and belvederes. Sections of the old city wall and gate are still intact, and the old Pisan **fortress** hangs over the town (not open to visitors). The palace of the Appiani may be seen on a narrow *vicolo* in the oldest part of town. Marciana's **Archaeology Museum** (10–12:30 and 4–7:30, closed Wed and from Oct–Mar) has a small collection of prehistoric and Roman objects found in the area. From Marciana a cable lift climbs to the summit of Elba's highest peak, **Monte Capanne**, with stupendous views over Corsica, the Tuscan archipelago, and the mountains of Tuscany itself.

Three churches outside of Marciana are of interest: the ruined Pisan **San Lorenzo**, the **Sanctuary of San Cerbone**, who escaped here from the troublesome Lombards (later his body was buried in a miraculous rainstorm, so the Lombards wouldn't see), and the **Sanctuary of the Madonna del Monte**, dating from the 11th century and one of the most important shrines on the island. Pagan Elbans may have worshipped on this site as well, as did Napoleon for two weeks, after a fashion, with his Polish mistress, Maria Walewska. Another mountain village, almost a twin of Marciana, is **Poggio**, just to the east. Poggio has a natural spring where the Elbans bottle their local *acqua minerale*—called Napoleone, of course. It's very good, but the Elbans keep it all to themselves.

On the rugged coast to the west and south of Marciana, there are yet more beaches and resorts: **Sant'Andrea, Patresi, Chiessi, Pomonte, Fetovaia** (a lovely stretch, protected by a rocky promontory), **Seccheto** and **Cavoli**. Seccheto has ancient granite quarries from which the stone was cut for the Pantheon in Rome.

Seven km east of Marciana stretches Elba's pocket-sized plain, the **Campo nell'Elba**, extending across the island from Procchio to Marina di Campo, separating the western mountains from the central range. Elba's small airport is here—it is the only place they could put it. Two old, pretty towns lie on the edge of the plain: **Sant'Ilario in Campo** and **San Piero in Campo**. San Piero's parish church of San Niccolò has interesting frescoes; it was built on the ruins of an ancient temple to Glaucus. Halfway between the two towns are the ruins of the Pisan church of **San Giovanni**, along with a Pisan watchtower. On the coast is **Marina di Campo**, Elba's first and perhaps largest resort, with the largest beach. The watchtower in the harbour was built by the Medici.

WHERE TO STAY (tel prefix 0565)

With more than 150 hotels around the island, Elba has something for everyone. The emphasis is on the not-too-expensive resort, attractive to family holiday-makers. Many hotels stay open all the year round, with substantial off-season discounts. Beware, however, that Elba is a big package-tour destination, and despite its scores of lodgings, book ahead to avoid disappointment.

If you want to stay in Portoferraio, an interesting possibility is the **Ape Elbana**, Via de'Medici 2, tel 92 245. The 'Elban Bee' is the oldest hotel on the island; it entertained Napoleon's guests (L60 000, all with bath). For something a little more up-to-date, ****Villa Ottone**, at Ottone, tel 966 042, is in a 19th-century villa right on the beach, with a shady garden and tennis, open all year (L200–230 000). Some of the city's hotels are near the beach of Le Ghiaie and the city park; one that is quite pleasant is the ***Villa Ombrosa**, Viale de Gasperi, no 3, tel 92 363 (L62–85 000, depending on the plumbing). The resorts begin where Portoferraio's suburbs end. Some areas within a few kilometres offer good value in lovely settings, such as the ***Mare**, at Magazzini, tel 966 069 (L80 000, all with bath); and **Tirrena**, also at Magazzini, tel 966 002, (L60 000, all with bath). Further out in peaceful Bagnaia, **Clara**, tel 961 077, a little hotel with a garden (L58 000, all with bath). South of Portoferraio at Acquabona is the ***Acquabona Golf Hotel**, tel 940 064, with Elba's only golf course—sorry, there's only room for 9 holes—as well as a swimming pool and tennis and comfortable, well-equipped rooms (L90–100 000).

At Cavo, on the east coast, prices tend to be slightly lower, and as Porto Azzurro tends to be crowded, there are plenty of campsites and holiday apartments there. The same is true of most of the beaches on the southeastern peninsula around Capoliveri, although many pleasant hotels are right on the beach like **La Voce del Mare**, at Naregno beach, tel 968 455 (L45–50 000 without bath, L55–65 000 with). The best beach on Elba may be at Cavoli, west of Campo nell'Elba; there you'll find **La Conchiglia**, tel 987 010, small and air-conditioned (L55–65 000, all rooms with bath). Of the resorts on the west end of the island, there are some smart establishments around Procchio, more modest hotels at Santa Andre and Pomonte, and some which are blissfully out of the way, like the **Andreina** at La Cala, west of Marciana Marina, tel 908 150 (L50 000 without bath, L65 000 with).

EATING OUT

In the long list of restaurants on the island, few really stand out. What does stand out is Elba's DOC wines; both *Elba rosso* and *Elba bianco* can hold their own with any in Tuscany. To start with, while you're waiting for the ferry at Piombino you might try the **Ristorante Terrazza**, above the bar in the port area, Piazza Premuda, tel (0565) 35 135, with delicious *spaghetti alle vongole* and a big picture window with a panoramic view of Piombino's steel mills (L22 000).

One of the most popular places to eat in Portoferraio, right in Piazza della Repubblica 22, is **La Ferrigna**, tel 914 129, offering some extravagant sorts of seafood antipasti, stuffed roast fish, and an Elban version of Livornese *cacciucco*; there are tables on the convivial piazza (L40 000; closed Tues). **La Bussola**, in Portoferraio at Le Ghiaie (the pebble beach north of town), tel 915 091, does tasty swordfish, and every other sort of grilled fish you can pronounce in Italian for a bargain L30 000 or so. In Capoliveri,

Chiasso, Via Nazario Sauro 20, tel 968 709, offers sole stuffed with shrimp and an Elban favourite that rarely travels to the mainland, *risotto al nero di seppia* (with cuttlefish in its own ink), (L50 000; closed Tues). In Portoferraio, **Arsa** is a good, honest, inexpensive trattoria by the port, at Via Manzoni 8 (L24–32 000). Pizzerias and seafood places abound in answer to demand, and one place where you can have both is the **Garden**, Via Vittorio Emanuele 14 (L40 000). In Porto Azzurro, among the many seafood restaurants on the beach, is the **Delfino Verde**, Lungomare Vitaliani, tel 95 197, built over the sea for a fine view (L45 000 and up). At Poggio, 3 km from Marciana, **Publius**, Piazza XX Settembre 13, tel 99 208, is as worth visiting for its lovely views as for its menu, with items you won't find elsewhere on the island: *pappardelle* in boar sauce, *fagioli al fiasco* (Tuscan beans), and game in season—as well as good fish dishes (L45 000).

Pianosa and Montecristo

Two other members of the Tuscan archipelago are included in Livorno province: one you won't want to visit, and the other you usually can't. **Pianosa** is the black sheep of the chain. Its name, taken from the Roman *Planasia*, explains why—it's as flat as a pool table. Like Gorgona, Pianosa's unhappy fate is to serve as a prison island. There are some substantial ruins of a Roman villa, from the days when Pianosa was the playground of Cornelius Agrippa, Emperor Augustus' great general, but to see them you'll need special permission from the prison authorities in Rome.

Likewise, don't count on visiting **Montecristo**, 40 km south of Elba. Once the hunting preserve of King Vittorio Emanuele III, the tiny island, no more than the cone of an ancient volcano poking above the sea, has recently been declared a nature reserve. Private boats, and day trips organized from Porto Azzurro on Elba are allowed to dock at Cala Maestra, one of the many coves around the island's coast, but visitors are only allowed to stay on the cove and its beach; the mountain, ruins of a medieval monastery, and the royal villa (now the custodian's house) are strictly out of bounds. In Roman times this was an important religious site, *Mons Jovis*, with a famous temple of Jupiter on the summit; not a trace of it remains. The early Church wasted no time Christianizing the place, renaming it Montecristo. The first monastic community was founded in the 6th century by San Mamiliano (see Giglio), who reportedly killed a dragon upon arrival. None of the action of the *Count of Montecristo* is really set here; like most of us, seeing the place on a map is probably as close as Alexandre Dumas ever got.

The Maremma

In a sense, this flat and lonely stretch of coast south of Piombino really belongs to Italy's south. As on the islands, history has been extraordinarily unkind to the Maremma, domain first of the Etruscans, later of the anopheles mosquito. Like so many of the southern coastal regions, the Maremma was a prosperous, happy agricultural region throughout classical times. The Romans gave it its name: the 'maritime' zone (recalled in place names like Massa Marittima) gradually mangled over the centuries into Maremma.

Historians sometimes give the Romans too much credit for capable governance; on the contrary, their grasping, bureaucratic state slowly corroded and destroyed the Italian economy. Many centuries of Roman misgovernment—impossible taxes, cheap imported grain and in this case, neglect of the Etruscans' system of drainage canals—doomed the Maremma to a slow death. When the drainage canals failed, much of the land was abandoned and reverted to swamps, breeding the malarial mosquitoes that made the Maremma of the Middle Ages a place of suffering and death, inhabitable only for the *butteri*, tough Maremma cowboys that tended the herds in the abandoned marshy pastures. A considerable body of folklore has grown up around the *butteri*, and the Maremma's proudest moment came in the last century when some of them defeated Buffalo Bill and his travelling Wild West show in a test of cowboy know-how. The first work of reclamation began with the Austrian Grand Dukes. The Italian Kingdom that followed them forgot all about the Maremma, and it was not until after World War II that the task was completed. The Maremma today is back on its feet, a new region and a little rough around the edges, but prosperous once again.

Follonica and Punta Ala

After Piombino, the coast bends eastwards into a broad arc, the Golfo di Follonica. Since the war, new resort towns have been popping up like toadstools all along the Tuscan coast. One of the biggest and least likeable is **Follonica**, 21 km east of Piombino, redeemed partially by the long pine groves that follow its crowded beaches. Forget the beaches; Follonica has other enchantments, notably the **Museum of Iron and Cast Iron**, in an old foundry of the 1830s where Elban iron once was smelted. On the promontory that closes the gulf, 14 km to the south, **Punta Ala** is a new, entirely synthetic resort, built in the suburban style of the Costa Smeralda. It's an attractive location, with a fine sandy beach and views around the gulf, and it attracts a very well-heeled clientele with unusual (for Tuscany) diversions like golf (at the Golf Hotel, Via del Gualdo) and polo (Polo Club, tel 922 013).

Castiglione della Pescaia, to the south, is just the opposite, a much less exclusive resort attached to an ancient fishing village. The beach isn't the best around, and the modern resort strip has a blowsy air, but the town itself, up on its hill, full of trees and ivy-covered walls, makes one of the more pleasant detours on this coast. The Spanish left behind a 16th-century castle, the Rocca Aragonese, and the church of San Giovanni has an interesting round tower that could pass for a Moorish minaret.

Grosseto

When Duke Cosimo I gobbled up Grosseto in 1559, along with the rest of the Sienese republic, he resolved to make it into a fortress town, guarding his southern borders against Spain and the pope. Following the manic geometry of the age, Cosimo's architects enclosed Grosseto in a perfect hexagon of walls. But as any good Chinese geomancer (or reader of Doris Lessing's *Shikasta*) could have told the Duke, one can't take such matters lightly. Maybe it was the wrong polygon for the prevailing telluric forces, but Grosseto (pop. 70,000) has certainly been suffering from some strange vibrations. Come to Grosseto, and you will find a city of Art Nouveau buildings and perverse teenagers, a city conducive to hallucinations, its streets alive with swirls of dust and flying plastic bags. Its citizens have a penchant for punk music and American football (the Grosseto 61'ers), also, so they claim, the highest rate of drug addiction in Italy. It is the only city in Italy, outside Calabria, where you cannot buy a decent slice of pizza.

GETTING AROUND

Trains depart regularly for Siena (73 km, 1 1/2 hrs), and on the coastal line for Livorno (134 km, 2 1/2 hrs) or Orbetello (22 km) and Rome (187 km, 3 hrs). The RAMA bus station, with connections to Siena and every town in Grosseto province, including Massa Marittima (see Hill Towns West of Siena p. 316), Arcidosso and Pitigliano (see Southern Tuscany p. 337) is a ramshackle nest of buildings on Via Oberdan, near the **post office**. Buses are likely to stop anywhere on the surrounding streets; get a few opinions in advance as to where yours might be.

TOURIST INFORMATION

On Corso Carducci, near the cathedral, tel (0564) 488 207.

Around La Vasca

Via Carducci leads you from the station towards the fearful hexagon, passing Mussolini's contribution to the city, a circular piazza called **La Vasca** (which can mean the 'tub' or the 'toilet bowl'); here the starring role is played by an exuberant Mussolini **post office**, with heroic statuary in travertine. The main gate is only a block away. Cosimo's walls are perfectly preserved, done in tidy, reddish brick festooned with Medici balls. Much of the old city looks very Spanish; the Art Nouveau pharmacies and shoe shops along the main street, Corso Carducci, contribute to the effect, as does the arcaded Piazza del Duomo, very like a Spanish *Plaza Mayor*. The **Duomo**, built 1190–1250, suffered grievously from over-ambitious restoration in the 1840s; the façade has more the appearance of a Hollywood prop than a genuine cathedral. Around the side, there is an interesting sundial, and in the piazza an allegorical monument to the Maremma's great benefactor, the Lorraine Grand Duke Leopold II; the woman he is raising up represents the suffering Maremma, and the snake he's crushing is Malaria.

Around the corner in Piazza Baccarini, the **Archaeology Museum of the Maremma** wants to show you something of life in this region before there ever was a Grosseto. Some parts of the Mediterranean coastline just can't stand still. Thousands of years ago, Grosseto and most of its surrounding plain were under water; by the time of the Etruscans, the sea had receded, leaving a large lake on the plain. Two wealthy Etruscan cities, Vetulonia and Roselle (see p. 281), stood on the hills above the lake, and they contributed most of the items here: cinerary urns with scenes from Homer, architectural fragments, and best of all the delicate terracottas, some preserving bits of their original paint. The collection is not a rich one, though well organized and relentlessly didactic. Up on the third floor, the city **Pinacoteca** has some good Sienese art, including an amazing *Last Judgement* scene by the 13th-century artist Guido da Siena (daily except Wed, 9–1, 4:30–8 pm; Sun 9–12:30; adm).

Just north of the museum, **San Francesco** church has an early work of Duccio di Buoninsegna, the crucifix above the high altar, and some good 13th-century frescoes with haunting eyes. From here, you can start a walk around the Medicean walls. After Italian unification, the bastions were landscaped into beautiful semi-tropical gardens; some are still well kept today, while others have decayed into spooky jungles. The liveliest part of Grosseto is in the shopping streets around the Piazza del Mercato; nearby, just outside the walls, the mornings see a large, almost picturesque street market.

Roselle and Vetulonia

In fact, you can learn much more about these two Etruscan towns from the Grosseto museum than from actually visiting the ruins. **Roselle**, 7 km north of the city, just off the main road to Siena, is the mother city of Grosseto. It survived Roman rule better than many other Etruscan cities, but writers of the 5th century report it being almost abandoned. Nevertheless, the bishops of Roselle hung on until 1178, when the seat was transferred to Grosseto. Like so many other Etruscan towns, Roselle stands atop a high plateau. Foundations of a few buildings are visible, along with the outline of the Roman amphitheatre, a medieval tower, and necropolises all around.

Vetulonia, 17 km from Grosseto, out in empty countryside west of the village of Braccagni, lives on in the modern city of Massa Marittima. Like Roselle, it lasted until the Middle Ages, and seems to have been destroyed in a 14th-century revolt against its Pisan overlords. The scanty ruins are more Roman and medieval than Etruscan, but the periphery has some interesting tombs, the massive **Tomba della Pietrera** and the unique tomb called 'Il Diavolino', a long corridor leading under a tumulus, with an arched burial chamber in the middle that had an opening to the sky.

WHERE TO STAY AND EATING OUT (tel prefix 0564)

If evil chance should find you spending time in Grosseto, at least there are some good restaurants for consolation. Hotels tend to be simple; the ***Appennino**, at Viale Mameli, tel 23 009, is plain and well kept (L38–45 000). Generally acclaimed as the best restaurant in the Maremma, **Enoteca Ombrone**, Viale Matteotti 69, tel 22 585, may be over the top in many respects (they have not only a wine list, but an olive oil list), but sincerely devoted to finding the best ingredients and preparing them with artistic balance and judgement. Both Maremma cuisine (dishes like *tortelli Maremmani*, filled with ricotta, beetroot and spinach or the local version of *cacciucco*, or maybe stewed boar) and international dishes; people come here from all over southern Tuscany (L65 000). For something less exalted, there is simple good cooking at **Dal Ghepa**, Via Vinzaglio 11, tel 22 239 (*tortelli alla Maremma* is a speciality) or the **Italiana** in Via Aurelia Saffi, tel 22 452, both in the L20 000 range.

There's an excellent seafood restaurant on at Via Vittorio Veneto 27 in Castiglione della Pescaia, tel 933 524. The dish to try at the **Miramare** is the *tesoro di Montecristo*, a delicious mixed grill of fish. All the dishes are innovative—like crêpes filled with prawns and baked spaghetti *al cartoccio* (L65 000).

Monti dell'Uccellina: The Maremma Nature Park

One side effect of the Maremma's long history of abandonment is a relatively unspoiled coastline. In the 1950s and 60s, developers followed the DDT wherever they could, but the Italian government managed to set aside a few of the best parts. The **Monti dell'Uccellina**, a ragged chain of coastal hills south of Grosseto, largely covered with groves of parasol pines, is a favourite rest stop for migratory birds between Europe and Africa, hence the name. For such a small area, about 5 by 15 km, the park has a lot to see: nine old Spanish, Sienese or grand-ducal defence towers, dozens of caves (one of which gave up bones of some of Italy's earliest inhabitants) and the ruins of an 11th-century monastery, **San Rabano**, retaining its campanile and some interesting early medieval stonecarving. Despite the park status, some people are still making a living here, herding cattle, cutting cork oak, and gathering pine nuts for Italy's pastry cooks.

The park's landscapes range from swamps to heather and rosemary-scented *macchia* (mixed Mediterranean scrub) to lovely pine groves, and it includes among its fauna herds of wild horses, deer, and boar, along of course with the *ucelline*—herons, eagles and falcons, ospreys and kingfishers, every sort of duck, and even that most overdressed of all waterfowl, the *cavaliere d'Italia*. (The park's visitors' centre is at Alberese, west of the coastal highway, the Via Aurelia (N. 1). At present, the park is open all year round, although some sections can only be visited by guided tour; it's best to call ahead, tel (0564) 407 098; also ask about guided tours in English during the summer; adm.)

Talamone

The Sienese republic never really had a port of its own, a great disadvantage for its foreign trade. Now and again, the Sienese would try to make one out of **Talamone**, a fishing village at the southern tip of the Monti dell'Uccellina. Unfortunately, the little harbour could not be kept clear, a continuing embarrassment for the republic; even Dante dropped a jibe about foolishly 'hoping from Talamone'. Garibaldi had better luck here. When he and his 'Thousand' decided to stop here instead of in Sardinia in 1860, they avoided the orders for their arrest that had treacherously been sent by Count Cavour; Garibaldi also found a cache of weapons in nearby Orbetello that came in handy during the conquest of Sicily.

Today the walled village on its rock has become a discreet, laid-back resort with a small marina. Above it, a blank, grey 16th-century Spanish castle sits like some sort of abstract modern sculpture. A new museum devoted to nature in the Monti dell'Uccellina is planned for it.

Monte Argentario

In the last decade or two, this curiosity of the Tuscan coast has become quite popular. It has a lot going for it: some attractive old towns, a genuine Mediterranean feeling and Mediterranean scenery, a standout attraction on the humdrum Tuscan coast. Once, perhaps thousands of years ago, Argentario was an island, the member of the Tuscan archipelago closest to the shore. No one seems able to explain just how it happened, but the Tyrrhenian currents gradually built up two sand bars, connecting the rugged, mountainous island to the mainland. In between, there was a peninsula with the Etruscan, then Roman city of Orbetello; the Romans built a causeway on to Argentario that split the natural lagoon in half. There's a story that sailors gave the Argentario its name in classical times, noticing the flashes of silver from the olive leaves that still cover the mountain slopes.

Most books on Italy that mention the Argentario describe Porto S. Stefano and Porto Ercole, its two resorts, as 'exclusive', even 'posh'. Not true. The Argentario attracts its share of the high life, but restaurants and hotels are not necessarily more expensive than other resorts. Neither has the peninsula become an overcrowded beach Babylon like Elba. However, the beaches are not special and Tuscany's art and other attractions are far away. On balance, though, if you're looking for the best place to spend a seaside vacation in Tuscany, the Argentario presents a pretty strong case.

GETTING AROUND

Orbetello is the centre for public transport around the Argentario, with a small bus station facing the northern lagoon, just off Piazza della Repubblica; buses leave regularly for Porto Ercole, Porto S. Stefano, Grosseto, and for the railway station, about 2 km east of town, a stop on the Grosseto-Rome coastal line. There are also daily buses to Capalbio and Pitigliano.

TOURIST INFORMATION

Orbetello: Piazza della Repubblica, tel (0564) 867 389.
Porto S. Stefano: Corso Umberto 55a, tel (0564) 814 208.

Orbetello

Go up to the northern tip of Orbetello's peninsula, near the causeway, and look over the edge of the water; in places, below the modern breakwater, you will see bits of ancient wall in huge irregular blocks. This is all that remains of Etruscan Orbetello, probably the biggest port of the Etruscan coasts. The easily defensible port has given the city at least a minor historical role over the centuries. The Byzantines held out longer here than anywhere else on the Tyrrhenian coast, and after them somehow the city fell into the hands of the Three Fountains Abbey in Rome, who passed it on to the pope—until 1980 the popes were also bishops of Orbetello. After the treaty of Câteau-Cambresis in 1559, settling political arrangements across Italy, Orbetello found itself the capital of a new state—the Spanish military *Presidio*, ruled by a viceroy directly responsible to the King of Spain.

The Spanish Presidio lasted only until 1707, but it left behind a strong influence in the buildings and the people of this area. Orbetello was something of a resort a century ago, a role now passed on to Porto Ercole and Porto S. Stefano; its most recent flash of glory came in the 1930s when Mussolini made it Italy's main seaplane base; Fascist hero Italo Balbo began his famous transatlantic flight here in 1933, landing at the opening of the Chicago World's Fair.

Confined on its narrow peninsula, with its palm trees and sun-bleached Spanish walls, Orbetello (pop. 13,500) is a charming town. Buses barely squeeze through the main gate in the land walls, decorated with the arms of the King of Spain. Off to the left, an unusual Spanish arsenal, the **Polveriera de Guzman**, now houses a small archaeological museum. Viale Italia is the main street, running down the centre of the peninsula. Just to the north, the **Cathedral** on Piazza della Repubblica has a beautiful façade with a sculpted portal and rose window from 1376; its interior was rebuilt in the 1600's. At the town hall, across the piazza, you can see the **Frontone di Talamone**, the pediment of an Etruscan temple, reconstructed from fragments found at Talamone; the reliefs portray mythological scenes of the Theban kings.

Orbetello's **lagoons**, on average about a yard deep, are partially used for fish farms, but most of the northern half has been declared a nature preserve, run by the World Wildlife Fund. Like the Monti dell'Uccellina, the area is an important breeding ground for marine birds, and also storks and a species of eagle, not to mention the stilt plover, the bee-eater, and the lesser hen harrier. When they're nesting, from April to October, the preserve is closed to humans; otherwise there is a visitors' centre and guides to show you around (on the coast road between Orbetello and Albinia; tours Thurs and Sun only at 10 and 2).

Porto Ercole and Porto Santo Stefano

Over the causeway from Orbetello on to Monte Argentario, you can go either north or south to begin the *gita panoramica*, the 24-km road (not completely paved) that circles the island. To the south, **Porto Ercole** wraps itself around a tiny fishing harbour, guarded on either side by Spanish fortresses. Forte Stella and Forte San Filippo were probably the last word in 16th-century military architecture, with low, sloping walls and pointed bastions draped over the cliffs; they present an ominous, surreal sight today. San Filippo is the most interesting, though you can't visit—it has been converted into holiday condominiums. Above the souvenir shops and seafood restaurants of the harbour, there is a fine old town, entered through a Gothic gate constructed by the Sienese. Little Piazza Santa Barbara is the centre, with the dignified 17th-century palace of the Spanish governor, and a view over the harbour below. Caravaggio was buried in the church of Sant'Erasmo in 1609 after washing up on the beach nearby. Beyond Porto Ercole, the coast road twists and turns under the slopes of Il Telegrafo, Argentario's highest peak (635 m). One feature of the *gita panoramica* is the many defence towers, some built by the Sienese, others by the Spaniards.

On the northern side of the Argentario, **Porto S. Stefano** makes a matching bookend for Porto Ercole. A bit larger and trendier than its sister town, this one also began as a sleepy fishing village, though now the fishing boats are elbowed off to the side of the port by speedboats, big, shiny yachts and the Giglio ferries, and the old town has become lost in the agglomeration of hotels and villas on the surrounding hills. There are really two harbours, the first, larger one has the ferries and the fish markets; the yachts—and some real dreadnoughts they are—call at the western harbour, at the other side of a small promontory.

WHERE TO STAY (tel prefix 0564)

For accommodation we'll get the extremes out of the way first. If you're travelling on a budget and just want to pass through for a look at the Argentario, the ***Piccolo Parigi** on Corso Italia 169, tel 867 233, is a delightful, very friendly and very Mediterranean establishment in the middle of Orbetello (L33–50 000, depending on season and plumbing). If, on the other hand, you've bushels of money to spend and like swilling gin with yachtsmen and Italian TV stars, try ******Il Pellicano**. This Relais & Chateaux hotel is located on Cala dei Santi, a cove near Porto Ercole, tel 833 801; all imaginable amenities are provided, along with a pool and beach, with possibilities for windsurfing and every other water sport, and tennis—not to mention the presence of a first-class restaurant—all this for only L350–550 000 (much less in the off season).

In between, there is a wider choice at Porto S. Stefano than at Porto Ercole, where the ***Don Pedro** has a nice location on the Via Panoramica, tel 833 914, but is some way off from the nearest beach (L70–85 000). Porto S. Stefano's best is the ***Girasole**, tel 812 647, with 20 rooms, close to the beaches at Poggio Calvella (L65–75 000). A simple hotel in the centre of the action around the harbour is the ***Alfiero**, tel 814 067 (L36–48 000). If you're planning an extended stay in the area, there's a hotel residence hidden away on the western tip of the peninsula. ****Torre di Calapiccola**, tel (050) 572 455, is an apartment complex in a great setting, with a beach and plenty of activities, or equal doses of peace and quiet if that's what you're looking for (L100–200 000, almost half that in low season).

EATING OUT

Orbetello: Here the local favourite is the **Pizzeria Gennaro** on Viale Italia, with solid home cooking, including seafood, for about L20 000 or less, or half that for pizza and drinks. And on the subject of pizza, just a bit down the block, Orbetello can claim the absolutely best *pizza a taglio* (by the slice) stand in all Tuscany; three toques and best wishes for continued success to the **Pizzeria Il Fornetto** (about L1200).

Porto Ercole: **La Lampara** is an outstanding restaurant right on the port, where the cooking is more or less Neapolitan—so of course there's pizza, too (Lungomare Andrea Doria 67, tel 833 024; outside tables, grilled fish for L35–40 000). For fancier seafood, like spaghetti with lobster sauce, at fancier prices, try the **Gambero Rosso** next door, tel 832 650—good *zuppa di pesce* on weekends (L50–60 000).

Porto S. Stefano: Some of the places here are almost too swank to be in such a little resort town: chief offender is the impeccably elegant **Dal Greco** on the yacht harbour, Via del Molo, tel 814 885. A *terrino di pesce* with vegetables is the star attraction, along with lobster and a wide choice of other dishes (L60 000). On the other harbour, at Piazzale Facchinetti, **Il Delfino**, tel 818 394, has semi-outdoor dining (pleasant, but a little close to traffic), and some more inventive seafood concoctions; they also pride themselves on their homemade desserts and ice cream (about L45 000). A less expensive place, and consequently very popular with the locals, is **La Formica**, tel 814 205, with a famous *risotto* involving caviar and prawns, and a bill of about L40 000; closed Wed. It's out at Pozzarello, about a 1.5 km east of town. Besides that, there's the **Mini Mouse Pub** on the yacht harbour, with some startling sandwiches (and very good, too), and every imaginable brand of beer from around the world.

Giglio and Giannutri

Giglio is the largest of the Tuscan islands after Elba, measuring about 21 km by 8. It is also second in population, with about 1600 souls, almost all of them in the three small villages, Giglio Porto, Giglio Castello and Campese. Like so many of the Italian islands, Giglio suffered grievously from deforestation and abandonment of the land in the last two centuries. Though much of it is still green and pretty, large sections have become almost barren. A remarkable change in the environmental consciousness of the Giglians seems to have taken place over the last few years; if the big signs posted all over the harbour are any indication, they've gone to the opposite extreme—no camping, no noise, no riding over the wild flowers, (and no collecting rocks—they're part of the island too!).

The word *Giglio* means lily, and the lily has become the island's symbol, although it has in fact nothing to do with the island's name. The Romans called it *Aegilium* or *Gilium*. Under them, Giglio like most of the other Italian islands was a resort for the very wealthy. Pisa, Aragon, and various feudal families held the island in the Middle Ages. Duke Cosimo seized it for Tuscany in the 16th century, but did little to protect it against its greatest danger, pirates. Fortunately, the Giglians had the holy right arm of San Mamiliano to protect them. This 6th-century Sicilian bishop, fleeing from the Arian heretics, became a hermit on Montecristo. When he died, a divine signal alerted fishermen from Elba, Giglio and even Genoa, who arrived at the same time and began to fight over the remains. In the true tradition of Christian brotherhood, they struck a deal and cut Mamiliano in three pieces. Giglio got the arm, which proved its worth by chasing away Turkish pirates in 1799. On other occasions it wasn't so helpful. The redoubtable pirate Barbarossa carried off most of the population in 1534, and his understudy Dragut came back for the rest in 1550.

GETTING AROUND

Porto S. Stefano is the main port for Giglio, a one-hour run twice daily, and more frequently in the summer on the TOREMAR line. The railway station for Porto S. Stefano, along the main Livorno-Rome line, is Orbetello Scalo; buses meet the trains to carry passengers to the port. Giannutri can be reached on a regular basis only in July and August, on a daily boat from Porto S. Stefano. On Giglio, buses run fairly regularly from the ferry dock to Giglio Castello and Campese.

TOURIST INFORMATION

In Giglio Porto at Via Umberto I 48, tel (0564) 809 265.

WHAT TO SEE

Giglio Porto, the island's metropolis, is a colourful place, with red and green light-houses to welcome the ferries, and pink and beige houses straggling up the hills. There are two beaches south of the town, at **Cala delle Canelle** and **Cala delle Caldane**, one to the north at **Punta Aranella**, all more or less developed, and in the town itself, the world's smallest beach, tucked behind the houses on the left side of the port. From Giglio Porto a difficult mountain road leads up to **Giglio Castello**, the only secure refuge in pirate days, and until recently the only real town. The fortress itself was begun by the Pisans and completed under the grand dukes. The picturesque town inside, all medieval alleys and overhanging arches, has plenty of gulls and swallows, a few lazy German tourists, and a small Baroque church with an odd tower where you can see the famous arm of San Mamiliano.

From Giglio Castello, a road leads southwards past **Poggio della Pagana**, the island's highest peak (530 m), through land largely reforested with pines to Punta del Capel Rosso, at the southern tip, then back along the coast to Giglio Porto. The main road from

Giglio Castello continues on to **Campese**, a growing resort area with an old watchtower and a large sandy beach.

Giannutri

Giannutri, the southernmost island of the Tuscan archipelago, is a rocky crescent about 5 km long, with little water and no fertile ground, and so little history to speak of. The ancient Greeks knew it as *Artemisia*, and the Romans as *Dianium*; perhaps the associations with the moon goddess came from the island's crescent shape. In Roman times it was an estate of the noble Ahenobarbus family, and substantial ruins of a **Roman Villa** (1st century AD) near Cala Maestra are visited by day trippers from Porto S. Stefano in the summer months. Though Giannutri has no permanent population, there are a tourist village and a few holiday cottages near the well-protected bay, **Cala Spalmatoio**, on the northern coast.

WHERE TO STAY AND EATING OUT (tel prefix 0564)

The number of tourists, and of hotels (13) on Giglio, seems to have stabilized in the last few years, leaving it not entirely overcrowded even in the summer months. Right in the port there's ***__Demo's__**, Via Thaon De Revel, tel 809 235, a little flash in the '60s Miami Beach style (L55–80 000), and the smaller, cosier **__La Pergola__** next door, tel 809 051, (L48–55 000). But persevere until you leave the Porto and you can enjoy the more serene ***__Arenella__**, close to the beach on Via Arenella 5, tel 809 340, with a pretty garden and a good restaurant (L55–80 000). And if you really want to get away from it all, your best chance on the entire Tuscan coast is **__Pardini's Hermitage__**. Located at a quiet cove called Cala degli Alberi, tel 809 034, this place can only by reached by boat (ask at the Giglio Sub shop on the port, but it's better to book as there are only ten rooms). They'll keep you busy with sports and nature activities if you want, or you can just enjoy the sea and mountains by yourself (prices for full board per person range from L90–120 000; basic double room is L50–60 000 with bath). A good, modern beach hotel off in Campese is the **__Campese__**, Via della Torre 18, tel 804 003 (L63–75 000).

Giglio Porto has its share of seafood restaurants around the harbour. **La Margherita**, tel 80–9 237, is probably the most popular; good fish and a terrace right on the beach (L30–40 000). The real find on the island, however, is up in Giglio Castello: **Da Maria**, on Via Casamatta, tel 806 062; not only good seafood (like stuffed squid or lobster flambé) but game dishes like the house speciality, wild rabbit *alla cacciatora* (L30–40 000).

Capalbio and the Giardino dei Tarocchi

Back on the coast, 8 km south of Orbetello, almost nothing is left of ancient **Ansedonia**, thoroughly destroyed by the Sienese in 1330. There's a long beach, a hotel or two, and some unusual souvenirs of the Etruscans, deep channels laboriously cut out of the solid rock; it is believed their purpose was to keep the small harbour from silting up. If it's ruins you're after, though, ascend the steep hill above Ansedonia to **Cosa**, a city founded by the Romans in the 3rd century BC, settled with loyal Roman citizens to keep an eye on the restless Etruscan cities nearby—and perhaps planned to help along their economic decline by draining off trade. Cosa never recovered after the Visigoths sacked it in the 5th century, but its recently excavated ruins (work is still under way) are enough to get an idea of what the city was like: a typical Roman rectangular circuit of walls, a strict grid of paved streets, a 'Capitoline' temple, and cisterns to catch rain water. There is also a small museum on the site.

Before the coastal highway (N. 1) passes from Tuscany into Lazio, it runs along the edge of another World Wildlife Fund project, a nature reserve at a narrow lagoon called **Lago di Burano**. Though small, the lagoon shelters the same impressive variety of birds as the Monti dell'Uccellina and the Orbetello lagoons; it is also the summer home of perhaps the only cranes (*fenicotteri*) left on the Italian mainland (tours Thurs and Sun at 10 am and 2 pm; closed in June and July when the birds are nesting).

Capalbio, 6 km inland, is one of the loveliest villages in southern Tuscany, a circular, walled hilltop enclave built around a castle of the Aldobrandeschi family. The pretty 12th-century parish church has some bits of frescoes inside. A few kilometres to the east, though, almost on the Lazio border, you can stop for a sneak preview of what may someday be one of the best-known sights in Tuscany.

The **Giardino dei Tarocchi**, still under construction, is the project of a French artist named Niki de Sant-Phalle. Someone is putting a lot of money into this place; the intention is to create a monumental sculptural work representing each of the 22 major arcana of the Tarot deck, a sort of garden for abstruse meditation. Already at least seven of them are completed, mad, brilliant works in concrete, brightly coloured ceramics and mirrors that show the strong influence of Antoni Gaudi's architecture in Barcelona. A few are over 12 m tall, glittering over the Maremma coast like some interplanetary Luna Park. The artist's symbolism is often obscure, but some works, like the broken *Tower*, are unmistakeable. (During construction, the site is open Sat and Sun only, 4–7:30 from June through September, 2–4:30 the rest of the year.)

Over the Border

If you're passing through here on the way to Rome, there are a few attractions in Rome's region of Lazio to distract you along the way. The biggest and richest Etruscan cities were here, not in Tuscany, and consequently the finest painted tombs can be seen along the north Lazio coast at **Tarquinia** and **Cervetri**. Not much has happened on this lonely shore since Etruscan times, but the town of **Tuscania** has two extremely unusual early medieval churches, an introduction to the styles of medieval southern Italy. Head a little further inland and you'll meet a chain of large lakes, including lovely, tranquil **Lake Vico**, and the medieval city of **Viterbo**, once the residence of the popes.

Part IX

SIENA

Cattedrale, Pavimento

Draped on its three hills, Siena (pop. 61,400) is the most beautiful city in Tuscany, a flamboyant medieval ensemble of palaces and towers cast in warm, brown, *Siena*-coloured brick. Its soaring skyline is its pride, dominated by the blazing black and white banner of a cathedral and the taut needle of the Torre di Mangia; and yet the Campo, the very centre of Siena, is only four streets away from olive groves and orchards. The contrast is part of the city's charm; densely built-up brick urbanity, and around the corner a fine stretch of long Tuscan farmland that fills the valleys within the city's walls.

Here art went hand in hand with a fierce civic pride to make Siena a world of its own, and historians go so far as to speak of 'Sienese civilization' in summing up the achievements of this unique little city.

Ancient Rivals

Few rivalries have been more enduring than that between Florence and Siena; to understand Tuscany take a moment to compare the two. Long ago, while Florence was off at university, busily studying her optics and geometry, Lady Siena spent her time dancing and dropping her scarf for knights at the tournament. Florence thought she had the last laugh in 1555, when Duke Cosimo and his black-hearted Spanish pals wiped out the Sienese Republic and put this proud maiden in chains. It's frustrating enough today, though, when Florence looks up in the hills and sees Siena, an unfaded beauty with a faraway smile, sitting in her tower like the Lady of Shalott.

For two towns built by bankers and wool tycoons, they could not have less in common. Siena may not possess an Uffizi or a David, but neither does it have to bear the marble antimacassars and general stuffiness of its sister on the Arno, nor her smog, traffic, tourist hordes and suburban squalor. Florence never goes over the top. Siena loves to, especially in the week around the race of the *Palio*, the wildest party in Tuscany, a worthy successor to the fabulous masques and carnivals, the bullfights and bloody free-for-alls of the Sienese Middle Ages. In fact, Florence has been clicking its tongue at Siena since the time of Dante, who inserted in his *Inferno* a sarcastic reference to a famous club called the *Brigata*—twelve noble Sienese youths who put up 250,000 florins for a year of nightly feasting; every night they had three sumptuously laid tables, one for eating, one for drinking, and the third to throw out the window.

But there's more to Siena than that. This is a city with its own artistic tradition (see 'Art' p. 59); in the 1300s, Sienese painters were giving lessons to the Florentines. Always more decorative, less intellectual than Florence, Siena fell behind in the quattrocento. By then, fortunately, the greatest achievement of Sienese art was already nearing completion—Siena itself.

History

Everywhere in Siena you'll see the familiar Roman symbol of the she-wolf suckling the twins. This is Siena's symbol as well; according to legend, the city was founded by the sons of Remus, Senius and Ascius. One rode a black horse, the other a white, and the simple comunal shield of black and white halves (the *balzana*) has been the other most enduring symbol of Siena over the centuries. It is most likely that somebody was living on these three hills long before this mythological pair. Excavations have found traces of Etruscan and even Celtic habitation. The almost impregnable site, dominating most of southern Tuscany, would always have been of interest. Roman-era *Sena Julia*, re-founded by Augustus as a colony for his veterans, never achieved much importance, and we know little about the place until the early 12th century, when the emerging *comune* began keeping written records. In 1125, an increasingly independent Siena electing its first consuls. By 1169, the *comune* wrested political control away from the bishop, and some ten years later Siena developed its own written constitution.

The political development is complex, and with good reason. 12th-century Siena was a booming new city; control over its rich countryside, supplying some of the best wool in Italy, helped start an important cloth industry, and a small silver mine, acquired from Volterra in the 1160s, provided seed capital for what was to become one of the leading important banking towns of Europe. Like so many other Italian cities, Siena was able early on to force its troublesome rural nobles to live within its walls, where they built scores of tall defence towers, fought pitched battles in the streets and usually kept the city divided into armed camps; in the narrowest part of the city, the *comune* once had to lay out new streets parallel to Via Camollia because of one particularly boisterous nobleman whose palace most Sienese were afraid to pass. Yet Siena was never completely able to bring its titled hoodlums under control. The businessmen made the money, and gradually formed their city into a sophisticated self-governing republic, but the nobles held on to many of their privileges for centuries, giving an anachronistically feudal tinge to Siena's life and art.

Like its brawling neighbours, medieval Siena enjoyed looking for trouble; in the endless wars of the 13th century they never had to look very far. Originally a Guelph town, Siena changed sides early to avoid being in the same camp with arch-rival Florence. Along with Pisa, Siena carried the Ghibelline banner through the Tuscan wars with varying fortunes. Its finest hour came in 1260, when a Florentine herald arrived with the arrogant demand that Siena demolish its walls and deliver up its large population of Ghibelline exiles from Florence. If not, the armies of Florence and the entire Guelph League—some 40,000 men—were waiting outside to raze the city to the ground. Despite the overwhelming odds, the Sienese determined to resist. They threw the keys of the city on the altar of the yet unfinished new cathedral, dedicating Siena to the Virgin Mary (a custom they have repeated ever since when the city is endangered, most recently just before the battle for liberation in 1944). In the morning, they marched out to the **Battle of Montaperti** and beat the Florentines so badly that they captured their *carroccio*.

After the battle Siena had Florence entirely at her mercy and naturally was anxious to level the city and sow the ground with salt. One of the famous episodes in the *Inferno* relates how the Florentine exiles, who made up a substantial part of the Sienese forces, refused to allow it. Unfortunately for Siena, within a few years Florence and the Tuscan Guelphs had the situation back under control and Siena was never again to come so close to dominating Tuscan affairs. Nevertheless the city would be a constant headache to Florence for the next three centuries. When things were quiet at the front, the Sienese had to settle for bashing each other. The constant stream of anti-Siena propaganda in Dante isn't just Florentine bile; medieval Siena had a thoroughly earned reputation for violence and contentiousness. The impressive forms and rituals of the Sienese Republic were merely a façade concealing endless, pointless struggles between the various factions of the elite. Early on, Siena's merchants and nobles divided themselves into five *monti*, syndicates of self-interest that worked like political parties only without any pretence of principle. At one point, this Tuscan banana republic had 10 constitutions in 27 years, and more often than not its political affairs were settled in the streets. Before the Palio was invented, Siena's favourite civic sport was the *Gioco del Pugno*, a general fistfight in the Campo with 300 on a side. Sometimes tempers flared, and the boys would bring out the axes and crossbows.

Siena's Golden Age

The historical record leaves us with a glaring paradox. For all its troubles and bad intentions, Siena often managed to run city business with disinterest and intelligence. An intangible factor of civic pride always made the Sienese do the right thing when something important was at hand, like battling the Florentines or selecting a new artist to work on the cathedral. The Battle of Montaperti may have proved a disappointment in terms of territorial ambitions, but it inaugurated the most brilliant period of Sienese culture, and saw the transformation of the hilltop fortress town into the beautiful city we see today. In 1287, under pressure from the Guelphs and their Angevin protectors, Siena actually allied itself with Florence and instituted a new form of government; the **'Council of the Nine'**. Excluding nobles from office, as Florence would do six years later, the rule of the Nine was to last until 1355, and it gave Siena a more stable regime than it knew at any other period.

Business was better than ever. The city's bankers came to rival Florence's, with offices in all the trading centres and capitals of Europe. A sustained peace, and increasing cultural contacts with France and Naples, brought new ideas and influences into Siena's art and architecture, just in time to embellish massive new building programmes like the

Cathedral (begun 1186, but not substantially completed until the 1380s) and the **Palazzo Pubblico** (1295–1310). Beginning with Duccio di Buoninsegna (1260–1319) Sienese artists took the lead in exploring new concepts in painting and sculpture and throughout the 1300s they contributed as much as or more than the Florentines in laying the foundations for the Renaissance. Contemporary records betray an obsessive concern on the part of bankers and merchants for decorating Siena and impressing outsiders. At the height of its fortunes, in the early 14th century, Siena ruled most of southern Tuscany. Its bankers were known in London, in the Baltic and in Constantinople, and its reputation for beauty and culture was matched by few cities in all Europe.

The very pinnacle of civic pride and ambition came in 1339, with the fantastical plan to expand the yet unfinished cathedral into the largest in all Christendom. The walls of that great effort, a nave that would have been longer than St Peter's in Rome, stand today as a monument to the dramatic event that snapped off Siena's career in full bloom. The **Black Death** of 1348 carried off one third of the population—a mortality not greater than some other Italian cities, perhaps, but the plague hit Siena at a moment when its economy was particularly vulnerable, and started a slow but irreversible decline that was to continue for centuries. Economic troubles led to political instability, and in 1355 a revolt of the nobles, egged on by Emperor Charles IV, who was then in Tuscany, overthrew the government of the Nine. Then in 1371, seven years before the Ciompi revolt in Florence, the wool workers staged a genuine revolution. Organized in a sort of trade union, the **Compagnia del Bruco**, they seized the Palazzo Pubblico and instituted a new government with greater popular representation.

The decades that followed saw Siena devote more and more of its diminishing resources to buying off the marauding mercenary companies that infested much of Italy at this time. By 1399 the city was in such straits that it surrendered its independence to **Giangaleazzo Visconti**, the tyrant of Milan, who was then attempting to surround and conquer Florence. After his death Siena reclaimed its freedom. Political confusion continued throughout the century, with only two periods of relative stability. One came with the pontificate (1458–63) of Pius II, the great Sienese scholar **Aeneas Silvius Piccolomini**, who exerted a dominating influence over his native city while he ruled at Rome. In 1487, a nobleman named **Pandolfo Petrucci** took over the government; as an honest broker, regulating the often murderous ambitions of the *monti*, he and his sons kept control of the republic until 1524.

The Fall of the Republic

Florence was always waiting in the wings to swallow up Siena, and finally had its chance in the 1500s. The real villain of the piece, however, was not Florence but that most imperious Emperor **Charles V**. After the fall of the Petrucci, the factional struggles resumed immediately, with frequent assassinations and riots, and constitutions changing with the spring fashions. Charles, who had bigger prey in his sights, cared little for the fate of the perverse little republic; he feared, though, that its disorders, religious toleration, and wretched financial condition were a disease that might spread beyond its borders. In 1530, he took advantage of riots in the city to install an imperial garrison. Yet even the emperor's representatives, usually Spaniards, could not keep Siena from sliding further into anarchy and bankruptcy on several occasions, largely thanks to Charles' war taxes. Cultural life was stifled as the Spaniards introduced the Inquisition and the Index.

Scholars and artists fled, while poverty and political disruptions made Siena's once proud university cease to function.

In 1550, Charles announced that he was going to build a fortress within the city's walls, and that the Sienese were going to pay for it. Realizing that even the trifling liberty still left to them would soon be extinguished, the Sienese ruling class began intrigues with Charles' great enemy France. A French army, led by a Piccolomini, arrived in July 1552. Inside the walls the people revolted and locked the Spanish garrison up in its own new fortress. The empire was slow to react, but inevitably, in late 1554, a huge force of imperial troops, along with those of Florence, entered Sienese territory. The siege was prosecuted with remarkable brutality by Charles' commander, the **Marquess of Marignano,** laying waste much of the Sienese countryside (which did not entirely recover until this century), torturing prisoners and even hiring agents to start fires inside the walls. After a brave resistance, led by a republican Florentine exile named **Piero Strozzi** and assisted by France, Siena was starved into surrendering in April 1555. Two years later, Charles' son Philip II sold Siena to Duke Cosimo of Florence, and the ancient republic disappeared into the new Grand Duchy of Tuscany.

If nothing else, Siena went out with a flourish. After the capture of the city, some 2000 republican bitter-enders escaped to make a last stand at Montalcino. Declaring 'Where the Comune is, there is the City', they established what must be the world's first republican government-in-exile. With control over much of the old Sienese territory, the **'Republic of Siena at Montalcino'** held out against the Medici for another four years.

With its independence lost and its economy irrevocably ruined, Siena withdrew into itself. For centuries there was to be no recovery, little art or scholarship, and no movements towards reform. The Sienese aristocracy, already decayed into a parasitic rentier class, made its peace with the Medici dukes early on; in return for their support, the Medici allowed them to keep much of their power and privileges. The once great capital of trade and finance shrunk rapidly into an overbuilt farmers' market, its population dropping from a 14th-century high of 60–80,000 to around a mere 15,000 by the year 1700. This does much to explain why medieval and Renaissance Siena is so well preserved today—for better or worse, nothing at all has happened to change it.

By the 'Age of Enlightenment', with its disparaging of everything medieval, the Sienese seem to have quite forgotten their own history and art, and it is no surprise that the rest of Europe forgot them too. During the first years of the Grand Tour, no self-respecting Northern European would think of visiting Siena. Few had probably ever heard of it, and the ones who stopped overnight on the way to Rome were usually dismayed at the 'inelegance' of its medieval buildings and art. It was not until the 1830s that Siena was rediscovered, with the help of literati like the Brownings, who spent several summers here, and that truly Gothic American, Henry James. The Sienese were not far behind in rediscovering it themselves. The old civic pride that had lain dormant for centuries yawned and stretched like Sleeping Beauty and went diligently back to work. Before the century was out, everything that could still be salvaged of the city's ancient glory was refurbished and restored. More than ever fascinated by its own image and eccentricities, and more than ever without any kind of an economic base, Siena was ready for its present career as a cultural attraction, a tourist town.

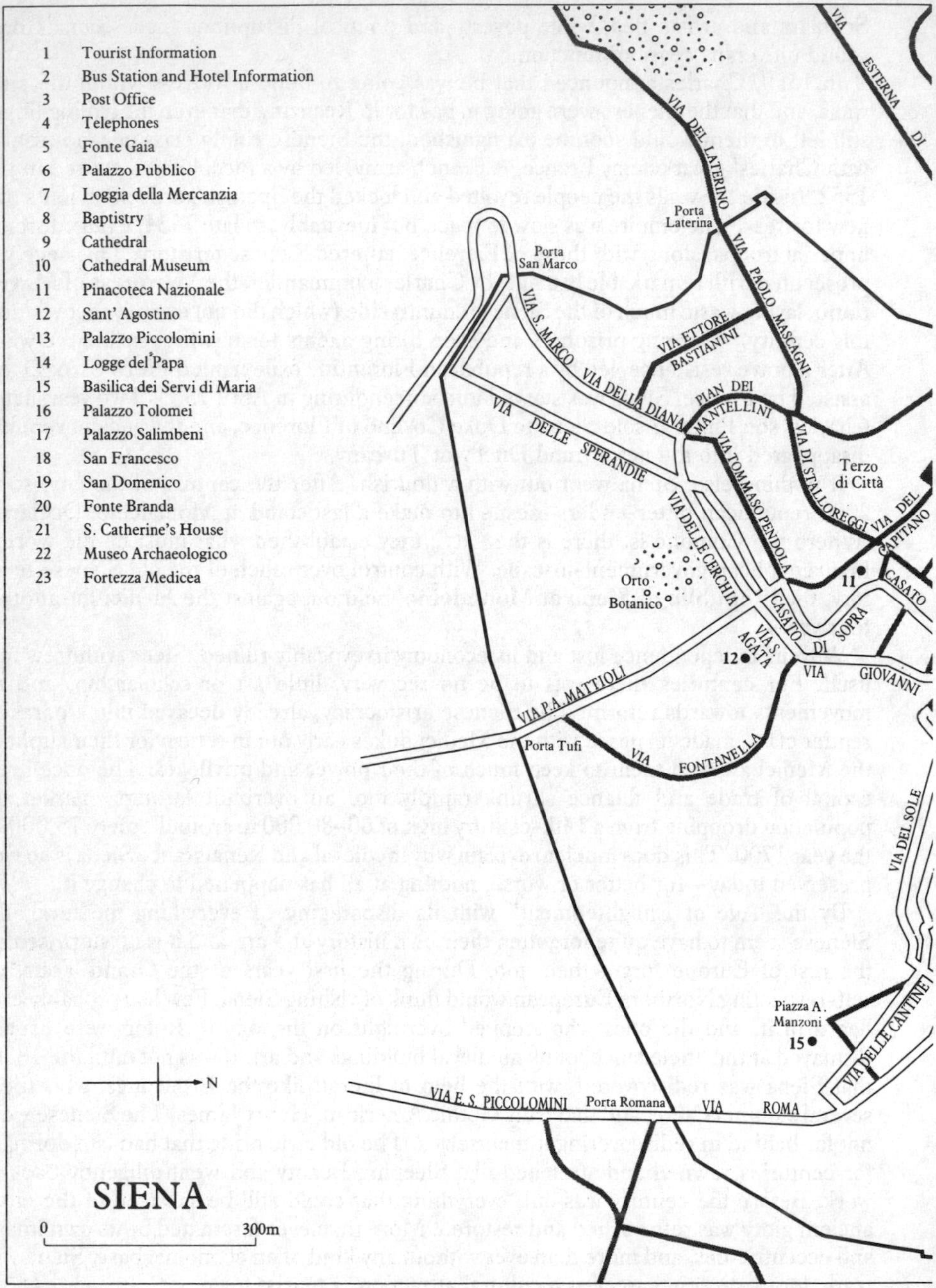
1 Tourist Information
2 Bus Station and Hotel Information
3 Post Office
4 Telephones
5 Fonte Gaia
6 Palazzo Pubblico
7 Loggia della Mercanzia
8 Baptistry
9 Cathedral
10 Cathedral Museum
11 Pinacoteca Nazionale
12 Sant' Agostino
13 Palazzo Piccolomini
14 Logge del Papa
15 Basilica dei Servi di Maria
16 Palazzo Tolomei
17 Palazzo Salimbeni
18 San Francesco
19 San Domenico
20 Fonte Branda
21 S. Catherine's House
22 Museo Archaeologico
23 Fortezza Medicea
VIA ESTERNA DI
VIA DEL LATERINO
Porta Laterina
VIA PAOLO MASCAGNI
Porta San Marco
VIA S. MARCO
VIA ETTORE BASTIANINI
VIA DELLA DIANA
PIAN DEI MANTELLINI
VIA DELLE SPERANDIE
VIA TOMMASO PENDOLA
VIA DI STALLOREGGI
Terzo di Città
VIA DEL CAPITANO
VIA DELLE CERCHIA
Orto Botanico
CASATO DI SOPRA
CASATO
11
12
VIA S. AGATA
VIA GIOVANNI
VIA P.A. MATTIOLI
Porta Tufi
VIA FONTANELLA
VIA DEL SOLE
Piazza A. Manzoni
15
VIA DELLE CANTINE
N
VIA E. S. PICCOLOMINI
Porta Romana
VIA ROMA
SIENA
0 300m

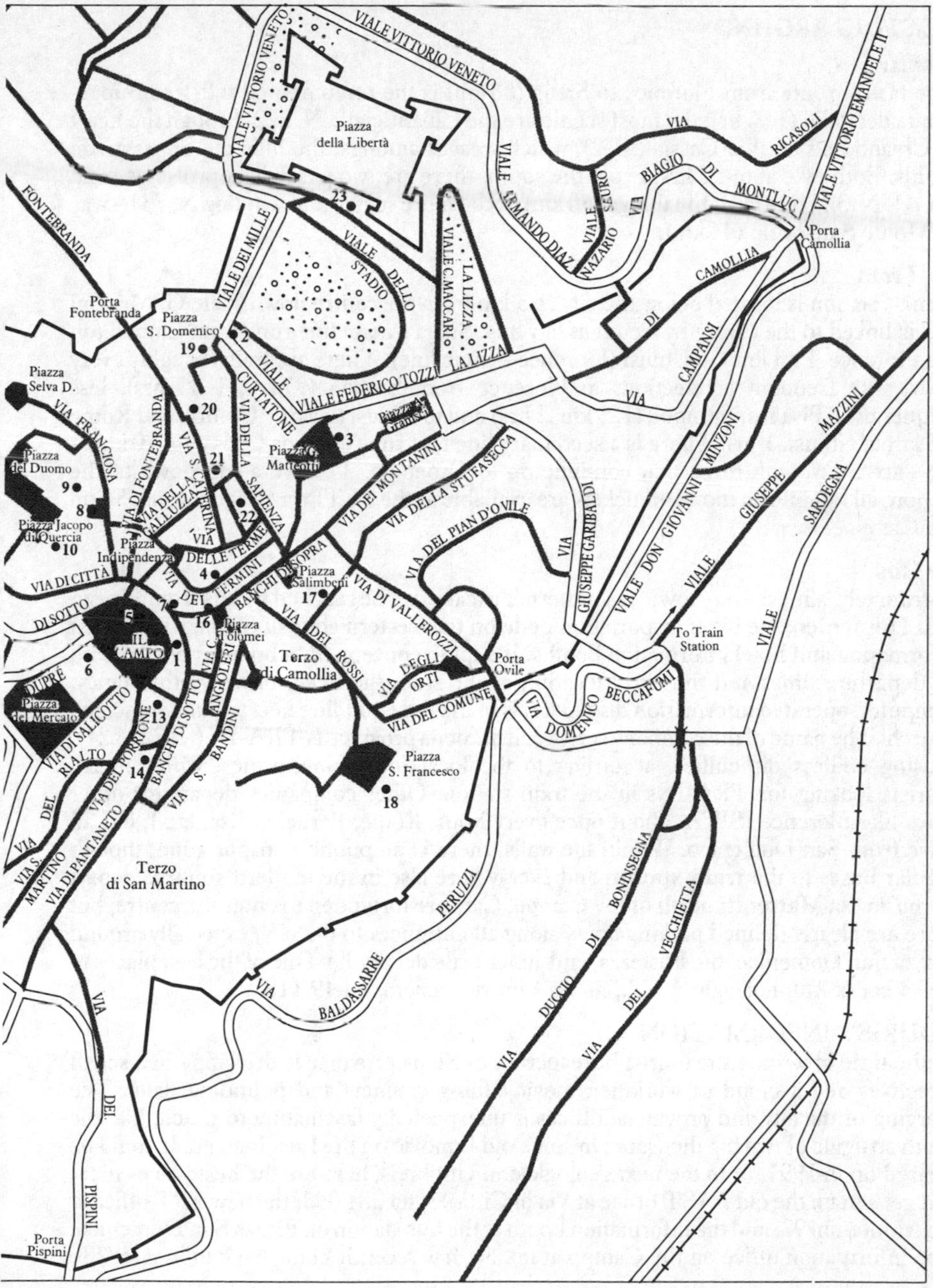

VIALE VITTORIO VENETO
VIALE VITTORIO VENETO
Piazza della Libertà
VIA RICASOLI
VIALE VITTORIO EMANUELE II
VIALE ARMANDO DIAZ
VIALE SAURO
VIA NAZARIO
VIA BIAGIO DI MONTLUC
Porta Camollia
FONTEBRANDA
VIALE DEI MILLE
23
VIALE DELLO STADIO
VIALE C. MACCARIO
LA LIZZA
DI CAMOLLIA
Porta Fontebranda
Piazza S. Domenico
2
19
VIALE CURTATONE
VIALE FEDERICO TOZZI
LA LIZZA
VIA CAMPANSI
MAZZINI
Piazza Selva D.
VIA FRANCIOSA
20
Piazza Gramsci
3
Piazza G. Matteotti
VIA DEI MONTANINI
VIA DELLA STUFASECCA
VIA GIUSEPPE GARIBALDI
VIALE DON GIOVANNI MINZONI
GIUSEPPE
SARDEGNA
VIALE
VIALE
Piazza del Duomo
9
8
VIA DI FONTEBRANDA
VIA DELLA GALLUZZA
VIA S. CATERINA
VIA DELLA SAPIENZA
21
22
Piazza Jacopo di Quercia
10
Piazza Indipendenza
VIA DELLE TERME
VIA DEI TERMINI
BANCHI DI SOPRA
Piazza Salimbeni
VIA DEL PIAN D'OVILE
VIA DI CITTÀ
4
17
VIA DI VALLEROZZI
DI SOTTO
5
7
IL CAMPO
1
16
Piazza Tolomei
VIA DEI ROSSI
To Train Station
6
Terzo di Camollia
VIA DEGLI ORTI
Porta Ovile
VIA DOMENICO BECCAFUMI
DUPRÈ
Piazza del Mercato
VIA DEL COMUNE
VIA DI SALICOTTO
13
VIA DEL PORRIONE
BANCHI DI SOTTO
VIA C. ANGIOLIERI
VIA S. BANDINI
RIALTO
DEL
14
Piazza S. Francesco
18
VIA S. MARTINO
VIA DI PANTANETO
Terzo di San Martino
VIA BALDASSARRE PERUZZI
VIA DUCCIO DI BONINSEGNA
VIA DEL VECCHIETTA
VIA DEI PISPINI
Porta Pispini

GETTING AROUND

By Car

The fastest route from Florence to Siena (68 km) is the unnumbered toll-free Superstrada del Palio (1 1/4 hr); the most scenic are the Chiantigiana N. 222 through the heart of Chianti and the Via Cassia (N. 2), which weaves amongst the hills the Superstrada avoids. Both take about 2 hrs. From the south, there are two possible approaches from the A1: N. 326 by way of Sinalunga (50 km) or the more scenic and winding N. 73 by way of Monte Sansovino (44 km).

By Train

Siena's station is located below the city, 1.5 km from the centre down Viale G. Mazzini and is linked to the centre by frequent city bus. Siena's main line runs from Empoli (on the Florence–Pisa line) to Chiusi (Florence–Rome line). There are trains roughly every hour, with frequent connections to Florence from Empoli (97 km, 1 1/2 hrs), less frequently to Pisa from Empoli (125 km, 2 hrs) and to Chiusi towards Umbria and Rome (65 km to Chiusi, 1 hr). There is a secondary line that runs towards Grosseto (70 km, 1 hr)—six a day, with three that continue on to Orbetello. To save a trip down to the station, all rail information and tickets are available at the SETI travel agency, no. 56 on the Campo.

By Bus

Fortunately, almost every town in southern Tuscany can be reached by bus from **Piazza San Domenico**, the big transportation node on the western edge of Siena, with tourist information and hotel information booths. It's quite convenient; a board is posted with all departure times and the exact location of the stop; the ticket office (with a fancy, computer-operated information dispenser) is in the little building next to San Domenico church. The name of the company serving all of Siena province is TRA-IN (tel 221 221), causing endless difficulties, according to the local tourist authorities, with English tourists looking for TRA-INs in the train station. Other companies depart for other cities like Florence (SITA, about once every hour, Rome, Perugia, Pisa, etc.), but all leave from San Domenico. Within the walls, there is no public transportation, though regular buses to the **train station** and everywhere else in the modern suburbs depart from **Piazza Matteotti** north of the Campo. Cars are forbidden to enter the centre, but there are clearly defined parking areas along all entrances to the city, especially around Piazza San Domenico, the Fortezza, and along Viale del Stadio. One of the best places to hire a car is Autonoleggio A.C.I., in Via Vittorio Veneto, tel 49 118.

TOURIST INFORMATION

At the time of writing the tourist bureaucracy of Siena province is drowning in a sea of directives and a cloud of workmen moving filing cabinets and pounding nails. The merging of the city and provincial offices is unexpectedly fascinating to watch, like the death struggle of two big dinosaurs in some old B movie on the Lost Plateau. It could be cleared up in 1991, or in the next geologic era. Until it is, here are the best places to try and get a map: the old AAST office at Via di Città 43, tel 281 093; the new EPT office at Via Montanini 92, and the information booth at the bus station on Piazza San Domenico. The information office on the Campo at no. 56, has recently come back to life, tel 280 551.

Next to the information booth at San Domenico, the city's hotelkeepers run a hotel info and reservations centre, very useful if you're arriving without a place to stay.
Post Office: Piazza Matteotti 1.
Telephones: Via dei Termini 40.

Orientation: *Terzi* and the *Contrade*

The centre of Siena, the site of the Palio and, importantly to the Sienese, the 'farthest point from the world outside', is the famous piazza called simply **The Campo**. From here, the city unfolds like a three-petalled flower along three ridges. It has been a natural division since medieval times, with the oldest quarter, the **Terzo di Città**, including the cathedral, to the southwest; the **Terzo di San Martino** the southeast; and the **Terzo di Camollia** to the north.

Siena is tiny, barely over a square mile in size. The density, and especially the hills, make it seem much bigger when you're walking. There are no short cuts across the valleys between the three *terzi*. Although there are no cars in the centre, taxis and ambulances (medieval Siena is full of medieval hospitals) will occasionally try to run you down.

CONTRADE

The Sienese have taken the *contrade* for granted so long that their history is almost impossible to trace. Basically, the word denotes the 17 neighbourhoods into which Siena is divided. Like the *rioni* of Rome, they were once the original wards of the ancient city—not merely geographical boundaries, but self-governing entities; the ancients with their long racial memories often referred to them as the city's 'tribes'. In Siena, the *contrade* survived and prospered all through classical times and the Middle Ages. More than anything else, they maintained the city's traditions and sense of identity through the dark years after 1552. Incredibly enough, they're still there now, unique in Italy and perhaps all Europe.

Once Siena counted over 60 *contrade*. Now there are 17, each with a sort of totem animal for its symbol:

Aquila (eagle), *Onda* (dolphin), *Tartuca* (turtle), *Pantera* (panther), *Selva* (rhinoceros), and *Chiocciola* (snail); all southwest of the Campo in the Terzo di Città.

Leocorno (unicorn), *Torre* (elephant), *Nicchio* (mussel shell), *Civetta* (owl), and *Valdimontone* (ram), in the Terzo di San Martino southeast of the Campo.

Oca (goose), *Drago* (dragon), *Giraffa* (giraffe), *Lupa* (wolf), *Bruco* (caterpillar), and *Istrice* (porcupine), all to the north in the Terzo di Camollia.

Sienese and Italian law recognize each of these as legally chartered communities; today a *contrada* functions as a combination social and dining club, neighbourhood improvement organization, religious confraternity, and mutual assistance fund. Each elects its own officials annually in May. Each has its own chapel, museum and fountain, its own flag and colours, and its own patron saint who pulls all the strings he can in Heaven twice a year to help his beloved district win the Palio.

Sociologists, and not only in Italy, are becoming ever more intrigued with this ancient yet very useful system, with its built-in community solidarity and tacit social control. (Siena has almost no crime and no social problems, except of course for a lack of jobs.)

The *contrade* probably function much as they did in Roman or medieval times, but it's surprising just what up-to-date, progressive, and adaptable institutions they can be, and they are still changing today. Anyone born in a *contrade* area, for example, is automatically a member; besides their baptism into the Church, they also receive a sort of 'baptism' into the *contrada*. This ritual isn't very old, and it is conducted in the pretty new fountains the *contrade* have constructed all over Siena in recent years as centrepieces for their neighbourhoods.

To learn more about the *contrade*, the best place to go is one of the 17 little *contrada* museums. The tourist office can give you a list of addresses. One of the best is that of the Goose in the Terzo di Camollia. Though the caretakers usually live close by, most of them ask visitors to call a day or two in advance. The tourist office also has details on the dates of the annual *contrada* festivals, and the other shows and dinners they are wont to put on; visitors are always very welcome.

The Palio

The thousands of tourists who come twice a year to see the Palio, Siena's famous horse race around the Campo, probably think the Sienese are doing it all just for them. Yet like the *contrade* which contest it, the Palio is an essential part of Sienese culture, something that means as much to the city as it did centuries ago. Here are the plain facts on Italy's best-known annual festival:

The oldest recorded Palio was run in 1283, though no one can say how far the custom goes back. In the Middle Ages, besides horse races there were violent street battles, bloody games of primeval rugby and even bullfights. (Bullfights were also common at Rome and there's an argument to be made that Italy is the place where the Spaniards got the idea, back in the 16th and 17th centuries when Spain's own medieval passion for such things had been almost forgotten.) At present, the course is three times around the periphery of the Campo, though earlier it was run on various routes through the city's main streets.

The *palio* (Latin *pallium*) is an embroidered banner, the prize offered for winning the race. Two races are held each year, on 2 July and 16 August, and the *palio* of each is decorated with an image of the Virgin Mary; after political violence the city's greatest passion was always Mariolatry. The course has room for only ten horses in each race. Some of the seventeen *contrade* are chosen by lot each race to ensure that everyone has a fair chance. The horses are also selected by lot, but the *contrade* are free to select their own jockeys. Although the race itself only lasts a minute and a half, there's a good hour or two of pageantry preceding the event; the famous flag-throwers or *alfieri* of each participating *contrada* put on a dazzling show, while the medieval *carroccio*, drawn by a yoke of white oxen, is pressed into service to circle the Campo, bearing the prized *palio* itself.

The Palio is no joke; baskets of money ride on each race, not to mention the sacred honour of the district. To obtain divine favour, each *contrada* brings its horse into its chapel on race morning for a special blessing (and if a little horse manure drops during the ceremony, it's taken as a sign of good luck). The only rule stipulates that you can't seize the reins of an opponent. There are no rules against bribing opposing jockeys, making alliances with other *contrade*, or ambushing jockeys before the race. The course around the Campo has two right angles. Anything can happen; recent Palii have featured not only jockeys but *horses* flying through the air at the turns. They say no one has ever been killed at a Palio. There's no reason to believe them. They wouldn't believe it themselves; it is an article of faith among the Sienese that fatalities are prevented by special intervention of the Virgin Mary. The post-Palio carousing, while not up to medieval standards, is still impressive; in the winning *contrada* the party might go on for days.

No event in Italy is as infectiously exhilarating as the Palio. There are two ways to see it, either from the centre of the Campo, which is packed tight and always very hot, or from an expensive (L85–175 000) seat in a viewing stand. Several travel agencies offer special Palio tours (see p. 19); otherwise book by April.

Walking in Siena

If you keep your eyes open while walking the back streets of Siena you'll see the city's entire history laid out for you in signs, symbols and a hundred other clues. You usually won't have trouble guessing which *contrada* you're in. Little ceramic plaques with the *contrada* symbol appear on many buildings and street corners, not to mention flags in the neighbourhood colours, bumper stickers on the cars, and the fountains, each with a modern sculptural work, usually representing the *contrada*'s animal.

Look for noblemen's coats-of-arms above the doorways; aristocratic, archaic Siena will show you more of these than almost any Italian city. In many cases they are still the homes of the original families, and often you will see the same device turning up on a dozen houses on one block, a reminder of how medieval Siena was largely divided into separate compounds, each under the protection (or intimidation) of a noble family. One common symbol is formed from the letters IHS in a radiant sun. Siena's famous 15th-century preacher, San Bernardino, was always pestering the nobles to forget their contentiousness and enormous vanity; he proposed that they replace their heraldic symbols with the monogram of Christ. The limited success his idealism met with can be read on the buildings of Siena today.

They don't take down old signs in Siena. One, dated 1641, informs prostitutes that the Most Serene Prince Matthias (the Florentine governor) forbids them to live on his street (Via di Salicotto). Another, a huge 19th-century marble plaque on the Banchi di Sotto, reminds us that 'In this house, before modern restorations reclaimed it from squalidness, was born Giovanni Caselli, inventor of the pantograph.' A favourite, on Via del Giglio, announces a stroke of the rope and a sixteen-lire fine for anyone throwing trash in the street, with proceeds to go to the accuser.

The Campo

There is no lovelier square in Tuscany, and none more beloved of its city. The Forum of ancient *Sena Julia* was on this spot, and in the Middle Ages it evolved into its present fan shape, rather like a scallop shell or a classical theatre. The Campo was paved in brick as early as 1340; the nine sections into which the fan is divided are in honour of the Council of the Nine, rulers of the city at the time. Thousands crowd over the bricks here every year to see the Palio, run on the periphery.

For a worthy embellishment to their Campo, the Sienese commissioned for its curved north end the **Fonte Gaia** from Jacopo della Quercia, their greatest sculptor, though what you see now is an uninspired copy of 1868. He worked on it from 1408 to 1419, creating the broad rectangle of marble with reliefs of Adam and Eve and allegorical virtues. It was to be the opening salvo of Siena's Renaissance, an answer to the Baptistry doors of Ghiberti in Florence (for which della Quercia himself had been one of the contestants). Perhaps it was a poor choice of stone, but the years have been incredibly unkind to this fountain; the badly eroded remains of the original can be seen up on the loggia of the Palazzo Pubblico.

No one can spend much time in Siena without noticing its fountains. The Republic always made sure each part of the city had access to good water; medieval Siena created the most elaborate engineering works since ancient Rome to bring the water in. Fonte Gaia, and others such as Fontebranda, are fed by underground aqueducts that stretch for miles across the Tuscan countryside. Charles V, when he visited the city, is reported to have said that Siena is 'even more marvellous underground than it is on the surface'. The original Fonte Gaia was completed in the early 1300s; there's a story that soon after, some citizens dug up a beautiful Greek statue of Venus, signed by Praxiteles himself. The delighted Sienese carried it in procession through the city and installed it on top of their new fountain. With the devastation of the Black Death, however, the preachers were quick to blame God's wrath on the indecent pagan on the Fonte Gaia. Throughout history, the Sienese have always been ready to be shocked by their own sins; in this case, with their neighbours dropping like flies around them, they proved only too eager to make poor Venus the scapegoat. They chopped her into little bits, and a party of Sienese disguised as peasants smuggled the pieces over the border and buried them into Florentine territory to pass the bad luck on to their enemies.

Palazzo Pubblico

If the Campo is like a Roman theatre, the main attraction on stage since 1310 has been this brick and stone palace, the enduring symbol of the Sienese Republic and still the town hall today. Its façade is the face of Siena's history, with the she-wolf of Senius and Ascanius, Medici balls, the IHS of San Bernardino, and squared Guelph crenellations, all in the shadow of the tremendous **Torre di Mangia**, the graceful, needle-like tower that Henry James called 'Siena's Declaration of Independence'. At 102 m (332 ft), the tower was the second tallest ever raised in medieval Italy (only the campanile in Cremona beats it). At the time, the cathedral tower up on its hill completely dominated Siena's skyline; the Council of the Nine wouldn't accept that the symbol of religious authority or any of the nobility's fortress-skyscrapers should be taller than the symbol of the republic, so its Perugian architects, Muccio and Francesco di Rinaldo, made sure it would be hard to beat.

There was a practical side to it, too. At the top hung the *comune*'s great bell, which had to be heard in every corner of the city tolling the hours and announcing the curfew, or calling the citizens to assemble in case of war or emergency. One of the first men to hold the job of bell-ringer gave the tower its name, a fat sleepy fellow named *Mangiaguadagni* ('eat the profits') or just Mangia for short; there is a statue of him in one of the courtyards. Climb the tower's endless stair for the definitive view of Siena—on the clearest days you'll also be able to see about half of the medieval republic's territory, a view that is absolutely, positively worth the slight risk of cardiac arrest (open daily 10–5:15; winter –2:15; adm). At the foot of the tower, the marble **Cappella della Piazza**, with its graceful rounded arches, stands out clearly from the Gothic earnestness of the rest of the building. It was begun in 1352, in thanks for deliverance from the Black Death, but not completed until the mid-15th century.

Most of the Palazzo Pubblico's ground floor is still used for city offices, but the upper floors have been made into the city's museum (daily 9:30–1:30, until 6:30 in summer; Sun 9–1; adm exp). Here the main attraction is the series of state rooms done in frescoes, a sampling of the best of Sienese art throughout the centuries. The first, the historical frescoes in the **Sala del Risorgimento** were done by an artist named A. G. Cassioli only in 1886: the meeting of Vittorio Emanuele II with Garibaldi, his coronation, portraits and epigrams of past patriots, and an 'allegory of Italian Liberty', all in a colourful and photographically precise style. If anything, it is a tribute to Sienese artistic conservatism; finally liberated after 300 years of Florentine rule, they immediately went back to their good old medieval habits.

Next on the same floor the **Sala dei Cardinali** offers some vigorous battle scenes from the 1300s by unknown artists. In the **Sala del Concistoro**, Gobelin tapestries adorn the walls while the great Sienese Mannerist Beccafumi contributed a ceiling of frescoes in the 1530s celebrating the political virtues of antiquity; that theme is continued in the vestibule to the **Chapel**, with portraits of ancient heroes from Cicero to Judas Maccabeus, all by Taddeo di Bartolo. These portrayals, along with more portraits of the classical gods and goddesses and an interesting view of ancient Rome, show clearly just how widespread was the fascination with antiquity even in the 1300s. Intruding among the classical crew, there's also a king-sized St Christopher covering an entire wall. Before setting out on a journey it was good luck to catch a glimpse of this saint, and in Italy and Spain he is often painted extra large so you won't miss him. In a display case nearby, some of the oldest treasures of the Sienese Republic are kept: the war helmet of the Captain of the People, and a delicate **golden rose**, a gift to the city from the Sienese Pope, Pius II.

The **Chapel** (*Cappella del Consiglio*) itself stays locked behind a lovely wrought-iron grille designed by Jacopo della Quercia; inside you can just make out more frescoes by Taddeo di Bartolo, an altarpiece by Sodoma, and some exceptional carved wood seats, by Domenico di Nicolò (*c.*1415–28).

THE ALLEGORIES OF GOOD AND BAD GOVERNMENT

When you enter the **Sala dei Nove** (or Sala della Pace), meeting room of the Council of the Nine, you'll understand at a glance why they ruled Siena so well. Whenever one of the councillors had the temptation to skim some cream off the top, or pass a fat contract over to his brother-in-law the paving contractor, or tighten the screws on the poor by raising the salt tax, he had only to look up at Ambrogio Lorenzetti's great frescoes to really feel like a worm. There are two complementary sets, with scenes of Siena under good government and bad, and allegorical councils of virtues or vices for each. Enthroned Justice rules the good Siena, with such counsellors as Peace, Prudence and Magnanimity; bad Siena groans under the thumb of one nasty piece of work, sneering, fanged Tyranny and his cronies: Pride, Vainglory, Avarice and Wrath among others. The good Siena is a happy place, with buildings in good repair, well-dressed folk who seem almost to be dancing in the streets, and well-stocked shops where the merchants appear to be making a nice profit. Bad Siena is almost a mirror image, only the effects of the Tyrant's rule are plain to see: urban blight, crime in broad daylight, buildings crumbling and abandoned, and business bad for everybody—a landscape which for many of us modern city dwellers will seem all too familiar.

Lorenzetti finished his work around 1338, probably the most ambitious secular painting ever attempted up to that time. Parts of the work will be under restoration for the next few years; fittingly, Good Government has survived in very good condition, while Bad Government has been mouldering away for some centuries now. Here, too, is Guido da Siena's large *Madonna and Child* (mid-1200s), the earliest masterpiece of the Sienese school. In the adjacent chamber, the **Sala del Mappamondo**, only the outline is left of Lorenzetti's cosmological fresco, a diagram of the universe including all the celestial and angelic spheres, much like the one in the Camposanto at Pisa. Above it, there is a very famous fresco by Simone Martini (*c.*1330), showing the redoubtable condottiere **Guidoriccio da Fogliano** on his way to attack the castle of Montemassi, during a revolt against Siena. Also by Martini is an enthroned Virgin, or *Maestà*, that is believed to be his earliest work (1315).

If you're not up to climbing the tower, at least take the long, unmarked stairway from the entrance that leads up to the **loggia**, with the second best view over Siena and the disassembled bits and pieces of della Quercia's reliefs from the Fonte Gaia, not particularly impressive in their worn and damaged state.

Around the Campo

Part of the beauty of the Campo lies in the element of surprise; one usually enters from narrow arcades between austere medieval palaces that give no hint of what lies on the other side. Two of Siena's three main streets form a graceful curve around the back of the Campo; where they meet the third, directly behind the Fonte Gaia, is the corner the Sienese call the **Croce del Travaglio** (a mysterious nickname: the 'cross of affliction'). Here, under the eternal scaffolding of bureaucratic restoration, sleeps one of Siena's landmarks, the three-arched **Loggia della Mercanzia**, in a sense Siena's Royal Exchange, the place where the Republic's merchants made their deals and settled their differences before the city's famed commercial tribunal. The Loggia marks the transition from Sienese Gothic to the early Renaissance style—begun in 1417, it was probably influenced by Florence's Loggia dei Lanzi. The five statues of saints around the columns are the work of Antonio Federighi and Vecchietta, the leading Sienese sculptor after della Quercia.

The three streets that meet here lead directly into the three *terzi* of Siena. All three are among the city's most beautiful streets, in particular the gracefully curving **Banchi di Sotto**, main artery of the Terzo di San Martino. Just beyond the Campo, this street passes Siena's most imposing *palazzo privato*, the **Piccolomini Palace**, done in the Florentine style by Rossellino in the 1460s. This palace now houses the old Sienese state archive—not a place you might consider visiting but for the presence of the famous *Tavolette della Biccherna* (the account books of the *Biccherna*, or state treasury). Beginning in the 1200s, the republic's custom was to commission the best local artists to decorate the covers of the *tavolette*; the most interesting show such prosaic subjects as medieval citizens coming in to pay their taxes, city employees counting their pay and earnest monks trying to make the figures square—all are Cistercians from San Galgano (see p.

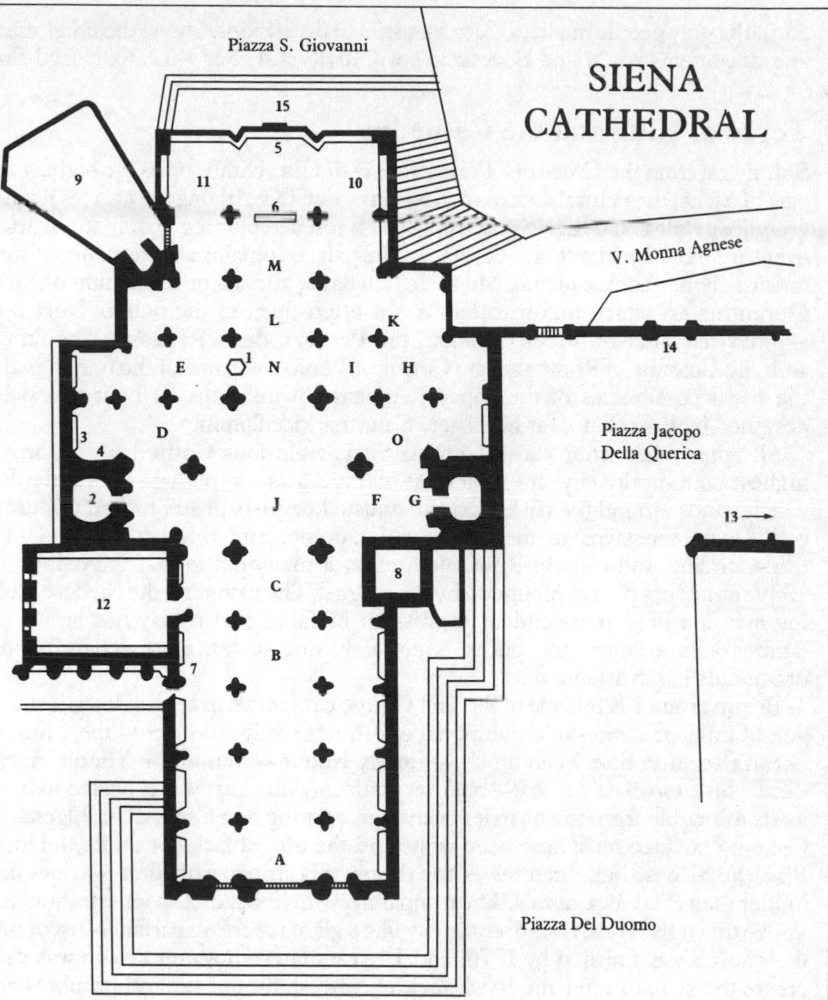

1 Pisano's Pulpit
2 Chapel Of St John Baptist
3 Tomb Of Cardinal Pecci (Donatello)
4 Tomb Of Cardinal Petroni (Tino Da Camaino)
5 Stained Glass Of Duccio
6 High Altar
7 Piccolomini Altar (Della Quercia, Michelangelo)
8 Campanile
9 Sacristy
10/11 Cantorie And Choir
12 Piccolomini Library
13 To Cathedral Museum
14 Cathedral Extension
15 Baptistry (Lower Level)

A Hermes Trismegistus
B Allegory Of Virtue
C Wheel Of Fortune
D Massacre Of The Innocents
E Judith Liberatino Bethulia
F Seven Ages Of Man
G Allegories Of Faith, Hope And Charity
H Story Of Absolom
I Emperor Sigismund On His Throne
J Sacrifice Of Elias, Killing Of The False Prophets
K Samson And The Philistines
L David The Psalmist
M Sacrifice Of Abraham
N Moses Receives The Commandments
O Story Of Jephta

335), the only people medieval Siena trusted to do the job. Among the other manuscripts and documents you'll find Boccaccio's will (daily 9–1, Sat 9–12:30, closed Sun).

Terzo di Città and the Cathedral

Southwest from the Croce del Travaglio, Via di Città climbs up to the highest and oldest part of Siena, the natural fortress of the Terzo di Città. Among the palaces it passes is the grandiose **Palazzo Chigi-Saracini**, with a wretched old tree, barely surviving, hanging over the street from its stony courtyard. The palace contains an internationally important music school, the Accademia Musicale Chigiana, and a large collection of Sienese and Florentine art which unfortunately is not often open to the public. Next door is yet another reminder of the Piccolomini, the **Palazzo delle Papesse**. The family, along with the Colonna of Rome and the Correr of Venice, was one of the first to really exploit the fiscal possibilities of the papacy; Aeneas Silvius (Pius II) built this palace, also designed by Rossellino, for his sister, Caterina Piccolomini.

All approaches from Via di Città to Siena's glorious **Cathedral**, spilling over the highest point in the city, are somewhat oblique. Easiest, perhaps, is Via dei Pellegrini, which winds around the back, past the unusual crypt-baptistry tucked underneath (see p. 307), up the steps to the Piazza del Duomo, and through a portal in a huge, free-standing wall of striped marble arches, a memorial to that incredible ill-starred 1339 rebuilding plan confounded by the plague. The cathedral the Sienese had to settle for may not be a transcendent expression of faith, and it may not be an important landmark in architecture, but it is certainly one of the most delightful, decorated ornaments in Christendom.

Begun around 1200, one of the first Gothic cathedrals in central Italy, it started in the good Gothic tradition as a communal effort, not really a project of the Church. There doesn't seem to have been much voluntary labour—even in the Middle Ages Italians were a little too blasé for that—but every citizen with a cart was expected to bring in two loads of marble from the quarries each year, earning him a special indulgence from the bishop. One load must have been white and the other black, for under the influence of Pisa, the Sienese built themselves one thoroughly striped cathedral—stripes darker and bolder than Pisa's or Lucca's. The campanile, with its distinctive fenestration, narrowing in size down six levels, rises over the city like a giant ice cream parfait. Most of the body of the church was finished by 1270, and 14 years later Giovanni Pisano was called in to create the sculpture for the lavish **façade**, with statues of Biblical prophets and pagan philosophers. The upper half was not begun until the 1390s, and the glittering mosaics in the gables are, like Orvieto's, the work of Venetian artists of the late 19th century.

The Interior: the Marble Pavement

This is a treasure-box of a cathedral, perhaps the only church in Italy that could keep a serious visitor busy for an entire day. Upon entering the main portal, the ferociously striped pilasters and the Gothic vaulting, a blue firmament painted with golden stars, inevitably draw the eye upwards. However, the most spectacular feature is at your very feet—the marble pavement, where the peculiar figure smiling up at you is **Hermes Trismegistus**, the legendary Egyptian father of alchemy (see Topics, p. 50), depicted in elegant *sgraffito* work of white and coloured marble. In fact, the entire floor of the cathedral is covered with almost 40,000 square feet of virtuoso *sgraffito* in 56 scenes including portraits, mystical allegories and events from the Old Testament. Like the Biccherna covers in the Palazzo Piccolomini, they are a tradition carried on over centuries. Many of Siena's best artists worked on them, beginning in 1369 and continuing into the 1600s; Giorgio Vasari claimed that Duccio di Buoninsegna himself first worked in this medium, though none of the pictures here are his.

Even in a building with so many marvels—the Piccolomini Library, Nicola Pisano's pulpit, Duccio's stained glass, works by Donatello, della Quercia, Pinturicchio, Michelangelo, Bernini and many others—this pavement perhaps takes pride of place. The greatest limitation of Sienese art was always the conservatism of its patrons, accustomed to demanding the same old images in the same old styles. Commissions from the Office of Cathedral Works, controlled by the state, were usually more liberal, allowing the artists to create such unique, and in some cases startling images, one of the greatest achievements of Renaissance Siena.

The Hermes on the cathedral pavement, by Giovanni di Stefano, was completed in the 1480s, a decade after Ficino's translation; it shows him together with Moses, holding a book with the inscription 'Take up thy letters and laws, O Egyptians'. On either side, all 10 prophetic *Sibyls* done by various artists at the same time decorate the aisles of the church. Nor are Hermes and the sibyls the only peculiar thing on this floor. Directly behind him begins a series of large scenes, including a Wheel of Fortune, with men hanging on to it for dear life, another wheel of uncertain symbolism, and emblems of Siena and other Tuscan and Latin cities. Oddest of all is a work by Pinturicchio, variously titled the *Allegory of Virtue* or the *Allegory of Fortune*; on a rocky island full of serpents, a party of well-dressed people has just embarked, climbing to the summit where a figure of 'Socrates' accepts a pen from a seated female figure, and another, 'Crates', empties a basket of gold and jewels into the sea. Below, a naked woman with a gonfalon stands with one foot in a boat, and another on land.

Unfortunately, many of the best scenes, under the crossing and transepts, are covered most of the year to save them from wear. You'll need to come between 15 August and 15 September to see the visionary works of Alessandro Franchi—the *Triumph of Elias* and other events in that prophet's life—and Domenico Beccafumi's *Sacrifice of Elias* and the *Execution of the False Prophets of Baal*. (Hasn't anyone in Siena ever heard of plexiglas?) Other works uncovered all year include *The Seven Ages of Man* by Antonio Federighi, scenes from the life of Moses by Beccafumi, Matteo di Giovanni's *Massacre of the Innocents* (always a favourite subject in Sienese art), and best of all the beautifully drawn *Judith Liberating the City of Bethulia*, a collaboration of Federighi, Matteo di Giovanni and Urbano da Cortona.

ELSEWHERE IN THE CATHEDRAL

Perhaps the greatest attraction above floor level is the great Carrara marble **pulpit** done by Nicola Pisano in the 1280s. Pisano started on it directly after finishing the one in Pisa; one of the assistants he brought here to help with the work was the young Arnolfo di Cambio. The typical Pisano conception is held up by allegorical figures of the seven liberal arts—more Sibyls, prophets, Christian virtues and saints tucked away in the odd corners, and vigorous, crowded relief panels from the Passion as good as the ones in Pisa. Nearby, in the left transept, the **Chapel of San Giovanni Battista** has frescoes by

Pinturicchio and a bronze statue of the Baptist by Donatello, who also contributed the **Tomb of Giovanni Pecci**, a 1400s Sienese bishop. Another tomb worth a look is that of Cardinal Petroni, an influential early Renaissance design from 1310 by Tino di Camaino.

Some of the **stained glass** in the cathedral is excellent, especially the earliest windows, in the apse, designed by Duccio, and the rose window with its cornucopia. Over the high altar is a bronze **baldachin** by Vecchietta, and in the north aisle, the **Piccolomini Altar** includes four early statues of saints by Michelangelo, and one by Torrigiani, the fellow who broke Michelangelo's nose and ended up in exile, working in Westminster Abbey. There is also a *Madonna* by Jacopo della Quercia. Throughout the cathedral, as everywhere else in Siena, be sure to keep an eye out for details—little things like the tiny, exquisite heads of the popes that decorate the clerestory wall. The Office of Works never settled for anything less than the best, and even such trifles as the holy water fonts, the choir stalls, the iron grilles and the candlesticks are works of genuine artistic merit.

THE PICCOLOMINI LIBRARY

This is the room with the famous frescoes by Pinturicchio maintained as part of the cathedral complex. It was built to hold the library of Aeneas Silvius, the greatest member of Siena's greatest noble family. The entrance is off the left aisle, near the Piccolomini Altar (open daily 10–1 and 2:30–5, until 7–30 in summer; adm).

Aeneas Silvius Piccolomini, eventually to become Pope Pius II, was the very definition of a Renaissance man. Probably the greatest geographer of his age, his works were studied closely by Columbus. Beyond that, and his activities as a poet, diplomat and historian, founder of Pienza and an important patron of artists and humanist scholars, he had, of course, a busy clerical-political career, working fitfully to reform the church of Rome and the constitution of his native city. In 1495, 31 years after his death, Cardinal Francesco Piccolomini, a man who would become Pope Pius III, decided his celebrated uncle's life would make a fine subject for a series of frescoes. He gave the job to Pinturicchio, his last major commission; among his assistants was the young, still impressionable Raphael—anyone who knows his *Betrothal of the Virgin* will find these paintings eerily familiar.

The 10 scenes include Aeneas Silvius at the court of James II in Scotland—a Scotland with a Tuscan fantasy landscape— where he served with an embassy. Later he is shown accepting a poet laureate's crown from his friend Emperor Frederick III, and presiding over the meeting of Frederick and his bride-to-be, Eleonora of Portugal. Another fresco depicts him canonizing St Catherine of Siena. The last, poignant one portrays a view of Ancona, and its cathedral up on Monte Guasco, where Pius II went in 1464, planning a crusade against the Turks. While waiting for the help promised by the European powers, help that never came, he fell ill and died.

Art historians and critics, following the snippish biography of the artist by Vasari, are not always kind to Pinturicchio. As with Gozzoli's frescoes for the Medici Palace in Florence, the consensus seems to be that this is a less challenging sort of art, or perhaps just a very elevated approach to interior decoration. Certainly Pinturicchio seems extremely concerned with the latest styles in court dress and coiffure. However, the incandescent colour, fairy-tale backgrounds and beautifully drawn figures prove irresistible. These are among the brightest and best-preserved of all quattrocento frescoes; the total effect is that of a serenely confident art, concerned above all with beauty for beauty's sake, even when chronicling the life of a pope. Aeneas Silvius' books have all been carted away somewhere but one of his favourite things remains, a marble statue of the Three Graces, a copy of the work by Praxiteles that was much studied by the artists of the 1400s.

THE MUSEO DELL'OPERA DEL DUOMO

Around the side of the cathedral, off the right transept, Piazza Jacopo della Quercia is the name the Sienese have given to the doomed nave of their 1330s **cathedral extension**. All around the square, the heroic pilasters and arches rise, some incorporated into the walls of later buildings. Beyond the big, blank façade, a little door on the right gives entrance to the **Museo dell'Opera del Duomo**, built into what would have been one of the cathedral transepts (daily 9–1:30, between 12 March and 31 Oct, 9–7:30; adm). This is the place to go to inspect the cathedral façade at close range. Most of the statues now on the façade are modern copies, replacing the works of great sculptors like Nicola Pisano, Urbano da Cortona and Jacopo della Quercia. The originals have been moved to the museum for preservation, and you can look the cathedral's marble saints right in the eye (if you care to; many of these remarkable statues, fairly alive with early Renaissance *prontezza* (alertness), seem ready to hop off their pedestals and start declaiming if they suspect for a minute you've been skipping Sunday mass).

Besides these, there are architectural fragments and leftover pinnacles, as well as some bits of the marble pavement that had to be replaced. On the first floor, a collection of Sienese paintings includes Duccio di Buoninsegna's masterpiece, the *Maestà* that hung behind the cathedral's high altar from 1311 until 1505. Painted on both sides, the main composition is a familiar Sienese favourite, the enthroned Virgin flanked by neat rows of adoring saints—expressive faces and fancy clothes with a glittering gold background. Among the other paintings and sculptures are works by Pietro and Ambrogio Lorenzetti, Simone Martini, Beccafumi and Vecchietta.

Among the works on the top floor is the *Madonna dagli Occhi Grossi* 'of the Big Eyes' by an anonymous artist of the 1210s, a landmark in the development of Sienese painting and the original cathedral altarpiece. There's a hoard of golden croziers, reliquaries, and crucifixes from the Cathedral Treasure, including another lovely golden rose from the Vatican—probably a gift of Aeneas Silvius. A stairway from here leads up to the top of the **Facciatone**, the 'big façade' of the unfinished nave, where you can contemplate lost ambitions and enjoy a view over the city .

THE BAPTISTRY

Outside the unfinished cathedral nave, a long, steep set of stairs leads down around the back of the church to Piazza San Giovanni. In this lower, but prominent setting the Office of Works architects squeezed in a baptistry, perhaps the only one in Italy situated directly under a cathedral apse. Behind its unfinished 1390s Gothic façade, this baptistry contains some of the finest art in Siena. It's hard to see anything in this gloomy cellar, though; bring plenty of coins for the lighting machines. Frescoes by Vecchietta, restored to death in the 19th century, decorate much of the interior. The crown jewel, however, is the **baptismal font**, a king-sized work embellished with some of the finest sculpture of the quattrocento. Of the gilded reliefs around the sides, *Herod's Feast* is by Donatello, and the *Baptism of Christ* and *St John in Prison* by Ghiberti. The first relief, with the annunciation of the Baptist's birth, is the work of Jacopo della Quercia, who also added the five statues of prophets above. Two of the statues at the corners of the font, the ones representing the virtues Hope and Charity, are also by Donatello.

Across the street from the baptistry, the Renaissance **Palazzo del Magnifico** by Cozzarelli was the family headquarters of the Petrucci, Sienese power brokers (and perhaps would-be rulers) in the late 15th and early 16th centuries.

Terzo di Città: the Pinacoteca

Opposite the old cathedral façade, one entire side of the piazza is occupied by the great **Ospedale di Santa Maria della Scala**, believed to have been founded in the 9th century and for centuries one of the largest and finest hospitals in the world. According to legend, the hospital had its beginnings with a pious cobbler named Sorore, who opened a hostel and infirmary for pilgrims on their way to Rome. (Siena was an important stop on medieval Europe's busiest pilgrimage route, the Via Francigiana.) Sorore's mother, it is said, later had a vision here—of babies ascending a ladder into heaven, and being received into the arms of the Virgin Mary—and consequently a foundling hospital was soon added. A meticulous attention to the health of its citizens was always one of the most praiseworthy features of Siena; even in the decadence of the 1700s advances in such things as inoculation were being made here. Today, old Siena is still full of hospitals. Only a part of this huge complex is still in use; the hospital and its chapel preserve some fine frescoes, and there has been some talk of making part of it into a museum.

The ancient quarter of steep narrow streets north of the cathedral is the *contrada* of the *Selva* (forest)—rhinoceros country. In its heart, Piazza della Selva, one of the most charming of the new *contrade* fountains has a bronze statue of the neighbourhood's rhinoceros symbol. Leaving the cathedral in the opposite direction, south down Via del Capitano, will lead you into the haunts of the dolphin and turtle (*Onda* and *Tartuga*). Where the street passes Via di Città, it changes its name to Via San Pietro, passing the 14th-century Palazzo Buonsignori, one of the most harmonious of the city's noble palaces, now restored as the home of the **Pinacoteca Nazionale** (daily 8:30–7; Sun 8:30–1; closed Mon; adm).

This is the temple of Sienese art, a representative sampling of this inimitable city's style; many of the works have been recently restored. The collection is arranged roughly chronologically, beginning on the ground floor with Guido da Siena and his school in the middle 13th century (Room 2), continuing through an entire room of delicate, melancholy Virgins by Duccio and his followers, reaching a climax with Duccio's luminous though damaged *Madonna dei Francescani* in Room 4. More Madonnas and saints fill room after room, including important works of Siena's greatest 14th-century artists; those of Pietro and Ambrogio Lorenzetti (*Madonna Enthroned* and the *Annunciation*, both in Room 7) and Taddeo di Bartolo (*Triptych*, in Room 9) stand out, with their rosy blooming faces and brilliant colour, a remarkable counterpoint to the relative austerity of contemporary painting in Florence. One element that is clearly evident in many of these paintings is Sienese civic pride; the artists take obvious delight in including the city's skyline and landmarks in the background of their works—even in nativities.

Sienese Renaissance painters are well represented, often betraying the essential conservatism of their art and resisting the new approaches of Florence: Domenico di Bartolo's 1433 *Madonna* in Room 9; Nerocchio and Matteo di Giovanni of the 1470s (Room 14); Sano di Pietro, the leading painter of the 1440s (Rooms 16–18). The first floor displays some of Il Sodoma's most important works, especially the great *Scourging of Christ* in Room 31 (1514); in Room 37 the *Descent into Hell* is one of the finest works by Siena's greatest Mannerist Beccafumi.

Around the Terzo di Città

Next to the Pinacoteca, the church of **San Pietro alle Scale** contains *The Flight into Egypt*, an altarpiece by Rutilio Manetti, the only significant Sienese painter of the Baroque era, a follower of Caravaggio. **San Giuseppe**, at the end of Via San Pietro, marks Siena's uneasy compromise with the new world of the 1600s. One of the city's first Baroque churches, it was nevertheless built not in Baroque marble or travertine but good Siena brown brick. This is the church of the *Onda* district; the *contrada*'s fountain is in front. Just around the corner, the gloomy bulk of **Sant'Agostino** conceals a happier Rococo interior of the 1740s by Vanvitelli, the Dutchman (born Van Wittel) who was chief architect for the Kings of Naples. Most of the building dates back to the 13th century, however, and there are surviving bits of trecento frescoes and altarpieces all around. In the north aisle, the Piccolomini Chapel has a fine painting by Il Sodoma, an *Epiphany*, and a *Massacre of the Innocents* by Matteo di Giovanni.

Via Pier Andrea Mattioli leads from here to the city walls and the Porta Tufi, passing along the way a path that leads to Siena's small **Botanical Gardens** (Mon–Fri 8–1, 3–5 pm; guided tours). Further west, the *contrada* of the *Chiocciola* (snail) centres on the church of **Santa Maria del Carmine**, a 14th-century church remodelled by Baldassare Peruzzi in 1517; inside is a painting of *St Michael* by Beccafumi and a grimly Caravaggiesque Last Judgement by an anonymous 16th-century artist.

Terzo di San Martino

Beginning again at the Croce del Travaglio and the Palazzo Piccolomini (p. 302), Banchi di Sotto leads into the populous eastern third of the city, passing the **Loggia del Papa**, a Renaissance ornament given to Siena by Aeneas Silvius Piccolomini in 1462. The most intriguing parts of this neighbourhood are found on the hillside behind Piazza del Mercato, old streets on slopes and stairs in the *contrada* of the *Torre*—one of the 'unlucky' *contrade* that hasn't won a *palio* in decades. Nevertheless they have a fine fountain with their elephant-and-tower emblem on pretty Piazzetta Franchi. One of the more characteristic streets in this part of town is **Via dell'Oro**, an alley of overhanging medieval houses, much like the ones in the Palazzo Pubblico's frescoes of Good and Bad Government. For something different, **Via Porta Giustizia** will lead you on a country ramble within the city's walls, down the valley that separates Terzo San Martino and Terzo di Città.

Some of the noteworthy churches in this Terzo are: **Santo Spirito** on Via dei Pispini, with another set of frescoes by Sodoma in the first chapel on the right; and **Santa Maria dei Servi**, to the south on Via dei Servi in the *contrada* of *Valdimontone* (ram). Here, in the north transept, is one of the earliest and best Sienese nativities, the altarpiece in the second north chapel by Taddeo di Bartolo. Among the many other good paintings in this church is a Madonna by Coppo di Marcovaldo and the *Madonna del Popolo* by Lippo Memmi. An interesting comparison can be made between two versions of that favourite Sienese subject, the *Massacre of the Innocents*: one from the early trecento by Pietro Lorenzetti, and another from 1491 by Matteo di Giovanni.

Nearby on Via Roma, the *Società Esecutori Pie Disposizioni* keeps an oratory and a small but good collection of Sienese art (call ahead, tel 220 400, daily 9–12, closed Sun). This Terzo also has two of the best surviving city gates, the **Porta Romana** at the end of Via Roma, and the elegant **Porta Pispini** on the road to Perugia. Once this gate was embellished with a painting of the Nativity by Sodoma, but only traces of it can be seen today.

Terzo di Camollia

Leading north from the Campo, **Via Banchi di Sopra**, a most aristocratic thoroughfare, lined with the palaces of the medieval Sienese elite, forms the spine of this largest and most populous of the *terzi*. The first important palace is also one of the oldest, that of the Tolomei family, a proud clan of noble bankers who liked to trace their ancestry back to the Greek Ptolemies of Hellenistic-era Egypt. The **Palazzo Tolomei**, begun in 1208, is the very soul of Sienese Gothic; it gave its name to Piazza Tolomei in front, the space used by the republic for its assembly meetings before the construction of the Palazzo Pubblico. Just a few blocks down Banchi di Sopra, **Palazzo Salimbeni** on Piazza Salimbeni was the compound of the Tolomei's mortal enemies; their centuries-long vendetta dragged Sienese politics into chaos on more than a few occasions. Together with the two adjacent palaces on the square, the Salimbeni is now the home of the *Monte dei Paschi di Siena*, founded in 1624, a remarkable savings bank with a medieval air about it that has a tremendous influence over everything that happens in southern Tuscany—they also have a good art collection, sometimes open to the public along with special exhibitions. A little further up the street, the plain brick **Oratory of Santa Maria delle Neve** is almost always locked up; if you should chance to see it open, stop in to see the altarpiece, the finest work of the late 1400s painter Matteo di Giovanni.

On the streets to the east of these palaces, in the neighbourhood of the *Giraffa* (giraffe), you'll find one of the last important churches to be built in Siena, the 1594 proto-Baroque **Santa Maria di Provenzano**, at the end of Via del Moro. This particular Virgin Mary, a terracotta image said to have been left by St Catherine (see p. 311), has had one of the most popular devotional cults in Siena since the 1590s; the annual *palio* is in her honour. The quiet streets behind the church, Siena's red-light district in Renaissance times, lead to **San Francesco**, begun in 1326, one of the city's largest churches. It's a sad tale; after a big fire in the 17th century, this great Franciscan barn was used for centuries as a warehouse and barracks. Restorations were begun in the 1880s, and the 'medieval' brick façade was completed only in 1913. The interior is still one of the most impressive in Siena, a monolithic rectangle with vivid stained glass (especially so in the late afternoon) and good transept chapels in the Florentine manner. A few bits of artwork have survived, including traces of frescoes by both the Lorenzettis in the north transept.

Next to San Francesco is the equally simple **Oratorio di San Bernardino**, begun in the late 1400s in honour of Siena's famous preacher. Its upper chapel, one of the monuments of the Sienese Renaissance, contains some fine frescoes by Beccafumi, Sodoma, and the almost forgotten, high Renaissance master Girolamo del Pacchia, few of whose works survive. (The oratory is not usually open, but ring for the doorkeeper.) The areas west of San Francesco, traditionally the solid working-class quarter, make up the *contrada* of *Bruco*, the caterpillar; their fountain is under the steps on Via dei Rossi. Bruco's name recalls the famous Compagnia del Bruco, the trade union that initiated the revolt of 1371 and at least temporarily reformed Siena's faction-ridden government. The workers paid a terrible price for it; while the revolution was underway, some young noble provocateurs started a fire that consumed almost the entire *contrada*. Today Bruco is the worst of the 'unlucky' neighbourhoods; it hasn't won a *palio* since 1955.

St Catherine, St Dominic and the Goose

In contrast to poor caterpillar, the equally proletarian *Oca* (goose) seems to have always been the best-organized and most successful of the *contrade*. On occasions during the Napoleonic Wars when the Tuscan and city governments were in disarray, the Oca's men temporarily took charge of the entire city. The goose's most famous daughter, Caterina Benincasa, was born here, on Vicolo del Tiratoio, in 1347. She was the last but one of twenty-five children born in the family of a wool dyer. At an early age the visions started. By her teens she had turned her room at home into a cell, and while she never became a nun, she lived like a hermit, a solitary ascetic in her own house, sleeping with a stone for a pillow. After she received the stigmata, like St Francis, her reputation as a holy woman spread across Tuscany; popes and kings corresponded with her, and towns would send for her to settle their disputes. In 1378, Florence was under a papal interdict, and the city asked Catherine to plead its case at the papal court at Avignon. She went, but with an agenda of her own—convincing Pope Gregory XI to move the papacy back to Rome where it belonged. As a woman, and a holy woman to boot, she was able to tell the pope to his face what a corrupt and worldly Church he was running, without ending up dangling from the top of the palace wall.

Talking the pope (a French pope, mind you) into leaving the civilized life in Provence for turbulent, barbaric 14th-century Rome is only one of the miracles with which Catherine was credited. Political expediency probably helped more than divine intervention—much of Italy, including anathemized Florence, was in revolt against the absentee popes. She followed them back, and died in Rome in 1380, at the age of only 33. Canonization came in 1460, and in our own century she has been declared co-patron of Italy (along with St Francis) and one of the Doctors of the Church. She and St Teresa of Avila are the only women to hold this honour; both of them for their inspired devotional writings and practical, incisive letters encouraging Church reform.

The *contrada* of the Goose stretches down steeply from Banchi di Sopra to the western city walls. At its centre, on Vicolo di Tiatoio, St Catherine's house is preserved as a shrine; the **Santuario e Casa di Santa Caterina** includes all of the Benincasa home and the dyer's workshop, each room converted into a chapel, many with frescoes by 15th- and 16th-century Sienese artists (open daily 9–12:30, 3–6 pm). The adjacent oratory is now the Oca's *contrada* chapel (note the goose in the detail of the façade).

Two blocks away, on Via della Sapienza, the **Museo Archeologico** contains a small collection of Etruscan and Egyptian artefacts (daily 9–2, Sun 9–1; adm).

Via Santa Caterina, the main street of the Oca, slopes down towards the city walls and **Fontebranda**, a simple pointed-arched fountain of the 13th century. It doesn't seem much now, but medieval and Renaissance travellers always remarked on it, an important part of Siena's advanced system of fountains and aqueducts. **San Domenico** church, on the hill above Fontebranda, similarly fails to impress, at least when you see it close up from the bus depot on Piazza San Domenico. From Fontebranda, however, the bold Gothic lines of the apse and transepts give a great insight into the straightforward, strangely modern character of much Sienese religious architecture. It's a long climb up to the church from here. Inside, the church is as big and empty as San Francesco; among the relatively few works of art is the only portrait of St Catherine, on the west wall, done by her friend, the artist Andrea Vanni. In this church, scene of so many incidents from the saint's life, you can see her head in a golden reliquary, though the real attraction is the wonderfully hysterical set of murals by Sodoma in the **Cappella Santa Caterina**, representing the girl in various states of serious exaltation.

The open, relatively modern quarter around San Domenico offers a welcome change from the dark and treeless streets of this brick city, in a shady park called **La Lizza** and the green spaces around the **Fortezza Medicea**. Though the site is the same, this is not the hated fortress Charles V compelled the Sienese to build in 1552; as soon as the Sienese chased the imperial troops out, they razed it to the ground. Cosimo I forced its rebuilding after annexing Siena, but to make the bitter pill easier to swallow he employed a Sienese architect, Baldassare Lanci, and let him create what must be the most elegant and civilized, least threatening fortress in Italy. The Fortezza, a long, low rectangle of Siena brick profusely decorated with Medici balls, seems more like a setting for garden parties or summer opera than anything designed to intimidate a sullen populace. The Sienese weren't completely won over; right after Italian reunification they renamed the central space of the fortress **Piazza della Libertà**. The grounds are now a city park, and the vaults of the munition cellars have become the **Enoteca Nazionale**, the 'Permanent Exhibition of Italian Wines'. Almost every variety of wine Italy produces can be bought here—by the glass or by the bottle; the Enoteca's purpose is to promote Italian wines, and it ships thousands of bottles overseas each year (open daily, 3 pm–midnight).

West of the fortress, beyond the Lizza and the city stadium, lie the twin centres of modern Siena, **Piazza Gramsci**, terminus for most city bus lines, and **Piazza Matteotti**. Continuing northwards towards the Camollia gate, you pass the little Renaissance church of **Fontegiusta**, just off Via di Camollia on Via Fontegiusta. Designed in 1482 by Urbano da Cortona, this church contains a fresco by Peruzzi (another Sibyl) and a magnificent tabernacle over the main altar—also a whalebone, according to local legend left here by Christopher Columbus. The **Porta Camollia**, in the northernmost corner of Siena, underwent the Baroque treatment in the 1600s. Here you will see the famous inscription 'Wider than her gates Siena opens her heart to you'. Old Siena was never that sentimental. The whole thing was added in 1604—undoubtedly under the orders of the Florentine governor—to decorate the visit of Grand Duke Francesco I, who wasn't really welcome at all.

Peripheral Attractions

From Porta Camollia, Viale Vittorio Emanuele leads through some of the modern quarters outside the walls. Soon after the Camollia gate it passes a pretty stone column, commemorating the meeting of Emperor Frederick III and his bride-to-be Eleonora of Portugal in 1451—the event captured in one of the Pinturicchio frescoes in the Piccolomini Library. Next looms a great brick defence tower, the **Antiporto**, erected just before the Siege of Siena, and rebuilt in 1675. Further down, the **Palazzo dei Diavoli**, built in 1460, was the headquarters of the Marquis of Marignano during that siege.

There isn't much to see on the outskirts of the city—thanks largely to Marignano, who laid waste lovely and productive lands for miles around. Some 2 km east of the city (take Via Simone Martini from the Porta Ovile), in the hills above the railway station, the basilica and monastery of **L'Osservanza** has been carefully restored after serious damage in the last war. Begun in 1422, a foundation of San Bernardino, the monastery retains much of its collection of 13th-and 14th-century Sienese art.

To the west of the city, the road to Massa Marittima passes through the hills of the Montagnola Sienese, an important centre of monasticism in the Middle Ages (see San Galgano, p. 335). Near the village of Montecchio (6 km), the hermitage of **Lecceto**, one of the oldest in Tuscany, changed much over the centuries but retains some Renaissance frescoes in the church and a 12th-century cloister; nearby, the hermitage of **San Leonardo al Lago** is mostly in ruins; the 14th-century church survives, with masterly frescoes (*c.* 1360) by Pietro Lorenzetti's star pupil, Lippo Vanni. Just outside the village of Sovicille (13 km), there is a Romanesque church of the 12th century, the **Pieve di Ponte allo Spina**. The village of Rosia (17 km) has another Romanesque church, and just to the south the Vallombrosan **Abbey of Torri** has much to show from its original foundation in the 1200s; there is a rare three-storey cloister, with three different types of columns.

A LITTLE SHOPPING

Siena, with its population of only 60,000, is blissfully short of designer boutiques and such. Even the usual tourist trinkets seem lacking—illuminated plastic models of the cathedral are harder to find every year! Nevertheless, a thorough search of the back streets will turn up plenty of unpretentious artisan workshops—almost all of them so unconcerned with tourism they don't even bother hanging out a sign. Some examples:

First and strangest, you can buy just about any kind of stuffed bird from the shop at Via San Martino 1. Brass and pewter shields of the *contrade*, and other paraphernalia of Siena's great obsession, can be had at Via S. Girolamo 15. Just off Piazza Independenza, at Via Galuzza 5, an artist with a distinctive modern style creates works in stained glass (most of them portable). Via di Città 94 sells interesting ceramic pieces, just down the street from Siena's best bookshop, the Libreria Senese, at no. 64.

WHERE TO STAY (tel prefix 0577)

Many of Siena's finest and most interesting hotels are outside the walls—out in the lovely countryside, or near the city gates, as close to the centre as cars can logically penetrate. What's left, in the centre, is simple but comfortable enough. In the summer, rooms are in short supply and it would be a good idea to book ahead. If you come without a reservation, your first stop should be the **Hotel Information Centre** run by the city's innkeepers, tel 288 084. It's conveniently located in Piazza San Domenico, the terminus of all intercity bus routes. If you arrive by train, take the city bus up from the station to Piazza Matteotti, and walk a block down Via Curtatone. Even at the worst of times, they should be able to find you something—except during the *Palio*, of course, when you should make your bookings several months in advance.

If you have a car, a number of hotels outside the walls have a rural Tuscan charm and views of the city that more than make up for the slight inconvenience. About 1 km southeast of the city, near the Porta Romana, ****La Certosa di Maggiano**, tel 288 180, is one of the most remarkable establishments in Italy. In this restored 14th-century Carthusian monastery, where there are only 14 rooms, the luxuries include a heated pool, air conditioning that works, a quiet chapel and cloister, a salon for backgammon and chess, tennis courts, an excellent restaurant, and a library that would be an antiquarian's dream. Of course all this doesn't come cheap (about L230 000). For a second choice, there are sunset views over Siena from the ****Villa Scacciapensieri**, 3 km north of the city at Strada Scacciapensieri 10, tel 41 442. This is a quiet country house divided into 29 spacious rooms; besides the view, it features a pool and a good restaurant with an outdoor terrace (L130–180 000).

Many of Siena's two and three-star hotels cluster around the entrances to the city. Just inside the walls, the ***Palazzo Ravizza**, tel 280 462, and its 25 rooms occupy an old town house on Pian dei Mantellini, near the Porta Laterina; the restaurant isn't anything special, but the rooms are cosy and there is a pretty terrace (L68–80 000). Closer to the centre, there are a number of choices, including the comfortably old-fashioned ***Continentale** near the Campo on Banchi di Sopra, tel 41 451 (L76–82 000); the ***Centrale**, around the corner at Via Calzolieri 24, tel 280 379 (L45 000 without bath, L60 000 with); and the **Chiusarelli**, a well-run establishment and a good bargain, on Via Curtatone near the bus station, tel 280 562 (L55–60 000). The **Piccolo Hotel il Palio** is a little way from the centre, at Piazza del Sale 19, tel 281 131, but it has the advantages of a quiet location and a friendly, English-speaking proprietress (L35–60 000).

Inexpensive places are a little hard to find—especially before terms when they're full of university students looking for a permanent place. Via delle Donzelle, a block from the Campo, has two pleasant ones: the cramped *Nuove Donzelle**, tel 288 088 (L35 000); and the more genteel *Tre Donzelle**, tel 280 358 (L36 000, some more expensive, with bath). The city of Siena runs its own youth hostel, the **Ostello della Gioventù Guidoriccio**, Via Fiorentina 17, tel 52 122, in Lo Stellino, 2 km from the city (buses no. 8 or 10, from the station or Piazza Matteotti). No cards are required, but good modern doubles and dorm rooms with breakfast for L12 000 a head; arrive early in July and August.

EATING OUT

Sitting between three of Italy's greatest wine-producing areas, the Chianti, the Brunello of Montalcino and the Vino Nobile of Montepulciano, there is always something distinguished to wash down the simple dishes of the Sienese table. This city's real speciality is sweets, and quite a few visitors to Siena find they have no room for lunch or dinner after repeated visits to the pastry shops for slices of *panforte*, an alarmingly heavy but indecently tasty cake laced with fruits, nuts, orange peel and secret Sienese ingredients, or *panpepato*, similar but with pepper in it. They are all artists—shop windows flaunt gargantuan creations of cakes and crystallized fruit in the shop windows, metres high, and as colourful as a Lorenzetti fresco, set out for all to admire before they are carted off to some wedding party, The **Enoteca** inside the Medici fortress (see p. 312) is another distraction; sometimes they organize special tastings, concentrating on one particular region of Italy. Siena being a university town, snacks and fast food of all kinds are common; a *cioccina* is Siena's special variation on pizza.

If you've survived the wine and the pastry shops, you'll appreciate the succulent risottos and pasta dishes at **Osteria le Logge**, just off the Campo at Via del Porrione 33, tel 48 013, with exotic second courses like stuffed guinea fowl (*faraona*) and a fine wine list (L45 000; closed Sun). Also near the Campo, **Taverna di Cecco**, Via Cecco Angioleri 19, tel 288 518, specializes in pasta dishes, meats, and nearly everything else done up with either truffles or *porcini* mushrooms. There is a L25 000 *presso fisso* menu, otherwise expect L35–40 000. **Tullio ai Tre Cristi**, tel 280 608, has been on Vicolo Provenzano since about 1830; perhaps the most authentic of Sienese restaurants, its menu includes things like *ribollita*, tripe with sausages, and roast boar from the Maremma. The *pici*, thick south Tuscan spaghetti, are home made. There are outside tables in the summer (about L35 000). On Via del Castoro, just off the Piazza del Duomo, **Al Marsili**, tel 47 154, is another of Siena's best, in a singularly elegant setting—not very traditional, with dishes like gnocchi in duck sauce, but it's hard to complain (L45 000 and up; closed Mon).

Less expensive places—and there are many good ones—are usually found a little further away from the Campo. **Da Mario** on Via Salicotto is always busy, offering home cooking for L14 000. **Trattoria da Dino**, Casata di Sopra 71, tel 289 036, makes a good *spiedini alle Senese* (about L25 000, or an L18 000 menu; closed Fri). The restaurant in the **Nuova Donzelle**, (see above), tel 42 069, is popular with students, has a choice of dinner menus for L10–14–16 000; closed Sun. One that has opened recently is the **Quikom** on Via dei Rossi 79 near San Francesco, tel 287 592: good local wines and an inventive kitchen with pasta dishes involving artichokes, asparagus and mushrooms (about L25–30 000, closed Sun).

Part X

HILL TOWNS WEST OF SIENA

Courtyard of Palazzo Comunale, San Gimignano

In the late Middle Ages, this dramatically diverse, often rugged countryside was a border region, both culturally and politically, its people alternately subject to the strong pull of Florence and Siena. Its towns do not have all that much in common: Poggibonsi is almost all new, while parts of Volterra go back to the Etruscans. San Gimignano presents its famous skyline of medieval skyscrapers, while parts of the Metal Hills show outlandish silhouettes of cooling towers from the ubiquitous geothermal power plants. San Gimignano and Volterra are the main attractions, both beautiful cities containing some remarkable works of art. Massa Marittima, often overlooked, has one of the finest cathedrals in Italy. Beyond that there is a doll-sized walled city, bubbling sulphurous pits, alabaster souvenirs, a Roman theatre, lonely moors, and a sword in a stone, not King Arthur's but someone else's.

Colle di Val d'Elsa and Poggibonsi

GETTING AROUND

The main routes between Florence and Siena—the Via Cassia (N. 2) or the Superstrada del Palio—have exits for Colle di Val d'Elsa (27 km/35 min from Siena, 49 km/1 hr from Florence) and Poggibonsi, 7 km further north on N. 68. Poggibonsi is a major bus junction in south Tuscany, with easy connections to Florence, Siena, San Gimignano, Volterra, and Colle di Val d'Elsa (TRA-IN buses if you're coming from Siena, SITA from Florence). Poggibonsi is also on the Empoli–Siena rail line, with a branch or bus beyond to Colle in 15 min.

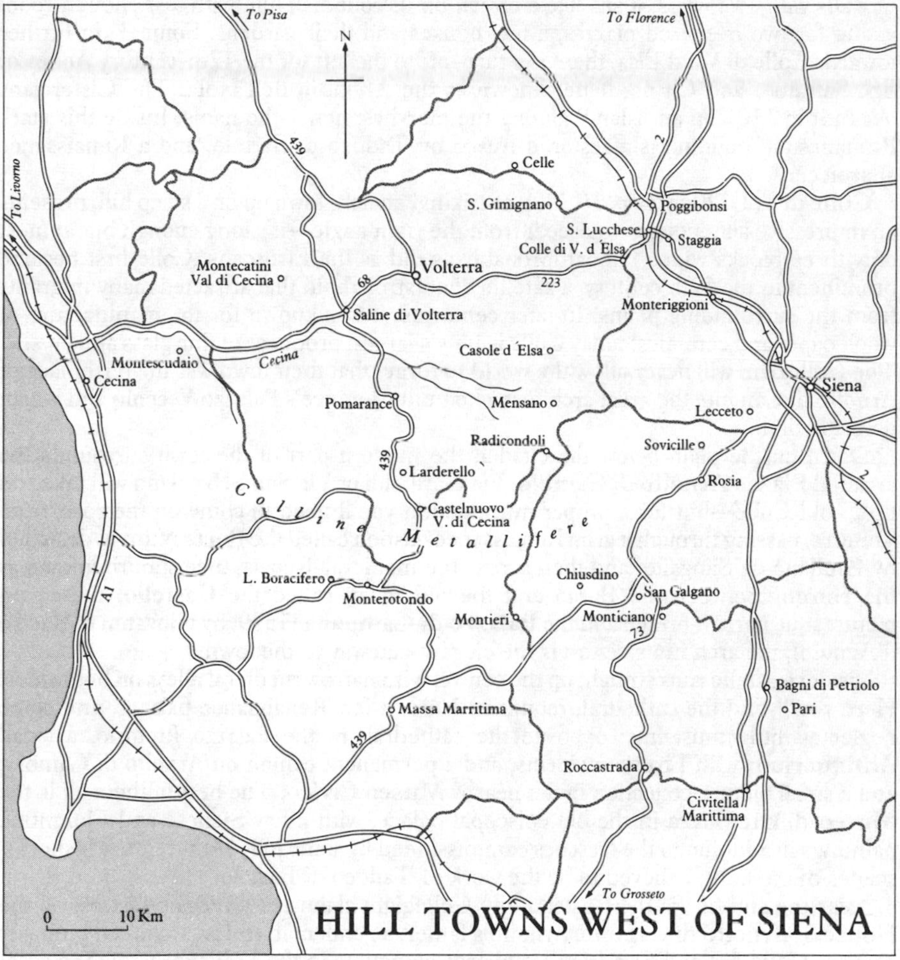

To Pisa
To Florence
N
To Livorno
439
2
Celle
S. Gimignano
Poggibonsi
S. Lucchese
Staggia
Colle di V. d Elsa
Montecatini
Val di Cecina
Volterra
68
223
Saline di Volterra
Monteriggioni
Montescudaio
Cecina
Casole d Elsa
Cecina
Siena
Pomarance
Mensano
Lecceto
Radicondoli
Sovicille
439
Larderello
Rosia
Colline Metallifere
Castelnuovo
V. di Cecina
2
A1
L. Boracifero
Chiusdino
Monterotondo
San Galgano
Montieri
Monticiano
73
Bagni di Petriolo
Pari
Massa Marritima
439
Roccastrada
Civitella
Marittima
To Grosseto
0
10 Km

HILL TOWNS WEST OF SIENA

Colle di Val d'Elsa

Eleven km north of Siena, the N. 2 passes a genuine curiosity, the tiny fortified town of **Monteriggioni**. For much of Siena's history, this was its northernmost bastion, often in the front lines in the wars with Florence after its construction in 1219. Now, a neat circle of walls with 14 towers, it sits like a crown on its roundish hill, with just enough room inside for two oversized piazzas, a few houses and their gardens. Some 3 km further towards Colle di Val d'Elsa, there is a turn-off to the left for the 12th-century Abbey of SS. Salvatore and Cirino, better known as the **Abbadia dell'Isola**. The Cistercians began it in 1101 on an 'island' among the marshes, hence the name. Inside this stark Romanesque building is a restored fresco by Taddeo di Bartolo, and a Renaissance altarpiece.

Colle di Val d'Elsa (pop. 16,300), a striking, ancient town up on a steep hill, presents an impressive silhouette if you see it from the right angle—it's long enough but at most only three blocks wide. Though probably as old as the Etruscans, Colle first became prominent in the 12th century, a safe fortified stronghold that attracted many migrants from the surrounding plains. In later centuries, it was known for the manufacture of wool, paper and ceramics; today Colle is Italy's largest producer of fine glass and crystal. The Collegiani will never allow the world to forget that their town was the birthplace of Arnolfo di Cambio, the great architect who built Florence's Palazzo Vecchio and began its Cathedral.

Down on the plain below the citadel, the modern part of the town surrounds the arcaded **Piazza Arnolfo di Cambio**. Via Garibaldi or Via San Sebastiano will take you up to old Colle—but for a proper introduction you'll need to come on the road from Volterra, passing through a grim Renaissance bastion called the **Porta Nuova**, designed by Giuliano da Sangallo, and then across the medieval-Renaissance suburb known as the **Borgo**. Between the Borgo and the old town, called the **Castello**, there is a picturesque narrow bridge and the **Palazzo di Campana** (1539, by Giovanni di Baccio d'Agnolo); the arch in its centre is the elegant gateway to the town.

Via del Castello runs straight up the centre, with narrow medieval alleys on both sides. Here you'll find the cathedral, rebuilt in 1603, a few Renaissance palaces, and some neglected little museums: opposite the cathedral, in the Palazzo Pretorio, a small **Antiquarium** with Etruscan objects, and a permanent exhibit on Arnolfo di Cambio; and a small picture collection in the nearby **Museo Civico**. The best of them all is the **Museo d'Arte Sacra** in the old episcopal palace, with a few Sienese and Florentine paintings in addition to the frescoes commissioned by some jolly 14th-century bishop—scenes of the hunt, believed to be the work of Taddeo di Bartolo.

Near the end of Via del Castello, the Collegiani claim an old tower-fortress as the **House of Arnolfo di Cambio**. Arnolfo's father, a gentleman and an architect, probably came to Colle di Val d'Elsa from Lombardy sometime in the 1230s, bringing the great tradition of the Lombard master-masons into Tuscany. Arnolfo himself may have received his initiation into the new (for Italy) Gothic style from studying works in nearby Siena or the new Cistercian abbey at San Galgano. He worked for Nicola Pisano on the Siena cathedral pulpit, and for Giovanni Pisano on the Fonte Maggiore in Perugia, and probably moved to Florence in the 1270s.

South of Colle, many of the villages in the hills retain their simple Romanesque churches from the 11th–12th centuries, beginning with the isolated **Badia à Coneo** a

Vallombrosan foundation of the 1120s (5 km, on an unpaved lane off the road to Casole). At **Casole d'Elsa** (15 km south, local bus) a town that took hard knocks in the last war, there is an interesting **Collegiata** church begun in the 12th century, with Sienese frescoes, two fine late 14th-century sepulchres by Gano da Siena, and terracottas by Giovanni della Robbia. Casole's Sienese **Rocca** held out into the 16th century, long after the rest of the Valdelsa flew the Florentine flag. South from Casole, the road winds through a pleasant green countryside leading up to the Colline Metallifere, the 'metal hills', and you can seek out more Romanesque churches in **Mensano** (7 km) and **Radicòndoli** (15 km, the church of San Simone).

Poggibonsi

If you spend enough time in Tuscany, sooner or later you are bound to pass through Poggibonsi (pop. 25,700), a major knot on the N. 2, N. 429 and Superstrada del Palio road links from Siena to Florence and Pisa. These days, residents of the pretty tourist towns of central Tuscany are not always above having a laugh at the expense of this homely, hard-working industrial centre. Poor Poggibonsi! Founded only in 1156, the original *Poggiobonizzo* grew rapidly. By 1220, it was probably one of the largest cities in Tuscany, with a population of some 15,000; in that year, Emperor Frederick II declared it a 'Città Imperiale' with special rights and privileges. Poggiobonizzo's Ghibelline politics and its Imperial favour, however, were to prove its undoing. In 1270, its neighbours San Gimignano and Colle di Val d'Elsa, along with the Florentines and the troops of Charles of Anjou, besieged and conquered the city, after which they razed it to the ground. Most of its citizens migrated elsewhere, but a number of the poorer ones stayed behind, refounding the town as a modest market village on the plain. Poggibonsi was thoroughly wrecked again during the battles of 1944, but has grown tremendously since to become the biggest town between Florence and Siena.

There isn't much to see: the 14th-century Palazzo Pretorio and the Collegiate Church on the main street recall at least something of the appearance of pre-war Poggibonsi. Nearby, the **Castello della Magione** is an interesting small complex from the 1100s; the Romanesque chapel and outbuildings form a little closed square, a fortified pilgrims' hospice said to have been built by the Templars. Above the town, an unfinished fortress begun by Lorenzo de' Medici covers much of the original city of Poggiobonizzo.

Just 2 km south of town near the N. 2, the austerely Franciscan **Basilica of San Lucchese** occupies an attractive site in the hills; inside are some good frescoes, including works of Taddeo Gaddi and Bartolo di Fredi. Not surprisingly, this strategically important corner of Tuscany has plenty of castles scattered about, including the 13th-century **Castello della Rochetta**, once the home of the famous *condottiere* Sir John Hawkwood, and the romantically ruined **Rocca di Staggia** (5 km south of Poggibonsi on the N. 2), built by the Florentines in the 1430s—a counterpart to Sienese Monteriggioni, just a few kilometres down the same road.

WHERE TO STAY (tel prefix 0577)

With the Superstrada del Palio running through these parts, roadside inns and quiet country hotels are not hard to find. A kilometre or so east of Colle di Val d'Elsa, at Località Belvedere near the Siena highway, the *****Villa Belvedere**, tel 920 966, is a pretty, old villa with a big garden, a restaurant and 15 simple rooms (L150 000). Up in the town itself, there is the *****Arnolfo**, a simple, comfortable place in the Borgo at Via Campana 8, tel 922 020 (L65–75 000).

EATING OUT

Heading from Florence to Siena, or from Siena to the west, a good place to stop for lunch is the little castle-village of Monteriggioni, and **Il Pozzo** on Piazza Roma 2, tel 304 127; they do some of the simpler dishes very well—bean soup and roast meats, but their real forte is fancy desserts (even crêpes suzettes) (L35–45 000 closed Sun eve and Mon). In Colle di Val d'Elsa, the **Villa Belvedere** hotel (see above) has a very popular restaurant (L40–60 000). For something lighter, the **Nuova Idea** on Via Salvagna has spaghetti and beer for about L5000. Out among the olive groves in the nearby hamlet of Mugnano, an old farm called the **Fattoria di Mugnano**, tel 959 023, has become a thriving business. The delightful restaurant offers local favourites but also Sicilian cuisine (L40 000); they'll also sell you some of the wine and olive oil they produce, or arrange horseback riding and tours of the countryside. If you're spending time in Poggibonsi, the restaurant of the **Hotel Alcide**, Viale Marconi 67a, tel 936 196, is one of the better places for seafood in this landlocked province, featuring dishes with a south Italian slant like Apulian *orecchiette* in a sauce with cuttlefish and several different varieties of maritime risottos (L55–75 000).

San Gimignano

In the miniaturist landscape of this corner of Tuscany, San Gimignano, Italy's best-preserved medieval city, is an almost fantastic landmark. From Poggibonsi, or from the Volterra road, its medieval towers, some of them over 50 m (150 ft) tall, loom over the surrounding hills. Once, almost every city in central Italy looked like this; more than just defensive strongholds in the incessant family feuds, these towers served as status symbols both for the families and the cities themselves, a visible measure of a town's power and prosperity, even if it also betrayed the bitterness of its internal divisions.

By the 16th century, most of Italy's towers had succumbed to age, decay, and particularly to the efforts of the urban *comuni*, which pruned and destroyed these symbols of truculent nobility at every opportunity. For whatever reason, this did not happen in San Gimignano, famous even in the 1300s as the '*Città delle belle torri*'. Originally there were at least 70 towers (in a town barely 1/8 of a square mile in size). Now only 15 remain, though enough, along with San Gimignano's beautiful streets, churches and public buildings, to give the impression of having been hermetically sealed in a time capsule from the Middle Ages.

History

According to legend, the town was originally called Castel della Selva. When the Gothic army of Totila passed through in the 550s, the townsfolk for some reason chose to pray to an obscure saint named Gimignano, a martyred bishop of Modena, for their salvation from what appeared to be a guaranteed sacking. Gimignano came through in style, looming down from the clouds in golden armour to scare away the besiegers.

Although it evidently must have been an important and prosperous place, San Gimignano does not cut much of a figure in the medieval chronicles. The city was an independent republic from the early 1100s until 1353, when it came under the rule of Florence. It certainly participated in the Guelph-Ghibelline strife, and in all the other troubles of the period, though today it is probably best remembered as the hometown of that excellent poet, Folgore of San Gimignano (*c.* 1250), famous for his lovely sonnets to the months of the year. As in so many other medieval towns, San Gimignano has the air of a false start, a free *comune* that could build a wall and defend itself, yet lacked the will or the money to make itself into a Siena or a Florence. When this city lost the wealth or the fierceness that briefly made it an important player on the Tuscan stage, it crystallised into its medieval form, a perfect preparation for a role as a tourist town. Today San Gimignano has a population of some 7500. On a good day in July or August it may see several times that in day-trippers.

Even during the Renaissance the town seems to have been a resort for the Florentines; Dante, Machiavelli and Savonarola all spent some time here, and artists like Ghirlandaio and Gozzoli were only too happy to come up for a small commission. Don't let the prospect of crowds keep you from coming. San Gimignano handles them gracefully; its fine art, elegant medieval cityscapes and the verdant rolling countryside right outside its gates make this one of the smaller towns of Tuscany most worth visiting.

GETTING AROUND

The railway station is 11 km away, an infrequent run on the Empoli-Siena line. Buses to the town *usually* coincide with the trains, but from either Siena or Florence you'll be better off taking the bus, which leaves you right at the Porta San Giovanni, the main entrance to the town. TRA-IN buses from Siena (38 km/45 min—the same bus that goes to Colle di Val d'Elsa) are very frequent, though for most you will need to change in Poggibonsi. Several daily SITA buses arrive from Florence (54 km/1 hr, 15 min) and there are four buses a day to nearby Certaldo.

If you're driving, San Gimignano is 11 km west of Poggibonsi, 13 km south of Certaldo, or 14 km from Colle di Val d'Elsa, each route more scenic than the last. Within the walls San Gimignano is almost always closed to traffic; the main car park is just outside **Porta San Giovanni**. You'll need to get a pass from the police if you want to take your car to one of the hotels inside.

TOURIST INFORMATION

Piazza del Duomo 1 (tel 940 008).

Piazza del Duomo and the Museo Civico

From the southern gate, Porta San Giovanni, the street of the same name leads towards the town centre, passing on the way the little churches of San Giovanni, built by the Knights Templar, and **San Francesco**, with a good Pisan-Romanesque façade, now deconsecrated and converted into a wine shop. Another ancient gate, the Arco dei Bacci, leads into the triangular **Piazza della Cisterna** and the adjacent **Piazza del Duomo**—a superbly beautiful example of asymmetrical, medieval town design, seemingly haphazard but really quite sophisticated. Piazza della Cisterna contains the town's well, whence the name, and some of its towers.

On Piazza del Duomo, two stout Gothic public buildings with Guelph crenellations and lofty towers compete with the Collegiata church for your attention. The **Palazzo del Podestà**, with its vaulted loggia, was begun in the 1230s by Emperor Frederick II at the height of imperial power for his *podestà*. Above it stands the Torre della Rognosa, with a small cupola on top; at 51 m (167 ft) it once marked the height limit for private towers—the *podestà* didn't want anyone putting him in the shade. Later, when the *comune* was able to wrest effective self-government from the emperors, it built an even taller tower for the **Palazzo del Popolo** across the piazza; the awesome 54 m (177 ft) Torre Grossa was completed about 1300 and the rest of the Palazzo about 20 years later.

Underneath this tower, an archway leads into the charming, thoroughly medieval **Cortile**, or courtyard, with bits of frescoes (one by Il Sodoma) and the painted coats-of-arms of Florentine governors from after 1353. A stair leads up to the **Museo Civico**, with an excellent collection of art from both Florentine and Sienese masters. One of the oldest works is a remarkable painted crucifix by Coppo di Marcovaldo (*c.*1270) that predates (and some might say surpasses) the similar, more famous crucifixes of Giotto. The museum has two sweet Madonnas by Benozzo Gozzoli, a pair of tondos by Filippino Lippi portraying the Annunciation, and a big, colourful enthroned Virgin of Pinturicchio's that looks like it strayed here from that artist's Piccolomini Chapel in Siena. Taddeo di Bartolo contributes a set of paintings with the definitive *Story of San Gimignano*, a saint worthy of having a town named after him judging by these scenes; he is pictured calming the sea, exorcizing a devil who had been inhabiting the daughter of Emperor Jovian, and succumbing to the flesh while saying mass—he has to pee, but when he sneaks out of church a winged devil attacks him; fortunate enough to have a cross on him, Gimignano drives it away without much difficulty.

To the San Gimignanese, the biggest attraction of the museum is the Sala del Consiglio, or **Sala di Dante**, where the poet spoke in 1299 as an ambassador of Florence, seeking to convince the *comune* to join the Guelph League. The frescoes on its walls include more works by Gozzoli, a glittering company of angels and saints in the *Maestà* of the Sienese artist Lippo Memmi, and some trecento scenes of hunting and tournaments. After this, contemplate a climb up the Torre Grosso—several hundred steps, but there's a view over San Gimignano and the surrounding countryside that is worth the effort (open daily except Mon; from April to end Sept, 9:30–12:30, 3:30–6:30 pm; from Oct to end March, 9:30–12:30, 2:30–5:30 pm; adm). These opening hours apply to all the city museums and one ticket is valid for all of them.

The Collegiata

The name Piazza del Duomo is a little misleading: San Gimignano doesn't have a cathedral any more, but a **Collegiata**, begun in the 12th century and enlarged in the 15th, which would make an impressive seat for any bishop. It turns a blank brick façade towards the world, but the interior is a lavish imitation of Siena cathedral, with its tiger striped arches and vaults painted with a firmament of golden stars. Its walls, however, out-shine the larger cathedral with first-class frescoes of the 14th and 15th centuries, mostly by artists from Siena.

In the north aisle, Bartolo di Fredi painted the Old Testament scenes in the 1360s. Note Noah with the animals, and the torments of Job (also how each scene is accompanied by a neat explanation in simple Italian, a fascinating example of the artists, and the Church, coming to terms with a newly literate public). Some of Bartolo's best work is in the lunettes off the north aisle: a medieval cosmography of the Creation, scenes of Adam naming the animals and a graphic view of the creation of Eve. New Testament pictures by Barna da Siena (about 1380) cover the south wall; his *Crucifixion* is an exceedingly fine work. On the west wall, over the entrance, is a well-punctured *Saint Sebastian* by Gozzoli and a real surprise, the most perverse *Last Judgement* in Italy. It isn't recorded what moved Taddeo di Bartolo, a most serendipitous painter of rosy Sienese Virgins, to this madness. You may think you have seen the damned suffering interesting tortures and indignities before; Italy has plenty of them. This is the first time, however, that delicacy forbids us to describe one. It's a little faded, unfortunately. Nearby stand two wooden figures of an *Annunciation* by Jacopo della Quercia.

THE CAPPELLA DI SANTA FINA

A ticket from the Museo Civico will get you into the **Chapel of Santa Fina**, off the south aisle, with an introduction to one of the most irritating hagiographies in Christendom. Little Fina was going to the well for water, according to the story, when she accepted an orange from a young swain. Upon returning home, her mother told her how wicked she was to take it, whereupon the poor girl became so mortified over her great sin that she lay down on the kitchen table and prayed forgiveness without ceasing for the next five years. Finally, St Anthony came down to call her soul up into heaven, and the kitchen table and all the towers of San Gimignano burst into bloom with violets. Domenico Ghirlandaio got the commission to paint all this; he pocketed the money and did a splendid job (1475) in the brightest springtime colours. In the last scene, note San Gimignano's famous towers in the background.

Just to the left of the Collegiata, there is a lovely small courtyard where musicians sometimes play on summer weekends. Here, on the wall of the Baptistry, you will see another fine fresco by Ghirlandaio, an *Annunciation* that has survived reasonably well for being outside for 500 years. The town's two other museums are here: the **Museo Etrusco** with a small collection of local archaeological finds, and the **Museo d'Arte Sacra**, which, besides the usual ecclesiastical clutter, has some good painted wood statues from the late Middle Ages.

Around the Town

From Piazza del Duomo, it's not too difficult a climb up to the **Rocca**, a somewhat ruined fortress of the 1350s that offers one of the best views of this towered town. Down Via di Castello, in the eastern end of town, the **Oratory of San Lorenzo in Ponte**, now unused, has quattrocento Florentine frescoes and an exhibit of finds from a 16th–18th-century pharmacy that once functioned in the nearby Hospital of Santa Fina. The busiest and finest street of San Gimignano, however, leaves Piazza del Duomo towards the north: Via San Matteo, lined with shops and modest Renaissance palaces. It begins by passing the three truncated **Salvucci Towers**, once the fortified compound of one of San Gimignano's most powerful families (the Salvucci were Ghibellines; the towers of their mortal enemies, the Guelph Ardinghelli, are the ones on the west side of Piazza della Cisterna).

The day trippers do not often venture into the quiet streets on the north side of town, and so usually miss the church of **Sant'Agostino**, famous for a series of frescoes by

Gozzoli on the *Life of St Augustine* on the walls behind the high altar. The merriest of all Renaissance painters has a good time with this one; many of the frescoes are faded and damaged, but not the charming panel where the master of grammar comes to drag sullen little Augustine off to school. Another well-preserved scene shows Augustine in Rome, with most of the city's ancient landmarks visible in the background. Gozzoli also contributed the *Saint Sebastian* on the left aisle. There is a haunting altarpiece, done by Piero Pollaiuolo in 1483 with an anticipatory touch of the El Greco to it, and some good trecento Sienese painting in a chapel off to the right. Across the piazza from Sant'Agostino, the little church of **San Pietro** has more Sienese painting of that era, but is hardly ever open. Via Folgore di San Gimignano leads off to the northeastern corner of the town; the church of **San Jacopo** stands under the town wall, another simple but interesting building left by the Templars.

Around much of San Gimignano, the countryside begins right outside the wall. There are plenty of opportunities for pleasant walks or picnics in any direction, and a few landmarks to visit along the way: the **Fonti**, arched medieval well-houses much like Siena's, can be seen just outside the Porta dei Fonti, south of San Jacopo. Further from town, the **Pieve di Cellole** is a pretty 12th-century church in a peaceful setting, 4 km west from the Porta San Matteo; its harmonious serenity amid the cypresses inspired Puccini's opera *Suor Angelica*. There are several ruined castles and monasteries within a few miles of the town, and every height offers a different view of San Gimignano's remarkable skyline.

SHOPPING

There isn't any particular artisan tradition here, but so many tourists visit that enterprising shopowners have assembled a host of interesting things—the town hasn't quite turned into a great trinket bazaar, but it's getting there. Some of the best buys are pretty, inexpensive things in alabaster from nearby Volterra—especially at the little shop at Via San Matteo 85, north of the Piazza del Duomo. Just within Porta San Giovanni is a 13th-century church now converted to a shop for local wine, olive oil and other farm products. Artists' studios and ceramics are everywhere, though nothing really stands out. This is an agricultural area, and its specialities are a formidable white wine called *Vernaccia* and a sweet called *mandorlato*, very much like the *panforte* of Siena. Many vineyards around this area would be glad to sell you a bottle of vernaccia—there's one right outside the Porta San Jacopo, the Cantina Molini.

WHERE TO STAY (tel prefix 0577)

All of the hotels in San Gimignano are in the L70–80 000 range, but the vacuum of low cost accommodation has been filled by a score of San Gimignanese who rent out rooms, usually about L25–30 000 (the family at the Il Pino Restaurant—see below—is among these; Via San Matteo 102, doubles without bath for L31–36 000; the tourist office can give you a list of the others). The two best hotels in town are both on Piazza della Cisterna: ***__La Cisterna__, tel 940 328, in a restored 14th-century palazzo, with many rooms enjoying unforgettable views over the surrounding countryside (L83 000, remember to ask for a room with the view if you book ahead). Across the piazza, the ***__Leon Bianco__, tel 941 294, has modern rooms for L74 000. If you would prefer the tranquillity of this very lovely patch of Tuscan countryside, there is *****Le Renaic** north of town at Pancale, about 7 km towards Certaldo, tel 955 044. The attractive modern building has a garden, pool, and tennis court (L80 000).

EATING OUT

With all the visitors it entertains, it should come as no surprise that San Gimignano is full of good restaurants. One of the most popular, as much for its panoramic views as for the cuisine, is **Le Terrazze** in the Hotel La Cisterna, tel 940 328. The breaded lamb chops with artichokes are a surprise treat, or else the *osso buco 'alla Toscana'*, following old house specialities like *zuppa sangimignese* and *pappardelle alla lepre* (wide noodles with hare sauce). Altogether it makes a memorable dinner for L620 000. Another possibility, at the opposite end of town at Via San Matteo 102, is **Il Pino**, tel 940 415. Here the main attraction is the inviting antipasti; a full dinner will cost about L30 000, L50 000 if you thoroughly indulge in the dishes with truffles that are Il Pino's pride. A separate room around the side serves spaghetti and beer for lots less.

The adventurous might like to try **Dorado**, on Vicolo del Oro 2, tel 941 862, where the chef claims to reconstruct Etruscan cuisine—game hen with juniper berries, and things stranger still (L40–50 000). Less extravagantly, **La Stella** is a fine trattoria down the street from Il Pino on Via S. Matteo 75, tel 940 444: good Tuscan *ribollita* and a succulent *stracotto alla Chianti* (L35 000 at the most).

Volterra

How you see Volterra may well depend on the cast of the skies when you come. On a good day in spring or summer, the sunshine illuminates elegant streets and piazze full of Volterrans going about their business, and bouncing holiday Germans come to buy alabaster cups and lampshades. A cloudy, windy day may remind you of fate and of the Etruscans, who arrived here some 2700 years ago. Like so many other cities in central Italy, the Etruscans founded Volterra on top of a steep hill with a flat top; from a distance you see only a dark silhouette looming over an eerie, empty landscape. The soil around Volterra (pop. 14,000) is a thin clay, not much good for vines or olives. Few trees grow here. It makes good pasture land—not as barren as it looks, but disconcerting enough among the green woods and well-tended gardens of this part of Tuscany.

History

Etruscan *Velathri*, one of the largest and most powerful cities of the Dodecapolis, grew up in the 9th or 8th century BC from an even earlier settlement of the Villanovan culture; it is undoubtedly one of the oldest cities in Italy. The attraction that has kept this hill continuously occupied for so many centuries is easily explained—sulphur, alum, salt, alabaster, lead and tin, the centre of one of the richest mining regions in Italy. In Etruscan days there was iron, too, and the people of Velathri did a thriving trade with the Greeks and Carthaginians.

Velathri reached the height of its prosperity in the 5th and 4th centuries BC, leaving as testimony three great circuits of walls; the largest is over 8 km (5½ miles) in length, enclosing an area three times the size of the present city. The Romans captured it sometime in the 3rd century, and Velathri began to decline. Along with most of Etruria, the city chose the populist side in the Social Wars, and was punished with a siege and sacking by Sulla in about 80 BC. Yet Roman *Velaterrae* remained an important town. It was the home of Saint Linus, successor to St Peter and the second pope. Even though many of the mines were giving out, Volterra survived the Dark Ages intact. The Lombards favoured it, and for a time it served as their capital. Medieval Volterra was ruled by its bishops, increasingly finding themselves in conflict with the rising middle class. An independent *comune* was established late in the 12th century, a good Ghibelline town that participated in most of the factional wars of the period, finally coming under the nominal control of Florence in 1361.

The Florentines were content with an annual tribute until the 'affair of the alum' in the 1470s, that wonderfully Italian ruckus that caused Pope Sixtus IV to plot the murder of Lorenzo de' Medici, excommunicate him, and finally declare war on him. Lorenzo had taken over a syndicate to mine here for alum, a key material used in dyeing cloth, on which the popes had a monopoly from their mines at Tolfa. Besides alarming the pope, Lorenzo also caused the Volterrans to revolt when they realized that he wanted to keep production down and prices high without letting any profit trickle down to them (the Medici Bank, not surprisingly, also controlled the sale of the pope's alum). Lorenzo eluded the pope with some difficulty (see Florence: History) and then hired the mercenary captain Federico di Montefeltro—none other than the famous broken-nosed Duke of Urbino, patron of artists and scholars—to subdue the Volterrans. This he did with a brutality quite unbecoming to the 'ideal Renaissance prince'. Lorenzo wept some crocodile tears over Volterra; after extinguishing the city's independence once and for all, he offered it the magnificent sum of 2000 florins in damages.

Fortunately for the Volterrans, the mining business was picking up again. Between 1400 and 1800, many pits that had been abandoned since Roman times were reopened. In particular, Volterra became Europe's centre for the mining and working of **alabaster**, a craft tradition that is still the city's biggest business today.

GETTING AROUND

Volterra lies 81 km/2½ hrs southwest of Florence by way of Colle di Val d'Elsa and winding N. 68; 50 km/1½ hrs west from Siena; and 61 km/2 hrs southeast of Pisa by way of Cascina and N. 439. It isn't the easiest town to reach if you don't have a car. The only train service gets as far as Saline di Volterra, 10 km southwest of the city. This is an infrequent branch line that goes to Cecina, 30 km to the west on the coast south of Livorno. Some trains continue on from Cecina to Pisa. (It wasn't like this in the old days: as late as the 20s, if old photographs are to be believed, a little steam train used to climb right up to the town.) Buses connect the Saline station with Volterra, but not always when you need them.

All **buses** leave from Piazza XX Settembre, just inside the walls. Inside the bar on the piazza with the 'Jolly Caffè' sign, you can get information and buy tickets to anywhere. There are plenty of buses direct to Pisa and Montecatini Terme, 4 a day to Florence and Siena (change at Colle di Val d'Elsa for Siena and San Gimignano), 3 to Livorno and 2 to Massa Marittima (usually change at Monterotondo).

TOURIST INFORMATION.
Palazzo dei Priori, Via Turazza 2, tel 86 150.

A Little Archaeology
Coming from Florence or Siena, the entrance to Volterra will be the eastern gate, the **Porta a Selci**, with a moving tribute to the *partigiani* of Volterra killed in 1944–5. Inside the gate, Via Don Minzoni leads towards the bus terminal at Piazza XX Settembre, passing along the way at no. 15 the **Museo Etrusco Guarnacci**, repository for finds from the Velathri necropolises (daily except Sat; from 16 March to 15 Oct, 9:30–1, 3–6:30 pm; rest of the year 10–2 pm; adm exp). Over 600 sculpted alabaster, travertine or terracotta cinerary urns make up the core of the collection, arranged in a number of galleries according to subject matter. These tend to be conventional—an Etruscan family would ask the artist for a scene from Greek mythology, from the Trojan war perhaps, or something like the death of Actaeon, or a daemon conducting the souls of the dead down to the underworld. Perhaps the artist already had one in stock. One rule of Etruscan art is its lack of rules. Expect anything: some of the reclining figures of the dead atop the urns are brilliant portraiture, while others could be the first attempts of a third grade crafts class. All, holding the little cups or dishes they carry down into Hades, look as serene and happy as only a defunct Etruscan can be.

As always, the Etruscans do their best to make you laugh. One terracotta, the *Urna degli Sposi*, portrays a hilariously caricatured couple who look as if they are about to start arguing over whose turn it is to do the dishes. Another Etruscan joke is the famous *Ombra della Sera* (evening shadow), quite a celebrity around Volterra, a small, carefully detailed bronze of a man with a quizzical expression and spidery, grotesquely elongated arms and legs. Also present are prehistoric finds, Roman mosaics from the baths and artefacts discovered in the theatre, and a collection of Etruscan jewelry.

The museum lies a stone's throw from Piazza XX Settembre, the bus terminal; from here Via Gramsci leads towards the town centre. Climb any of the alleys to the south of

Etruscan Urna degli Sposi, Volterra

the museum, however, and you'll reach Volterra's **Parco Archeologico** just inside the walls. There isn't much archaeological about it—some Etruscan foundations and a huge ancient cistern called the *Piscina* (swimming-pool) *Romana*—but the park is a marvel, a lush English garden of manicured lawns and shady groves unlike anything else in Tuscany. Above the park stretches an exceptionally long and elegant castle, the **Fortezza Medicea**, begun in 1343 and completed by Lorenzo de' Medici in 1472. You can't get in; it has been a prison almost from the day it was built, perhaps the fanciest in this nation of fancy calabooses.

Piazza dei Priori

It's a fine little republican piazza, surrounded by plain, erect palazzi that call your attention ever so discreetly to the sober dignity of the *comune*. The **Palazzo dei Priori**, of 1208, is said to be the oldest such building in Tuscany, the model for Florence's Palazzo Vecchio and a score of others. Its tower has been closed to visitors for several years, but if you ever find it reopened, climb up for a view that literally takes in all of Tuscany; on a clear day you'll see Monte Amiata, all the coast from La Spezia to the Argentario, and Corsica and Elba as well. Across the square, the simple **Palazzo Pretorio** is almost as old; next to it, the rakishly leaning **Porcellino Tower** takes its name from the little pig sculpted in relief near the base, just barely visible after almost seven centuries.

The Cathedral and the Etruscan Arch

Just to the right of the Palazzo dei Priori, a bit of green and white striped marble façade peeks out between the palaces. This is the back of the archiepiscopal palace, located around the corner in the **Piazza del Duomo**. Quiet and dowdy, the contrast of this square with well-built Piazza dei Priori is striking, a lasting memory of the defeat of Volterra's medieval bishops by the *comune*. Its octagonal **Baptistry**, begun in 1283, has its marble facing completed only on one side. Within, there is a fine baptismal font sculpted by Andrea Sansovino in the early 1500s, an altar by Mino da Fiesole, and a holy water dish carved out of an Etruscan boundary stone. Unfortunately, bits of the cornice have been dropping down on the Volterrans lately, and the baptistry is closed indefinitely until it can be restored.

The **Cathedral** façade isn't finished either. This forlorn mongrel of a building was begun in the Pisan Romanesque style in the 1200s, and worked on fitfully for the next two centuries. The campanile went up in 1493, and the interior was entirely redone in the 1580s when the blatant Medici coat-of-arms was placed over the high altar. Do not pass this old Duomo by; the works of art inside are few in number, but of an exceptionally high quality. As this is Volterra, fittingly some of the windows are made of thin-sliced alabaster, a stone that was also used in the intricate, Renaissance **tabernacle** by Mino da Fiesole over the high altar. The chapels on either side have excellent examples of Tuscan woodcarving: a late one by the Sienese Jacopo della Quercia off to the left, the *Madonna dei Chierici*, and to the right, a polychromed *Deposition* with five separate, full-sized figures among the best of 13th-century Pisan sculpture. Another chapel off to the right contains fragments of some unusually good anonymous trecento frescoes of the *Passion of Christ*, very much ahead of their time in composition, in the figures and the folds of the draperies—even Giorgio Vasari might have liked it.

In the left aisle, the **pergamo** (pulpit) is one of the lesser-known works of the Pisanos, less spectacular than the ones in Pisa, Siena and Pistoia, but still showing something of the vividness and electric immediacy seen in the best Pisan sculpture. Guglielmo Pisano did the fine relief of the Last Supper (note the faces of the Apostles, and the sly metaphorical monster sneaking under the table). The pulpit's supporting columns rest on two lions, a bull and one unclassifiable beast, all by Bonamico Pisano. In the oratory, off the left aisle near the entrance, there is a small fresco of the *Adoration of the Magi*, said to be by Benozzo Gozzoli, though perhaps because of its deterioration or early date, it lacks Gozzoli's usual charm.

Just around the corner in the Archiepiscopal Palace, there is a small **Museo d'Arte Sacra**, with some sculpture and architectural fragments, and a della Robbia terracotta of St Linus, Volterra's patron (daily exc. Mon; 9:30–1 pm, in summer also 2:30–4:30 pm; adm).

From the Duomo, if you retrace your steps back towards Piazza dei Priori and turn down Via Porta all'Arco, you'll find the most quaint old relic in Volterra, the **Arco Etrusco**. The Etruscans built the columns at least, though the arch above them was rebuilt in Roman times. Set into this arch are three primeval black basalt sculpted heads from the original gate, *c.* 600 BC, believed to represent the Etruscan gods Tinia (Jupiter), Uni (Juno) and Menvra (Minerva). Some of the features of Juno are barely traceable; 2700 years of wind and rain have worn all three into great black knobs—carved out of the voussoirs, they resemble nothing so much as garden slugs.

The Pinacoteca

Just off Piazza dei Priori, the intersection of Via Roma and Via Buonparenti is one of the most picturesque corners of Volterra, with venerable stone arches and tower houses such as the 13th-century Casa Buonparenti, or the house at Via Ricciarelli 14 with the tiny windows near the floors, supposedly added for the children.

On Via dei Sarti, the elder Antonio da Sangallo's Palazzo Solaini (note the elegant arcaded courtyard) has been restored to hold Volterra's **Pinacoteca**, another small but choice collection. Trecento Sienese painting is well represented, including a glorious altarpiece of the *Madonna and saints* by Taddeo di Bartolo. To complement the remarkable 1300s wood sculptures in the Duomo, the Pinacoteca has two figures portraying the *Annunciation* by a local artist named Francesco di Domenico Valdambrino. Neri di Bicci was a quattrocento Florentine, but his *St Sebastian* here looks entirely Sienese—probably at the request of the customer. Among the works of other Tuscans, there is a big shiny altarpiece by Ghirlandaio, and two by Luca Signorelli (or his workshop): a *Madonna and saints* and an *Annunciation*. Only tantalizing fragments are left of another altarpiece by Giuliano Bugiardini (1475–1554) a little-known Florentine with a very distinctive style.

For all that, the prize of the collection is the *Deposition* of Rosso Fiorentino, dated 1521 and perhaps his greatest work in Italy. Even out here in the boondocks of Volterra, it attracts considerable attention from the art scholars, a seminal work and one of the thresholds from the Renaissance into Mannerism, with all of the precision and clarity of the best quattrocento work, yet also possessing an intensity that few works had ever achieved. The Descent from the Cross is a starkly emotional subject; in Rosso's work it is terror and disarray, a greenish Christ and a small, nearly hysterical crowd dramatically illuminated against a darkening deep blue sky. You'll find little that this painting has in common with Rosso's contemporaries, not even with his fellow madman Pontormo (who did his own, quite different *Deposition* in Florence's S. Felicità)—but oddly enough it could almost be mistaken for the work of Goya. The Pinacoteca has nothing that can follow this one, but if you plod through to the last room there is a collection of delightfully absurd 18th-century portraits, one with eyes that follow you around the room (daily 10–1, 3–6 pm, closed Mon; adm).

San Francesco and the Roman Theatre

On the corner east of the Pinacoteca, the church of **San Michele** has a Pisan Romanesque façade. If you go in the other direction, towards the Porta San Francesco on the western edge of town, you will pass through back streets dusty with alabaster workshops and finally arrive at the church of **San Francesco** on Via San Lino. Here the attraction is off to the right of the altar, the **Chapel of the Holy Cross**, completely frescoed in 1410 by a Florentine artist whose name seems to be Cenni di Francesco di Ser Cenni—a rare soul, indeed, with a sophisticated, wonderfully reactionary medieval sense of composition and his own ideas about Christian iconography, done in a bold style that in places almost seems like modern poster art. The Legend of the Cross frescoes generally follow those of Gaddi at Santa Croce in Florence (see p. 145), and there are also scenes of St Francis, the Passion, and the Massacre of the Innocents, many with fantasy city backgrounds. Note the *Dream of Constantine* (or of Heraclius), in his tent adorned with the Imperial Eagle; naturally the artist had never seen a Roman eagle, but he painted a very nice medieval German one instead.

Just to the right of San Francesco, a pedestrian passage under the walls takes you out to Viale Francesco Ferrucci, home to a lively outdoor **market** on Saturday mornings. Beneath the walls, ancient Volaterrae's large **Roman theatre** has been excavated. Not much of the cavea is intact, but enough marble slabs and columns survived for the archaeologists to reconstruct part of the stage building, an impressive witness to the importance of the city long ago. Behind the theatre are ruins of **baths** and a large rectangular **palestra**, a yard for exercise and gymnastics.

The Balze

Leaving Volterra from the San Francesco gate, you pass the Borgo San Giusto, with the ruins of the 12th-century Pisan Romanesque church of **Santo Stefano**. The road to Pisa exits through the outer circuit of the **Etruscan walls**; though barely more than foundations they are traceable for most of their length around the city, and easily visible here.

Some 2 km beyond these, decorating the lonely moors are the *balze*, barren eroded gullies that may have begun as Etruscan mining cuts. They have been growing ever since; chronicles from the Middle Ages report them gradually gobbling up farms and churches around the city. No one has yet discovered a way to stop the inexorable growth of these deep clay-walled chasms. In the 1700s the *balze* tried to atone for their appetite, uncovering some of the most important Etruscan necropolises yet discovered, contributing their urns to the Guarnacci Museum. Now even most of these necropolises have disappeared completely. On the edge of one steep cliff you will see the **Badia**, an 11th-century Camaldolensian abbey now half-devoured by the *balze*.

Alabaster, and where to find it

Archaeological evidence has the Villanovan culture in Tuscany finding creative uses for the *pietra candida*, alias $CaSO_4 2H_2O$, as early as 800 BC. The Etruscans made good use of this luminous, easily worked mineral in their funeral urns and everyday objects. During the Dark Ages, the locals appear to have forgotten about it, though now and then some artist would turn a chunk into a vase or cup (the Medici, with their insatiable lust for dust magnets, bought quite a few). The craft of carving alabaster revived dramatically in the last two centuries. Volterra today is full of small workshops, and even a few large firms that turn the stone into vases, figurines, ashtrays and everything else that's serviceable or collectable. Many of the alabaster workers are genuine artists, turning out one-of-a-kind pieces at high prices; the city runs a contest each year for the best. Others produce vast numbers of attractive little baubles from £1 and up.

There are shops selling alabaster in every corner of Volterra; you'll do well to seek them out, and avoid the temptations of the big glossy establishments in the most prominent places. Paolo Sabatini, who has won several prizes in the annual competition, has his shop at Via Porta all'Arco 45, with some of the most original creations in town. Just down the street, there are some unusual alabaster miniatures at no. 26. More of the best can be found on Via di Sotto: simple, elegant vases and lamps at no. 2 and at the shop 'Come una Volta' at no. 6. The avant-garde is represented by Via Guarnacci 26, with some splashy modern work in coloured alabaster. Beyond these, there's the city Artisans' Cooperative on Piazza dei Priori, and some conservative, well-crafted pieces at Giuseppe Bessi, Via San Lino 52; just next door at no. 46 there is a shop specializing in carved olive wood. For really serious alabaster—say, complete bathrooms, or life-size copies of the Trevi Fountain—try the big shops with big parking lots around the outskirts of town.

WHERE TO STAY AND EATING OUT (tel prefix 0588)

Volterra does not see as many tourists as San Gimignano, but is nevertheless just as expensive—at least, doubles under L40 000 are almost impossible to find. Students aren't entirely out of luck; there's the hostel, **Ostello Volterra** on Via del Pozzetto, tel 85 577, near the Porta a Selci; institutional atmosphere for L12 000 a person. The *****Villa Nencini** is a 16th-century villa with lovely views, just north of the city centre on Borgo S. Stefano, tel 86 386 (L70 000; some cheaper without bath). Within the walls, the *****San Lino** stands out only for being the only place with parking; simple accommodation for L100 000 (Via San Lino 26, near Porta San Francesco, tel 85 250). Closer to the centre, the *****Etruria** at Via Matteotti 32, tel 87 377, has one of Volterra's best restaurants—roast boar and game dishes in season (rooms L67 000 with bath; meals L40 000).

Most restaurants in Volterra, for that matter, specialize in roast boar and the like, good medieval cuisine entirely in keeping with the spirit of the place. The menu at **Il Porcellino**, Via delle Prigione 8, tel 86 392, combines seafood and familiar Tuscan favourites with local treats like roast pigeon and boar with olives; a good bargain at L30–35 000. After a morning in the Etruscan museum, you can regale yourself for about the same price at the **Ristorante La Pace** just inside the gate at Via Don Minzoni 29, tel 86 511; roast boar or lamb, as well as rabbit cooked in Vernaccia; the *spaghetti alla boscaiola* for starters is a good choice. Not too many tourists make it to the **Tre Scimmie** (three monkeys) on Via del Mandorlo, tel 86 047, a small, delightful place where the usual boar and bunny are an even better bargain (L25–30 000). Another alternative offering hearty Tuscan fair, is **La Tavernetta**, Via Guarnacci 16, tel 87 630 (L25–35 000).

One of the restaurants most popular with the Volterrans is outside the town: **A Biscondola**, about 3 km away on the SS 68, tel 85 197. The country setting is plain enough, but the cooking is superb; lots of ducks—lasagna with duck sauce is the inspired speciality, also duck *alla cacciatora* and game dishes in season (L25–30 000).

The Val di Cecina and the Metal Hills

In the romantic emptiness of the Volterran hills, there are not many other attractions. For a complete change in scenery, take N. 68 west along the valley of the river Cecina from Volterra as far as Guardistallo, a lovely, rolling valley with the pines and cypresses in just the right places—a suitable Tuscan background for any Renaissance painting. **Montecatini Val di Cecina**, in the hills just to the north, is a quiet medieval village with a 12th-century castle. Further west, a big wine-producing area extends around **Montescudaio**: Montescudaio (both red and white) is a distinguished, though lesser-known dry variety with a DOC label.

The best road from Volterra the N. 439 leads south, over the **Colline Metallifere** towards Massa Marittima and the coast. These 'metal hills', along with the iron mines of nearby Elba, did much to finance the gilded existences of the ancient Etruscans. Several of the mines are in operation today, though driving through these hills you may see little but oak forests and olive groves along the way. **Pomarance**, a town that has retained some buildings from the Middle Ages and Renaissance, holds few surprises, but wait until you get to **Larderello**, the self-proclaimed 'World Centre of Geothermal Energy'. This is the northern boundary of volcanic Italy; that extinct volcano, Monte Amiata, and the ancient crater lakes of Umbria and Lazio are not far away. This far north, the only subterranean manifestations are benign little geysers and gurgling pools of sulphurous mud. Larderello is a growing town; huge ugly cooling towers of the type that would signify a nuclear power plant anywhere else are all over the landscape wherever there is a geothermal source worth tapping. Near the centre, there is a strange, post-modernist parish church designed in the 1950s by Michelucci, the architect of Florence's rail station, and also the little **Museo Lardarel**, which may explain something of this overheated little town's career.

After Larderello, and almost as far as Monterotondo, the landscape is downright uncanny. It smells bad, too; miniature geysers and steam vents (*soffioni*) whistle and puff away by the roadside, while murky pits bubble up boric salts amidst yellow and grey slag piles. Follow the yellow road signs of the 'itinerario dei soffioni' to see the best of it. Despite the sulphur and borax, the cooling towers and occasional rusting hulks of old mining equipment, the Metal Hills are really quite winsome, especially south of Larderello (still on N. 439) around the medieval village of **Castelnuovo di Val di Cecina**, surrounded by chestnut groves and the pass of the *Ala dei Diavoli*, or 'Devils' Wing' at the crest of the hills. **Monterotondo Marittimo**, further south, has more than its share of subsurface curiosities; nearby **Lago Boracifero** is the centre for borax mining in Italy. And in some places the ground is covered with strange webs of steam pipes, ever since the *comune* discovered its unique resource could power almost everything in town for free.

Massa Marittima

This lovely, ruggedly hilly area is part of the coastal district of the Maremma only in name; as early as Roman times it was considered part of the 'maritime' province. And for just as long, Massa Marittima has been making its living from the mines, though today its 10,000 people are not nearly enough to fill the space within the medieval walls. Small as it may be, its brief period of prosperity left it a beautiful little city, with two good reasons for visiting: first, to see the second city of the Sienese Republic, like Siena a lesson in urban refinement in a small place; and second, an enormous, exquisite Cathedral that is one of the great medieval monuments of Tuscany.

This mining town appeared as a free *comune*, the *Repubblica Massetana*, about 1225, just at the time it was beginning a dizzying period of prosperity from the discovery of new silver and copper deposits nearby. Unfortunately, this wealth had a fatal attraction for Massa's bigger neighbours. Pisa and Siena fought over the little republic for a century, and it finally fell to the latter in 1337. It wasn't long before the mines gave out, putting Massa into a decline that lasted for centuries. Malaria was a problem from the 1500s, and not until the Lorraine dukes drained the wet places and reopened some of the mines did things start looking up.

GETTING AROUND

Massa is only 22 km off the coastal Via Aurelia at Follonica, absolutely worth the diversion if you are passing that way; direct from Siena it's a not particularly captivating 65 km/1 hr 20 min drive on N. 73 (passing by San Galgano) and N. 441. If you are using public transport, there are 3 or 4 buses a day from Volterra (change at Monterotondo), 5 to nearby Follonica, and frequent bus and train connections from there to Grosseto (Massa is in Grosseto province) also 2 a day to Florence and Siena, and 1 direct to Grosseto: information and tickets for all of them at the *Agenzia Massa Veternensis* opposite the Duomo. Most buses stop on Via Corridoni, behind and a little downhill from the Duomo.

TOURIST INFORMATION

Also opposite the Duomo—the town museum in the Palazzo del Podestà also functions as an information office, tel 902 289.

The Duomo

It's quite a sight, rising up incongruously on its stepped pedestal above the little town, its effect greatly heightened by its brilliant setting, above and at an angle to Massa's main square, **Piazza Garibaldi**, a *tour-de-force* of medieval town design. Massa began its cathedral around 1200, reconstructing a smaller cathedral of the 11th century, and finished it in 1250. Some additions were made later; note the striking contrast between the original Pisan Romanesque building, with its blind arches and lozenges, and later Sienese work like the campanile, added about 1400. Some of the best features of the building are the Gothic windows, capitals and carved grotesques on the façade and the left side.

The interior, under massive columns with delicately carved capitals, each one different from the others, has a few trecento frescoes, including one of St Julian tending the sick near the entrance. On the left side, there is a luminous *Madonna* by Duccio (1318) and a unique collection of reliefs from the original 11th-century church: staring priests and apostles in a vigorous, cartoon-like style. On the right side hangs the *Nativity of Mary* by the last and most peculiar great Sienese artist, Rutilio Manetti (*d.* 1639): woebegone ladies and a jellicle cat attend a pug-nosed, thumb-sucking, very un-beatific baby Mary. Nearby is a fine baptismal font with reliefs by Giraldo da Como (*c.* 1250) and a Renaissance tabernacle added in 1447. A wooden crucifix by Giovanni Pisano hangs over the high altar; behind it, in the impressive Gothic apse, is the *Ark of San Cerbone* with more good early reliefs (1324) of the life of Massa's patron saint.

Up and Down Massa

Next to the cathedral on Piazza Garibaldi, the 1230 **Palazzo Pretorio** now holds Massa's town museums, including a well-organized but not especially interesting **Archaeology Museum** (the Medici dukes carried the best local finds off to Florence long ago), and a small **Pinacoteca**, in which the best work is a full-hallelujah *Maestà* by Ambrogio Lorenzetti, aglow with rosy faces, flowers and golden trim, worthy to have hung over the high altar of the cathedral. Note the angel with the distaff and spindle in the centre—a sure sign that the local wool guild paid for the painting (daily exc. Mon; April–Oct, 10–12:30, 3:30–7 pm; Nov–Mar, 9–1, 3–5 pm; adm). The present-day city offices are in the **Palazzo Comunale** across the square, a group of connected tower-houses from the 13th and 14th centuries. Note the inscription above the door of another old building on the piazza: MASSA VETERNENSIS CELEBRIS VETULONIA QUONDAM. Just as Grosseto thinks of itself as the successor to Etruscan Roselle, Massa is the heir to lost Vetulonia, the once-great city of the Dodecapolis whose ruins can be seen on the coast (see p. 281).

Piazza Garibaldi is a lively place, often crowded with Teutons perching on the steps of the Duomo or swilling beer in the two outdoor café-pizzerias. Via Libertà leads off into the older quarter of town, a tiny, tidy nest of arches and alleys that hasn't changed much over the centuries. Like Siena, Massa is divided into three *terzi*; this is the terzo of Civitavecchia. Another street, Via Moncini, climbs up to the **Città Nuova**, a 14th-century suburb behind some unusual Sienese fortifications; the street ends at Piazza Matteotti, with the 1330 **Torre del Candaliere**, or Torre dell'Orologio, connected to the fortifications by a long, slender walkway called the **Sienese Arch**; it's a beautiful ensemble, built more for show than for any military consideration, à la Siena (daily exc. Mon; April–Oct 10–12:30, 3:30–7; Nov–Mar 9–1 and 3–5; adm). Across the piazza, the Palazzo delle Armi has a small **Museum of the Art and History of Mining**. Up Corso Diaz, the modest main drag of the Città Nuova, the big church of **Sant'Agostino** was completed in 1313; inside are more paintings by Rutilio Manetti.

Finally, no visit to Massa would be complete without a trip to the **Mining Museum**, behind the Duomo on Via Corridoni. Mining, after all, is what Massa is all about (if you go to the city library and ask them politely, they may show you the city's great treasure, the 1310 *Codice Minerario Massetano*, modern Europe's first code of laws concerning mining rights). The entrance of the museum leads down into nearly a half-mile of old mine tunnels, with exhibits to show how the job was done from medieval days to the present (daily exc. Mon; guided tours every half hour; April–Sept, 10–12:30, 3:30–7 pm; Oct–Mar, 11–1, 4–5 pm; adm).

WHERE TO STAY AND EATING OUT (tel prefix 0566)
Massa seems to be becoming an increasingly popular spot—especially with the Germans and Swiss—and the town's hotel capacity of 38 rooms is often stretched to the limit. Two of the three hotels are just below the town centre on the Via Massetana, both in lovely settings with gardens and views over the countryside (Massa lies on a rather steep hill), both in modern buildings with simple trattorie. In fact, the ****Duca del Mare**, Piazza Alighieri 1, tel 902 284 and the ****Girafalco** are nearly impossible to tell apart— both have doubles for the same prices (L45–55 000). In town, on Via Capellini, the ***Cris**, tel 903 830, is adequate enough for L35 000. Dining in Massa is uncomplicated; on the square in front of the Duomo, two places with outside tables compete for the visitor's attention: the **Vanni** and the **Tre Archi**; at either a pizza or plate of spaghetti with drinks goes around L10 000. For something more substantial, **Da Alberto**, Via Parenti 35, tel 902 093, does hearty Tuscan favourites like boar and more delicate pasta dishes (L25 000); or try the **Taverna del Vecchio Borgo**, Via Parenti 12, tel 93 950, which has been highly recommended, not only for its food but its extensive list of lyrical grappas (L20–25 000).

San Galgano and the Sword in the Stone

The N. 73 east from Massa to Siena skirts the southern edge of the Colline Metallifere, through quiet landscapes that in the Middle Ages saw a great flowering of domestic and foreign monasticism. The monks are mostly long gone, but they left behind one of the most unusual, least-visited sights in Tuscany, the ruined Cistercian **Abbey of San Galgano**, some 2 km north of the village of Palazzetto. In some of the older paintings in Siena's Pinacoteca, you will notice the oddly Arthurian figure of a man apparently drawing a sword out of a stone. This is San Galgano, and in fact he is putting the sword in. Galgano Guidotti, born in the nearby village of Chiusdino, was a dissolute young soldier who one day had a vision of St Michael, here on the slopes of Montesiepi, commanding him to change his ways. Thrusting his sword into a rock as a symbol of his new life, Galgano became a holy hermit. For this and a long career of miracles that followed, he was canonized only a few years after his death in 1181.

Almost from the start, the community he founded on Montesiepi was associated with the Cistercian Order, attracting monks from France as well as new members from around Siena. For three centuries, they played an extremely important role in the life of the community, draining swamps, building mills and even starting up a small textile industry. The Republic of Siena came to find them indispensable as architects; administrators—and especially as accountants. Many of the painted *Biccherna* covers in the Siena archives show white-robed Cistercians puzzling over the books or handing out workers' pay. With its immense wealth, and its French architects eager to initiate the backward Italians in the glories of the new Gothic style, the order began its great **Abbey Church** in 1218. The Cistercians were already in a bad way when the abbey was dissolved in 1600; not too long after their departure the roof, the marble façade and the campanile collapsed, leaving the grandest French Gothic building in Tuscany a romantic ruin. Its beautiful travertine columns and pointed arches remain, with the sky for a roof and a green lawn for a floor.

Parts of the monastery survive, now in the care of Olivetan nuns. On a hill above the abbey, St Michael appeared again, just after Galgano's death, to command his followers to build the **Cappella di Montesiepi** over the sword in the stone. The curious round chapel, one of very few in Italy, was begun in 1185. The sword is still there, sticking up from its rock right in the centre of the chapel; as with all the sites associated with St Michael, it is a reminder of a branch of medieval mysticism that while not entirely lost, is hardly well understood. Note the altar, with a cross of the type often seen on buildings of the Knights Templar, and the shallow dome of the ceiling, done in a pattern of 22 concentric white stripes, perhaps a representation of the heavenly spheres of the medieval cosmology (as in the famous fresco in Pisa's Camposanto). In a chamber off to the side is a series of frescoes by Ambrogio Lorenzetti on the life of the saint.

In the silent land around San Galgano, possible detours include the mildly tortuous routes 8 km west to **Chiusdino**, the dense, sleepy medieval village where San Galgano was born, or **Monticiano**, south on N. 73, just as old, where the Romanesque church of Sant'Agostino has frescoes by Bartolo di Fredi in its adjoining cloister.

Along Route 223

Possibly the least interesting of the roads south from Siena is the one for Grosseto, passing through the prosperous and fertile but nearly empty valley of the River Merse. Once over the border into Grosseto province it becomes even emptier, though there are a few towns which are worth a visit: **Bagni di Petriolo**, an old walled town with thermal springs that will relieve your gout; **Civitella Marittima**, a hill town with the Romanesque church of San Lorenzo al Lanzo, and perhaps the best, **Pagànico**, a charming village that retains its Sienese walls and gates. Its parish church of San Michele has some excellent, well-preserved frescoes by the trecento Sienese painter Bartolo di Fredi.

Part XI

SOUTHERN TUSCANY

Tempio di San Biagio, Montepulciano

Not counting the coastal Maremma around Grosseto, the old territories of the Sienese Republic make a complete and coherent landscape, rolling hills mostly given over to serious farming and pastureland. It isn't as garden-like as some other parts of Tuscany, though tidy vineyards and avenues of cypresses are not lacking. Hill towns, ready landmarks, poke above the horizon—Montepulciano off to the east, Pienza a bit to the left, while that castle on the left of the road must be Castiglione d'Orcia. At times it seems the whole region is laid out before you, bounded on one side by the hills around Siena, on the other by the cones of Monte Amiata and Radicófani.

In the little tourist offices in these towns, they remark that not too many English or Americans pass through, which is a pity. It's beautiful country, the food and wine are among the best in Tuscany, and there are delightful towns with charming souvenirs from the Renaissance and Middle Ages.

Asciano

N. 326 from Siena heads east, and its main purpose is to get you out to Cortona (p. 377) and then Lake Trasimeno and Perugia (p. 387). Before it leaves Siena province, the road passes the village of **Montaperti**, where the Sienese won their famous victory over Florence in 1260, and **Rapolano Terme** (27 km), a small spa that retains some of its medieval walls. Besides the hot springs there is a surplus of natural gas in the area, some of it pumped out from wells, and some just leaking out of the ground—don't drop any matches. **Asciano**, 10 km south of Rapolano, has walls built by the Sienese in 1351, and a good collection of Sienese art in the **Museo d'Arte Sacra**, next to the Romanesque church of the Collegiata. From Etruscan necropolises in the area, finds have been

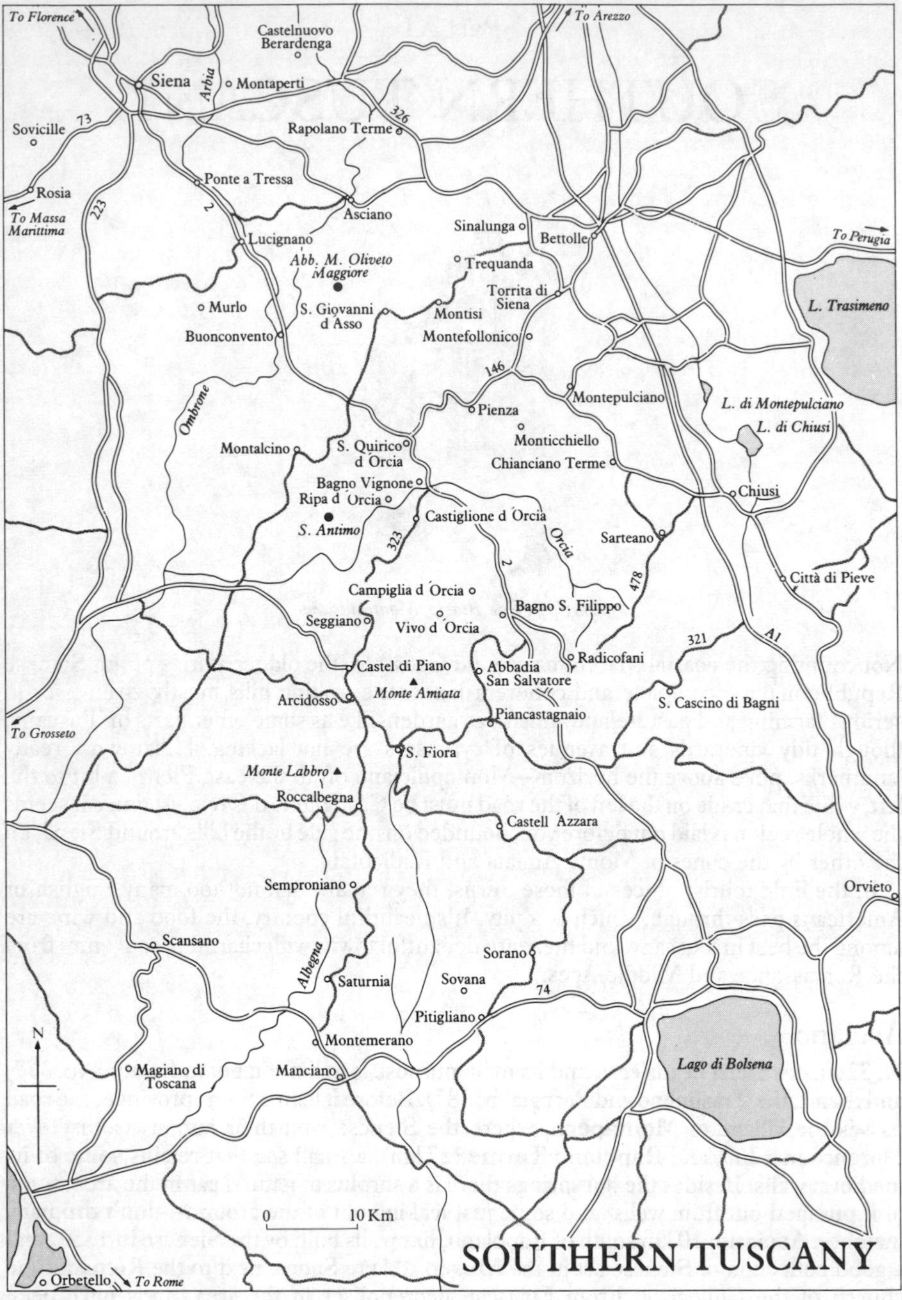

SOUTHERN TUSCANY

assembled in the church of San Bernardino, a modest **Museo Etrusco**. In a house at Via del Canto 11, there are some recently discovered Roman mosaics; ask at the pharmacy on Corso Matteotti for a visit.

The countryside around Asciano is dotted with *biancane*, knobby chalk hills exposed when the soil above erodes away, that often appear in the backgrounds of 14th- and 15th-century Sienese and Florentine paintings. This has always been sheep country, and it suffered much in the changes after World War II, when many of the men went off to look for work in the cities. Today, immigrants from Sardinia make up a large minority of the population, born shepherds who are trying to get the business back on its feet. Old **Sinalunga**, up on its hill, is the next town (22 km west), but offers little to detain you; the main square is named after Garibaldi, to commemorate his arrest here in 1867, at the orders of King Vittorio Emanuele, who was afraid his volunteers were about to attack Rome. **Torrita di Siena**, 6 km southwest of the junction with the A1 from Florence to Rome, takes its name from the tall towers of its old walls, some of which remain.

The Crete and Monte Oliveto Maggiore

South of Siena, lovely N. 2 makes its way towards Rome, roughly following the routes of the Roman *Via Cassia* and the medieval pilgrims' path to Rome, the *Via Francigena*. Along the way, it passes **Lucignano d'Arbia** (16 km), a charming, tiny village with a medieval church, and **Buonconvento** (27 km), a gritty industrial town that hides a miniature, walled, medieval town at its centre. The walls, no longer very proper and military, are peppered with windows of the houses that have been built against them. There are two fine gates at either end of the main street, and in the middle the 14th-century parish church with an altarpiece by Matteo di Giovanni; across the street from the church, the **Museo d'Arte Sacra** has a small collection of choice Sienese paintings by the likes of Matteo, Sano di Pietro and Bartolo di Fredi.

East of Buonconvento, the valleys of the Ombrone and the Asso enclose the country of the *crete*. Like the *biancane* and the *balze* of Volterra, these are uncanny monuments to the power of erosion; in the broken, jumbled hills south of Asciano, austere green meadows alternate with ragged gullies and bare white cliffs. At the centre of these *crete*, in the bleakest and most barren part, there is a huge grove of tall, black cypresses around **Monte Oliveto Maggiore** (9 km from Buonconvento on N. 451). Some of the great gentlemen of Siena's merchant elite founded this monastery, including Giovanni Tolomei and Ambrogio Piccolomini, both jaded merchants and sincere Christians who retired here in 1313 to escape the fatal sophistication of the medieval city. Their new Olivetan Order was approved by the pope only six years later.

With such wealthy backers, Monte Oliveto became a sort of elite hermitage for central Tuscany. An ambitious building programme carried on throughout the 1400s made it a complete, though little-known monument of quattrocento architecture and art. In its isolated setting, Monte Oliveto is a marvel of Renaissance clarity and rationality, expressed in simple structures and good Siena brick. The beautiful, asymmetrical **gatehouse**, decorated with a della Robbia terracotta, makes a fitting introduction to the complex. Inside, the well-proportioned brick **Abbey Church** (finished in 1417) has an exceptional set of wooden *intarsia* choirstalls by the master of the genre, Fra Giovanni da Verona, among the best work of this kind in all Italy. The monastery's greatest treasure, however, is the **Great Cloister**, embellished with 36 frescoes of scenes from the life of St Benedict (whose original rule Tolomei and the Olivetans were trying to restore). The first nine of these are by Luca Signorelli, with formidable ladies and bulky, white-robed monks in the artist's distinctive balloonish forms and sparing use of colour. All the rest are the work of Il Sodoma (1505–08)—some of his best painting, ethereal scenes of pre-Raphaelite ladies and mandarin monks, with blue and purple backgrounds of ideal landscapes and cities. If you are of that persuasion, popular enough a century ago, that it was with Raphael and Michelangelo that the Renaissance started to go wrong, you owe a visit here. Sodoma, not a Florentine or really even a Sienese (he was from Vercelli in the north), wrote the last word to the mainstream tendency of Florentine painting before the excesses of Mannerism. Mr Sodomite himself appears in the scene '*Come Benedetto risaldò lo capistero che era rotta*' (How Benedict repaired the broken sieve); he's the dissipated fellow on the left with the white gloves. Look carefully—not only did Sodoma paint himself in, but also his pet badgers, of which he was very fond. The badgers and other of Sodoma's many pets appear in various other frescoes as well.

Unlike so many great Tuscan art shrines, Monte Oliveto, isolated here in the Sienese hills, retains something of its original aloof dignity. Although Napoleon himself suppressed the monastery in 1810, a group of talented brothers still works here, specializing in the restoration of old books (daily 9–12:45, 3–7 pm; adm).

In the *crete* around Monte Oliveto, the village of **San Giovanni d'Asso** (8 km southeast) is built around a Sienese fortress; the church of San Pietro in Villore is from the 12th century, with an ambitious, unusual façade. From here a by-road east leads to **Montisi** (7 km) and **Trequanda** (12 km), two other fine little villages, seldom visited; the latter has a 13th-century castle and another Romanesque church.

WHERE TO STAY AND EATING OUT (tel prefix 0577)

Accommodation isn't always easy to find in this quiet corner of Tuscany. Often, towns and villages have only one real hotel, or none. Quite a few restaurants have rooms to rent, and there are always a few private homes with rooms to rent that don't advertise. Don't be shy; ask around and you'll find something. The closest rooms to Monte Oliveto Maggiore are in Buonconvento, the simple ****Albergo Ristorante Roma**, on the main street of the old town, tel 806 021, (L50 000 with bath, L40 000 without). For something really special, reserve far in advance for one of the seven rooms at the ******Locanda dell'Amorosa**, 2 km south of Sinalunga at Locazione L'Amorosa, tel 679 497. More than an inn, this is a tiny, medieval hamlet, complete with a manor house and frescoed church. There are no particular amenities—but beautiful rooms, in a memorable setting, and a prize-winning restaurant. The menu follows the seasons, but usually includes fresh water fish dishes (Lake Trasimeno isn't far away) such as the *ravioli di pesce*; for the seconds, try stuffed pigeon or the big Florentine steaks (rooms L250 000, but dinner is a better bargain, about L60–70 000; closed Mon, Tues lunch and Feb). A simpler restaurant near Sinalunga (Loc. Bettole, Via di Vittorio 12, tel 624 192) is **Al Cacciatore**. As the name implies, expect some game dishes—boar with *porcini* mushrooms, little birds on the spit, also grilled fish (L30–40 000).

Montalcino

Beautifully situated on a hill inhabited since Etruscan times, swathed in vineyards and olive groves, the walled village of Montalcino (pop. 5400) dominates the serene countryside 14 km south of Buonconvento. Its major attraction is liquid—Brunello di Montalcino, a dark pungent red that holds a proud place among Italy's finest wines.

Every year at the Palio in Siena, there is a procession of representatives from all the towns that once were part of the Republic. The honour of leading the parade belongs to Montalcino, for its loyalty and for the great service it rendered in 1555 after the fall of Siena (see Siena: History p. 293). During the siege, a band of diehard republicans escaped from Siena to the nearly impregnable fortress of Montalcino, where they and the local populace established the 'Republic of Siena at Montalcino', holding out against the Medici until 1559. Today, Montalcino tries hard to be up to date (signs on the outskirts proclaim it a 'comune of Europe' and a 'denuclearized zone'); in reality it's a friendly, resolutely sleepy town where people often forget to wind the clocks.

GETTING AROUND

There are regular buses from Siena (41 km/1 hr), a few involving a change at Buonconvento, near the N. 2 crossroads for Montalcino. Buses stop at Piazza Cavour on the eastern end of town; tickets and perhaps information can be obtained at the bar on the piazza. There are no convenient buses to take you to Sant'Antimo.

TOURIST INFORMATION

A Pro Loco office, open now and then, is on Via Mazzini near Piazza Cavour, tel 848 242.

Within the Walls

Right on Piazza Cavour is one of Montalcino's modest museums: the small **Archaeology Museum**, set in a former hospital pharmacy with detached frescoes by a student of Il Sodoma. Via Mazzini leads west to the Piazza del Popolo, and the attractive **Palazzo Comunale**, begun in the late 13th century, with a slender tower that apes the Torre di Mangia in Siena. Nearby, **Sant'Agostino** is a simple Sienese church, preserving some original frescoes from the 1300s. The **Diocesan and Civic Museum** around the corner has a collection of Sienese painting and polychromed wood statues, including some of the earliest successes of Sienese art, an illuminated Bible and painted crucifix, both from the 12th century. Besides some minor works of the 14–15th-century Sienese masters, there is a collection of locally produced majolica from the same period (daily exc Mon, summer 10–12, 3–7 pm, winter 10–12, 3–5; adm).

Just down Via Ricasoli, at the eastern end of Montalcino, the impressive 14th-century **Rocca** was the centre of the fortifications that kept the Spaniards and Florentines at bay. This citadel means a lot to Italian patriots; it was the last stronghold not only of the Sienese, but symbolically of all the medieval freedoms of the Italian cities, blotted out in the bloody, reactionary 1500s. Near the entrance is a plaque with a little poem from the 'Piedmontese Volunteers of Liberty', extolling Montalcino's bravery in 'refusing the Medici thief'. Now a city park, with views that on a clear day stretch over half the province, the Rocca itself (9–1 and 3–8) contains the last battle standard of the Sienese republic and an **Enoteca** where you can become better acquainted with Montalcino's venerable Brunello and other local wines such as Moscadello and Rosso di Montalcino.

Following inside the city walls through the north side of the city, you pass through neighbourhoods made largely of orchards and gardens—Montalcino isn't nearly as busy a place as it was in the 1400s. The **Cathedral**, on Via Spagni, was largely rebuilt in the 1700s. Follow that street past the Baroque church of the Madonna del Soccorso, and you come to the city park, the 'Balcony of Tuscany', with views over Siena and beyond.

Sant'Antimo

A few of the vineyards that produce the famous Brunello di Montalcino are on the road south for Sant'Antimo. Two of them welcome visitors: the Azienda Agricola Greppo, and the Cantine dei Barbi (tel, respectively, 848 087 and 848 277; ring first if you plan to visit). **Sant'Antimo** itself, about 10 km south of Montalcino, is worth the detour. One of the finest Romanesque churches in Tuscany, it originally formed part of a 9th-century Benedictine monastery founded, according to legend, by Charlemagne himself. The present building, begun in 1118, includes parts of the Carolingian works, including the crypt.

This half-ruined complex could easily serve as the set for *The Name of the Rose*. An important monastic community once flourished here; what buildings remain are now used as barns. The church, though, is exquisite, with its elegant tower and rounded apse. Some of the stone inside, on the capitals and elsewhere, is luminous alabaster from Volterra. The sophistication of the architecture is impressive—in particular the Byzantine-style women's gallery, and the ambulatory behind the apse with its radiating chapels. The caretaker does not live on site, but he is usually around in the mornings; alternatively, seek out the sacristan in Castelnuovo dell'Abate.

WHERE TO STAY AND EATING OUT (tel prefix 0577)

There are two hotels in the town centre of Montalcino, the ****Giardino**, right by the bus stop on Piazza Cavour, tel 848 257 (L55 000, or L43 000 without bath), or ****Il Giglio**, Via Salomi 48, tel 848 167 (same price for same plumbing). **Idolina**, also on Piazza Cavour, rents out well-furnished rooms in her charming house for about L28 000.

Besides wine, Montalcino is known for its honey, which comes into its own in early September at the National Honey Fair. Some of it goes into the desserts served at **Cucina de Edgardo**, Via Saloni 9, tel 848 282, serving some of the best and most creative *cucina nuova* this side of Siena; be sure to reserve, especially in the summer (L35 000).

Pienza

Some 50 km south of Siena on N. 2, turning left at San Quirico d'Orcia (see p. 351) you'll come across a perfect, miniscule core of Renaissance order and urbanity, surrounded by a village of about 2500 souls. Pienza is a delightful place, even if it does get more than its share of tourists. Like Monte Oliveto Maggiore, it is a small dose of the best of the Renaissance, a jewel set among some of the best, most archetypical of Tuscan landscapes.

During a period of political troubles, common enough in Renaissance Siena, the great family of the Piccolomini had chosen to exile itself temporarily in one of its possessions, the village of Corsignano. Aeneas Silvius Piccolomini (see p. 306) was born there in

1405; later, as Pope Pius II, he became determined to raise his country birthplace into a city. No historian has ever discovered any compelling economic or military reason for a new town here. Architect Bernardo Rossellino designed it, with some help from Pius, the pennies of the faithful paid for it, and Pius named it after himself, Pienza. No one knows if Rossellino merely meant to build the pope a monument, or was consciously creating a model city of Renaissance town planning. Perhaps fortunately, after the first wave of papal patronage Pienza was nearly forgotten. The strict grid of streets that was to extend over the Tuscan hills never materialized, and only the central piazza with a new cathedral and a Piccolomini palace were ever completed—enough, at least, to reveal something of the original intention.

TOURIST INFORMATION

There is a Pro Loco office on Piazza Pio II, tel 748 502, offering occasional guided tours of the town.

Piazza Pio II

Piazza Pio II, the heart of Rossellino's design scheme, is a simple, decorous square, displaying the chief buildings of the town without any of the monumental symmetricality of the later Renaissance, seemingly relying on proportion alone to tie the ensemble together. Such a square suggests that despite all its paintings of ideal buildings and streetscapes, the early Renaissance had little interest in city design. Compared with the sophisticated planning of the Middle Ages, Piazza Pio as this looks somewhat austere.

Rossellino designed a truly elegant façade for the **Cathedral** (1462), capturing the spirit of the times by omission—there is no hint anywhere on this façade that it belongs to a Christian building, though the arms of the Piccolomini and the papal keys are prominently carved on the pediment. The interior, though equally elegant, is a surprise: it's done in a squarish, tamed Gothic—as if this bold Renaissance architect were a slightly embarrassed humanist who believed that only Gothic truly suited a church. Rossellino also carved a marble altar and baptismal font; in addition, some of the leading Sienese artists contributed altarpieces: Sano di Pietro, Matteo di Giovanni, Vecchietta and Giovanni di Paolo. Nothing in this cathedral has been changed, or even moved, since the day it was completed; Pius' papal bull of 1462 expressly forbade it. See it while it lasts. The cathedral, built on the edge of a slight cliff, has been subsiding almost since it was built. Occasionally sulphurous fumes seep up from the floor. If you walk around the left side of the building, there is a fine outlook over the surrounding countryside, also a glimpse of the fearfully large cracks that have been developing in the apse. No one has yet discovered a way to shore it up, and it could collapse, at least partially, at any time. The cathedral has a small **Museum** in the adjacent Canon's House (daily 10–1, 2–4 pm; adm).

Next to the cathedral, the columned **well**, a favourite sort of Renaissance urban decoration, is also by Rossellino. So is the **Palazzo Piccolomini**, a rehash of the more famous Palazzo Rucellai in Florence, built by the architect after designs by Alberti. The best part of the design is in the rear, where a fine three-storey loggia overlooks a 'hanging garden' on the edge of the cliff. The interior of the palace and gardens are open to visitors (daily exc Mon 10–1, 3–6 pm, 2–4 pm in winter; adm). Other buildings on the piazza include the **Archbishops' Palace** and the Gothic **Palazzo Comunale**. Behind the Palazzo Piccolomini, the church of **San Francesco** predates the founding of Pienza; there are some 14th–15th-century frescoes inside including one small work attributed to Luca Signorelli.

Few people visit the 11th-century **Pieve** of old Corsignano, 1 km west of the town. This unusual church, where Aeneas Silvius was baptised, has some even more peculiar carvings over its entrance. Mermaids, or sirens, turn up with some frequency in Romanesque tympana and capitals, and here are several—one spreading its forked tail to display the entrance to the womb, flanked by others, a dancer and a musician, with dragons whispering into their ears. Such symbols are steeped in medieval mysticism, not entirely inaccessible to the modern imagination. Some scholars interpret this scene as a cosmic process: the sirens, representing desire, as the intermediary by which nature's energy and inspiration (the dragons) are conducted into the conscious world. It has been claimed that they betray the existence of an ecstatic cult, based on music and dance and descended from the ancient Dionysian rituals.

SHOPPING

Corso Rossellino leads from the centre of the village to Porta Murello and the bus terminus, passing trendy artisan shops selling ceramics and leatherwork, antique shops and health food stores. Pienza for some reason has dozens of these, offering among other things the very good, locally made honey and preserves. And if Renaissance architecture leaves you cold, you can at least come for the sheep cheese, maybe Italy's best. Pienza's variety of *cacio* is mild, even delicate in taste; this self-proclaimed 'capital of sheep cheese' has been making it at least since the time of the Etruscans.

WHERE TO STAY AND EATING OUT (tel prefix 0578)

In Pienza, choices are few; the modern, but comfortable ***Corsignano** in Via della Madonnina 11, tel 748 501, is the only hotel in town (L60 000), although near the bus stop, at Piazza Dante 7, tel 748 551, the **Ristorante del Falco** has quite a few spartan rooms for rent (L38 000 a room; meals L25 000). Across the piazza at no. 25, the **Del Prato**, tel 748 601, is the best place to stop for a bite—outside tables in the little garden and a huge menu of simple local dishes, featuring homemade *pici* (thick spaghetti), also crêpes filled with ricotta cheese or other delights (L25–30 000). In the village centre, the **Sperone Nudo** in Corso Rossellino offers wine and *bruschetto*, sandwiches and snacks.

Montepulciano

Two graceful hill towns linger south of Siena, both with a distinguished past and both best known for wine—Montepulciano and Montalcino. Montepulciano is larger (pop. 14,500) and livelier, with some fine buildings and works of art. Old Montalcino was a home-from-home for the Sienese, while Montepulciano usually allied itself with Florence. And this town's *Vino Nobile di Montepulciano*, while perhaps not as celebrated as Montalcino's *Brunello*, was being praised by connoisseurs over 200 years ago, and can certainly contend with Italy's best today.

Inhabitants of this town, which began as the Roman *Mons Politianus*, are called *Poliziani*, and that is the name by which its most famous son is known. Angelo

Ambrogini, or Poliziano, scholar at the court of Lorenzo de' Medici and tutor to his children, was one of the first Renaissance Greek scholars, also an accomplished poet and critic. Botticelli's mythological paintings may have been inspired by his *Stanza per la Giostra*. Today's Poliziani are a genteel and cultured lot, still capable of poetic extemporization and singing. The town's biggest festival is the *Bruscello*, a partly improvised play on medieval and Renaissance themes in music and verse, acted by the townspeople in the Piazza Grande each August. Montepulciano's other festival requires no poetry but plenty of sweat: the *Bravio delle Botti*, also in August, when teams from the various neighbourhoods race up the steep main street pushing huge barrels.

GETTING TO AND AROUND

Montepulciano is 12.5 km/20 min east of Pienza on N. 146, 66 km/1½ hrs from Siena, and 16 km/30 min west of the Chiusi exit on the A1. The rail station (Florence–Rome line) is far out in the countryside, irregularly served by buses to town, and usually only local trains stop; a better possibility is to use the station at Chiusi-Chianciano, which has bus connections up to Chiusi town, to Chianciano Terme, Montepulciano and occasionally Pienza. The bus station in Montepulciano is just outside the Porta al Prato, the main gate into the city. There are several buses a day to Pienza, and to Chianciano Terme–Chiusi–Chiusi Station; one each in the morning and afternoon for Siena (via Pienza and San Quirico), also daily connections to Abbadia San Salvatore, Montalcino, Perugia and Arezzo. There is an LFI bus information booth inside the train station at Chiusi; outside, besides the buses mentioned above, there are infrequent LFI connections to Cortona, Arezzo, Perugia, Orvieto and Città della Pieve.

TOURIST INFORMATION

There's a very helpful office at Via Ricci 9, just off the Piazza Grande, tel 716 935.

Palazzi and Pulcinella

Entering the city through the **Porta al Prato**, the first monument you encounter will be a stone column bearing the *marzocco*, a symbol of Montepulciano's longtime attachment to Florence. Though nominally under Florentine control, the city was allowed a sort of independence up to the days of Cosimo I. The main street, called here Via di Gracciano del Corso, climbs and winds in a circle up to the top of the city (if you follow it all the way, you'll walk twice as far as you need to, and end up thinking Montepulciano is a major metropolis). This stretch of it is lined with noble palaces; the **Palazzo Avignonesi** at no. 91 and the **Palazzo Tarugi** at no. 82 are both the work of the late Renaissance architect Vignola, famous for his Villa Giulia in Rome and the Farnese Palace in Caprarola (Lazio). Further up, at no. 73 the **Palazzo Bucelli** has the most unusual foundation in Italy—made almost entirely of rectangular Etruscan cinerary urns, filled with cement and stacked like bricks, many still retaining their sculpted reliefs. Montepulciano was an Etruscan settlement, though most likely the urns came from nearby Chiusi.

Piazza Michelozzo, where the street begins to ascend, takes its name from the Florentine architect of the **Sant'Agostino** church, with an excellent, restrained Renaissance façade, similar in attitude to the cathedral in Pienza though much more skilfully handled. Michelozzo also contributed the terracotta reliefs over the portal. Across the Piazza, note the figure atop the old **Torre del Pulcinella**. To anyone familiar with

Naples, the white *Commedia dell'Arte* clown banging the hours on the town bell will be an old friend. There's a story that a Neapolitan bishop was once exiled here for some indiscretions with the ladies back home, and when he returned he left this bit of Parthenopean culture as a remembrance, and also to thank the Poliziani for their hospitality.

Continuing along the main street, you pass a dozen or so more palaces, reminders of what an aristocratic city this once was. There is one florid Baroque interior, in the **Gesù Church** by Andrea Pozzo. Further down the street curves around the medieval **Fortezza**, now partially residential, part of a fascinating quarter of ancient alleys, the oldest part of Montepulciano.

Piazza Grande

In these times, when even the stalwart citizens of the Italian hill towns are becoming a little too spoiled to walk up hills, the old centres of towns sometimes become quiet, out-of-the-way places. So it is in Montepulciano, where the **Piazza Grande** is the highest point in the city. On one side, Michelozzo added a rusticated stone front and tower to the 13th-century **Palazzo Comunale** to create a lesser copy of Florence's Palazzo Vecchio. Opposite, there is a pretty Renaissance well in front of the **Palazzo Contucci**, built by the elder Antonio da Sangallo. On the west side of the piazza, a tremendous pile of bricks, a sort of tenement for pigeons, proclaims the agonizing unfinishability of the **Cathedral**, victim of a doomed rebuilding that began in 1592. Like the toad, believed by medieval scholars to conceal a precious jewel in its brain, this preposterous building hides within its bulk a single transcendent work of art. Atop a marble Renaissance altar adorned with putti stands an *Assumption of the Virgin* by Bartolo di Fredi, quite possibly the greatest of all 14th-century Sienese paintings. Set in glowing, discordant colours—pink, orange, purple and gold, this is a very spiritual Madonna, attended by a court of angel musicians. Don't miss the predella panels beneath; each is a serious, inspired image from the Passion, including one panel of the *Resurrection* that can be compared to Piero della Francesca's more famous version in Sansepolcro.

The **Museo Civico**, just down Via Ricci, has a somewhat disappointing collection—some della Robbia terracottas from the dissolved convent that was once downstairs, a *Crucifixion* from the workshop of Filippino Lippi, an *Assumption* by the Sienese Jacopo di Mino, an odd work by Girolamo di Benvenuto—baby Jesus as an *objet d'art*—and even more peculiar, an inexplicable *Allegory of the Immaculate Conception* by one Giovanni Antonio Lappoli (d. 1552). Continue down Via Ricci and you will find the church of **Santa Lucia**, with a small *Madonna* by Luca Signorelli in a chapel off to the right.

Antonio da Sangallo's San Biagio

One of the set pieces of Renaissance architecture was the isolated temple, a chance to create an ideal building in an uncluttered setting, often on the edge of a city. Giuliano da Sangallo's Santa Maria delle Carceri in Prato was the first and worst, followed by Bramante's San Pietro in Montorio in Rome and the Tempio della Consolazione in Todi (Umbria) by one of his followers. Montepulciano's fine example of this Renaissance genre lies just south of the city (a long walk downhill, and back, if you don't have a car) near the road junction for Chianciano; a stately avenue of cypresses, each over a small marker commemorating a local soldier who died in the first World War, leads to the site.

Antonio da Sangallo, long in the shadow of his less talented brother Giuliano, left his masterpiece here. **San Biagio** stands in a small park, a central, Greek cross church of creamy travertine. As with so many other Renaissance churches, there is more architecture than Christianity in the design, a consciously classical composition, using not the Doric, but an adaptation of the 'Tuscan' order on the ground level, then Ionic on the second and finally Corinthian on the upper storeys of the campanile, gracefully fitted into one of the corners of the Greek cross. The interior, finished in fine marble and other expensive stones, is equally symmetrical and rational and impressive, appealing to an entirely different side of the religious sensibility than do the flowering Gothic churches or the soaring histrionics of the Baroque. Over the handsome altar, a Latin inscription proclaims '*Hinc deus homo et homo deus. Immensum Concepti—Aeternum Genuit*'. The beautiful **Canon's House**, with its double loggia, is also the work of Sangallo.

Around Montepulciano

There are some beautiful villages on the hills around Montepulciano, beginning with **Montefollonico** (8 km northwest), a walled town with a frescoed parish church and Palazzo Comunale, both from the 13th century. **Monticchiello**, 7 km southwest on a back road leading towards Pienza, hangs languorously on its hillside; here there is another 13th-century church, with an altarpiece by Pietro Lorenzetti.

Vino Nobile, and Other Delights

Montepulciano and environs are full of *cantine*, and each of these is full of people ready for long discussions on the virtues of this famous wine. After two years, it carries the bouquet of unknown autumn blooms, a perfume that confounds melancholy; its colour is a mystery of faith. Certain writers are known to be very fond of it. A wine tour of Montepulciano should begin with the **Cantine Cantucci**, on the Piazza Grande, where they might show you the salon with frescoes by Baroque artist Andrea Pozzo. The **Cantina Gattavecchia**, next to the church of Santa Maria on the southern end of town, has a cantina dating back to the 1500s; and don't neglect the venerable cellar built into the embankment beneath Piazza Grande, next to the Teatro Poliziano. *Vino Nobile* isn't the only variety of wine made in these parts. There is a version of Chianti—*Chianti Colli Senesi*, a creditable white *Valdichiana* and a sweet dessert *Vin Santo*. And on those evenings when quantity means more than quality, try any of the mass-produced Montepulciano red sold all over Italy; a more honourable plonk is hard to find.

Besides wine, Montepulciano has some local surprises to offer—**jams, preserves, honey** and other farm specialities have all recently become prominent in this corner of Tuscany, where the ideology of natural food has become just as popular as in the trendiest neighbourhoods of New York. You'll find them in almost any grocer's. Montepulciano has some very good **antique** stores on its back streets, and a sound **crafts** tradition, especially in woodcarving. On Piazza Grande, there is a **School of Mosaics**, with a permanent exhibition and some pretty examples of the craft on sale—even if you're not buying, take a peek at the mosaic fountain in the courtyard.

WHERE TO STAY AND EATING OUT (tel prefix 0578)

Montepulciano puts out the welcome mat at a few very amiable hotels, especially the **Marzocco**, tel 757 262, an airy and serendipitous family-run establishment next, of course, to the Marzocco on Piazza Savonarola, just inside the main gate (L45 000 without bath, L55 000 with). Up near the cathedral, ****La Terrazza**, Via Pie al Sasso 16, tel 757 440, has pretty rooms in a centuries-old house, some with views over the town (L48–60 000). Cheaper rooms for L30 000 can be had at the **Ristorante Cittino**, Vicola Via Nuova, tel 757 335 (meals L20 000). If you can't find a room in town, there are millions of them a few miles south at Chianciano Terme (see below) and at a pinch in Sant'Albano, 3 km from Montepulciano—seven hotels, all in the L40–50 000 range, stuck bizarrely in the middle of nowhere; there are more thermal baths nearby.

The best restaurants in Montepulciano are outside town. In the lovely village of Montefollonico, with panoramic views back towards Montepulciano, **La Chiusa** in Via Madonnina, tel 669 668, closed Tues, has been acclaimed as the best restaurant in southern Tuscany, where typical local cuisine is raised to transcendent heights, and there is an exhaustive wine list for those not satisfied with mere Vino Nobile from nearby. Many of the products are grown on the premises, but not the olive oil: La Chiusa is located in an old *frantoio* (olive press) unfortunately closed since a big frost not long ago killed off most of the trees in these parts. You might wish to sample the seven-course *menu degustazione* (L70 000, but can easily rise to L100 000—your best bet for a big splurge in this half of Tuscany). If that's too extravagant, try **Il Pulcino**, 3 km down the road to Chianciano, tel 757 905, specializing in grilled meats and fish for L30–50 000. Montepulciano itself has a few restaurants, but none particularly stand out. Why not have a picnic? Stock up on some of the fine local products—honey and preserves, pecorino cheese, ham or boar salami and a case of Vino Nobile; the back roads off N. 146 will eventually take you to an ideal spot.

Chianciano Terme

TOURIST INFORMATION

Piazza Italia 67, tel 63 167, and in Piazza Gramsci at the gate into Chianciano Vecchio, tel 31 292.

Chianciano—fegato sano

This is the slogan you see everywhere in Chianciano Terme (pop. 7500): on the signs that welcome you to town, on the municipal buildings, even on the garbage trucks. 'Chianciano, for a healthy liver'. And after rotting yours on too much Montepulciano wine, how convenient to have one of Italy's most attractive spas close at hand to flush it out and get it pumping again. The waters here were known to the Etruscans, but only in the last 50 years have they been exploited in a big way. There is an old walled town, *Chianciano Vecchio*, with a medieval clock tower and a small Museo d'Arte Sacra; at the gate is the bus station and information booth. Beyond it, modern Chianciano stretches out for miles down its one main street, Viale della Libertà, passing hundreds of hotels, lovely gardens with clipped lawns, and bathhouses in a clean, modern style from the 1950s.

Everything is just as pleasant as it could be, and besides repairing your liver, Chianciano has mineral mud packs for your acne, hot aerosol douches and plenty of other medically respected treatments for whatever is wrong with you: they'll lock you in a room full of gas for a collective dry nebulization, throw you in the hydro-gaseous bath and then hand you over to the masseuses (this for patients suffering from trauma), or put you face to face with the sulphurous sonic aerosol spray. They can make hot mineral water go up one of your nostrils and come out the other. 'Ah', said the Italian in seeming despair: 'The English never come. They simply do not understand the baths...'

Chiusi

If anyone, when you were a child, ever read you Macaulay's rouser about Horatio at the Bridge, you will remember the fateful name Lars Porsena of Clusium, leading the Etruscan confederation and their Umbrian allies to attack Rome in the brave days of old. Thanks to Horatio, of course, Rome survived and made a name for itself; you can come here to see what happened to Clusium—or *Camars*, as the Etruscans actually called it. Many of its 9500 citizens live down in the newer districts by the railway station (see Montepulciano: Getting Around), but the charming hill town up on the site of Lars Porsena's capital is still doing well.

TOURIST INFORMATION
Pro Loco at Via Porsena 67, tel 227 667.

Archaeological Museum

From the brave days of old, Chiusi retains at least an excellent **Archaeological Museum.** As with so many other Etruscan collections, here the main attraction is the large number of cinerary urns, and as usual the Etruscans are able to produce a bewildering variety of styles and themes. Large urns with thoughtful, reclining figures are common, as well as mythological battle scenes with winged gods in attendance. Not all the tombs contained the well-known rectangular urns; some Etruscans chose to be buried in 'canopic' jars, surmounted by a terracotta bust of the deceased. Other sculptures and terracottas include a strange horse-headed serpent and a few alert sphinxes with curving wings. Camars was a wealthy town, and the excavations at its necropolises unearthed a large amount of Greek pottery, some of it very fine work—note the urn with Achilles and Ajax playing at dice, and the Dionysiac scenes with sexy maenads and leering satyrs. Many Etruscan imitation vases are present; it's easy to believe the local talent could have done as well as the Greeks, had they only possessed thinner paintbrushes. To end the collection, there is a glittering hoard of nice barbaric trinkets from some 6th–7th-century Lombard tombs on the Arusa hill just outside town (open daily exc Mon, 9–1:40, Sat 9–12:40; adm).

Etruscan Tombs and Tunnels

If you're interested in seeing some of the **Etruscan tombs** (5th–3rd century BC) where these items were discovered, mention it to the museum guards, who arrange guided tours—in fact they'll probably ask you first. These are the only good painted tombs in Tuscany; the best of them, the **Tomba della Scimmia**, contains paintings of wrestlers and warriors, in addition to the monkey that gives the tomb its name. The Tomba della Pellegrina and the Tomba del Granduca are also interesting, as is the Tomba Bonci Casuccini, in a different necropolis east of town. Ask the guards if there's any way to get into the **Etruscan tunnels** that honeycomb the ground under Chiusi. The huge **Roman cistern**, built in the 1st century BC under what is now the cathedral, is usually opened for visitors; the rest of the tunnels, several centuries older, are something of a mystery. Whatever their original purpose, some of them were converted into **catacombs** by the early Christian communities, the Catacomb of Santa Mustiola and the smaller catacomb of Santa Caterina.

The Cathedral

Across the street from the museum, Chiusi's **Cathedral** is the oldest in Tuscany. Only parts of it—the recycled Roman columns in the nave—go back to the original 6th-century building. The cathedral was rebuilt in the 12th century and again in the 19th. Have a look at the mosaics that cover the walls inside. Astounding works they seem at first, an unknown chapter in early Christian art. Then you'll notice they have a touch of Art Nouveau about them—and finally you'll realize they aren't mosaics at all, but skilfully sponged-on squares of paint, a crazy masterpiece of mimicry completed in 1915. The small **Cathedral Museum** contains Roman fragments and some beautiful 15th-century illuminated choir books.

Around Chiusi: Lakes, Sarteano and the *Crete*

Just northeast of Chiusi, the **Lago di Chiusi** and the **Lago di Montepulciano** are pretty patches of blue on the border between Tuscany and Umbria, the smallest in the chain of lakes that begins with nearby Lago Trasimeno. Lago di Chiusi in particular makes a nice place for a picnic, not too far from the autostrada if you're on your way from Florence to Rome or Orvieto.

Nine km south of Chianciano or Chiusi, **Sarteano** is a smaller resort-spa, attached to a fine old hill town with some Renaissance palaces, a squarish medieval fortress, and the church of **San Martino in Foro**, with an *Annunciation* that is one of the best works of the Sienese Mannerist Beccafumi. Another 6 km south of Sarteano, just off the ruggedly scenic N. 321, lies **Cetona**, a small, untouristed gem of a town, while along the N. 478 from Sarteano towards Monte Amiata you'll pass one of the loneliest, most barren regions of *crete* en route to the Val d'Orcia (see p. 351).

WHERE TO STAY AND EATING OUT (tel prefix 0578)

Chianciano: You may not be ready to entrust yourself to the thermal torture of the spa, but Chianciano can be a very useful place in July or August when hotels are booked solid everywhere else. The Azienda Autonima di Cura on Viale Roma 67 offers help with accommodation. Almost all of Chianciano's hotels were built in the last 30 years—nothing special, but there's a place to stay in every price range.

In Chiusi, most of the hotels are down by the railway station in Chiusi Scalo, unremarkable places like the *****Centrale**, Piazza Dante 3, tel 20 118, with modern rooms for L60 000. Chiusi has a famous restaurant; plenty of Italians in the know make the long detour off the Rome-Florence autostrada to **Zaira**, up at Via Arunte 12 in the oldest part of Chiusi, tel 20 260. They come for the speculative 'Etruscan cuisine'. Surely the Etruscans, so often portrayed with plates of food on their funerary urns, had some tasty dishes, but every restaurant that tries imaginatively to reconstruct an Etruscan menu comes up with something different. No matter; it's a useful fancy, and with dishes here like the *pasta del lucumone* (with ham and three different cheeses), duck cooked in

Vino Nobile, and pheasant *al cartoccio* it's hard to complain. Zaira takes special pride in the wine list; they have one of the largest cellars in Tuscany. Prices are reasonable—usually around L40 000.

If your car can't climb the hill up to Chiusi, take it out to Lago di Chiusi to the north—at Conciarese al Lago, **La Fattoria**, tel 21 407, is an old house with views over the lake, specializing in fresh fish from it, and every sort of roast and pasta dish made with *porcini* mushrooms (L35 000). Down in Sarteano (6 km southwest of Chiusi), at Viale Europa 1, tel 265 511, **La Giara** is usually crowded with Sartanese, and with its homemade pasta, roast duck, and lamb chops for a bill under L25 000, it's no surprise.

The Val d'Orcia

San Quirico d'Orcia, a humble little agricultural centre where the N. 146 from Pienza joins the N. 2, still has some of its medieval walls. The **Collegiata Church**, begun in the 1080s, is the only reason for a visit; it has an exceptional façade and portals from the 1200s, sculpted with lions and telamones. There are a couple of points of interest nearby: **Ripa d'Orcia**, a hamlet with a stately castle of its own, 7 km south on a white road, and **Bagno Vignoni**, a small, modern spa town just to the south.

Before the modern N. 2 was built, the old Via Francigena traversed the valley of the Orcia, passing a patch of castles and fortified towns that began in the early Middle Ages. **Castiglione d'Orcia** (9 km south of S. Quirico) is as medieval-looking a town as you could ask for (though its cobbled piazza and fountain are from the 1600s). The parish church has Madonnas by three great Sienese artists, Martini, Pietro Lorenzetti, and Il Vecchietta. The ruined fortress overlooking the town was built by the Aldobrandeschi family, who controlled much of southern Tuscany as late as the 1200s. If you're spending time around Castiglione, get in touch with the Centro Agriturismo 'I Lecci', tel 887 287. They can arrange horses for tours of the countryside, hunting trips and nature excursions.

Another 15 km south of Castiglione, **Vivo d'Orcia** began as a Camaldolensian monastery in 1003; when the monastery withered the village gradually replaced it, leaving only the pretty Romanesque Cappella dell'Ermicciolo in the woods above the town. **Bagni S. Filippo**, some 8 km east of Vivo, circling back towards the N. 2 may go into the books as the world's smallest thermal spa—a telephone booth, a few old houses, an outdoor spring with glistening limestone formations, and one small hotel. It takes its name from San Filippo Benizi, a holy hermit of the Middle Ages who hid here when he heard there was a movement to elect him pope.

Radicófani

Some wonderfully rugged countryside lies in the valley of the Orcia, east of this chain of villages, especially along the roads approaching **Radicófani**, a landmark of southern Tuscany, with its surreal, muffin-shaped hill topped by a lofty tower. The ruined fortress around it, originally built by Pope Adrian IV (the Englishman Nicholas Breakspear), served in the 1300s as headquarters for the legendary bandit Ghino di Tacco, solid citizen of Dante's *Inferno* and subject of a story in the *Decameron* (day 10, number 2), about how he imprisoned the Abbot of Cluny in this tower. The elegant loggias on the highway, just outside town, belong to the 17th-century Palazzo La Posta, once the only good hotel between Siena and Rome; most of the famous on the Grand Tour stopped on their way through.

Abbadia San Salvatore and Monte Amiata

A thousand years ago, you might have heard of this town, home of the most important monastic centre in Tuscany and a fair-sized city in its own right. History passed Abbadia San Salvatore by a long time ago; today it makes a modest living as a mountain resort, the gateway to nearby Monte Amiata.

GETTING AROUND

Transportation isn't always easy around these towns if you don't have a car. Don't try to get there by train; there's a 'Monte Amiata station' on an infrequent branch line from Siena, but it's really some 40 km on the other side of the mountain, near Castiglione d'Orcia. Buses stop on Viale Roma in the centre of Abbadia S. Salvatore (tickets and schedules in the toy store behind the information booth)—a few daily to Siena (79 km/2½ hrs), Montepulciano—Chiusi (48 km/1½ hrs) and Arcidosso (25 km/1 hr). Note that Arcidosso and the other towns on the west slope of Amiata are in Grosseto province; almost all the buses there go on to Grosseto.

TOURIST INFORMATION

In Abbadia S. Salvatore, Via Mentana 95 (2nd floor), tel 778 608, also a little booth (on Viale Roma by the bus stop) for information on Monte Amiata.

Abbadia San Salvatore

Abbadia (pop. 7900) at first glance seems a modern town, but just behind Viale Roma a narrow gateway leads into the grey, quiet streets of the **medieval centre**. It isn't very large, and there are no buildings of particular interest, but it is as complete and unchanged as any medieval quarter in Tuscany. Note the symbols carved into many of the doorways: coats-of-arms, odd religious symbols (a snake, for example) or signs like a pair of scissors that declare the original owner's profession.

The **Abbey Church** is outside the centre, a few blocks north in Via del Monastero; in the Middle Ages it must have been open countryside. According to legend—there's even a document telling the story, dated the Ides of March, 742—the Lombard King Rachis was on his way to attack Perugia when a vision of the Saviour appeared to him. Rachis not only founded the monastery, but retired to it as a monk. Historians think the whole business a convenient fabrication, but by 1000 the abbey had achieved considerable wealth and influence, ruling over a large piece of territory and waging occasional wars with the Bishop of Chiusi. In 1036, the present church was begun, an excellent Romanesque work that may seem plain to us, but was undoubtedly one of the grandest sights in Tuscany when it was new.

Behind the twin-steepled façade, the church is surprisingly long; the eastern end consists of a raised chancel, leading to a series of arches over the altar and choir; here is a series of quirky frescoes by an early 1700s artist named Nasino, telling the story of King Rachis. The **crypt**, under the chancel, was the original 8th-century church. The proportions and even the shapes of the arches are thoroughly Byzantine, with stone vaulting and oddly-carved columns and capitals, no two alike.

South of Abbadia San Salvatore, **Piancastagnaio** is a smaller mountain resort. It has a **castle** of the Aldobrandeschi, with a small museum inside, and, as its name implies, lots of chestnut trees.

WHERE TO STAY AND EATING OUT (tel prefix 0577)

Abbadia San Salvatore has become a popular place, not just for winter skiing, but also as a cool retreat in the summer. There are a dozen or so hotels in town, including the ***Adriana**, a few blocks north of the centre at Via Serdini 76, tel 778 116 (L50 000 without, L75 000 with bath) and the brand new ***San Marco**, on Via Matteotti, tel 778 089 (L50 000). The San Marco has a ristorante-rosticceria with a good L18 000 menu; just down the street, **Da Aldo** has a L15 000 menu—but you'd do better to go for L25 000 à la carte—good *pici* and *tortelli* (big south Tuscan ravioli), and roast meats. The menu seems to include beaver *scottiglia di castoro*!

Monte Amiata

Monte Amiata, 13 km west of Abbadia, an extinct volcano a bit over a mile high (1738 m), is impressive enough in its setting. With no real competition west of the Apennines, it has become a skiing and hiking centre, a popular resort in both summer and winter. The presence of Europe's second largest mercury mine (a complex that has been putting dinner on the table for Abbadia San Salvatore since the Middle Ages) does not detract from the natural beauty of the area. The lower slopes, where they are not cultivated, are largely covered in chestnut and beech forests—beautiful mature forests, at the higher altitudes, without so much of the usual Italian prickly underbrush and vipers. They turn colour marvellously in the autumn.

If you take the panoramic route around Amiata, here are some of the towns and villages you'll encounter: **Seggiano**, 20 km northwest of Abbadia, where there's an unusual 16th-century church with a square cupola, the Madonna della Carità; pretty **Castel del Piano**, 7 km south of Seggiano, with a lower town and upper *borgo*; and **Arcidosso**, another 4 km south, the largest town (pop. 4500) on the Grosseto side of Amiata. Arcidosso has been around for a long time; there's one church outside town, the triple-apsed Pieve di Lamulas, begun in the 900s. The town is best known, however, for the strange career of David Lazzaretti, a millenarian prophet gunned down by the Carabinieri during a disturbance in 1878. People in this area still talk about Lazzaretti; his movement, combining reformed religion and plain rural socialism (in an age when land reform was Italy's biggest social issue), spread widely in southern Tuscany. Before Lazzaretti's murder, his followers had started a sort of commune on **Monte Labbro**, 10 km south. The church they built on Monte Labbro still stands, and a small number of the faithful occasionally hold 'Giurisdavidical' services there.

Above Arcidosso, another strong medieval **castle** testifies to the power of the Aldobrandeschi family. **Roccalbegna**, 20 km south on N. 323, has another one, and a small collection of mostly Sienese art in its Oratorio del Crocifisso. The Aldobrandeschi also built at **Santa Fiora**, a pleasant town 7.5 km south, with della Robbia terracottas in its three churches.

ACTIVITIES

As one of the few good skiing areas close to Rome, Monte Amiata can be a busy place when the snow flies. The pistes begin almost at the very summit of Amiata (decorated by the obligatory giant crucifix); to reach them there are 2 chair lifts and 15 ski lifts. The 15 runs (longest 1500 m) are connected by paths through the forest. There is also a ski school. For snow news and other information, call the tourist office in Abbadra San Salvatore, 778 608. With a perfect landscape for it, cross-country skiing and hiking are also very popular here. A whole network of hiking trails have been marked, extending as far as Castiglione d'Orcia.

WHERE TO STAY AND EATING OUT (tel prefix 0577)

For skiing, there are pleasant new facilities; the ***Rifugio Cantore**, tel 789 704, stays open all year for summer mountaineering; it is located at 'secondo rifugio 10' along the road from Abbadia; a little further up, at Vette Amiata, there is the cosy ***La Capannina**, tel 789 713 (open 15 Dec–Easter, also July–Sept, L64 000). The hotel restaurant is probably the best in the area; lots of dishes with mushrooms (including *polenta*, that northern Italian alternative to pasta that is also popular around here); also stuffed pigeon (L35 000).

The Lost Corner of Tuscany

Not many readers, we suspect, will be planning to spend some of their holiday in Saturnia or Pitigliano this year. Only a true connoisseur of regional obscurity would appreciate the inland reaches of Grosseto province, the largest stretch of territory in Italy (north of the Abruzzo) without a single compelling attraction. Once part of the Etruscan heartland, these towns have been poor and usually misgoverned ever since—by Romans, the Aldobrandeschi, the popes and the Tuscan dukes. Some people don't consider the area part of Tuscany at all, and it does seem to have more in common with the Lazio towns just to the south.

Southeast 20 km from Santa Fiora, **Castell'Azzara** takes its name from a medieval game of dice (the word similar to our *hazard*); one of the Aldobrandeschi won it in a crap shoot. **Sorano**, a grim, grey town to the south, clings tenaciously to its rock. Bits of it have been sliding down into the surrounding valleys for centuries; after a big landslide the town was declared uninhabitable and largely abandoned, though efforts to restore it have been undertaken. Sorano is dominated by two equally grim castles; the larger is the 15th-century Rocca degli Orsini.

Sovana

Sovana, 10 km west, with its population of about 190, is another medieval time capsule, a town almost perfectly preserved in its 13th- or 14th-century appearance. Sovana was an Etruscan city, and in the 11th century it was thriving as the family headquarters of the Aldobrandeschi. This powerful clan, controlling much of southern Tuscany and northern Lazio, played a role in politics on a European level. The zenith of its influence came with the election to the papacy of one of its members in 1073. Gregory VII (his common

Sovana

name *Hildebrand* betrays the Aldobrandeschis' Teutonic origins) made a great reforming pope, the man who defeated the Emperors in the great struggle over investiture, but he also took good care of the family interests.

On Sovana's humble main street, the Via di Mezzo, you can see the 13th-century Palazzo del Pretorio, with only a clock and bifore windows to betray its civic dignity. There is some interesting early Christian and medieval sculpture preserved in the 12th-century church of S. Maria, and the **Duomo**, just outside the village, has an octagonal dome from the 900s, a crypt 200 years older, and some sculptural work on the façade that may have been recycled from a pagan temple. Just west of town, there is perhaps the best **Etruscan necropolis** in Tuscany—no paintings, but many architectural details carved out of the living rock have survived, notably in the temple-like construction called the 'Tomba Ildebranda'.

Pitigliano

Just 8 km away is Pitigliano, another ominous-looking place that could be Sorano's twin. Pitigliano makes a memorable sight, its grey houses perched along the edges of the cliffs; underneath are countless holes in the cliff faces that once were Etruscan tombs, now often used as stables or storehouses. Its city walls are built on Etruscan foundations. Piazza della Repubblica, the centre of Pitigliano, has a big fountain and the 14th-century palace of the Orsini, the powerful Roman family that aced the Aldobrandeschi out of many of their holdings in southern Tuscany. There is another picturesque medieval centre, and a 16th-century aqueduct, like the one in Perugia, running across Via Cavour. The alleys around Vicolo Manin, where a ruined synagogue still stands, were once Pitigliano's Jewish ghetto; the centuries-old Jewish community was decimated in 1945.

Saturnia

Little **Saturnia**, 25 km west of Sovana, sits all by itself above the Val d'Albegna, claiming nothing less than to be the first city ever founded in Italy—by Saturn himself, in fact, during the Golden Age. The present village has the form of a Roman settlement, but fragments of monolithic, pre-Etruscan walls can be seen, and aerial photography has discerned traces of an older city beneath the Roman level. There are hot sulphur springs in the neighbourhood, still in use as they evidently were throughout antiquity; ruins are everywhere. **Manciano**, 12 km to the south, has a Sienese fortress and not much else.

To the west on N. 323, **Magliano in Toscana** was given a fine set of walls by the Sienese. The city, heir to the Etruscan town of Heba, has a Sienese style Palazzo dei Priori, and the church of San Giovanni Battista, with a Renaissance façade. Its best known attraction, though, is the **Ulivo della Strega** (the witches' olive), a weirdly gnarled tree well over a thousand years old, said to be the site of ritual dances in pagan days, and still haunted today. The tree is just outside the town's Porta San Giovanni, near the Romanesque **Annunziata** church, with some good Sienese frescoes inside. About 2 km southeast, on the road for Marsiliana, are the ruins of the 12th-century abbey of San Bruzio.

WHERE TO STAY AND EATING OUT (tel prefix 0564)

Real pioneers passing through this region will find reasonable food and accommodation throughout—though usually they'll have to look hard to find it. The region produces some good but little-known wines, notably Morellino di Scansano, a severe dry variety with a beautiful deep red colour. Just outside Pitigliano, the ****Corano**, Via Maremaro, tel 616 112, has 29 modern rooms and a pool (L55 000). In town, the ****Guastini** on Piazza Petruccioli, tel 616 065, (rooms L40–55 000)has the most popular restaurant in the area; homemade pasta, Bianco di Pitigliano wine, and 'Etruscan style' dishes like *biglione d'agnello*, well worth L30–35 000. In Sovana, there's the Dark Ages ambience of the Piazza Pretorio and the **Taverna Etrusca**, tel (yes, a telephone) 615 539; roast boar and the other south Tuscan favourites for L30 000; pleasant, simple rooms upstairs for L26 000 (double that, though, for the high season, July–Sept). Saturnia, being a spa of sorts, has a wider choice of restaurants. The best is in the ******Hotel Terme di Saturnia**, tel 601 061. It's hard to imagine anyone paying L250 000 for a hotel room up here, but the restaurant, at about L45 000, repays a visit with fresh seafood, including a good *risotto marinaro*, besides game dishes like quails with olives.

Part XII

AREZZO AND ITS PROVINCE

Castello dei Conti Guidi, Poppi

Between Florence and Umbria lies a lovely region of nature and art, most of which is included in the province of Arezzo. Watered by the newly born Arno and Tiber rivers (at one point they flow within a mere 15 km of each other), it occupies a keystone position in Italy, not only geographically but as amazingly fertile ground for 'key' Italians: Masaccio and Cosimo il Vecchio's humanist Greek scholar and magician, Marsilio Ficino, were born in the Arno Valley; Petrarch, Michelangelo, Piero della Francesca, Paolo Uccello, Luca Signorelli, Andrea Sansovino, Vasari, the great satirist Aretino, Guido Monaco (inventor of the musical scale), Pietro da Cortona, and the Futurist Gino Severini were born in Arezzo or its province. Many of them left some of their art behind, which adds to the region's charms. Because of its strategic location battlefields dot the countryside, and castles, yet here, too is St Francis' holy mountain of La Verna, where he received the stigmata.

There are two possible routes between Florence and Arezzo: the quick one, following the trains and Autostrada del Sole down the Valdarno, while the second, through the Passo della Consuma or Vallombrosa, takes in the beautifully forested areas of Pratomagno and the Casentino.

The Valdarno: Florence to Arezzo

If a Tuscan caveman ever sang 'O give me a home, where the giant mammoth roam' he would have wanted to live in what is now the Arno Valley. In the Pliocene age the valley was a lake, a popular resort of ancient elephants, and farmers are not surprised when their ploughs collide with fossils. The typically Tuscan towns of the Valdarno, however,

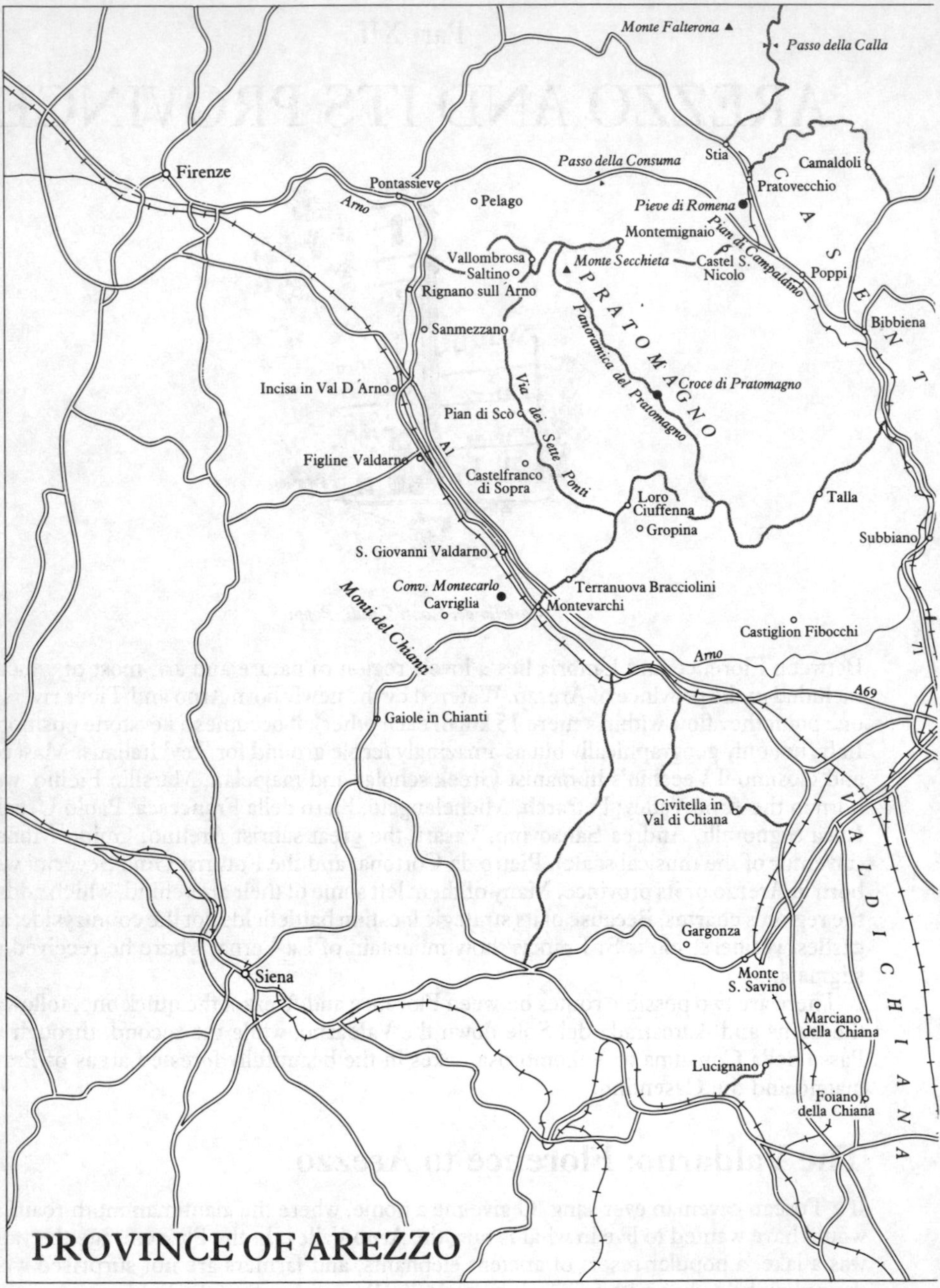

PROVINCE OF AREZZO

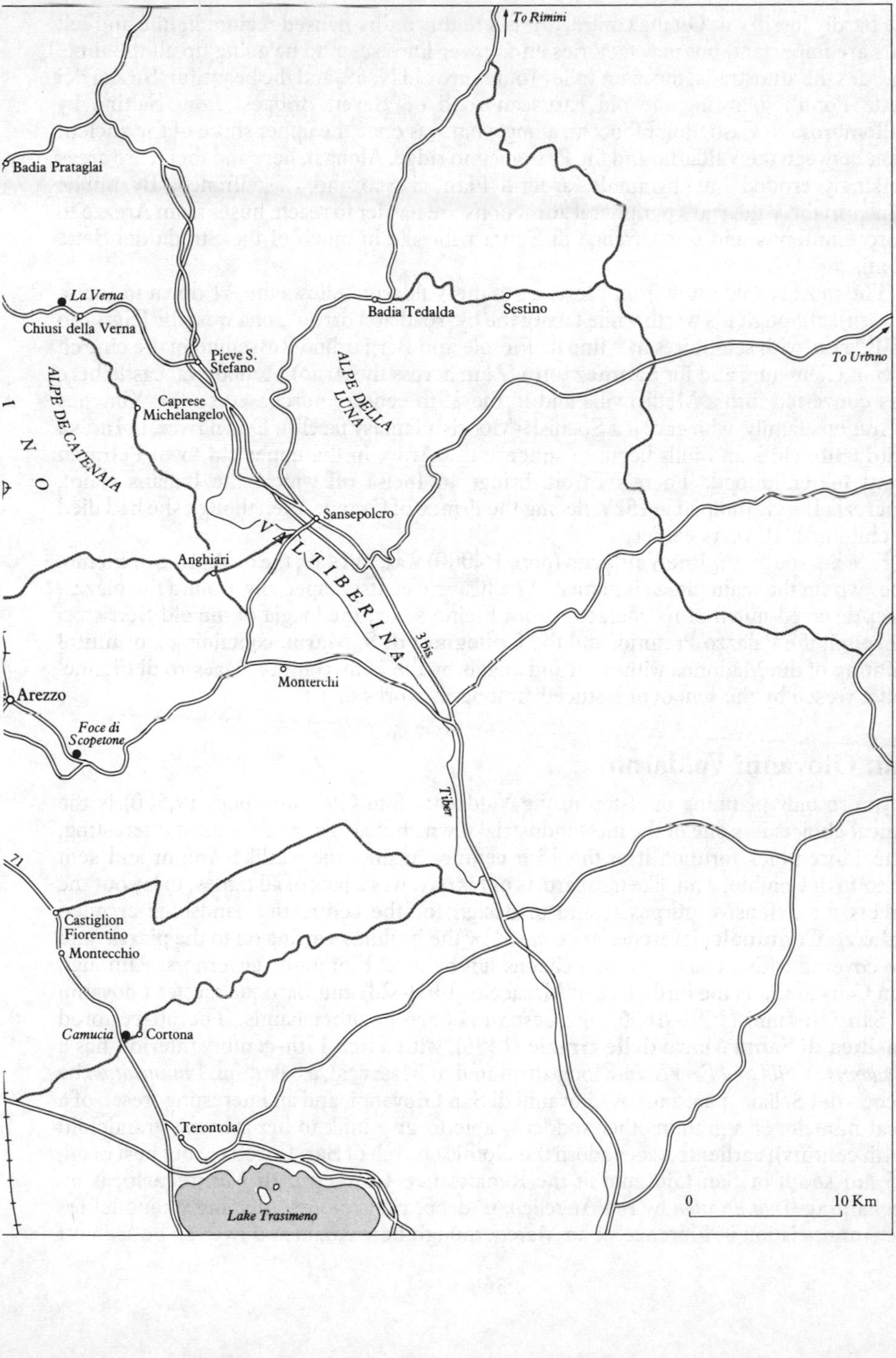

To Rimini
Badia Prataglai
La Verna
Chiusi della Verna
Pieve S. Stefano
Caprese Michelangelo
ALPE DE CATENAIA
ALPE DELLA LUNA
Badia Tedalda
Sestino
To Urbino
Sansepolcro
VALTIBERINA
Anghiari
3 bis
Monterchi
Arezzo
Foce di Scopetone
Tiber
71
Castiglion Fiorentino
Montecchio
Camucia
Cortona
Terontola
Lake Trasimeno
0
10 Km

are hardly fossilised. On the contrary, it is a highly industrialised region: lignite and felt hats are important, but new factories and power lines seem to be going up all the time. Besides the autostrada, the main valley routes are old N. 69, and the beautiful 'Strada dei Sette Ponti', following the old Etruscan road of 'Seven Bridges' from Saltino by Vallombrosa to Castiglion Fibocchi, along what was once the upper shore of the ancient lake, between the Valdarno and the Pratomagno ridge. Along it, here and there, are areas strikingly eroded into pyramids, around Pian di Scò and Castelfranco. By public transport the Valdarno's peripheral attractions are harder to reach; buses from Arezzo to Loro Ciuffenna and Castelfranco di Sopra will take in much of the Strada dei Sette Ponti.

The most scenic route from Florence to the Valdarno follows the A1 down to Incisa (23 km), although it's worth while taking the by-road at Torre a Cona west for **Rignano sull'Arno**, with sculptures by Mino da Fiesole and Bernardino Rossellino in the church of San Clemente, and for **Sanmezzano** (2 km across the Arno). A medieval castle here was converted into a Medici villa and in the 19th century purchased by the Ximenes d'Aragona family, who gave it a Spanish-Moorish fantasy facelift. Down river, at **Incisa Valdarno**, cliffs and hills begin to squeeze the Arno; in the upper old town Petrarch spent his childhood. There's an old bridge in Incisa off which, the Italians claim, Lucrezia Borgia jumped in 1529, fleeing the Prince of Orange, even though she had died in childbirth 10 years earlier!

Five km south, **Figline Valdarno** (pop. 16,000) was, in 1439, the birthplace of Ficino, after whom the main piazza is named. The historic centre, especially around the piazza, has preserved much of its character from Ficino's day: the loggia of the old Serristori Hospital, the Palazzo Pretorio, and the **Collegiata di S. Maria**, containing a beautiful painting of the Madonna with child and angels by the 14th-century 'Maestro di Figline' and a fresco by the school of Botticelli among its works of art.

San Giovanni Valdarno

If you're only planning one stop in the Valdarno, San Giovanni (pop. 19,500) is the logical choice: it is one of the most industrial towns but also one of the most interesting. The Florentines fortified it in the 13th century against the warlike Aretini and sent Arnolfo di Cambio, who, like most artists of his day, was a jack of all trades, to lay out the streets for defensive purposes, and to design for the centre the handsome arcaded **Palazzo Comunale**; its arches are echoed by the buildings giving on to the piazza, and are covered with a collage of escutcheons left by local Florentine governors. Although San Giovanni was the birthplace of Masaccio (1401–28) and Baroque master Giovanni di San Giovanni (1592–1636), the best works are by other hands. The oft-restored **Basilica di Santa Maria delle Grazie** (1486), with a rich 17th-century interior, has a *Madonna, Child and Four Saints*, long attributed to Masaccio, a beautiful *Annunciation* by Jacopo del Sellaio, paintings by Giovanni di San Giovanni, and an interesting fresco of a local miracle, of a grandmother suddenly able to give milk to her starving grandchild (14th century); earlier frescoes adorn the Gothic church of **San Lorenzo**; but best of all, 2.5 km south of San Giovanni at the Renaissance **Convento di Montecarlo**, is an enchanting *Annunciation* by Fra Angelico, in deep, rich colours, seemingly a model for the Annunciation in Florence's San Marco, though here Adam and Eve can be seen off to the left, fleeing the Garden of Eden. From the convent the road continues to the Monti del Chianti by way of **Cavriglia**, but instead of vineyards the hills here are scarred with the amphitheatres of open lignite mines. Yet not all the earth here is exploited; Cavriglia is also the site of a Nature Park, where modern deer and buffalo roam in the company of other animals from around the world.

The Valdarno also offers a look at former animals, especially the large *elephas meridionalis* in the **Museo Paleontologico** in **Montevarchi** (9–12 and 4–7, Sun 10–12, closed Mon and Aug). Montevarchi is a major marketing centre of the region, famous for its hats and chickens; in its ancient core, you can trace the oval medieval street plan. In the centre of town stands the old **Collegiata di San Lorenzo**, which had a complete facelift in the 18th century. Within it is an unusual reliquary 'of the holy milk', brought from a cave in the Holy Land where the Holy Family is said to have rested and where a fountain of milky water flows; a small museum holds a quattrocento **Tempietto** covered inside and out with Andrea della Robbia's cherub friezes. In Rendola, 6 km south, there's a **riding stable** open late September to early June (Rendola Riding, tel 987 045). Across the Arno, **Terranuova Bracciolini** is an old Aretine fortress town, its walls still standing.

Along the Road of Seven Bridges

East of the Arno, the panoramic Strada dei Sette Ponti passes several medieval towns en route to Arezzo. **Regello** (8 km east of Sanmezzano) stands amid its famous olive groves in a beautiful setting; some of its streets retain their medieval arcades, and the 12th-century parish church of **San Pietro a Cascia** has good, early Romanesque columns. **Castelfranco di Sopra**, 12 km south, was another Florentine military town laid out by Arnolfo di Cambio, with fine palaces, and to the north at Pulicciano, a landscape eroded into pyramidical forms, or *balze*, more common around Volterra. Oddly-named **Loro Ciuffenna** offers some picturesque medieval corners, a Romanesque bridge and tower, and a triptych by Lorenzo di Bicci in **S. Maria Assunta**. Best of all is the tiny 12th-century parish church of **Gròpina** (from the Etruscan *Kropina*), 2 km away, an excellent example of rural Romanesque. Although it was referred to in the 8th century, the current church was built in the early 1200s. Dominated by its huge campanile, the façade is simplicity itself, while the three naves and little semicircular apse have never been altered; the columns are carved with primitive tigers, eagles, etc., while the round marble **pulpit** is a bizarre relic of the Dark Ages, carved with archaic figures raising their arms over a marble knot; over them is a kind of totem pole, geometrical and floral decorations, and a sexy siren with a snake whispering sweet nothings in her ear. **Castiglion Fibocchi**, 13 km from Arezzo, is another typical town where little has changed, except for the industry on its outskirts.

WHERE TO STAY AND EATING OUT (tel prefix 055)

In Figline Valdarno, you can have a memorable stay in the ****__Castello di Sanmezzano__**, at Leccio, tel 867 911; 18 rooms, garden, Mozarab-Hollywood atmosphere, with Byzantine and peacock rooms (L250 000). The best restaurant in the area is the elegant **Vicolo del Contento**, in Castelfranco di Sopra, Loc. Mandri 38, tel 914 9277, where the cuisine matches the decor: delicious ravioli filled with crab meat, well-prepared meat and fresh fish, followed, perhaps, by a slice of *pecorino from Pienza. Fine Chianti and other wines (menu degustazione* L65 000 with wine).

At Montevarchi, *****Delta**, Via Diaz 137, tel 901 213, is the best hotel in town, with a garage, air conditioning and TV in each room (L65 000). At tiny **Adriano**, in Piazza Masaccio 15, San Giovanni Valdarno, tel 92 470, you can dine on the local stew *stufato alla sangiovannese*, homegrown roast chicken, homemade desserts and wines from all over Tuscany (L25 000).

Pratomagno and Vallombrosa

The Strada dei Sette Ponti skirts the west rim of Pratomagno, not a big meadow as its name suggests, but a forested mountain ridge. Its highest peak, Croce di Pratomagno (1591 m), is due north of Loro Ciuffenna; winding roads from Loro let you explore the tiny mountain hamlets on the slopes, while the Loro-Talla route crosses over into the Casentino.

Other roads from the west into the Casentino are much further to the north. The two routes from Florence, both taking in fine, wooded scenery, are N. 70 over the **Passo della Consuma** (1025 m), a favourite Italian rest stop, and the secondary route through **Vallombrosa** ('Shady valley'), famous for its abbey founded by San Giovanni Gualberto of Florence, and still the headquarters of his Vallombrosan order. The abbey itself has gone through enlargements and remodellings in the 15th and 17th centuries and is mainly of interest for its splendid position, while **Saltino**, a kilometre away, is a small summer resort, surrounded by firs, where most people end up, an excellent base for walking or motoring excursions. One of the most beautiful is the road up to the Monte Secchieta (1449 m), affording views over most of north-central Italy; in the winter the skiing facilities spring into action. For a longer outing, drive or walk along the newly opened **Panoramica del Pratomagno**, which crosses nearly the entire Pratomagno to join the Strada dei Sette Ponti near Castiglion Fibocchi.

The Casentino: North to South

The Casentino's blue mountains, pastoral meadows and velvet valleys have long been Tuscany's spiritual refuge. Since the 18th century, travellers have trickled into the area, attracted initially by its famous monasteries, then charmed by one of the loveliest and most peaceful regions not only in Tuscany, but in Italy.

The Arno, such a turgid, unmannerly, creature in its lower reaches ('the emblem of Despair', Norman Douglas called it once), is a fair, sparkling youth near its source at Monte Falterona (1658 m); one of the classic excursions is to take the trail up and spend the night, to witness the sunset over the Tyrrhenian sea and dawn over the Adriatic. **Stia** (pop. 3000), the first town the Arno meets, is a pretty medieval town, centred about large porticoed Piazza Tanucci and **S. Maria Assunta**. The 17th-century façade hides a fine Romanesque interior, with some curious, primitive capitals, a triptych by Lorenzo di Bicci and a Madonna by Andrea della Robbia. Wool—the thick, heavy, brightly coloured *lana del Casentino*—is the main industry; in the old days Stia was the market for the Guidi counts, whose ruined **Castello** at Porciano guarded the narrow Arno valley from the 10th century. Near this (4 km north of Stia) is the **Sanctuary of S. Maria delle Grazie**, a 14th-century church with frescoes, works attributed to Luca della Robbia, and a painting by Lorenzo di Niccolò Gerini. This road continues into the Mugello, while the N. 310 from Stia goes around the other side of Monte Falterona towards the **Passo la Calla** and Emilia-Romagna; near the pass the Alpine pasture **Burraia** (15 km from Stia) is a good place for a cool summer picnic.

Down river from Stia, **Pratovecchio** was the birthplace of Paolo Uccello, and chances are he'd recognize its narrow, porticoed lanes if he were to see it again. A couple of kilometres from the centre is the most beautiful Romanesque church of the Casentino, **San Pietro di Romena**, founded in 1152, which has retained its original lines in spite of several earthquakes and subsequent repairs. Although the façade is plain, the apse has two tiers of blind arcades, pierced by narrow windows. Inside, the well-preserved capitals are decorated with a medieval menagerie of people, animals, and monsters. Among the works of art, dating back to the 1200s, is a Madonna by Maestro di Varlungo. Nearby, the Guidi's **Castello di Romena**, high on its hill, was one of the most powerful in the Casentino, with its three sets of walls and 14 towers (now reduced to three), and dominating views down the Casentino. Dante mentioned it in the *Inferno*, as well as the **Fonte Branda**, the ruins of which are close by.

Dante knew this region well; at the age of 24 he fought with the Guelphs against the Ghibellines of Arezzo and its allies at the Battle of **Campaldino** (1289), a small plain just to the south of Pratovecchio. The victory was of paramount importance for Florence; it made her the leading power in Tuscany, and from there she went on to conquer Pisa and Arezzo. A column commemorating the battle was erected near the crossroads in 1921. At the head of the plain, just off the N. 70, Countess Matilda's **Castel S. Nicolò** and the wee medieval hamlet of **Strada**, and its little Romanesque church, form a picturesque ensemble in the wooded hills.

Poppi and Camaldoli

Between 1000 and 1440 the Casentino was ruled by the Counts Guidi, who had their headquarters in the compact little bump of a hill town of **Poppi** (pop. 5800), set above a charming landscape of low rolling hills. From miles around you can see the Guidi's stalwart and erect **Castello**, modelled on the Palazzo Vecchio in Florence. The best-preserved medieval castle in the region, it has a magnificent courtyard, emblazoned with coats-of-arms and stairs that zigzag to and fro with a touch of Piranesi. If you ask the custodian, he'll show you the grand hall, with Florentine frescoes of the 1400s, the frescoed chapel, and the commanding views from the tower.

The centre of Poppi is made up of ancient porticoed lanes, winding around a small domed chapel with a train station clock; at the end of Poppi's long, arcaded, main street is the Romanesque church of **San Fedele**, with a 13th-century Madonna and child. Shops selling locally made copperware line the main street of lower Poppi (or Ponte a Poppi), and there's the little **Zoo Fauna Europea** for the kids.

A beautiful road northeast leads up from Poppi to the ancient hermitage and monastery of **Camaldoli**, founded in 1012 by St Romualdo. Romualdo was a Benedictine monk who sought to found a community of hermits, similar to those of the early

Christians, and was given this forest by Count Maldolo (hence the name 'Camaldoli'). A conflict, however, began even during the lifetime of Romualdo, for the piety of the hermits soon attracted pilgrims and visitors who interfered with their solitary meditations. Romualdo's solution was ingenious: to found another community lower down, a monastery with a more relaxed rule, whose sole purpose was to entertain visitors and care for the forest domains that belonged to the order. Perhaps of all monastic orders, the Camaldolese are the most ecologically minded; self-sufficient vegetarians whose rule orders them to plant at least 5000 new trees every year. Little remains of San Romauldo's original foundation, except for portions of the 11th-century cloister, the rich library, and the 16th-century pharmacy, where the monks sell their balsams, herbal remedies and liqueurs. Some 300 m further up, a beautiful hour's walk, is the **Eremo**, or Hermitage (only men admitted past the gate), with its 20 cottages in an amphitheatre of pines, each with its own chapel and walled kitchen garden, where the hermits live silent and solitary existences, meeting only on certain feast days and in the church, which was decorated inside by Vasari and has two marble tabernacles by Desiderio da Settignano.

Badia Prataglia, 10 km from Camaldoli, is the region's most popular secular retreat, a summer resort spread out among the trees and hills, with beautiful walks along streams and waterfalls leading off in all directions.

Bibbiena and La Verna

Only a few kilometres from Poppi, the modern Casentino's chief town, **Bibbiena**, has been enveloped in sprawl and lacks Poppi's quaint charm, though in its heart it retains its old Tuscan feel. Few buildings stand out—a good Renaissance palace, **Palazzo Dovizi**, and the church of **San Lorenzo**, where there are some excellent polychrome terracottas by Andrea della Robbia. From Bibbiena, N. 208 crosses east over into a range of hills, bravely called the Alpi di Catenaia, that divides the Arno from the Tiber valleys, to the famous Franciscan monastery of **La Verna**, high up on a bizarre, rocky outcrop, which, according to one of St Francis' visions, had been rent and blasted into its wild shape at the moment of the Crucifixion. The land was given to Francis in 1213 by another pious nobleman, Count Orlando, and the saint at once built some mud huts here for a select group of his followers. He found La Verna a perfect spot for meditation, and came to his holy mountain on six different occasions. During the last, on 14 September 1224, he became the first person ever to receive the stigmata—an event pictured in the frescoes of Assisi and elsewhere—after which he could only walk in extreme pain. The churches, chapels, and convent at La Verna are simple and rustic, though the main church, the chapel of Stigmata and St Francis' tiny church of **S. Maria degli Angeli** are decorated by the most transcendently beautiful blue, green, and white terracottas Andrea della Robbia ever made. You can also visit the **Sasso Spicco**, Francis' favourite retreat under a huge boulder, and **La Penna** (1283 m), on a sheer precipice, with romantic views of the Arno and Tiber valleys. The nearby village of Chiusi della Verna is a small resort and there are many summer homes in the area.

WHERE TO STAY AND EATING OUT (tel prefix 0575)

In Stia, **Canto della Rana** is big and popular and mobile—in the winter it's in Piazza Tanucci 28, and in the summer at Canto la Rana, although the 'phone is always 58 631.

Among the specialities are antipasto with *prosciutto del Casentino*, one of Italy's finest hams, as well as game dishes (L25–30 000).

In Poppi, the ***Casentino**, Piazza Repubblica, tel 529 090, right opposite the castle, is a shady little *pensione*—the only one up in the old town (without bath L38 000, with bath L48 000). Down in the lower town, Ponte a Poppi, ***Campaldino**, Via Roma 95, tel 529 008, is a little inn in business since 1800. There are 10 simple rooms, none with bath (L38 000); in the pretty, old-fashioned dining room upstairs you can dine on tasty local prosciutto, ravioli filled with vegetables and ricotta, and succulent lamb and chicken, and for dessert, *semifreddi* made *in casa* (L30 000). A couple of kilometres from the monastery at Camaldoli, *****Il Rustichello**, Via del Corniolo 14, tel 556 020, is a small but modern resort hotel, a great place to bring the kids with tennis, mini golf, and walks in the woods (L70 000, all rooms with bath). The hotel's restaurant is a good place to stop even if you're not staying, featuring great pasta dishes from nearby Emilia-Romagna, grilled meats, and Casentino cheeses (L30 000).

Arezzo

Strategically located on a hill at the convergence of the valleys of the Valdarno, Casentino, and the Valdichiana, Arezzo (pop. 92,000) is an ancient city, one of the richest of the Etruscan Dodecapolis. Modern Arezzo is still one of the wealthiest cities in Tuscany—it has one of the biggest jewellery industries in Europe, with hundreds of small firms stamping out gold chains and rings, and bank vaults full of ingots. Its second, most notable industry, one that fills the shops around its main Piazza Grande, is furniture making and marketing antiques; the first Sunday of each month the entire square becomes an enormous antique curiosity shop.

Arezzo itself is a bit of an antique curiosity shop. It had only a brief, but remarkable, moment in the Renaissance sunshine, though in the Middle Ages it was a typical free *comune*, a Ghibelline rival to Florence and a city of great cultural distinction. It was the birthplace of Guido Monaco (or Guido d'Arezzo), around the year 1000, inventor of musical notation and the musical scale, of the 13th-century painter Margarito, an important figure in the transition from the Byzantine to the Italian styles, of Petrarch (1304–74), son of a banished Florentine Black Guelph and the 'first modern man', and of Spinello Aretino, one of Tuscany's trecento masters. Arezzo was at its most powerful in the early 1300s, when it was ruled by a remarkable series of warrior bishops. One died in the Battle of Campaldino; another, the fierce Guido Tarlati, ruled the city 1312–1327. He expanded its territory, built new walls, settled internal bickerings, renewed warfare with Florence and Siena, and was excommunicated. After Bishop Guido came the deluge—his brother sold the city for a brief period to Florence, family rivalries exploded, the plague carried away half the population, and to top it all, in 1384 the French troops of Louis d'Anjou sacked the city and brought it to its knees, refusing to move on until Arezzo paid 40,000 florins. Florence came up with the ransom money, and in effect purchased Arezzo's independence. It became an economic backwater, on the fringe of the Renaissance, although it managed to produce two leading players for the stage: Giorgio Vasari and Pietro Aretino, the uninhibited writer and poet whose celebrated poison pen allowed him to make a fortune by *not* writing about contemporary princes and popes—the most genteel extortionist of all time.

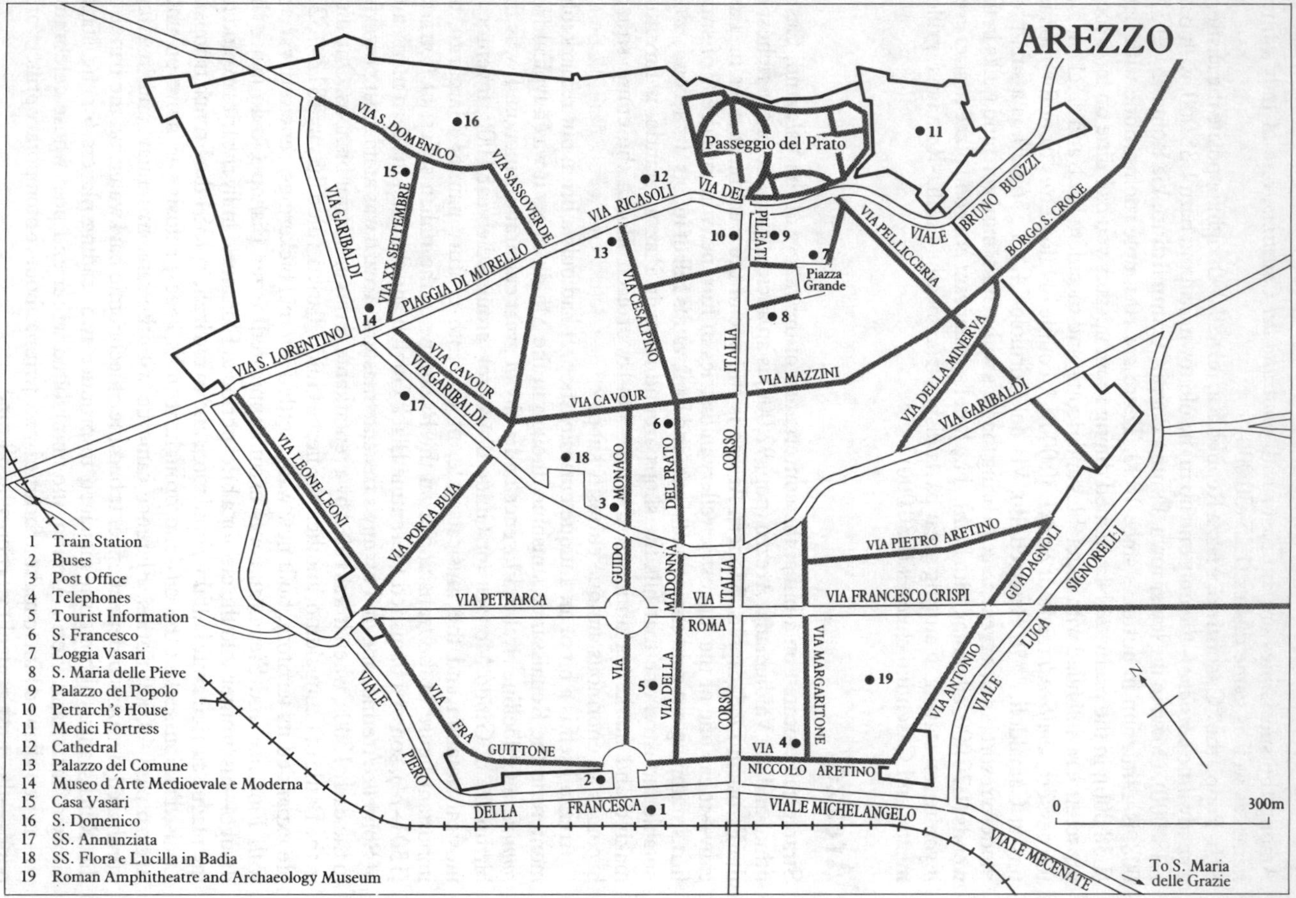
AREZZO
Passeggio del Prato
Piazza Grande
VIA S. DOMENICO
VIA GARIBALDI
VIA XX SETTEMBRE
VIA SASSOVERDE
VIA RICASOLI
VIA DEI PILEATI
PIAGGIA DI MURELLO
VIA S. LORENTINO
VIA CAVOUR
VIA GARIBALDI
VIA CESALPINO
CORSO ITALIA
VIA MAZZINI
VIA PELLICCERIA
VIALE BRUNO BUOZZI
BORGO S. CROCE
VIA DELLA MINERVA
VIA GARIBALDI
VIA LEONE LEONI
VIA PORTA BUIA
VIA GUIDO MONACO
VIA MADONNA DEL PRATO
VIA PETRARCA
VIA ROMA
VIA FRANCESCO CRISPI
VIA PIETRO ARETINO
GUADAGNOLI
SIGNORELLI
VIALE LUCA
VIA DELLA
CORSO
VIA MARGARITONE
VIA ANTONIO
VIA NICCOLO ARETINO
VIA FRA GUITTONE
VIALE PIERO DELLA FRANCESCA
VIALE MICHELANGELO
VIALE MECENATE
To S. Maria delle Grazie
N
0
300m
1 Train Station
2 Buses
3 Post Office
4 Telephones
5 Tourist Information
6 S. Francesco
7 Loggia Vasari
8 S. Maria delle Pieve
9 Palazzo del Popolo
10 Petrarch's House
11 Medici Fortress
12 Cathedral
13 Palazzo del Comune
14 Museo d'Arte Medioevale e Moderna
15 Casa Vasari
16 S. Domenico
17 SS. Annunziata
18 SS. Flora e Lucilla in Badia
19 Roman Amphitheatre and Archaeology Museum

GETTING AROUNDFrom Florence (75 km/1½ hrs), Perugia (73 km/1½ hrs), and Cortona (32 km/45 min), the train is the easiest way to reach Arezzo; the station is at the southern end of town, where Via Guido Monaco crosses Viale Piero della Francesca and the old city walls. Buses for Cortona and other towns in Arezzo province, as well as for Siena, leave from the station directly opposite on Viale Piero della Francesca, tel 382 169. The little LFU trains from Arezzo to the Casentino are being restored like everything else in Italy, and at the time of writing only go as far as Subbiano, where buses meet the train.

TOURIST INFORMATION
Piazza Risorgimento (one block north of the station, and one block to the right from Via Guido Monaco), tel (0575) 23 952. For information on any aspect of Arezzo's gold industry: Consorzio Orafi Aretini, tel 300 761.

San Francesco
If you arrive by train or bus, Via Guido Monaco leads up to the old centre of Arezzo by way of a stern statue of musical monk Guido, and passes on the left one of Italy's prettiest post offices with an ornate ceiling, before ending in Piazza San Francesco, site of **San Francesco** (open 8–1 and 4–7). This dowdy barn of a Franciscan church contains the star attraction in Arezzo: Piero della Francesca's frescoes on the popular pseudo-Classical/Christian subject of the *Legend of the Cross*, the most riveting cycle of frescoes of the 1400s and the gospel of Renaissance painting, the ideal—other works seem mere commentary. Piero literally wrote the book on the new science of artificial perspective, and yet as strictly as these frescoes obey the dictates of the vanishing point they make no concessions to realism; simplified and drawn with geometrical perfection, Piero's beings are purely spiritual creatures. It is fascinating that Piero and Uccello, the two artists most obsessed with perspective and space, should have created the most transcendent art; few compositions are as haunting as Piero's *Dream of Constantine*, a virtuoso piece of night lighting, colouring, and perspective, the angel swooping down from the upper left-front of the scene—and yet all is uncannily still, the scene of the dream itself like a dream; the soldiers stand guard, woodenly unaware, the sleeping emperor's attendant gazes out with a bored expression.

So much for the good news; the bad is that the frescoes will be under a much-needed restoration until 1992, the 500th anniversary of Piero's death.

Piazza Grande
Few *piazze* in Italy have the eclectic charm of Arezzo's **Piazza Grande**, surrounded by a collection of diverse private and public buildings that make the perfect backdrop for the monthly antique fair and the *Giostra del Saracino* in early September. On this occasion, the town sports from the four quarters of Arezzo don 13th-century costume to re-enact an event that was first documented in 1593, a celebration of the feats of arms against Saracen pirates who menaced the Tyrrhenian coast, and penetrated inland even as far as Arezzo. Revived in 1932, the festival begins with a parade of costumes and flag tossing by the *sbandieratori*, and is followed by a test of individual prowess between eight knights, two representing each quarter, who tilt against a wooden figure named 'Buratto, king of the Indies' for the prize of a golden lance.

Piazza Grande

On one side of the piazza is the **Loggia del Vasari**, a large building Vasari designed for his hometown in 1573, with the idea of replicating a Greek stoa, with little shops and workshops under the portico. Vasari also designed the clock tower of the **Palazzo della Fraternità dei Laici**, the old ornate building, half Gothic and half by Renaissance master Bernardo Rossellino. Although it looks like a town hall, the palazzo is really the home of a lay brotherhood founded in the 1200s. Arezzo's old Palazzo del Popolo exists only in ruins, behind Vasari's loggia on Via dei Pileati. Like Pisa's, it was destroyed by the Florentines after they captured the city.

Santa Maria della Pieve

Perhaps most impressive on Piazza Grande is the round, Romanesque arcaded apse of Arezzo's great 12th-century church of **Santa Maria della Pieve**; rather eccentrically it turns its back on the piazza, while directing its unusual Pisan-Lucchese façade towards narrow Via dei Pileati, where it's hard to see well. Few things in Tuscany look as ancient as these four tiers of shallow arcades, rough hewn and eroded like a vertical stone cliff. Each tier of arches is successively narrower, in a unique rustic style with no two columns or capitals alike. The campanile 'of a hundred holes' has so many neat rows of double mullioned windows it resembles a primitive skyscraper, complete with a protruding elevator shaft.

Under the arch of the front portal, note the interesting early medieval *reliefs of the twelve months*: April with her flowers, February with his pruning hook, and the pagan two-headed god Janus for January. The dim interior has an early Romanesque relief of the *Three Magi* on the entrance wall and finely decorated capitals in the nave. Like many early churches, the presbytery is raised above the low crypt, the most ancient part of the church, with primitive capitals—human faces mingling with rams, bulls, and dragons. On the left wall there's another primitive relief of the Nativity and Christ's Baptism, while above in the choir is a beautiful polyptych by Pietro Lorenzetti (1320), which has been recently restored to its glimmering original appearance, featuring a very well-dressed Madonna and saints modelling the latest Tuscan fashions and fabrics.

Below Santa Maria descends Corso Italia, Arezzo's main evening parade, while above, Via dei Pileati continues up into the oldest quarter of the city, passing by way of **Petrarch's House**, a replacement for the original, bombed in the last war; it stands near the picturesque 14th-centruy **Palazzo Pretorio**, decked with coats-of-arms of imperial and Florentine governors.

The Cathedral

Narrow streets from the Piazza Grande lead up to the **Passeggio del Prato**, a big English-style park with lawns, trees, a café, and a big white elephant of a Fascist monument to Petrarch. All of Arezzo slopes gradually upwards from the railway station, ending abruptly here; from the cliffs on the edge of the Prato there is a memorable view over the mountains, extending towards Florence and Urbino. Overlooking the park is a half-ruined Medici fortress of the 1500s; at the other end is the back of the **Cathedral**, with a lovely Gothic bell tower (less than a hundred years old). The cathedral, built in bits and pieces over the centuries (1276–1510), has a nondescript façade but several great works of art in its sombre, dimly lit Gothic naves, not the least of which are its stained-glass windows, created by the greatest 16th-century master of the art, the Frenchman Guillaume de Marcillat, seeming almost like illuminated frescoes by a Gozzoli or a Luca Signorelli. The magnificent marble Gothic High Altar is dedicated to San Donato, and there are impressive tombs—the first is of Pope Gregory X (1205–1276) with a canopy and 4th-century sarcophagus, holding the mortal dust of the pope who holds the record for taking the longest to be elected; the enclave, in Viterbo, lasted from 1268–1271, and only ended when the Viterbans starved the cardinals into deciding. The second, even more impressive, is the 1327 **Tomb of Bishop Guido Tarlati**, a fascinating early predecessor of the heroic sculptural tombs of the Renaissance, perhaps designed by Giotto. The tomb is divided into three sections, with a relief resembling a miniature theatre and a Ghibelline eagle like a party badge on top; below lies the battling bishop's effigy; and below that, 16 fine relief panels that tell the story of his life, his battles, and his good works. Near it is Piero della Francesca's rather mysterious fresco of the *Magdalene* holding an empty glass box—a curious iconography that brings to mind the ancient legend that it was the Magdalene who brought the Holy Grail to Marseilles. The **Museo del Duomo** contains detached frescoes by Spinello Aretino and his son Parri di Spinello, a terracotta *Annunciation* by Bernardo Rossellino, and paintings by 13th-century master Margarito d'Arezzo, Signorelli, and Vasari (Oct–Palm Sun, Thurs, Fri and Sat 9–12; otherwise 9–12 Mon–Sat).

Art Museum

Diagonally opposite the cathedral stands Arezzo's Ghibelline **Palazzo del Comune** with its distinctive tower; from here Via Ricasoli descends, past the birthplace of Guido Monaco (with a plaque of Guido's do-re-mi), to the **Museo d'Arte Medioevale e Moderna** (9–7, Sun 9–1:30; adm), where you can get to know some local medieval and Renaissance artists not often seen elsewhere. The collection is housed in a medieval palace, remodelled in the Renaissance, perhaps by Bernardo Rossellino, and later used as a customs house. All is arranged chronologically: the attractive courtyard contains medieval columns and capitals, a fine sculpted horse's head and gargoyles, while the two rooms on the ground floor contain sculptural details from the cathedral façade and a fine

10th-century *pluteo* carved with peacocks. Among the works on the first floor are a stylized, Byzantine *St Francis* by Margarito d'Arezzo, painted just after the saint's death and an *Enthroned Virgin* by Guido da Siena, studded with chunky, plasticky gems. Next you'll find detached frescoes by Spinello Aretino, the city's greatest trecento artist, and by his son, Parri di Spinello (1387–1453), whose ghostly battle scene, the *Sconfitta di Massenzio*, was discovered in the Badia after the war; the museum also has one of his beautifully dressed Madonnas. Another native of Arezzo, Bartolomeo della Gatta, painted the plague saint San Rocco praying to liberate the city from the Black Death. Also on the first floor is a fresco attributed to Signorelli; a huge busy canvas by Vasari of Esther's wedding banquet; a collection of small Renaissance bronzes, including a bear with a monkey on his head; beautiful ceramics from Urbino, Deruta, Montelupo and a plate by Master Giorgio of Gubbio with his secret red. On the second floor there's a strange painting by Angelo Cacoselli (d. 1652) called the *Maga*, of an enchantress with her animals, a small room of 18th-century Neapolitan *presepi* figurines, and some splashy Mannerist canvases by Vasari, Allori, and the great Rosso Fiorentino.

Vasari, Cimabue, and more Vasari

Around the corner, on Via XX Settembre, is the **Casa Museo Giorgio Vasari** (9–7, Sun 9–1, ring bell). Vasari was so fond of his own brand of spineless Mannerism that he was not content to leave it all for Duke Cosimo, but decorated his own house with the same fluff. Mediocrity attracts mediocrity; besides the frescoes there are several rooms of nondescript paintings, of which three stand out: the most repugnant St Sebastian ever committed to canvas, a terracotta portrait of Galba, one of Rome's ugliest mugs, by Sansovino, and a painting, by a follower of Santi di Tito, of Christ and the Apostles dining in a 17th-century greasy spoon.

From Vasari's house, Via S. Domenico will take you to the 13th-century church of **San Domenico**, with a simple asymmetrical exterior and a fine stone Gothic chapel (1360s) on the right wall, while the rest of the walls are covered with frescoes that overlap like the funny colour pages mouldering on the bottom of a canary cage. The main altar has a crucifix by Cimabue (*c.* 1265); the chapel to the left contains a fine triptych of the Archangel Michael by the 'Maestro del Vescovado'.

Via Garibaldi from the art museum returns to the centre by way of **SS. Annunziata**, Arezzo's late response to Brunelleschi, begun by Bartolomeo della Gatta in the 1490s and completed by Antonio da Sangallo; the fourth altar has a painting by Pietro da Cortona and in the choir there's a stained-glass window by Marcillat. Further up, off Via Porta Buia, stands **SS. Flora e Lucilla in Badia**, a 13th-century church, with an unusual interior remodelled by Vasari. He also designed the unusual altar, with reliefs from the Gospel of St Matthew on the front and St George slaying the dragon on the back. Over the presbytery the impressive cupola is actually a masterful fake by 17th-century *trompe l'oeil* master P. Andrea Pozzo. On the entrance wall there's a good fresco of St Lawrence by della Gatta; the fine cloister is by Giuliano da Maiano, a student of Brunelleschi (entrance no. 2, Piazza della Badia).

Roman Amphitheatre and the Archaeology Museum

On the southern edge of Arezzo, near the station on Via Margaritone, the remains of a small **Roman Amphitheatre** have become a quiet city park. A former monastery, built on a curve over the amphitheatre's foundations, has been restored to house the **Museo Archeologico** (9–2, Sun 9–1, closed Mon; adm). Not much has survived of the thriving Etruscan and Roman city of *Arretium*, but there are some mosaics and sarcophagi, Etruscan urns and Greek vases, examples of the Roman era red *corallino* vases and an excellent portrait of a rather jaded-looking middle-aged Roman, worked in gold.

Finally, you can take a 15-minute walk from Via Mecenate out through Arezzo's southern suburbs to see a simple but exceptionally pretty Renaissance church, **Santa Maria delle Grazie**, finished in 1444 and given a delicate jewel of a loggia by Benedetto da Maiano, in 1482. On the main altar, in a colourful tabernacle by Andrea della Robbia, is Parri di Spinello's *Madonna della Misericordia* (1430).

WHERE TO STAY (tel prefix 0575)

No hotels in Arezzo really stand out; unlike some of Tuscany's art cities, the forces of tourism have yet to convert old villas into modern accommodation. What the city does have is clean, comfortable, and up-to-date, but nothing to tempt you into lingering. If you're travelling by car, ***__Minerva__, Via Fiorentina 6, tel 27 891, may be the most convenient; it's a few blocks west of the city walls, but besides pleasant rooms, TV and air conditioning, it can offer you a parking place. It also has an excellent, unpretentious restaurant (rooms, L92 000 all with bath, dinner L35 000). In town, most of the rooms are close to the station. You may enjoy contemplating the towers and red rooftops from the roof terrace of the ***__Continentale__, a fine, older hotel in Piazza Guido Monaco 7, tel 20 251 (all rooms with bath, L95 000). Its competitor, ***__Europa__, Via Spinello 45, tel 357 701, is just across from the station, and is similarly modern and plain, but many of its rooms are air-conditioned (L95 000).

Budget hotels are a bit cheaper than their counterparts in Tuscany, and by the beginning of 1989, a new youth hostel should be open in the city—check at the tourist office for details. Alternatively, near the station, *__Michelangelo__, Viale Michelangelo 26, tel 20 673, is one of the best, friendly and well-kept (L35 000 without bath, L42 000 with). **__Truciolini__, Via Pacinotti 6, tel 380 219, has parking, air conditioning, and a private bath in each room (L60 000).

EATING OUT

Arezzo isn't going to blind you with science in the kitchen (though while you wait for the train you can enjoy Tuscany's best railway cuisine in the station bar). One restaurant that tries hard (it even has a piano bar, which may seem a little incongruous after a day in medieval Arezzo) is **Le Tastevin**, Via de' Cenci 9, tel 28 304; *carpaccio*, also good *penne* with pepper sauce; wines from around the world (L35–55 000). Tourists favour the **Buca di San Francesco**, opposite Piero's frescoes in Piazza Umberto 1, tel 23 271, but don't let that discourage you—the Buca has an honest-to-goodness medieval atmosphere and tasty Tuscan cooking to match, though slightly adapted for the uninitiated (L45 000). The restaurant in the hotel **Continentale** (see above) serves *zuppa del Tarlati*—chicken soup prepared according to a 12th-century recipe—as well as a tender turkey breast with truffles (L40 000). For a meal in the country, one of the best restaurants near Arezzo is the **Osteria La Capannaccia**, Loc. Campriano 51/c, tel 361 759, where the specialities are those of the Aretine countryside—simple dishes like *minestra di pane*, roast meats, and wines from the Colli Aretini—and the price is equally unpretentious, L28 000 at the most. Another fine country place offering traditional dishes, *Al Principe*, Via Giovi 25, tel 362 046 (near the Arno, between Arezzo and Subbiano), still serves the eels in a *piccante* tomato sauce, once but no longer fished out of the Arno itself, as well as homemade spaghetti (*pici*), also *minestra di pane*, and good local wines (L24 000).

The Valtiberina

The Valtiberina, or upper valley of Old Father Tiber, is a luminous patchwork of pasturelands and pine and beech woodlands, and the birthplace of Michelangelo and Piero della Francesca.

GETTING AROUND

LFU buses from Arezzo serve the area efficiently if not especially frequently. Sansepolcro is the terminus of Umbria's FCU line, which can slowly whisk you down to Città di Castello (16 km/25 min), Umbertide, Perugia, Todi, and Terni. Buses from Sansepolcro (station just outside the walls) go to Città di Castello, Caprese Michelangelo (26 km/45 min), Arezzo (38 km/1 hr), Florence, and Pieve Santo Stefano.

Caprese Michelangelo

Michelangelo's father, a minor noble of Florence, was podestà in the tiny town of Caprese (pop. 1850) when his wife gave birth to little Michelangelo. As was the custom in those days, the baby was sent into the countryside to be nursed, in this case by the wife of a mason. 'If my brains are any good at all, it's because I was born in the pure air of your Arezzo countryside,' Michelangelo later told Vasari. 'Just as with my mother's milk I sucked in the hammer and chisels I use for my statues.' Although he only returned once to the Valtiberina, to select sturdy firs to float down the Tiber for the scaffolding in the Sistine chapel, Caprese does not let any opportunity slip by to remind us of its most famous son, even changing its name to **Caprese Michelangelo**. The artist's purported birthplace, the 14th-century **Casa del Podestà**, has been restored and now houses a museum in his honour, with photographs and reproductions of his works. Caprese's medieval castle contains questionable tributes from modern sculptors. From here it's only a few bumpy kilometres into the Alpi di Catenaia and La Verna (see p. 364).

Caprese to Sestino

East of Caprese the countryside is the biggest attraction; between **Pieve Santo Stefano** (Roman *Sulpitia*, mostly rebuilt after World War II) and **Badia Tedalda** (a small summer resort) lie the rolling Alpi della Luna, the Mountains of the Moon. From Badia N. 258 is the main highway to **Rimini** and the Adriatic coast (see p. 466).

Sestino (from the Roman woodland god Sextius), Tuscany's easternmost *comune* on the border of the Marches, was ruled by the Montefeltro dukes of Urbino until 1516. It has been the agricultural centre for its area since Roman times and preserves many medieval buildings. Near its little Romanesque parish church, the **Antiquarium** will show you the headless 'Venus of Sestino' and other local finds. The church, built in the 8th century, shows the influence of Ravenna, Byzantine capital of the west; its 13th-century altar sits on a Roman boundary stone. From Sestino a secondary road heads east to Urbino (see p. 459).

Arezzo to Sansepolcro

Although Michelangelo took fresh air and stone-flavoured milk from his native place, Piero della Francesca carried the light and luminous landscape along the Tuscan-Umbrian frontier with him throughout his career, and left more behind in his native haunts than Michelangelo. From Arezzo, it's a pretty 41-km drive to Sansepolcro, especially along SS73, which ascends through the Foce di Scopetone (with panoramic views back towards the city) then continues another 17 km to the short turn-off for **Monterchi**. Dedicated to Hercules in Roman times, Monterchi is a tiny triangle of a medieval town; while strolling its lanes, don't miss the curious underground passageway around the apse of the parish church, dating back to the Middle Ages but of uncertain purpose. Monterchi is most famous, however, for Piero della Francesca's extraordinary fresco in the little chapel at the cemetery. The *Madonna del Parto* (1445) is perhaps the first (and last?) portrayal of the Virgin in her ninth month, a mystery revealed by twin angels who pull back the flaps of a tent, empty but for Mary, weary and melancholy, one eyelid drooping, one hand on her hip, the other on her swollen belly, almost painful to see—one of the most psychologically penetrating paintings of the quattrocento. Unfortunately, the fresco, like Piero's works in Arezzo, will be under restoration until 1992.

Anghiari (pop. 6200), between Monterchi and Sansepolcro, is a fine old town located on a balcony over the Valtiberina. Once a property of Camaldoli and later of the Tarlati family, it was the site of a 1440 victory of the Florentines over the Milanese, a decisive victory in corking up Visconti ambitions over Tuscany and the rest of Italy. Leonardo da Vinci chose it as his subject matter in the Battle of the Frescoes in Florence's Palazzo Vecchio—one of the Renaissance's greatest un-happenings, though the cartoons left behind by the master were often copied and one of the inspirations of Florentine Mannerism. In Anghiari's Renaissance Palazzo Taglieschi at Via Mameli 16, the **Museo delle Arti e Tradizioni Popolari dell'Alta Valle del Tevere** has exhibits relating to traditional crafts of the Upper Tiber Valley. Just over one km to the southwest, there's the pretty Romanesque **Pieve di Sovara**, and on the Sansepolcro road, you can still make out the 8th-century Byzantine origins of **Santo Stefano**.

Sansepolcro

Sansepolcro (pop. 16,000) is the largest town of the Valtiberina, famous for its lace, its pasta (the Buitoni spaghetti works is just outside the city), and for Piero della Francesca. The painter was born here sometime between 1410 and 1420, and given his mother's name as his father died before his birth. Although he worked in the Marches, Arezzo, and Rome, he spent most of his life in Sansepolcro, painting and writing books on geometry and perspective until he went blind at the age of 60.

Sansepolcro was founded around the year 1000, and like Anghiari belonged to the monks of Camaldoli until the 13th century. The historic centre, with its crewcut towers, has plenty of character, though a bit dusty and plain after several earthquakes and rebuildings. It is enclosed within well-preserved walls, built by the Tarlati and given a Renaissance facelift by Giuliano da Sangallo. **Piazza Torre di Berta** is the centre of town, where on the second Sunday of September crossbowmen from Gubbio come to challenge the home archers in the Palio della Balestra, an ancient rivalry. Along Via Matteotti are many of the city's surviving 14th–16th-century palaces, most notably the Palazzo delle Laudi and the 14th-century palace housing the **Museo Civico** (daily 9:30–1 and 2:30–6; adm). Here you can see Piero della Francesca's masterpiece, the *Resurrection*, an intense, almost eerie depiction of the solemnly triumphant Christ stepping out of his tomb surrounded by sleeping soldiers and a sleeping land, more autumnal than springlike. It shares pride of place with one of Piero's early works, the *Misericordia Polyptych*, a gold-background altarpiece dominated by a serene, giant goddess of a Madonna, sheltering under her cloak members of the confraternity (note the black hood on one) who commissioned the picture, and a damaged fresco of San Giuliano. Other works are by his greatest pupil, Luca Signorelli, a *Crucifixion* (with two saints on the back), Pontormo (*Martyrdom of San Quintino*), Santi di Tito, Mannerist Raffaellino del Colle, and the 16th-century Giovanni de' Vecchi, also of Sansepolcro, whose *Presentation of the Virgin* is interesting for its unusual vertical rhythms. You can see a 16th-century scene of Sansepolcro in the *Pilgrimage of the Company of the Crucifix of Loreto*, a relic of the days of the Black Death, as are the wooden panels of Death (one showing a fine strutting skeleton). Downstairs, a room contains sculptural fragments gathered from the town, including a rather mysterious 12th-century frieze of knights from a local palace; upstairs there's a collection of detached frescoes.

Sansepolcro also has a couple of pretty churches: near the museum is the Gothic church of **San Francesco**, with a fine rose window and portal. The **Duomo** on Via Matteotti was built in the 11th century but has been much restored since; among the art inside is a fresco by Bartolomeo della Gatta and a polyptych by Matteo di Giovanni. Another church, **San Lorenzo**, has a *Deposizione* by Rosso Fiorentino.

WHERE TO STAY AND EAT (tel prefix 0575)

Up in the Alpe Faggeto, above Caprese Michelangelo, ***__Fonte Galletta__**, tel 793 925, is a pleasant little mountain hotel and restaurant, in a lovely forested landscape. The hotel has simple rooms, all with bath (L45–55 000); the restaurant uses local ingredients—chestnuts, mushrooms, truffles, game, mountain hams—to create tasty dishes. The pasta is excellent, as are the homemade *semifreddi* (L30–35000). **Locanda al Castello di Sorci**, near Anghiari at San Lorenzo, tel 789 066, is a country beanery located in a former tobacco barn; the fare is simple and rustic, much of it (the wine and meats) coming from the farm annexe (L20 000). In Sansepolcro, ***__Fiorentino__**, Via L. Pacioli 60, tel 76 033, has been the town inn since the 1820s; rooms provide the basics, and there's a garage for your car (L35 000 without bath, L50 000 with). The restaurant, however, is Sansepolcro's best; it's a good place to try Italian onion soup; other local specialities are especially well prepared, and there's a wide assortment of local cheeses (L35 000; closed Fri). Other hotels in Sansepolcro: ****__La Balestra__**, Via del Montefeltro 29, tel 735 151, with modern, comfortable rooms and parking for L65 000; it also has a good restaurant, with delicious homemade pasta; for seconds try the lamb chops with courgette flowers (L25–35 000). The friendly budget ***Nuova Stella**, Via XX Settembre 2, tel 76 541, has seven rooms for L34 000, all with bath.

South of Arezzo: the Valdichiana

The flat Valdichiana south of Arezzo is the largest, broadest valley in the Apennines, rimmed by hills and old towns that surround it like a walled garden. The Etruscans, headquartered at Cortona, were the first to drain its marshlands, making it their breadbasket, so rich, it is said, that even after Hannibal's troops pillaged and burned on their way to Lake Trasimeno, there was still more than enough to feed the army and its elephants. By the Middle Ages, however, the valley had reverted to a swamp, forcing the inhabitants back into the hills. And so it stayed, until the beginning of the 19th century, when the Lorraine Grand Dukes initiated a major land reclamation scheme. Now, once again, prosperous farms are the main feature of the Valdichiana. The equally prosperous-looking cattle you may notice are of a prized breed called the Chianina, named after the valley, and descendants of the primal herds, whose fossils were discovered in the vicinity.

Monte San Savino and Lucignano

But there is more to the Valdichiana than farms and *bistecca alla fiorentina* on the hoof. On both sides of the valley are some of the most beautiful villages in this part of Tuscany. Cortona is the most famous, but there are others, like **Monte San Savino** (21 km from Arezzo, on the west side of the valley), the birthplace of Andrea Contucci, better known as Andrea Sansovino (1460–1529), artistic emissary of Lorenzo de'Medici to Portugal and one of the heralds of the High Renaissance; his Florentine pupil Jacopo adopted his surname and went on to become chief sculptor and architect in Venice in its Golden Age. Monte San Savino, spread out on a low hill on the west rim of the Valdichiana, is an attractive town with a mélange of medieval and fine Renaissance palaces. Andrea Sansovino left his home town an attractive portal of the church of **San Giovanni**, terracottas (along with others by the della Robbia) in the little church of **Santa Chiara**, and the lovely cloister of **Sant'Agostino** (13th-century, with a small rose window by Guillaume de Marcillat); Antonio da Sangallo the Elder designed the beautiful and harmonious **Loggia dei Mercanti**, with its grey Corinthian capitals (early 1500s, also attributed by some to Sansovino), and the simple, partly rusticated **Palazzo Comunale**, originally the home of the Del Monte family, whose money paid for most of Monte San Savino's Renaissance ornaments. Foremost among the medieval monuments, the **Palazzo Pretorio** was built by the Perugians, while the city walls are the work of the Sienese.

On a cypress-clad hill 2 km east, **S. Maria della Vertighe** was built in the 12th century and restored in the 16th; within it holds a 13th-century triptych by Margarito d'Arezzo and from the next century, works by Lorenzo Monaco. Some 7 km to the west there's the pretty hamlet of **Gargonza**, with its mighty tower dominating a tight cluster of houses on a wart of a hill, the whole of which is now a hotel (see p. 377). Best of all, perhaps, is cheerful little **Lucignano**, south of Monte San Savino, unique in the annals

Lucignano

of Italian hill towns for its street plan—it will literally run you round in circles; Lucignano is laid out in four concentric ellipses, like a kind of maze, with four picturesque little *piazze* in the centre. One piazza is dominated by the Collegiata, with a theatrical circular stair, another by the 14th-century **Palazzo Comunale**, now the Museo Civico, containing a good collection of 13th–15th-century Sienese works, a Madonna by Signorelli, and most famously, a 14th-century masterpiece of Aretine goldsmiths, a delicate reliquary *Albero di Lucignano*. There are more good Sienese paintings in the little tiger-striped church of **San Francesco**. Outside the centre there's a 16th-century Medici fortress, and the **Madonna delle Querce**, a Renaissance temple sometimes attributed to Vasari, with a fine Doric interior.

Marciano della Chiana, 6 km northeast of Lucignano, is another old fortified village with an impressive main gate, which also does time as clock and bell tower. **Foiano della Chiana**, just to the south, is encompassed by newer buildings, but in its **Collegiata** has a good *Coronation of the Virgin* by Signorelli and a terracotta by Andrea della Robbia. Between Marciano and Foiano, keep an eye open for the curious octagonal church of **Santa Vittoria**, built by Ammannati for Cosimo I.

Castiglion Fiorentino

Across the Valdichiana to the east, **Castiglion Fiorentino** was known as Castiglion Aretino until the Florentines snatched it in 1384. Within its walls it has retained its medieval street plan, with some Renaissance touches—the 16th-century **Logge del Vasari** and the **Palazzo Comunale**. The latter houses yet another small Pinacoteca Civica (Mon–Sat 8–2), where the prized pieces are a gilded silver reliquary bust and the *Stigmata of St Francis* by Bartolomeo della Gatta. The old Gothic church of **San Francesco** was frescoed within by 14th-century Florentines, and has a painting by Margarito d'Arezzo (1280). Like many a larger Tuscan town, Castiglion Fiorentino built a little Renaissance geometric temple in an isolated position below the walls, the charming, octagonal **Madonna della Consolazione**, untampered with since the 16th century; inside there's a fresco called the *Maestà di Geppe*, attributed to Signorelli. Dilapidated castles from the bad old days are all around Castiglion, most impressively at **Montecchio Vesponi**, 4 km south, with its tall honey-coloured tower and walls, a landmark visible all over the Valdichiana. For a while in the 1400s it was the stronghold of the *condottiere* Sir John Hawkwood, he of the famous 'monument' by Uccello in Florence cathedral.

WHERE TO STAY AND EATING OUT (tel prefix 0575)

The top place in the Valdichiana, at least for peace and quiet and medieval atmosphere, is the ****Castello dei Gargonza**, an entire walled village near Monte San Savino, with 20 rooms in restored houses, a pool, and forests all around; the restaurant, with local specialities, is also very popular (just off SS 73, tel 847 021; L130 000). In the very centre of Lucignano, ****Da Totò**, Piazza del Tribunale 6, tel 836 763, is the best (and only) place to sleep and eat (L50 000 without bath, L70 000 with); the menu proposes an unusual variety of tastes, in dishes like *pici* in duck sauce, or *pappardelle* with boar, and rabbit with fennel (L25 000).

Cortona

Seemingly floating high above the Valdichiana plain, on terraced slopes covered with olives and vines, Cortona (pop. 22,600) may not be entirely undiscovered, but it is still one of the real jewels among hill towns. Some 600 m above sea level, sweeping down a spur of Monte Sant'Egidio, the town's crooked, cobblestone streets climb precipitously to the old fortress—even halfway up, if there's a space between the houses, you can see as far as Lake Trasimeno in Umbria. It produced three celebrated artists: Luca Signorelli; Baroque painter Pietro Berrettini (1596–1669), better known as Pietro da Cortona, master of the rooms in the Pitti Palace; and Futurist-Impressionist-mosaicist Gino Severini (1883–1966), all of whom left works in Cortona.

Cortona's remarkable site brought it notoriety early on; according to popular tradition, the city is nothing less than the 'Mother of Troy and Grandmother of Rome'—founded by Dardanus, who according to legend was fighting against a neighbouring tribe when he lost his helmet (*corythos*) on the hill, thus giving the name *Corito* to the city that soon grew up. Dardanus went on to Asia to found Troy and give his name to the Dardanelles. Like all myths from the mists of time, there is apparently a germ of truth in it, in an important Etruscan-Anatolian connection. The mysterious Etruscans themselves always claimed to have come from Western Anatolia (perhaps around the year 900 BC), and inscriptions very similar to Etruscan have been found on the Greek island of Lemnos, near Troy; artefacts from the Iron Age found in Anatolia and Tuscany suggest cultural affinities. Cortona was an important Etruscan city, one of the Dodecapolis and one of the largest in the north; the ragged, monolithic Etruscan stonework can still be seen in the foundations of its walls. These are over three kilometres in perimeter, but still cover only two thirds of the area of the original Etruscan fortifications. As a medieval *comune*, Cortona held its own against Perugia, Arezzo, and Siena, while internally its Ghibellines and Guelphs battled until the Ghibellines came out on top, and when that fight was settled the ruling family, the Casali, spent the 14th century knocking off each other. The typical Tuscan orgy of self-destruction ended in 1409, when King Ladislas of Naples captured the city and sold it to the Florentines at a good price.

GETTING AROUND

Cortona is just off the main Florence–Arezzo–Rome railway line; the nearest station is Camucia, 5 km west; however, if you're coming up from Umbria, the station is Teròntola, 10 km south. Both stations have frequent LFI buses up to Cortona. There are also LFI bus connections to Arezzo (34 km/50 min), Castiglion Fiorentino, Foiano della Chiana, and Castiglione del Lago on Lake Trasimeno (22 km/30 min); schedules for both buses and trains, and tickets for the former are posted in the office in Via Nazionale, near the bus terminus and parking lot in panoramic Piazzale Garibaldi. Bicycles may be hired at Santa Caterina from G. S. Fratta, tel 603 009.

TOURIST INFORMATION

Via Nazionale 72, tel (0575) 603 056.

Palazzo Casali—Museo Civico

The heart of Cortona, the **Piazza della Repubblica**, is a striking asymmetrical square, with lanes leading off in all directions. Dominant here is **Palazzo Comunale**, a 13th-century building with a tower from 1503, its monumental steps a favourite place to dally away the early evening. Just behind it is Cortona's most impressive medieval palace, the 13th-century **Palazzo Casali**, home of the city's former lordlings and now the seat of the Etruscan Academy and the **Museo Civico** (9–1 and 3–5, May–Sept 9–1 and 4–7; adm). This has a fascinating eclectic collection; 15th-century ivories with court scenes; a good set of Etruscan bronzes; Greek vases, attesting to the city's wealth and trading contacts of long ago; Egyptian mummies and a doll-like Egyptian funeral bark; and Cortona's most famous relic, an Etruscan bronze chandelier with 16 lamps dating back to the 5th century BC, found in a field nearby. Each of the lamps is a squatting male or female figure, while in the inner circle there's a ring of stylized waves and dolphins, and in the centre, an archaic gorgon—the total effect resembles an Aztec calendar stone. There is also a fine collection of paintings, the oldest of which is a Roman portrait of the Muse Polyhymnia. Other works include *Two Saints* by Niccolò di Pietro Gerini, a 12th-century mosaic of the Madonna, a Madonna by Pinturicchio, and another by Signorelli, who portrays her in the company of the patron saints of Cortona, with a nasty-looking devil laid low. Other rooms contain souvenirs of a Knight of Malta from Cortona, ivory chess sets, old globes, costumes, some out-of-the-ordinary ceramics, Etruscan urns, works by Gino Severini, and a fine Roman alabaster Hecate, the queen of the night.

Museo Diocesano

Behind the civic museum signs point the way back to the **Duomo**, an 11th-century church unimaginatively rebuilt in 1560, probably by Giuliano da Sangallo; inside there's a mosaic by Gino Severini. However, across the piazza in the deconsecrated church of Gesù there's the excellent **Museo Diocesano** (April–Sept 10–1 and 4–7, Oct–March 9–1 and 3–5, closed Mon; adm) with one of Luca Signorelli's finest works—a *Deposition*, with background scenes of the Crucifixion and Resurrection (the latter composition inspired by his master Piero della Francesca) and a beautiful, luminous *Annunciation* by Fra Angelico, in which the angel appears to be gently whispering. Other works include a 14th-century Crucifix by Pietro Lorenzetti, a triptych by Il Sassetta, a fine Sienese Madonna by the school of Duccio di Buoninsegna, and a Roman sarcophagus with reliefs of the Battle of Lapiths and Centaurs that was closely studied by Donatello and Brunelleschi. Don't miss the fine coffered wooden ceiling of the church itself. Below the Piazza del Duomo is one of Cortona's most picturesque lanes, the medieval Via Jannelli (or del Gesù); here and around Cortona you'll see *porte del morto* (doors of the dead), more common in medieval Umbria than in Tuscany. Other especially picturesque streets around town are Via Ghibellina, Via Guelfa, and Via Maffei, with its town palaces.

Up and down Cortona

You'll need your climbing shoes to see the other monuments of Cortona, although **San Francesco** is only a short walk up from Piazza della Repubblica. St Francis' controversial lieutenant Brother Elias was a native of Cortona and founded this little church at an interesting angle in 1245; it still retains its original façade and one side. Both Brother Elias and Luca Signorelli are buried here, and on the left wall is a fine fresco of the *Annunciation*, the last work of Piero da Cortona. On the high altar is a relic of the Holy Cross brought back from Constantinople by Brother Elias, housed in an ivory reliquary that Byzantine emperor Nicephoras Phocas took with him to battle against the Saracens in the 960s, as described in the Greek inscription on the back. From here Via Berrettini continues up to Piazza Pozzo and Piazza Pescaia and the medieval neighbourhood around **San Nicolò**, a handsome little Romanesque church, built by an anachronistic architect in the 1440s; it was the seat of San Bernardino da Siena's Company of St Nicholas, for whom Luca Signorelli painted a magnificent standard of the *Deposition*, still hanging in the church.

You can reach the loftiest church of them all, the **Santuario di Santa Margherita**, from San Nicolò or by way of Via S. Margherita and the Via Crucis from Piazzale Garibaldi. The Via Crucis was built in 1947 by the people of Cortona to thank their patron saint Margherita for sparing their city from the war; it is lined with mosaic shrines by Severini. The views become increasingly magnificent, until you reach the pretty 19th-century neo-Romanesque Sanctuary. The original church here was built in the 1200s by Santa Margherita, who is buried here in a silver urn on the high altar; her fine but empty Gothic sarcophagus on the left wall has been attributed to Giovanni Pisano. To the right of the altar are standards and lanterns captured from the Turks in 18th-century sea battles, donated by a local commander. The overgrown **Medici Fortress** above occupies the site of the old Etruscan acropolis.

As in many Etruscan and Roman towns, Cortona's four gates are oriented to the four points of the compass. The northern **Porta Colonia** has an Etrusco-Roman arch and is near some well-preserved remains of the Etruscan walls; from here it's a 15-minute walk to the late Renaissance church of **Santa Maria Nuova**, one of the more serene works to come out of the Counter-Reformation, designed in a Greek cross, emphasising the vertical, and crowned by a dome. Outside the southern gate, at the end of Via Nazionale and beyond Piazzale Garibaldi, the Gothic **Church of San Domenico** has just been restored; in its elegant interior there's a grand altarpiece by Lorenzo di Niccolò Gerini, given to the Dominicans by Lorenzo de' Medici; and in the apse there's a Madonna with angels by Signorelli. Nearby is a good stretch of Etruscan wall and the beginning of the pretty Passeggiata Pubblica through Cortona's shady public gardens, **Il Parterre**, with more great views of the Valdichiana. Halfway down the hill, in an isolated position, stands **Santa Maria delle Grazie al Calcinaio** (1485–1513), done in perfect and elegant Renaissance symmetry by Sienese architect Francesco di Giorgio Martini—a simple central plan with an octagonal drum. The stained glass is by Guillaume de Marcillat; the harmonious interior, done in Brunelleschian dark and light accents, is light and airy and pure.

Environs of Cortona

Not surprisingly, a number of Etruscan tombs have been discovered around and below Cortona. Among the best-preserved is the circular **Tanella di Pitagora**, down near Camucia, named after Pythagoras (from an ancient confusion of Cortona with Croton in Calabria, where the philosopher lived), prettily surrounded by cypress trees, with an unusual vault over its rectangular funeral chamber. Very near the Camucia station is a large tumulus called the **Melone di Camucia**, 200 m in perimeter, with two doors of uncertain purpose; in a place called Il Sodo (3 km north, from the western Porta S. Maria) there are two other 'melons', the first of which is especially impressive, with a corridor leading into the five mortuary chambers.

Beyond Santa Maria Nuova the road continues for another 3.5 km along the slopes of Monte Sant'Egidio to the **Convento delle Celle**, founded by St Francis in 1211 in a beautiful setting. Little has changed in subsequent years; its simple rustic buildings have preserved their Franciscan spirit better than many others—the humble founder's cell retains the saint's stone bed.

ACTIVITIES

Antiques are big business in Cortona; besides the offerings in the town's shops, the national antique furniture market is held here at the end of August and September. Another speciality is handmade copperware, given its own show and market in April. 15 August is the time of the *Sagra di Bistecca*—the festival of the beefsteak, with a huge outdoor grilling of the Valdichiana's main product. From June–Oct Italian language and cultural courses help bring this ancient hill town to life. Cortona's public swimming-pool is at Il Sodo; horses from Centro equitazione Casale, on Via Teverina 134, tel 616 088.

WHERE TO STAY (tel prefix 0575)

In Cortona, available lodgings have yet to catch up with demand, especially since the town is the site of both a language school and a University of Georgia art programme. ***__San Luca__, Piazza Garibaldi 2, tel 603 787, is simple but comfortable; many of the rooms enjoy wonderful views (L80 000). In town ***__San Michele__, Via Guelfa 15, tel 604 348, is a comfortable hotel on a medieval street (L52 000 without bath, L75 000 with). High up in the old town, the *__Athens__, Via S. Antonio, tel 603 008, (named after Athens, Georgia, not Greece) is a good budget choice with spacious rooms in an older building (L40 000 without bath, L45 000 with). The youth hostel, **Ostello San Marco**, Via Maffei 57, tel 601 392, is one of Italy's more pleasant, and a viable option if all is full—though an IYHF card is required (open March–Oct, a long walk up from Piazza Garibaldi, L8500, inexpensive meals available).

EATING OUT

Cortona's restaurants are not fancy, but make a point of using local ingredients—homemade pasta, *salumeria* and beefsteaks from the Valdichiana, mushrooms and truffles in season, and the local white wines, called *Bianchi vergini* (the white virgins). **La Loggetta**, Piazza Pescheria 3, tel 603 777, is a pretty little restaurant where you can try some of these prepared *alla Cortonese* (L40 000). **Tonino**, Piazza Garibaldi, tel 603 100, is Cortona's most elegant restaurant, with wonderful hot and cold antipasti, followed by traditional pasta dishes and the Valdichiana's tender beef (L60 000, closed Tues). Far simpler, **Trattoria dell'Amico**, Via Dardano 12, tel 604 192, offers well-prepared à la carte meals for around L25 000, and a good tourist menu for L16 000; even simpler is the 'Gastronomia' snack bar in Via Nazionale, with pizza and other traditional treats.

Part XIII

PERUGIA AND NORTHERN UMBRIA

Piazza IV Novembre, Perugia

Umbria is often called 'Tuscany's little sister', and although historically the paths of these two sisters seldom crossed they bear more than a casual family resemblance. The timeless, transcendent landscapes, medieval hill towns, beautiful frescoes, good wine and olive oil, are as much in Umbria as Tuscany, though often in a less polished form. Long ruled by papal indifference, Umbria was never as wealthy as Tuscany, and its contributions to Western civilization were spiritual rather than intellectual. It is the land of saints extraordinaire, beginning with St Benedict, the founder of monasticism, to St Francis, the most gentle, synonymous with Umbria itself, and patron of all Italy.

Green is the mystic colour, and the colour of Umbria even in midsummer; the 'Green Heart of Italy' is its tourist slogan. It is the only region in the country to neither touch the sea nor share a frontier with a foreign land. Isolated from outside influence, introspective, scarcely touched by contemporary events, Umbria in its miniature time warp tends to be conservative and complacent, but also kind, sweet-tempered and hospitable—even Italians from other regions are taken aback to see the villagers leaving keys in their front doors. 'Umbria speaks in silences,' said a nun on the bus, and such silence and stillness is its greatest gift to the world-weary; far more than Tuscany it's a place to be rather than to do.

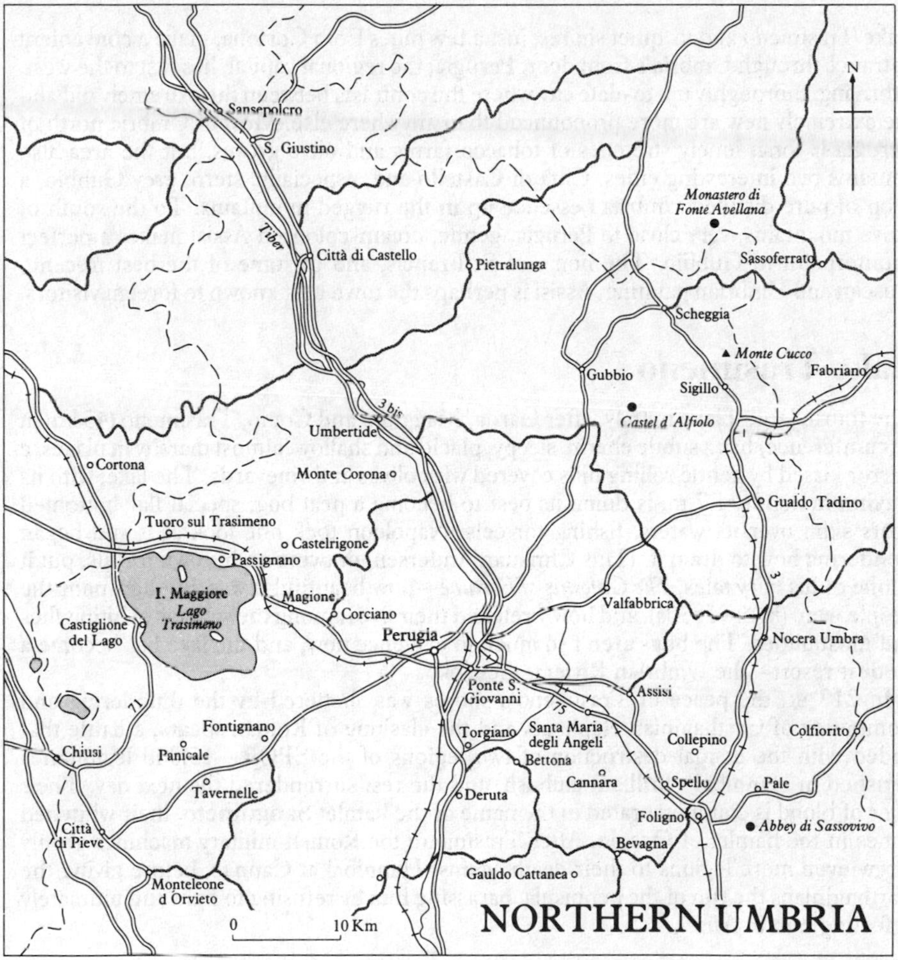
NORTHERN UMBRIA
N
Sansepolcro
S. Giustino
Monastero di Fonte Avellana
Tiber
Città di Castello
Pietralunga
Sassoferrato
Scheggia
Monte Cucco
Gubbio
Sigillo
Fabriano
Castel d'Alfiolo
3 bis
Umbertide
Cortona
Monte Corona
Gualdo Tadino
Tuoro sul Trasimeno
Castelrigone
Passignano
I. Maggiore
Lago Trasimeno
Magione
Valfabbrica
3
Castiglione del Lago
Corciano
Perugia
Nocera Umbra
Ponte S. Giovanni
Assisi
75
71
Fontignano
Torgiano
Santa Maria degli Angeli
Colfiorito
Chiusi
Panicale
Bettona
Collepino
Cannara
Tavernelle
Deruta
Spello
Pale
Foligno
Abbey di Sassovivo
Città di Pieve
Bevagna
Gauldo Cattanea
Monteleone d Orvieto
0
10 Km

Northern Umbria

Lake Trasimeno and its quiet shores, just a few miles from Cortona, make a convenient entrance through Umbria's front door. Perugia, the regional capital, lies just to the west, a thriving, thoroughly up-to-date city where the contrasts between the extremely old and the extremely new are more pronounced than anywhere else. Most of Umbria north of Perugia is long, lonely stretches of tobacco farms and olive groves, but the area also contains two interesting cities, Città di Castello and, especially, stern, grey Gubbio, a drop of pure distilled Umbrian essence up in the rugged mountains. To the south of those mountains, very close to Perugia, gentle, cream-coloured Assisi makes a perfect counterpoint to Gubbio. The home of St Francis, and of some of the best trecento Tuscan and Umbrian painting, Assisi is perhaps the town best known to foreign visitors.

Lake Trasimeno

The fourth largest lake in Italy, after Garda, Maggiore and Como, Trasimeno (45 km in circumference) has a subtle charm, sleepy, placid and shallow, almost marshy in places, a mirror kissed by gentle rolling hills covered with olives and vineyards. The lake, with its maximum depth of 7 m, is doing its best to become a peat bog; special flat-bottomed boats skim over its waters, fishing for eels. Napoleon took one look at it and began wondering how to drain it. Hans Christian Andersen, drawing on his own travels, put it in one of his fairy tales, *The Galoshes of Fortune*—how beautiful it was, but how poor the people were (in the 1830s), and how wretched their lives among the swarms of biting flies and mosquitoes. The bugs aren't so much in evidence now, and the lake has become a modest resort—the Umbrian Riviera, they joke.

In 217 BC the peace of Trasimeno's shores was shattered by the thundering and trumpeting of Carthaginian elephants and the clashing of Roman spears, a battle that ended with the dismal destruction of two legions of the SPQR—15,000 legionaries perished in Hannibal's brilliant ambush, and the rest surrendered the next day. Their river of blood is commemorated in the name of the hamlet **Sanguineto**, their whitened bones in the hamlet of **Ossaia**. After Trasimeno the Roman military machines grimly threw even more legions to their death against Hannibal at Cannae, before giving the Carthaginians the run of the peninsula, harassing him by refusing to fight and ultimately defeating him in Africa.

GETTING AROUND

Lake Trasimeno lies 37 km south of Arezzo, 13 km south of Cortona, 69 km east of Siena, and 30 km west of Perugia. Approaching by A1 from the north, take the Val di Chiana exit for the spur of the autostrada that skirts the north shore en route to Perugia; from the south, the Chiusi exit will bring you near the N. 71 to Castiglione on the lake or Città della Pieve. Train travel can be awkward: on the main Florence-Rome line change at Teròntola for Perugia and the north-shore towns of Tuoro and Passignano; from Siena or the south, change at Chiusi for Castiglione del Lago. Perugia is the main bus terminus for the area; connections from Cortona and Siena are less frequent.

By boat
Lake ports are Castiglione, Tuoro, and Passignano, linked to one another and to Isola Maggiore. Connections are frequent in the summer, but diminish to only one or two a day in winter; for sailing times, tel 827 157.

TOURIST INFORMATION
Castiglione del Lago: Piazza Mazzini 10, tel (075) 952 184.

Around the Lake

Among the olive groves along the west bank of Trasimeno juts the picturesque promontory of **Castiglione del Lago** (pop. 13,500), the lake's biggest resort with its ruined medieval castle and beach. There are views over the lake from **Piazza Ducale**, site of Castiglione's 16th-century **Palazzo Comunale**, former headquarters of the della Corgna dukes who controlled the lake into the 17th century; some of the palazzo's rooms retain late Renaissance frescoes by the Roman school. In the church of the **Maddalena**, there's a lovely *Madonna col Bambino* (1500), by a follower of Perugino.

On the north shore, the smaller resort of **Passignano** enjoys a favoured position on its own promontory. Clustered within its walls is an attractive old quarter; below lies the nearest port to **Isola Maggiore** (20 min), Trasimeno's only inhabited island, with its little fishing village and women famous for their lacemaking. In 1211 St Francis visited the island, and made a lasting impression by throwing back a pike a fisherman had given him, only to be followed across the lake by his grateful 'Brother Fish' until the saint blessed him—events commemorated in the island's church of **San Michele**. A pretty path encircles the island, offering good picnicking sites on the way. Besides the lake ferries, a Passignano company called *Trasimeno Viaggi* offers afternoon and evening cruises around the lake, with seafood dinners, music and dancing (call 953 969 for schedules).

From here a road, with fine views over the lake, ascends to **Castel Rigone**, a restful little village with a fine Renaissance church called the Tricine. From Trasimeno it's 30 km to Perugia; if you snub the fast company of the autostrada you can visit a castle built in 1420 by the Knights of Malta at **Magione**, 8 km southwest of Passignano.

Città della Pieve

From Castiglione del Lago it's a diversion of some 27 km to **Città della Pieve** (pop. 6500), famous as the birthplace of Pietro Vannucci (1446–1523), called Il Perugino for the years he spent working in Perugia. He did leave several paintings in his home town; Greatest among these is a lovely fresco of *The Adoration of the Magi* in Santa Maria dei Bianchi, portraying the birth of the Saviour in an Arcadian springtime—a world that seems hardly to need a redeemer at all. Other works of his can be seen in the **Duomo**, across the piazza from the grandiose **Palazzo Mazzuoli**, built by the Perugian artist Galeazzo Alessi in 1551, and in **San Pietro** outside town near the hospital.

Perugino is a disturbing character. To Giorgio Vasari, he committed the unpardonable sin of not being born in Tuscany; if there is anything to Vasari's nasty biography, the teacher of Raphael was perhaps the most bitter artist of the Renaissance. Born into a desperately poor family, success made him an untrusting miser, and he would ride out from Città della Pieve from job to job with his saddlebags full of money. About midpoint in his career he became an atheist; even so he mechanically cranked out two more decades ot richly rewarded but vacuous Madonnas and religious scenes before dying, stubbornly unconfessed and unabsolved on his deathbed—an extremely rare event in the 16th century—rejecting any future with the sweet-faced angels he depicted for others.

Around Città della Pieve

Italian writers have often commented that Città della Pieve looks more like a Sienese town than an Umbrian one; in fact, the Tuscan border is only a few miles away, with interesting towns like Chiusi and Montepulciano (see Part XI). But if you're going towards Perugia, there is more Perugino to entertain along the way. In **Panicale**, a 5-km detour north of the main N. 220, the master left two frescoes in the church of **San Sebastiano**, a *Coronation of the Virgin* and a *Martyrdom of St Sebastian*. Panicale is an old walled town, with a good Baroque church, **San Michele**, and some peculiar carvings and coats-of-arms on the walls of its 14th-century **Palazzo Pretorio**. In the nearby village of **Tavernelle**, just off the N. 220, there is a stately domed Renaissance temple, the **Sanctuary of Mongiovino**, with cinquecento frescoes by Pomerancio and others. Perugino died of the plague in **Fontignano** in 1523; his tomb and his last fresco can be seen in the parish church.

N. 220 continues to Strozzacapponi (13 km from Perugia), turn off for **San Mariano**, near Umbria's only **golf course**, at the 9-hole Golf Ellera, tel 79 704, and two **riding stables**, Cape Horse at Capocavallo, tel 605 858, and Santa Sabina, tel 780 198, with riding lessons available.

WHERE TO STAY AND EATING OUT (tel prefix 075)

Not many Italians think of Trasimeno as a beach resort—the water isn't very good, but there's still fishing and boating to keep you busy. There are modest vacation hotels around Castiglione, Passignano and Magione, but perhaps the most unusual possibility is out on Isola Maggiore—the best place in Umbria to really get away from it all; the island's only hotel is called the ****Sauro**, Via Guglielmi, tel 826 168, a gracious, uncomplicated place (only 11 rooms) with a brilliant restaurant that naturally specializes in fish from the lake: eels, carp and such, along with more traditional Umbrian dishes. A good bargain altogether (L55 000 for a double with bath, or L54 000 per person full board). Hotels in Castiglione are quite simple, but the *****Trasimeno**, Via Roma 16/a, tel 887 875, has just what you need if you want to take a swim—a pool—also bar and TV in some rooms (L65 000). In San Feliciano, a lakeside hamlet 7 km south of Magione, ***Da Settimio**, Via Lunga Lago 1, tel 849 104, is another small charmer, with peaceful rooms for L48–55 000 and a simple but good fish restaurant (L25 000). 7 km north of Città della Pieve, at Po Bandino, ***Villa Maraska**, N. 71, no 50, tel (0578) 20 524, has 7 quiet rooms in a garden setting for L48 000. For stays in local farmhouses, get in touch with the Agriturismo Azienda La Dogana, Via Dogana 107, Tuoro del Trasimeno 06100, tel 846 011.

Medieval Perugians were so fond of fish from Trasimeno that Nicola Pisano jokingly sculpted some on his famous fountain in front of the cathedral there. Today the catch isn't really big enough to send too much outside the lake area, but you can still try some at the little restaurants around the lake, most of them unpretentious places with bargain prices. In Castiglione del Lago, **La Cantina,** Via Vittorio Emanuele 89a, tel 952 163, makes good pasta dishes with a ragù of fish or eels; their other speciality is game dishes like pheasant and quails, when in season (L30 000 or less; closed Mon).

PERUGIA

'What a town for assassinations!'

—H. V. Morton

Balanced on a commanding hill high over the Tiber, Perugia (pop. 140,000) is a fascinating medieval acrobat able to juggle adroitly several roles at the same time; that of an ancient hill town, a magnificent *città d'arte*, and a slick cosmopolitan modern city. It is a fit capital for Umbria, with splendid monuments from the Etruscan era to the Late Renaissance stacked next to one another; its gallery contains the region's finest art, but in the alleyways cats sleep undisturbed. Yet its sun-filled present is haunted by sinister shadows from the past. Three medieval popes died in Perugia. One did himself in—stuffing his gut with Lake Trasimeno eels—but for the other two the verdict was poison. And then there were the Baglioni, the powerful family that ruled this city for a time; they were so dangerous they nearly exterminated themselves. Blissful Assisi, perfumed with the odour of sanctity, may be only over the next hill, but Perugia in the old days was as full of trouble as a town could be. As so often in medieval and Renaissance Italy, creativity and feistiness went hand in hand, and the Umbrian capital has contributed more than its share to Italian culture and art.

A strange thing happened to Perugia in the middle of its rough-house career. The great cities of Tuscany also suffered in the political changes of the 1500s, but to Perugia fell the singular privilege of becoming a part of the Papal States. Art, scholarship, trade and civic life quickly withered, and the town's traditional penchant for violence was rocked to sleep under a warm blanket of Hail Marys. Look at Perugia now, a little over a hundred years after liberation—its people famed for their politeness, urbanity, and good taste; Perugians dress more sharply than the Florentines for half the money and effort. They make their living on chocolates and ladies' shoes, and teaching Italian language and culture to foreigners. Maybe a few centuries under the pope was just what they needed. Perugia is a bustling university town, remarkably bright and alive compared with any other city in this book. Their biggest annual event is a jazz festival. Just as remarkable as the people is the stage they act on: the oldest, most romantically medieval streets and squares in Italy.

History

Gubbio, Perugia's longtime rival, liked to claim it was one of the first cities founded by Noah's sons after the flood. Naturally the Perugians had to top that, and one of the city's medieval chroniclers records that Noah himself, at the age of 500 or so, pitched his tents on Perugia's mountain. That would probably have been news to the Etruscans, who had settled *Pieresa* by the 5th century BC and probably much earlier. Pieresa was the easternmost city of the Dodecapolis, and maintained its freedom until the Roman conquest of 309 BC.

Never entirely happy under Roman rule, the city staged several revolts in the republican era. In the years after Caesar's assassination, it chose the wrong side with catastrophic results; Octavian's troops besieged it for seven months, and after the capitulation an Etruscan diehard decided to commit suicide rather than surrender—unfortunately his funeral pyre started a conflagration that took the rest of the city with him. Some years later Octavian, by then **Emperor Augustus**, decided to rebuild the city and rename it after himself—*Augusta Perusia*. Almost nothing is known of the city's passage through the Dark Ages. Totila the Goth took it from the Byzantines around 545, after a (probably apocryphal) siege of seven years, but the Exarchs of Ravenna were still contending for it with the Lombards fifty years later.

Among the constantly changing alliances of medieval Italian states, Perugia found itself in a fortunate position, out of the turbulent mainstream, with no large and dangerous neighbours, and an attractive ally (when it suited Perugia) of pope, emperor, or any of the contentious cities over in Tuscany. As a result, the Perugians, though they never established a republic like Florence or Siena, were almost always able to manage their own affairs. Mostly, they spent their time subjugating neighbours: Lake Trasimeno towns in 1130, Città di Castello not long after, then Assisi and Spello. Foligno, another bitter enemy, fell in 1282. Almost always a Guelph city, Perugia maintained a special relationship with Florence and the popes—it had allies, certainly, but friends, never. Even fierce, factional cities like Florence and Siena were careful to walk wide of this wildcat which was constantly molesting its neighbours when not itself convulsed in civil wars. Siena had its annual festive punch-up, the *Gioco del Pugno*, but the Perugians enjoyed spending their holidays at the *Battaglia de' Sassi*, the 'battle of stones' in the Piazza del Duomo, with usually a dozen or so fatalities each year. Not even in religion could Perugia behave itself; besides being a graveyard for popes, Perugia gave a cold shoulder to most of the early revivalists and reformers. Even St Francis, who before he became a preacher spent a year in a Perugian dungeon, couldn't make the city mend its ways. One product of Perugian piety cannot be denied: the medieval mass-psychosis of the **Flagellants** began with the hallucinations of a monk here in 1265; within ten years it spread across Europe.

In principle, Perugia has been a part of the papal dominions, the 'Patrimony of St Peter', since the days of Charlemagne. Few popes, though, were able to exercise much control over such a volatile city. After 1303, the Priors of the ten major guilds established their rule, although noble families like the **Oddi** and the **Baglioni** remained extremely influential. In the 1360s and 70s, when **Cardinal Albornoz** was raising armies and building castles to reassert papal authority over central Italy, Perugia revolted. Pope Urban VI paid a visit in 1387 to make up—a wild dove perched on his shoulder as he passed through the city gate, which the Perugians took as a good omen.

Unfortunately, the rebellion only took the lid off a cauldron of conflicting ambitions that had long been ready to boil over, and Perugia's three big factions—the nobles, the *Raspanti* (the wealthy merchant class) and the commons—leapt to each other's throats. In 1393, with the connivance of the pope, a noble named **Biondo Michelotti** seized power. Five years later (again the pope was involved) Michelotti was murdered on his wedding day by the Abbot of S. Pietro. In the resulting confusion, Giangaleazzo Visconti of Milan was able to grab the city for a time (1400–02), followed by a period under the rule of King Ladislas of Naples (1400–14). After Ladislas, the celebrated Perugian *condottiere* **Braccio Fortebraccio** ('Arm Strongarm', the Popeye of the Renaissance judging by his name and the spinach in a helmet portrayed on his escutcheon), won the city by defeating another *condottiere*, Carlo Malatesta of Rimini, at the Battle of Sant'Egidio. Fortebraccio, soon master of all Umbria and 'Prince of Capua', had king-sized ambitions and potent friends—according to contemporary gossip he owned a crystal with a genie imprisoned inside who gave him good advice. After conquering most of the Marches, Fortebraccio had dreams of ruling a united Italy, but his luck ran out in 1424, when he died at the hands of another Perugian during the siege of L'Aquila, in the Abruzzo.

In the aftermath, Pope Martin V took control of Perugia though he could do nothing to stop the increasingly bloody fighting between the noble clans. In 1488 the Oddi were exiled from the city and the Baglioni became rulers of Perugia. This meteoric family, with their legendary good looks, pet lions, and tendency towards fratricide, blazed through Perugia's history like the House of Atreus. In 1520 an even bigger shark, the Medici Pope Leo X, tricked **Gianpaolo Baglioni**, the last family tyrant of Perugia, into coming to Rome, where he was imprisoned and murdered. The remaining Baglioni found employment as *condottieri* around Italy. One, Malatesta Baglioni, distinguished himself by betraying Florence to the Medici and Charles V in the siege of 1530. Another, Rodolfo, murdered a papal legate in revenge for the death of his uncle Gianpaolo, giving **Pope Paul III** an excuse to intervene. Over the centuries it had become customary for popes reasserting their authority to make a formal visit; contemporaries record Paul, father of the Inquisition and one of the kinkiest and most corrupt of all popes, requiring all the nuns of the city to queue up and kiss his feet, an experience which left him 'very greatly edified'.

To put an end to Perugia's independence for ever, Paul needed yet one more provocation: he found it in 1538, raising the salt tax a year after promising not to. The Perugians revolted again, initiating the '**Salt War**', but were immediately crushed by a huge papal force of mercenaries and Spaniards. Government was handed over to officials entitled Preservers of Ecclesiastical Obedience; its trade ruined and its streets full of monks, nuns, and Jesuits, Perugia began a precipitous economic decline that would not be reversed until the Risorgimento.

Until then, the only event in the conquered city was to be the Napoleonic occupation: the emperor's troops sent the hordes of monks and nuns packing, but also packed much of Perugia's art—some of the best Peruginos included—back to the Louvre. In 1859, during the disturbances of the Risorgimento, Perugia rebelled once more against the pope. Pius IX sent his **Swiss Guard** to quell them—some 2000 Switzers forced the city, burning, looting, and butchering citizens in the streets. After that, the final liberation a year later was greeted with delirium. King Vittorio Emanuele's army had to protect the retiring Swiss Guards from massacre at the hands of the Perugians.

GETTING AROUND

By Air

Perugia's airport, Sant'Egidio-Perugia, is 13 km west of the city towards Assisi and at the time of writing has connections only with Milan; for information, tel 692 9447.

By Train

Because Perugia is up on a hill, its two train stations are both some distance from the centre. The main **FS station**, on Piazza V. Veneto, tel 70 980, lies about 3 km from the centre in the lower suburb of Fontevegge; it has connections for Florence (154 km/2½ hrs) and Arezzo (78 km/1½ hrs) all via Terontola junction on the northern shore of Lake Trasimeno; for Siena (147 km/3½ hrs) another change is required, at Chiusi. Another line passes through Assisi (26 km/25 min), Spoleto (47 km/70 min), Foligno, and Terni on the way to Rome (3 hrs). For other destinations in Umbria, you'll find the **FCU** handy, tel 29 121; the narrow-gauge Ferrovia Centrale Umbria has its main station in Perugia—Stazione Sant'Anna, halfway up Perugia's hill, just off Piazza dei Partigiani. The FCU goes north to Città di Castello (45 km/1 hr) and Sansepolcro (60 km/1½ hrs) and south to Todi (41 km/1 hr) and Terni. Regular city buses (nos. 26, 27 and 36) connect the FS station with Corso Matteotti or Piazza Italia in the centre; many of them pass the FCU station.

By Coach

Perugia's **bus depot** is near the FCU station in Piazza dei Partigiani, linked to Piazza Italia by a system of steps and escalators (*scala mobile*; see below). ASP buses, tel 61 807, serve all the villages in Perugia province (roughly the northern two-thirds of Umbria), also two a day to Rome, and one a day to Orvieto and Siena (also to Urbino, the Renaissance town in the Marches). There are about a dozen buses a day to Assisi, Todi and Lake Trasimeno; also five a day to Chiusi, that important rail stop on the Florence–Rome line, and one a day to Massa Marittima. Connections in this part of Italy are always complicated; plan your trip before you start.

By Car

Perugia may be quickly reached by the Florence-Rome A1, on the N. 75bis spur that begins at the Val di Chiana junction, although from Rome you can save toll money by exiting at Orte, picking up the major highways (N. 204 and N. 3bis) up to Perugia. Parking in the city can be a headache; most of the city is closed to traffic, and peripheral garages and car parks are few and usually charge by the hour. Car parks nearest the centre are at Piazza Italia, Piazza Piccinino, Piazza Pellini, the Mercato Coperto, and Piazza dei Partigiani, all connected to the centre by elevator or escalator. You can **hire a car** from AVIS at the airport, tel 692 9796, or near the centre at Paolini Paoletti, Piazza Dante 28, or a **motor scooter** at Easy Bike, Via Marconi 27.

Walking

Walking in Perugia is a delight, though you'll often find yourself out of breath. In the oldest parts, densely packed and half-covered with arches and passageways, Perugia often seems like one big building. Its difficult topography has been mastered with some cleverness—there always seem to be stairs, elevators or escalators to carry you from one part to another. Many of these are on the edges, where some truly beautiful parks have been strung along the cliffs to take advantage of unusable land. Pay attention to the street names—Via Curiosa *Curious* Street, Via Perduta *Lost* Street, Via Piacevole *Pleasant* Street, Via Pericolosa *Dangerous* Street, among many others. And look for medieval details—carved symbols and coats-of-arms. One local peculiarity is the *Porta del*

Mortuccio, 'Death's door', used only to carry out the dead, and bricked up the rest of the time—where death has once passed, the superstition went, he might pass again.

TOURIST INFORMATION

Corso Vannucci 96, tel (075) 23 327; Via Mazzini 21, tel 25 341, and at the FS station, tel 71 660. But why talk to human beings when you can consult the *Digiplan* computerized information system, which never lies and (when it's working) is always right. This planet's most sophisticated mechanical tourist information office is found on the *scala mobile*, just up the escalator from the Piazza dei Partigiani; it will print out details on almost any hotel, restaurant or sight in town, or anything else you want to know.
Post Office: Piazza Matteotti.
Telephones: AAST, Piazza Matteotti, open till midnight; SIP, Via Marconi 21, until 9:30 pm.

Piazza IV Novembre

Magnificent time-worn Piazza IV Novembre, the heart and soul of Perugia, is also the central node of its meandering streets. As in so many Umbrian towns, the old town hall, symbol of the *comune*, entirely upstages the cathedral. Here, the two face each other with one of Italy's most beautiful fountains in between, the circular **Fontana Maggiore**, designed in the 1270s by a little-known monk named Fra Bevignate to hold the water from Perugia's first aqueduct. For the occasion, the Priors commissioned Nicola and Giovanni Pisano to sculpt 48 relief panels around the basin. Twelve of these portray that favourite medieval conceit, the months and their occupations, each accompanied by its zodiacal sign; in between are scenes from Roman legend, Aesop's fables, and saints' lives, personifications of the sciences and arts, altogether a complete, circular image of the medieval world. Above them, 24 saints keep company with three water nymphs, all by later sculptors.

Surveying the piazza, high up on the wall of the **Palazzo dei Priori** perch a Guelph lion and Perugia's totem, the famous brass griffin, an emblem you will see at least once on every street in town. The scrap iron dangling beneath it is said to be chains and bolts from the gates of Siena, captured after a famous victory in 1358 (but no—the real war trophies, whatever they were, disappeared two centuries ago; these chains were simply there to hold them up). This Gothic, asymmetrical complex, crowned with toothsome crenellations, was recently cleaned to look as sharp and new as when it was begun in 1297, about the same time as the civic palaces of Florence and Siena. The first floor, still used for the city offices, has two rooms usually open to the public, the **Sala dei Notari**, with interesting early 13th-century frescoes, and the **Sala del Malconsiglio** ('bad counsel'), so called because it was here in the 1360s that the Priors decided to release some prisoners—almost the entire English mercenary company of Sir John Hawkwood. The very next year Hawkwood's men defeated Perugia at the Battle of Ponte San Giovanni. The Perugians learned their lesson; they were never nice to anyone again.

Galleria Nazionale

In the Palazzo dei Priori, but entered from Corso Vannucci, the **Galleria Nazionale dell'Umbria** is the finest and largest collection of Umbrian paintings anywhere (lift up to the third floor, open 9–2, Sun 9–1, closed Mon; adm, expensive). Not all the best

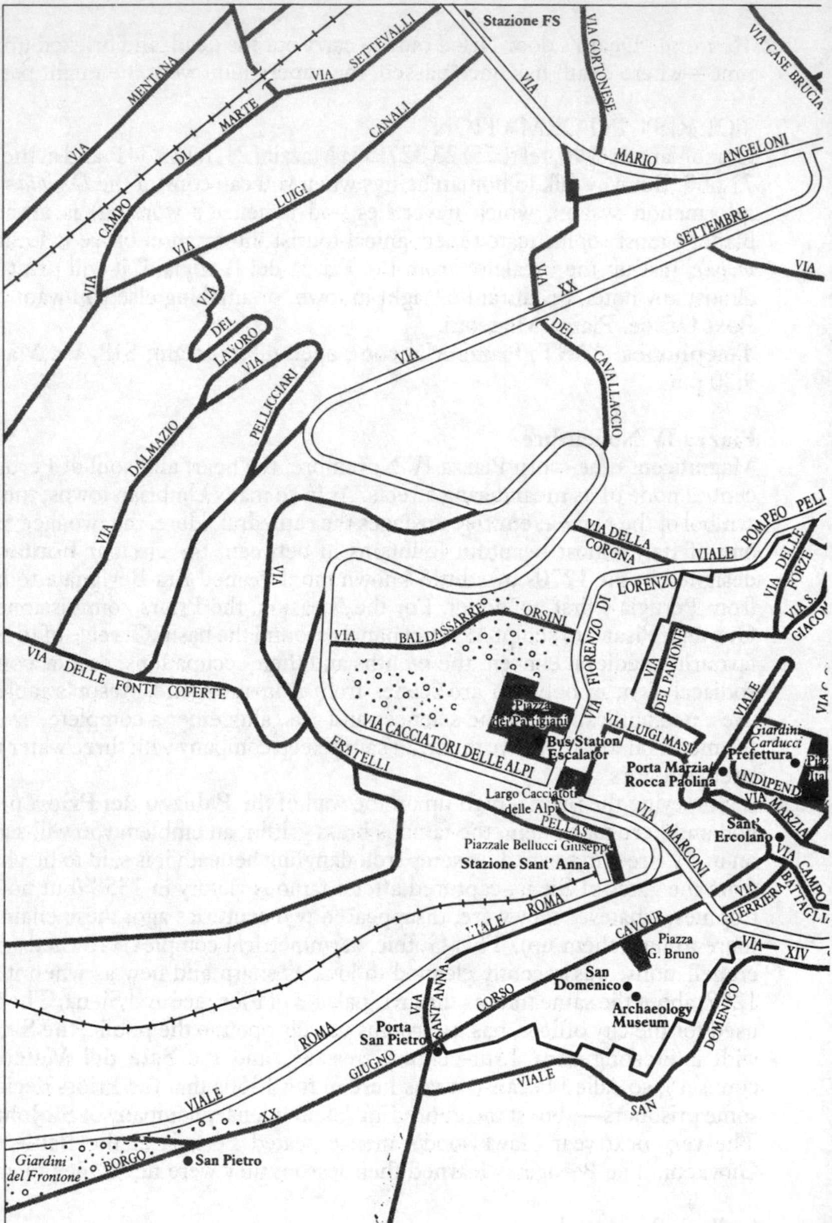
Stazione FS
VIA CORTONESE
VIA MENTANA
VIA SETTEVALLI
VIA CAMPO DI MARTE
VIA CANALI
VIA LUIGI
MARIO ANGELONI
VIA XX SETTEMBRE
VIA DEL LAVORO
VIA PELLICCIARI
VIA DALMAZIO
VIA DEL CAVALLACCIO
VIA DELLA CORGNA
VIA FIORENZO DI LORENZO
VIA DELLE FORZE
VIA BALDASSARRE ORSINI
VIA DELLE FONTI COPERTE
Piazza dei Partigiani
Bus Station Escalator
VIA CACCIATORI DELLE ALPI
FRATELLI PELLAS
Largo Cacciatori delle Alpi
Piazzale Bellucci Giuseppe
Stazione Sant' Anna
VIA MARCONI
VIA DEL PARIONE
VIA LUIGI MASI
VIALE
Giardini Carducci
Prefettura
Porta Marzia Rocca Paolina
VIA MARZIA
Sant' Ercolano
VIA CAMPO BATTAGLIA
VIA GUERRIERA
VIALE ROMA
CAVOUR
Piazza G. Bruno
San Domenico
Archaeology Museum
VIA XIV
CORSO
VIA SANT' ANNA
Porta San Pietro
VIALE ROMA
GIUGNO
VIALE SAN DOMENICO
VIALE XX
BORGO
San Pietro
Giardini del Frontone

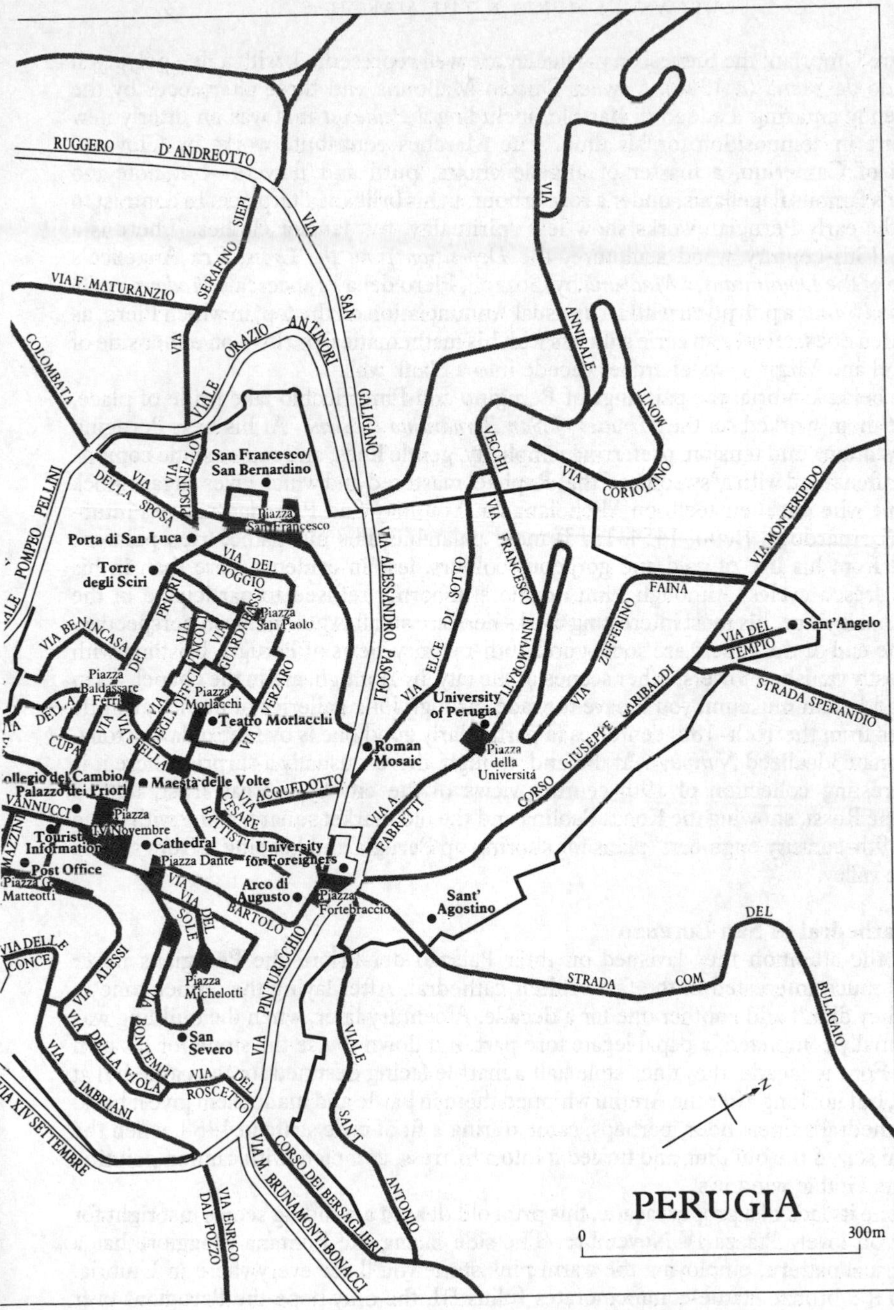
PERUGIA
0
300m
N
RUGGERO D'ANDREOTTO
VIA SERAFINO SIEPI
VIA F. MATURANZIO
VIA SAN GALIGANO
VIALE ORAZIO ANTINORI
VIA PISCINELLO
COLOMBATA
POMPEO PELLINI
VIA DELLA SPOSA
VIA ANNIBALE
MONTI
VIA CORIOLANO
VIA FRANCESCO INNAMORATI
VIA VECCHI
VIA ELCE DI SOTTO
VIA ALESSANDRO PASCOLI
VIA MONTERIPIDO
VIA ZEFFERINO FAINA
VIA DEL TEMPIO
STRADA SPERANDIO
CORSO GIUSEPPE GARIBALDI
VIA A. FABRETTI
VIA DEL POGGIO
VIA DEI PRIORI
VIA BENINCASA
VIA DELLA CUPA
VIA VINCIOLI
VIA GUARDABASSI
VIA DEGLI OFFICI
VIA SELLA
VIA VERZARO
VIA ACQUEDOTTO
VIA CESARE BATTISTI
VANNUCCI
MAZZINI
VIA BARTOLO
VIA DEL SOLE
VIA ALESSI
VIA DELLE CONCE
VIA DELLA VIOLA
VIA IMBRIANI
VIA BONTEMPI
VIA DEL ROSCETTO
VIA XIV SETTEMBRE
VIA PINTURICCHIO
VIALE SANT ANTONIO
CORSO DEI BERSAGLIERI
VIA M. BRUNAMONTI BONACCI
VIA ENRICO DAL POZZO
STRADA DEL COM
BULAGAIO
San Francesco/
San Bernardino
Piazza San Francesco
Porta di San Luca
Torre degli Sciri
Piazza San Paolo
Piazza Baldassare Ferri
Piazza Morlacchi
Teatro Morlacchi
University of Perugia
Piazza della Università
Sant'Angelo
Roman Mosaic
Collegio del Cambio
Palazzo dei Priori
Maestà delle Volte
Piazza IV Novembre
Tourist Information
Cathedral
Piazza Dante
Post Office
Piazza G. Matteotti
University for Foreigners
Arco di Augusto
Piazza Fortebraccio
Sant' Agostino
Piazza Michelotti
San Severo

works are Umbrian; the Sienese in particular are well represented, with a fine polyptych by Guido da Siena (*c.* 1360), a sweet Duccio Madonna and three altarpieces by the consistently amazing Taddeo di Bartolo, including a *Pentecost* that was an utterly new adventure in composition for his time. The Marches contribute works by Giovanni Boccati of Camerino, a master of angelic choirs, putti and flowers—but note too Perugia's famous flagellants, under a rose arbour, in his brilliant altarpiece. In contrast to these, the early Perugian works show less spirituality, but fancier clothes. There is a serene, 13th-century wood sculpture, the *Deposition from the Cross*, Fra Angelico's triptych of the *Dominicans*, a *Madonna* by Gozzoli, Piero della Francesca's *Madonna with Angels and Saints* a polyptych with an unusual Annunciation on the top, in which Piero, as he so often does, creates an eerie stillness with his mathematical purity—on either side of the angel and Virgin rows of arches recede into a blank wall.

This being Umbria, the paintings of Perugino and Pinturicchio take pride of place. Both of them worked on the *Miracles of San Bernardino of Siena*. At his best Perugino eschews drama and tension, preferring simplicity, gentle lines, and rather static compositions often filled with a 'sweetness' that Raphael mastered and which gives sugar-shock to people who cut their teeth on Michelangelo. You may find Perugian native Pinturicchio (Bernardo di Betto, 1454–1513) more palatable. His nickname, 'rich painter', derived from his use of gold and gorgeous colours, less in evidence here than in his famous fresco cycles. Although Pinturicchio stubbornly refused to participate in the High Renaissance, his most interesting works here are small experiments in perspective. Near the end of the gallery are some good 16th-century views of Perugia, bristling with now mostly vanished towers; other scenes of the city, by Bonfigli, are in the chapel. As in any good Italian museum, you'll have to wade through long galleries of numb, gigantic canvases from the 16th–18th centuries (a particularly good one is by Pietro da Cortona, the ultimate idealized *Nativity*). At the end, though, there's usually a surprise; here it is an interesting collection of 19th-century views of the city by a local artist, named Giuseppe Rossi, showing the Rocca Paolina and the old market square, along with some of the 19th-century engineers' plans for shoring up Perugia and keeping it from sliding into the valley.

The Cathedral of San Lorenzo

For all the attention they lavished on their Palazzo dei Priori, the Perugians never seemed much interested in the fate of their cathedral. After laying the cornerstone in 1345, they didn't add another one for a decade. A century later, when the building was substantially completed, a papal legate tore part of it down to use the stone for his own palace. For the façade, they once stole half a marble facing destined for the cathedral at Arezzo, but not long after the Aretini whipped them in battle and made them give it back. The cathedral's finest hour, perhaps, came during a fit of civic strife in 1488, when the Baglioni seized the building and turned it into a fortress, complete with cannon pointing out of its Gothic windows.

Despite its lack of a proper façade, this prim old dear of a building seems just right for its post on lovely Piazza IV Novembre. The side facing the Fontana Maggiore has a geometrical pattern, employing the warm pink stone you'll see everywhere in Umbria. Next to it a bronze statue commemorates Julius III, the only pope the Perugians ever liked. The unfinished pulpit on the façade was built for the great charismatic revivalist

San Bernardino of Siena, who preached to vast crowds in the piazza, finally persuading them to stop at least the *Battaglia de' Sassi*. The best feature of the façade, however, is the elegant **Loggia di Braccio Fortebraccio**, added by the *condottiere* in 1423. The interior is unimpressive, supported by columns badly painted to simulate marble. In the first chapel on the right, the Chapel of S. Bernardino, the tomb of a bishop, by Urbano da Cortona, stands across from a saccharine *Descent from the Cross* by the 15th-century Urbino painter Federico Barocci.

On the left side, near a pair of reliefs by Agostino di Duccio, the Perugians keep their most prized relic, nothing less than the wedding ring of the Virgin Mary. Many stories have grown up around this prodigy, a big onyx stone that seems to change colour according to the person looking at it. To keep out thieves and sceptics, the ring is usually kept in fifteen nested cases under fifteen locks, the keys to which are each held by a different notable citizen. A Perugian woman stole it from Chiusi back in the Middle Ages, and the townspeople have never stopped worrying that the Chiusini might try to get it back. The relic indirectly inspired Raphael's finest painting, the *Betrothal of the Virgin* now in Milan; Raphael had the idea from a painting by his master Perugino that hung in this chapel before Napoleon spirited it off to France—the emperor always had a weakness for doe-eyed Virgins; Perugino was one of his favourite painters.

Behind the cathedral, the cloister of the **Canonica** witnessed four conclaves of cardinals between 1124 and 1305. Among the popes elected here was Clement V, who began the 'Babylonian Captivity' by moving the papacy to Avignon. The cloister now contains the **Museo dell'Opera del Duomo**, with a small collection of art, starring Luca Signorelli's 1484 *Madonna enthroned with saints and the donor* and a pot-bellied angel tuning a lute, with a supporting cast of reliquaries and hymnals (open apparently when someone wants to see it; ask at the sacristy; adm). The cathedral's campanile, right over your head, projects some quite impressive bell-ringing each day at noon.

Corso Vannucci and Underground Perugia

To complement the excellent Piazza IV Novembre, Perugia has a truly noble main street. The Corso is named after the city's most famous son, Pietro Vannucci, better known as Perugino; it is always closed to traffic, and the citizens stroll it every evening in central Italy's liveliest *passeggiata*. On the Corso, next to the Palazzo dei Priori, Perugino received a commission in 1499 to decorate the **Collegio del Cambio**, headquarters of Perugia's bankers' guild. He and his assistants adorned the hall with allegorical figures, fashionably clothed in High Renaissance *haute couture*. Among these, Perugino painted a self-portrait in the middle of the left wall, and his most famous pupil Raphael, then a mere pup of 17, contributed the figure of Fortitude. The frescoes in the bankers' Chapel are by another of Perugino's students, Giannicola di Paolo (Nov–Feb 8–2, otherwise 9–12:30 and 2:30–5:30, Sun 9–12:30, closed Mon; adm). The ticket is also valid for the adjacent **Collegio della Mercanzia**, the merchants' guild's hall, decorated with almost Moorish-style 15th-century carvings and inlays.

Continuing down the Corso, past the hotels and formidable Perugian pastry shops, you pass from the Middle Ages to 19th-century Neoclassical in the twinkling of an eye at **Piazza Italia**, dominated by the bulky, 1870s **Prefettura**, emblazoned with the Perugian griffin; behind it, the balustrades of the **Giardini Carducci** offer a splendid view over the Perugian suburbs and the distant countryside. To find out why there are no old buildings on this piazza, take the down escalator, unobtrusively hidden under the colonnades of the Prefettura, into a Perugia that for over 300 years was lost to view and almost forgotten. Only days after the end of the Salt War, Paul III found a way to intimidate the Perugians into obedience until Judgement Day while obliterating the Baglioni family at the same stroke. The quarter of town he demolished for his famous **Rocca Paolina** was the stronghold of the Baglioni, and it included all of their palaces. Most of the buildings were not completely demolished, only because Paul's architect, Antonio da Sangallo, needed them to give the new fortress a level foundation. It was always looked upon as a loathsome symbol of oppression, of the grisly terror that came to Italy in the 1500s. No enemy ever attacked it, and throughout the centuries of papal rule its only real use was as a prison—a prison from which few that entered ever found their way out again. As soon as Perugia was liberated from the Swiss Guards in 1860, the Perugians gleefully began tearing it down; the workmen, with their dynamite, found themselves joined by the entire populace, including women and children, some with pickaxes, some with their bare hands.

In a way it's a pity the Rocca Paolina no longer stands. The old paintings and prints in the Palazzo dei Priori show it as a startlingly modern building, beautiful in a way, designed by one of the best Renaissance architects. After demolishing it, the Perugians built the Neoclassical ensemble of the Piazza Italia and the Carducci Gardens over it; few even knew about the medieval streets and buildings underneath. Recently, the city has made use of these buried streets to create a quick pedestrian passage down to Piazza dei Partigiani, convenient, and also one of the most fascinating things to visit in Perugia. At the bottom of the escalator, you'll be at the medieval street level, among the brick palaces of the Baglioni and their unfortunate neighbours, all roofed over by the arches and vaults of Sangallo. There are many interesting corners to explore off the beaten track, including parts of Rocca Paolina bastions (open 9–1 and 4–7) where you can peek out through the pope's gun slits over peaceful Viale Indipendenza below. The entrance to this part is outside, on Via Marzia, where you can also see the remains of the **Porta Marzia**, the best surviving piece of Etruscan architecture anywhere that isn't a tomb. Antonio da Sangallo was so impressed with it that he carefully reassembled it here after destroying the original walls. The five sculpted panels, now almost completely eroded away, probably represented five gods; the Perugians have a strange old story that they are a Roman family that died from eating poisonous mushrooms.

Perugia's West End: Down Via dei Priori

On the Corso Vannucci side of the Palazzo dei Priori, a little archway, easy to overlook, leads into this street and Perugia's west end, a quiet and lovely part of the city. The first sight you'll encounter along this street is the church of **St Philip Neri**, rebuilt from an earlier church in the 1630s. Perugians used to call this impressive Baroque building the 'Chiesa Nuova'; its interior, full of florid paintings, seems to be made of dirty ice cream, an echo of the Roman Baroque out in the papal provinces. Further down, stop for a look at the charming **SS. Stefano e Valentino**, a vaulted medieval church almost hidden among the surrounding houses: the altarpiece is a fine *Crucifixion* by the 16th-century Perugian artist Alfani. Next, in the shadow of the lofty 13th-century **Torre degli Sciri**, Perugia's only surviving tower-fortress, the huge **S. Teresa** (always locked) was an ambitious Renaissance project that was never finished. In the little piazza by the **Porta Trasimena**, built in the Middle Ages on Etruscan foundations, the church of the **Madonna della Luce** has a good Renaissance façade and an altarpiece by another little-known Perugian artist, Bartolomeo Caporali (d. 1499). The church commemorates a miracle: a barber, playing cards in front of his shop, cussed so hard after losing a hand that a wooden Madonna in a nearby street-corner shrine shut her eyes, and didn't open them for four whole days.

San Bernardino and San Francesco

Turn right at the Madonna della Luce for green Piazza San Francesco, formerly located outside the walls, and since 1230 the site of **S. Francesco al Prato**. Once the finest and most richly decorated church in Perugia, it suffered a partial collapse in a mud slide in 1737 and a thorough looting by Napoleon's soldiers; the elegant façade remains, in patterns of pink and white stone. Next door, **San Bernardino** commemorates the 15th-century Sienese saint who made such an impression on the Perugians. 'Little St Bernard' must certainly have been a crafty preacher to affect this nest of pirates. Just coincidentally, his celebrated powers of persuasion, and in particular his famous dictum: 'Make it clear, make it short and keep to the point', have earned him a difficult posthumous responsibility—a recent pope has declared him Patron Saint of Advertising. The chapel was begun in 1461, not long after the saint's death, and placed on this site because Bernardino, himself a Franciscan, always stayed at the adjacent convent of S. Francesco during his frequent visits.

Agostino di Duccio, that rare Florentine sculptor whose best work is in the Malatesta Temple of Rimini, was commissioned to do the façade, and he turned the little chapel into Umbria's greatest temple of pure Renaissance art. At first, the glaring pink and green marble may seem hopelessly jarring, but Agostino's reliefs are deserving of a close look: beatific angel musicians, scenes of miracles from the life of the saint, and allegorical virtues, Mercy, Holiness and Purity on the left, Religion, Mortification and Penance on the right. One of the panels on the lower frieze portrays the original Bonfire of Vanities, held in front of the cathedral after a particularly stirring sermon from Bernardino—which may have given Savonarola in Florence the idea. Inside, the chapel's altar is a late Roman sarcophagus, perhaps that of a Christian; it seems to be portraying the story of Jonah and the whale.

The Arch of Augustus

Quite a few old tales start with a little boy going around a church widdershins (counterclockwise) and ending up in fairyland. Try it with Perugia's cathedral, and you'll find yourself transported immediately back to the Middle Ages, a half-vertical cityscape of dark, grim buildings and overhanging arches, some incorporating bits of Gothic palaces and Etruscan walls, a set no movie director could possibly improve upon. And they are as old as they look. Via Ulisse Rocchi, leading down to the old northern gate, used to be called Via Vecchia; traditionally the oldest street in town, Perugians have been walking it for at least 2500 years. Once through the north gate, look round to see another fabulous relic of the city's past, the **Arco di Augusto**. The huge stones of the lower levels are Etruscan; above them rises a perfectly preserved Roman arch built during the emperor's refounding of *Augusta Perusia*. The city's new name is inscribed with typical Imperial modesty: 'Augusta' in very large letters, 'Perusia' in tiny ones. The portico atop the Roman bastion, an addition that makes this gate one of the most beautiful in Italy, was added in the 16th century. The arch faces Piazza Fortebraccio and the 18th-century Palazzo Gallenga Stuart, home of the **University for Foreigners**, founded in 1921 as a centre for studies in Italian language and culture and attended by students from all over the world.

The University and Borgo Sant'Angelo

Another itinerary through this ancient district would begin west from behind the cathedral down into a jumble of interwoven medieval arches and asymmetrical vaults that lead down to Via Battisti. Near Via Battisti, a long stairway descends through the Roman-Etruscan walls into the **Borgo Sant'Angelo**, Perugia's medieval suburb that once was a proletarian quarter, the centre of popular resistance to the Baglioni and the popes, and now is the seat of the city's famous university. Walk over the **'Acquedotto,'** a long stone footbridge carried over the housetops on graceful arches to the precincts of the **University**, founded in 1307 and still one of the most prestigious in Italy. The central University buildings are found on Via Fabretti, in an Olivetan monastery liquidated by Napoleon in 1801. In the Institute of Chemistry, on Via S. Elisabetta, you can see a **Roman mosaic** of the 2nd century, discovered during recent construction. The scene represents Orpheus charming the wild animals with his lyre—not mere decoration, but one of the key religious images of the late classical world. It's open whenever the chemistry building is; whenever classes are not in session you'll have to be content with the view from the street through the basement windows (or call 22 882 for the custodian).

Beyond the University quarters, Corso Garibaldi runs northwards through the old working-class neighbourhoods of the Borgo Sant'Angelo, passing the bulky church of **Sant'Agostino**; here the main attraction is the set of extravagantly carved choirstalls by Baccio d'Agnolo, from designs by Perugino. There are some frescoes by students of Perugino, but the real prize, a five-part altarpiece by the master himself, was looted by Napoleon. Its panels are now scattered across France, except for the Madonna herself, who took a cannonball on the nose in Strasbourg during the Franco-Prussian war. Around the corner, on Via Pinturicchio, the church of **Santa Maria Nuova** has a curiosity of Umbrian art, a *gonfalon* painted by Bonfigli (1472) with a view of Perugia in the background. Further up Corso Garibaldi, you will see a plaque commemorating the meeting of St Francis and St Dominic, both in Perugia to visit Pope Honorius III; contemporary accounts have the two saints embracing and going their separate ways, without more than a word or two.

At the end of the street, one of the highest points in the city was graced in ancient times by a circular temple, dedicated to either Venus or Vulcan. Christians turned it into a church of **Sant'Angelo** in the 5th century, replacing the outer circle of columns with a plain stone wall. Many legends grew up around this singular church in the Middle Ages—some writers referred to it as the 'pavilion of Roland'. Today, with tons of Baroque frippery cleared away in a recent remodelling, the church has returned to something like its original appearance. Some scholars doubt there really was a temple here: the 16 Corinthian columns do come in a wild variety of styles, and some were undoubtedly brought from other buildings. Still, this oldest church in Umbria casts its quiet spell, especially in the early hours when the sunlight streams through the little window in the apse. The tall **Porta Sant'Angelo** behind the church, a key point in Perugia's medieval defences, was built by Braccio Fortebraccio.

On *Perusia*'s Acropolis

The streets to the east of the cathedral, while not quite as dramatic, are just as ancient and intractable as those to the north and west. One of the few breathing spaces in the whole crowded district is **Piazza Matteotti**, the former marketplace and field for burning witches, just east of the cathedral. In the old days it was called Piazza Sopramura, being actually built on top of a section of the Etruscan-Roman walls. The west side of the piazza is shared by the Post Office and an old Perugian institution, a brightly decorated kiosk with an eccentric owner who sells nothing but bananas. Opposite them stand the 17th-century Gesù Church, the 15th-century **Palazzo del Capitano del Popolo**, and the original quarters of the University.

If you care to climb a bit, a tour of this area will take you to such sights as the **Via delle Volte**, an ancient vaulted tunnel of a street just east of the cathedral; and the churches of Santa Fiorenza and Santa Maria Nuova, each of which has one of Bonfigli's bizarre *gonfalons*; these painted banners, among the earliest works of the Umbrian school of painting, were intended to be carried during mournful *misericordia* processions in the streets, invoking God's mercy during plagues, famines, or the frequent attacks of communal guilt to which the Perugians were always subject.

Further up, on Via Raffaello (or up Via del Sole from Piazza Danti next to the cathedral) you'll find **San Severo**, founded in 1007 by Camaldolese monks; the story goes that this high ground was ancient *Augusta Perusia*'s acropolis, and that the monks built their church over the ruins of a Temple of the Sun. Only one chapel survived a Baroque remodelling of the 1750s, but it contains a celebrated fresco of the *Holy Trinity and saints* by Raphael; underneath are more saints by his master Perugino, ironically done long after Raphael's death when Perugino was in a noticeable artistic decline. **Piazza Michelotti**, nearby, is an attractive spot and the highest point in the city. Long before the Rocca Paolina, the popes built their original fortress here. And like the work of Paul III, this castle was also destroyed by the Perugians. In the rebellion of 1375, the people besieged it; after bribing off Sir John Hawkwood, the paid protector of the papal legate, they knocked down the walls with the aid of a fearsome homemade catapult called the *cacciaprete* (priest-chaser).

Archaeology Museum and San Pietro

From Piazza Matteotti, Via Oberdan descends to Perugia's oddest church, **Sant'Ercolano** (1326), a tall octagonal building with a train station clock and lace curtains in the upstairs window. From here, the city extends itself along a narrow ridge, following Corso Cavour to another colossal, ambitious, woefully unfinished church, **San Domenico**. The Gothic rose window is claimed as the biggest in all Italy, and inside there is the fine *Tomb of Pope Benedict XI*, attributed to Giovanni Pisano. Poisoned figs did Benedict in, during a visit in 1304, but surprisingly the Perugians had nothing to do with it; prime suspects included the Florentines and King Philip the Fair of France. Around the back, the equally grandiose and unfinished convent now houses the **Museo Archeologico Nazionale dell'Umbria**, with an excellent collection of material from prehistoric and

Etruscan Umbria. A large part of it comes from the Etruscan cemeteries around Perugia—a lovely incised bronze mirror (an Etruscan speciality, 3rd century BC), intricate gold filigree jewellery, sarcophagi, a famous stone marker called the *Cippus Perusinus*, with one of the longest Etruscan inscriptions ever found, bronzes, armour and weapons. Among the funeral vases and urns there is one portraying a hero who looks just like a dentist about to examine a monster's teeth (daily 9–2, Sun 9–1; adm).

Corso Cavour leaves the city at the **Porta San Pietro**, designed by Agostino di Duccio while he was working on S. Bernardino. Changing its name to Borgo XX Giugno, the street continues to the end of the ridge, where there's an 18th-century park, the **Giardino del Frontone**, main venue of the Umbria Jazz Festival, and facing it, **San Pietro**, the most gloriously decorated church in Perugia, almost entirely covered inside with frescoes and canvases. The Perugians have always taken good care of it—especially since 1859, during the sack by the Swiss Guards, when the monks of San Pietro shielded the leaders of the revolt from the papal bloodhounds. As the story goes, they cut down their bell-ropes by night, and used them to lower the fugitives down the cliffs to safety. Among the acres of painting, there's a Pietà by Perugino (in the north aisle) and several works of his pupil, Eusebio di San Giorgio. The best works, however, are the wooden choirstalls, from the 1520s, and other woodwork in the sacristy, the work of craftsmen from Bergamo. The sacristy also has paintings of four saints by Perugino, all that remains of an altarpiece looted by Napoleon. A door in the choir gives out onto a little balcony with a memorable view over Assisi and Spello.

Ipogeo dei Volumni

As you leave Perugia, Via XX Settembre, the twisting boulevard down to the train station, passes the 13th-century church of **Santa Giuliana**, with a beautiful campanile, one of Perugia's landmarks, and cloisters from the 1200s and 1300s. A new business centre is growing up in the flatlands around the station; one of the new developments has a post-Modernist office block with a small piazza, one of the slickest new buildings in Italy.

Near the Ponte San Giovanni, just east of Perugia, signs lead to Perugia's finest Etruscan tomb, the **Ipogeo dei Volumni**, sheltered by a modern yellow building (9–6 summer, 9–5 winter, Sun 9–1, closed Mon; adm). Dating from the 2nd century BC, the hypogeum is shaped like an Etruscan house, with an underground 'atrium' (under a high gabled roof carved in the rock), and surrounded by small rooms, the main one holding the travertine urns containing the ashes of four generations of the family. The oldest one, that of a man named Arnth, is a typical Etruscan tomb with a representation of the deceased on the lid, while that of his descendant, the 1st-century AD Pulius Voluminius, demonstrates Perugia's rapid Romanization. Unlike most other Etruscan tombs, the Volumni has no paintings, but unusual high-reliefs in stucco.

ACTIVITIES

The principal Perugian occupation in the evening is the *passeggiata* down Corso Vannucci, with a stop for a tantalizing bite at the **Bar Ferrari** (no. 43), full of Perugia's famous chocolate *Baci* and other confections, or perhaps an ice cream at the **Gelateria Veneta** (no. 20) before loitering in Piazza IV Novembre. The city also holds a market with a view, the **Mercato della Terrazza**, with clothes and shoes, near the Kennedy escalator, off Piazza Matteotti. Other activities include July's **Umbria Jazz Festival**, which draws lights like Miles Davis, Stan Getz, and Wynton Marsalis to Perugia and other towns; pick up tickets at Piazza della Repubblica. There are performances in the city's cloisters and squares in the *Teatro in Piazza* festival in July and August. Summer courses in painting and sculpture are offered by the Accademia di Belle Arti Pietro Vannucci, Piazza S. Francesco al Prato 5, tel 29 106, or you can take Italian in the summer at the University for Foreigners; write in advance for details (Palazzo Gallenga, Piazza Fortebraccio 4, tel 64 344). In September the *Sagra Musicale Umbra* features sacred music in Perugia's churches. At other times the large student population brings in numerous concerts, films, and other performances, advertised on posters and bulletin boards around the universities.

If you're travelling with children, Perugia has a large brightly lit Fun Fair and Umbria's modest but sincerely meant 'Disneyland,' the **Città della Domenica**, just west of the city, with a miniature Africa, a serpentarium, bumper cars, and more (tel 754 941, open daily April–Sept, and weekends Oct–Mar). The nearest swimming-pool to the centre is at Via Pellini, tel 65 160.

WHERE TO STAY (tel prefix 075)

Perugia has several good hotel choices: *****__Brufani__, Piazza Italia 12, tel 62 541, is a renovated, traditional 19th-century hotel with fine views over the countryside and an attractive central courtyard. There's a private garage downstairs, and each very comfortable room is furnished with TV, frigo-bar and air conditioning (L250 000, up to L350 000 for a suite). Also in Piazza Italia, ****__La Rosetta__, tel 20 841, is another older hotel, deservedly popular, with a wide variety of rooms from various periods and remodellings. The hotel has a celebrated restaurant, and dining in the garden in the summer; the rooms, either modern or furnished with antiques, are cosy and quiet (L70 000 without bath, L120–150 000 with). Just below Piazza Italia, ***__Excelsior Lilli__, Via L. Masi 9, tel 20 241, is a fine, modern hotel with a garage, conveniently located near the escalators; rooms have optional air conditioning (L65 000 without bath, L85 000 with). When Goethe passed through Perugia he checked in at the ****__Della Posta__ on Corso Vannucci 97, tel 61 345, the oldest hotel in town, with an ornate exterior and pleasant, renovated rooms. It, too, has a private garage, and a frigo-bar and radio in each room (L100–280 000, depending on season). Also enjoying a good location just off Corso Vannucci, the ****__Fortuna__, Via Bonazzi 19, tel 22 845, has more comfort than charm; all rooms have bath and TV, and there's a garage (L100–140 000). The friendly and convenient **__Aurora__, Viale Indipendenza 21, tel 24 819, is only a minute's walk from Piazza Italia, on the main road up from the station. Rooms are rather spartan, but comfortable enough for a short stay (L40 000 without bath, L60 000 with). *__Etruria__, Via della Luna 21, tel 23 730, is a simple place just off Corso Vannucci (L32 000 without bath). Young people can check in at the **Centro Internazionale Accoglienza per Giovani**, near San Severo on Via Bontempi 13, tel 22 880, with bunk beds for L10 000 a night.

There are a couple of special places outside the city. Between Perugia and Deruta, Torgiano is the site of a Relais & Chateau inn called *****__Le Tre Vaselle__, Via Garibaldi 48, tel 982 447. A lovely villa set in the vineyards of the Lungarotti family, it is an exquisite place, though often frequented by conferences and symposiums. One of its attractions is a magnificent wine museum, run by the wife of the owner and open for visits (daily 9–12 and 3–7; adm); another is one of the finest gourmet restaurants in Umbria, serving the villa's own label of wine with its delicious meals; lovely, comfortable rooms, with air conditioning, frigo-bar, baby-sitting service, etc. (L200–270 000). Corciano, between Perugia and Lake Trasimeno, is the site of the ****Colle della Trinità, Loc. Fontana, tel 795 048, a pretty hotel in a fine setting, with a garden and tennis; each finely furnished room has a private bath, TV, and frigo-bar (L150 000).

EATING OUT

Besides the restaurant in the Hotel La Rosetta, Perugia has several fine places to eat. On 'Witch Street', Via delle Streghe, in the medieval quarter west of Corso Vannucci, **La Taverna**, tel 61 028, has an atmosphere matching its surroundings, and simple dishes from Umbria as well as the rest of Italy like succulent roast lamb, and a wide variety of pasta dishes with truffles and mushrooms (L35 000, closed Mon). Another fine old inn, **Falchetto**, Via Bartolo 20, tel 61 875, is near the cathedral. The kitchen features Umbrian specialities—salumeria, *crostini* (paté on toast), tagliatelle with truffles, *pasta e fagioli*, grilled lamb and trout, all well prepared and followed by tasty desserts (L35 000, closed Mon). **Priori**, in Via Vermiglioli off Via dei Priori, has very nice antipasti: ham and melon, *crostini con funghi*, before roast meats *all'arancia* (about L30 000, also a L16 000 menu). **Il Cantinone**, Via Ritroto 6, just behind the cathedral, tel 64 430, offers mostly simple things: spaghetti all'amatriciana, beans and sausage, also *filetto tartufato* (L25–30 000). Just off Piazza Italia on Via Cesare Caporali, **Trattoria Calzoni** is run by a kindly grandmother, and will take old-time travellers to Italy back with its plastic tablecloths and holy pictures, and simple but tasty meals for around L15 000. Another neighbourhood place, **Osteria del Pozzo**, Via Pinturicchio, tel 23 938 has *agnolotti* (semicircular ravioli) and other simple stuff on an L18 000 menu. In the same price range you can also have a jovial student atmosphere at **Fratelli Brizi**, Via Fabretti, near the Arco Augusto.

If you're not that hungry, you can go for a beer and banana break at the stands on Corso Matteotti, or go a-wine tasting of Umbrian vintages at the **Enoteca Provinciale** on Ulisse Rocchi 16, behind the cathedral, tel 24 824. **Pasticceria Sandri**, on Corso Vannucci, may be the fanciest pastry shop in Italy, with a pretty frescoed ceiling and divinely artistic confections; their window has more colours than the Pinacoteca across the street.

Città di Castello

From Perugia, most people travel on to Assisi or Spoleto. To be contrary, consider the opposite direction, northwards up the valley of old Father Tiber. Route 3 (bis), following the Tiber and the ancient Via Flaminia, carries you up into an enchanting, very Umbrian landscape of rolling hills and tobacco barns. Halfway to Città di Castello, **Umbertide** is a sprawling modern industrial town with a small but charming old centre, including a castle from the 1300s, the octagonal Renaissance church of S. Maria della Reggia, and pretty bridges over the Tiber. Just south of town, at the foot of Monte Corona, the **Badia di San Salvatore** is an interesting 12th-century building with an unusual campanile and some frescoes from the 1300s.

Città di Castello (pop. 38,000), the northernmost town of Umbria, started as a city of the ancient Umbrians, but reached the peak of its fortunes under the early Roman Empire, when as *Tifernum Tiberinum* it controlled trade in the upper Tiber valley. Medieval bishops built it into a fortress town, called at first *Castrum Felicitatis*. In the 1400s and 1500s, under the enlightened tyranny of the Vitelli family, the city attracted some of the best Renaissance artists to help in its decoration. Today, behind its 16th-century walls, it makes a living from industry and tobacco farming.

Within those walls, Città di Castello is a neat rectangle, still roughly following the street plan of ancient Tifernum. It offers the surprises of any little town in central Italy—for example the fine 1890s Art Nouveau bank building on Corso Cavour, just a block from the **Duomo**, which has exactly one half of a harmonious Baroque façade; most of the building went up in the 1400s, though parts of the original Romanesque cathedral remain, especially an intriguing round campanile, inspired by the ancient towers of Ravenna (and just as tilted as any of them). Inside, the mystical altarpiece of the risen Christ is by Rosso Fiorentino, who took refuge here with the Vitelli during the sack of Rome in 1527. The cathedral museum has objects from the 6th-century 'treasure of Canoscio' and a lovely 12th-century altarpiece (daily 8–12, 3–dusk; adm). The little Piazza in front of the Duomo faces a small park, built on the site of a demolished papal fortress, and also the **Torre Civico**, an old tower-fortress with the city's medieval prisons (daily exc Mon, 10–1, 3:30–6 pm; adm).

The Pinacoteca

Despite all the good pictures in this unique little museum, the people who run it are still in mourning for their lost Raphaels—works like the *Betrothal of the Virgin* and several more, stolen by Napoleon; one Raphael remains, a half-ruined, barely competent early canvas that would never have been noticed without the famous name. Don't let that discourage you; there are plenty of other attractions, beginning with the building itself, built in the 1520s by Antonio da Sangallo the Younger and decorated with *sgraffito* by Giorgio Vasari—a very nice façade, facing the inner gardens, suggesting that Vasari could do a good job on things he didn't take too seriously. (The former Vitelli gardens are now the yard of the museum keeper; mind the dog.)

Many of the oldest paintings here show a Sienese or Venetian influence, such as the residual 14th-century Gothic Madonnas of Antonio Vivarini and Giovanni d'Alemagna. Florence's Lorenzo Ghiberti puts in a rare guest appearance with an equally Gothic golden reliquary. From the Renaissance, there is a *Coronation of the Virgin* from the workshop of Domenico Ghirlandaio, a strange Virgin by an unknown follower of Pontormo, altarpieces by a local boy, Francesco Tifernate, and a good comical kitsch piece, an anonymous *Quo Vadis*. Probably the best of the lot is the *San Sebastiano* by Luca Signorelli and his workshop—a fascinating work with fantasy Roman ruins and a truly surreal treatment of space (or were Signorelli's students just practising random backgrounds?).

The sculpture collection includes some fine early medieval woodcarving, or mixtures of painting and wooden sculpture; especially an altarpiece of the Crucifixion with the Virgin Mary and the Magdalene, the sun and moon—the wooden crucifix has disappeared, but the work is strangely suggestive without it. Some parts of the original palace remain, including a painted ceiling on the stairs, and a frescoed room with period furnishings from the 1400s (the museum is on Via della Canoniera 22, on the southern end of town; daily exc Mon 10–12, 4–5; adm). Watch out for another 'museum' in town, devoted to the works of a contemporary painter named Alberto Burri.

North of the town, the next stop in the Tiber Valley is Sansepolcro in Tuscany (see p. 373). Just before that town, **San Giustino** has a beautiful castle, the **Castello Bufalini**, begun in the 1200s and converted into an elegant seignorial mansion by Vasari.

WHERE TO STAY AND EAT (tel prefix 075)

The central *****Tiferno**, Piazza R. Sanzio 13, tel 855 0331, is the best place to stay and dine in Città di Castello, with good comfortable rooms, a private garage, and one of the best restaurants in the area, with dishes like ravioli with shrimp in orange sauce, or pigeon with white grapes—not perhaps, for everyone! (rooms L45 000 without bath, L75 000 with, meals L40 000 maybe more.) If the Tiferno is too much, try the **Pizza & Griglio** on Via Angelari (L13–16 000 for pizza or hamburgers). Umbertide has a simple central hotel with an equally simple restaurant, the ****Capponi**, Piazza 25 Aprile 2, tel 932 256; rooms L38–55 000 depending on private bath.

Gubbio

In a way, Gubbio (pop. 33,000) is what Umbria has always wanted to be: stony, taciturn and mystical, a tough mountain town that fought its own battles until destiny and the popes caught up with it—also a town of culture, one that had its own school of painters. For a city over 2500 years old it still seems like a frontier town, an elemental city that sticks in the memory: the green mountainside, a rushing stream, straight rows of rugged grey stone houses. On Gubbio's windy mountainside, the delicate hills and subtle towns of Tuscany seem a world away. Somehow, though, the hard-edged brilliance of the Italian Middle Ages seems much closer.

Panorama, Gubbio

History

Unlike Perugia, Gubbio really was a city of the ancient Umbrians, perhaps their political and religious centre. In Roman times it flourished, under the name *Iguvium*, but unsolicited visits by the Goths, Huns, and Avars left the place in such a mess that the surviving Eugubians decided to move their town to a more defensible site on the nearby hillside. As soon as the wall was up, they began annoying their neighbours; the chronicles paint a picture of medieval Gubbio as a tough, querulous town, a fitting rival for Perugia. At one point, in the 1150s, no less than twelve Umbrian cities under Frederick Barbarossa combined to put an end to Gubbio; the city was saved from destruction by its bishop, now San Ubaldo, who persuaded the emperor to leave in peace.

The chroniclers also claimed for Gubbio a population of 50,000—probably double the real figure but still quite large for a medieval town. As in every other city, there was continuous conflict between the *comune* and ambitious nobles. One of them, Giovanni Gabrielli, became *signore* of the town in 1350, but only four years later Cardinal Albornoz and his papal army snatched it away from him. In 1387, it fell to Urbino's Dukes of Montefeltro, who ruled it well until their line became extinct in 1508. Gubbio remained part of the Duchy of Urbino until 1624, when it became part of the Papal State.

One famous visitor to Gubbio was Saint Francis, who found the city plagued by wolves, one of which in particular was ravaging the countryside and terrorizing the populace. St Francis heard of it while in town, and ignoring the townspeople's pleas for his safety, went out and had a word with the wolf, brought it to town, and made a public agreement that it would stop terrorizing Gubbio in exchange for regular meals, an agreement sealed with a shake of the paw. The wolf kept its part of the bargain, and is immortalized in a bas-relief over the door of a little church on Via Maestro Giorgio. A few years ago, while workmen were repairing another church, the skeleton of a giant wolf was discovered buried under a slab.

Gubbio has retained some exceedingly medieval festivals that fill its solemn streets with colour and exuberance, most tumultuously the famous festival of the *Ceri*, held every 15 May in honour of San Ubaldo, Gubbio's patron. The festa is first documented a couple of years after Ubaldo saved the city from Emperor Frederick, although it seems to have been adapted from a pagan celebration. The *Ceri* (or 'Candles') are three tall, wooden and rather phallic towers, each topped by a wax saint—San Ubaldo, San Giorgio, and Sant'Antonio Abate, each representing a clan. The *Ceri* are baptized wtih a jug of water, and then carried on supports by teams of 10 men. The climax of the day is when the teams race pell-mell through the crowds up to the mountaintop church of San Ubaldo, a steep race that San Ubaldo invariably wins (and what could be more Italian than a fixed race?). On the last Sunday in May, crossbowmen from Sansepolcro come to compete in the *Palio della Balestra*, a contest and fierce rivalry dating back to 1461.

GETTING AROUND

There are no trains, but some 10 ASP coaches along beautiful N. 298 to Perugia (40 km/1 hr) from the central Piazza Quaranta Martiri where schedules are posted. Also buses to the closest train station, 20 km south at Fossato di Vico, on the Foligno-Ancona line, to Rome, and a line to Città di Castello-Arezzo-Florence. There is a bus and train information office for all of the above at Via della Repubblica 13, tel 927 1544.

TOURIST INFORMATION
Piazza Oderisi, tel (075) 927 3693.
Post Office: Via Cairoli 11.
Telephones: Via della Repubblica 13.

Gubbio, from the bottom up

Approaching Gubbio from the west, the first thing you see is the large, well-preserved 1st-century AD **Roman Amphitheatre**; besides the seats, much of the arcades remains standing. The theatre is used these days for summer performances of ancient Greek and Roman plays and Shakespeare. Once this was the centre of Roman Iguvium, now open pastureland. The view of Gubbio from here is better than the one from up on Monte Ingino; the city's stone houses climb the slope in neat parallel rows, with the tall Palazzo dei Consoli on its massive platform dominating the centre. Gubbio proper is entered by way of the green **Piazza Quaranta Martiri**, the most important square in the lower town, named in memory of the 40 citizens gunned down on this spot by the Nazis in reprisals for partisan activities. To the west, the church of **San Francesco** has a distinctive Gothic design with a triple apse and an octagonal campanile; it is the work of the Perugian architect Fra Bevignate, and it closely resembles some of the churches of Ascoli Piceno in the Marches. Some good frescoes are inside, especially the 15th-century series on the Madonna in the left apse, by Gubbio's greatest painter, Ottaviano Nelli (1375–1440). On the other side of the piazza is the **Tiratoio**, or Weaver's Loggia, a 14th-century arcade under which newly woven textiles could be stretched to shrink evenly—one of the few such loggias to survive.

Palazzo dei Consoli

From the piazza the streets ascend past picturesque medieval lanes on the banks of the rushing Camignano. Many of the houses and modest palazzi date back to the 13th century, here and there adorned with carved doors or windows, or 'Death's doors' as in Perugia. The main street, the Via dei Consoli, passes by the 13th-century **Bargello**, the combined police station and governor's office; its fountain used to be Gubbio's main water source. Further up, the street widens to form the magnificent **Piazza della Signoria**, occupying a ledge of the hill, its belvedere hovering over a steep drop and a stunning view of the town below. The king of the piazza is the beautiful **Palazzo dei Consoli**, a lofty, graceful town hall begun in 1332 by Gubbio's master architect Gattapone (*consolo*, a word derived from the Roman *consul*, was a common title for an officer of a free medieval *comune*). Supported on the hill by a mighty substructure of arches, the palazzo is graced with an elegant loggia, a slender campanile, square Guelph crenellations, asymmetrically arranged windows and arches. Inside are the town museums (9–1 and 3–5, summer 9–12:30 and 3:30–6; adm): first the **Museo Civico**, a cluttered, fascinating place that resembles an indoor flea market, with archaeological odds and ends, tombstones, and crossbows deposited every which way. There is a Roman inscription—Governor Gnaeus Satirus Rufus bragging how much he spent to embellish the town—and a collection of seals and coins from the days when Gubbio minted its own. One unique treasure, the bronze *Eugubine Tables*, the only inscriptions ever found in the Umbrian language, were discovered in the 15th century beside the

Roman theatre. Partly written in the Latin alphabet, partly in the Umbrian, these tables are codes of religious observances and ritual; one of them instructs apprentice augurs on how to take readings from the livers of sacrificed animals and the flight of birds.

The **Pinacoteca** upstairs is just as quirky and charming, though there are few really good pictures: a 13th-century diptych, in a Byzantine-style portable altar, a *Tree of Jesse* by an unknown cinquecento Gubbio artist, the beautiful *Madonna del Melograno*, a quattrocento Florentine painting, and an anonymous work of the 1600s called the *Last Night of Babylon*. It's one of the best crazy paintings in Italy, and it deserves a good cleaning. The rooms of the Pinacoteca are an attraction in themselves; some haven't seen any remodelling since the 1500s.

At the top of the town stands Gubbio's simple **Duomo**, built in the 13th century and most notable for the unusual pointed wagon vaulting of the nave, a Eugubine speciality, and for its 12th-century stained-glass windows. Many Gubbio artists are represented in the paintings in the side chapels, along with a *Nativity* by Pinturicchio's student Eusebio di San Giorgio. Perhaps the best works are in the **museum**: a damaged 14th-century fresco of the *Crucifixion* and a beautiful 16th-century Flemish cope, magnificently embroidered and presented to the cathedral by Pope Marcellus II, a native of Gubbio. The **Palazzo Ducale**, facing the cathedral, was designed for Federico da Montefeltro by Luciano Laurana, as a more compact version of the ducal palace in Urbino. The courtyard is well worth a look, even though the rest of the palace is at the time of writing closed for restoration (9–2, closed Mon). Around the corner on Via Ducale, you can peek into an old cellar under the cathedral to see the **Botte dei Canonici**, a house-sized barrel from the 1500s that once held some 40,000 litres of wine, a masterpiece of the cooper's art (it was made without nails) and a winebibber's impossible dream.

Some other Eugubine attractions: on the western end of town, the 13th-century **Palazzo del Capitano del Popolo**, a no-nonsense Romanesque structure; nearby are one of the equally simple city gates and a surviving medieval tower-fortress. Two blocks to the south, on Piazza S. Martino, **San Domenico** is an earlier Romanesque church taken over by the Dominicans in the 1300s. Only bits of the trecento frescoes remain, along with an exceptional Renaissance intarsia reading stand. Two churches on the eastern end of town, near the Porta Romana, contain works by Gubbio's Ottaviano Nelli. In **Santa Maria Nuova** is the joyous, worldly *Madonna del Belvedere*, while the 13th-century **Sant'Agostino**, just outside the gate, has more works by Nelli and his followers, including a *Last Judgement* and a series on the life of St Augustine. Finally, the spot where Francis met the wolf, just south of town on Viale della Vittorina, is marked by the **Vittorina** church; the charming interior has another odd nave with pointed vaulting and some early frescoes undisturbed by the remodelling in the 1500s.

On Monte Ingino

From the cathedral you can make the stiff climb up Monte Ingino to the church of **San Ubaldo**, but it's much easier to take the **funivia** up from the Porta Romana on the southeast side of town. In San Ubaldo, you can't take a close look at the three *Ceri*, without wondering that the Eugubini need a considerable amount of Dutch courage to run up the mountain lugging these towers on their shoulders. There's a café where you can while away the afternoon, or you can walk a bit further up for even more spectacular views from the **Rocca** (888 m).

SHOPPING

Medieval Gubbio made its living from ceramics, a craft that's still flourishing today. In the 16th century, this tradition produced a real artist, Mastro Giorgio Andreoli, who discovered a beautiful ruby glaze for his majolica plates (you'll notice the absence of red in most painted ceramics; for some reason it's very hard to do). Mastro Giorgio's secret died with him, but Gubbio's artist-craftsmen still turn out some of the most beautiful ceramic ware in Italy, carefully hand-painted in colourful, original floral designs. Some of their best work is too big to fit in your suitcase—majolica lamps and telephone stands, for example—but there are simple plates in every size for a souvenir. Perhaps the most artistic work is done at the **Fabbrica Ranimi** and at the **Fabbrica Mastro Giorgio**, both on Via dei Consoli. The shop down the street at no. 44 has some less extravagant work; beautiful plaques and plates at lower prices.

WHERE TO STAY (tel prefix 075)

Though not yet in the same league as Assisi, Gubbio gets its share of visitors; day trippers from Perugia looking for the essential Umbria make reservations in July and August essential—otherwise you're bound to be disappointed. A good place in central Gubbio, the ***Bosone**, Via XX Settembre 22, tel 927 2008, is conveniently located in a picturesque setting. Rooms are comfortable, though not brilliant, and there's a private garage for your car (L70–85 000, all with bath). *****San Marco**, Via Perugina 5, tel 927 2349, has modern comforts and a pretty garden terrace at the back. All rooms have bath and there's parking nearby (L68 000). ****Dei Consoli**, Via dei Consoli 59, tel 927 3335, near the Piazza della Signoria, is small and simple, but enjoys an excellent location (L60 000 with bath). It also has a good restaurant in a medieval cellar, with tasty *spiedini* (meat on a spit) for L30 000. ****Gattapone**, Via G. Ansidei 6, tel 927 2489, is another pleasant locale in the central medieval zone. All rooms have private bath, and there's a small garden at the back (L55–65 000). ***Locanda Galletti**, Via Ambrogio Piccardi 1, overlooking the river, tel 927 4247, has rooms for L33–48 000. There's a restaurant here, with outdoor tables in a beautiful setting—roast duck and lamb for L25 000.

EATING OUT

Gubbio has no good wines, but there are local poisons like Amaro Iguvium and Liquore Ingeno to top off a meal. For a taste of tradition in Gubbio, dine at the **Fornace di Mastro Giorgio**, in the workshop where the master ceramist once created his famous ruby glaze (Via della Fornace di Mastro Giorgio, tel 927 5740). The cuisine combines the best traditions of Apulia and Umbria, with seafood (rare in Umbria) on Thursday and Friday and pungent delicacies like *tagliolini alle alici* (with anchovies) or Umbrian pigeon with olives, topped off by delicious desserts (L30 000, or L40 000 for a gourmet *menu degustazione*; closed Mon). Another classic eatery recalls the legend of St Francis: the **Taverna del Lupo**, Via Ansidei 21a, tel 927 4368, a beautifully medieval place, where you can dine on such traditional fare as boar sausage, game in the autumn, and *risotto dei tartufi* (Gubbio, like Piedmont, is a land of white truffles, which are even more expensive than the black truffles of the Valnerina in southern Umbria), as well as delicious pasta dishes like lasagne with prosciutto and truffles and *Frico*, a local speciality of mixed meats with cress (L35–40 000). On a clear day, the restaurant **Funivia**, on Monte Ingino, tel 927 3464, is an exceptional dining experience, offering fabulous views as well as delicious pasta with truffles or porcini mushrooms, and tasty secondi like grilled lamb or stuffed pigeon. Good desserts and local wines (L35 000; closed Wed). **Del Peppe**, on the west end of Via dei Consoli, features dishes like *anatra in porchetta* and green gnocchi on Fridays and spaghetti with vegetables (*all'ortolana*), for around L35 000. **Ristorante Pizzeria S. Francesco e Il Lupo**, Via Cairoli 24, tel 927 2344 features local products, including prosciutto, porcini mushrooms, and truffles for around L30 000, or a L17 000 menu—or you can just order pizza. **Del Bargello**, Via dei Consoli 37, at Largo Bargello, tel 927 3724, is another ristorante-pizzeria, offering good choices with polenta (quite popular in this corner of Umbria), *agnolotti, agnello scottadito* (burn-your-fingers lamb) and other grilled meats (L30 000, also a L13 000 menu).

Excursions from Gubbio

This is not a densely populated part of Umbria: long stretches of empty space punctuated by an occasional half-ruined castle or monastery, and with the very plainest of mountain villages. East (22 km on N. 298) of the city, **Monte Cucco** (1567 m) is a popular spot with the Eugubini on summer weekends, with pretty mountain meadows and beech forests in the area of Pian di Ranco. There's also a cave full of stalactites and stalagmites, the **Grotto di Monte Cucco**, reached by a long iron stair (bring a torch). **Sigillo**, south on the N. 3, the village where the more southerly mountain road begins, has some frescoes by the local painter Matteo da Gualdo (see below) in its church of S. Anna, and remains of a small single-arch Roman bridge. Two interesting monasteries in the area: the **Hermitage of Fonte Avellana** (30 km east, off N. 360) is really just over the border in the Marches, in an isolated mountain setting above Sassoferrato. This was an important centre of learning in the Middle Ages (Dante and Guido Monaco of Arezzo both visited), and almost nothing has changed since the 12th century. Perhaps unique in Italy, it preserves the *scriptorium* where books were copied. The second, the **Castel d'Alfiolo**, 6 km south of Gubbio on N. 219, was converted from a family fortress to a Benedictine abbey in the 1100s; most of the buildings were redone in the 16th century, but the chapel and the main building conserve some good stonecarving from the 1200s.

Down the Via Flaminia

The ancient Via Flaminia (N. 3) was a Roman road of conquest in the old days; even in the Dark Ages the Goths and Lombards kept it in repair, an important highway linking Ravenna, Spoleto, and Rome. For all that, there's little to see on this mountainous stretch. **Gualdo Tadino**, an ancient Umbrian town mentioned in the Eugubine tables, was called *Tadinum* in Roman times. The squat but well-proportioned **Duomo** has a good façade of 1256, and a small **Pinacoteca** has been installed in the old church of San Francesco (they keep the key at the police station). Here some of the best works are frescoes by Matteo da Gualdo, a local boy of the quattrocento given to brilliant colouring (and, as critics liked to sniff a century ago, 'incorrect drawing'). Another of his paintings, a glowing triptych, can be seen in the church of **S. Maria** on Piazza XX Settembre. Gualdo's castle, the **Rocca Flea**, was begun by Emperor Frederick II, and is considerably larger than its name suggests.

More Matteo da Gualdo can be seen in the Pinacoteca (8–2, 3–7; adm) in **Nocera Umbra**, a town that ships fizzy mineral water all over Italy, and still has enough left over for two small spas outside town. The **Pinacoteca**, like Gualdo Tadino's, is in a church of San Francesco, and contains another excellent *Nativity* by L'Alunno, the master of nearby Foligno, as well as works by Matteo da Gualdo and a set of Roman milestones.

ASSISI

Visible for miles around, Assisi (pop. 25,000) sweeps the flanks of Monte Subasio in a broad curve like a pink ship sailing over the green sea of a valley below. This is Umbria's most famous hilltown, and one of its loveliest, but there's more to it than just St Francis. A wealthy Roman *municipium* that survived the invasions intact, the city came into prominence again in the Middle Ages as another of Umbria's battling *comuni*, mostly saving its bile for incessant wars with arch-rival Perugia. The 13th century, the century of St Francis and the great religious revival he helped begin, was also the time of Assisi's greatest power and prosperity, leaving behind a collection of beautiful buildings any Italian city could be proud of. Nevertheless, it was Francis who made all the difference to Assisi. Five million pilgrims and tourists crowded its narrow streets for Francis's 500th birthday year, 1982, and on any day this summer you'll see (besides an overflow of tourists) flocks of serene Franciscans and enthusiastic, almost bouncy nuns from Africa or Missouri or Bavaria, having the time of their lives visiting a place that, much more than Rome, is the symbol of a living faith.

Regardless of all that happened before or since, St Francis illuminated this city with his clear and remarkable faith, and despite all the efforts of the Church and the souvenir sellers to turn it into a Disneyland of the faith, this is still his city. Something simple and good has survived these seven centuries in Assisi, something that would edify the soul of any cynic who cares to linger—the great joyousness Francis bequeathed Assisi along with his piety. Recently, the city has been host to some unusual demonstrations of faith that could never have happened in Rome, or anywhere else—in 1986, when the Pope hosted his inter-faith World Day of Prayer, complete with Tibetan lamas, Zoroastrians, and American Indian medicine men, and most recently during the 1988 Umbria Jazz Festival, when black gospel choirs from New Orleans sang in the upper church of San Francesco. The friars in charge would only let them sing for fifteen minutes at a time, sincerely fearing that the rhythm might bring down the roof and Giotto's frescoes with it. Providence saw that the building came to no harm, and by the end the cheerful Franciscans were clapping their hands along with everyone else.

St Francis of Assisi

The man who started it all was the son of a wealthy Assisi merchant, Pietro Bernardone, and his Provençal wife, Madonna Pica. Some say Pietro was the richest man in town; he travelled often through the south of France, buying and selling fine cloth, and he named his son Francesco after the country he loved so well. His wealth financed a merry and dissipated youth for Francesco; according to his first biographer, an early Franciscan convert named Celano, he was 'the first instigator of every evil, and behind none in foolishness'. He was also a poet, a troubadour, his French upbringing giving him an early

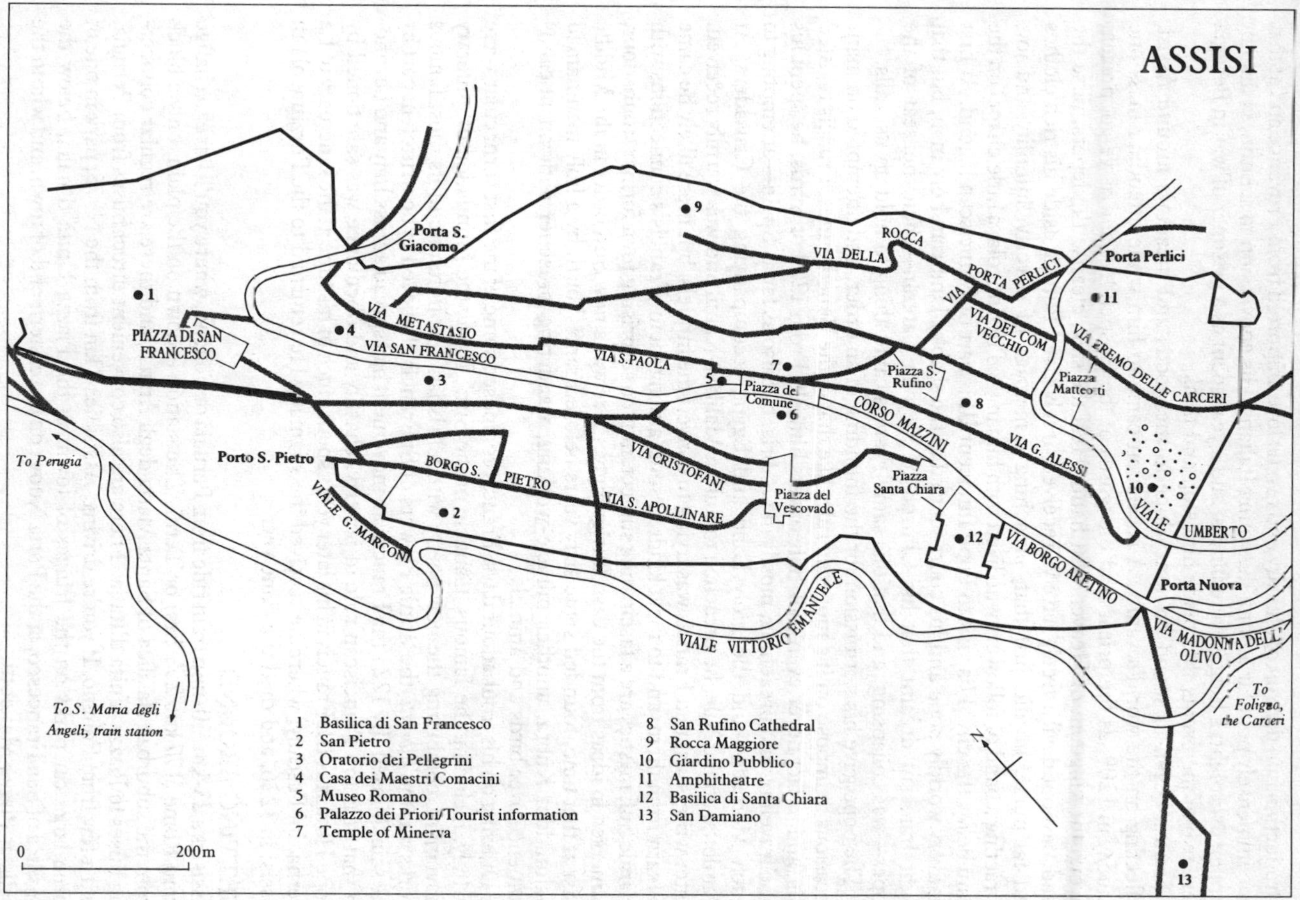
ASSISI
Porta S. Giacomo
Porta Perlici
PIAZZA DI SAN FRANCESCO
VIA METASTASIO
VIA SAN FRANCESCO
VIA S.PAOLA
VIA DELLA ROCCA
VIA PORTA PERLICI
VIA DEL COM VECCHIO
VIA EREMO DELLE CARCERI
Piazza S. Rufino
Piazza Matteotti
Piazza del Comune
CORSO MAZZINI
VIA G. ALESSI
Porto S. Pietro
BORGO S. PIETRO
VIA CRISTOFANI
Piazza del Vescovado
Piazza Santa Chiara
VIA S. APOLLINARE
VIALE G. MARCONI
VIALE UMBERTO
VIA BORGO ARETINO
Porta Nuova
VIALE VITTORIO EMANUELE
VIA MADONNA DELL' OLIVO
To Perugia
To S. Maria degli Angeli, train station
To Foligno, the Carceri
N
0
200m
1 Basilica di San Francesco
2 San Pietro
3 Oratorio dei Pellegrini
4 Casa dei Maestri Comacini
5 Museo Romano
6 Palazzo dei Priori/Tourist information
7 Temple of Minerva
8 San Rufino Cathedral
9 Rocca Maggiore
10 Giardino Pubblico
11 Amphitheatre
12 Basilica di Santa Chiara
13 San Damiano

introduction into the cult of chivalry and mystic love, imported from Provence and at that time immensely popular among the young Italians. His conversion to saintliness did not happen overnight; a long, severe illness, and a year spent as a prisoner of war in Perugia were two of the events that made him stop and think.

Francis began to spend his time alone in the woods and meadows around Assisi, reflecting on the world's vanity. A revelation came to him while attending mass one Sunday in 1209, as the priest read the words of the Gospel: '. . . and as ye go, preach, saying, the kingdom of Heaven is at hand. Heal the sick, cleanse the lepers, raise the dead, cast out devils: freely have ye received, freely give.' Putting aside his rich clothes and fat purse, he did just that, preaching a message of poverty, humility and joy, attracting a band of followers who lived with him in the Porziuncola, a little chapel on the plain below the city. His visit to Pope Innocent III is part of Franciscan legend. At first that very worldly pope and his court scoffed at the shabby Umbrian holy man, but that night Innocent dreamt that his Church of St John Lateran—then the seat of the popes—was collapsing, and that this same Francis came along to hold up its walls.

The pope gave his permission for the founding of an order, and attempted on many occasions to impose on it a monastic rule, like that of the Benedictines. Francis resisted this, and in fact never even took holy orders himself. From 1209 onwards, he spent his time travelling and preaching, mostly in Umbria, but also as far as Spain—attempting to reach Morocco—and the Holy Land and Egypt, accompanying the Crusaders. At Damietta, on the Nile, he preached to Sultan Malik el-Kamil and was warmly received. Later writers claimed Francis was trying to convert the infidels, but more likely he came to learn from them, and to meet kindred souls among them. Francis's connections with Islamic Sufi mystics are a fascinating subject, not too surprising for a former troubadour, immersed in ideas from the east. Intriguingly, there was a new Sufi order in the Middle East at that time, founded some sixty years before Francis' birth by a holy man named Najmuddin Kubra, another miracle-working, wandering preacher with an uncanny influence over birds and animals

Drawing on his troubadour days, Francis composed some of the first vernacular verse in Italy, including the famous 'Canticle of the Sun'. It was the foundation of a literary movement, combining the new poetry with Christian devotion; one of its most famous works was the *Fioretti*, the 'Little Flowers of St Francis', believed to be written in part by the saint himself. By 1221 the Franciscan movement had spread across Italy and beyond. In that year the Franciscan rule of poverty, chastity and obedience was sanctioned by Pope Honorius III. Francis in his later years spent much of his time at the sanctuary of La Verna, in Tuscany, where he received the stigmata. He returned to the Porziuncola in Assisi in 1226, and died the same year.

GETTING AROUND

Assisi is a 23-km/30-min train ride from Perugia or Foligno, where you'll have to change from Rome (177 km/2½ hrs) or Terni. The station is down on the plain, only a block from the suburban Basilica of Santa Maria degli Angeli, and there are regular connecting buses to Piazza Unità d'Italia. There are also convenient direct buses from Perugia, and a few from Foligno. If you're driving, Assisi lies 7 km from the N. 75; park in one of three large car parks on the fringes of town: in the Piazza Unità d'Italia, below the Basilica of San Francesco, at the Porta Nuova on the eastern end of town, and within the walls at Piazza Matteotti.

TOURIST INFORMATION

Piazza del Comune 12, tel (075) 812 450.

The Basilica of San Francesco

Although the popes were originally mistrustful of the spontaneous, personal approach to faith preached by Francis and his followers, they soon realized that this movement would be better off within the Church than outside it. In transforming the Franciscans into a respectable, doctrinally safe arm of the Church, they had the invaluable aid of Francis's successor, Brother Elias, Vicar-General of the Order, a worldly, businesslike man, something of an epicurean and a friend of Emperor Frederick II. Elias's methods caused the first split within the Franciscans, between those who enjoyed the growing opulence of the new dispensation and those who tried to keep to the original simplicity and poverty of St Francis. This monumental building complex, begun the day after Francis's canonization in 1228, was one of the biggest causes of contention. Nothing could have been further removed from the philosophy and intentions of Francis himself; on the other hand, nothing could have been more successful in perpetuating the memory of Francis and his teaching. And with its remarkable frescoes, by Giotto and many other trecento masters, the Basilica is one of the greatest monuments of Italian art.

From the beginning, the popes were entirely behind the effort. They paid for it by promoting a great sale of special indulgences across Europe. There's a story that Brother Elias himself supplied the design—maybe he did, for the building does have an amateurish, clumsy form, one of the less successful attempts to transplant the Gothic style on Italian soil. As in many Assisi churches, the façade projects above the roofline like a storefront in a wild west town, to make the building look more imposing. The usual approach to the basilica is from the Piazza Inferiore, lined with arcades where medieval pilgrims bought their souvenirs before returning home. The grandest entrance is the one to the Lower Church, with a Renaissance portico of 1487 covering a fine Gothic portal.

THE LOWER CHURCH

With its low dark vaults, it seems at first to be a simple crypt, though once your eyes adjust to the dim light you can see that they are covered with beautiful frescoes by the masters of the 13th and 14th centuries (bring plenty of L100 coins and a torch to illuminate them). In the first chapel to the left are relics of the saint—an autographed letter, his humble habit and sandals, and Honorius III's Papal Bull authorizing the Franciscan Rule. The first chapel to the left of the frescoed nave contains magnificent frescoes on the *Life of St Martin* by Simone Martini, painted around 1322, while the third chapel on the right contains frescoes on the *Life of Mary Magdalene*, attributed to Giotto (1314). All of the frescoes attributed to Giotto in Assisi, dating from 1295, constitute one of the longest-raging controversies in the history of art. The Italian faction is convinced that the frescoes in the lower and upper churches are the climax of Giotto's early career, while most foreign scholars believe Giotto didn't paint them at all. Whatever the case, Martini's 'International Gothic-style' poses are a serious artistic challenge to the great precursor of the Renaissance. This master of line and colour, whom Berenson called the 'most lovable painter of the pre-Renaissance', creates a wonderful narrative of St Martin's life; the Gaulish soldier and wastrel who ended up as a bishop and split his cloak to give half to a beggar seems a perfect foreshadowing of St Francis.

Giotto is also credited with the four beautiful *allegorical frescoes* over the high altar, depicting Poverty, Chastity, Obedience, and the Glory of St Francis. Note the *Marriage of St Francis with Lady Poverty*, one of the most striking images ever to come out of the 13th-century religious revival. In the left transept are fine works by Pietro Lorenzetti of Siena, among the best in the basilica, especially the lovely *Madonna della Tramontana* ('of the sunset') *with St Francis and St John*, a *Crucifixion* and a *Descent from the Cross*. In the right transept is Cimabue's *Madonna and Saints*, with a famous portrait of St Francis (1280), believed to be an accurate likeness; a serious-looking female saint nearby, by Simone Martini, is believed to be St Clare.

In the **Crypt** lie the bones of St Francis and four of his closest followers, discovered only in 1818. Brother Elias, worried that the Perugians would come to steal the saint's body, hid it with exceeding care, behind tons of stone. His fears were not unfounded; when Francis was coming back from La Verna to die, the Perugians (who never listened when Francis came to preach) were waiting to kidnap him along the road; Brother Elias had the foresight to direct Francis on a longer route. From the transepts, stairs lead up to a terrace and the **Museo-Tesoro della Basilica** (9:30–12:30 and 2:30–6, closed Mon and Nov–Mar; adm), containing what wasn't pillaged or pinched from the treasury through the centuries—a beautiful Venetian cross, a French ivory Madonna from the 13th century, a Flemish tapestry with St Francis, and more.

THE UPPER CHURCH

In comparison with the lower church, the **Upper Church**, facing its emerald-green lawn, is strikingly bright and airy, and dazzles with its colour. Here, under the azure, star-spangled ceiling are two major series of medieval frescoes, the lower set on the *Life of St Francis* by Giotto or his school, and the upper, with *Old and New Testament scenes*, attributed to Rome's Pietro Cavallini. What makes most Italian scholars attribute the St Francis frescoes to Giotto is the artist's mastery of composition; Giotto amazed his contemporaries with his ability to illustrate the physical and spiritual essentials of a scene with simplicity and drama, cutting directly to the core of the matter. The scenes begin with the young *St Francis honoured by the simple man*, who lays down his cloak and foretells the saint's destiny (note Assisi's Temple of Minerva in the background); Francis returns his clothes to his father, who in his anger and disappointment has to be restrained; Pope Innocent III has a dream of Francis supporting the falling Church; the demons are expelled from Arezzo by Brother Sylvester; Francis meets the Sultan of Egypt; he creates the first Christmas crib, or *presepio*, at Greccio; he preaches to the attentive birds, and then to Pope Honorius III; he appears in two places at the same time, and next, receives the stigmata from a six-winged cherub; he dies, bewailed by the Poor Clares, and is canonized.

The transepts were painted by Giotto's master, Cimabue, though the works have deteriorated into mere shadows, or negatives of their former selves. Look especially at the *Crucifixion* on the left, a faded masterpiece still radiating some of its original drama and feeling. Behind the basilica, propped up on huge arches, the enormous convent is now used as a missionary college.

To the Piazza del Comune: the Temple of Minerva

On entering Assisi, through the main road from the car park, you may have noticed the excellent façade of **San Pietro**, just inside the gate of the same name (down Via Frate Elia from the piazza of the lower basilica). This Benedictine church was built in the 1200s, though Assisi's chroniclers date the original building back to the 2nd century; relics of Assisi's first bishop, San Vittoriano, are kept inside.

From the upper basilica, Via San Francesco leads up past many fine medieval houses to the centre of Assisi. On the way there are several buildings of note: no. 14, the Masons' Guild, or **Casa dei Maestri Comacini** (since most of those who built the basilica came from Como); no. 11, the pretty frescoed **Oratorio dei Pellegrini**, a 15th-century gem surviving from a hospice built for pilgrims; some of the chapel's frescoes are by Matteo da Gualdo. At no. 3, the **Monte Frumentario** began as a 13th-century hospital, later converted into a granary. Next to it is a 16th-century fountain, still bearing the warning that the penalty for washing clothes here is one *scudo* and confiscation of laundry. Near the entrance of the Piazza del Comune is the **Museo Romano**, located in the crypt of a now-vanished church, with a small collection of Etruscan urns. A passageway from the museum leads into the ancient **Roman forum**, which lies directly under the piazza. Currently work is going on to excavate the forum entirely underground—leaving the piazza above intact.

Piazza del Comune

This long attractive square, the medieval centre of Assisi, is embellished with 13th-century buildings of the old *comune*: the **Torre and Palazzo del Comune**, the **Palazzo del Capitano del Popolo**, and what at first looks like a decrepit bank building but is in reality a Roman **Temple of Minerva**, its Corinthian columns and travertine steps incorporated into what is now the church of Santa Maria. When Goethe (a muddle-headed classicist who felt a national embarrassment whenever he heard the word 'Gothic') came to Assisi it was to see this—and nothing else. It is the best surviving Roman temple façade on the Italian peninsula, sitting on its square in the exact position it had in the ancient forum, as good as any ruin in Rome for helping your imagination conjure up the classical world. Only the façade remains from the original work; inside you'll be treated to some eccentric Baroque.

The Palazzo del Comune contains the **Pinacoteca Civica** (9–12, also winter and Sun 4–7, closed Mon), with a sleepy collection of Umbrian Renaissance art. To the left of the Palazzo, the **Chiesa Nuova** was built by Philip III of Spain on property owned by St Francis's father; the **Oratorio di San Francesco Piccolino** (of 'Little baby St Francis') is believed to mark the saint's birthplace.

Upper Assisi: the Cathedral and Castle

Most visitors labour under the mistaken impression that the Basilica of St Francis is Assisi's cathedral, and never find their way up Via di S. Rufino from the Piazza del Comune to the real **Cattedrale di San Rufino**. This has a huge campanile and a beautiful Romanesque façade, the finest in Assisi, designed by Giovanni da Gubbio in 1140 and adorned with fine rose windows and the kind of robust medieval carvings of animals and saints that Goethe so disdained. Inside, it houses the porphyry font where SS. Francis and Clare were baptized, as well as Emperor Frederick II, who was born nearby in Jesi, in the Marches. It is an amazing coincidence that the two leading figures of the 13th century should have been baptized in the same place; the holy water must have had a special Moslem essence to it, to connect these two figures so profoundly influenced by the East. The rest of the interior was restored in the 16th century, and still waits for an unrestoration to clear all the clutter and bring it back to its original state. The cathedral has a small **Museum** (9–1 and 4–7; adm), with paintings by Matteo da Gualdo and L'Alunno; the same ticket lets you explore the ancient crypt and cloister. Don't miss the Roman cistern directly under the cathedral's campanile.

From the cathedral, it's a bracing walk up to the **Rocca Maggiore**, Assisi's well-preserved castle, built in 1174 and used by Conrad von Luetzen (who cared for the little orphan Emperor Frederick II), and then destroyed and rebuilt on several occasions; it offers excellent views of Assisi and the countryside (open summer 9–12 and 2–6, otherwise upon request).

East of the cathedral you can visit more of Roman *Assisium*—the **theatre** in Via del Torrione, flanking the cathedral, and the remains of the **amphitheatre**, off Piazza Matteotti and Via Villamena. The **Porta Perlici** near the amphitheatre dates from 1199, and there are some well-preserved 13th-century houses on the Via del Comune Vecchio. The **Giardino Pubblico**, with its pavilions and goldfish ponds, is an exquisite city park, a fine place to have a picnic after a hard day's sightseeing. Roman Assisi had up-to-date plumbing; you might be able to pick out parts of the Roman drain between the amphitheatre and the Giardino Pubblico, built to carry off water after the amphitheare was flooded for mock sea battles.

Basilica di Santa Chiara

When Santa Chiara (St Clare, 1182–1226) was 17 she ran away from her wealthy and noble family to become a disciple of St Francis, and later head of the Franciscan order for women, the Poor Clares. Whatever the later Church mythology, gratifying rumours were never lacking that there was more to her relationship with Francis than practical piety. Gentle, humble, and well loved, she once had a vision of a Christmas service in the Basilica of St Francis while at the monastery of San Damiano, over a kilometre away, a feat that brought Pope Pius XII in 1958 to declare her the patron of television. (Unfortunately, the plastic, reception-guaranteeing statues of St Clare, with two holes in the back for your TV antenna, are now hard to find among the souvenir shops of Assisi.)

Her basilica, below the Piazza del Comune by way of Corso Mazzini, is a pink and white striped beauty with a lovely rose window and huge flying buttresses that support its outward side, masterpieces of medieval abstract art that seem structurally unnecessary, but create a memorable architectural space below. The basilica was built on the site of old San Giorgio, where Francis attended school and where his body lay for two years awaiting the completion of his own basilica. The interior of Santa Chiara is decorated with fine frescoes by followers of Giotto, unfortunately mostly fragments today. The main chapel on the right contains the famous *Crucifix of San Damiano* that spoke to St Francis, commanding him to 'Rebuild my church', while the adjacent chapel of the Holy Sacrament has fine Sienese frescoes; these two chapels survive from the original church of San Giorgio. The nearby portrait of St Clare, with scenes from her life, is by the Byzantinish, 13th-century Maestro di Santa Chiara, while St Clare's body, darkened with age, lies like Snow White in a crystal coffin down in the neo-Gothic crypt.

From Santa Chiara, Via Sant'Agnese leads to the very simple 1163 church of **Santa Maria Maggiore**, built on the site of the Roman Temple of Apollo, traces of which are still visible in the crypt. Near here the house of Sextus Propertius, the Roman poet of love (46 BC– AD14), was discovered, complete with wall paintings, but for lack of funds it has yet to be arranged for the public to visit. Between here and the Piazza Unità d'Italia, stroll along Via Cristofani and Via Fontebella, the latter adorned with wrought-iron dragons and another old fountain.

On the outskirts of Assisi

The seminal events of Francis' life all took place in the countryside around Assisi, all easily visited by car, though **San Damiano** is a pleasant 1-km walk down from Santa Chiara, a simple, asymmetrical little church where Francis heard the voice from the crucifix (see p. 416) that changed his life. While staying here he composed his masterful *Canticle of All Things Created.* He brought Santa Chiara here in 1212, and here she and her sisters passed their frugal, contemplative lives.

Another Franciscan shrine more in the spirit of the saint than the great art-filled basilicas, the peaceful **Eremo delle Carceri**, lies along the scenic road up Monte Subasio, a beautiful walk or drive 4 km east of Assisi. This was Francis' forest hermitage, where he would retreat to walk through the woods, and where he preached to the birds from a simple stone altar; here you can see his humble bed hollowed from the rock. The handful of Franciscans here live a traditional Franciscan existence on the alms they receive.

The real centre of early Franciscanism, however, was the chapel called the Porziuncola ('the little portion'), where angels were wont to appear, down on the plain near the train station (convenient for Francis when he wanted to begin one of his wandering preaching missions). St Francis, in return for the use of the chapel, owed a yearly basket of carp from the river Tescio to the Benedictines, still faithfully paid by the Franciscans. In 1569, a monumental basilica called **Santa Maria degli Angeli** was built over the

Santa Maria degli Angeli, Assisi

Porziuncola. The building, not completed until 1684, is an excellent piece of nostalgic Baroque—most of it rebuilt after an 1832 earthquake, and the surprisingly elegant façade not added until 1927.

In the austere interior, the Porziuncola stands out like a jewel box, dolled up with 19th-century frescoes. The rugged stone of the original chapel can be seen inside (it may be as old as the 6th century), along with some fine 1393 frescoes of St Francis's life by Ilario da Viterbo, this artist's only known work. Remains of the original Franciscan monastery have been partially excavated under the high altar; here St Clare took her vows of poverty as the spiritual daughter of Francis; here Francis died 'naked on the bare earth' in the convent's infirmary, now the **Cappella del Transito**, with some unusual frescoes by the Umbrian painter Lo Spagna, along with a statue of St Francis by Andrea della Robbia. The garden contains the roses that St Francis threw himself on while wrestling with a severe temptation, staining their leaves red with blood, only to find that they lost their thorns on contact with his body. Still thornless, they bloom every May. Francis's cell has been covered with the frescoed Cappella del Roseto, and there's an old pharmacy and museum (9–12:30 and 2:30–6:30) with a portrait of St Francis by an unknown 13th-century master, another one sometimes attributed to Cimabue, a Crucifix by Giunta Pisano, and items relating to Franciscan missionary work.

ACTIVITIES

Assisi is Umbria's both spiritual and shopping centre, overflowing with little ceramic friars, crossbows, local ceramics and glass, textiles, and serious art galleries. Spello (see p. 420) produces some of the region's finest olive oil; you can visit an olive press, or *Frantoio*, in action in July–Aug or Dec–Jan (Cianetti, Via Bulgarella 10, tel in advance, 652 781 or 652 834). Annual festivals in Assisi include the medieval May Day celebrations of *Calendimaggio* during the first 10 days of May, commemorating St Francis' troubadour past with song, dance, torchlit parades, competitions between Lower and Upper Assisi and beautiful costumes. Easter week is busy with activities—on Holy Thursday there's a mystery play on the Deposition from the Cross, followed by processions on Good Friday and Easter Sunday; 1–2 August sees the *Festa del Perdona* ('Feast of Pardon') at the Porziuncola, initiated by St Francis, who once had a vision of Christ asking him what would be most helpful for the soul. Francis replied forgiveness for anyone who crossed the threshold of the chapel; indulgences are still given out on the day. In July and early August the *Festa Musica Pro* sponsors concerts throughout the city, often including early Italian music.

WHERE TO STAY (tel prefix 075)

Tourists have been coming to Assisi for longer than to any town in Umbria, and it does its best to please. There are plenty of rooms, but still not enough for Calendimaggio, Easter, and at times in July and August, when you should strive to book in advance. Two hotels compete for luxury top billing: the traditional, formal ****__Subasio__, Via Frate Elia 2, tel 812 206, linked to the Basilica of St Francis by the portico. Many of the rooms have views over the famous mystical countryside from vine-shaded terraces, and it has a private garage and an attractive medieval vaulted restaurant. St Francis never slept here, but the King of Belgium and Charlie Chaplin did (L145–160 000). ****__Hotel Fontebella__, Via Fontebella 25, tel 812 883, is a bit nearer the centre, housed in a 17th-century palazzo.

Rooms are comfortable, public rooms elegant; a garden and garage are added attractions (L100–145 000). The ***Umbra, near Piazza del Comune at the end of a narrow alley, Via degli Archi 6, tel 812 240, is a real charmer, a little family-run inn; quiet, sunny, and friendly with a little walled garden in front. Rooms can be a bit small but serendipitous, and many have balconies overlooking the countryside. The Umbra's restaurant deserves special mention as one of the most attractive in Assisi, with the best of regional cuisine (like *risotto* with white truffles from Gubbio) and a cellar full of excellent wine; in good weather meals are served in the garden. Parking can be a minor problem, however—the nearest car park is by S. Chiara (rooms L48 000 without bath, L80 000 with; meals around L35 000). ****Giotto, Via Fontebella 41, tel 812 209, has very pleasant modern rooms near the Basilica, as well as a garage and garden terraces for relaxing (L60 000 without bath, L100–130 000 with).

Nearly a kilometre away—a 10-minute walk to the west gate of Assisi—in a pretty country setting, the old stone **Country House**, S. Pietro Campagna 178, tel 816 363, has lovely rooms furnished with items from the owner's antique shop on the ground floor (L60 000, all rooms with bath; breakfast only). Near the amphitheatre, at Piazza Matteotti 1, the **Ideale per Turisti**, tel 813 570, has a name that says it all: a fine, small hotel with a garden, views, and baths in every room (L60 000). American sisters run **S. Antonio's Guest House**, Via G. Alessi 10, tel 812 542, in a 12th-century villa, with pleasant rooms and three meals for L55 000 a person, L65 000 with private bath, but beware the early curfew. ***Anfiteatro Romano**, Via Anfiteatro 4, tel 813 025, is a good quiet choice near Piazza Matteotti, with only seven rooms (L33 000 without bath, L50 000 with). If everything is full, try the large pilgrimage houses in Santa Maria degli Angeli, especially the **Cenacolo Francescano**, Via Piazza d'Italia 70, tel 804 1083, with 130 adequate rooms, all with private bath, a short walk from the train station (L55–60 000).

Further afield, at Ospedalicchio di Bastia (SS 147 towards Perugia), the very friendly ***Lo Spedalicchio**, Piazza B. Buozzi 3, tel 801 0323, is a hotel converted from a medieval fortified house, nicely restored and preserving many of its original features, but with added creature comforts like private baths, telephones and televisions; there's a garden and an excellent restaurant (L80 000). In the same area, 12 km northwest of Assisi at San Gregorio, ***Castel San Gregorio**, Via S. Gregorio 16, tel 803 8009, offers 12 rooms in a restored 13th-century castle, set in a pretty garden (L80–115 000). A local 'Agriturismo' agency, Le Silve, at Armenzano, tel 812 659, has a listing of cottages and farmhouses to rent in the Assisi area.

EATING OUT

Besides the Umbra, mentioned above, Assisi has the well-known **Buca di San Francesco**, Via Brizi 1, tel 812 204, below street level in a cavernous medieval cellar. Served here are delicious cannelloni, homemade pasta with meat and porcini mushrooms, pigeon cooked Assisi style, or *filet al Rubesco*. Good wines from Umbria and other regions; closed most of July (L40–45 000, closed Mon). Another venerable choice, **Il Medioevo**, Via dell'Arco dei Priori 4, tel 813 068, has an elegant medieval atmosphere and tasty antipasti with Umbrian prosciutto, pasta with truffles, and sweet and sour rabbit (L40 000, closed Wed). **La Fortezza**, Via della Fortezza (near the Piazza del Comune), tel 812 418, has delicious *cappelletti al tartufo nero o funghi* (truffle or mushroom filled pasta caps), roast guinea hen (*faraona alla Fortezza*), or rabbit in asparagus sauce (L30–35 000; closed Thurs). For pizza, try the popular pies and imported beers at **Il Pozzo Romano**, Via Sant'Agnese near Santa Chiara (L5500–8000). For a treat, try one of the rich strudels or chocolate-and-nut breads in the speciality bakery in Piazza del Comune, near the Temple of Minerva, or at the Santa Monica, Via Portica 4.

Spello

It could be Assisi's little sister, lounging on the same sort of gentle hillside, 13 km to the southeast above the N. 75. Spello is linked by rail and bus to Assisi, Perugia, and Foligno. Like Assisi, Spello is a beautiful town, done in the same prevailing pink and cream Umbrian stone. It has a similar history, first as an Umbrian settlement, then as the Roman city of *Hispellum*, and in the Middle Ages as a *comune* that fought to keep free of Assisi the same way Assisi resisted domination by the Perugians. There's so much to see in Assisi that few tourists find their way up here, but like most little sisters Spello has some charms of her own.

Spello has three excellently preserved Roman gates, including the main entrance to the town, the **Porta Consolare**, with three well-worn statues from the time of the Roman republic. Beyond it, there is an interesting open chapel, the **Cappella Tega**, with faded Renaissance frescoes, and a little further, the church of **Santa Maria Maggiore**. Behind the simple façade, retaining the campanile and some stonecarving from the original Romanesque building, is Spello's treasure, the Baglioni Chapel with its brilliant frescoes by Pinturicchio. The three scenes, an *Annunciation*, *Nativity*, and *Dispute in the Temple*, are a delight, as full of colour and incident as the more famous Pinturicchios in Siena's Piccolomini Library. Note the floor, made entirely of 16th-century painted ceramics from Deruta. More work by the same artist can be seen in the chapel opposite, along with a late fresco of Perugino. Another chapel has been converted into a **Museum** with woodcarving from the 13th and 14th centuries (daily exc Sun 8–12, 3–6; adm). For yet more Pinturicchio (he spent all of 1501 in Spello) the nearby church of **Sant'Andrea** has a fresco of the Madonna and saints.

Souvenirs of Roman *Hispellum*

Walking the medieval streets of Spello is a joy, though they're a bit steep; press on past the attractive Piazza della Repubblica, where the **Palazzo Comunale** bears some traces of its original work from the 1200s; just off the piazza, **San Lorenzo** (*c.* 1160) has an unusual façade full of bits from Roman and early medieval buildings. Ambitious climbers will manage to find the lovely view from the **Belvedere**, at the end of Via Belvedere, and perhaps even the 14th-century **Rocca**, at the highest point of the city. The small **Roman Arch** nearby was the entrance to *Hispellum*'s acropolis, ruins of which are still lying around. A circumnavigation of the city's walls will show you the other two Roman gates: the **Porta Urbica** and, best of all, the **Porta Venere**, a beautiful, almost perfectly preserved monumental gate flanked by tall cylindrical towers, a relic even more remarkable than the famous Arco di Augusto in Perugia.

The gate is plainly visible from the road to Assisi and Perugia. Look the other way and you'll see the ruins of the **Amphitheatre**, perhaps more impressive when seen from the Belvedere up in the city than from ground level. Just to the north is charming, resolutely asymmetrical Romanesque **San Claudio**, and 2.5 km further on the same road, set in the lovely countryside around Spello, the **Chiesa Tonda**, or S. Maria Rotonda, another geometric Renaissance temple (1517), less ambitious than the ones in Todi and Montepulciano, but with quirky Umbrian frescoes by Mezzastris inside. A kilometre northeast of Spello, **San Girolamo** is another good Renaissance church (1474) decorated inside by various students and followers of Pinturicchio. The S. Girolamo road continues up on to the slopes of Monte Subasio to the walled medieval village of **Collepino**; the Romanesque parish church, San Silvestro, has an interesting crypt and an altar carved out of a Roman sarcophagus.

Spello celebrates Corpus Domini in June with the *Infiorata*, when the streets are decked with intricately designed carpets of flowers—get there in the early morning to see them at their best.

WHERE TO STAY AND EATING OUT (tel prefix 0742)

Four moderate hotels are the offerings in Spello, of which ***__La Bastiglia__**, Via Salnitraria 17, tel 651 277, stands out, not only for its pleasant rooms but for its beautiful terrace and views; rooms L80 000, all with bath. If it's full, try ****Julia**, Via S. Angelo 22, tel 651 174, with similar rooms for L60–80 000.

In central Spello dining is *bello* and mellow under the vaulted ceiling at **Il Molino**, in Piazza Matteotti, tel 651 305—try the homemade pasta or traditional Umbrian meats cooked over the flames with a few glasses of Spello's own wines (L40 000; closed Tues).

Part XIV

SOUTHERN UMBRIA

Ceremonial Procession, Orvieto

In the green heart of Italy, more than anywhere else, all roads lead to Rome. This chapter, covering perhaps some of the least travelled territory in this book, follows the two most important routes south from Assisi and Perugia. First, the old Roman Via Flaminia (N. 3), beginning at Foligno in the sunny Valle Umbra, passing towns that deserve to be better known, such as Bevagna, Montefalco and Trevi, as well as the unique relic of the dark ages called the Tempio del Clitunno; Spoleto follows, a genuine capital in those times, now among the trendiest of art towns thanks to its famous music festival.

The second route (N. 3bis, N. 448 and the A1) follows the lovely valley of the Tiber, from Perugia through the proud hill towns of Todi, with its medieval and Renaissance monuments, and Orvieto, with its spectacular cathedral and memories of the days when the popes made it a favoured retreat. Finally, there's the little-known section called the Valnerina, on Umbria's southern borders, with a double helping of mountain scenery and more than a few curiosities, one of tourism's last frontiers in central Italy.

Foligno

Not many people stop for Foligno (pop. 54,000); in a sense the town is a victim of its post-war prosperity, and the ring of factories and modern suburbs that surrounds it is enough to discourage most travellers. What they're missing is one of the most distinctive Umbrian towns, not as archaic or as cute as Assisi, but memorable in its own way, a minor medieval capital with a pinch of grandeur and an air of genteel dilapidation. Ancient Roman *Fulginum* popped back up in the 12th century as a free *comune* with strongly

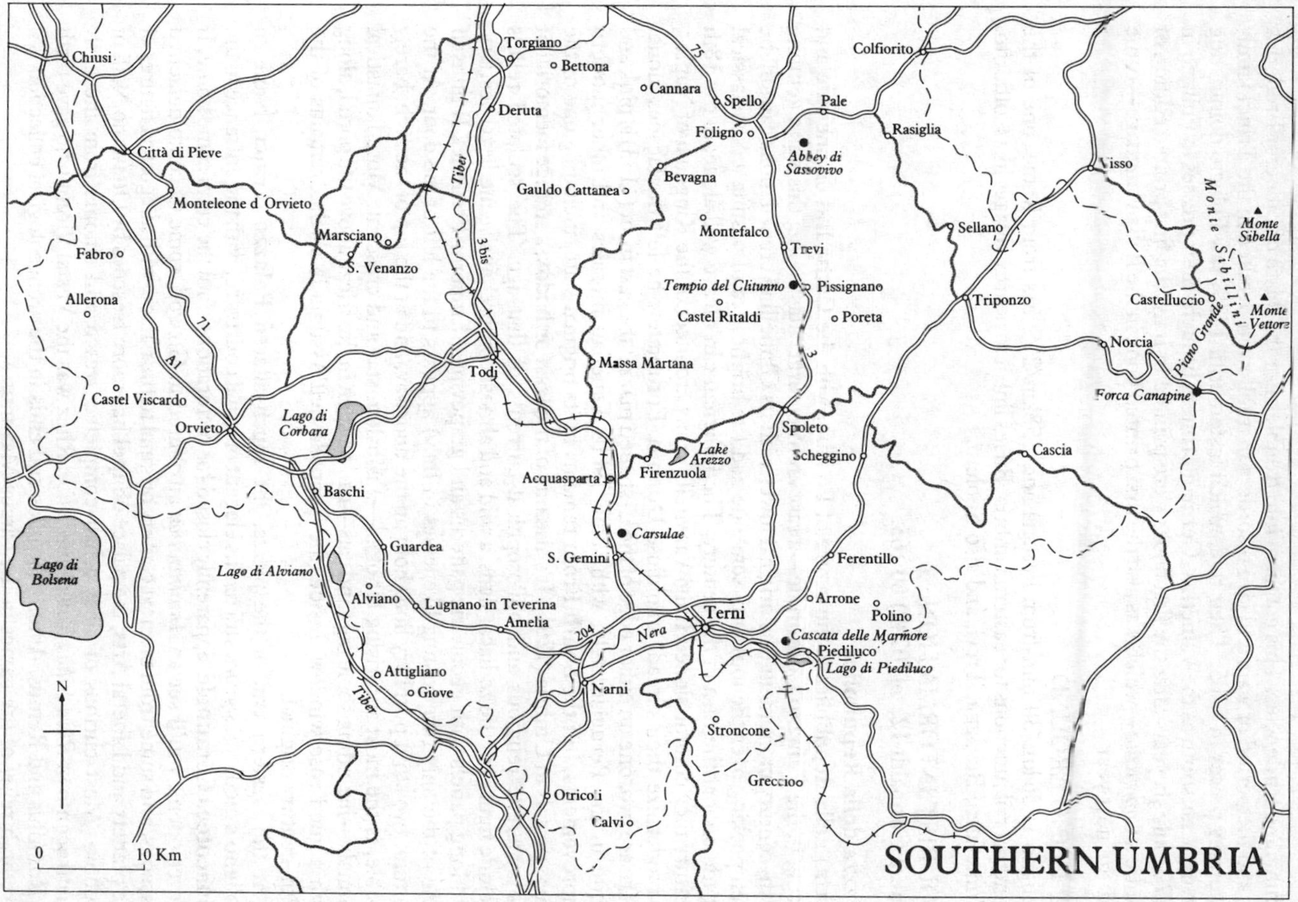
SOUTHERN UMBRIA
Chiusi
Città di Pieve
Monteleone d'Orvieto
Fabro
Allerona
Castel Viscardo
Orvieto
A1
71
Lago di Bolsena
Lago di Corbara
Lago di Alviano
Baschi
Guardea
Alviano
Lugnano in Teverina
Amelia
Attigliano
Giove
Tiber
Marsciano
S. Venanzo
Torgiano
Bettona
Deruta
3 bis
Todi
Gauldo Cattanea
Cannara
Spello
Foligno
Bevagna
Montefalco
Trevi
Tempio del Clitunno
Pissignano
Castel Ritaldi
Poreta
3
Massa Martana
Lake Arezzo
Firenzuola
Acquasparta
Carsulae
S. Gemini
204
Nera
Terni
Narni
Otricoli
Calvi
Stroncone
Greccio
Colfiorito
Pale
Rasiglia
Abbey di Sassovivo
75
Sellano
Spoleto
Scheggino
Ferentillo
Arrone
Polino
Cascata delle Marmore
Piediluco
Lago di Piediluco
Triponzo
Cascia
Visso
Norcia
Castelluccio
Piano Grande
Forca Canapine
Monte Sibillini
Monte Sibella
Monte Vettore
N
0
10 Km

Ghibelline tendencies. This got them into trouble after the death of Emperor Frederick II, and the period of wars and civil disorders that followed resulted in the Trinci family assuming power in 1305. Their rule, which lasted until 1339, saw Foligno dominating towns as far south as the Valnerina. German printers brought their presses to Foligno in 1470, only six years after the first books were printed in Italy; the first printed edition of Dante's *Commedia*—which was also the first printed book in the Italian language—came out the next year.

GETTING AROUND

Foligno is 36 km/30 min from Perugia and 158km/2½ hrs from Rome, one of the principal rail junctions for eastern Umbria. Buses link it to nearby villages like Colfiorito, Montefalco, Bevagna, Trevi, and also Spoleto.

TOURIST INFORMATION

Piazza Garibaldi 12, tel (0742) 60 165.

Piazza della Repubblica

Piazza della Repubblica is the centre of Foligno, with the **Cathedral** on one side and facing it, the **Palazzo Comunale**—a rare architectural catastrophe; this was a genuine 12th-century monument (the original tower with its Ghibelline crenellations can still be seen peeking over the top) until someone had the bright idea of pasting a Neoclassical façade on it at the turn of the century. The Folignati can't leave well alone; in the 18th century they commissioned Luigi Vanvitelli, court architect of the Kingdom of Naples, to modernize their already grandiose **Duomo**. Fortunately he left the façades alone; there are two, one on either edge of the L-shaped piazza: the east front (1133) is pink and white in the Perugian style, with some 1900s Venetian mosaics and other modern improvements, but the **South Front** remains in its original state, including one of the finest portals in Umbria (1201). It's also one of the least orthodox, a strange memorial of the syncretic religious and philosophical currents of that age. The sculpted reliefs include figures of the zodiacal signs, a wild and almost comprehensive medieval bestiary, and long panels with geometric patterns and grapevines. Emperor Frederick II himself (one of the only two existing likenesses in Italy) appears to the left of the door. At the bottom, two stout porphyry lions hold up the doorway, and at the top of the arch, barely visible, is the most surprising bit of all—a Moslem star and crescent. More fantastical animals—including some pigs and cats—can be seen in the frieze above the portal, along with a good rose window. Inside, the Cappella dell'Assunta is all that remains of the 12th-century original.

At the western end of the piazza, the much-altered **Palazzo Trinci**, home to Foligno's medieval *signori*, still has its elegant original courtyard, with the entrance to the **Pinacoteca Comunale**, apparently closed for restorations until the cows come home. If it ever opens, you'll see an *Annunciation* attributed to Gozzoli, some trecento detached frescoes, and some from the next century original to the palace, with allegorical figures of the planets and Liberal Arts; the palace **chapel** has more frescoes by Ottaviano Nelli of Gubbio. Most curious of all is a half-completed fresco and sinopia from the early quattrocento of *Rhea Silvia being buried alive*; Rhea was the Vestal Virgin who gave birth to Romulus and Remus. Among the odds and ends in the archaeological collection is a rare high relief of the games in the Circus Maximus.

Down Viale Ammaniti

Palazzo Trinci is only the last of a long line of Folignati palaces, stretching down Viale Ammaniti from the piazza. Most of the noble residences were built in the 1500s, and most are under restoration after long years of neglect. At the small piazza at the other end, **S. Maria Infraportas** is one of Foligno's oldest churches, with unusual 12th-century windows and portico, and medieval frescoes inside. Foligno's other churches are well endowed with art: **San Niccolò** with virtuoso (but not always interesting) works by Foligno's own Nicolò di Liberatore, better known as L'Alunno; the **Nunziatella** nearby has a fresco by Perugino.

Up the Menotre Valley

Directly east of Foligno, you can penetrate the valley of the little Menotre river into the mountains, a beautiful but seldom visited corner of Umbria that extends as far as the border with the Marches. N. 77 follows the valley, but just after it crosses the Via Flaminia there is a side road to the left that in 5 km reaches the **Abbazia di Sassovivo**, an 11th-century Benedictine abbey with a remarkable cloister; its variegated double columns are reminiscent of some in Rome (St Paul's outside the walls). The main road twists up into the mountains, passing some interesting caves and a pretty waterfall on the Menotre at **Pale**, 8 km from Foligno. On the mountain heights, just before the regional border, it levels out at the broad meadow of Colfiorito, where there are some green marshlands, oddly a thousand feet above sea level; you'll pass a rugged 11th-century church, **S. Maria di Plestia**, with porticoes on two sides to accommodate the country fairs held here in the Middle Ages. A side road before Colfiorito (24 km) heads south into pristine mountain scenery around Rasiglia, where the little church of **Madonna delle Grazie** has walls covered with well-preserved, colourful quattrocento frescoes.

ACTIVITIES

Foligno jousts every second and third Sunday in September at the *Giostra della Quintana*, a festival accompanied by plays performed in 17th-century Umbrian dialect (of which you won't understand a word) and a more accessible historic cooking competition between the various quarters of the city. Besides jousting, Foligno is Umbria's gliding and hang-gliding centre (contact the Aeroclub, tel 670 201); there's a riding stable as well in the suburban hamlet of S. Bartolomeo (Società ippica, tel 50 461). Shoppers can browse through the permanent display of local ceramics next to the tourist information office.

WHERE TO STAY AND EATING OUT (tel prefix 0742)

In Foligno: *****Villa Roncalli**, Via Roma 25, tel 670 291, is a fashionable, central villa-hotel in a shady garden, with garage, and comfortable rooms for L85 000. The ****Posta**, Via Oberdan 1, tel 56 379, has good rooms and an even better restaurant, with a menu that changes according to the season—in summer *penne* with aubergine and peppers, truffles in autumn, *tegame* in the winter (L45 000 without bath, L55 000 with; full meals L30 000; closed Sun). Foligno is also the site of the region's modest youth hostel, the **Ostello Fulginium**, Piazza San Giacomo 11, tel 52 882 (bus no. 1 from the station), open Mar–Sept (L10 000 a head, including showers). **Da Remo**, Viale C. Battisti 11, tel 50 079, serves a tasty *strangozzi* (fat, homemade spaghetti) and roast kid cooked in Montefalco's Sagrantino wine (L25–30 000); while up in the mountains at Colfiorito, ****Lieta Sosta**, Via Adriatica 228, tel 681 127, offers fine country dining Umbrian style, with grilled lamb and *strangozzi* with truffles (about L30–35 000), and rooms with bath for L60 000.

The Valle Umbra: Bevagna

Between Assisi and Spoleto spreads one of the largest patches of open country in Umbria. The **Valle Umbra**, actually the valleys of the Teverone and the Topino ('River Mouse'), has much in common with parts of southern Tuscany; the landscape seems almost consciously arranged by some geomantic artist to display each olive grove, vineyard, city and town to the best advantage. In Roman times, this was a prosperous region, and its centre was *Mevania*, an old foundation of the Umbrians that has survived as **Bevagna**, a sunny, sleepy town (pop. 4600) that merits a detour for two of Umbria's best Romanesque churches.

Little Bevagna was a free *comune* through much of the Middle Ages, and its central Piazza Silvestri shows that it tried hard to keep up with its bigger neighbours. The impressive **Palazzo Comunale** of 1270 now functions as a theatre as well as housing the town offices. An archway connects it to **San Silvestro**, a work by an architect named Maestro Binello. The simple façade incorporates bits of Roman buildings, and an 1195 inscription to Emperor Henry VII. The interior is essentially Romanesque, all muscular stone and subtle geometry. Like many 12th-century buildings (e.g. Tuscany's Abbadia S. Salvatore), it features a raised presbytery, leaving room for twin pulpits (*ambones*, now vanished) on either side of the steps, and a small crypt underneath. The real surprise is the style of the capitals—they're in the Egyptian order, representing papyrus leaves the way Ionic and Corinthian capitals recall the leaves of the acanthus. Such columns are common in this area, but their presence has never been explained. One possible guess: that they were copied from the ruins of some Roman-era temple to Isis or Serapis.

Across the piazza, the big church of **S. Michele** also has a few Egyptian capitals, recycled from older buildings. Maestro Binello built this one about the same time as S. Silvestro, and to the same interior plan. St Michael and his dragon figure prominently on the façade, along with some re-used Roman friezes, a Cosmatesque arch, and a menagerie of cows, cats, and such, similar to the portal in Foligno. The third church on the piazza, **SS. Domenico e Giacomo**, has a Baroque interior with what must be the biggest alabaster window in Italy behind the altar. Of the church's original decoration, little remains but a radiant trecento Virgin of the Annunciation. From here, a block down Corso Matteotti leads to the new town hall, with a small **Pinacoteca** (daily 8–2; adm) and a collection of medieval manuscripts and Roman coins. More remnants of Roman *Mevania* can be seen a few blocks further, a **Roman Temple** partially conserved when its columns were bricked in long ago, a picturesque circle of houses built over the seats of the amphitheatre, and a marine **mosaic** featuring a big lobster, once part of the baths (ring the bell at Via Porta Guelfa 2).

Montefalco

TOURIST INFORMATION

Corso Mameli 68, in the Palazzo Comunale, tel (0742) 79 122.

Montefalco (pop. 5600), high on a hill at the edge of the Valle Umbra, only 7 km from Bevagna, has been known since the earliest times as the 'Ringhiera (balcony-rail) d'Umbria'; some points around the town offer splendid prospects as far as Assisi and sometimes Perugia. The pride of this town is the collection of frescoes in the church of **San Francesco**, now converted to a museum (daily except Thurs, 10–1 and 3:30–6:30; adm), located a block north of the central Piazza della Repubblica. Benozzo Gozzoli spent two years here (1450–52), painting the apse with some of his best work, the *Life of St Francis*. Montefalco's Franciscans did not let Gozzoli put in many of his usual fancies—though there are a few moppet children grinning out from the corners. Gozzoli does indulge in his favourite city-scapes, including views of Montefalco (where Francis visited after preaching to the birds around Bevagna), and of Arezzo (where he cast out the devils). The panels along the bottom of the apse show portraits by Gozzoli of great Franciscans—a distinguished company, including philosopher Duns Scotus. The other Renaissance fresco here is by Perugino, a not-too-inspired *Nativity*. The aisles contain some fine trecento painting, including a vivid and unique version of the *Temptations of St Anthony*; there are two fond paintings of a local favourite, the Madonna del Soccorso, about to whack a devil with a big club, and an ancient marble statue of Hercules found in the town.

Montefalco's people are a cheerful lot, contentedly looking down from their balcony over the rest of Umbria. Most of them live in tiny low houses jammed into narrow lanes; when it's nice they sit out front in garden chairs fostering Umbria's leading industry—talking about the weather. After San Francesco, sights are few; two other churches contain frescoes by Umbrian painters—**Sant'Agostino** and **S. Illuminata**. **S. Fortunato**, just over 1 km to the southeast, a simple Renaissance building Baroqued inside, contains another fresco by Gozzoli. Montefalco retains its medieval walls, including the two interesting gates of **S. Agostino** and **Federico II**.

At Montefalco a range of hills begins, separating the Valle Umbra from the Tiber. There isn't much to entice you any deeper into this region; truly rustic centres like **Massa Martana** (a rather pretty 25 km southwest on N. 316, turning left at Bastardo) with its medieval walls and three plain Romanesque churches, and **Gualdo Cattaneo** (15 km west of Montefalco). At Bruna, near the village of **Castel Ritaldi** (14 km south), there's an unusual Renaissance church in the shape of a trefoil, **S. Maria della Bruna**; also near Castel Ritaldi, the 1140 parish church of **S. Gregorio** with a charming sculpted façade.

Trevi and the Tempietto del Clitunno

No small town in Umbria makes a grander sight than **Trevi** (pop. 7400), a nearly vertical village reminiscent of Positano on the Amalfi coast, hung on a steep and curving hillside above the Via Flaminia 9 km south of Foligno. If you were wondering, there's no connection with the Trevi Fountain in Rome, only that both appeared at the junction of three roads—*tre vie*. Halfway up the road to Trevi's centre, the quattrocento church of the **Madonna delle Lacrime** contains a fresco of the *Adoration of the Magi* by Perugino.

Trevi too was a free *comune* in the Middle Ages, as evidenced by its small but proud Palazzo Comunale, now home to a **Pinacoteca** housing a Madonna by Pinturicchio, a fine *Deposition* by the school of Sodoma, and works by local Umbrian artists.

Just south of Trevi, Umbrians and tourists alike speed down the Flaminia without noticing the remarkable relic just to the side of the road. This area, at the source of the Teverone, was sacred to the river god Clitumnus in Roman times and probably long before, famous for the big snow-white oxen raised here, not to pull ploughs but to serve as temple sacrifices. The Roman villas and temples that once stood here are long gone, but bits of them were reassembled in a mysterious little building called the **Tempietto**. Two centuries ago, this was commonly believed to be a pagan temple converted to Christian use; Goethe, almost alone in his opinion, dissented, believing it to be an original Christian work. For once this most misinformed of all geniuses got it right. The most recent studies put the Tempietto somewhere in the 6th century, or even as late as the 8th—making this obscure, lovely building in a way the last work of classical antiquity, Christian enough, but an architectural throwback to a world that was already lost.

The little track that runs below the temple was the original Roman Via Flaminia; travellers between Ravenna and Rome would look up and see the beautiful façade, with its two coloured marble columns and ornate pediment, in an exotic, half-oriental late Roman style. The entrance, however, is around the side, leading into the portico and from there to the tiny sanctuary, decorated with Byzantine frescoes of the 700s: SS. Peter and Paul flanking the altar, and above them two unforgettable, very spiritual angels, gazing inscrutably out at you from the depths of the Dark Ages (daily exc Mon 9–12, in summer also 4–7 pm; ring the bell).

The **Fonti del Clitunno**, a little to the south, was not only a sacred place in pagan times, but one of the beauty spots of Italy. A score of underground springs rise here, forming a landscape of lagoons and islands, planted with weeping willows and poplars. Virgil mentioned it in his *Georgics*, and Byron devoted a few stanzas of *Childe Harold's Pilgrimage* to the place (Canto 4), but today the proximity of the busy highway and railroad tracks keep it from being quite the paradise evoked by the poets. It's still a popular resort for the locals, though, and well stocked with trout for those who follow that favourite Umbrian pastime of beating the prices at the local fish market.

WHERE TO STAY AND EATING OUT (tel prefix 0742)

Bevagna offers an attractive lunch stop; **Da Nina**, Piazza Garibaldi, tel 360 161, has more truffles, and good pasta dishes with porcini mushrooms—fancy dining for these parts (L30 000).

Besides Gozzoli, Montefalco is perhaps best known for a couple of red wines, *Sagrantino* and *Rosso di Montefalco*. Sagrantino is a bit special, with a delicate aroma of blackberries; both are sold in many shops around town. There isn't a lot of accommodation—***Ringhiera Umbra**, Via G. Mameli, tel 79 166, pretty, with an inexpensive restaurant (rooms L33 000 without bath, L48 000 with; meals L25 000). The little ****Nuovo Mondo**, Via delle Vittorie, tel 79 243, has one of the few swimming-pools in the region and a garden, as well as cosy rooms, all with bath (L60–75 000). **Coccorone**, off the central square at Vicolo Fabbri, tel 79 535, is an elegant, quiet and understated place with tempting crêpes and *tagliatelle al tartufo* for primo and dishes like *faraona ai salmi* and grilled pigeon for seconds (L35–40 000.)

Trevi: ****Cochetto**, Via Dogali 13, tel 78 229, has fine views, pleasant rooms, and the most popular restaurant in town (L40–60 000, depending on the plumbing; L30 000 for dinner, more if you order truffle dishes).
Campello sul Clitunno: Besides its own virtues, Clitunno is a quiet alternative to Spoleto if you've come for the festival. ****Le Fontanelle**, Via d'Elci 1, tel 521 091, is a lovely hotel and restaurant surrounded by refreshing greenery. Rooms are comfortable, and all equipped with bath (L65 000); the restaurant serves Umbrian specialities like country prosciutto, *strangozzi* and platters of tender lamb, chicken, pigeon, etc. (L35 000). At the Fonti del Clitunno, ****Ravale**, Via Virgilio, tel 521 320, has simple rooms for L55–60 000 as well as a modestly priced ristorante-pizzeria. In Poreta di Spoleto, 3 km from Campello, **Casaline**, tel 520 811, is a good, old-fashioned Umbrian inn in the country, specializing in game and truffle dishes in season, wild asparagus in the spring, and delicious pasta all year round (L35 000; closed Mon).

Spoleto

When composer Giancarlo Menotti was dreaming up the Festival of Two Worlds in the 1950s, he spent some months travelling across central Italy looking for just the right spot, some pretty town where the best of modern culture could be displayed against a background that recalled the best of the past. Spoleto was almost unknown then, a town of some 40,000 buried in one of the most obscure corners of darkest Umbria. But more than any Umbrian city, this one has a remarkable past behind it. From its prominence in classical times, there are Roman relics lying about everywhere. And at the beginning of the Middle Ages, Spoleto became the seat of one of the most powerful states in Italy. After a long, long sleep, Spoleto was ready for Menotti and the thousands who come each year for the music. More than ready, perhaps; even after the musicians pack their instruments and go, they leave behind a Spoleto full of special exhibitions and art workshops, its streets littered with jarring chunks of abstract sculpture. This experimental marriage of trendy art and the medieval hill town is not always a happy one, but it's done Spoleto no harm.

History

The ancient Umbrian *Spoletium* was resettled by the Romans in 242 BC, a few decades before an over-confident Hannibal came knocking at the gates, expecting an easy victory after his rout over the legions at Lake Trasimeno. But Spoletium held firm and repulsed him, and Hannibal, who intended to move on to Rome from there, took his elephants to graze in the Marches instead. With its strategic location on the Via Flaminia between Ravenna (the late Imperial capital) and Rome, Spoleto prospered in the twilight of empire. Emperor Theodoric built it up, as did the Byzantines under Justinian's general, Belisarius. The Goths under Totila made the city into a fortress, while the Lombards, arriving in 569, made it the base of their power, a duchy that at its height in the 700s controlled most of central Italy. In 890, after Charlemagne, Duke Guido III made an armed play for the Imperial crown, but had to be content with crowning himself King of Italy at Pavia. In the 11th century, the popes began to lean on Spoleto, claiming authority

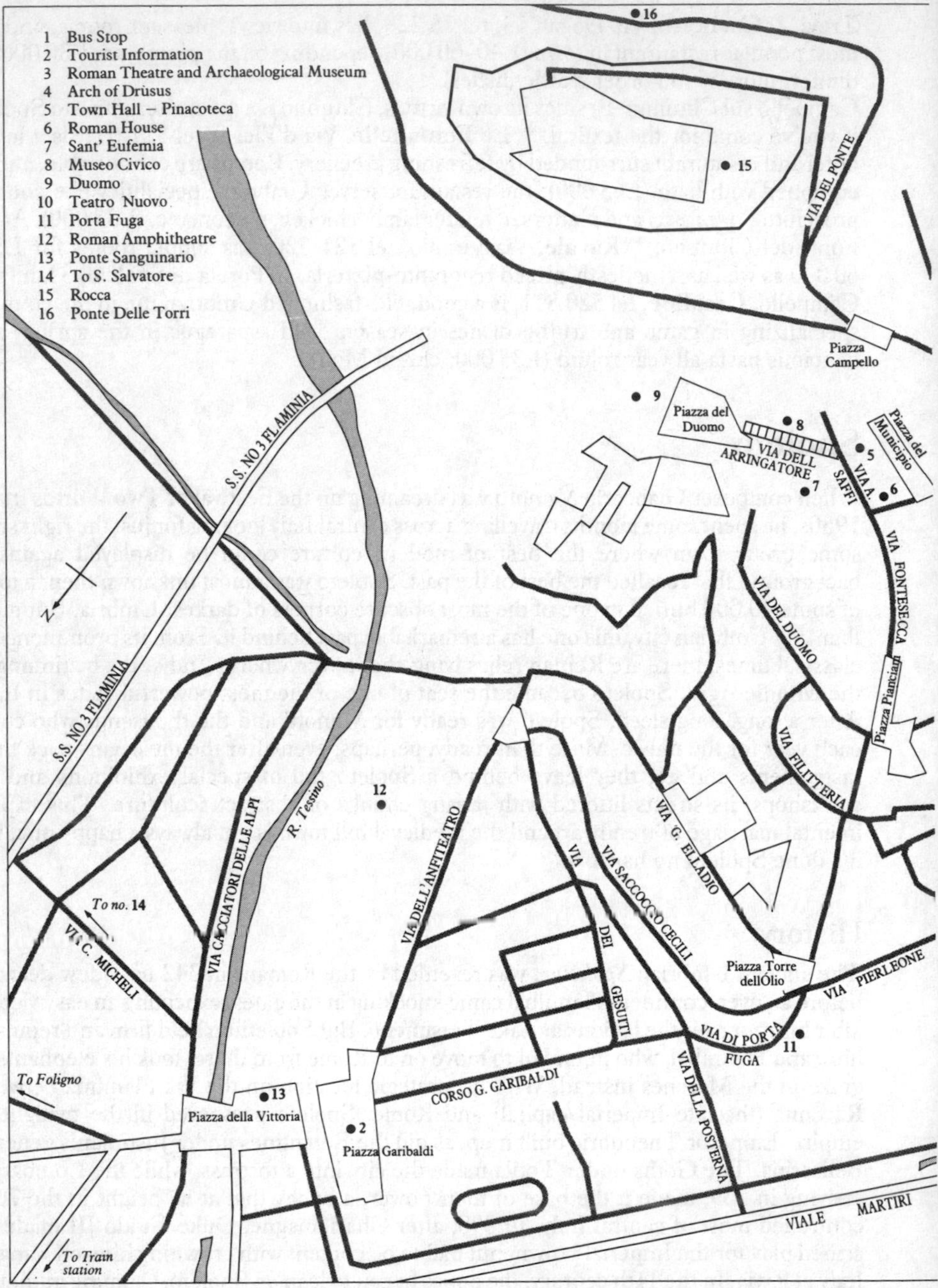
1 Bus Stop
2 Tourist Information
3 Roman Theatre and Archaeological Museum
4 Arch of Drùsus
5 Town Hall – Pinacoteca
6 Roman House
7 Sant' Eufemia
8 Museo Civico
9 Duomo
10 Teatro Nuovo
11 Porta Fuga
12 Roman Amphitheatre
13 Ponte Sanguinario
14 To S. Salvatore
15 Rocca
16 Ponte Delle Torri
VIA DEL PONTE
Piazza Campello
Piazza del Duomo
VIA DELL ARRINGATORE
Piazza del Municipio
VIA A. SAFFI
VIA FONTESECCA
VIA DEL DUOMO
Piazza Pianciani
VIA FILITTERIA
S.S. NO 3 FLAMINIA
N
R. Tessino
VIA CACCIATORI DELLE ALPI
VIA DELL'ANFITEATRO
VIA G. ELLADIO
VIA SACCOCCIO CECILI
VIA DEI GESUITI
Piazza Torre dellÓlio
VIA PIERLEONE
VIA DI PORTA FUGA
VIA DELLA POSTERNA
CORSO G. GARIBALDI
To no. 14
VI. C. MICHELI
To Foligno
Piazza della Vittoria
Piazza Garibaldi
VIALE MARTIRI
To Train station

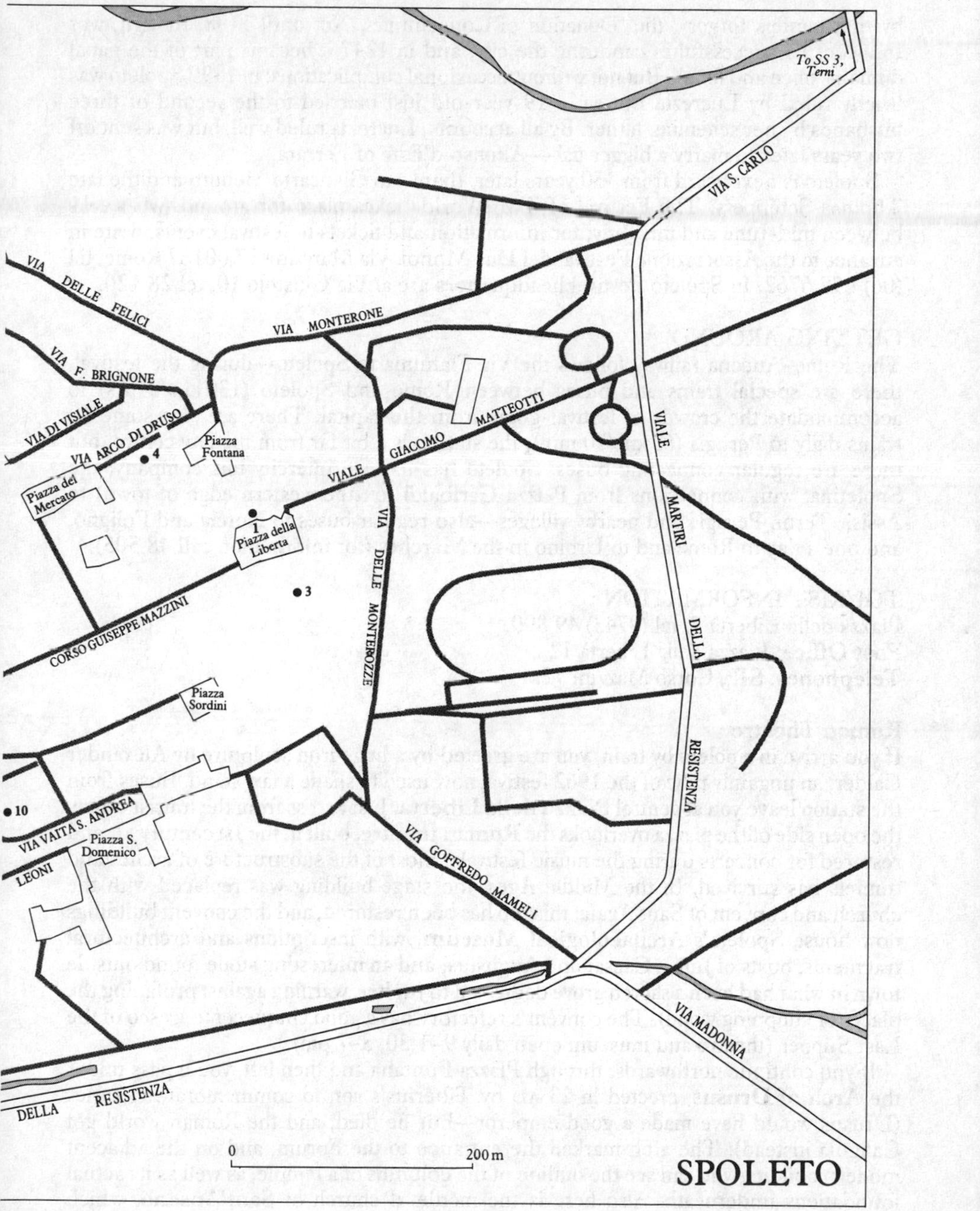
To SS 3, Terni
VIA S. CARLO
VIA DELLE FELICI
VIA MONTERONE
VIA F. BRIGNONE
VIA DI VISIALE
VIA ARCO DI DRUSO
Piazza Fontana
4
Piazza del Mercato
VIALE GIACOMO MATTEOTTI
1
Piazza della Liberta
3
VIA DELLE MONTEROZZE
VIALE MARTIRI DELLA RESISTENZA
CORSO GIUSEPPE MAZZINI
Piazza Sordini
10
VIA VAITA S. ANDREA
Piazza S. Domenico
LEONI
VIA GOFFREDO MAMELI
VIA MADONNA
DELLA RESISTENZA
0
200 m
SPOLETO

by that famous forgery, the 'Donation of Constantine'. Not until 1198, though, was Innocent III successful in capturing the city, and in 1247 it became part of the papal domains once and for all. But not without occasional complications; in 1499 Spoleto was briefly ruled by Lucrezia Borgia, a 19-year-old just married to the second of three husbands by her scheming father. By all accounts, Lucrezia ruled well, but was sent off two years later to marry a bigger fish—Alfonso d'Este of Ferrara.

Spoleto is next heard from 450 years later, thanks to Giancarlo Menotti and the late Thomas Schippers. The Festival of Two Worlds takes place for around two weeks between mid-June and mid-July; for information and tickets to festival events, write in advance to the Associazione Festival dei Due Mondi, Via Margutta 17,00187 Rome, tel (06) 679 6762. In Spoleto Festival headquarters are at Via Giustolo 10, tel 28 120.

GETTING AROUND

The Rome–Ancona railway follows the Via Flaminia to Spoleto—during the festival, there are special trains and buses between Rome and Spoleto (130 km/2 hrs) to accommodate the crowds of festival-goers from the capital. There are also some 10 trains daily to Perugia (63 km/70 min); the station is a bit far from the city centre, but there are regular connecting buses. Spoleto has its own intercity bus company, the Spoletina, with connections from Piazza Garibaldi (on the western edge of town) to Assisi, Terni, Perugia and nearby villages—also regular buses to Norcia and Foligno, and one a day to Rome and to Urbino in the Marches (for information call 48 505).

TOURIST INFORMATION

Piazza della Libertà 7, tel (0743) 49 890.
Post Office: Piazza della Libertà 12.
Telephones: SIP, Corso Mazzini 72.

Roman Theatre

If you arrive in Spoleto by train, you are greeted by a huge iron sculpture by Alexander Calder, an ungainly relic of the 1962 festival now used to shade a taxi stand. Buses from the station leave you at central **Piazza della Libertà**. Just across from the tourist office, the open side of the piazza overlooks the **Roman theatre**, built in the 1st century AD and restored for concerts during the music festivals; most of the substructure of arches and tunnels has survived. In the Middle Ages, the stage building was replaced with the church and convent of Sant'Agata; this too has been restored, and the convent buildings now house Spoleto's **Archaeological Museum**, with inscriptions and architectural fragments, busts of Julius Caesar and Augustus, and an interesting stone found outside town in what had been a sacred grove dedicated to Jupiter, warning against profaning the place (or chopping wood). The convent's refectory has a good cinquecento fresco of the Last Supper (theatre and museum open daily 9–1:30, 3–7 pm).

If you continue northwards, through Piazza Fontana and then left, you'll pass under the **Arch of Drusus**, erected in 23 AD by Tiberius's son to commemorate victories (Drusus would have made a good emperor—but he died, and the Roman world got Caligula instead). The arch marked the entrance to the Forum, and on the adjacent modern building you can see the outline of the columns of a temple, as well as its actual foundations underneath. Also here is the medieval church of **Sant'Ansano**, which incorporates more ancient fragments; its **Crypt of San Isacco**, built in the 12th century, has some unusual early medieval frescoes. Via Arco di Druso empties into the **Piazza del Mercato**, where the bright, glistening tomatoes and aubergines compete for your attention with the 18th-century **fountain**, a little provincial version of Rome's Trevi fountain that was a present from the popes.

Piazza del Municipio

From the fountain, walk north past some more questionable modern sculpture into the narrow Piazza del Municipio. Enter the town hall, report to the Spoleto Police, in an office on the right, and they'll sell you a ticket for the **Pinacoteca** on the first floor (daily exc Tues, 9:30–12:30, 3–6; adm). The star of this small, unlabelled collection is probably an *Adoration of the Magi* by Perugino, but there are also works by Spoleto-born Lo Spagna and other Umbrian painters, a lovely trecento *Annunciation* and other frescoes and woodcarving taken from Spoleto churches, portraits of the Teutonic dukes of long ago and coins from the days of the Lombard duchy. Close readers of that classic conspiracy book, *Holy Blood, Holy Grail* may want a look at an odd painting of the Magdalene, by Guercino. Plans are to move this museum into the Rocca (see below) when restorations are completed; this could be in 1990 or later.

The police, or the museum attendant, can also find you the custodian for the **Roman House**, around the corner on Via di Visiale, believed, perhaps fancifully, to have been the address of Emperor Vespasian's mother. The atrium, bedrooms and bath survive along with some mosaic floors.

Sant'Eufemia and the Duomo

Behind the Municipio, on Via Saffi, an archway leads into the small courtyard of the bishop's palace, facing one of the finest Umbrian Romanesque churches: **Sant'Eufemia**, completed about 1140, has a plain façade, but a remarkable interior in luminescent white stone. Fragments of Roman buildings are built into the walls and columns in surprising ways, but the really unique feature is the *matroneum*, the Byzantine-style second-floor gallery where women were segregated during mass. The altar is a good piece of Cosmatesque work, with symbols of the four Evangelists surrounding the Paschal lamb.

Via dell'Arringo, a grand, shallow stairway behind Sant'Eufemia, opens into the Piazza del Duomo. One can't help thinking it was this ensemble that sold Menotti on Spoleto as a site for the Festival; it doubles perfectly as an auditorium for the concerts held in front of the cathedral portico, with the cathedral façade and the Umbrian hills for a backdrop. Sharing the square with the cathedral is Spoleto's **Museo Civico**, housed in a Renaissance palace (9:30–12:30 and 3–6, closed Tues), with an interesting collection of sculpture extending up to the 14th century, as well as the **Teatro Caio Melisso**, also used for festival events.

The elegant **Duomo** was consecrated in 1198 by the most powerful of medieval popes, Innocent III, the year he captured Spoleto. Rebuilding was necessary after Emperor Frederick Barbarossa, the greatest of papal enemies, had razed its predecessor. It has several unusual features: eight rose windows of varying sizes, like buttons, adorn its horizontally divided façade, surrounding a gold-ground Byzantine-style mosaic of 1207. The lower middle *rosone* is an exceptional example of the Cosmati work imported from

Rome—stone or enamel chips arranged in sinuous, intricate patterns—that is so common in this part of Umbria. Its campanile is built out of Roman odds and ends and very un-Italian flying buttresses help to hold it up, although the interior was unfortunately redone in the 17th century. It contains several treasures, most notably the fine Cosmati pavement, and most piously the *Santissima Icone*, with a picture of the Madonna believed to have been brought to Spoleto from Constantinople.

Pinturicchio, not on one of his better days, painted the frescoes in the first chapel, the Eroli, and in the apse are the richly coloured frescoes on the *Life of the Virgin* by Fra Filippo Lippi, who portrayed himself and his assistant among the mourners in the scene of the Virgin's death. The fun-loving monk from Florence died in Spoleto while working on the project, and it was finished by his chief helper, Fra Diamanti; when Lorenzo de' Medici asked that Lippi's body be returned to Florence, the Spoletini refused, claiming they had no notable dead while Florence had so many and Lorenzo had to be content with ordering a fine Florentine tomb for him, now in the right transept (frescoes now under restoration, and Our Lady only knows when they'll be finished).

Lower Spoleto

On the opposite side of town (Via del Duomo to Via Filitteria) there's another grand theatre, the **Teatro Nuovo**, used both for the Two Worlds festival and for the even older September Festival of Experimental Opera. Nearby, the colourful church of **San Domenico** was built in the 13th century, and contains some interesting if fragmentary 13th–15th-century frescoes. From San Domenico walk down to the tall-towered 13th-century **Porta Fuga**, and then along Via Cecili, where you can take in an excellent stretch of Spoleto's **walls**, an intriguing record of the town's history, beginning at the 6th-century BC 'Cyclopean' base of huge polygonal rough blocks built by the ancient Umbrii, all the way up to the 15th-century additions on the top. The street ends in Piazza Cairoli; from here Via dell'Anfiteatro descends past the ruined **Roman amphitheatre**, turned into a fortress by Totila the Goth and even now part of a military barracks (the soldiers can sometimes be persuaded to show you around it); further down, on Piazza Garibaldi there's the fine 12th-century church of **San Gregorio** and the Roman **Ponte Sanguinario** ('bloody bridge'), so called after all the Christians supposedly martyred here.

From the bridge, signs point the way to the cemetery church of **San Salvatore**, a 15-minute walk away. San Salvatore is Spoleto's most ancient church, built in the 4th century. It has an unusual façade, and preserves much of its original vertical lines and simplicity despite subsequent rebuildings. The elegant, fluted Corinthian columns in the interior were incorporated from a Roman temple.

The Rocca and the Ponte delle Torri

From Piazza del Municipio, Via Saffi climbs up to the Piazza Campello, with another good fountain, the 17th-century **Mascherone**, where the water shoots from the mouth of a huge, grotesque face. Above this looms the **Rocca**, the impressive, six-towered castle built by Gattapone, the master architect from Gubbio, for the 14th-century papal legate, Cardinal Albornoz. Built of third-hand stone, first used in the Roman amphitheatre, it was secondly cannibalized by the Goth Totila for his fortress. The Rocca was a popular papal country resort, frequented by Julius II, accompanied on occasion by Michelangelo, who loved the peace of the surrounding hills. Until 1983 the Rocca was used as a prison, and once its current restoration is completed, it will hold Spoleto's Pinacoteca. For now, the best thing to do is stroll along the garden walk that encircles the Rocca and enjoy the views of Spoleto below.

The **Porta della Rocca** leads down to Master Gattapone's unique masterpiece, and one of the greatest engineering works of the trecento, the **Ponte delle Torri**, a bridge and aqueduct of 10 towering arches linking Spoleto with the slopes of Monteluco, spanning the 80-m deep ravine of the Tessino river far below. Gattapone built the bridge on a Roman foundation; it leads to the towers that gave it its name, and to the road for Monteluco's San Pietro and San Francesco.

Monteluco

Beautiful, forested Monteluco is Spoleto's holy mountain, lying just to the east of town, attainable by car, by bus departing from Piazza della Libertà, or by walking from the Ponte delle Torri. If you're walking, take the right-hand fork in the road for the great Romanesque church of **San Pietro**, only a few minutes away, with a romp of a façade dating from the days of the Dukes of Spoleto; if you've ever visited the medieval cathedrals in the north, you'll recognize the vigorous animals, real and imaginary, that the Lombards delighted in portraying: here is a fox playing dead to capture some too-curious chickens, battles with lions, oxen, peacocks, eagles, a wolf in monk's clothing, and devils contesting souls, along with a relief of St Michael slaying his dragon.

The other (left) fork in the road demands some serious walking through beautiful ilex (holm oak) forests to reach the 12th-century **Church of San Giuliano**, with a façade incorporating some 6th-century elements of its predecessor. In the 7th century anchorites and hermits, refugees from the wars in the Holy Land, settled here and set up early monasteries; in the 13th century St Francis and later St Bernardino of Siena came to meditate here, at the tiny monastery of **San Francesco** near the summit of Monteluco, a serene spot enjoying a lovely view of the surrounding countryside. Monteluco now has more summer villas and hotels than hermitages, but it's still a cool and tranquil place to spend an afternoon.

WHERE TO STAY (tel prefix 0743)

During the Festival of the Two Worlds accommodation is tight in Spoleto and in the surrounding area from Foligno to Terni, so reserve months in advance. The tourist office in Spoleto has a list of private rooms to rent, but again, don't count on finding one on the spot: plan ahead. Spoleto itself has several fine hotels, of which the most spectacular is the tiny ****Gattapone**, Via del Ponte 6, tel 36 147, located in a stone house, clinging to the slope near the Rocca and the Ponte delle Torri, with fabulous views; even during the festival rush it remains serene. Its eight rooms are spacious and finely furnished; another house next door contains the restaurant (L100–110 000). Another very comfortable choice, ***Dei Duchi**, Viale Matteotti 4, tel 44 541, is centrally located near the Piazza della Libertà, yet enjoys fine views over Spoleto. Popular among visiting artists and performers, it is a well-designed contemporary hotel (L100–150 000). ***Nuovo Clitunno**, Piazza Sordini 6, tel 38 240, is a good, fairly central hotel (L66–85 000, all rooms with bath). At Monteluco, the ***Parco Ipost, tel 36 141, is a pleasant resort hotel, with a garden, tennis, pool, great views and peace and quiet (L75 000, all rooms with bath). ***Dell'Angelo**, Via Arco di Druso 25, tel 32 185, offers six good double rooms near the centre of the action (L32 000 without bath, L48 000 with).

EATING OUT

Good Umbrian truffle dishes are the speciality at **Il Tartufo**, Piazza Garibaldi 24, tel 40 236, utilizing the black truffles of the Valnerina in various forms of pasta and eggs; other dishes include grilled lamb and kid, and veal. Prices depend on whether or not you indulge in the tasty tuber (L40–50 000; closed Wed). **Sabatini**, Corso Mazzini 54, tel 37 233, has good traditional Umbrian fare, served indoors and out (L24 000). For a good glass of wine and tasty snacks and spaghetti, try **La Cantina**, Via Filitteria 10a, tel 44 475 (L24 000 for a snack and a bottle of wine; L30 000 for a full meal). Up on Monteluco, near the church of San Giuliano, **Trattoria S. Giuliano**, tel 47 797, is a lovely place overlooking Spoleto, with seasonal Umbrian dishes like *bruschetto, strangozzi*, asparagus omelettes, mushrooms, and game dishes (L30 000 at the most). Outside Spoleto, on the N. 33 to Terni, the **Madrigale**, tel 54 144, offers a gourmet *menu degustazione* of Umbrian specialities; just sit down and a tasty array of pasta and meat courses will arrive at your table, all for about L45 000. There are also three lovely rooms to rent, with pretty views.

South of Perugia: The Tiber Valley

From Perugia, long modern N. 3bis follows the Tiber to Todi with only a few possible distractions along the way. **Torgiano**, 15 km south, has one of Umbria's best-known vineyards and an excellent wine museum (see Perugia: Where to Stay); it stands near the turn off for **Bettona**, 7 km to the east, a compact, nearly elliptical hill town, but big enough to have a long history as an Etruscan city and Roman *municipium*. Unfortunately all the art and artefacts found here have been carted off to Rome's Villa Giulia museum. At the northern end of the walls you can still see the monolithic stones of the original Etruscan fortifications. The humble **Palazzo Podestarile** (1478) in the central Piazza Cavour has a small picture collection open on request; chief works are Peruginos's *Madonna rolamo* and Dono Doni's *Nativity*.

Deruta

TOURIST INFORMATION

Piazza dei Consoli 4, tel (075) 971 1559.

If there's room in your suitcase, stop and buy a plate in the tiny hill town of **Deruta** (pop. 7500), 20 km from Perugia just off the Via Flaminia. Along with Gubbio, Deruta has been Umbria's centre for ceramics and majolica since the Middle Ages. All through the town, shops hang out displays of colourful majolica ware. If there's no room in your grip, you can still admire the works of past artisans in the **Museo delle Ceramiche** (open by request, 9–1, closed Sun), housed in the medieval **Palazzo Comunale**, along with a small Pinacoteca that features the modest talents of Nicolò Alunno. The Palazzo stands in Deruta's fine central square, Piazza dei Consoli, as does 14th-century **San Francesco**, its interior embellished with contemporary Sienese and Umbrian frescoes. Another church, **S. Antonio Abate**, has frescoes by Bartolomeo Caporali of Perugia.

In the fortified village of **Castellone**, a few km east in the hills, the frescoes in the parish church were done by Matteo da Gualdo. More unusual are the decorations in little **Madonna del Bagno**, 2 km south of Deruta along N. 3bis: it's full of colourful ceramic votives made in the 17th and 18th centuries, the heyday of majolica art. Across the highway to the south, there is a 12th-century castle at **Marsciano**, and several more ruined ones in the hills around **San Venanzo**, though it's unclear why the medieval barons found this lonely country worth all the trouble.

Todi

Todi (pop. 17,200) may be small, but it has everything it needs to rate as a self-respecting central Italian hill town. There's the hill, of course, a cathedral upstaged by exceptional medieval public buildings, one great Renaissance monument, a long and tortuous history, a saint (uncanonized, this time), and a proud communal escutcheon, a fierce eagle over the inevitable device *SPQT*. And since 1986, it has added the latest fashionable ingredient: a Festival di Todi, which brings the town opera, ballet and stage companies in the first ten days of September.

History

It was the eagle that showed the ancient Umbrians where to build the city they called *Tuter*, high atop what is now the Rocca. Later, the Etruscans founded a settlement lower down, around the Piazza del Popolo; according to legend, one day they slaughtered many of their Umbrian neighbours and enslaved the rest. As *Colonia Julia Fida Tuder*, the town prospered through Roman times, and its nearly impregnable site kept the barbarians out remarkably well; there's no evidence that Todi ever was part of the Lombard duchy of Spoleto, and indeed it may have maintained its independence all along. By the 1200s, Todi had accumulated a little empire, including Terni and Amelia, and its soldiers kept in trim by constant dust-ups with their peers in Spoleto, Narni and Orvieto. By the end of the century both the government and the political effectiveness of the free *comune* were failing. The Atti family established themselves as *signori* in the early 1300s, and then the pope gobbled up the town for the Papal State in 1330.

But Todi's prosperous and successful 13th century, besides embellishing the city with its finest buildings, also contributed its best-known son: **Jacopone dei Benedetti** (1228–1306), the greatest of the *laudesi*, or medieval Franciscan poets, who like St Francis, sang songs of praise to cheer the people. Jacopone, before becoming 'Christ's clown', was a wealthy lawyer. When he caught the Franciscan spirit, though, he turned into such an eccentric that the Franciscans at first refused him admission. In the end, however, he found his niche with the Spirituals, the most unworldly branch of the order, living in a monastery at Collazzone, near Perugia, where he is believed to have composed the famous Latin *Stabat Mater Dolorosa* and the *Stabat Mater Speciosa*—as well as some of the first Christmas carols.

Modern Todi is a sophisticated little place, famous for its carpentry and woodworking. In April it hosts one of Italy's major antique fairs, and in August and September the *Mostra Nazionale dell'Artigianato*, a national crafts fair.

GETTING AROUND

Todi is linked by bus with Terni (33 km/45 min), Perugia (41 km/1 hr), and Rome (130 km/2½ hrs), and by the FCU's little choo-choo-trains from Perugia or Terni. There are two stations: Stazione Ponte Rio is closer and more convenient to town, where a city bus meets the train to take you uphill. Unfortunately there's only one bus a day between Todi and Orvieto, a route that takes in the lovely scenery over the Tiber valley. If you're driving, Todi is just off N. 3bis; of the two roads linking Todi and Orvieto, the N. 79bis is the more dramatically scenic—also the longer and more difficult.

TOURIST INFORMATION

Piazza Umberto 6, tel (075) 883 395.

Piazza del Popolo

Todi's streets converge on its magnificent 13th–15th-century **Piazza del Popolo**, the centre of civic life since the Etruscans. The piazza is a medieval pageant in grey stone, though now its great palazzi glare down with haughty contempt on the rows of parked Fiats jammed onto their noble doorsteps. Sternest of them all, the **Palazzo dei Priori** (1293–1337) has square battlements with a chunky tower, while the **Palazzo del Popolo** (1213), with the swallowtail crenellations, and its adjacent **Palazzo del Capitano** (1290) are all grace by comparison; these two, connected by a grand Gothic stairway, make a remarkable composition, one of the best medieval town halls in Italy. Up on the fourth floor of the Palazzo del Capitano, there's a small **Museo Etrusco-Romano** and **Pinacoteca** that you can take in if it decides to rain (8–2, Sun 9–1, closed Mon; adm) and an impressive Gothic hall with frescoes.

On the far side of the piazza, the squarish **Duomo** is enthroned atop a distinguished flight of steps. Begun in the 12th century, its façade has a fine rose window and delicately decorated portal, while the interior is embellished with good Romanesque capitals and an arcade with a 14th-century altarpiece; parishioners who turned around to gossip during Mass were confronted by a not-too-terrifying vision of the *Last Judgement* by a north Italian artist, Farraù da Faenza. You can also visit the crypt for its cryptic charm. Before leaving the piazza, have a look over the balcony behind the civic palaces for a view over much of central Umbria.

San Fortunato and the Rocca

Todi's medieval lanes invite aimless roaming, but if you're pressed for time, head straight along Via Mazzini to the almost out of scale Franciscan church of **San Fortunato**, built in 1292, located up a broad stair in a prominent position. A bronze statue of Jacopone stands near the foot of the steps; his locally revered tomb is in San Fortunato's crypt. In front of the church are three recessed Romanesque portals, the central one especially lovely with its carvings of acanthus leaves and little human figures near the base. But the façade remains unfinished; according to legend, when the Orvietani heard that Todi had commissioned Lorenzò Maitani to decorate it, they had the sculptor murdered to prevent Todi from having a church as good as their cathedral. Through Romanesque doors awaits an airy, luminous Gothic interior, one of the best in central Italy. It contains Todi's greatest work of art, a fresco of the *Madonna and Child* by Masolino, who came from the nearby town of Panicale, south of Lake Trasimeno. The fine wooden choir in the apse is by Antonio Maffei of Gubbio (1590).

Above San Fortunato, crowning the town is the massive round tower of the **Rocca**—all that remains of Todi's 14th-century citadel—public park, and magnificent belvedere, offering an unforgettable view of the valley of the Tiber and the Tempio della Consolazione. Of Roman Todi, little remains but some bits of the amphitheatre, near the eastern Porta Romana, and in Piazza Mercato Vecchio, a series of imposing arches with a Doric frieze above, called the **Nicchioni** (niches); they are believed to be the wall of an Augustan era basilica.

Tempio della Consolazione

Of the three major attempts in Tuscany and Umbria to create a perfect Renaissance temple, one is nearly perfect (Montepulciano), one a disaster (Prato), and the third a modest success—naturally, that is the one in Umbria. The impressive, ivory-coloured **Tempio della Consolazione**, designed by Cola da Caprarola in 1508, shows the strong influence of Bramante, who may indeed have helped with the design. It was not completed until 99 years later. By that time every celebrity architect of the late Renaissance had had his say in the work: Sangallo the Younger, Peruzzi and Vignola among others. But unlike St Peter's in Rome, too many cooks did not spoil this broth. The Tempio's purity of form, geometrically harmonious restraint, and careful proportions came out as if the work of a single architect. Its setting, alone amid the wooded hills and farmlands, lends it a special charm; the fine dome and four semi-domes enclose an equally white classical interior, in the symmetrical form of a Greek cross, containing good Baroque statues of the twelve Apostles.

WHERE TO STAY AND EAT (tel prefix 075)

For motorists, the pick of Todi's small selection of hotels is the ****__Bramante__, Via Orvietana 48, tel 884 8381, a 13th-century convent beautifully restored, located just outside town. Rooms have air conditioning, baths, and frigo-bars, while outside you can play tennis in the garden, or leave the children with the hotel's babysitting service (L140–160 000). ***__Villa Luisa__, Via A. Cortesi 147, tel 884 8571, is a pleasant place nearer the centre, with parking and a garden; most rooms have TVs as well, and all have private bath (L70–80 000). **__Cavour__, Corso Cavour 12, tel 882 417, is a simple older hotel very conveniently located in the centre (L40 000 without bath, L60 000 with). Local specialities in the kitchen range from the usual pigeon, lamb, and *porchetta*, though here the homemade fat spaghetti is called *ombricelli*, served by preference *alla boscaiola* (tomatoes, piquant black olives, and hot peppers); the wine to look for, dating back to the days of the Roman Republic, is the dry white *Grechetto di Todi*. For fine Umbrian cuisine with an enchanting Umbrian view, eat at—where else?—the **Umbria**, under the stone arches just off the Piazza del Popolo at Via S. Bonaventura 3, tel 882 390. Meals begin with a delicious variety of antipasti, followed perhaps by *spaghetti alla tudertina*, and succulent grilled *secondi*, ranging from trout to boar (L30–35 000). Otherwise, try **Jacopone**, in Piazza Jacopone, tel 882 366, with similar Umbrian specialities for L30 000.

Acquasparta and San Gemini

From Todi, you have the choice of following the Tiber down to Orvieto, or the highway down to Terni and the valley of the Nera. This latter route passes two little towns known for their waters since the Etruscans: **Acquasparta** (Latin *Ad Aquas Partas*) can show you a small zoo and the 1565 Palazzo Cesi, with Renaissance frescoes. Normally peaceful and very Umbrian, the town alarms its neighbours every summer by hosting, of all things, a German *lieder*-singing competition. From Acquasparta, you can duck down to visit **Montecastrilli**, a traditional Umbrian hamlet, or follow a pretty mountain road, N. 418, which will lead you across to Spoleto—just don't think you've got lost and gone back to Tuscany when you see signs for Arezzo and Firenzuola. There are pleasant picnic spots along the way overlooking deep-set **Lake of Arezzo**, and near that a Romanesque church with an unusual portico at a country crossroads called **Firenzuola**.

San Gemini, another quiet spot to sort out your digestive problems, has its spa in a pretty park full of old oaks. The old centre is essential Umbrian hilltown, despite being wrecked on two occasions, by the Saracens in 882, and by the Imperial army of the Constable of Bourbon in 1527, practising for the sack of Rome. Just outside town, the church of San Francesco has a 12th-century carved portal; another country church, S. Nicolò, keeps fragments of its original painting of the 1200s. And to the north, you can see the small but interesting ruined Roman city of **Carsulae**, never rebuilt after its destruction in the 800s. A simple arch, built by Trajan, remains from the walls, with a long stretch of the original paved Via Flaminia passing underneath. The foundations in the town centre have been excavated, including a theatre and amphitheatre, as well as temples and a basilica around the forum. One of the temples was rebuilt into the medieval chapel of S. Damiano.

Along the Tiber and N. 448 towards Orvieto, you'll pass the **Lago di Corbara**, backed up into the hills by a modern dam, but primarily of interest for its nationally famous restaurant (see p. 445).

Orvieto

Orvieto (pop. 23,000) owes much of its success to an ancient volcano. First it created the city's magnificent pedestal—a 325-m sheer crag of tufa, resembling a mesa in the American southwest. The same volcano enriched the hillsides below with a special mixture of minerals that form part of the secret alchemy of Orvieto's famous white wine. Although new buildings crowd the outskirts of Orvieto's unique hill, the medieval town on top, crowned by its stupendous cathedral, looks much the same as it has for the last 500 years. The scaffolding you see around the cliffs, however, is part of a recent effort to shore it up; human progress isn't as much of a threat to the old centre as are such natural forces as erosion and landslides.

Attracted by Orvieto's incomparable defensive position, the Etruscans settled it early and named it *Volsinium*. It was one of the twelve cities of the Etruscan confederation, and one that fought frequently with the Romans until those upstarts laid it waste in 280 BC. It must have been a wealthy place; historians record the Romans as carrying home some 2000 statues after the sack. The Etruscans departed in a huff and founded a new *Volsinium* on the shores of Lake Bolsena, leaving behind their old city (*Urbs Vetus*, hence 'Orvieto'). Orvieto in the Middle Ages was an important stronghold of the Papal States—important primarily for popes who could take refuge here when they were on the outs in Rome.

GETTING AROUND

Orvieto lies on the main railway between Florence (152 km/2 hrs) and Rome (121 km/2 hrs); from Perugia it's 86 km and just over an hour. Orvieto is also linked by coach with Terni and Todi (48 km/2 hrs), a magnificently scenic journey down N. 79bis made only once a day, and far more frequently with Viterbo in Lazio (see p. 447), all departing from Piazza XXIX Marzo. Bus no. 1 from the station makes the steep trip up, though Orvieto is repairing its aged funivia from the station to the top of the town. If you're driving, Orvieto's an exit off the A1; there's usually plenty of parking in Piazzale Cahen, next to the Fortezza.

TOURIST INFORMATION

Piazza Duomo 24, tel (0763) 41 772.
Post Office: Via Cesare Nebbia, just off Corso Cavour.
Telephones: Valentino's Bar, Piazza Fracassini 11, just off Corso Cavour, closed Fridays, has metered phone boxes.

The Cathedral

The 13th century may have been an age of faith, but it certainly wasn't an age of fools. The popes were having trouble putting over the doctrine of transubstantiation, an archaic, genuinely pagan survival that many in the Church found difficulty in accepting. It was during one of Orvieto's papal visits (Pope Urban IV) in the 1260s, that the necessary miracle occurred. A Bohemian priest named Peter, while on his way to Rome, was asked to celebrate mass in the town of Bolsena, just south of Orvieto. Father Peter had long been sceptical about the doctrine of the Host becoming in truth the body of Christ, but during this mass the Host itself answered his doubts by dripping blood on the altar linen. Marvelling, Peter took the linen to the Pope in Orvieto, who declared it a miracle and instituted the feast of Corpus Christi. Thomas Aquinas, also in Orvieto at the time, was asked to compose a suitable office for the new holy day, while Urban IV promised Orvieto (and not poor Bolsena!) a magnificent new cathedral to enshrine the blood-stained relic. The cornerstone was laid in 1290, and though begun in the Romanesque style, its plan was transformed into the new-fangled Gothic by master architect Lorenzo Maitani of Siena in 1310. Subsequent architects included such luminaries as Andrea Pisano, Orcagna, and Sammicheli. But even then the mighty edifice, visible for miles around, wasn't completed until the 17th century.

The end result is one of Italy's greatest cathedrals, with a stunning, sumptuous façade resembling a giant triptych. This is Maitani's masterpiece, a creation that earned the church its nickname, the 'Golden Lily of Cathedrals'. As you approach, you are struck first by dazzling, technicolor hues of its mosaics, and then by the elaborate, prickly spires and tracery, and as you draw near, by the richness and beauty of the sculptural detail. It is said that 152 sculptors worked on Orvieto cathedral, but it was Maitani himself who contributed the best work—the remarkable design and execution of the celebrated **bas-reliefs** on the lower pilasters that recount the story of the Creation to the Last Judgement, a Bible in stone that captures the essence of the stories with vivid drama and detail. Maitani's *Last Judgement*, in particular, is enough to make the fresco in Todi Cathedral look as dire as a soft-touch greeting card. Maitani also cast the four bronze figures of the Evangelists' symbols, the ox, eagle, man, and winged lion, all ready to step right off the façade. He also did the angels in the lunette over the central portal, who pay homage to a Madonna by Andrea Pisano. The magnificent rose window is by Orcagna, and the controversial bronze doors, portraying the *Works of Mercy*, are by Emilio Greco, completed in 1965.

THE INTERIOR

In contrast with the soaring vertical lines of the façade, the cathedral's sides and interior (closed between 1 and 2:30) are banded with horizontal zebra stripes, a handsome contrast. In the muted light of the interior, filtered through alabaster windows, the stripes merge into shadows. The lack of clutter does much to reveal the cathedral's proportions and the sense of height. The columns of the nave support rounded arches, and above them runs a fine clerestory. Among the works of art in the nave, the most notable are Gentile da Fabriano's 1426 fresco of the Madonna, near the baptismal font, and the 1579 *Pietà* by Ippolito Scalza, a native of Orvieto.

The greatest treasures, however, are in the chapels. Bring plenty of coins to illuminate them, especially the **Cappella della Madonna di San Brizio**, painted with one of the finest fresco cycles of the Renaissance. The project was begun in 1447 by Fra Angelico, with the assistance of his pupil Benozzo Gozzoli. The Angelic One finished two sections—the serene *Christ in Judgement* with the prophets, while Gozzoli contributed the hierarchies of angels. Before he could finish, however, Fra Angelico was summoned to Rome. Orvieto then commissioned Perugino to complete the work, but he never got around to it, and finally, in 1499, the city hired Luca Signorelli, who completed the vaults according to Fra Angelico's design. The walls, however, are Signorelli's masterpiece: his breathtaking and awesome compositions of the *Last Judgement*, the *Preaching of the Antichrist* (a most unusual subject), and the *Resurrection of the Dead* are generally acclaimed to be the inspiration for Michelangelo's *Last Judgement* in the Sistine Chapel. Yet it is hard to say that Michelangelo surpassed them; Signorelli's remarkable fore-shortening skills, draughtsmanship, and ability to simplify nature and architecture into the essential geometrical forms, give the frescoes tremendous power. Far to the left of the figure of the preaching Antichrist, Signorelli has portrayed himself and Fra Angelico, both listening solemnly, as does Dante standing amidst a crowd including Petrarch and Christopher Columbus, while in the background chaos and catastrophe are busy at work. Signorelli's mistress jilted him while he painted this, and he painted her in the scene as a prostitute taking money to the right of the Antichrist. Then the world ends, the darkened sky shot with streaks of fire, the earth shakes, and in literal detail the dead re-emerge from the earth, skeletons pulling themselves out of the ground, forming new coats of flesh. Some are met by Charon, who rows them across to Renaissance hell, to keep company with Signorelli's mistress, caught in the embrace of a blue devil. Below the frescoes Signorelli painted medallions of Homer, Dante, Virgil, Ovid, Horace, Lucan and pre-Socratic philosopher Empedocles, and scenes from the *Divine Comedy*.

The left arm of the cathedral crossing houses the **Chapel of the Corporale** (of the blood-stained linen cloth), frescoed with scenes of the *Miracle of Bolsena* by Ugolino of Siena (1360s), and on the right wall there's the 1339 *Madonna dei Raccomandati* by Lippo Memmi. On the altar, a Gothic tabernacle shelters the Corporale's fabulous **reliquary**, made in 1338 by Ugolino di Vieri. Before leaving, take a look at the cathedral's organ, built in the late 16th century and the second largest in Italy; for a real ear-opener, attend a musical mass.

Around Piazza del Duomo

Rising up on the north side of the piazza is a colourful clock tower, where a bronze figure named **Maurizio** strikes the hours, as he has done since 1351; the cathedral builders timed their workday by his clanging. Across from the cathedral, in the Palazzo Faina, the **Museo Civico** (9–1 and 2:30–4:30 winter afternoons, 3–7 summer, closed Mon) contains Orvieto's excellent Etruscan collection: items found in local tombs, with numerous Greek vases (and Etruscan imitations) among the jewellery and terracottas. The top floor of the palace enjoys one of the best views of the cathedral. On the south side of the cathedral, the **Palazzo Papale**, or Pope's palace, built by Urban IV and finished in 1304, contains the **Museo dell'Opera del Duomo** (May–Aug 9–1 and 3–6, otherwise 9–12 and 2:30–4:30; closed Mon; adm), with works of art that once filled the cathedral—statues by grand masters like Arnolfo di Cambio and Andrea Pisano, and grand statues by little-known hands, especially the colossal *Apostles*. Paintings include a *Crucifixion* by Spinello Aretino, a *Magdalene* by Signorelli (very much like the one painted by his master Piero della Francesca, in Arezzo cathedral), and most beautiful of all, two lovely, richly coloured Madonnas by Simone Martini.

Smaller Churches

In contrast to its heavenly cathedral (even Pope John XXIII said that on Judgement Day the angels would bear it up to Paradise), the rest of Orvieto is unpretentious and worldly, a solid, bourgeois, medieval town. On Via del Duomo stands the medieval **Torre del Moro**, and further on, the pretty 12th-century **Palazzo del Popolo**, a tufa palace with mullioned windows and arches; the little piazza in front is the site of a colourful vegetable market. From here, Via della Pace leads back to the narrow church of **San Domenico**, built in 1233, just after St Dominic's canonization—the first Dominican church ever built. Another saint, Thomas Aquinas, taught here at the former monastery and is recalled with several mementoes; don't miss the elegant *Tomb of Cardinal de Braye* by Arnolfo di Cambio.

Piazza della Repubblica

From Via del Duomo Orvieto's main Corso Cavour leisurely winds through 16th-century palazzi and medieval homes to the main **Piazza della Repubblica**. On the corner, the historic 12th-century church of **Sant'Andrea** has an unusual 12-sided campanile, pierced by mullioned windows and topped by bellicose crenellations. The site is ancient: the ruins of a 6th-century church were discovered underneath Sant' Andrea and on an even lower level an Etruscan street and buildings (the sacristan has the key to the excavations). Sant'Andrea, decorated with 14th-century frescoes, basks in the memory of the important events that took place within its walls: here Innocent III proclaimed the Fourth Crusade, and here in 1281 Charles of Anjou and his glittering retinue attended the coronation of Martin IV. Piazza della Repubblica is the site of the 13th-century **Palazzo Comunale**, hidden by a late Renaissance façade, and the starting point for exploring some of Orvieto's most ancient streets, like Via Loggia dei Mercanti, lined with tufa houses; follow Via Filippeschi back to the northwesternmost corner of the town, site of the church of **San Giovenale**, begun in 1009 and full of frescoes of the 12th–15th centuries.

Orvieto claims yet one other noteworthy church, **San Lorenzo de Arari**, reached by Via Maitani from the Piazza Duomo, or on Via Scalza from Corso Cavour. Built in the 14th century, San Lorenzo shelters a cylindrical Etruscan altar under its Christian high altar, all of which are protected by a lovely 12th-century stone canopy. Byzantine-style frescoes cover the walls, with elongated figures and staring eyes; one set depicts the life of San Lorenzo, who retains his sense of humour even while being toasted on the grill.

Pozzo di San Patrizio

Orvieto's northeastern end (near the upper station of the funivia) is dominated by a citadel built in 1364 by the great papal legate, Cardinal Albornoz. Only the walls, a gate, and a tower survive, encompassing a pretty little garden of parasol pines. There are good views from the ramparts, stretching from the shallow Paglia river all the way to the Tiber valley.

Next to the citadel lie the foundations of an **Etruscan temple** and the **Pozzo di San Patrizio** (St Patrick's well), designed in the 1530s by Antonio da Sangallo the Younger on the orders of the calamitous Medici Pope Clement VII. After surviving the sack of Rome—and sneaking out of the city disguised as a greengrocer—Clement became understandably paranoid about the security of the papal person. He commissioned this unique work of engineering to supply Orvieto in the event of a siege; to reach the spring below, Sangallo had to dig down the equivalent of seven storeys; to haul the water to the surface he built two spiral stairs of 248 steps, which never cross—one for the water-carriers and their donkeys going down, another for going up. The stairs are dimly lit by windows on the central shaft; think twice before you descend; you have to get back up again under your own steam (summer 8:30–1 and 3–dusk, winter 10–1 and 2–dusk; adm). Despite the labour that went into its construction, the well was never needed. But it didn't harm the Church as much as another decision the hapless Clement made in Orvieto—his refusal to annul Henry VIII's marriage to Catherine of Aragon.

Down below Orvieto's northern cliffs, along the road that leads towards the rail station there are several **Etruscan tombs**, nothing special compared with the tombs of Chiusi or Tarquinia. None are decorated; they seem almost like a street of low houses, each sparsely furnished with a pair of benches where the urns of the departed were arranged—the most impressive is the 4th-century BC **Necropoli del Crocifisso**, the austerity of its large tufa blocks relieved by velvety moss. Also outside the city, about 5 km south from the Porta Romana, there is the 12th–13th-century Benedictine abbey of **SS. Severo e Martirio** (now partly a hotel), retaining much of its original work—a Cosmatesque pavement and some trecento frescoes, as well as another strange dodecagonal campanile like the one at S. Andrea within the city.

Wine and Song

Orvieto Classico, Umbria's most famous wine, comes from 16 designated areas in Terni and Viterbo provinces, and consists of a careful mixture of different grapes, with Tuscan Trebbiano and Verdello dominant. The resulting wine, either dry (Orvieto *secco*) or moderately sweet (*abboccato*, often served with dessert), is a delicious, light straw-coloured wine; there are plenty of places in Orvieto to try it, beginning with the wine shops and bars around the cathedral; the Antinori label is one of the best, but don't neglect the others. Besides the solemn procession of the *Corporale* at Corpus Domini in early June, Orvieto hosts a series of concerts in August, leading up to the cracking **Festa della Palombella** on the 15th, with simultaneous noon fireworks explosions in front of the cathedral and church of San Francesco, ignited by an iron dove on a wire.

WHERE TO STAY (tel prefix 0763)

Orvieto's hotels have more character than many, most stunningly ****La Badia**, located in the hills 5 km south on the road towards Bagnoregio, tel 90 359, with views up to the tufa-crowned citadel. A 12th-century abbey, renovated in the 19th century, it preserves much of its original ambience; the rooms are lovely and comfortable, and in the grounds there's a pool and tennis court, although it doesn't come cheaply (L165–200 000). Up in Orvieto itself, ****Maitani**, Via Maitani 5, tel 42 011, is a fine hotel just opposite the cathedral, where the comfortable rooms all have bath, air conditioning, and TV, and there's parking as well (L135 000). The ***Grand Hotel Reale**, Piazza del Popolo 25, tel 41 247, was one of the town's first hotels, an old dear full of personality and atmosphere if not modern amenities (L50 000 without bath, L80 000 with). Just around the corner, **Antico Zoppo**, Via Marabottini 2, tel 40 370, is a recently renovated hotel with the best rooms in its price range (L35–40 000 without bath, L55–60 000 with).

EATING OUT

Orvieto often sees bus-loads of day-trippers from Rome, who help keep its mediocre and often expensive restaurants in business. A triad of real choices among the pretenders are: **Le Grotte del Funaro**, Via Ripa Serancia 41, tel 43 276, located in one of Orvieto's prettier corners. This elegant restaurant occupies a set of tufa caves and dishes up good, solid Umbrian cuisine, with especially good pasta and mixed grilled meats (L40 000; closed Mon). **Del Pino da Cecco**, Via di Piazza del Popolo 15/21, tel 42 661, has a lovely terrace with views over the oldest part of town, where you can also enjoy appetizing specialities like *cannelloni alla Ducale* or tagliatelle with artichokes, or *bistecca in intingolo* (beef in a savoury sauce), accompanied by the delicious dry wines of Orvieto (L30–35 000). The best bargain in town is the tasty homecooked meals at **Da Anna**, Piazza I. Scalza 1, tel 41 098, for L20 000.

Southeast at Civitella del Lago, 13 km from Orvieto on artifical Lake Corbara, you can splurge at a restaurant gourmets rank as one of Italy's top five: **Vissani**, tel (0744) 950 296. In this almost passionately religious inner sanctum of *cucina altissima*, you may dip your fork (but only if you've diligently reserved a table in advance) into such marvels as oysters with roast onions and thyme sauce, suckling pig with bilberries, or lobster in broccoli leaves, to mention only a fraction of the master's dishes, each dish accompanied by a specially prepared bread. A fabulous array of Italian and French cheeses and exquisite wines will help make your meal unforgettable. The *menu degustazione* is around L100 000; with a rare wine, somewhat more; closed Wed. If these prices ruin your appetite, you can also eat very well nearby at **Il Padrino**, also on the lake on N. 448, tel (0744) 950 206, where chef Vissani got his start. The pasta with seafood or asparagus in season is lovely, and the *secondi* are classics rarely seen (or prepared very well) in Italy, like Chateaubriand, scampi Newburg, coq-au-vin, and sole Colbert (a palatable L50 000 or so; closed Wed).

Southwest Umbria

TOURIST INFORMATION
Amelia: Via Orvieto 1, tel (0744) 981 453.

North of Orvieto

The rather empty territory to the north of Orvieto isn't one of the more exciting regions, even by Umbrian standards. **Castel Viscardo**, in an isolated setting to the northwest, takes its name from a really fancy castle, an archaic sort of family palace built for the Mondaldeschis of Orvieto in the 1400s. **Fabro**, 23 km north just off the A1, had a more serious castle until the Germans made it into a stronghold during the campaigns of 1944; both castle and town suffered greatly. **Allerona**, 17 km northwest of Orvieto, is another out-of-the-way spot, and the westernmost *comune* in Umbria, where you can see some well-preserved stretches of a minor Roman aqueduct. Finally, before you get to Città della Pieve (p. 385), there is another pleasant hill village, its houses packed densely over the surrounding cliffs, called **Monteleone d'Orvieto**.

South of Orvieto

This is another sleepy corner on the Umbrian frontier; it hasn't many surprises to offer, although there is some splendid scenery along the N. 205, high over the valley of the Tiber. Some 20 km south of Orvieto, along N. 205 medieval **Alviano** is dominated by a strong and perfectly preserved castle built by the feudal Liviani family not in the Middle Ages, but in 1506. The Tiber has been dammed up here to create another small artificial lake, **Lago di Alviano**; its banks are nothing to look at now, but come back in a century or so. Walled **Lugnano in Teverina** (pop. 1650), built along a ridge 4 km south, is by far the most interesting town in these parts, and it attracts a few Romans and even foreigners for summer 'villeggiatura' (country holidays). Its main attraction is one of the finest, most exotic-looking Romanesque churches around, the 12th-century **S. Maria Assunta**, with a columned portico (derived from the form of some secular ancient Roman basilicas), a rose window, and some interesting carved details on the capitals; inside are *ambones* (twin pulpits), an iconostasis, and Cosmati-work *transennas*. Ten km south of Lugnano are two game but crumbling medieval villages overlooking the Tiber, **Attigliano** and **Giove**, the latter with an imposing and really rather elegant 16th-century palace-fortress of the Mattei, a great Roman family.

Amelia, and a Detour into Lazio

About 11 km east of Lugnano on N. 205, the gritty and lately prosperous hill town of **Amelia** (pop. 11,100) was claimed by Roman writers like Pliny and Cato to be among the oldest Italian cities—perhaps founded in the 12th century BC; impressive portions of its megalithic walls remain, along with bits of Roman masonry and columns in some of the houses. The Renaissance sculptor Agostino di Duccio is buried here, in San Francesco, and there are some characteristic bas-reliefs of his followers in the **Cathedral**, almost completely rebuilt in 1640. **Sant'Agostino** church has a good, squarish Gothic façade. Perhaps the best thing to do is hire a horse from the stables of the Circolo Ippico Amerino, at Via Rietta 15, and explore the lovely *terra incognita* to the north, between Amelia and Todi: hamlets like Dunarobba, Montenero, Camerata, and Umbria's petrified forest.

Most of the truly remarkable sights in these parts are over the border in Lazio—**Viterbo** is only 22 km from Attigliano, with its papal palace from the Middle Ages; on the way you shouldn't miss the **Monster Park** in the woebegone village of Bomarzo, a mad garden of colossal cinquecento sculptures that brings the neurosis of late Renaissance Italy right to the surface. Just to the south, the pretty Cimino hills shelter fine towns like **Soriano al Cimino** and **S. Martino nel Cimino**, as well as beautiful, unspoiled **Lake Vico**, an ancient volcanic crater. **Caprarola**, nearby, sits in the shadow of one of the greatest, strangest and most arrogant of all Renaissance palaces, the Farnese, built with papal booty by villainous Paul III.

Narni

High over the river Nera, a convenient stop on the Via Flaminia, Narni (pop. 21,000) is a fine old hill town and one of Umbria's best-kept secrets. Originally Etruscan *Nequinum*, it changed its name to *Narnia* and its allegiance to Rome in 299 BC, and was later the birthplace of Emperor Nerva (AD32). Today Narni, despite its dramatic position and

Via del Monte, Narni

fine medieval churches and palaces, is defended, so to speak, by its modern industry and electro-carbon plant in the river valley; most people never get past these to discover one of the most pleasant of Umbria's hill towns.

GETTING AROUND

Narni is easily reached by train from Rome (89 km/1 hr), Terni, Spoleto, or Assisi on the main Rome-Ancona line; it is only 15 km from the main Florence-Rome rail and autostrada junction at Orte. Frequent buses link the railway station with the city on the hill. Other buses make connections to Amelia, Terni, and surrounding hamlets; you can hire a car at Auto Maggiore, Via Tuderte 10, tel 737 997.

TOURIST INFORMATION

Piazza dei Priori 18, tel (0744) 715 362.

To and Around Piazza Garibaldi

The sight in Narni that most engaged the Grand Tourist of the past two centuries is the romantically ruined **Bridge of Augustus**, visible from the bridge near lower, industrial Narni Scalo; if you're coming by train, you'll pass right by its great arches, just south of the station. Many of the old city gates are intact, especially the eastern **Porta Ternana**, with its twin round towers, where the Via Flaminia enters Narni proper. This ancient road leads shortly into the main crossroads of Narni, the colourful, irregularly shaped **Piazza Garibaldi**. Narrow lanes from here wind up through a medieval quarter to the great foursquare **Rocca Albornoz**, built in the 1370s by the indefatigable Cardinal Albornoz, whose task it was to repair the Papal States after the 'Babylonian captivity' in Avignon. Though the Rocca is permanently being restored, the great views are worth the walk or drive up. The Via Flaminia itself continues through Piazza Garibaldi and skirts the steep promontory, offering a fine view over the narrow river canyon of the Nera, a river Virgil described as 'pale'; near Narni it takes on a natural if peculiar shade of robin's egg blue from the copper deposits in the surrounding soil.

The Duomo and Piazza dei Priori

From Piazza Garibaldi, Via Garibaldi, the main street of Narni, squeezes around the corner to the front of the **Duomo**, embellished with a quattrocento portico adorned by a classical frieze. Consecrated in 1145, with remnants of its original frescoes, the Duomo contains in its south aisle a statue of S. Antonio Abate by the Sienese Vecchietta, two 15th-century marble pulpits and the ancient marble screen, or **Sacello dei SS. Giovenale e Cassio**, pieced together in the Renaissance of palaeo-Christian and Romanesque reliefs and Cosmati work; the mosaic of the Redeemer dates from the 9th century. Across the narrow street from the cathedral is the Palazzo del Vescovile, with a **Roman arch** behind it.

From here, Via Garibaldi widens to form narrow Piazza dei Priori, address of the **Palazzo del Podestà** (14th–15th centuries), built over an old tower-house and decorated with four medieval bas-reliefs depicting a joust, a lion and dragon, the beheading of Holofernes, and a hunt with falcons. The atrium contains Roman and medieval remains, and in the Sala del Consiglio is Narni's great painting, a *Coronation of the Virgin* (1486) by Ghirlandaio. Across the street is the loggia and tower of the **Palazzo dei Priori**, built by

Gubbio's Matteo Gattapone; note the exterior pulpit, built for San Bernardino's sermons. Adjacent, at the head of Via Mazzini, is the pretty 12th-century Romanesque façade of **S. Maria in Pensole**. All around you'll see iron fixtures in the walls to hold torches for Narni's medieval May pageant, the *Corsa dell'Anello*, the Tournament of the Ring, in which knights from the three areas of Narni compete in piercing a ring with their lances at full gallop.

Further down palace-lined Via Mazzini, there's another 12th-century church, the large **San Domenico**, now used as the municipal art gallery, with an *Annunciation* by Gozzoli among the clutter of frescoes and paintings salvaged from local churches (open 8–2). From the garden behind there are more good views over the Nera and the nearby Romanesque Abbey of S. Cassiano. From the end of Via Mazzini and Piazza Marcellina, a street leads down to the **house of Gattamelata**, the 'honeyed cat', who was born with the name Erasmo da Narni to a baker here in 1370, and who went on to achieve fame and fortune as a great *condottiere* for the Republic of Venice and received the highest honour the Venetians ever bestowed on a mercenary commander: a paid funeral and an equestrian statue by Donatello, the first since Roman times and one of the jewels of the city of Padua, where it stands before the Basilica of Sant'Antonio. Two other Narnian churches have interesting quattrocento frescoes—**Sant'Agostino** on the eastern edge of town (with a fine Renaissance wooden Crucifix) and **San Francesco** on the western edge of Narni.

Otricoli

South of Narni, the ancient Via Flaminia (N. 3) continues towards the Rome of the Caesars, no longer the main highway of Empire, but a back road in one of the more obscure corners of Umbria. At about the 83 km mark, it passes through a small plain with rugged cliffs near the road, an ancient holy site that has somehow acquired the name **Grotte d'Orlando** (cave of Roland). Some badly worn Roman reliefs can be made out on the rocks, and there are remains of an altar called 'Roland's Seat'. Where the road branches off for Calvi, you'll see scanty remains of another Roman bridge, the **Ponte Sanguinario. Otricoli** (16 km from Narni), once the thriving Roman city of *Ocriculum*, now is reduced to a little, walled hill town with medieval-looking streets; the ruins of the old city, including an amphitheatre and baths with a good mosaic are just outside town, overlooking the Tiber.

Beyond that, the attractions on Umbria's southern borders are mostly scenery; oak forests around **Calvi** (11 km east of Otricoli, and the pretty, old village of **Stroncone** (east along some confusing back roads from Narni, or 8 km due south of Terni) which lies at the crossroads up to a big series of alpine meadows called **I Prati**, a popular resort of the Ternani on hot summer weekends.

WHERE TO STAY AND EATING OUT (tel prefix 0744)

In Lugnano in Teverina the best (and only) place to stay and eat is ****La Rocca,** Via Cavour 60, tel 902 129, a small, pleasant little inn in the centre, with parking. All rooms have private bath (L65 000), with good home-style cooking in the restaurant (L30 000). In Narni, most of the hotels are down by river and station at Narni Scalo; the finest is ******Dei Priori**, Vicolo del Comune 4, tel 726 843, located in a medieval palace on a narrow lane, with very comfortable rooms (L100–120 000); its restaurant, **La Loggia** (tel 722 744), pre-dates the hotel and has long been on the maps of visiting gourmets, featuring an amazing variety of country-based fare and local specialities, with unusual surprises that don't cost a bomb (L30–35 000; closed Mon). For something on the outskirts and a touch of the Arabian Nights, ***Minareto**, Via Cappuccini Nuovi 32, tel 726 343, has 10 pretty rooms near a tiny lake and garden (L80 000).

The Valnerina

The river Nera, one of the main tributaries of the Tiber, flows from the slopes of the mighty Monti Sibillini of the Marches along the southern edge of Umbria. Many of its sights are still Italian secrets: its black truffles, waterfall, and saints enjoy national reputations, but the rest is touristically *terra incognita*.

GETTING AROUND

N. 209 from Terni to Visso is the main thoroughfare of the Valnerina; for Norcia and Cascia, turn off at either Sant'Anatolia di Narco or Triponzo, the latter offering the prettier routes, N. 320 to Cascia and N. 396 to Norcia. Both towns have frequent buses to Spoleto. From Terni ACT provincial buses, tel 59 541, leave from the lot near the station for Narni, the Cascata delle Marmore, Piediluco, Arrone, Ferentillo, Spoleto, Orvieto, Viterbo, and Scheggino; another bus picks up passengers along N. 209 daily to Rome. Terni is the terminus of the FCU line through Todi, Perugia, Città di Castello to Sansepolcro, tel 415 297, and a stop on the FS's Rome-Ancona line, though from Rome you'll often have to change at Orte; coming from Assisi and points east usually requires a change at Foligno (for FS information, tel 401 283).

TOURIST INFORMATION

Terni: Viale C. Battisti 7a, tel (0744) 43 047.

Terni

Sprawling, mouldering, modern—you won't want to spend much time in southern Umbria's provincial capital, but at least some respect for its accomplishments is in order. In the 1800s, Terni (pop. 111,200) stole all the water out of Europe's highest waterfall for cheap hydroelectric power, starting Italy's first steel mill and lurching the nation into the Industrial Revolution. In the 1920s Terni scientists astounded the world with the first practical plastic. Terni also has an armaments works (the rifle that killed John Kennedy was manufactured here); these three industries together proved enough of an attraction during the last war for Allied air forces to smash the place flat. They also keep Terni an ardently Communist town, and a fun place to be on 1 May, occasion for a big parade of humorous floats made by towns in the province. By some quirk of fate, Terni's martyred first bishop, St Valentine, became the patron saint of lovers and the greeting-card industry. At the **Basilica di San Valentino**, 2 km south of the centre, his reunited remains are still honoured with a festival and market each 14 February—the mummified head was stolen in 1986 and found three years later, wrapped in newspaper under a park bench at the Cascata delle Marmore.

For the visitor, Terni has little to offer besides trains and buses to other places, and shots of viper juice (Vipero, the local *aperitivo* with all the excitement of a flat rum and Coke). Despite a history of over 2500 years the city has nothing to show for it. The Etruscans came first. During the original building of the steelworks the bulldozers uncovered an important Etruscan necropolis, though all the finds have been carted off to Rome's Villa Giulia museum. The ancient Romans called the city *Interamna Nahars*—a real mouthful that was traditionally considered the birthplace of the historian Tacitus, although scholars now quibble that Terni actually produced a more meagre Tacitus, Claudius Tacitus, emperor for a day.

Of Roman Terni only part of the **amphitheatre** remains, now employed as a pensioners' *bocce* (bowls) court in the city's prettiest area, in the public gardens off the main Corso del Popolo. Visible from the Corso and the amorphous Piazza Europa, the charming round church of **San Salvatore** was built in the 5th century, with a nave added in the 12th and early fresco fragments inside. Nearby stands the **Palazzo Spada** (1546) by Antonio da Sangallo the Younger and perhaps his least inspired effort. There are a couple of other churches worthy of note: the Knights of Malta's 12th-century church of **Sant'Alò**, off Via Cavour, and the 13th-century **San Francesco**, on the other side of Via Cavour. Its landmark 14th-century campanile with colourful ceramic edgings is by Angelo da Orvieto, and inside, to the right of the altar, is a 15th-century fresco based on the *Divine Comedy*.

From Piazza San Francesco, Via Fratini is the address of the 17th-century Palazzo Fabrizi, where the **Pinacoteca Comunale** has recently been arranged (open 10–1 and 4–7, closed Mon). Most of its paintings are by Anonymous (a strange 16th-century Circumcision; a portrait of St Charles Borromeo, bright light of the Counter-Reformation, but here almost caricatured, with an enormous nose; and then in the same Counter-Reformation vein, a neurotic, nightmarish scene of martyrdoms in the Low Countries). There's a *Marriage of St Catherine* by Gozzoli, not one of his better efforts, an anti-plague standard from Siena, and small works by Chagall, Carrà, Gino Severini, Joan Mirò, Kandinsky, and Léger. Best of all, a large collection of the works of Terni's own Orneore Metelli (1872–1938), a shoemaker who spent his evenings painting under a 100-watt bulb, drinking quarts of coffee and painting, as Bernard Berenson said, the most naive of naive art. Metelli is Umbria's Grandma Moses, and the two rooms of his paintings here make a trip to this industrial city worth while: disarming, colourful scenes of Terni, its steel mill and its surroundings, of shoemakers, of Mussolini's motorcade, of Dante, even the Venus of Terni. Apparently all of his paintings not in this gallery are in Tokyo.

Cascata delle Marmore and Lake Piediluco

From Terni it's 6 km up the Valnerina to the 126-m green and misty **Cascata delle Marmore**, one of Europe's tallest and most photographed waterfalls—when it's running. Surprisingly, the Cascata is an artificial creation; in 271 BC Curius Dentatus, best known as the conqueror of the Sabines, first dug the channel to drain the marshlands of Rieti, diverting the river Velino into the Nera. Although the falls are usually swallowed up by hydroelectric turbines, the thundering waters are let down on the following schedule (after dark they are brilliantly illuminated): from Nov–15 Mar on Sun and holidays from 3–6; from 16 Mar–April and Sept–Oct, Sat 6–9 and Sun 10–12 noon and 3–9 pm; from May–Aug, Sat 5–9 pm, and Sun from 10am–1 pm and 3–11 pm; from 15 July to 11 Aug, also every weekday from 5–6:30 pm.

There are two places from which to view the falls—from down below on the N. 209, or from the belvedere on top, in the village of Marmore. A path through the woods connects the two, though it's steep, prone to be muddy in the off season, and much nicer to walk down than up (the path at the bottom begins 100 m downstream from the falls). There are some pleasant places to swim near the bottom, but you can't use them when the falls are on. Both top and bottom of the falls are easily reached by bus from Terni.

Up near Marmore, lovely **Lago di Piediluco** zigzags in and out of wooded hills, one of which is crowned by a 12th-century fortress. There are a couple of beaches, but unfortunately the lake is better to look at than swim in—the water is cold, rather dirty, and has dangerous undercurrents. There are other diversions; in recent years the lake has become the centre for sport rowing in Italy and the site of international competitions. Perched high above the east shore of the lake is the lovely pale village of **Labro**, former nest of noblemen on the run, and now reoccupied by Belgians after a Belgian architect purchased and restored the entire place. Below the lake, the Arrone road passes by **Villalago**, which has an outdoor theatre used for summertime events.

WHERE TO STAY AND EATING OUT (tel prefix 0744)

Terni is dull but can be a good base for visiting the Valnerina if you're dependent on public transport; it's a good place to look for lodgings if Spoleto is filled up for the Two Worlds festival. The best hotel is in the centre, the ****__Valentino__, Via Plinio il Giovane 3, tel 55 246, with very comfortable modern rooms, all air-conditioned (an important consideration here in the summer) and furnished private bath, frigo-bar, and TV (L100–150 000). It also has one of Terni's classiest restaurants, the **Fontanello**, with a menu featuring fresh, natural ingredients in tasty and imaginative dishes (L40 000). Near the motorway exit, the contemporary ****__Garden__, Via Bramante 6, tel 300 041, is Terni's prettiest hotel, with plant-filled balconies and a pool; the comfortable rooms come equipped with private baths, frigo-bars, and TVs (L100–135 000; meals L30–35 000). A block from the station, ***__Hotel de Paris__, Viale Stazione 52, tel 58 047, is nondescript but convenient, and air-conditioned, too (L68–80 000). Near the Nera and the Corso del Popolo, **__Brenta II__, Via Montegrappa 51, tel 273 957, has nice modern rooms, all with bath, in one of Terni's shady, anonymous neighbourhoods (L55 000). It's easy to eat cheaply in Terni, where the pizza-by-the-slice and snack competition is fierce; try the **Pizzeria del Secolo** across from UPIM on Corso Tacito, or for more variety the place on the Piazza Tacito. Up at Lake Piediluco, the posh place to stay is ***__Casalago__, tel 68 421, a largish hotel with a garden overlooking the water (L65 000).

Up the Valnerina: Mummies and Crayfish

TOURIST INFORMATION

Cascia: Via G. da Chiavano 2, tel (0743) 76 630.

Arrone and Ferentillo

After the Cascata, N. 209 passes under a pretty hill townlet of **Torre Orsina** and the more substantial and picturesque village of **Arrone**, spilling over its isolated rock. In the old days Arrone and its neighbours indulged in some fierce C Division warfare; the feudal lordlings of Arrone, who built the town's picturesque tree-planter tower, were the bitter enemies of the lords of **Polino**, Umbria's tiniest *comune*, located up a pretty 10-km winding road from Arrone that passes under a Mussolini aqueduct; it too has its feudal tower and monumental Baroque fountain. Above Polino, a pretty road leads to the Colle Bertone (1232 m), a very modest winter sports and summer picnicking area.

The biggest rival of the lords of Arrone were the powerful Abbots of **Ferentillo**, the next town up the Valnerina, whose twin 14th-century citadels dominate the town and narrow valley like matching bookends. In **Precetto**, the oldest quarter of town, the crypt of Santo Stefano contains something most people don't expect to find in Umbria: **mummies**. Accidentally preserved by the soil and ventilation, a desiccated vulture mummy points the way inside with its wing to the poor mummified Chinese newlyweds (minus a head, swiped perhaps by the same mummy fetishist who got St Valentine's) who came here in the last century for a honeymoon and got cholera instead, two gruesome French prisoners who were hanged in the Napoleonic wars, and a pyramid of skulls. Sad to relate, the mummies have recently been imprisoned in glass display cases, ruining much of their charm.

The abbey of Ferentillo is located 4 km further up the valley: **San Pietro in Valle**, founded in the 8th century by Faraoldo II, Duke of Spoleto. He chose a lovely spot, with views across the valley to the abandoned citadel that once helped it defend the Valnerina—this is **Umbriano**, the legendary first city of Umbria. Today it can only be reached by mule. San Pietro in Valle's church has a lovely 12th-century campanile embedded with Roman bits, and a two-storey cloister, with a Roman sacrificial altar in the centre. Inside, the nave is covered with frescoes of Old and New Testament scenes from 1190, an unusual example of the Italian response to the Byzantine style. The altar is an equally rare example of Lombard work, sculpted on both the front and back; one of their early saints is interred to the right in a lovely 3rd-century Roman sarcophagus. On either side of the altar are good 13th-century frescoes by the school of Giotto, with a pretty Madonna. At the back there's a cylindrical Etruscan altar, now used for monetary rather than animal offerings. Among the stone fragments arranged on the wall is a real rarity—a bas-relief of a monk with oriental features, brought over by refugees from Syria, perhaps in the 7th century.

Scheggino, the next town along the Nera, is laced with tiny canals full of trout and a rare species of crayfish (*gamberettini*) imported from Turkey; it is also the fief of Italy's truffle tycoons, the Urbani family. **Cascia** sees more pilgrims than truffles, who come to the shrine of Santa Rita, the matronly 'Saint of Impossibilities' who was born near here in 1381, but had to wait until the impossible Fascist era for her sanctuary. Poor Rita! After a wretched marriage and wretched offspring, she became a nun, only to develop such a foul-smelling sore in the middle of her forehead that none of the other sisters would come near her. According to a well-informed Catholic lay critic, her shrine is the most vulgar in Christendom, complete with a dirty plastic dust sheet over the coffin, but is nonetheless fervently worshipped at every year by tens of thousands of unhappily married women. Once you've done Rita, there's a little picture gallery in the church of **Sant' Antonio**, and 1461 frescoes by Nicola da Siena.

Norcia

TOURIST INFORMATION
Piazza San Benedetto, tel (0743) 816 701.

St Ben's Home Town

Little Norcia (pop. 4800) gave the world St Benedict (480–543), the father of monasticism, and his twin sister St Scholastica. It has also been known at times for witches (there seems to have been a sort of sorcerers' college here in the Middle Ages), surgeons (who, it was claimed in the 18th century, were the only ones capable of properly castrating a boy with operatic potential), Umbria's best cheeses, and bristling boar hams. An ancient place, mentioned by Virgil, Norcia resembles a Spanish town more than an Italian, and though earthquakes have slapped it around it retains several historic monuments, most of them in the central Piazza San Benedetto. This has a stern statue of St Benedict for a centrepiece, the church of **San Benedetto**, built over the late Roman house where the famous twins were born, and the handsome **Palazzo Comunale**, with a 13th-century campanile and door, next to the boar and truffle gastronomic speciality shops. These are Norcia's real attraction for the Italians: turd-like whole truffles, tough crusty hams and cheeses (*Two years old and never been in a refrigerator!* proclaims one sign). The other side of the piazza is occupied by the **Castellina**, designed in 1554 by Vignola for Pope Julius III, now housing a museum of Umbrian art, at the time of writing closed for restoration.

And to end your trip through Umbria, there's the most unique, poetic bit of landscape in all these many pages. Above Norcia, in a regional nature park, lies the beautiful **Piano Grande**, an unusual flat meadow measuring 16 square km and surrounded by rolling hills and mountains that seem covered with velvet in the late spring, when the meadow blooms into huge swathes of colour. It is a rarefied landscape (used by Franco Zeffirelli in his Franciscan film *Brother Sun, Sister Moon*) where herds graze and fields produce the famous minute lentils of **Castelluccio**, the old village occupying an upper corner of the plain. Castelluccio had 700 inhabitants in 1951 and now has around 40; winter conditions are so bad that the village is often cut off. From the summit of **Monte Vettore** (2476 m), the tallest peak in the area, you can see both the Adriatic and Tyrrhenian seas on a clear day. In the winter there's skiing at the dramatic **Forca Canapine**, on the south side of Piano Grande; from here the road gradually winds down to Ascoli Piceno and the sea (see p. 480).

WHERE TO STAY AND EATING OUT
Up the Nera, ****Rossi**, N. 209 near Arrone, tel (0744) 788 372, has 16 modern rooms (L54–60 000, all with bath) and one of the best restaurants in the area, with excellent *crostini*, spaghetti with truffles, the usual grilled meats and a wide variety of trout dishes (not more than L30 000, closed Fri). On the other side of Arrone, on the Polino road, keep your eyes peeled for the **Rema**, tel 78 292, a little trattoria with outdoor picnic tables and an outdoor grill, the usual Umbrian fare with a flare and prices that cheapskates like; try the *ciriole* (homemade spaghetti) with mushrooms, the grilled lamb, or the *Desirée farcita* (L20–25 000, closed Mon). Back on N. 209, towards Ferentillo in the *comune* of Montefranco, *****Fontegaia**, tel (0744) 788 621, has the most pretensions in the Valnerina; rooms are very comfortable, and there's a playground for the children

(L80 000); the restaurant is a favourite for locals going out for a special occasion, if a bit heavy-handed with the cream sauces (L35 000).

Further up the valley, quiet Scheggino has one hotel, the charming little ****Del Ponte**, Via Borgo 15, tel (075) 61 131, right on the Nera river, offering 12 rooms with bath (L60 000), and in the restaurant, delicious meals based on Scheggino's two specialities, crayfish and truffles. For a trip to Umbrian heaven, try the fettuccine with a sauce that combines both ingredients (L35–50 000; closed Mon). In Cascia, the top place to stay and eat is the *****Cursula**, Via Cavour 3, tel (0743) 76 206, with extremely pleasant rooms, all with bath (L70–80 000) and good Umbrian specialities in the restaurant (L35 000). Less expensively, though 5 km west in Roccaporena, the ****Casa del Pellegrino**, tel (0743) 71 205, has pretty rooms in a garden setting, open April–Oct (L56 000).

Norcia (tel prefix 0743): The *****Posta**, Via C. Battisti 10, tel 816 274, is a fine hotel and restaurant, where the pleasant rooms all have bath (L80 000) and they serve the famous, hearty, robust fare of Castelluccio lentils, boar salami, *tortellini alla norcina* (with ricotta), lamb with truffles, topped off, if you dare, by a tumbler of Norcia's nasty grappa flavoured with black truffles (L25–30 000). *****Grotta Azzurra**, on Via Alfieri, tel 816 590, is Norcia's other hotel of any size, and offers equally good rooms with showers (L68–80 000) but a different approach to local culinary traditions in its restaurant: a lighter touch, perhaps, its mandatory truffled dishes competing with a tasty risotto with crayfish from the Nera, or fettuccine with trout, or delicious grilled mushrooms (L30–35 000). **Dal Francese**, Via Riguardati 16, tel 816 290, is the ideal place for a bumper meal in this corner of Umbria, where the truffle is king. Try the smoked turkey and homemade salami for antipasto, followed by a pasta medley of *tris al tartufo, gnocchi al tartufo* or *tortellini con crema di tordi* (thrushes) *e tartufi*; for a main course choose between trout dishes, tender grilled lamb or the unusual *braciola in agrodolce con tartufi* (chop in sweet-and-sour sauce with truffles). Good wine list (L40 000). Up in Castelluccio you can spend a rural medieval interlude at the only hotel in town, the ***Sibilla**, tel 870 113, which also boasts the sole restaurant. Its 7 rooms each have private showers (L48 000).

Part XV

THE MARCHES

S. Maria della Piazza, Ancona

Meglio un morto in casa che un marchegiano fuori della porta.

—old Italian saying

'Better a corpse in the house than a man from the Marches at the door.' Now what could the inhabitants of this placid little region could have done to earn such opprobrium from their countrymen? They aren't so bad, really; the saying comes from the old days when many of *marchegiani* served across the Papal States as the pope's tax collectors. Since then, their neighbours have more often ignored than insulted this obscure patch of territory along the Adriatic.

A *march*, or *mark*, in the Middle Ages meant a border province of the Holy Roman Empire, usually an unsettled frontier held by one of the Emperor's fighting barons. With no better name than that, one might expect this Italian region to be somewhat lacking in personality. In fact, this has always been the odd bit of central Italy. In ancient times too it was a border zone, shared by Umbrians, Gauls, Sabines and the Piceni, a stout-hearted little tribe that had for its totem the *picus*, or woodpecker. Unencumbered by art and culture, they occupied much of the central Adriatic; their name lives on in their old capital, Ascoli Piceno. Today, the Marchegiani still have a little identity problem, but it doesn't keep them awake at night. Their land, tucked between the Apennines and the sea, is one of the greenest, prettiest, and most civilized corners of Italy, with two lovely Renaissance art towns in Urbino and Ascoli Piceno, lots of beaches, and scores of fine old towns in the valleys that lead up to the impressive snowy peaks of the Sibilline Mountains, one of the highest sections of the Apennines.

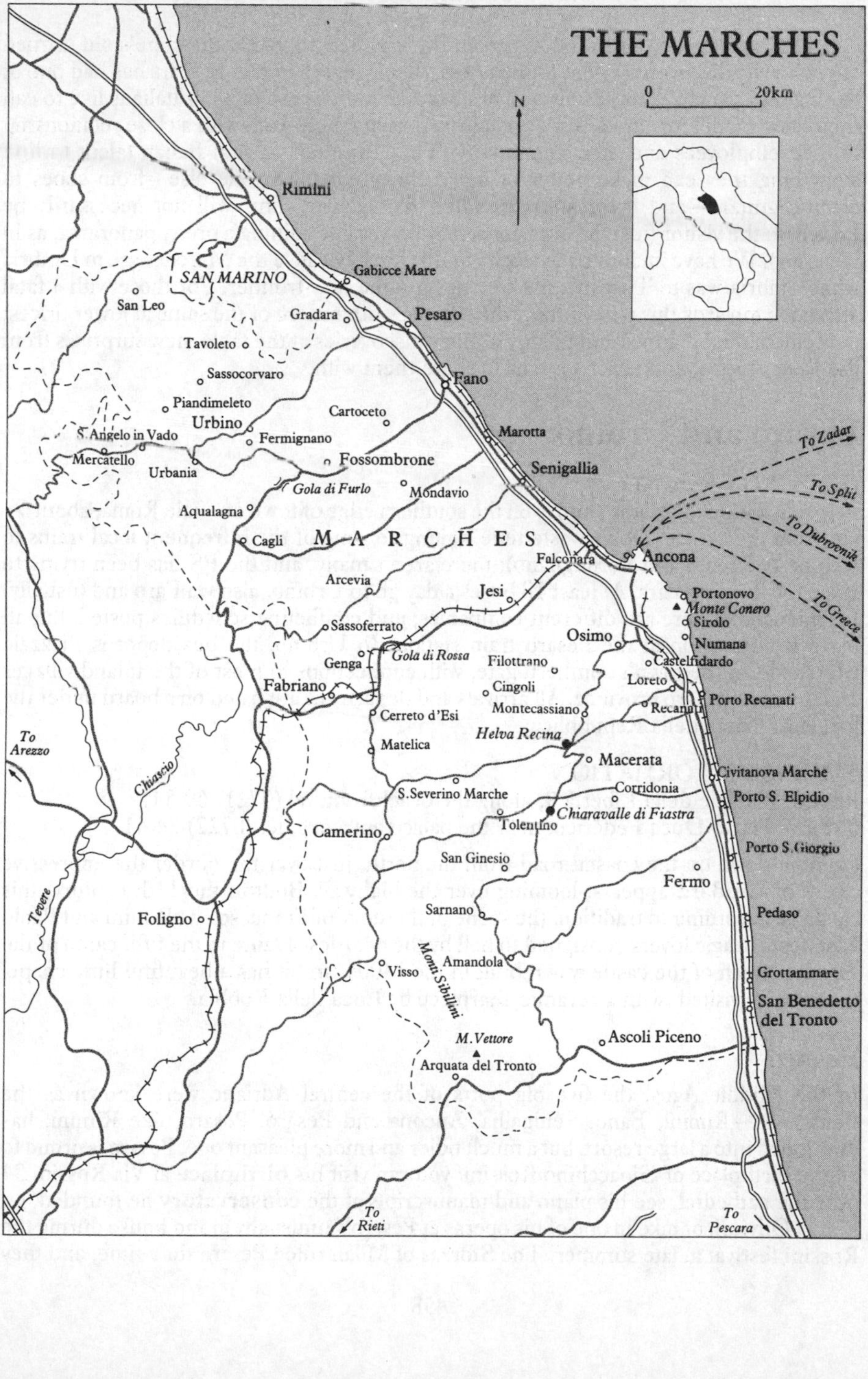
THE MARCHES
0
20km
N
Rimini
SAN MARINO
San Leo
Gabicce Mare
Gradara
Pesaro
Tavoleto
Sassocorvaro
Fano
Piandimeleto
Cartoceto
Urbino
S. Angelo in Vado
Fermignano
Marotta
Mercatello
Urbania
Fossombrone
Senigallia
Gola di Furlo
Mondavio
Aqualagna
Cagli
M A R C H E S
Falconara
Ancona
Arcevia
Jesi
Portonovo
Monte Conero
Sirolo
Sassoferrato
Osimo
Numana
Genga
Gola di Rossa
Filottrano
Castelfidardo
Loreto
Fabriano
Cingoli
Porto Recanati
Montecassiano
Recanati
Cerreto d'Esi
Helva Recina
Matelica
Macerata
Civitanova Marche
Corridonia
S. Severino Marche
Porto S. Elpidio
Chiaravalle di Fiastra
Tolentino
Camerino
Porto S. Giorgio
San Ginesio
Fermo
Sarnano
Foligno
Pedaso
Amandola
Visso
Monti Sibillini
Grottammare
San Benedetto del Tronto
M. Vettore
Ascoli Piceno
Arquata del Tronto
To Zadar
To Split
To Dubrovnik
To Greece
To Arezzo
Chiascio
Tevere
To Rieti
To Pescara

Today, what every Italian knows about the *marchegiani* is that the pope's old taxmen have a newly discovered talent for business. Their region in recent years has had one of the highest growth rates in Italy and has become a showcase of what Italians like to call their 'new model for capitalism': small firms, often family-run, with a close relationship to their employees and their community. They use their natural Italian talent to find something they can make better or more cheaply than anyone else—from shoes to electric guitars—and the results are often spectacular. This will not necessarily be evident to the visitor (just the occasional new power line ruining a pretty panorama, as in Tuscany). We have included the region in this book because the Marches are to Umbria what Umbria was to Tuscany, not so long ago: the new frontier. For those with a fatal attraction towards this part of Italy, the Marches offer more of the same at lower prices: new emerald landscapes and hill towns, new discoveries at the table, new surprises from the Renaissance, and fewer tourists to share them with.

Pesaro and Urbino

GETTING AROUND

Pesaro's station (all trains stop) is on the southern edge of town on Viale Roma, about 1/2 km from the centre. Don't waste time waiting for one of the infrequent local trains to Urbino (via Fano and Fermignano); there aren't many, and the FS has been trying to close the line for years. At least 10 buses a day go to Urbino, also via Faro and (usually) Fermignano. There are different companies, and conflicting schedules posted, but all leave from or stop at the Pesaro train station. In Urbino, the bus depot is Piazzale Mercatale, at the town's southern gate, with connections to most of the inland villages and towns in Pesaro province. All arrivals and departures are listed on a board under the loggia in Piazza della Repubblica

TOURIST INFORMATION

Pesaro: Piazzale della Libertà 9, along the beachfront, tel (0721) 69 341.
Urbino: Piazza Duca Federico, near the palace entrance, tel (0722) 24 41.

Coming down on the coastal road from the north, just over the border the impressive castle of **Gradara** appears, looming over the highway. Built in the 11th century, this castle is, according to tradition, the scene of the story of Francesca da Rimini and Paolo Malatesta, tragic lovers consigned to hell by the heartless Dante in the fifth canto of the *Inferno*. Much of the castle was rebuilt in the 1400s, and it has a beautiful little chapel that can be visited, with a ceramic altarpiece by Luca della Robbia.

Pesaro

In the Middle Ages, the five big ports of the central Adriatic were known as the Pentapolis—Rimini, Fano, Senigallia, Ancona and Pesaro. Pesaro, like Rimini, has developed into a large resort, but a much tidier and more pleasant one. Pesaro is proud to be the birthplace of Gioacchino Rossini; you can visit his **birthplace** at Via Rossini 34 near the cathedral, see his piano and manuscripts at the **conservatory** he founded, on Piazza Olivieri, or take in one of his operas at Pesaro's unusually grand house during the Rossini festival in late summer. The Sforzas of Milan ruled Pesaro for a time, and they sold it to the della Rovere, the family of Julius II, in 1512. The big **Palazzo Ducale** in the centre of town was completed in 1510. In those years Pesaro rivalled Faenza as a producer of fine ceramics; you can see examples at the **Museo Civico**, on Via Toschi Mosca (open daily 8:30–1:30, Sun 9:30–12:30; from April–Sept daily 9–12:30, 4–6:45 pm, Sun 9:0–12:30; adm). Besides the majolica plates there are a few good pictures—and one very great one, a *Coronation of the Virgin* by Giovanni Bellini. Another museum, the **Museo Oliveriano**, has exhibits from the Romans and the various tribes who lived in the Marches before them (weekdays 9:30–12; July and August, weekdays, 4–7 pm).

Though it doesn't have many exceptional monuments, Pesaro is none the less a lovely town to to walk through, both in its older quarters and in the new streets by the beach. These are full of trees and little villas from the 19th century—many in the Liberty style, including one small but outrageous house right on the centre of the beach front, with its cornice supported by terracotta lobsters, designed by an architect named Oreste Ruggiero in 1907. Pesaro's castle, the **Rocca Costanza** near the sea, was built by Laurana, the designer of the palace at nearby Urbino. Ask at the tourist office about visits to the **Villa L'Imperiale**, on a hill some 2 km north of the city. Though damaged in the last war, this is a real surprise, a big villa, built for the Sforzas and enlarged by the della Rovere that includes a park and 'secret garden' along with a wealth of often startling Mannerist frescoes—voluptuous nymphs in Dosso Dossi's *Sala delle Cariatide*, an allegory of *calumny* by Raffaellino del Colle, after the famous one by Botticelli, and works by Bronzino and Perin del Vaga.

Urbino

From Pesaro—and almost nowhere else—it is easy to reach the isolated mountain setting of Urbino. With its celebrated Ducal Palace, and the memory of the honourable and refined Duke Federico who built it, Urbino is one of the monuments of the Italian Renaissance. Today its boosters go perhaps too far—'the ideal city of the Renaissance' and 'most beautiful palace in the world', and on and on, a lack of modesty that probably would have disappointed Federico da Montefeltro. Even so, Urbino does represent more clearly than any Italian town a certain facet of the Renaissance: elegance, learning, and intelligent patronage combined in a small place. Urbino's golden age may not have long outlasted the reign of Duke Federico, but, as an example of what a community can be, it exerts a fascination even today.

History

Throughout the Middle Ages, Urbino's fortunes were attached to those of the house of Montefeltro, mountain warlords from around San Leo who gradually extended their influence in the northern Marches. Most of them were *condottieri* working throughout Italy, serving various masters. In 1443, Oddantonio da Montefeltro earned the title of Duke for his services. His half-brother and successor, Federico (reigned 1444–82), was the most successful of all the family *condottieri*, a crafty and respected warrior who earned the money for his famous palace serving the cause of the Pope and Alfonso of Naples. In his later days, with more of a chance to stay at home, Federico became one of the quattrocento's great patrons, as well as a slow but close student of the Classics and the new humanities; he learned Greek and Latin, and the library he assembled was one of the best in Europe. Much of the legend of Urbino in Federico's time comes from Baldassare Castiglione, in whose book *The Courtier* Urbino's court was idealized as the height of civilized existence.

There was a bad side to Federico—his brutal sack of Volterra while serving Lorenzo de' Medici was only one of his indiscretions on the job—but he ruled Urbino paternally and well, always liberal to those of his subjects in need, peering into every detail of his little state's economy and social life, and educating the sons of the poor. It is also said that he banished gambling and cursing, and made the people of Urbino exert themselves mightily to keep the place clean. His admirable wife, Battista Sforza, was a Duchess beloved of her subjects, a lady capable of delivering an impromptu speech in impeccable Latin to welcome any surprise visitor. Their son, Guidobaldo I, was as enlightened a ruler as his father, and clever enough to survive and prevail after an occupation by Cesare Borgia's Papal army in 1497. When Guidobaldo died without an heir, the duchy fell to a nephew of Pope Julius II. The last della Rovere Dukes willed Urbino to the Popes in 1626.

Urbino had a moment of high drama in 1944. Many of the works of art of central Italy had been brought there for safekeeping near the end of the War. During the retreat in August, a spiteful German commander planted enough explosives under the town walls to blow the whole place to kingdom-come. Only a small number went off, and the remainder were defused by the British after the liberation—a job that took over a week.

Palazzo Ducale

So many architects helped Federico build his dream house, it is difficult to divide the credit. Alberti may have been an original adviser, and the Dalmatian Luciano Laurana is generally given credit for most of the work, but the finest part of it, the twin-turreted façade, is by Ambrogio Barocchi, and no one is quite sure who did the elegant arcaded courtyard. That every Italian schoolboy should know this to be 'the most beautiful palace in the world' is an interesting reflection both on the Italians and on the quattrocento. Federico's palace is not finished, not symmetrical, and not really even very grand; its aesthetic is utterly foreign to the tastes of the centuries that followed. For all that, it is a great building, and a test of one's faith in the genuine Renaissance—the 15th-century high noon of life and art, as opposed to the cinquecento of Spaniardism, surrender, and neurotic excess. Many critics have regarded it, though unfinished, as the culmination of Renaissance architecture, not yet entirely enslaved to perspectivism or imitation of the ancients, but a creation of freedom and delight. The palace was comfortable for the Montefeltri to live in, and an exquisite decoration for the city of Urbino.

The palace **façade**, overlooking the hills on the edge of town, consists of three levels of balconies between two slender towers; the decorative trim is done in a fine Dalmatian limestone that eventually hardens to look like marble. To enter the palace today, you'll need to go round the back through the courtyard, called the **Cortile d'Onore**, a prototype for so many other palace courtyards around the western Mediterranean. Inside, much of the palace is occupied by the **Galleria Nazionale delle Marche**, a splendid collection whose finest works were originally the property of Duke Federico (daily 9–2, Sun, 9–1; adm).

Piero della Francesca's amazing *Flagellation* is perhaps the best-known work in Urbino, an endlessly disturbing image that has troubled art scholars for centuries.

Standing before a pavilion of fantasy classical architecture, three gentlemen in contemporary dress hold a serious discussion, indifferent to the scourging of Christ going on behind them—a bloodless scourging, for that matter. Piero had already written one of the great Renaissance treatises on theoretical perspective; a complex system of foreshortening here is the major feature of the work. The combination of a surreal, dream-like scene and a dryly scientific visual presentation gives the painting its enigmatic quality—as critics have often noted, this is one of the places where art crosses the line into sorcery. Almost as strange a display of perspectivist wizardry is another work, often attributed to Piero or Laurana, the *Ideal City*. The scene is a broad, paved square, lined with buildings in the new style, dominated by a large circular temple in the centre. Here again, perspective is the star of the work. Disturbingly, there are no people present—no living things at all save a few potted plants on the balconies.

Not to be outdone by Piero, Paolo Uccello offers a similarly mysterious *Miracle of the Profaned Host*, and Luca Signorelli is represented by two inspired paintings, the *Crucifixion* and *Pentecost*. Other paintings not to miss: a *Crucifixion* by Antonio Alberti de Ferrara, taking care to show off contemporary fashions, in armour as well as court dress; the *Annunciation* of Vicenzo Pagani (and a pagan-looking work it is, too); *La Muta*, a portrait of a lady by Raphael; also fine works by Luca della Robbia, Giovanni Santi, Crivelli, Verrocchio and the Venetian Alvise Vivarini. The Spanish artist Pedro Berruguete contributes the famous *portrait of Duke Federico*: the tough old warrior, with his broken nose, symbolically still wears his armour as he pores over a heavy book, with his little son Guidobaldo at his knee; note the badge of the Order of the Garter, conferred on Federico by King Edward IV.

Some of the surviving interior decoration of the palace is wonderful—carved mantelpieces and window frames in many rooms, and, above all, the intarsia (inlaid wood) **Study** of Duke Federico. Some of the designs are said to be by Botticelli, and they portray the 'Life of a Scholar' with many interesting *trompe l'oeil* effects. The paintings above, representing philosophers and illustrious men, are by Berruguete. Nearby, reached by a spiral staircase inside one of the façade's towers, are the **Cappella del Perdono**, with an ornate ceiling of hundreds of angel heads in stucco, and an equally fancy chamber called the **Tempietto delle Muse**. The palace's upper floor has lots of rooms full of 16th- and 17th-century paintings, and many portraits of the poor Italians dressed in black like their Spanish overlords. Some chiaroscuros of the *Life of St Paul* by Claudio Ridolfi, colourful 18th-century ceramics, and surprisingly good woodcuts by a Marchegiano artist of the 1900s named Adolfo di Carolia, make the climb upstairs worth while. The palace's basement has recently been opened, with displays on the difficult job of restoring the palace after the vandalism and neglect of papal rule. They have bits of the duke's plumbing and cooking pots on exhibition, with other curiosities found during the restoration, such as the sundial-birdbath from the roof garden (no longer extant), and a big book with a conspicuous dedication to *James III, Re di Gran Bretagna*; the Old Pretender was a guest here twice in the 1700s.

Urbino today is above all a university town, despite its small size a lively place full of students from many countries. Though its streets and roads are often steep, the town and its surrounding hills make an enchanting spot for walks. Adjacent to the Ducal Palace, the **Cathedral** is a work of the 1790s, completely rebuilt after an earthquake that caused the collapse of its dome; there is a small collection of religious art and artefacts in the

Urbino

Museo Diocesano Albani (daily 9–12:30, 2:30–7, by request in the winter). On Via Barocci (south of Via Mazzini, the street that leads up from Urbino's main gate), the little **Oratorio di San Giovanni** has strikingly colourful frescoes by the brothers Iacopo and Lorenzo Salimbeni (1416), artists from the little town of San Severino Marche who show a distinctive approach to the early Renaissance, still heavily under the influence of Giotto. Their work includes a Crucifixion, an enthroned Madonna, and a cycle on the life of John the Baptist (daily 10–12 and 3–5; adm). On the same street, the **Oratorio di San Giuseppe** has a carved *presepio* by an artist from Urbino, Federico Brandani. Raphael (Raffaello Sanzio) was from Urbino, and his birthplace is now restored as a museum. The **Casa di Raffaello** has works by other artists, and a *Madonna* attributed to Raphael himself (daily 9–1, 3–7; adm). On Via Bramante, there is a small **Botanical Garden** with tropical plants (daily 9–12, 3–6)

All of Urbino's 16th-century walls are still intact, and the garden enclosed by one of the corner bastions, the **Fortezza Albornoz**, has a fine view of the palace and town. A pleasant half-hour walk out from the western end of town will take you to the pretty church of **San Bernardino**, attributed by some to Bramante, another son of the Urbino area; inside are the simple but impressive black marble tombs of the Montefeltro Dukes.

WHERE TO STAY AND EATING OUT

Pesaro (tel prefix 0721): At first sight Pesaro looks a refined, perhaps exclusive, resort; it comes as a pleasant surprise to find that prices are on a level with Rimini, and often a little lower. There's only one fine old establishment at the top of the list—the ****Vittoria**, Piazzale della Libertà 2, tel 34 343, a renovated century-old villa at the centre of the beach strip; all rooms have TV and air conditioning (L200 000). Beyond that, Pesaro's speciality is the modern, understated three-star hotel, all of which seem to cost (high season) exactly L60–65 000—maybe one fellow owns them all. It's difficult to recommend one over the other: the ***Principe**, Viale Trieste 180 (quite a distance from the centre), tel 30 222, has a very good and popular restaurant (L60–65 000). There is also a wide selection of one- and two-star places, most in the L40–46 000 range, both along the beach and on the side streets behind it; try ****Liana**, Viale Trieste 102, tel 68 330 (L46 000 with bath). For a fine fish dinner by the seaside, there's **Da Carlo**, at Viale Trieste 265, tel 31 453, with an outdoor terrace—often crowded, and not without reason (up to L40 000). Or else, in the centre of the old town, **Lo Scudiero** at Via Baldassini 2, tel 64 107, occupies the cellar of a 17th-century palace. Specialities include some imaginative dishes with seafood and pasta—ravioli with sole, or *tagliatelle marine*. Roast kid is another dish they do well (L40 000 average). **Daniela e Umberto**, at Loc. S. Veneranda, tel 452 325, offers hearty dishes for the hungry—gnocchi in duck sauce, rabbit and porchetta, and for the more picky digestions, frogs, snails, and pigeon (L35–40 000, closed Wed). For some more modest but delectable home cooking, try **Bibo e Biba**, Via G. Bruno 37 behind the post office; for L20 000 you can enjoy dishes such as *polenta con funghi* or *farfalle al salmone*—also pizza.

Urbino (tel prefix 0722): Hotels in Urbino can be extremely crowded in the summer, and even springtime. There aren't many of them, and it would always be wise to book ahead. Even so, this isn't a town you can spend many lire in, even if you try. Much of the civilized air of Duke Federico's time seems to have survived into our own. Urbino is full of clean, attractive, inexpensive hotels and restaurants with disarmingly friendly proprietors—you may end up staying longer than you planned. Sitting on the walls of the city, the most luxurious place in town short of the palace itself is the ******Bonconte**, Via delle Mura 28, tel 2463 (L95 000). A good, central hotel is the ****Italia**, Corso Garibaldi 32, tel 2701, a block from the Ducal Palace (L37 000 without bath, L47 000 with); another is the ****San Giovanni**, Via Barocci 13, tel 2827 (L28–32 000 without bath, L33–40 000 with), in an old palazzo with a good restaurant. Dining is similarly modest at the **Trattoria Leone**, tel 329 894, right in Piazza della Repubblica, average meals go for L20 000, with surprise specialities like *coniglio al porchetto* on the menu. **Il Nuovo Coppiere**, at Via Porta Maja 20, tel 320 092, is a charming little spot behind the cathedral (also about L20 000). If you want to spend more, you can do so in a fancy restored granary: **Vecchia Urbino**, Via dei Vasari 3, tel 4447; specialities include tagliatelle with sole or truffles, and a savoury *millefoglie ducale*, and a list of good local wines (L35 000, closed Tues).

Towns Around Urbino

If you have the time, Urbino can be used as a base for excursions to a number of interesting towns and villages in the rolling hills and mountains of the northern Marches—towns as serene and lovely as those in Tuscany, though much less known. **Fermignano**, where Bramante may have been born (Urbania also claims that honour), is one of the best and most convenient, about 9 km south of Urbino. At its centre, under a graceful medieval tower and bridge, there is a little waterfall on the Metauro river.

From Fermignano, you can follow the Metauro valley to the east to **Fossombrone**, a Roman foundation that takes its name, *Forum Sempronii*, from the famous reformer Sempronius Gracchus. The dukes of Urbino built a palace here, the **Corte Alta**, or Palazzo Ducale, with remarkable Renaissance pavements and ceilings; it now houses a small archaeological museum with busts and fragments of Roman sculpture, ceramics and coins (open by request). Baroque **Sant'Agostino**, the finest of the town's churches, has a Nativity inside by Taddeo Zuccari. Fossombrone has a number of other Renaissance palaces and churches, as well as a small collection of 19th century and modern Italian painting, the **Museo Cesarini** on Via Pergamini (open by request, tel 71 650).

The Gola del Furlo

Southwest from Fossombrone, a little stream called the Candigliano passes through a steep gorge called the **Gola del Furlo**, with wild, rocky landscapes that provide a striking contrast to the gently sculpted farmlands beyond. A road has traversed the gorge since ancient times, including a small tunnel cut in the rock that may have been built by the Etruscans. Under the Romans, it became a stretch of the busy Via Flaminia; a larger tunnel built by Emperor Vespasian is still in use. Despite the traffic, the Furlo is a home to wildlife, including a few specimens of Italy's rare *aquila reale*('royal eagle').

Mussolini built the tall dam and power plant at the end of the Furlo; later on, passing through in one of his endless trips around Italy in his red Alfa Romeo, he became enamoured of the region and stopped in often for short vacations. To make him feel at home, the local fascists sculpted one of the Furlo's cliffs into the dictator's profile. It can still be seen, from a point near the village of Acqualagna—though a bit hard to make out, since resistance fighters blew his nose off with dynamite after the war. Acqualagna is famous for truffles, both black and white, the speciality of the region. **Cagli**, to the south, is known for craft work in wrought iron. It has its modest collection of monuments—late Gothic details in the cathedral and church of San Francesco, a Renaissance portal by the Roman architect Vignola on S. Angelo Minore, and another palace of Duke Federico, now the town hall. They make for a pleasant ensemble, all in the shadow of the huge **Torrione**, Cagli's landmark, an elliptical defence tower built for the Montefeltro dukes by Francesco di Giorgio Martini. **Monte Petrano** overlooks the town from the south, near the border with Umbria; a detour on the side road up to it will bring you to some green alpine meadows, full of wild flowers in the spring and sheep in the summer.

West of Urbino

In the upper Metauro valley, just southwest of Urbino, **Urbania** was another sometime residence of the dukes; originally called Castel Durante, it was renamed after Pope Urban VIII. Urbania retains a smaller **Ducal Palace**, a properly elegant castle overlooking the Metauro valley that holds a small museum, a picture gallery, and the remains of Duke Federico's famous library, with many antique globes and maps.

Beyond Urbania, in all directions towards the summits of the Apennines, villagers dream of the truffles they will find in the autumn, just like their counterparts over the mountains in Umbria. The 'Sagra del Tartufo' in October is the big event of the year in **Sant'Angelo in Vado**, another exceptionally pretty village on the Metauro; originally called *Tifernum Metaurensis* (to distinguish it from *Tifernum Tiberensis*, nearby Città di Castello in Umbria), it was the home of the Zuccari brothers, late Renaissance painters whose best works are in Rome. The small octagonal church of **San Filippo** has a wood statue attributed to Ghiberti.

From here the SS73 climbs over the mountains to Sansepolcro and Arezzo passing the village of **Mercatello**; here one of the earliest Franciscan churches (13th century) has been converted into a museum with a small collection of late medieval works. North of Sant'Angelo, continuing this long circle around Urbino, **Piandimeleto**,

Sassocorvaro, and **Tavoleto** are three villages built around rather genteel Renaissance castle-palaces; Sassocorvaro's is an unusual round one, also built by Francesco di Giorgio Martini, with a small museum with paintings and exhibits on country life and crafts in the region.

San Leo

The best of all the Montefeltro castles can be found northwest of Tavoleto overlooking the lilliputian republic of San Marino. **San Leo** was founded by a companion of Marinus (who founded San Marino), according to legend, but lost its independence long ago. The rough-walled, 10th-century church called the **Pieve** is one of the earliest Romanesque works in the Marches, but San Leo's real attraction is the **castle**, built by Martini for the Montefeltro dukes of Urbino in the 15th century. Like their palace at Urbino, this fortress is a perfect representative building of the Renaissance, balanced, finely proportioned in its lines, a building of intelligence and style. It is also impregnable, hung on a breathtakingly sheer cliff. Once this mount held a temple of Jupiter; as *Mons Feretrius* (referring to Jove's lightning) it gave its name to the Montefeltro family. An earlier fortress on this site was briefly 'capital of Italy' in the 960s, during the undistinguished reign of King Berengarius II. This one, under papal rule, became a prison; among its guests, in the 1790s, was the famous swindler Cagliostro. Now there is a small picture gallery in the castle—it's a stiff climb up if you don't have a car (daily, 9–12, 2–4:30; in summer 9–12, 2–6:30; adm)

San Marino

Not far from San Leo, you can take some pretty back roads through the hills to visit the world's only sovereign and independent roadside attraction. Before nearby Rimini became the Italian Miami Beach, the 50,000 citizens of San Marino had to make a living peddling postage stamps. Now, with their medieval streets crowded with day-trippers, the San Marinese have been unable to resist the temptation to order some bright medieval costumes, polish up their picturesque mountain towns, and open up some souvenir stands and 'duty free' shops. Their famous stamps, though nothing like the exquisitely engraved numbers of 40 years ago, are still prized by collectors, and recently the country has begun to mint its own coins again after a lapse of 39 years; nevertheless, the citizens of San Marino, who may just have the highest national average income in Europe, are making their living almost entirely from tourism.

TOURIST INFORMATION
In San Marino, there is one tourist office for each 7 sq. m.
San Marino town: Contrada del Collegio, tel (0549) 992 059.
Dogana: Piazza Tini tel 905 414.
Tavolucci: Via XXVIII Luglio, tel 902 701.

The World's Smallest Republic

Also the oldest republic. According to legend, San Marino was founded as a Christian settlement on the easily defensible slopes of Monte Titano by a stonecutter named Marinus, fleeing from the persecutions of Diocletian in the early 4th century. 'Overlooked', as the San Marinese charmingly put it, by the empire and various states that followed it, the little community had the peace and quiet to evolve its medieval democratic institutions; its present constitution dates from 1243, when the first pair of 'consuls' was elected by a popular assembly. The consuls are now called Captains Regent, but little else has changed in 700 years. Twice, in 1503 and 1739, the Republic was invaded by papal forces, and independence was preserved only by a little good luck. Napoleon, passing through in 1797, found San Marino amusing, and half-seriously offered to enlarge its boundaries, a proposal that was politely declined. The republic felt secure enough to offer refuge to Garibaldi, fleeing from Venice after the end of the Roman revolt of 1849, and as an island of peace during World War II, it distinguished itself by taking in thousands of refugees.

San Marino last made world news in the 70s, when the Communists were threatening to win the elections. The San Marino government decided that even emigrants were still citizens, with the right to vote. Of course the government felt obliged to assist them; thousands of San Marinese descendants in places like New Jersey were given free holidays at government expense to help tip the election.

Most visitors enter San Marino from Rimini, at the hamlet called Dogana (though there are no border formalities now). The main road passes through a string of villages. San Marino, no midget like the Vatican City, is all of 12 km long at its widest extent. At the foot of Monte Titano, rising dramatically above the plain, is **Borgomaggiore**, the largest town, with a cable car up to the capital and citadel of the republic, also called **San Marino**. Here, among medieval streets and squares, there are wonderful views over Rimini and the coast. Nothing is really as old as it looks; the **Palazzo del Governo**, full of Ruritanian guardsmen in brass buttons and epaulettes, is a reconstruction of 1894. Here the Grand Council meets, and the Captains Regent have their offices. Some new museums have been conjured up for the tourists—a Stamp and Coin Museum, Garibaldi Museum, and a Museum of Weaponry, but the best thing to do is walk the paths through Monte Titano's forests to the three (rebuilt) medieval **tower fortresses** on the three peaks that give San Marino its famous silhouette—famous to philatelists anyhow, and long the symbol of the republic.

Rimini and the Malatesta Temple

If you have travelled all the way to Urbino on a Renaissance sentimental journey, you should also consider a short detour over the border into the Romagna to Italy's biggest and most outrageous resort. Rimini's 15 km of beaches and teenagers may not be your cup of tea, but behind them lies an attractive old city, with a Roman bridge, an Arch of Augustus, street scenes that recall Fellini's *Amarcord* (it's his home town), and a good small museum with works by Ghirlandaio and Giovanni Bellini. Best of all, Rimini can show you one of the essential buildings of the Renaissance, the **Malatesta Temple**.

Sigismondo Malatesta ('headache'), the pagan, perverse local tyrant immortalized when Pope Pius II accorded him the unique honour of a canonization to Hell, built this mysterious, unfinished work in 1461. Converted from an old Franciscan church, its classical exterior was designed by Leon Battista Alberti, with an austere, incomplete façade based on the Augustan arch nearby, and niches around the sides meant to hold Malatesta family tombs. Inside, the major feature is the series of sculptural reliefs by Agostino di Duccio, among the most exquisite productions of the quattrocento: angels and child musicians that recall the Florence *cantorie* of Donatello and della Robbia, allegories of the Arts and Sciences, St. Michael, Sigismundo himself, and the Triumph of Scipio. The best are the allegorical panels of the signs of the zodiac and the planets, including an enchanting lunar goddess in her silver car. As with Botticelli's mythological paintings, or the pavement of Siena cathedral, here you can feel close to the subversive undercurrents of the early Renaissance, steeped in classical humanism and Pico della Mirandola's natural magic. Malatesta's temple will always be something of a puzzle, partly a personal monument but also a reminder of the pervasive mysticism of a supposedly rational era.

The Valle dell'Esino

The mountain valleys, stretching down to the sea in parallel lines, neatly divide the Marches' geography; south of the Metauro, the next valley is that of the Cesano. At **Mondavio**, it passes another castle fit for a Duke, the Rocca Roveresca, long a possession of the della Rovere. The indefatigable Francesco di Giorgio Martini began it in 1482; its studied elegance is only emphasized by what must be the queerest-shaped defence tower in all Italy. There's a collection of old arms and armour inside (daily 8:30–12:30, 2:30–7:30; adm).

The Esino is the next important valley, most easily reached from Ancona or Gubbio. From Ancona, the first town is **Jesi**, once the Roman *Aesis*, set on a narrow ridge between crumbling, picturesque Renaissance walls with houses built on and over their tops. Jesi was the birthplace of none other than Emperor Frederick II; on the entrance of the **Palazzo del Comune** is engraved the text of a letter from Frederick confirming the town's ancient privileges. Adjacent to it, the 16th-century **Palazzo Ricci** has an odd waffle-iron façade like the Gesù Nuovo in Naples. Two blocks west, the **Palazzo della Signoria** is another fine building of the same period, with a small museum of paintings and archaeological finds. Jesi's real treasure, however, is a set of paintings by Lorenzo Lotto, some of his finest work, in the **Pinoteca Comunale**, located in the Palazzo Pianetti on Via XX Settembre (daily exc Mon 9–12:30, 4–7, Sun 10–12:30). Outside the walls, the **San Marco** church has some fine 14th-century frescoes in the manner of Giotto. In the hills to the south, some 14 km from Jesi, is the village of **Filottrano.** Here, at the **Museo del Biroccio** on Via Beltrami, a collection of antique carts and wagons shares space with artefacts of Mississippi Indian tribes, including a calumet, or 'peace pipe'; a local gentleman named Giacomo Beltrami collected them in the 1820s, while in exile for having served in the revolutionary government during the Napoleonic wars (tel 33 037 to arrange a visit).

Further up river, after another limestone gorge, the **Gola di Rossa**, a road off to the right leads to the village of **Genga** and the series of recently discovered caves called the **Grotte di Frasassi**; one of these, already a popular attraction, is the 'cave of the winds', with a spectacular display of glistening pastel stalactites and calcareous pools that go on for over half a kilometre. Another cave, called the **Grotto del Santuario**, has an octagonal 18th-century chapel built in it. Nearby, close to the Genga railway station, is **San Vittore**, an impressive building from the 10th century. This church shows an unusual combination of Romanesque and Byzantine influences, square in shape, decorated with Lombard blind arcades, a triple apse and corner towers, an octagonal cupola and a huge, squat campanile. Another rather difficult 17 km past Genga takes you to the lovely hill village of **Arcevia**, where there is an altarpiece by Luca Signorelli in the church of San Medardo.

Fabriano, near the border with Umbria and a stop on the Rome-Ancona railway, was famous in Renaissance times as a centre of papermaking (the watermark was invented here), and as the home of a school of painting, following Francesco di Gentile da Fabriano, an important artist of the early quattrocento. Some of Fabriano's artists can be seen in the picture gallery in the **Pinacoteca Civica** on Piazza Umberto di Savoia, along with a good collection of late medieval and Renaissance works (daily exc Mon, 10–12:30, 4–7, Sun 10–12:30; winter hours 9:30–12:30, Sun 10–12:30). The centre of town is a fine arcaded square, the **Piazza del Comune**, with a Palazzo del Comune and fountain strangely reminiscent of the ones in Perugia. Nearby **San Domenico**, Fabriano's most important church, has interesting frescoes by local artists of the 1300s, most notably those in the Chapel of S. Orsola. San Domenico's convent has been restored to hold the **Museum of Papermaking** (tel 3073 for information). Typical of the tenacity of craftwork in many Italian towns, Fabriano still makes its living from paper, using modern methods as well as the old-fashioned way. The most important use for speciality paper is, of course, banknotes; besides supplying the Italian treasury, Fabriano paper changes hands each day from Kashmir to the Congo. At the museum, much of the equipment of the old craft has been assembled, and they'll give a demonstration of how they do it.

To get really off the beaten track, press on south to **Matelica**, with another fine town square and a picture gallery, the **Museo Piersanti**, with an exceptional triptych by Antonio da Fabriano and some saints of Giovanni Bellini (daily 10–12). **Cerreto d'Esi** has remains of a Byzantine gate and a leaning tower, said to be built in the time of Justinian.

WHERE TO STAY AND EATING OUT

In this cosy corner of Italy, almost any small town can provide you with a comfortable night's lodging. Urbino, of course, makes a good base for seeing the northern Marches, but if you wish to spend a night or two elsewhere, there's Fermignano's ***Serra Alta**, Via Serra Alta, tel (0722) 54 173, which has a pool and garden, and 15 cosy rooms, most with bath (L60 000), as well as an excellent restaurant with a view; try the *ravioloni* or *raviolini*, duck or guinea fowl, and in the autumn, mushrooms and truffles (L35 000). Or if you just want a simple place to sleep, ***La Pace**, tel 54 401 (L30 000, none with bath).

In Urbania, *****Bramante**, Via Roma 92, tel (0722) 319 562, is a pleasant hotel and good value, too (L37 000 without bath, L45 000 with). The place to eat in town is **Big Ben**, tel (0722) 319 795—a name the locals have borrowed for their own tower. Porcini mushrooms, truffles, and meat, but no fish (L25–30 000, closed Wed).

In Jesi, the choice is between a posh country inn, the ******Federico II**, just outside town on the Via Ancona, tel (0731) 543 631; pool, gardens, and TV—elegant enough, but a bit dear at L140–200 000, or the more central *****Italia**, Viale Trieste 28, near the station, tel (0731) 4844 (L85 000). Or spend less at ****Mariani**, Via Orfanotrofio 10, tel 52 396, where a room with bath is L50 000. On Via Mura Occidentali 5, **Galeazzi**, tel 57 944, has been the best restaurant in town for a long time, and well worth the bill of about L30 000, closed Mon. *****Alle Terrazze**, Via Rocchi, tel (0731) 9391, in a lovely setting just outside Arcevia, with a pool and a chance for a stroll in the woods (L60–90 000).

This establishment also has the town's best restaurant, a good place to savour the area's culinary treasure—truffles; when they're in season it will be *spaghetti con tartufi*, everything else *con tartufi*, and you won't mind a bit (L25–30 000). There are simpler hotels and trattorie in the town itself. Anywhere in this district, try bottle of the dry, almost greenish-white Verdicchio, considered by many to be the only really distinguished wine from the Marches. Some of the best is produced around Jesi, and in Matelica.

Fabriano makes a good stop if you're travelling over the mountains; the ***Mastro Marino** on the outskirts at Piazzale XX Settembre 32, tel (0732) 5382, is air-conditioned and has a pool (L95 000); or the *****Aristos**, Via Cavour 103, tel (0732) 22 308, a similar resort hotel (L100 000). There are no first-class restaurants, but you can get a perfectly agreeable dinner at the **Trattoria Marchegiana** on Piazza Cairoli, tel 23 284 (L25 000).

Back on the Coast: Fano and Senigallia

TOURIST INFORMATION

Fano: Viale Cesare Battisti 10, tel (0721) 803 534.

Senigallia: Piazza Morandi 2, tel (071) 792 2725. Both concern themselves mostly with helping you find a hotel in the summer.

South of Pesaro, the string of Adriatic resorts continues through these two towns. Fano and Senigallia are not merely resorts, however, but fine old towns, both members of the medieval Pentapolis. Older even than the Romans, **Fano** takes its name—once *Fanum Fortunae*—from a famous temple of the goddess Fortuna. Under Roman rule it became the most important of the Marches' coastal cities, the terminus of the Via Flaminia from Rome. Today, in the central Piazza XX Settembre, a statue of Fortune from the 1500s decorates the Fontana della Fortuna. Behind it, the elegant loggia belongs to the **Palazzo Malatestiano**, a palace built in the 1420s and enlarged in 1544, when Fano was ruled by the tyrants of Rimini. Inside, there is a small but good picture collection, including a fine quattrocento polyptych by Venetian artist Michele Giambono, works by Renaissance tail-enders Guido Reni and Guercino, and some small bronzes of the ancient Piceni (daily except Mon 9–12, 4:30–7:30; Sun 9–12; in winter open mornings only).

In the church of **Santa Maria Nuova**, two blocks south on Via dei Pili, there are altarpieces by Giovanni Santi and Perugino, with a small predella panel attributed to the young Raphael. From Roman days, Fano preserves a stately gate of the year AD 2, the **Arco di Augusto**. San Michele Church, to the right of the gate, has a relief carved on its façade showing how the arch looked before being heavily damaged in 1463. The besieging *condottiere*, eventually successful, who bombarded it was none other than Duke Federico of Urbino, working at that time for the pope; the defender was Sigismundo Malatesta of Rimini.

Fano's **Lido**, modern and a little overbuilt, is typical of the resorts on the Adriatic, but the long broad beach continues down the coast for miles, through the resort suburbs of Torrette and Marotta, and there's room for all. **Senigallia**, the next town on the coast, was the site of an important trade fair in the Middle Ages. Besides its long 'velvet beach', one of the nicest on the Adriatic, its landmark is an elegant though serviceable fortress, the **Rocca Roveresca**, built by the della Rovere in 1480.

WHERE TO STAY AND EATING OUT

There aren't any special choices in Fano or Senigallia—pretty standard beach hotels, all less than 30 years old. In Fano (tel prefix 0721) the *****Excelsior**, Via Simonetti 21, tel 803 558, (L60 000, some cheaper without bath), *****Piccolo**, Viale Cairoli 1, tel 803 305 (all with bath, L47 000) and the ****Astoria**, Viale Cairoli 86, tel 803 474 (L45 000) are three pleasant hotels near the centre of the action, on the nicest part of the beach. Fano has some good restaurants—heading the list is one place on the beach where you can put away an enormous pile of little fishes for less than L22 000—**Pesce Azzurro**, on Lungomare Sarsonia (*pesce azzurro*—'blue fish'—by the way, is something you'll see all along the Adriatic, not one specific variety, but really many kinds of small fish common in these waters, very tasty though! The degradation of the Adriatic makes them harder to find with each passing year). Even more than Fano, Senigallia has a huge choice of modern hotels. *****La Vela**, Piazza N. Bixio 35, tel (071) 60 135, is a nice place with garden and tennis; its biggest advantage, though, is that it's the furthest hotel from the railway line (L60–75 000). Senigallia, unlike Fano, has its beach chopped into bits, all owned by the hotels.

Ancona

Just before the city, the mountains once more reach the sea, giving the mid-Adriatic's biggest port a splendid setting, a crescent-shaped harbour under the steep promontory of Monte Guasco; here colonists from Syracuse founded the city in the 5th century BC. It was the furthest north the Greeks ever went in the Adriatic, and the colony was never a great success until Roman emperors, especially Trajan, built it up. Ancona recovered from the bad centuries to become the leading city of the Pentapolis in the 12th century, and lived on quietly thereafter, coming under papal rule in 1532. Our own century, however, has been murderous to Ancona. The Austrians bombarded it in 1915, and the British and Americans did a much more thorough job in 1944. Then came a major flood, a serious earthquake in 1972, and after that a landslide that caused the abandonment of parts of the old town. For all its troubles, Ancona has come up smiling. The port is prospering, and even though most of the population now lives in newer districts to the south and west, the city is finally devoting its attention to the restoration of the historic centre.

GETTING AROUND

Ancona lies at the intersection of two major railway lines—the Adriatic coast route and Ancona-Rome, with no long waits for trains in either direction. The station is west of the port on Piazza Roselli (take bus No 1 or 3 to or from Piazza Repubblica by the port). Some trains, but not many, continue to Ancona Marittima station on the port itself. Buses to Portonovo and the Conero Riviera, to Bologna, Rome, and towns in the province all leave from the station on Piazza Stamira, just west of Piazza Cavour, tel 23 339, many buses also stop at the railway station. Ancona's two air terminals are both nearby—at Corso Stamira 80 (ATI, tel 31 801) for Bari, Tàranto, and Venice and on Piazza Roma (Italia, tel 53 696) for Bologna, Crotone, Foggia, Genoa, Milan, Pescara, Turin, and Rome. Raffaello Sanzio Airport is 5 km away at Falconara.

If you're not up to making the long climb up to the cathedral, the No 11 bus from Piazza Cavour or Piazza Repubblica will save you the trouble.

Ferries: Plenty of lovely big ferries, ready to bustle you off to Greece or Yugoslavia. If you're heading to Greece from Rome or anywhere north of Rome, taking the ferry from here is a moderately better bet than making the long train trip down to Brindisi, Bari, or Otranto. Fares are only slightly higher, and in both cases it will be an overnight trip. For Yugoslavia, there's little difference between northern and southern ports; fares from both are much more expensive than they should be, considering the distance. All fares rise dramatically in the high season, and there are usually discounts for students. To Yugoslavia (Zadar or Split), fares can range from L40 000 for deck passage in low season all the way up to L200 000 for a nice cabin in the high season (July and Aug). To Greece, the same range is L60 000–290 000, whether you get off in Igoumenitsa or Patras.

Several lines operate from Ancona. To Yugoslavia: **Adriatica**, Corso Garibaldi 43, tel 29 250, and **Jadrolinija**, Via XXIX Settembre 4, tel 201 933. Both go to Zadar and Split, and Adriatica also visits Dubrovnik in the summer. The Jadrolinija line, slightly cheaper, is the better bet. To Greece: **Minoan Lines**, Via XXIX Settembre 4, tel 201 933, has the nicest boats but also slightly higher fares; **Karageorgis Lines**, Via XXIX Settembre 18, tel 201 080 and **Strintzis Lines**, Piazza Roma 21, tel 58 292, also make the trip. Of course, which line you take will probably depend on what day you wish to travel. The tourist office in the port has all the information, but especially in the summer you'll want to book your ticket in advance.

Besides these, a good bargain but probably a trip you'll never forget is the four-day **Turkish Maritime Lines** cruise to Izmir, run at weekends during the summer (Piazza S. Maria 2, tel 91 234). In summer there may also be cruises to Israel and Cyprus.

TOURIST INFORMATION

Ancona has information offices in the railway station, tel (071) 41 703, and in the Palazzo Provincia on Corso Stamira, tel 29 882. There's a booth in the port, open summer months only, tel 201 183, and also in summer, offices in the Conero resorts of Numana (Piazza Santuario, tel 936 142) and Sirolo (Piazza V. Veneto, tel 936 141).

Falconara Marittima (the rail junction just north of Ancona): Via Cavour 3, tel (071) 910 458.

Around the Port

Most of Ancona's monuments have survived the recent misfortunes, though many are a little the worse for wear. The business centre has gravitated a few blocks inland, around the broad **Piazza Cavour**; from here Corso Garibaldi leads down to the sea. At its western end, the long curve of the port is anchored by the **Mole Vanvitelliana**, a pentagonal building that resembles a fortress, but really served as Ancona's lazaretto in the 18th century. At the other end, the tall, graceful **Arch of Trajan** was built in AD 115, in honour of Ancona's imperial benefactor; even though the sculptural reliefs have disappeared, it is one of the better preserved in Italy. Nearby, the 18th-century Pope Clement XII imitated Roman glory by having an arch put up to himself; the **Arco Clementino**, like the lazaretto, was the work of Vanvitelli, the court architect of the Bourbons at Naples, best known for his palace at Caserta. At the centre of the port, the 15th-century Venetian Gothic **Loggia dei Mercanti**, the merchants' exchange, is the best souvenir of Ancona's heyday as a free maritime city.

To see the oldest quarters of Ancona you'll have to climb a little, starting up Via Gramsci and under the Renaissance decorative arch of the **Piazza del Governo**. Off on a little square to the left, the church of **Santa Maria della Piazza** has a fine late Romanesque façade with figures of musicians and soldiers and odd animals carved by a 'Master Phillippus'. Another two blocks up takes you to **San Francesco delle Scale**, with another Gothic portal, and a late Renaissance palace that houses a small collection in the **Pinacoteca Comunale**. Here is a masterpiece of the eccentric but endearing Carlo Crivelli, tidiest of all Renaissance painters: a *Madonna col Bambino*, complete with Crivelli's trademark apples and cucumbers hanging overhead. Other Madonnas on the wall include one in a *Sacra Conversazione* by Lotto, formerly in the Santa Maria church, and one of Titian's, floating smugly on a cloud (daily exc Mon 10–7; Sun 9–1)

On Monte Guasco

Further up, the street changes its name to Via del Guasco, in an area where bits of decorative brickwork from Roman Ancona's theatre peek out between and under the buildings. This was the area hardest hit by the earthquake and landslide, and restorations are going on everywhere. One building that may never be finished is the one on Via Ferretti that houses the **Museo Nazionale delle Marche**, an important archaeological collection with some exceptional Greek vases, sculpture, and metalwork. The wartime bombings blew up its first home, and the second was jolted severely in the earthquake. It has been closed since 1972, and no one who works there has any idea when, or if, it will reopen. Also damaged in 1972 was the 13th-century **Palazzo del Senato**, around the corner, Ancona's capital when it was a self-governing *comune*.

Ancona's **Cathedral** crowns Monte Guasco, a site that in antiquity held a famous temple of Venus. To reach it, either climb the long garden stairway, the **Scalone Nappi** (or drive up from the port, where an ugly new road has replaced the neighbourhoods lost in the landslide). Unusually for a church this far north, the 11th-century cathedral shows a strong influence from the Apulian Romanesque, and but for the long, rounded transepts the building would not look out of place in any of the cathedral towns around Bari. The sculpted portals and detached campanile were both added about 1200. Inside, there isn't much to see; the marble columns come originally from the Temple of Venus, and there is an unusual carved altar screen from the 12th century. The cathedral is dedicated to St Cyriacus, an early bishop and martyr—not a real martyr, but a clever piece of propaganda from the time of the virtuous but non-Christian Emperor Julian the Apostate. There is a small diocesan museum, expected to reopen soon, with a fine 4th-century Christian sarcophagus, reliquaries and architectural fragments from the cathedral (9th–12th centuries).

The Conero Riviera

The same arm of the Apennines that stretches down to shelter Ancona's port also creates a short but uniquely beautiful stretch of Adriatic coast. South of Ancona, the cliffs of Monte Conero plunge steeply into the sea, forcing the railway and coastal highway to bend inland, and isolating a number of beautiful beaches and coves only a few kilometres from the centre of Ancona.

From the city, the Conero road is a narrow thread between sea and mountain, passing after some 7 km the cliff of Trave, so called for a rock formation that resembles a beam (*trave*), dropping sheerly down to the sea. A little further on, a side road to the left leads to the little resort town of **Portonovo**, a white, sandy bay, clean and unspoiled despite being only a half hour from Ancona on the city bus line. Besides the beach, there is a church of the 1030s in the same style as Ancona cathedral. **Santa Maria di Portonovo**, with the same blind arcading around the roofline and a distinctive cupola in the centre, is one of the better Romanesque churches in the north; Dante mentions it—'the House of Our Lady on the Adriatic coast' in the 21st canto of the *Paradiso*. Also in Portonovo are a small fortress, the Fortino Napoleonico (now restored as a hotel: see below), and a watchtower built by Pope Clement XII in 1716—even at that late date, there was worry about pirates. Much earlier in history, some of the local pirates hung out at the nearby **Grotta degli Schiavi**—*schiavi* in this case meaning Slavs, not slaves, refugees from across the Adriatic. The grotto faces a sheltered cove popular with divers and fishermen.

South of Portonovo, the main road curves inland around **Monte Conero** proper. On its slopes, remains of a Camaldolese monastery include yet another church of the mid-11th century: **San Pietro**, with some interesting carved capitals. A track leads to the summit of the mountain, worth the trouble for spectacular views down the steep cliffs overlooking the sea. On its opposite slope Conero is green and luxuriant; in this direction the view takes in a wide stretch of the Apennines, as far south as the Gran Sasso d'Italia in Abruzzo. Somebody, apparently, was enjoying it 100,000 years ago; near the summit archaeologists dug up the oldest traces of human settlement yet discovered in the Marches.

On the southern slope of Conero are two attractive but often very crowded resorts; **Sirolo**, the first of them, is a medieval village on the cliffs high above the sea. There is a 15th century church, and a former Franciscan convent; near its entrance are two holm oaks, planted by St. Francis himself in 1215. Almost adjacent to Sirolo, **Numana** was once an important town, a bishopric from the 5th to the 15th centuries. At its centre, Piazza del Santuario, the **Santuario del Crocifisso**, has become a pilgrimage site for the presence of a miraculous icon, a crucifix painted by St. Luke and St. Nicodemus (a less pious opinion calls it a Byzantine-inspired work from 13th-century Poland). Numana also has an **Antiquarium**, with displays recounting the evolution of the ancient Piceni culture (daily exc Mon 9–2, Sat and Sun 9–2, 4:30–6:30). Both Sirolo and Numana have beaches nearby, but the best ones are places that can only be reached by small boat, like the beach of **Due Sorelle** or the stretch of jagged white cliffs called **Sassi Bianchi**.

WHERE TO STAY (tel prefix 071)

With all the ferry passengers passing through, Ancona has a wide choice of accommodation. The finest in the city is the ****Grand Hotel Palace** on Lungomare Vanvitelli 24, tel 201 813, by the port near Trajan's Arch, a comfortable small hotel with a good restaurant and a roof garden with views over the port (L140–180 000). For a little tranquillity and lower prices, the **Viale** is nearly a kilometre from the centre at Viale della Vittoria 23, tel 201 861 (L70 000). Near the railway station, the recently upgraded ***Rosa**, Piazza Fratelli Rossini 3, tel 41 388, has rooms for L75–90 000 with bath, or there's **Gino**, Via Flaminia 4, tel 43 333 (L45 000 with bath, less without). Out in Portonovo, ****Fortino Napoleonico**, tel 801 124, as its name implies, incorporates part of a fortress built during the Napoleonic Wars; it's quiet and modern, and has its own beach and a pool (L100 000 all year round, but if you check into the 'Josephine suite', L160–200 000). How the hotel keepers in Numana get away with charging what they do is a mystery—L70–90 000 for some pretty dismal spots thrown up in the recent building boom. One that's worth the bill is the ***Gigli Eden**, tel 936 182—nice rooms with a view, two pools, tennis, and acres of ground with plenty of trees. There's a secluded private beach, but it's a bit of a climb to get back from it (L75–90 000). Another choice is **Teresa a Mare**, Via del Golfo 26, tel 936 153 (L75 000, with bath). At Monte Conero, ***Monte Conero**, tel 936 122, is in a relaxed setting on the lush green headland (L70–100 000).

EATING OUT

Ancona's famous restaurant, **Miscia**, was long a legend for the eccentricities of its owner, a former boxer, and the enormous, unending dinners. Since Miscia's demise, the place has become more than a little pricey, but they still make first-class seafood—and tons of it, on a no-choice prix-fixe menu that can last four hours (in the port, Molo Sud 44, tel 201 376, menu L70 000, all-inclusive). **Passetto**, on Piazza IV Novembre, tel 33 214, is another excellent seafood place, claimed by some to be the best in Italy—*zuppa di balleri*, made from a kind of mussel that only lives around the Conero coast, is the speciality (L60 000 and up). **La Moretta**, Piazza Plebiscito 52, tel 58 382 has long been a favourite with the townspeople for its excellent stoccafisso and spaghetti agli scampi (L30 000, closed Sun). Like any self-respecting port, Ancona has dozens of trattorie where you can put away some less grandiose marine delights at inconceivably low prices: the **Osteria del Pozzo**, on Via Bonda, tel 50 396, at the centre of the port, is one (good mixed fry; average L15 000), and **La Cantineta**, around the corner on Via Gramsci, tel 201 107, another, that offers a foretaste of Greece if you're hopping on a ferry, complete with Greek seamen fingering worry beads. It is one of most popular places in town, though certainly not for its decor; delicious stoccafisso, and oddly enough, lemon sorbet (L20 000). Or try **Pekino**, one of two Chinese restaurants on Viale Marconi, up from the station (L20 000). On the way out of Ancona, to the north at Torrette, **Da Carloni**, Via Flaminia 247, tel 888 239, is another hot spot for its seafood, but the restaurant sits right on the tracks and rattles your mussels when trains pass (L30 000).

In Portonovo, the aforementioned **Fortino Napoleonico** is one of the finest places to dine in the region, with two beautiful dining rooms and immaculate service; be sure to notice the painting at the entrance, depicting the manager, staff, and guests decked out in Napoleonic costume—the big black dog in the picture is the one that comes out to greet you. For L80 000 they'll indulge you with eight superb courses, including stuffed olives and scampi, sole stuffed with spinach, cream and smoked salmon, shrimps with fennel and orange, gnocchi with caviare, and more. If your budget won't stretch to the Fortino, just around the corner on the beach is the **Emilia**, tel 801 109, with a sea terrace and pleasant views if you ignore the colour of the water. All fish, with a good seafood risotto for L40 000. Also in Portonovo, **Da Anna**, right on the beach, tel 801 343, is a restaurant not to be missed if you're anywhere near the Conero. The proprietor goes out daily to catch the fish; his wife does the cooking. The atmosphere and the cuisine couldn't be better—hit it soon before they realize they could be charging twice what they are now—about L30 000 on the average (open from Easter to the end of Oct).

The Southern Marches: Down the Coast

TOURIST INFORMATION
Porto San Benedetto: Viale delle Tamerici 5, tel (0734) 22 37.
Porto San Giorgio: Via Oberdan 8, tel (0734) 378 461.
Fermo: Piazza del Popolo, tel (0734) 23 205.
Loreto: Via Solari 3, tel (071) 977 139.

After Monte Conero, the Adriatic won't show you another stretch of beautiful coastline until the Gargano peninsula in Apulia. All through the southern Marches, the coast is dotted with humble but growing resort towns, all pleasant enough but nothing special: **Porto Recanati, Civitanova Marche, Porto Sant'Elpidio, Porto San Giorgio, Pedaso, Grottammare** and **San Benedetto del Tronto**. If you're looking for a chance to dip inland, the best place would be **Fermo**, a fine old town 6 km west of Porto San Giorgio. The Sabine town of *Firmum*, later a close ally of Rome, has gained importance and lost it several times; during the 10th century it was the capital of a duchy that included all the southern Marches, and later it was the seat of a university. A singular relic of Roman times can be visited under the Via degli Aceti: the **Piscina Epuratoria** is an enormous underground reservoir of 30 chambers, designed to both hold and clarify rain and spring water. The 15th-century façade of the **Palazzo Comunale** is adorned with a mildly eerie statue of Pope Sixtus V, once Fermo's bishop, inviting you in to a fine collection of art in the **Pinoteca Civica**, including a moving and intense *Nativity* of Rubens; local records recall a Fermo priest commissioning it in 1608 for the grand sum of 1700 scudi. Other works include a painting of Jacobello del Fiore and a 15th century Flemish tapestry (daily exc Sun mornings and Mon, 9–12:30, 5–8; winter 10–12, 4–7; adm). In the museum of the 14th-century **Cathedral**, they'll show you a chasuble of Moorish silk that belonged to St Thomas à Becket—but they can't really explain how they got it.

Sweet Music: Castelfidardo and Osimo

Many of the inland towns of this area can provide object lessons in the growth and strength of the 'new model' small-scale economy. Fermo, for example, and the villages around it produce a quarter of all the shoes made in Italy. South of Ancona, the town of **Castelfidardo** lives almost entirely on the manufacture of accordions. This most catholic of musical instruments was invented here, in the 1870s, so they say, and there is an **Accordion Museum** to fill in any gaps in your accordion knowledge (on Via Mordini; daily exc Mon afternoon 10:30–12:30, 3:30–7:30; adm). In 1860, the accordion capital witnessed a comic-opera skirmish that would have been worthy of an accordion accompaniment. The Battle of Castelfidardo, where King Vittorio Emanuele II vanquished the ragtag legions of the pope, allowed the Piedmontese to look heroic in completing Italy's year of unification—after all the hard work had been done by Garibaldi and his Thousand. A monument to the Piedmontese General Cialdini, set on a cypress-lined avenue, commemorates the event.

Osimo, 3 km up the road, began life as a capital of the Piceni, later becoming Roman *Auximum*. It may be much older than Castelfidardo, but musically at least it tries to be more up-to-date; the town makes most of Italy's electric guitars and organs. Its neighbours aren't impressed; they call people from Osimo 'senza teste' because the twelve headless Roman statues that decorate the town hall. Osimo has a small **museum** in its Palazzo Campana, with a retro (for the late 1400s) polyptych by the Vivarini brothers of Venice (daily exc Wed, 4–6 pm). Another museum is attached to its 13th-century **cathedral**, with some surprising paintings by little-known local Renaissance artists (open on request).

Loreto

The inventor of the accordion, the story goes, got his inspiration when an Austrian pilgrim on his way to **Loreto** left behind a button-box as a gift after lodging for the night. This town, hardly even half the size of Osimo or Castelfidardo, is one of the most popular pilgrimage sites in Europe, and has been since the 1300s.

Even though the town of Loreto puts up billboards all over Italy inviting us to visit, few foreigners apart from the devout ever take the hint. That is a pity, for like Urbino, Loreto is a small but concentrated dose of fine art from the Renaissance. Its story is a mystery of the faith. During the 1200s, the Church found itself threatened on all sides by heretical movements and free-thinkers. The popes responded in various subtle ways to assimilate and control them; creating the Franciscan movement was one, and the encouragement of the cult of the Virgin Mary another. Conveniently enough, a legend of a miracle in the Marches gained wide currency. Mary's house in Nazareth, after being divinely transported to a hill in Istria, decided to fly off again in 1294, this time landing in these laurel woods (*loreto*) south of Ancona. Supposedly the house had bestirred itself in protest over Moslem reoccupation of the Holy Land; the popes were thumping the tub for a new Crusade, and Loreto was just coincidentally located on the route to the Crusader ports on the Adriatic. Before dismissing this as silly business, though, consider that among the devout pilgrims to make their way here were Galileo and Descartes.

Loreto's Santuario della Santa Casa

Beginning in the 1460s, the simple church originally built to house the *Santa Casa* was reconstructed and embellished in a massive building programme that took well over a century to complete. Corso Boccalini, lined with the inevitable souvenir stands, leads from the town centre up to the Sanctuary—a very sudden surprise, when you turn the corner and enter the enclosed **Piazza della Madonna**, with the church, a great fountain by Carlo Maderno, one of the architects of St Peter's, and an elegant **loggia** by Bramante, enclosing the square. This being a papal production—a big bronze statue of Sixtus V, in front of the church doors, dominates the piazza—many of the most important figures in the Roman art world had a hand in the work.

The sanctuary's understated façade is typical early Roman Baroque, though a little ahead of its time (1587); no one is perfectly sure to whom to ascribe it, since so many architects had a hand in the work. Giuliano da Sangallo built the cupola, almost a copy of Brunelleschi's great dome in Florence, Bramante did the side chapels, and Sansovino and Sangallo the Younger also contributed. One of the best features is the series of reliefs on the bronze doors, by the Lombardos and other artists; another is the circle of radiating brick **apses** on the east end, turreted like a Renaissance castle; be sure to walk around for a look. Apparently the original architects really did intend the back of the church, overlooking the town walls, to function as part of the fortifications. The only unfortunate element in the ensemble is the ungainly Neoclassical **campanile**, topped with a sort of bronze-plated garlic bulb. Luigi Vanvitelli designed it in the 1750s. Don't blame the architect for the proportions; the tower had to be squat and strong to hold the 15-ton bell, one that has little trouble making itself heard in Ancona once it gets going.

Chapels line the walls inside, embellished by the faithful from nations around the world; two of the more recent are those of the USA and Mexico. The sedate Spanish chapel is one of the better ones, and the English chapel holds a memory of the lyric poet Richard Crashaw, a refugee from Protestant intolerance who served as canon here until his death in the 1640s. A good deal of Loreto's art was swiped by Napoleon, and consequently most of the paintings in the interior are from the last two centuries; the two **sacristies** on the right aisle have fresco cycles by Melozzo da Forli and Luca Signorelli. The left-aisle sacristies have a number of della Robbia lunettes. Under the dome you'll see the object of the pilgrims' attention. The **Santa Casa**, a simple brick building with traces of medieval frescoes inside, was sheathed in marble by Bramante to become one of the largest and most expensive sculptural ensembles ever attempted (in size and plan it is rather like Michelangelo's original project for the famous tomb of Pope Julius II); its decoration includes beautiful reliefs by Sansovino, Sangallo, della Porta, and others, showing scenes from the *Life of Mary*.

Next to the sanctuary, there is a small **museum** (daily exc Mon, 9–1 and 3–6, closed afternoons in winter; adm) with a number of works by Lorenzo Lotto, who spent his last years in Loreto. In the walls, at the Porta Marina, a **Museum of Antique Arms** has recently been opened(daily 10–12:30, 3–5; closed Dec–February; adm).

WHERE TO STAY AND EATING OUT

If you're stopping at Fermo, there is a comfortable hotel in the town's lovely historic centre, facing the cathedral and town park, the ***__Casina delle Rose__ on Piazzale Girfalco, tel (0734) 32 236 (L68 000) or **__Regina Mundi__, out of the centre at S. Petronilla, tel (0734) 212 100 (L55 000 with bath). **Da Nasò**, run by a genial proprietor who doesn't mind being called 'big nose', is the place for dinner, with good wine, local food and lots of it, at Via Crollalanza 45, tel (0734) 229 661 (L30 000), closed Mon. If you're passing through San Benedetto, **Al Gambero**, Via Galilei 3, tel (0735) 5184, is a good place to stop for fish without breaking the bank. Try the *brodetto di San Benedetto* and maccheroni al sugo di pesce for L30–35 000.

In Castelfidardo, ****__Del Parco__, Via Donizetti 2, tel 783 605, has most modern comforts, but no pool, for L110 000, or try the *__Piccolo Ranch__, Via Adriatica 22, tel 782 385, which has a restaurant (L48 000 with bath).

Hotels in Loreto are invariably clean, quiet, and respectable, with a crucifix above every bed. A good many of them are run by religious orders—Ursulines, Franciscan Sisters, the Holy Family Institute of Piedmont—inexpensive accommodation for pilgrims: ***__Casa del Clero Madonna di Loreto__ is a typical example, with 30 rooms, all with bath for L80 000. For a slightly more secular atmosphere, try the **__Centrale__, tel (071) 970 173 (L45 000). It might be worth a stay for dinner at Loreto's one outstanding restaurant. At **Orlando Barbani**, Via Villa Constantina at Loreto Archi, tel 977 696, you won't see a humdrum everyday menu; roast small game—quail, pigeon, and thrushes, are a speciality, along with snails or *coniglio con porchetta* (a good bargain too, at L30–35 000, closed Wed).

The Pocket Province of Macerata

TOURIST INFORMATION
Macerata: Piazza Libertà 12, tel (0733) 45 807.
Tolentino: Piazza Libertà 18, tel (0733) 973 002.
Camerino: Vico del Comune 6, tel (0733) 25 34.

You won't find a more out-of-the-way corner in central Italy. Although this hilly enclave lacks great attractions, all of its towns put up a good front, with stout medieval walls or a gay Romanesque tower to lure you in for a short stop. Many of its villages and towns also have fine works of art in their little museums. **Recanati**, 9 km south of Loreto, was the birthplace of Italy's greatest modern poet, Giacomo Leopardi. They have made a discreet cottage industry out of him, and you can visit his birthplace in the **Palazzo Leopardi**, along with a small museum and library. The town's **Pinacoteca** is full of relics of another favourite son, the great tenor Beniamino Gigli; there is an altarpiece and three other works by Lorenzo Lotto as well, including what may be the silliest *Annunciation* ever painted (daily except Sun, 9–12 and 5–6; adm). Serious opera buffs may visit Gigli's tomb, a fair-sized pyramid with full *Aida* trappings, in the town cemetery. Recanati enjoys an elevated site, and there are wonderful views as far as Loreto and the Adriatic from the town and its surroundings.

To the southwest, route 77 takes you to **Macerata**, the modest provincial capital, and a pleasant medieval-looking town of 45,000. About one-sixth of them can fit into the town's major landmark, a huge colonnaded hemicycle and outdoor theatre called the **Arena Sferisterio**, built in the 1820s—maybe the grandest setting for opera south of Verona. Macerata makes good use of it in their opera festival in July, one of the most popular summer music events in Italy. On Piazza Vittorio Veneto, the **Museo Civico** complex has another Madonna by Crivelli (no cucumbers, but a lovely work just the same), archaeological finds from a nearby Roman town called *Helvia Ricina*, and a museum of carriages (daily 9–12:30, 4–6). If you're fond of *presepi* (carved Italian Christmas cribs) and can't make it to Naples, Macerata has a little private museum of them, the **Museo Tipologico del Presepio**. It's on Via Maffeo Pantaleoni; call Cavaliere Cassese on 49 035 if you'd like to see his collection. Some of Helvia Ricina survives, a romantically overgrown ruin with remains of a theatre and amphitheatre, 4 km north on the SS361 towards Osimo; press on a little further and you'll pass the walled medieval village of **Montecassiano**, with a church designed by Antonio Lombardo.

South of Macerata, the valley of the Chienti carries you deeper into the province, towards the Monti Sibillini. At **Corridonia**, near Macerata, there is an interesting Byzantine church off Route 485, **San Claudio al Chienti**, from the 6th century, with a pair of round campaniles like those of the churches in Ravenna. Corridonia's **Pinacoteca** (open on request), in an 18th century Neoclassical church, has another remarkable Madonna of Carlo Crivelli, enclosed in a wreath of angels.

Tolentino

Continuing up the valley of the Chienti on the SS77, a side road to the south for Mogliano leads to the **Chiaravalle di Fiastra**, an 11th-century French Romanesque church, part of a Cistercian abbey (like San Galgano in Tuscany); Chiaravalle is a translation of *Clairvaux*, where the Cistercians began. Now a bit over-restored, it retains some 15th-century frescoes. A foundation runs it, with a museum of country life and crafts, local flora and fauna, a working cantina and an archaeological exhibit (daily 8:30–12:30, 4–8). Nearby, at Urbisaglia, there are some extensive ruins of a Roman town, *Urbs Salvia*, including an amphitheatre (daily 8–2 pm). Back on SS77, you will pass the Renaissance **Castello della Rancia**(1357) just before the outskirts of **Tolentino**. This is one of the larger towns, prosperous and modern and not much to look at until you reach the medieval centre, with the 13th-century **Devil's Bridge** leading to the **Basilica of San Nicola** from the 1300s. This church has an impressive portal (1430s) by the Florentine Nanni di Bartolo; inside, an artist long known only as the 'Maestro di Tolentino' (now believed to be a certain Giuliano da Rimini) left a beautiful series of frescoes in the Cappellone Gotico: intense, inspired work that bears comparison with the best trecento painting in Tuscany. Around the garden cloister, there is a series of **museums** displaying ceramics (Italian and foreign, from many periods), archaeology (Greek and Etruscan ceramics and bronzes), and art from Tolentino's churches—including an exquisite carved wood nativity tableau from the quattrocento, a Madonna by Simone de Magistris, and interesting painted ex-votos (the Basilica was a pilgrimage site) as old as the 1400s (daily 9–12, 3:30–7); adm).

Tolentino has a fascinating **clock tower**, next to the church of San Francesco in the Piazza della Libertà, one that will tell you the phases of the moon, the canonical hour, and the day, among other things. There are more early frescoes in San Francesco and the nearby **Cathedral**, which also has the Roman sarcophagus of Tolentino's patron, San Catervo. For something different, Tolentino has opened the world's first **Museum of Caricatures** in the Palazzo Bezzi, with hundreds of cartoons from around the world (daily, in summer 9–12, 4:30–7:30; Sun 9–12:30, 4–8). This was a little private collection that grew into a big affair; Tolentino now hosts an annual *International Festival of Humour in Art*.

Some other towns around Tolentino: **San Ginesio**, to the south, with another picture gallery, installed in its 15th-century church of San Sebastiano, and a *collegiata* church with a peculiar Gothic façade; the walls still stand, and outside the main gate is a large medieval stone pilgrims' hospice. Further south, **Sarnano** is a small spa offering all the important mud, water and aerosol tortures, plus yet another tiny *Pinacoteca*, on Via Leopardi; look for the *Last Supper*, an exceptional work by the truly obscure Simone de Magistris, *c.* 1600, and a Madonna (with cucumber) by Carlo Crivelli's brother Vittore (Tues, Thurs, Sat, 8–1, 3–7; Wed and Fri 3–6 pm). Northwest of Tolentino, **San Severino Marche** hasn't been awakened from its slumbers since Totila the Goth sacked it; the oldest parts of town, in the medieval Castello, are almost abandoned. In the early Renaissance, though, the town was a minor artistic centre, home town of Iacopo and Lorenzo Salimbeni. And right on Via Salimbeni, you can inspect some of their work at the town **Pinacoteca**—one of the best of these little galleries, with three Pinturicchio Madonnas, an elegant polyptych by Paolo Veneziano (a great pre-Renaissance Venetian; this is his only work south of the Veneto), and many others, along with an archaeological collection (daily 9–1; in summer also 4:30–6:30).

Camerino, up-river, passed the time during the Middle Ages in endless fighting with arch-enemy Fabriano just to the north. Today a mere shadow of the proud and thriving town of those times, Camerino has two good picture galleries, the **Museo Diocesano**

and the **Museo Civico**; in both the best works are from a local quattrocento painter named Girolamo di Giovanni. The ruined castle east of town is the **Rocca Varano**, from the 1200s. After Camerino there are only two-lane mountain roads over the Apennines to Foligno and Spoleto in Umbria.

Towards the southern corner of the Marches the mountains grow higher, reaching a climax in the dark, dramatic range called the **Monti Sibillini**, with the second highest peak in the Apennines; **Monte Vettore** (2476 m) often has snow until June. Around these mountains there are popular skiing areas at **Ussita** and **Arquata del Tronto**, both with a wide choice of long runs. Arquata del Tronto, a lovely village under a hilltop castle, lies along the surest route over the mountains, an often spectacular, twisting road from Ascoli Piceno through a 1500 m pass, the **Forca Canapine** over to Norcia in Umbria, by way of the spectacular mountain meadow called the Piano Grande (see p. 454). The route is a balcony over all the southern Apennines, and full of wild flowers in the spring. No one is sure how the 'Mountains of the Sibyls' got their name. Ancient writers record no such oracular priestesses in these parts (the closest were at Cumae, near Naples, and at Tivoli). Italy, though, is full of stories about them, and supposedly these mountains gave birth to the legend of Wagner's *Tannhäuser*.

WHERE TO STAY AND EATING OUT (tel prefix 0733)

Macerata is a perfectly fine place to stop for the night or during the opera festival. ****Da Rosa**, Via Armaroli 94, tel 49 670 (L64 000) and ******Motel AGIP**, Via Roma 149, tel 34 246, with the usual trimmings but no pool for L130–180 000, are two of its modest, comfortable hotels. For something really special, though, drive the 9 km north of town to Montecassiano and the ******Villa Quiete**, an 18th-century country house in beautiful grounds with a pool; rooms furnished with antiques and decorated with a masterful eye. If they could pick it up and move it to Tuscany, they could charge three or four times the L110 000 room rate (at Frazione Valle Cascia outside Montecassiano, tel 599 559; the hotel has a fine restaurant, too, costing about L50 000 for dinner). Another choice in Montecassiano is the *****Roganti**, Fraz. Palazetto, tel 598 639, with comfortable rooms and a garden, for L90 000. Macerata is the place to try *vincisgrassi*, a dish with many variations, a more refined version of lasagna, sometimes with béchamel sauce. Before you get out your Latin dictionary, know that the name comes from the Austrian General Windischgratz (from the Napoleonic Wars) who must have liked it a lot. Macerata's best restaurant is **Da Secondo** on Via Pescheria Vecchia, tel 44 912, where besides *vincisgrassi* you can order the famous *fritto misto* of lamb and vegetables—do book, as it's always crowded (L40 000).

Ascoli Piceno

Urbino, at the northern end of the Marches, and Ascoli, at the southern, compete for your attention as almost polar opposites. Urbino gets most of the praise, and partisans of Ascoli may find that somewhat unfair. Unlike the northern town, paternalistically led by its enlightened, aesthetic Dukes, Ascoli with its long heritage as a free *comune* has always had to do for itself. The difference shows; Ascoli is a beautiful city, but beautiful in a gritty, workaday manner like Florence. It has taken some hard knocks in its 2500 years, which have helped make it a city of character.

History

Ascoli, as its name implies, had its beginnings with the Piceni, and it probably served as the centre of their confederation. To the Romans, *Asculum Picenum* was an early ally, but later a major headache. Asculum fought Rome in the Samnite Wars, and actually initiated the pan-Italian revolt of the Social Wars.

The Romans took the city in 89 BC and razed it to the ground, soon afterwards refounding it with a colony of veterans. The street plan of Ascoli today has hardly changed since then; it is one of the most perfect examples in Italy of a rectilinear Roman *castrum*. In the Dark Ages, Ascoli's naturally defensible position between the steep ravines helped avert trouble. Its citizens, too, showed admirable determination, defeating Odoacer's Goths on one occasion, and the Byzantines and Saracens on several others. Despite periods under the rule of others—Lombards, Franks, Normans, and various feudal lords—Ascoli emerged by the 1100s as a strong free *comune*. Reminders of this most glorious period of the city's history are everywhere, in the 13th-century Palazzo del Popolo, the clutch of tall, noble towers like those of San Gimignano, and in Ascoli's famous festival, the **Quintana**, a jousting contest the rules of which were laid down in the statutes of 1378. Ascoli lost its freedom immediately, and its prosperity gradually, with the coming of papal rule in the 15th century, only recovering some of its wealth and importance in the last 100 years.

GETTING AROUND

Ascoli is not the easiest place to reach. The only train service is a dead-end branch off the Adriatic coast line, from San Benedetto del Tronto. The station (several trains a day), is on Viale Marconi in the new town. Buses, for Pesaro, Ancona, and Rome, leave from Viale Alcide di Gasperi behind the Cathedral; all information on both can be obtained from the Brumozzi Travel Agency on Corso Trieste, near Piazza del Popolo. For the Rome bus, see the Cameli Agency, Via Dino Angelini 127 west of the Cathedral.

TOURIST INFORMATION

Piazza del Popolo, tel (0736) 53 045

Piazza del Popolo

Like Rome, Ascoli is built of travertine. Also like Rome, it has more traffic than it can handle, and consequently the first impression will be of a grey, sooty town that shows its age. It's more wonder, then, that the central **Piazza del Popolo** can be so nonchalantly, so effortlessly one of the most beautiful squares in all Italy. This is no grand architectural ensemble, not monumental, not even symmetrical. But the travertine paving shines almost like marble; the low arcades that surround it give the square architectural unity and a setting for two fine buildings. The first, the 13th-century **Palazzo del Popolo**, was begun in the 1200s and redone in the late 16th century, with a façade by Ascoli's best known artist, Cola dell'Amatrice (next door to it stop at the Art Nouveau **Bar Meletti** for a coffee or a home-made *amaretto*; it's quite a place, one of the few bars in Italy to resist trashing itself by modernization). At the narrow end of the Piazza, the church of **San Francesco** (*c.* 1260) turns its back on the square—not really an insult, since the apse and transepts are the best part of the building, a classic, austere ascent of Gothic bays and towers under a low dome added in the late 15th century. Over the south door is a statue of Pope Julius II. The façade, around the corner, isn't much to look at; a strange, flat square of travertine decorated with a tiny plain rose window, like a wall with an electrical outlet on it. It does have a good sculpted portal, guarded by a pair of sarcastic-looking lions. Inside, there are only grand and simple Gothic vaults to look at, Outside, the southern end of the façade adjoins the **Loggia dei Mercanti**, built by the Wool Corporation—a typical medieval-style manufacturers' cooperative—in the early 1500s.

On the northern side, the old Franciscan cloister has become Ascoli's busy and colourful **market**. The street running in front of San Francesco is the centre of activity in Ascoli, the **Via del Trivio**; follow it northwards to Ascoli's oldest and prettiest neighbourhoods, on the cliffs above the River Trcnto. Most of the city's surviving **towers** are here. Ascoli has as many of these medieval family-fortresses as San Gimignano in Tuscany, though they are not as well known; the tallest is the **Torre di Ercolani** on Via Soderini. You can see many of them from **Via della Luna**, a lovely walk that follows the route of the old walls, around the northern edge of town overlooking the river. Piazza Ventidio Basso, the medieval commercial centre, has two interesting churches: **SS. Vicenzo ed Anastasio**, with an unfinished Renaissance façade, and the Gothic **San Pietro Martire**. The former is famous for a miraculous well in the crypt (it'll cure your leprosy). At the northern tip of Ascoli, a doughty single-arched Roman bridge, the 1st-century **Ponte di Solesta**, still carries traffic across to the northern suburbs without a creak or a groan. If you cross it, and walk along the river bank to the east, you will see signs for the church of **S. Emidio della Grotta**, on the street of the same name, an elegant 1623 Baroque façade that closes the front of a cave; here San Emidio, Ascoli's patron, was martyred, and the site became the city's earliest place of Christian worship.

All around the northern edge of Ascoli, the lovely valley of the Tronto makes a perfect picnic spot. Parts of Ascoli's walls, still visible in many places, still show the characteristic diamond-shaped brickwork of Roman construction, and at the western entrance to town, on Corso Mazzini, a Roman gate survives, the **Porta Gemina**. On the fringes of the city, Roman remains are everywhere; just south of the Porta Gemina, on Via Angelini, there is a Roman **theatre**, near the remains of a fortress built by the popes in 1564; continuing back to Corso Mazzini through this quarter you will pass the medieval churches of the Annunziata and S. Angelo Magno, and finally San Gregorio, built over a Roman temple of Vesta, just behind Ascoli's town hall and cathedral.

Piazza Arringo

Ascoli's **cathedral**, dedicated to Sant'Emidio, is a 12th-century building similar to San Francesco, but with a new façade from the 1530s, also by Cola dell'Amatrice. In a chapel on the south side you can see the inevitable cucumber in an altarpiece by Carlo Crivelli, badly in need of restoration but still one of his finest. The **Museo Diocesano**, in the adjacent archbishop's palace, has works by Cola dell'Amatrice, but here a mid-1500s painter from Vicenza, Marcello Fogolino, steals the show with a room of unusual Old Testament frescoes (Mon, Thurs, and Sat only, 10–12). The 10th-century octagonal **baptistry**, off to the side of the cathedral, stands resolutely in the middle of Ascoli's busiest street. Facing the cathedral, behind the fierce dragons in the twin Renaissance fountains, there are works by Cola dell'Amatrice and other local artists, as well as Simone de Magistris, Titian and Guido Reni, and collections of ceramics and musical instruments, in the Pinacoteca of the **Palazzo Comunale**, an imposing Baroque façade that hides the original 13th-century town hall (summer 10–1, 4:30–6:30, Sun 10–12; winter 9–1, Sun 9–12). Across the square, the **Musco Archaeologico** has some good bronzes of the ancient Piceni, Roman mosaics and a plan of the city in Roman times, as well as Lombard jewellery and relics from a recently discovered medieval necropolis (daily exc Mon 9–1; adm).

A walk through the streets north of Piazza Arringo will take you past some of the palaces of medieval Ascoli, with many curious carvings and inscriptions on the old houses; one, the **Palazzo Bonaparte** on Via Bonaparte, was built by a prominent family of the 1500s that local legend claims as the ancestors of the famous Bonapartes; Napoleon himself said he didn't know if it was true or not. The **Palazzo Malaspina** on Corso Mazzini is one of the fancier buildings.

WHERE TO STAY AND EATING OUT (tel prefix 0736)

One of Ascoli's attractions, of course, is that it is largely undiscovered, but that also means choices for accommodation are few. One thoroughly pleasant hotel, on the edge of the old town near the Cathedral, is the *****Gioli**, at Via Alcide di Gasperi 14, tel 52 450, with parking—a real blessing in this crowded town—and a small garden (L55–75 000). ****Pavoni**, Via Nazionale 135, tel 47 501, has ten simple rooms for L40 000 without bath, L48 000 with. Ascoli also has a very friendly youth hostel—the **Ostello dei Lombardi** is located in the tallest of the medieval towers on the northern edge of town (Via Soderini 26, tel 50 007).

Forget about jousting and Crivelli madonnas—to most Italians Ascoli means one thing, *olivi ripieni*. These breaded and fried stuffed olives are wonderful, but one of the most tedious dishes imaginable to prepare; you won't find them often outside Ascoli. The best place to try them is the **Cantina Al Pennile (Da Mario)** on Via Spalvicri, tel 42 504, in the eastern suburbs, a long-time Ascoli institution (a real bargain at about L25–35 000). Closer to the centre, olives and other specialities *all'Ascolana* await you at **Tornasacco**, Via Tornasacco 27, off Piazza Arringo, tel 54 151, such as tagliatelle with lamb sauce, also very good local cheeses and charcuterie (L25–35 000; closed Fri). **Kursaal**, Corso Mazzini 221, tel 53 140, in the centre has a variety of risotto dishes—with asparagus, salmon and caviare, or truffles, and other local specialities for L35 000. Ascoli is a fine town for inexpensive family-run trattorie; you can pick one out at random, or seek out **Da Giovanna** on Rua Marcolini a block west of Piazza Arringo, a typical place where you can have an agreeably satisfying dinner for L15 000.

ARCHITECTURAL, ARTISTIC AND HISTORICAL TERMS

Acroterion: decorative protrusion on the rooftop of an Etruscan, Greek or Roman temple. At the corners of the roof they are called *antefixes*.

Ambones: twin pulpits in some southern churches (singular: *ambo*), often elaborately decorated.

Ambulatory: an aisle around the apse of a church.

Atrium: entrance court of a Roman house or early church.

Badia: *abbazia*, an abbey or abbey church.

Baldacchino: baldachin, a columned stone canopy above the altar of a church.

Basilica: a rectangular building, usually divided into three aisles by rows of columns. In Rome this was the common form for law courts and other public buildings, and Roman Christians adapted it for their early churches.

Borgo: from the Saxon *burh* of S. Spirito in Rome: a suburb.

Bucchero ware: black, delicately thin Etruscan ceramics, usually incised or painted.

Calvary chapels: a series of outdoor chapels, usually on a hillside, that commemorate the stages of the Passion of Christ.

Campanile: a bell-tower.

Campanilismo: local patriotism; the Italians' own word for their historic tendency to be more faithful to their home towns than to the abstract idea of 'Italy'.

Camposanto: a cemetery.

Cardo: transverse street of a Roman *castrum*-shaped city.

Carroccio: a wagon carrying the banners of a medieval city and an altar; it served as the rallying point in battles.

Cartoon: the preliminary sketch for a fresco or tapestry.

Caryatid: supporting pillar or column carved into a standing female form; male versions are called *telamones*.

Castrum: a Roman military camp, always neatly rectangular, with straight streets and gates at the cardinal points. Later the Romans founded or refounded cities in this form, hundreds of which survive today (Lucca, Aosta, Florence, Pavia, Como, Brescia, Ascoli Piceno, Ancona are clear examples).

Cavea: the semicircle of seats in a classical theatre.

Cenacolo: fresco of the Last Supper, often on the wall of a monastery refectory.

Chiaroscuro: the arrangement or treatment of light and dark areas in a painting.

Ciborium: a tabernacle; the word is often used for large, freestanding tabernacles, or in the sense of a baldacchino.

Comune: commune, or commonwealth, referring to the governments of the free cities of the Middle Ages. Today it denotes any local government, from the Comune di Roma down to the smallest village.

Condottiere: the leader of a band of mercenaries in late medieval and Renaissance times.

Confraternity: a religious lay brotherhood, often serving as a neighbourhood mutual-aid and burial society, or following some specific charitable work (Michelangelo, for example, belonged to one that cared for condemned prisoners in Rome).

Contrapposta: the dramatic, but rather unnatural twist in a statue, especially in a Mannerist or Baroque work, derived from Hellenistic and Roman art.

Convento: a convent *or* monastery; it's the same word in Italian.

Cosmati work: or *Cosmatesque*: referring to a distinctive style of inlaid marble or enamel chips used in architectural decoration (pavements, pulpits, paschal candlesticks, etc.) in medieval southern Italy. The Cosmati family of Rome were its greatest practitioners.

Crete: in the pasturelands of southern Tuscany, chalky cliffs caused by erosion. Similar phenomena are the *biancane*, small chalk outcrops, and *balze*, deep eroded ravines around Volterra.

Cupola: a dome.

Cyclopean walls: fortifications built of enormous, irregularly polygonal blocks, as in the pre-Roman cities of Latium.

Decumanus: street of a Roman *castrum*-shaped city parallel to the longer axis, the central, main avenue called the Decumanus Major.

Dodecapolis: the federation of the twelve largest and strongest Etruscan city-states (see 'History').

Duomo: cathedral.

Ex-voto: an offering (a terracotta figurined, painting, medallion, silver bauble, or whatever) made in thanksgiving to a god or Christian saint; the practice has always been present in Italy.

Forum: the central square of a Roman town, with its most important temples and public buildings. The word means 'outside', as the original Roman Forum was outside the first city walls.

Fresco: wall painting, the most important Italian medium of art since Etruscan times. It isn't easy; first the artist draws the *sinopia* (q.v.) on the wall. This is covered with plaster, but only a little at a time, as the paint must be on the plaster before it dries. Leonardo da Vinci's endless attempts to find clever shortcuts ensured that little of his work would survive.

Ghibellines: one of the two great medieval parties, the supporters of the Holy Roman Emperors.

Gonfalon: the banner of a medieval free city; the *gonfaloniere*, or flag bearer, was often the most important public official.

Graffito: originally, incised decoration on buildings, walls, etc.; only lately has it come to mean casually-scribbled messages in public places.

Greek cross: in the floor plans of churches, a cross with equal arms. The more familiar plan, with one arm extended to form a nave, is called a *Latin Cross*.

Grisaille: painting or fresco in monochrome.

Grotesques: carved or painted faces used in Etruscan and later Roman decoration; Raphael and other artists rediscovered them in the 'grotto' of Nero's Golden House in Rome.

Guelphs (see *Ghibellines*): the other great political faction of medieval Italy, supporters of the Pope.

Intarsia: work in inlaid wood or marble.

Loggia: an open-sided gallery or arcade.

Lozenge: the diamond shape—along with stripes, one of the trademarks of Pisan architecture.

Lunette: semicircular space on a wall, above a door or under vaulting, either filled by a window or a mural painting.

Martroneum: the elevated women's gallery around the nave of an early church, a custom adopted from the Byzantines in the 6th and 7th centuries.

Narthex: the enclosed porch of a church.

Naumachia: mock naval battles, like those staged in the Colosseum.

Opus Reticulatum: Roman masonry consisting of diamond-shaped blocks.

Palazzo: not just a palace, but any large, important building (though the word comes from the Imperial *palatium* on Rome's Palatine Hill).

Palio: a banner, and the horse race in which city neighbourhoods contend for it in their annual festivals. The most famous is at Siena.

Pantocrator: Christ 'ruler of all', a common subject for apse paintings and mosaics in areas influenced by Byzantine art.

Pieve: a parish church, especially in the north.

Pietra Dura: rich inlay work using semi-precious stones, perfected in post-Renaissance Florence.

Podestà: in medieval cities, an official sent by the Holy Roman Emperors to take charge; their power, or lack of it, depended on the strength of the *comune*.

Predella: smaller paintings on panels below the main subject of a painted altarpiece.

Presepio: a Christmas crib.

Putti: flocks of plaster cherubs with rosy cheeks and bums that infested much of Italy in the Baroque era.

Quattrocento: the 1400s—the Italian way of referring to centuries (*duecento, trecento, quattrocento, cinquecento*, etc.).

Sbandieratore: flag-thrower in medieval costume at an Italian festival; sometimes called an *alfiere*.

Sinopia: the layout of a fresco (q.v.), etched by the artist on the wall before the plaster is applied. Often these are works of art in their own right.

Stele: a vertical funeral stone.

Stigmata: a miraculous simulation of the bleeding wounds of Christ, appearing in holy men like St Francis in the 12th century, and Padre Pio of Apulia in our own time.

Telamone: see *caryatid*.

Thermae: Roman baths.

Tondo: round relief, painting or terracotta.

Transenna: marble screen separating the altar area from the rest of an early Christian church.

Travertine: hard, light-coloured stone, sometimes flecked or pitted with black, sometimes perfect. The most widely used material in ancient and modern Rome.

Triptych: a painting, especially an altarpiece, in three sections.

Trompe l'oeil: art that uses perspective effects to deceive the eye—for example, to create the illusion of depth on a flat surface, or to make columns and arches painted on a wall seem real.

Tympanum: the semicircular space, often bearing a painting or relief, above the portal of a church.

Voussoir: one of the stones of an arch.

LANGUAGE

The fathers of modern Italian were Dante, Manzoni, and television. Each did his part in creating a national language from an infinity of regional and local dialects; the Florentine Dante, the first 'immortal' to write in the vernacular, did much to put the Tuscan dialect in the foreground of Italian literature. Manzoni's revolutionary novel, *I promessi sposi* (The Betrothed), heightened national consciousness by using an everyday language all could understand in the 19th century. Television in the last few decades is performing an even more spectacular linguistic unification; although the majority of Italians still speak a dialect at home, school, and work, their TV idols insist on proper Italian.

Perhaps because they are so busy learning their own beautiful but grammatically complex language, Italians are not especially apt at learning others. English lessons, however, have been the rage for years, and at most hotels and restaurants there will be someone who speaks some English. In small towns and out of the way places, finding an Anglophone may prove more difficult. The words and phrases below should help you out in most situations, but the ideal way to come to Italy is with some Italian under your belt; your visit will be richer, and you're much more likely to make some Italian friends.

Italian words are pronounced phonetically. Every vowel and consonant (except 'h') is sounded. Consonants are the same as in English, except the *c* which, when followed by an 'e' or 'i', is pronounced like the English 'ch' (*cinque* thus becomes cheenquay). Italian *g* is also soft before 'i' or 'e' as in *gira*, pronounced jee-ra. *H* is never sounded; *z* is pronounced like 'ts'. The consonants *sc* before the vowels 'i' or 'e' become like the English 'sh' as in *sci*, pronounced shee; *ch* is pronouced like a 'k' as in *Chianti*, kee-an-tee; *gn* as 'ny' in English (*bagno*, pronounced ban-yo; while *gli* is pronounced like the middle of the word million (*Castiglione*, pronounced Ca-steely-oh-nay).

Vowel pronunciation is: *a* as in English father; *e* when unstressed is pronounced like 'a' in fate as in *mele*, when stressed can be the same or like the 'e' in pet (*bello*); *i* is like the i in machine; *o* like 'e', has two sounds, 'o' as in hope when unstressed (*tacchino*), and usually 'o' as in rock when stressed (*morte*); *u* is pronounced like the 'u' in June.

The accent usually (but not always!) falls on the penultimate syllable. Also note that in the big northern cities, the informal way of addressing someone as you, *tu*, is widely used; the more formal *lei* or *voi* is commonly used in provincial districts.

Useful words and phrases

yes/no/maybe	si/no/forse
I don't know	Non lo so
I don't understand (Italian)	Non capisco (italiano)
Does someone here speak English?	C'è qualcuno qui chi parla inglese?
Speak slowly	Parla lentamente
Could you assist me?	Potrebbe aiutarmi?
Help!	Aiuto!
Please	Per favore
Thank you (very much)	(Molto) grazie
You're welcome	Prego
It doesn't matter	Non importa
All right	Va bene
Excuse me	Scusi
Be careful!	Attenzione!
Nothing	Niente
It is urgent!	E urgente!
How are you?	Come sta?
Well, and you?	Bene, e lei?
What is your name?	Come si chiama?
Hello	Salve *or* ciao (both informal)
Good morning	Buongiorno (formal hello)
Good afternoon, evening	Buona sera (also formal hello)
Good night	Buona notte
Goodbye	Arrivederla (formal), arrivederci, ciao (informal)

What do you call this in Italian	Come si chiama questo in italiano?
What	Che
Who	Chi
Where	Dove
When	Quando
Why	Perchè
How	Come
How much	Quanto
I am lost	Mi sono smarrito
I am hungry	Ho fame
I am thirsty	Ho sede
I am sorry	Mi dispiace
I am tired	Sono stanco
I am sleepy	Ho sonno
I am ill	Mi sento male
Leave me alone	Lasciami in pace
good	buono/bravo
bad	male/cattivo
It's all the same	Fa lo stesso
slow	piano
fast	rapido
big	grande
small	piccolo
hot	caldo
cold	freddo
up	su
down	giù
here	qui
there	lì

Shopping, service, sightseeing

I would like ...	Vorrei ...
Where is/are ...	Dov'è/Dove sono ...
How much is it?	Quanto viene questo?/Quante'è/Quanto costa questo?
open	aperto
closed	chiuso
cheap/expensive	a buon prezzo/caro
bank	banca
beach	spiaggia
bed	letto
church	chiesa
entrance	entrata
exit	uscita
hospital	ospedale
money	soldi
museum	museo
newspaper (foreign)	giornale (straniero)
pharmacy	farmacia
police station	commissariato
policeman	poliziotto
post office	ufficio postale
sea	mare
shop	negozio
room	camera
telephone	telefono
tobacco shop	tabaccaio
WC	toilette/bagno
men	Signori/Uomini
women	Signore/Donne

TIME	
What time is it?	Che ore sono?
month	mese
week	settimana
day	giorno
morning	mattina
afternoon	pomeriggio
evening	sera
today	oggi
yesterday	ieri
tomorrow	domani
soon	presto
later	dopo/più tarde
It is too early	E troppo presto
It is too late	E troppo tarde
DAYS	
Monday	lunedì
Tuesday	martedì
Wednesday	mercoledì
Thursday	giovedì
Friday	venerdì
Saturday	sabato
Sunday	domenica
NUMBERS	
one	uno/una
two	due
three	tre
four	quattro
five	cinque
six	sei
seven	sette
eight	otto
nine	nove
ten	dieci
eleven	undici
twelve	dodici
thirteen	tredici
fourteen	quattordici
fifteen	quindici
sixteen	sedici
seventeen	diciassette
eighteen	diciotto
nineteen	diciannove
twenty	venti
twenty-one	ventuno
twenty-two	ventidue
thirty	trenta
thirty-one	trentuno
forty	quaranta
fifty	cinquanta
sixty	sessanta
seventy	settanta
eighty	ottanta
ninety	novanta
hundred	cento
one hundred and one	cento uno
two hundred	duecento
thousand	mille

two thousand	due mila
million	milione
a thousand million	miliardo

TRANSPORT

airport	aeroporto
bus stop	fermata
bus/coach	auto/pulmino
railway station	stazione ferroviaria
train	treno
platform	binario
port	porto
port station	stazione marittima
ship	nave
automobile	macchina
taxi	tassi
ticket	biglietto
customs	dogana
seat (reserved)	posto (prenotato)

TRAVEL DIRECTIONS

I want to go to...	Desidero andare a...
How can I get to...?	Come posso andare a...?
Do you stop at...?	Ferma a...?
Where is...?	Dov'è...?
How far is it to...?	Quanto siamo lontani da...?
When does the... leave?	A che ora parte ...?
What is the name of this station?	Come si chiama questa stazione?
When does the next ... leave?	Quando parte il prossimo...?
From where does it leave?	Da dove parte?
How long does the trip take...?	Quanto tempo dura il viaggio?
How much is the fare?	Quant'è il biglietto?
Good trip!	Buon viaggio!
near	vicino
far	lontano
left	sinistra
right	destra
straight ahead	sempre diritto
forward	avanti
backward	in dietro
north	nord/settentrionale
south	sud/mezzogiorno
east	est/oriente
west	ovest/occidente
around the corner	dietro l'angolo
crossroads	bivio
street/road	strada
square	piazza

DRIVING

car hire	noleggio macchina
motorbike/scooter	motocicletta/Vespa
bicycle	bicicletta
petrol/diesel	benzina/gasolio
garage	garage
This doesn't work	Questo non funziona
mechanic	meccanico
map/town plan	carta/pianta
Where is the road to...?	Dov'è la strada per...?
breakdown	guasto *or* panna

driving licence	patente di guida
driver	guidatore
speed	velocità
danger	pericolo
parking	parcheggio
no parking	sosta vietato
narrow	stretto
bridge	ponte
toll	pedaggio
slow down	rallentare

Italian menu vocabulary

Antipasti

These before-meal treats can include almost anything; among the most common are:

Antipasto misto	mixed antipasto
Bruschetto	garlic toast
Carciofi (sott'olio)	artichokes (in oil)
Crostini	liver pâté on toast
Frutta di mare	seafood
Funghi (trifolati)	mushrooms (with anchovies, garlic, and lemon)
Gamberi al fagioli	prawns (shrimps) with white beans
Mozzarella (in carrozza)	buffalo cheese (fried with bread in batter)
Olive	olives
Prosciutto (con melone)	raw ham (with melon)
Salame	cured pork
Salsicce	dry sausage

Minestre e Pasta

These dishes are the principal typical first courses (*primo*) served throughout Italy.

Agnolotti	ravioli with meat
Cacciucco	spiced fish soup
Cannelloni	meat and cheese rolled in pasta tubes
Cappelletti	small ravioli, often in broth
Crespelle	crepes
Fettuccine	long strips of pasta
Frittata	omelette
Gnocchi	potato dumplings
Lasagne	sheets of pasta baked with meat and cheese sauce
Minestra di verdura	thick vegetable soup
Minestrone	soup with meat, vegetables, and pasta
Orecchiette	ear-shaped pasta, usually served with turnip greens
Panzerotti	ravioli filled with mozzarella, anchovies, and egg
Pappardelle alla lepre	pasta with hare sauce
Pasta e fagioli	soup with beans, bacon, and tomatoes
Pastina in brodo	tiny pasta in broth
Penne all'arrabbiata	quill shaped pasta in hot spicy sauce
Polenta	cake or pudding of corn semolina, prepared with meat or tomato sauce
Risotto (alla Milanese)	Italian rice (with saffron and wine)
Spaghetti all'Amatriciana	with spicy sauce of salt pork, tomatoes, onions, and chilli pepper
Spaghetti alla Bolognese	with ground meat, ham, mushrooms, etc.
Spaghetti alla carbonara	with bacon, eggs, and black pepper
Spaghetti al pomodoro	with tomato sauce
Spaghetti al sugo/ragu	with meat sauce
Spaghetti alle vongole	with clam sauce
Stracciatella	broth with eggs and cheese
Tagliatelle	flat egg noodles

Tortellini al pomodoro/panna/in brodo	pasta caps filled with meat and cheese, served with tomato sauce/with cream/in broth
Vermicelli	very thin spaghetti

Second courses–Carne (Meat)

Abbacchio	milk-fed lamb
Agnello	lamb
Animelle	sweetbreads
Anatra	duck
Arista	pork loin
Arrosto misto	mixed roast meats
Bistecca alla fiorentina	Florentine beef steak
Bocconcini	veal mixed with ham and cheese and fried
Bollito misto	stew of boiled meats
Braciola	pork chop
Brasato di manzo	braised meat with vegetables
Bresaola	dried raw meat similar to ham
Capretto	kid
Capriolo	roe deer
Carne di castrato/suino	mutton/pork
Carpaccio	thin slices of raw beef in piquant sauce
Cassoeula	winter stew with pork and cabbage
Cervello (al burro nero)	brains (in black butter sauce)
Cervo	venison
Cinghiale	boar
Coniglio	rabbit
Cotoletta (alla Milanese/alla Bolognese)	veal cutlet (fried in breadcrumbs/with ham and cheese)
Fagiano	pheasant
Faraono (alla creta)	guinea fowl (in earthenware pot)
Fegato alla veneziana	liver and onions
Involtini	rolls (usually of veal) with filling
Lepre (in salmi)	hare (marinated in wine)
Lombo di maiale	pork loin
Lumache	snails
Maiale (al latte)	pork (cooked in milk)
Manzo	beef
Osso buco	braised veal knuckle with herbs
Pancetta	rolled pork
Pernice	partridge
Petto di pollo (alla fiorentina/bolognese/sorpresa)	boned chicken breast (fried in butter/with ham and cheese/stuffed and deep fried)
Piccione	pigeon
Pizzaiola	beef steak with tomato and oregano sauce
Pollo (alla cacciatora/alla diavola/alla Marengo)	chicken (with tomatoes and mushrooms cooked in wine/grilled/fried with tomatoes, garlic and wine)
Polpette	meatballs
Quaglie	quails
Rane	frogs
Rognoni	kidneys
Saltimbocca	veal scallop with prosciutto and sage, cooked in wine and butter
Scaloppine	thin slices of veal sautéed in butter
Spezzatino	pieces of beef or veal, usually stewed
Spiedino	meat on a skewer or stick
Stufato	beef braised in white wine with vegetables
Tacchino	turkey
Trippa	tripe
Uccelletti	small birds on a skewer
Vitello	veal

Pesce (Fish)

Acciughe or Alici	anchovies
Anguilla	eel
Aragosta	lobster
Aringa	herring
Baccalà	dried cod
Bonito	small tuna
Branzino	sea bass
Calamari	squid
Cappe sante	scallops
Cefalo	grey mullet
Coda di rospo	angler fish
Cozze	mussels
Datteri di mare	razor (or date) mussels
Dentice	dentex (perch-like fish)
Dorato	gilt head
Fritto misto	mixed fried delicacies, usually fish
Gamberetto	shrimp
Gamberi (di fiume)	prawns (crayfish)
Granchio	crab
Insalata di mare	seafood salad
Lampreda	lamprey
Merluzzo	cod
Nasello	hake
Orata	bream
Ostriche	oysters
Pesce spada	swordfish
Polipi/polpi	octopus
Pesce azzurro	various types of small fish
Pesce di San Pietro	John Dory
Rombo	turbot
Sarde	sardines
Seppie	cuttlefish
Sgombro	mackerel
Sogliola	sole
Squadro	monkfish
Tonno	tuna
Triglia	red mullet (rouget)
Trota	trout
Trota salmonata	salmon trout
Vongole	small clams
Zuppa di pesce	mixed fish in sauce or stew

Contorni (side dishes, vegetables)

Asparagi (alla fiorentina)	asparagus (with fried eggs)
Broccoli (calabrese, romana)	broccoli (green, spiral)
Carciofi (alla giudia)	artichokes (deep fried)
Cardi	cardoons, thistles
Carote	carrots
Cavolfiore	cauliflower
Cavolo	cabbage
Ceci	chickpeas
Cetriolo	cucumber
Cipolla	onion
Fagioli	white beans
Fagiolini	French (green) beans
Fave	broad beans
Finocchio	fennel
Funghi (porcini)	mushroom (boletus)
Insalata (mista, verde)	salad (mixed, green)

Lattuga	lettuce
Lenticchie	lentils
Melanzana (al forno)	aubergine/eggplant (filled and baked)
Mirtilli	bilberries
Patate (fritte)	potatoes (fried)
Peperoni	sweet peppers
Peperonata	stewed peppers, onions, etc. similar to ratatouille
Piselli (al prosciutto)	peas (with ham)
Pomodoro	tomato(es)
Porri	leeks
Radicchio	red chicory
Radice	radishes
Rapa	turnip
Sedano	celery
Spinaci	spinach
Verdure	greens
Zucca	pumpkin
Zucchini	zucchini (courgettes)

Formaggio (Cheese)

Bel Paese	a soft white cow's cheese
Cascio/Casciocavallo	pale yellow, often sharp cheese
Fontina	rich cow's milk cheese
Groviera	mild cheese (gruyère)
Gorgonzola	soft blue cheese
Parmigiano	Parmesan cheese
Pecorino	sharp sheep's cheese
Provalone	sharp, tangy cheese; *dolce* is more mild
Stracchino	soft white cheese

Frutta (Fruit, nuts)

Albicocche	apricots
Ananas	pineapple
Arance	oranges
Banane	banana
Cachi	persimmon
Ciliege	cherries
Cocomero	watermelon
Composta di frutta	stewed fruit
Dattero	date
Fichi	figs
Fragole (con panna)	strawberries (with cream)
Frutta di stagione	fruit in season
Lamponi	raspberries
Macedonia di frutta	fruit salad
Mandarino	tangerine
Melagrana	pomegranate
Mele	apples
Melone	melon
More	blackberries
Nespola	medlar fruit
Pera	pear
Pesca	peach
Pesca noce	nectarine
Pompelmo	grapefruit
Prugna/susina	plum
Uve	grapes

Dolci (Desserts)

Amaretti	macaroons
Cannoli	crisp pastry tubes filled with ricotta, cream, chocolate or fruit

Coppa gelato	assorted ice cream
Crema caramella	caramel topped custard
Crostata	fruit flan
Gelato (produzione propria)	ice cream (homemade)
Granita	flavoured ice, usually lemon or coffee
Monte Bianco	chestnut pudding with whipped cream
Panettone	sponge cake with candied fruit and raisins
Panforte	dense cake of chocolate, almonds, and preserved fruit
Saint Honore	meringue cake
Semifreddo	refrigerated cake
Sorbetto	sorbet/sherbet
Spumone	a soft ice cream
Tiramisù	cream, coffee, and chocolate dessert
Torrone	nougat
Torta	cake, tart
Torta millefoglie	layered pastry with custard cream
Zabaglione	whipped eggs and Marsala wine, served hot
Zuppa inglese	trifle

Bevande/beverages

Acqua minerale con/senza gas	mineral water with/without fizz
Aranciata	orange soda
Birra (alla spina)	beer (draught)
Caffè (freddo)	coffee (iced)
Cioccolata (con panna)	chocolate (with cream)
Gassosa	lemon flavoured soda
Latte	milk
Limonata	lemon soda
Succo di frutta	fruit juice
Tè	tea
Vino (red, white, rosé)	wine (rosso, bianco, rosato)

Cooking terms, miscellaneous

Aceto (balsamico)	vinegar (balsamic)
Affumicato	smoked
Aglio	garlic
Alla brace	on embers
Bicchiere	glass
Burro	butter
Caccia	game
Conto	bill
Costoletta/Cotoletta	chop
Coltello	knife
Cotto adagio	braised
Cucchiaio	spoon
Filetto	fillet
Forchetta	fork
Forno	oven
Fritto	fried
Ghiaccio	ice
Griglia	grill
Limone	lemon
Magro	lean meat/or pasta without meat
Mandorle	almonds
Marmellata	jam
Menta	mint
Miele	honey
Mostarda	candied mustard sauce
Nocciole	hazelnuts
Noce	walnut

Olio	oil
Pane (tostato)	bread (toasted)
Panini	sandwiches
Panna	fresh cream
Pepe	pepper
Peperoncini	hot chilli peppers
Piatto	plate
Pignoli/pinoli	pine nuts
Prezzemolo	parsley
Ripieno	stuffed
Rosmarino	rosemary
Sale	salt
Salmi	wine marinade
Salsa	sauce
Salvia	sage
Senape	mustard
Tartufi	truffles
Tazza	cup
Tavola	table
Tovagliolo	napkin
Tramezzini	finger sandwiches
Umido	cooked in sauce
Uovo	egg
Zucchero	sugar

FURTHER READING

Carmichael, Montgomery, *In Tuscany* (Burns & Oates, 1910).

Goethe, J. W., *Italian Journey* (Penguin Classics, 1982). An excellent example of a genius turned to mush by Italy; good insights, but big, big mistakes.

Hutton, Edward, *Florence, Assisi*, and *Umbria Revisited*, in *Unknown Tuscany*, and *Siena and Southern Tuscany* (Hollis & Carter). Modern travel classics.

McCarthy, Mary, *The Stones of Florence* and *Venice Observed* (Penguin, 1986). Brilliant evocation of Italy's two great art cities, with an understanding that makes many other works on the subject seem sluggish and pedantic; don't visit Florence without it.

Morton, H. V., *A Traveller in Italy* (Methuen & Co, 1964). Among the most readable and delightful accounts of Italy in print. Morton is a sincere scholar and a true gentleman.

Raison, Laura (ed), *Tuscany: An Anthology* (Cadogan, 1983) An excellent selection of the best by Tuscans and Tuscan watchers.

Williams, Egerton R., *Hill Towns of Italy* (Smith, Elder, 1904). An Englishman goes exploring in Tuscany and Umbria.

History

Burckhardt, Jacob, *The Civilization of the Renaissance in Italy* (Harper & Row, 1975). The classic on the subject (first published 1860), the mark against which scholars still level their poison pens of revisionism.

Gardner, Edmund G., *The Story of Florence, The Story of Siena*; also Gordon, Lina Duff, *The Story of Assisi* and *The Story of Perugia* and Ross, Janet, *The Story of Pisa* (J. M. Dent, 1910s). All part of the excellent and highly readable Medieval Towns series.

Hale, J. R., editor, *A Concise Encyclopaedia of the Italian Renaissance* (Thames and Hudson, 1981). An excellent reference guide, with many concise, well-written essays. Also *Florence and the Medici: The Pattern of Control* (1977) which describes just how the Medici did it.

Hibbert, Christopher, *Rise and Fall of the House of Medici* (Penguin, 1965). One of the classics—compulsive reading.

Hook, Judith, *Siena* (Hamish Hamilton, 1979). A little weak on art, but good on everything else.

Masson, Georgina, *Frederick II of Hohenstaufen* (London, 1957).

Origo, Iris, *The Merchant of Prato* (Penguin, 1963). Everyday life in 14th-century Tuscany with the father of modern accounting, Francesco di Marco Datini. Also *Images and Shadows; War in the Val d'Orcia*, about a Tuscan childhood and life during the war.

Procacci, Giuliano, *History of the Italian People* (Penguin, 1973). An in-depth view from the year 1000 to the present—also an introduction to the wit and subtlety of the best Italian scholarship.

Symonds, John Addington, *A Short History of the Renaissance in Italy* (Smith, Elder, 1893). A condensed version of the authority of a hundred years ago, but still fascinating today.

Boccaccio, Giovanni, *The Decameron* (Penguin, 1972). The ever-young classic by one of the fathers of Italian literature. Its irreverent worldliness still provides a salutary antidote to whatever dubious ideas persist in your mental baggage.

Cellini, B., *Autobiography of Benvenuto Cellini* (Penguin, trans. by George Bull). Fun reading about the vicious competition of the Florentine art world by a swashbuckling braggart and world-class liar.

Clark, Kenneth, *Leonardo da Vinci* (Penguin).

Dante, Alighieri, *The Divine Comedy* (plenty of good translations). Few poems have ever had such a mythical significance for a nation. Anyone serious about understanding Tuscany or Italy and their world view will need more than a passing acquaintance with Dante.

Ghibert/Linscott, *Complete Poems and Selected Letters of Michelangelo* (Princeton Press, 1984).

Leonardo da Vinci, *Notebooks* (Oxford, 1983).

Levey, Michael, *Early Renaissance* (1967) and *High Renaissance*, both by Penguin. Old-fashioned accounts of the period, with a breathless reverence for the 1500s—but still full of intriguing interpretations.

Murray, Linda, *The High Renaissance* and *The Late Renaissance and Mannerism* (Thames and Hudson, 1977). Excellent introduction to the period; also Peter and Linda Murray, *The Art of the Renaissance* (1963).

Petrarch, Francesco, *Canzionere and Other Works* (Oxford, 1985). The most famous poems by the 'First Modern Man.'

Vasari, Giorgio, *Lives of the Artists* (Penguin, 1985). Readable, anecdotal accounts of the Renaissance greats by the father of modern art history.

GENERAL INDEX

Note: Page references in **bold** are to maps; those in *italics* are to illustrations.

INDEX OF ARTISTS & ARCHITECTS

Note: Page references in **bold** are to maps; those in *italics* are to illustrations.

INDEX OF ARTISTS AND ARCHITECTS

ANSWERS TO 'A FLORENTINE PUZZLE' *Page 48*

1 Façade, S. Miniato
2 Baptistry, interior apse
3 Windows at the rear of S. Iacopo sopr'Arno, visible from S. Trinita bridge
4 Windows, Orsanmichele
5 Façade, S. Croce (inspired by Orcagna's tabernacle in Orsanmichele
6 Baptistry doors (Pisano's and Ghiberti's first set); portico of the Bigallo, interior apse, S. Croce
7 Loggia dei Lanzi
8 Rucellai Chapel, S. Pancrazio

Other Cadogan Guides available from your local bookshop or from the UK or the USA direct:

From the UK: Cadogan Books, Mercury House, 195 Knightsbridge, London SW7 1RE.
From the US: The Globe Pequot Press, 138 West Main Street, Chester, Connecticut 06412.

Title

Australia .... ☐
Bali .... ☐
The Caribbean (available November 1990) .... ☐
Greek Islands (Update) .... ☐
India (Update) .... ☐
Ireland (Update available January 1991) .... ☐
Italian Islands (Update) .... ☐
Italy .... ☐
Morocco .... ☐
New York .... ☐
Northeast Italy .... ☐
Northwest Italy .... ☐
Portugal .... ☐
Rome .... ☐
Scotland (Update) .... ☐
South Italy .... ☐
Spain (Update) .... ☐
Thailand & Burma .... ☐
Turkey (Update) .... ☐
Tuscany, Umbria & The Marches..................... ☐
Venice (available September 1990) .... ☐
☐

Name ....

Address ....

.... Post Code ....

Date .... Order Number ....

Special Instructions ....

....

Please use these forms to tell us about the hotels or restaurants you consider to be special and worthy of inclusion in our next edition, as well as to give any general comments on existing entries. Please include your name and address on the order form on the reverse of this page.

Hotels

Name ....

Address ....

Tel.. Price of double room ....

Description/Comments ....

....

....

Name ....

Address ....

Tel.. Price of double room ....

Description/Comments ....

....

....

Name ....

Address ....

Tel.. Price of double room ....

Description/Comments ....

....

....

Name ....

Address ....

Tel.. Price of double room ....

Description/Comments ....

....

....